Toward a New U.S. Industrial Policy? ☆ ☆ ☆

☆ ☆ ☆ ☆ ☆ ☆ ☆ ☆ ☆ ☆ ☆ ☆ ☆

Edited, with an Introduction, by
Michael L. Wachter and
Susan M. Wachter

University of Pennsylvania Press
Philadelphia   1983

★ ★ ★ ★ ★ ★ ★ ★ ★ ★ ★ ★ ★ ★ ★

Toward
a New
U.S. Industrial
Policy?

THIS BOOK IS BASED ON
THE WHARTON/RELIANCE SYMPOSIUM
COSPONSORED BY THE WHARTON SCHOOL OF THE UNIVERSITY OF PENNSYLVANIA
AND RELIANCE GROUP, INCORPORATED,
WITH A GRANT FROM
RELIANCE INSURANCE COMPANY

Library of Congress Cataloging in Publication Data

Main entry under title:

Toward a new U.S. industrial policy.

   Proceedings of a symposium cosponsored by the
Wharton School of the University of Pennsylvania
and Reliance Group, Inc., and held in Philadelphia,
March 1981.
   Bibliography: p.
   1. Industry and state—United States—Congresses.
2. United States—Economic policy—1971-   —Congresses.
I. Wachter, Michael L.   II. Wachter, Susan M.
III. Wharton School.   IV. Reliance Group.
HD3616.U47T68   338.973   81-16060
ISBN 0-8122-7819-4   AACR2
ISBN 0-8122-1142-1 (pbk.)

Printed in the United States of America

CONTENTS

PREFACE

This volume is the result of the Wharton/Reliance Symposium cosponsored by the Wharton School of the University of Pennsylvania and Reliance Group, Incorporated. The symposium, held in Philadelphia in March of 1981, brought together approximately 300 business, labor, government, and academic leaders to discuss the major issues in the nation's industrial policy or evolving government-business relationship. The papers presented in this book were prepared for and discussed at that symposium. The comments of the discussants represent their remarks at a panel discussion on the respective topic areas; the summary comments attempt to provide some insight into the nature of the debate that took place. The stress of the Symposium was not on developing consensus views, but rather on encouraging an open debate among diverse viewpoints.

Funding for the Symposium and the volume was provided by a grant from Reliance Insurance Company.

The Symposium and this volume represent the work of many individuals. Certainly, as coeditors, our job would not have been possible without the ongoing support of Dean Donald C. Carroll and Karen Freedman of the Wharton School; Saul P. Steinberg of Reliance Group; Reginald H. Jones of the General Electric Corporation; Daniel Yankelovich and Larry Kaagan of Yankelovich, Skelly and White; and William A. Pollard and Richard J. Guilfoyle of Reliance Insurance Company. Finally, many thanks are owed to those, too many to name, without whose help both the Symposium and the book would never have become realities.

MICHAEL L. WACHTER
SUSAN M. WACHTER

Philadelphia, Pennsylvania

LIST OF PARTICIPANTS

F. GERARD ADAMS is Professor of Economics and Finance and Director of the Economics Research Unit at the Wharton School of the University of Pennsylvania. He also serves as Senior Consultant and Secretary of Wharton Econometric Forecasting Associates.

BERNARD E. ANDERSON is an economist now serving as Director of the Social Services Division of the Rockefeller Foundation. He is on leave from the faculty of the Wharton School where he is a Professor of Industry.

R. JAMES BALL is Professor of Economics and Principal of the London Business School. He has served on many national boards in Great Britain such as the Committee to Review National Savings and was Chairman of the Treasury Committee on Policy Optimization.

MARK A. BLOOMFIELD is the Executive Director and a member of the Board of Directors of the American Council for Capital Formation. Recently he served as Secretary of President Reagan's Transition Tax Policy Task Force.

MARSHALL E. BLUME is Howard Butcher Professor of Finance at the Wharton School of the University of Pennsylvania. He currently serves as Associate Director of the School's Rodney L. White Center for Financial Research and he is a past Managing Editor of the *Journal of Finance.*

WILLIAM H. BRANSON is Professor of Economics and International Affairs at Princeton University. He is Director of Research in International Economics and Research Associate at the National Bureau of Economic Research, and is coeditor of the *International Journal of Economics.*

THEODORE F. BROPHY is Chairman and Chief Executive Officer of General Telephone and Electronics Corporation. He is Co-Chairman of the Business Roundtable and serves as Chairman of the Roundtable's Taxation Task Force.

EDWARD J. CARLOUGH has been General President of the Sheetmetal Workers International Association since 1970.

ROBERT CARSWELL is a former Deputy Secretary of the Treasury. Prior to his government service, Carswell was a partner in the New York law firm of Shearman and Sterling. Presently he is the Thomas A. O'Boyle Visiting Distinguished Practitioner and Adjunct Professor of Finance at the Wharton School.

FINN M. W. CASPERSEN is Chairman of the Board and Chief Executive Officer of the Beneficial Corporation. He is a Trustee of the Committee on Economic Development, and Director of the American Council on Foreign Diplomats.

SOL C. CHAIKIN has been President of the International Ladies' Garment Workers' Union since 1975. He has served on numerous governmental boards and commissions, most recently the Council on Wage and Price Stability.

JEAN A. CROCKETT is Professor of Finance and Chairman of the Finance Department of the Wharton School of the University of Pennsylvania. She is Deputy Chairman of the Board of Directors of the Federal Reserve Bank of Philadelphia, and Director of the American Finance Association.

PETER F. DRUCKER is Clarke Professor of Social Science and Management at Claremont Graduate School. He served for many years as Visiting Professor of Management at the Wharton School. In addition to his academic role, he is a management consultant and a writer on management topics.

JOHN T. DUNLOP is Lamont University Professor at the Harvard Graduate School of Business Administration. He was formerly U.S. Secretary of Labor, and he is an arbitrator and member of numerous government boards. He is presently Coordinator of the recently-formed Labor-Management Group.

GEORGE C. EADS is a senior economist in the Washington office of The Rand Corporation. He served as a member of President Carter's Council of Economic Advisers. Prior to joining the Council, he headed Rand's Research Program in Regulatory Policies and Institutions.

OTTO ECKSTEIN is Chairman of Data Resources, Inc. He served as a member of President Johnson's Council of Economic Advisers. He is also the Paul M. Warburg Professor of Economics at Harvard University.

BARBARA HACKMAN FRANKLIN is former Vice Chairman of the U.S. Consumer Product Safety Commission. She is a Senior Fellow in Public Management at the Wharton School and a member of the faculty of the Department of Legal Studies and Public Management.

BENJAMIN M. FRIEDMAN is Professor of Economics at Harvard University. He also serves as Program Director of Monetary Economics and Financial Markets, at the National Bureau of Economic Research.

IRWIN FRIEND is Edward J. Hopkinson Professor of Finance and Economics at the Wharton School of the University of Pennsylvania and Director of its Rodney L. White Center for Financial Research. He is past president of the American Finance Association.

JACK GUTTENTAG is Professor of Finance and Robert Morris Professor of Banking at the Wharton School of the University of Pennsylvania. He formerly was Chief of the Domestic Research Division of the Federal Reserve Bank of New York.

WILLIAM W. HOGAN is Director of the Energy and Environmental Policy Center, John F. Kennedy School of Government, Harvard University, and Professor of Political Economy. He is Chairman of the Steering Committee of the Energy Modeling Forum.

ROBERT C. HOLLAND is President of the Committee for Economic Development. He was a member of the Board of Governors of the Federal Reserve System, and is an Overseer of the Wharton School.

LACY H. HUNT serves as Senior Vice President and Economist of The Fidelty Bank in Philadelphia. He authors the bank's monthly *Economics Bulletin* and *Econometric Forecast.*

JERRY J. JASINOWSKI is Senior Vice President and Chief Economist of the National Association of Manufacturers. Prior to joining NAM he served as President Carter's Assistant Secretary for Policy at the Department of Commerce, and before that as Senior Research Economist for the Joint Economic Committee.

REGINALD H. JONES joined the General Electric Company on graduation from the Wharton School in 1939. He was named Chairman and Chief Executive Office of General Electric in 1972, and retired in the spring of 1981. He served as Co-Chairman of the Business Roundtable and Chairman of the Business Council. Mr. Jones has been a trustee of the University of Pennsylvania since 1963 and also chairs the Wharton School's Board of Overseers.

JOHN T. JOYCE became President of the International Union of Bricklayers and Allied Craftsmen in November, 1979, after serving 13 years on the Union's Executive Board as Treasurer and then Secretary.

LARRY KAAGAN is Senior Associate and Assistant to the Chairman of Yankelovich, Skelly and White, Inc. His current research focuses on the public opinion context of tax, regulatory, and economic affairs and foreign policy making. He served on the planning committee of the Wharton/Reliance Symposium.

LANE KIRKLAND was elected President of the AFL-CIO in 1979. Previously, he served for ten years as Secretary-Treasurer. He has spent 30 years in various positions within the organized labor movement.

LAWRENCE R. KLEIN, winner of the 1980 Nobel Prize in Economics, is Benjamin Franklin Professor of Economics at the Wharton School of the University of Pennsylvania. He is the founder of Wharton Econometric Forecasting Associates, Inc.

MARVIN H. KOSTERS is Resident Scholar and Director, Center for the Study of Government Regulation, American Enterprise Institute. Formerly, he was Senior Economist for the Council of Economic Advisers, and Associate Director of the Cost of Living Council.

IRVING B. KRAVIS is Professor of Economics of the University of Pennsylvania. A member of the Research staff of the National Bureau of Economic Research since 1962, he is currently Chairman of the Council, International Association for Research in Income and Wealth.

MALCOLM R. LOVELL, JR., has been President of the Rubber Manufacturers' Association since 1973. Before entering the rubber industry, he was Manpower Administrator and Assistant Secretary of Labor for Manpower from 1969 to 1973.

WILLIAM LUCY was elected International Secretary-Treasurer of the American Federation of State, County and Municipal Employees (AFSCME), AFL-CIO in 1972. He was a founder and is the president of the Coalition of Black Trade Unionists.

J. PAUL LYET is Chairman and Chief Executive Officer of Sperry Corporation. A Trustee of the University of Pennsylvania, he is a member of the President's Export Council, the Business Council, and the Emergency Committee for American Trade.

ROBERT MCCLEMENTS, JR. became Executive Vice President of Sun Company, Inc. in 1977. Previously, he was President of Sunoco Energy Development Company (SUNEDCO). He is a member of Sun's Board of Directors.

WILLIAM A. MARQUARD is Chairman of the Board, President, and Chief Executive Officer of American Standard, Inc. He serves as a Trustee of the University of Pennsylvania, and as a member of the Wharton School's Board of Overseers.

D. QUINN MILLS is Albert J. Weatherhead Professor of Business Administration at the Harvard Business School. He helped administer wage and price controls during the Nixon and Ford Administrations in 1971–74. He is a labor arbitrator and consultant to corporations.

MICHAEL H. MOSKOW is Executive Vice President of International Jensen, Inc., a subsidiary of Esmark, Inc. He entered industry after a career in government service and in academia.

ROBERT H. MUNDHEIM is University Professor of Law and Finance at the University of Pennsylvania. Recently, he served as General Counsel for both the U.S. Treasury Department and the Chrysler Loan Guarantee Board.

ROBERT R. NATHAN is Chairman of the Washington economic consulting group that bears his name. He served in the U.S. government as an economist and planner from 1933 to 1945, and he is a member of the Board of Overseers of the Wharton School.

RUDOLPH A. OSWALD was appointed Director of Research for the AFL-CIO in 1976. He has long experience with the trade union movement, and has served on a number of governmental advisory committees.

NORMA PACE is Senior Vice President of the American Paper Institute, which she joined in 1973. Before joining API, she was Vice President of the economic consulting firm of Lionel D. Edie and Company.

DONALD E. PETERSEN is President and Chief Operating Officer of Ford Motor Company and a member of its Board of Directors. He is a member of the Foreign Policy Association, and the Economic Policy Council of the United Nations Association.

ESTHER PETERSON served as Special Assistant to President Carter for Consumer Affairs, and as Special Assistant to President Johnson for Consumer Affairs. She also served as Assistant Secretary of Labor under Presidents Kennedy and Johnson.

ALMARIN PHILLIPS is Professor of Economic Law and Public Policy at the University of Pennsylvania. He was Co-Director of the President's Commission on Financial Structure and Regulation from 1970–71. He was a member of the National Commission on Electronic Funds Transfer.

ROBERT S. PINDYCK is Professor of Applied Economics in the Sloan School of Management at M.I.T. Dr. Pindyck has been a consultant to the Federal Reserve Board, the Federal Energy Administration, and the World Bank, as well as a number of private and public organizations.

DONALD T. REGAN is President Reagan's Secretary of the Treasury. The former Chairman and Chief Executive Officer of Merrill Lynch and Co., he began as an account executive with Merrill Lynch in 1946, and spent his entire career with the firm. He served as Chairman of the Board of Trustees of the University of Pennsylvania from 1974 to 1978.

HENRY S. REUSS, Democratic Congressman from Wisconsin's Fifth Congressional District, has served in the House since 1955. He is Chairman of the Joint Economic Committee, and the ranking majority member and former Chairman of the House Committee on Banking, Finance and Urban Affairs.

F. M. SCHERER is Professor of Economics at Northwestern University. His current research studies the relationship between research and development and productivity growth. He was director of the Bureau of Economics at the Federal Trade Commission from 1974 to 1976.

ANITA A. SUMMERS is Associate Chairperson and Adjunct Professor in Public Management at the Wharton School of the University of Pennsylvania. She was Research Officer and head of Urban Research at the Federal Reserve Bank of Philadelphia.

ROBERT TANNENWALD is a consultant for the Center for Employment and Income Studies at the Florence Heller Graduate School, Brandeis University. He was formerly an economist in the U.S. Macro Service of Data Resources, Inc. and for the Congressional Research Service. He is a member of the Committee on Federal Taxation of the National Tax Association.

MICHAEL L. WACHTER is a Professor of Economics and Management, the Wharton School of the University of Pennsylvania. He is currently a commissioner on the Minimum Wage Study Commission, a member of the National Council on Employment Policy and a Senior Adviser to the Brookings Panel on Economic Activity.

SUSAN M. WACHTER is Associate Professor of Finance, the Wharton School of the University of Pennsylvania. She has served as consultant to the Council of Economic Advisers, the Federal Trade Commission, and the Department of Housing and Urban Development. She is an Associate Editor of the Housing Finance Review.

CHARLS E. WALKER, Former Deputy Secretary of the Treasury, heads his own Washington-based consulting firm. He serves on President Reagan's Economic Policy Advisory Board, and is an Overseer of the Wharton School.

DANIEL YANKELOVICH is founder and president of Yankelovich, Skelly and White, Inc. He is the author of many works on foreign affairs, the labor market, youth attitudes, and the social implications of economic policy making. In 1975, Yankelovich was co-founder of the Public Agenda Foundation.

INTRODUCTION

Michael L. Wachter   Susan M. Wachter

The term industrial policy has many connotations. To many individuals it is an ideologically loaded phrase describing a policy of formal government planning of business or a national planning effort. Interpreted in this fashion, some will be either for or against industrial policy. More recently, this term has taken on a new meaning and it is in this new sense that we are using the term. Specifically, the term industrial policy indicates the relationship between business and government on a microeconomic level: that is, the level of the decision-making of the firm. Virtually all industries are already affected by industrial policies and indeed most of these policies are complex, involving a number of government agencies. For example, all industries that are regulated by specific Federal government agencies—banks, insurance companies, airlines, and trucking are involved in an industrial policy with considerable government intervention. All industries are also affected to varying degrees by antitrust policies of the government. Industrial policy also includes government trade policy, especially the import control of certain products, government stockpiling of "strategic" materials, and the occasional use of those stockpiles to influence the pricing decisions of the industries involved; government procurement policies ranging from fighter aircraft to business forms and the ability to alter the behavior of potential industrial suppliers who are interested in government business; and the new so-called social regulations of industry implemented by the Equal Employment Opportunity Commission, Occupational and Safety and Health Administration, and Environmental Protection Agency.

The important issues of industrial policy are twofold: first, the optimal or proper level of intervention of government in the affairs of business; second, the types of business decisions that should or should not be affected by government policies of different types.

The past decade has seen a transformation in the public's attitude toward government and economic policy. In the aftermath of the Great Depression, the public began to believe that government policy was capable of dampening recessions, reducing poverty, increasing economic growth rates, and bringing about a new, higher quality-of-life. Recent events have proven disappointing. For the public, declining economic growth rates have meant an end to the period of rising standards of living.

In a society with steadily growing income levels, the different interest groups could all benefit from a division of the gains. Once the growth in income stopped, a gain for one group meant an actual decline for others. This, in turn, had led to a breakdown in the liberal consensus which supported the proactivist industrial policies of the past several decades.

There is widespread agreement on the unsatisfactory performance of the U.S. economy and the need for a new industrial policy direction. There is less agreement on the policies that we should pursue.

To address this issue requires an understanding of what government policy can accomplish and how best it can achieve desired ends. To make useful and not counterproductive policy, government must respond to what it is referred to in economic jargon as "market failure." This focuses the debate on competing goals and the disagreement within the attainable set of policy choices. With an understanding of the trade-offs, a new consensus can begin to develop to replace the consensus of the past.

In evaluating policy options to achieve the goals of economic growth, quality-of-life, and income distribution, it is possible to distinguish between two polar cases: where the policy option being pursued is inefficient, in the sense that it is dominated by alternative options that can achieve the same ends at lower economic cost; and where the policy is efficient, in the sense that any changes would require trading-off one goal (for example, economic growth) against the others. Most policy issues involve both a potential move to a more (or less) efficient policy and also a trade-off among alternative goals.

In the development of a new consensus, the evolving relationship between business and government plays a pivotal role. The current debate, like the historic one, diverges between those who want more and those who want less government involvement.

Current government policies advocate a supply-side approach. The organizational structure of the government-business relationship or the "rules of the game" are retained, but specific policies are altered. Supply-side policies are specifically those that encourage faster growth through market mechanisms and through an increase in the ratio of investment to GNP. Various supply-side policies have been suggested;

the version favored by the Reagan administration is but one of several variants. The themes of supply-side economics include the following:

First, over the past two decades there has been an inappropriate and inadvertent government policy tilt toward private consumption and government expenditures and away from private investment. The solution to this problem, however, does not require substantive institutional changes. It is argued that the government, acting within the current context, should alter the tax and expenditure bases to yield the desired increase in private sector investment. Relevant policies include accelerated depreciation, higher investment tax credits, indexing the personal income tax structure in real terms, lowering tax rates on interest savings and capital gains, and stablizing or lowering the overall share of government expenditures as a percentage of GNP.

Second, it is argued that there is a need to increase the rate of growth of the economy compatible with stable inflation rates and improve the rate of productivity growth. By accomplishing this, the rate of growth of real wages and standards of living would be increased. More jobs would be created in the process and presumably the higher income levels could be shared with the nonworking poor through increased transfer payments. In this way, the benefits of increased supply-side growth would be shared by all groups.

Third, to the extent that supply-side initiatives, especially in the micropolicy area, are oriented toward the market mechanism, they could introduce alternative rules that involve less burdensome government intervention. In the extreme, the position argues for a return to a laissez-faire relationship between business and government. In this view, if government would only "get off the back" of business, economic conditions would be just fine.

The supply-side approach may be contrasted to a preferential approach which advocates a more direct, active involvement of the government in the economy and the targeting of government assistance and tax advantages to specific sectors. In this approach, the government is involved in the allocation of investable funds. Although this is currently being done on an *ad hoc* basis, as in the cases of Chrysler, Lockheed, New York City, and the First Pennsylvania Corporation, a further step is recommended; the development of a mechanism to accomplish certain investment goals as agreed upon by either a government-business or other group.

The preferential strategy in which the government allocates investable funds can be approached in several ways: (1) using the Japanese model, in which the government attempts to anticipate which industries have a natural competitive advantage; (2) favoring specific industries that are part of the old industrial base (that is, steel and automobiles) to revitalize them by granting tax advantages and easier access to invest-ment funds; and (3) singling out geographic regions for specific new industrial development—tax subsidies, additional resources, and the like; presumably this would be aimed at the Northeast and industrial-ized Midwest. Although the Reagan government has rejected a system-atic adoption of the preferential approach, the push towards imposing voluntary control of the Japanese automobile exports, and the need for a policy to deal with the savings and loan industry, makes it clear that this issue remains unresolved. In addition, tax and expenditure type policies, although they may appear to be generally applicable, and hence supply-side, may be quite preferential in nature. Obviously closely targeted investment subsidies to specific industries can be clothed in supply-side jargon.

These different strategies—the supply-side and the various sectoral approaches—may all lead to quite different distributional and quality-of-life results. Although faster economic growth is a goal in some of these proposals, even in these cases, the rewards are reaped in the longer run, when the higher levels of investment lead to potentially higher standards of living. In the immediate, short run, the various suggested tax policies that govern the increased level of investable funds will force different groups to cut back their consumption by different amounts. It is generally held that tax policies will tend to favor the wealthy and the owners of capital. This would lead to an increase in the wealth disparity among groups and even cause an absolute decline in income if certain regions, industries, or economic groups are particularly hard hit. A similar argument is made that progrowth policies tend to slight quality-of-life concerns.

The differing income distribution and quality-of-life aspects of the high growth strategies have obviously affected their popularity in com-parison with those proposals that seek to maintain and strengthen the current industrial base. However, most of these distributional and qual-ity-of-life questions have not been explored in a rigorous, systematic fashion. Must higher rates of economic growth lead to a change in the distribution of wealth or a lower quality-of-life? Could not tax and transfer programs disconnect any predetermined linkage between a par-ticular growth strategy and its assumed, straightforward income distri-bution and quality-of-life results?

The theme of this book is to identify the shape that a new industrial policy should take. In Part One, government, business, and labor leaders Reginald H. Jones, Lane Kirkland, Henry S. Reuss, and Donald T. Regan present their views on alternative economic policies from their differing political prospectives.

In Part Two, researchers examine areas where policy changes may be called for to achieve the goals of economic growth, equity, and quality-of-life. Specific topic areas are capital formation, energy, international trade, retraining of workers, regulation, and the political experience of allocating funds. In each, the authors consider what may be the market failure or current government policy failure that necessitates the need for new policies. In addition, in each the authors address the trade-offs among growth, quality-of-life, and income distribution goals.

Part Three explores the question of building a consensus on a new industrial policy. John T. Dunlop describes the mechanisms for achieving consensus, and R. J. Ball reports on lessons from the British experience on the building of a consensus. In conclusion, the extent of the current agreement and disagreement on goals and policies is examined by Daniel Yankelovich and Larry Kaagan.

★ ★ ★ ★ ★ ★ ★ ★ ★ ★ ★ ★ ★ ★ ★

PART ONE

VISIONS OF A NEW
INDUSTRIAL POLICY
FOR THE 1980s

1.

TOWARD A NEW
INDUSTRIAL POLICY

Reginald H. Jones

The Wharton School of the University of Pennsylvania was founded 100 years ago in a period of extraordinary optimism about the future —especially the nation's economic future. Thomas Edison's electrifying inventions were only the most widely publicized of a series of techno- logical innovations which did more to change the lives of ordinary people than anything since the agricultural revolution 10,000 years ago. It was the beginning of a century in which the United States rose swiftly to a position of economic, military, and political leadership in the world. And that rise was supported, in fact driven, by a broad consensus on the rightness of our goals, values, policies, and actions. We were a confident people.

What is the scene that greets us 100 years later, in the centennial year of Wharton's founding?

You know as well as I. What a sorry contrast there is between yesterday's optimism and today's pessimism; yesterday's faith and today's skepticism; yesterday's unity and today's dissension. There will always be differences in a democracy, but today our only shared belief is that America is over the hill. And judged objectively by our declining competitiveness in world markets, our loss of influence in world affairs, and our inability to deal with the most obvious national perils such as the energy problem, it is hard to disagree with the world opinion that the United States is not what it used to be.

So the 1980s clearly are going to be a time of decision. If we continue to drift as aimlessly as we did in the 1970s, our pessimism about the American future will become a self-fulfilling prophecy. But if we can build a new consensus on what is needed to restore the nation's vitality, the 1980s will be a memorable moment in our history—a vindication of the faith of Washington and Lincoln and so many other people here and abroad that the United States is indeed a nation with a special destiny, worthy of emulation and respect by any nation that aspires to human progress.

The outlook is not wholly pessimistic. It is better than it was just a year ago because the 1980 elections showed that the people are ready for a major change of direction. They voted in the minority party, and voted out many of the leading spokesmen for the liberal-welfare philosophy that has dominated national politics ever since the New Deal. And President Reagan has moved quickly to signal a real change of course —a significant slowdown in the growth of the Federal government and a shift of resources from government to the private sector.

But as Reagan knows better than anyone else, while there is a great tide of emotion behind the desire to "get the country moving again," there is by no means a broad public or political consensus on his program to get it done. He has to *build* a consensus. The *nation* has to build a consensus on a workable, acceptable program of specific policies and actions that will restore our economic health.

STRUCTURAL CHANGES

As a first step, let's take a look at the deep structural changes—economic, social, and political—that have precipitated this crisis in our national life.

For many years, our country was united by an unspoken consensus that the economic imperatives should prevail over all other competing values. When Calvin Coolidge said, "The business of society is business," he was expressing a widely held truth. While the Great Depression opened the door to Keynesian economics and governmental manipulation of economic life, it certainly reinforced our sense that economic matters had to have top priority. But the general prosperity of the 1950s and most of the 1960s led many to believe that we could at last take our economic growth for granted, and give higher priority to other values —the elimination of inequities in society, the preservation of the environment, the enhancement of what is called the "quality-of-life." And these noneconomic objectives did in fact take priority, with expanding government and a redirection of resources as a direct consequence.

While these changes of values were expressing themselves in national policy, there were major discontinuities in the international structure. We saw the rise of powerful industrial competitors in Europe and Japan; the emergence of the Third World, with all its growing pains; the OPEC cartel, and the massive transfer of wealth to the oil-rich nations.

Here in the United States, we suddenly found our productivity advances slowing down, then stopping altogether. We found ourselves

A New Industrial Policy for the 1980s

with chronic unemployment, enormous trade deficits, slower economic growth, and inflation at double-digit levels.

But the economic changes were only part of the story. Social tremors also shook the ground beneath us. Changing moral values and lifestyles have had profound effects. Consider the family—the bedrock of social organization. The traditional Norman Rockwell picture of an American family is a breadwinning husband, a stay-at-home wife, and a couple of children. Three decades ago, that accurately described 70 percent of the American households. Today, barely 15 percent fit the mold. The divorce rate has doubled, and single-parent households, childless marriages, people living alone, people living together, and househusbands have turned the idea of family into a bewildering series of options. Working women have changed the character of the labor force.

There have been structural changes in our political life, too. Until the 1970s, there was a broad consensus on the importance of a strong two-party system of government, with the party disciplines that brought experienced people to nomination and pushed essential legislation through the Congress. But in the 1970s, the disciplines of party politics and congressional committees were "reformed" out of existence, and we saw the rise of individual political entrepreneurs who depended on their own personal organizations and media expertise to get elected. Government, in response to the maneuvers of narrow and competing special interests, replaced the consensus government of the two-party system. The result has been a highly volatile and unstable political process, lurching suddenly in response to temporarily contrived majorities, or paralyzed by the contradictory pressures of conflicting special interests.

THREE VISIONS OF THE FUTURE
With such deep structural changes altering our economic, social, and political landscape, we have leaders pointing in every direction, and consensus could not have survived. Instead, as Daniel Yankelovich[1] has observed, we now have three competing ideologies—three visions of America's future, each with its own priorities and supporters.

One he calls the industrial vision. Those who hold this vision strongly endorse economic growth, greater emphasis on capital formation, reinvestment in productive plant and technology, improved competitiveness abroad, and efforts to improve productivity. They believe that without economic growth, none of our other national objectives can be achieved because we will not have the wherewithal to expand or even sustain our social programs. Those who hold this vision are mostly in the business and financial communities and in the business schools. They are strong advocates of market economics, limited government, and the private enterprise system. And their views necessarily come in conflict with those who hold another vision—the vision of an egalitarian society.

The egalitarian perspective is held by those who are faithful to the ideals of the welfare state. This would include people in the academic community, in social service professions, in minority groups, civil rights and activist organizations, and in civil service—essentially the people who are receiving or dispensing government checks. Their priorities are on an equitable redistribution of the wealth that the American society has produced, and they define social justice in terms of rights and entitlements. They tend to be mistrustful of both corporate ideology and the market mechanism, and favor instead a planned economy. As Yankelovich puts it, among the partisans of this view, "there is an image of historical and contemporary America as a land awash with prejudice and discrimination, where social mobility is but a cruel myth propagandized to the poor, and where hard work and motivation count for little in the face of the great corporate-industrial machine."[2]

In addition to the industrial and the egalitarian ideologies, Yankelovich sees a third ideology which has the vision of a "quality-of-life" society. This is the "small is beautiful" crowd, the people who greet our slowing economy and our energy problems with some secret delight, because they truly believe that we are all too materialistic anyway and should settle for a more frugal, aesthetically-oriented life. For them, material incentives, technological advances, and nose-to-the-grindstone work habits have been replaced in large part with an emphasis on leisure, physical and psychological fitness, self-fulfillment, and a new, more respectful harmony with the biosphere. They are suspicious of industry and technology, and their attitudes toward regulation move beyond market control mechanisms into the realm of disciplinary regulation and extensive "zero risk" prohibition of dangerous products.

Now, it's the contention of Mr. Yankelovich that the leaders of these three ideologies—the industrial, the egalitarian, and the quality-of-life ideologies—see their priorities not merely as desirable goals, but as moral imperatives that must not be compromised. And it is their passionate advocacy, and their willingness to stand as veto groups which will not allow any concession to those with another vision, that has kept us from achieving a national consensus.

But the people are not ideologues. They want a little of all three visions. They want jobs and higher real incomes and relief from inflation—the industrial vision. They also want to keep a safety net down there for the losers, and they are certainly not going back to the smoke and pollution of yesteryear. What they want is a workable, vigorously pursued program that pulls us out of the traffic jam of conflicting ideologies and onto the broad highroad of national progress.

Let us now go back and examine the economic discontinuities referred to earlier, the changes that have precipitated our present economic problems.

ECONOMIC DISCONTINUITIES

First of all, the decline in productivity. Since 1973, real output per hour (in private non-farm businesses) has risen only 0.4 percent per year, compared with about 2.5 percent a year during the preceding 25 years. And productivity has actually declined in the past three years. Since we can only consume what we produce, this means that real income has declined—and will continue to do so until we can resume our productivity advances.

Competitors in other nations, whose productivity has been increasing faster than our own, have rushed in to fill the gap and take over markets once proudly served by U.S. industry. The consequences in the steel and auto industries are too recent and too painful to need retelling. But when foreign competitors surpass us in productivity, quality, and innovation, the impact on jobs and tax revenues and stricken communities creates severe social and political tensions.

One basic cause of declining productivity is the sharp decline in capital formation —another discontinuity. From 1948 to 1965, the stock of physical capital per worker in this country—the plant and equipment—increased at an average rate of 2 percent a year. Then the increase slowed down, and since 1973 our capital equipment per worker has actually been declining. Business investment averaged only 10.3 percent of real GNP in the period from 1975 to 1980, compared with the 12 percent to 13 percent various government and academic studies have concluded is necessary to provide us with the needed industrial capacity, productivity improvement, and new energy sources.

A third structural economic change is that our economy is becoming increasingly internationalized. The international sector of the U.S. economy—the amount of goods we import and export—has grown twice as fast as the GNP in the past 10 years. As late as 1970, our exports and imports amounted to only 12 percent of the national economy. In 1980 they amounted to 24 percent.

The fourth discontinuity, of course, is that OPEC has ended the long era of cheap energy that fuelled our spectacular growth in the postwar period. Our oil import bill climbed from $5 billion in 1972 to an estimated $105 billion this year, and is headed still higher. The adjustment to this tremendous tax on our national income has been very painful indeed. It has been a major contributor to inflation, it has drained off much of the real income of our people, and it has rendered much of U.S. industrial capacity—built in an era of cheap energy—obsolete.

The fifth structural change is chronic inflation. As measured by the Consumer Price Index, inflation averaged only 1 percent a year from 1960 to 1965. But in the five years just past it averaged 9 percent. Even more disturbing is the volatility of the inflation rate—going from 11 percent in 1974 to 6 percent in 1976 and back up to 13.5 percent in 1980. This greatly increases the level of risk and uncertainty that inhibits all business planning, not to mention the planning of individuals for their own future.

A sixth structural change has been the explosion of regulations, and the huge burden of compliance. The Council on Environmental Quality estimates that the cumulative cost of compliance with existing environmental regulations will reach $478 billion during the decade from 1978 to 1987. And of course there is the inhibiting effect of regulations on industrial expansion—the inhibition of our much-needed expansion of the coal industry, for example.

All of these structural changes, most of them self-inflicted wounds, I might add, come on top of the normal dynamics that are inevitable in an evolving industrial society—the long trend toward services, the demographic effects, the shifts of comparative advantage in world trade, the changing consumer preferences and social objectives that change our mix of industries and send some regions into sharp decline while others surge ahead.

INDUSTRIAL POLICY—TWO APPROACHES

Responding to these changes is a difficult challenge, and we have not been up to it in the past decade. So we face now the need for a new industrial policy—a combination of approaches that is workable, equitable, and capable of generating the public consensus needed to overcome the inevitable political obstacles.

Two basic approaches have emerged from public discussion thus far. One approach is the targeted approach by which government offers incentives and subsidies to certain chosen industries and locations. These could either be sunset industries, industries that are declining, or sunrise industries, those that seem to have some prospect for growth. But political reality suggests that the sunrise industries don't want or need the bureaucratic hand of government to help them along, and government does not have any particular wisdom in selecting future winners, any more than the speculators in the stock market. In any contest for government funds, the sunset industries, which are usually mature industries with high employment in old established locations, are sure to win. They will have the high numbers of employees laid-off, the big plants closed down, the communities threatened with all the social and economic problems of industrial change. They have the votes and the claims to public sympathy. So an industrial policy structured around high government intervention into the economy by way of targeted incentives and subsidies is bound to direct the nation's limited resources toward the industries that have lost the ability to compete. It may be argued that these industries have only temporarily lost the ability to compete and need only temporary subsidies and protection until they can return to a position of competitive leadership. But this approach has the high risk that we will be backing history's losers, immobilizing our resources in industries that should be pulling back, consolidating, closing up shop if necessary, while their employees move to the growth industries and the growth locations of the future.

The other approach to industrial policy is the nontargeted approach —a package of broad macroeconomic measures that encourage savings, investment, innovation, exports, and productivity increases in our whole industrial and service structure, with market forces determining the winners and losers. In this approach, generally known as "supply-side economics," the taxpayers pay the social cost of foregoing some consumption in order to encourage investors and restore economic vitality. But individual investors, rather than the whole nation, take the risks involved in making choices among companies, locations, and industries. In today's highly competitive worldwide economy, I have the feeling that this approach would be most likely to direct our resources toward the companies and locations that have the best chance of making it— providing jobs and building a worldwide customer base against foreign competition.

But here I am stating a personal preference. The postulates of supply-side economics and targeted-incentive economics must be measured against each other, and also against the standards of those with other priorities—the egalitarians with their concern for social justice, and the quality-of-life people with their concerns about excessive industrialization. If sacrifices are called for, and they do seem inevitable if inflation is to be brought under control, how do we keep the sacrifices from falling too heavily on those already struggling desperately to make ends meet? If risks to our environment are involved in a program of expanded industrialization, what trade-offs are acceptable to the general public?

I am confident that a consensus can be built. The 1980 elections showed that we have an electorate that is ready to try new approaches. There is a broad recognition that our economy is sick and needs new medicine. There is evidently a growing recognition that we cannot meet our moral commitments to our poor and underprivileged, and we cannot afford more headway against environmental pollution, unless we rebuild our economy to the point where personal incomes and government revenues are growing at a healthy rate, without the distortion of inflation. The public is ready for a vigorous debate that will lead to consensus on a new industrial policy. What we need is a set of ideas that can be combined into a coherent and workable policy.

Britain's Iron Lady was here in the United States a few weeks ago. While we may not all agree with her particular policies, I think we would agree with the sentiments Mrs. Thatcher expressed at Georgetown University when she said, "The road to recovery is paved not with good intentions but with hard decisions."[3]

NOTES
1. Yankelovich (1980), pp. 18–24.
2. *Ibid.*, p. 21.
3. Margaret Thatcher [at Georgetown University], *New York Times*, February 28, 1981.

BIBLIOGRAPHY
Yankelovich, Daniel. *The Economy and the President: 1980 and Beyond*, edited by Walter E. Hoadley. Englewood Cliffs: Prentice-Hall, Inc., 1980.

2.

PEAS, PEOPLE, AND THE ECONOMY

Donald T. Regan

It was ten years ago that I ventured into the literary world by writing a book about certain stock market events that occurred in 1970 and 1971. Since then some pundits have unhesitatingly quoted various passages from that book which turned out to be slightly different from my present positions. However, I would like to quote at least one paragraph which still holds true. I noted then that, "the strength and the momentum of inflation and inflationary expectations (in 1970) had clearly been underestimated. The belief that the same can of peas would cost more next year than this year was ingrained by that time. And no quick turn in the economy could root out that belief in a short time."

I should have said can of worms instead of peas, because none of the policies of the past decade have succeeded in changing that situation. Inflation now plagues us at an even higher rate. Inflationary psychology is still a major problem. And we know that quick turns in the economy won't root out the basic disease.

But there is one big difference. We now have an economic recovery plan that rejects the mistakes of the past in favor of a bold and innovative new philosophy. The plan rejects the quick turns, easy answers, and fast food approach to economic change in favor of an integrated economic plan for long term improvement. It is comprehensive enough, and bold enough, and thoughtful enough to provide the American people with a realistic promise for change—a reason for them to start believing that the cost of a can of peas can go down.

Indeed, we are seeing remarkable signs of public support. A recent NBC-Associated Press poll showed 61 percent of the American people support spending cuts and 71 percent support tax cuts. Other polls show even higher support. The White House has received over 30,000 letters on the economic program and they are running 100 to 1 in support of the effort.

These are very encouraging signs, not only because this is a political program that requires congressional approval, and not only because every political leader wants and needs public support. It is encouraging because if we are to beat the inflation problem, only the American people can do it. Only the people themselves can reverse the inflationary mentality make the necessary saving and investment decisions that will increase productivity, and make the personal initiatives toward more production, getting a better job, upgrading their professions, and generally increasing their living standards.

Our task is to provide the governmental policies that will let those forces go to work. We believe in the people of this country and we want to put the economy back in their hands. The Presidential election, and every public opinion poll since then, indicates that the people are ready to accept that responsibility. In light of this, here are excerpts from some recent letters to the Treasury:

- A telegram from New York says: "I earn $47,000. I work very hard for my salary, but taxes destroy my American dream. Please don't decrease my share of your tax cuts. You promised a break for hardworking, productive people like me."

- A Dallas secretary writes to list all of her monthly expenses and then subtracts them from an $11,000 annual salary. Very little is left.

Her bottom line on inflation was: "Where will it all end?" My bottom line is: "It should end right here, right now."

Whether it is taxes, or waste and abuse in government spending, or unwarranted regulatory meddling, people are fed up with business-as-usual solutions. This Administration is not satisfied with that approach either. The President's program provides a dramatic change from existing policies, but perhaps that change isn't so great within historical context. The nation's political reporters have draped it with words like "new, adventuresome, experimental, modern, untested, and pioneering." In fact, it relies on the oldest and most proven economic principles known to this country. It restores our faith in the private enterprise system, in personal initiative, in individual prerogative and in the traditions of personal saving and investment that have built everything from log cabins to high-rise apartments.

Specifically, the program has four parts:

- Spending restraint, to keep government from absorbing and controlling an ever increasing share of the goods and services produced by the people each year, and to free up those resources for use by the private sector;

- Tax rate reductions, to encourage private saving and work effort, and business tax changes to promote investment by business in expanding and modernizing our factories, farms, and mines;
- Monetary stability, to reduce inflation and stabilize interest rates at levels people can afford; to restore confidence in the currency and preserve the value of people's savings; and
- Regulatory reform, to reduce the infuriating and ruinously expensive burden of government regulation by restricting government intervention to cases where it is absolutely necessary, and to regulate in a sensible and cost effective manner.

It used to be that economic policy bounced from one extreme to another: all policy levers on "stop" to fight inflation, or all levers on "go" to fight unemployment. The result was the worst of both worlds, with ever increasing government intervention in the economy. The importance of the President's proposal lies in the fact that it is a mixture of policies, all mutually reinforcing, that can curb inflation while promoting the expansion of real production and employment at the same time. As one corporate leader said recently: "It is vital that . . . [these programs] proceed simultaneously and in step with one another. To generate results in the future we must begin now—we must keep the economy moving forward even while reducing the size of government. This is the essence of the plan."

He is absolutely right that all elements of the program are integrated. As an example of this integration, consider monetary policy: Inflation is primarily a monetary phenomenon. Stable prices are impossible if the rates of money growth consistently increase faster than the growth of goods and services as they have done, on average, for more than a decade. There is substantial evidence both at home and abroad that serious inflation and high interest rates can be reduced only if monetary growth is consistently restrained. The prerequisite for slowing inflation is curbing the growth in money supply.

This Administration clearly recognizes the importance of the independence of the Federal Reserve System, and that independence will be maintained. A common objective is shared by both, however. That objective is the control of inflation. A steady, slow rate of growth in the money supply is important to that objective. Accordingly, the Administration will regularly consult with the Federal Reserve Board on the full range of its economic program, and will pursue budget policies that will facilitate the task of the Federal Reserve in assuring slow and steady monetary growth. Through this effort we hope to assure a slow, steady growth in the money supply. With a program successful in achieving a stable and moderate growth pattern for the money supply, both inflation and interest rates will recede, thereby restoring vigor to our financial institutions and markets.

Marginal tax rate reduction is aimed primarily at encouraging real growth, yet it has beneficial impacts on restraining inflation. Marginal rate cuts raise after-tax wages, interest, and dividends, and encourage work effort and saving. Accelerated depreciation and a higher investment tax credit increase the rate of return on investment. Output will rise. Yet this rising output will itself help to restrain prices, as will increased productivity.

The increase in personal saving will help to finance both an investment boom and the Federal deficit, reducing the pressure on the Federal Reserve to increase the money supply. In fact, we expect the marginal rate cuts to reinforce monetary policy by stimulating saving, producing "crowding in" instead of crowding out.

Our projections show an average personal savings rate of 7 percent over the 1981–86 period, which is substantially higher than the 5.7 percent rate in the 1976–80 period. Business saving is expected to increase gradually to 13.3 percent of GNP in the 1984–86 period under the spur of the Accelerated Cost Recovery System, from the average 12.8 percent of GNP experienced from 1976–80.

I might add that there is historical precedent for the new savings projections in the Kennedy–Johnson rate cuts of 1964–65: The response was dramatic then. The labor force participation rate reversed a downward drift from the mid-1950s to a steady and prolonged rise which began in 1965. The unemployment rate fell sharply below 5 percent in 1965 and declined to 3.5 percent by 1969. The personal saving rate rose markedly from a range of 5.4 percent to 6.3 percent in the preceding 5 years, to 6.7 percent in 1964, and it rose to 7 percent or higher in 9 of the next 11 years, and was 8 percent or higher in 6 of those years.

This experience, as well as sound economic analysis, argue forcefully that the personal saving response to the marginal rate reductions President Reagan has proposed will be at least as pronounced as those following the 1964–65 tax cuts.

Finally, all income taxes, personal and corporate, are part of the wage and capital costs a business must pay and the prices it must charge.

Spending restraint is of obvious antiinflationary benefit, yet it fosters real growth as well. Resources employed by the people for their own gain are generally used more efficiently, and are far more likely to go for productivity-enhancing investment than are resources used by the government.

A reduced regulatory burden also has the duel impact of increasing output and reducing costs. In addition, if the cost of meeting government regulations is lowered by several billions of dollars, that too reduces both private borrowing and pressure on the Federal Reserve to print more money.

With that scenario in mind, let me discuss some of the specific results we expect from the program. A Federal Reserve policy of reducing the growth of the monetary base and monetary aggregates through 1986 should cut inflation at least in half by 1986: the rate of growth of the CPI falling from 11 percent in 1981 to just over 4 percent in 1986, and the GNP deflator falling from 9.9 percent in 1981 to 4.9 percent in 1986. Concomitently real GNP should grow at least between 4 and 5 percent each year from 1982 through 1986. As a result of past developments, however, 1981 may be a sluggish year with overall growth of about 1 percent.

The program will generate substantial increases in employment, principally in the private sector. Total employment in 1986 is expected to be approximately 11.8 million greater than in 1981; the unemployment rate is expected to decline steadily from 7.8 percent in the current year to less than 5.7 percent in 1986.

As a result of the expansion of saving and capital formation, significant improvements in productivity will accompany these employment gains. Growth in real output per worker should average over 2 percent per year from 1982 through 1986. In real terms, plant and equipment outlays are expected to rise at an average annual rate of 11.0 percent from 1981 through 1986.

Substantial resources will be diverted from the public to the private sector. The ratio of receipts to GNP will drop from 21.1 percent in fiscal year 1981 to 19.3 percent in fiscal 1984. Over the same period, spending will fall from 23.3 percent of GNP to 19.3 percent. And as a result, the budget should be balanced in 1984.

Finally, this strengthened domestic economy will be the foundation of a strengthened American position in the international economy. The decontrol of oil prices will discourage U. S. consumption and encourage domestic production, thereby reducing American demands on the international oil markets. Increased productivity will help make U.S. products more competitive internationally. Price stability will restore confidence in the dollar as a medium of international exchange and as a store of value. And a stable, vigorous rate of economic growth will reduce protectionist pressures at home, even while providing growing markets for products from developing and industrialized countries.

I believe that President Reagan's program will begin to bear fruit even before it is enacted. The Federal Reserve has already moved to lower the growth of the money supply. Inflationary expectations and interest rates are already coming down. As people see the program unfold, as permanent changes in spending programs and tax rates move through Congress and are enacted into law, and as the regulatory burden is reduced, we expect the public will respond.

This will not be some sort of mystical response based on faith and psychology. The expectations we are referring to are the public's logical computation of what they expect to happen in the future. People know what to do when government spending explodes, tax rates soar, and the printing presses roll. They consume more and save less. They behave exactly as the public has behaved over the past few years.

That same logical public will know what to do when the printing presses slow, tax rates fall, and the spending juggernaut is halted. Savings will rise. Real investment will increase. Interest rates will fall.

These changes in behavior will occur quickly, because the public looks and plans ahead. They can see that we have a real change of policy, and they will respond. This means that we have a real chance of bringing down inflation without the sort of major economic slowdowns that seemed to be necessary in the past. In the past, the public quite rightly refused to believe that government had changed its ways.

3.

CAN AMERICAN INDUSTRY BE BORN AGAIN?

Henry S. Reuss

The Wharton School could hardly find a better theme on which to celebrate 100 years of excellence than this—what kind of policy should we adopt toward American industry?

We have just passed through a decade of economic turmoil. We have not come close to solving our chief economic problems: high inflation, high unemployment, high interest rates. The rate of economic growth has slowed, and the rate of productivity growth has stopped. International economic competition has taken over a substantial portion of the American market for a wide range of industrial goods—from steel and autos to the newer high technology industries.

Many proposals to resuscitate American industry are on the table:

(1) Backing losers—bailing out troubled firms or industries by government subsidies, refundable tax credits, orderly marketing agreements, renegotiated wage contracts, new Federal banks.

(2) Picking winners—selecting individual industries, firms, or product lines for a broad range of government support, as in Japan's effort to foresee world trends.

(3) The Reagan program—tight money, a reduced Federal sector by slashing spending, and massive cuts in marginal personal income tax rates heralded to encourage "work, savings, and investment."

(4) The March 2, 1981 report of the Joint Economic Committee Democrats—building upon our earlier supply-side work to develop a comprehensive strategy for investment and jobs.

Let us look at each of the four proposals:

BACKING LOSERS

Backing losers has been a popular governmental occupation, but not all of the government's rescue attempts have ended in failure. The $250 million of loans guaranteed to Lockheed have been repaid, and the company survives. On a smaller scale, the Small Business Administration, the Economic Development Administration (EDA), and the Farmers Home Administration have given financial assistance to hundreds of struggling firms, most of which remain in business.

But too often the bail-out approach simply sends good money after bad. EDA guaranteed over $50 million of loans to Wisconsin Steel in 1979 to finance modernization and pollution control equipment at an aging Chicago plant. Within months a lengthy strike at International Harvester, Wisconsin Steel's largest customer, drove the company into bankruptcy.

EDA fared even worse on a series of loans it guaranteed to the Seatrain Shipbuilding Corporation for building large tankers in the old Brooklyn Navy Yard. As the cost overruns mounted, so did the infusions of guaranteed credit. By the time Seatrain had sold two tankers, the market had dried up. Seatrain finally filed for bankruptcy this February, leaving EDA with $60 million of debts.

And fifteen months after Congress bailed out Chrysler, the company is still teetering on the edge of collapse. The arguments that the bail-out would save hundreds of thousands of jobs and billions of dollars in transfer payments were quickly proven false. Chrysler has had to close plants and fire more than half its 120,000 workers anyway. On top of a general slump, the combination of high car prices and high interest rates continue to undermine the company's recovery.

Already, Chrysler has used $1.2 billion of the $1.5 billion of Federally-guaranteed credit. Its best hope of averting bankruptcy is to attract new equity through a merger or foreign joint venture. This could have happened without the taxpayers risking $1.5 billion to give the current management another chance. I reluctantly supported the Chrysler loan guarantees because they were the only game in town. A far more useful governmental role would have been to provide retraining and supportive services to workers displaced in a Chrysler reorganization.

These *ad hoc* governmental tinkerings would not, in my judgment, be much improved by regularizing them into a new Reconstruction Finance Corporation to salvage the losers. Advocates of an RFC hope to free it from the kinds of political pressure that dominated the debate on Chrysler. I am not at all sure that transferring the decision-making power to an RFC would purge the process of the politics that polluted Wisconsin Steel and Seatrain. Worse, I fear that an RFC would only institutionalize the process of government bail-outs, sink even greater resources into inefficient, noncompetitive industries, and thus simply postpone the structural reforms that our economy needs.

PICKING WINNERS

Can our Federal government do a better job than the market in deciding what products, firms, and industries will prosper in the future? I doubt it.

The advocates of picking winners usually point to the industrial policies of foreign countries, but the record is not particularly encouraging. Despite the commitment of vast sums of money and a near monopoly of the government market, the British are still struggling to break into the world computer market. The Germans and French have been equally unsuccessful. In the case of Japan, the government favored some industries, and those industries have prospered. But so have a number of industries that were not the targets of government largesse.

Agriculture is the one area in which the United States government has played a broad-based role. Building on our rich base, the government influences everything from the course of agricultural research to the actual marketing of farm products overseas. It is the one area in which we have become most Japanese.

But we are ill-prepared by either our philosophy or our past to embark on a path of detailed intervention across the industrial spectrum. Not that the government has not had a major impact on the nature and size of U.S. industry. Major postwar expenditures on defense and space contributed a great deal to the evolution of the domestic aircraft and computer industries. Subsidies, tax benefits, and trade protection have benefited many industries. However, this military-space experience, where government is the market, has not prepared the government to judge the vagaries of changing technology or shifting markets. When it comes to picking private sector winners, humility becomes us.

THE REAGAN PLAN

Mainly, the Reagan program proposes to increase saving and investment through a massive personal income tax cut, largely to the affluent. The beneficiaries of the tax cut, we are told, will not divert the cuts to inflationary personal expenditures, particularly of luxury imports. Nor will they use the proceeds to bid up the price of existing real estate, commodities, and collectibles. Instead, the tax cut will somehow be channeled into the productivity-enhancing inflation-fighting new plant and equipment that we clearly need.

Let us give the proposal the benefit of an enormous doubt. Let us assume that it will by itself bring about large-scale new business fixed investment. We still have to ask two questions:

First, why will not the high interest rates resulting from the President's and the Federal Reserve's restrictive monetary policy, and from the continued budget deficit, in large part undo the proinvestment effect of the income tax cut?

Second, can hyped-up business fixed investment succeed unless it is accompanied by those very structural programs—a good infrastructure, training for real jobs, support for research and development—that the Reagan budget would weaken?

The Reagan program, then, makes contact with the problem of reindustrialization in only the most preliminary way.

A COMPREHENSIVE STRATEGY
FOR INVESTMENT AND JOBS

This brings us to the last, best hope of earth—the strategy for industrial regeneration of the Joint Economic Committee Democrats. This strategy moves us away from an exclusive focus on any one element of the economy. Even something as vital as new plant and equipment is only part of the picture. After all, the latest robot is only as good as the trained programmer hired to run it. What is needed is a many-sided approach:

NEW PLANT AND EQUIPMENT

Our need for new capital has been rising. America's capital stock has been growing older. Almost half our industrial plant and equipment was built before the oil shock in 1973, and much of the rest was designed on the assumption of cheap, abundant oil. Moreover, the labor force has grown rapidly as the baby boom came of working age and more women entered the labor market. With more workers, we need more and better machines if economic opportunity is to be open to all.

In addition growing international competition has forced many domestic industries to run faster if they want to continue to run at all— and that often means more or better or newer capital equipment. However, despite the evident need, we actually invested a smaller proportion of our national income in the 1970s than we did in earlier decades. It is no wonder that our productivity performance has been so poor.

In the recent 1981 annual report, Democrats and Republicans alike urge that firms be allowed to depreciate their equipment more rapidly. In my view, such a true supply-side measure is needed today, not in the sweet bye-and-bye when Congress can make up its mind on the cosmic implications of Kemp-Roth.

RESEARCH AND DEVELOPMENT

We should be equally concerned about the current trend in our commitment to research and development. Working smarter, bringing new products and processes to the world market are crucial elements in maintaining the competitive strength of the U.S. economy. Again, the key word is comprehensive. We need to maintain the public commitment to funding basic research and updating the quality of our research facilities. The recently established industry technology centers in the Department of Commerce can help focus the efforts of academic researchers on the particular challenges facing American industry. The challenge is there. For many years we led the industrial world in the share of national income devoted to commercial research and development. That has changed. Germany and Japan now devote a higher percentage of their total resources to research and development than we do, and France and Britain are not far behind.

The Administration's program does take one small step in the right direction by allowing research equipment to depreciate over three years, with a 6 percent investment tax credit. However, research and development, both public and private, need far greater support.

DEVELOPING NEW MARKETS

A comprehensive approach to investment and jobs is the key element in an effective U.S. international trade policy. New factories will help meet foreign competition; new products will bring new customers to our door.

In a competitive era, we will have to do more. We need to take our better mousetraps to the world's door and make sure that door is open to American products. We have a definite interest in the economic health of our trading partners. Slow growth in Europe or the developing world will have a severe effect on U.S. exports.

INFRASTRUCTURE

Our industrial development depends on an adequate and properly maintained infrastructure, including roads, bridges, railroads, ports, sewer and water systems, utilities, and other physical support systems. That infrastructure has been allowed to deteriorate, particularly in our older cities. One in five American bridges should be replaced, and more than half of the nation's roads require major repairs. The future costs of water and sewage treatment are astronomical.

Despite the urgency of the needs, state and local governments have reduced their investment in infrastructure over the last decade. Financially strapped cities have increasingly chosen to delay new construction or repairs on existing facilities.

Before the accumulated effects of such postponements overwhelm us, we must strengthen the ability of state and local governments to respond to their infrastructure needs. Your ideas for encouraging such investments could be of great value to us.

HUMAN RESOURCES

Similarly, investment in human resources must be a central focus of a comprehensive investment strategy. Millions of potential workers now fail to find stable employment in the private sector. Some lack the most basic educational skills. Others, the victims of poverty and discrimination, are trapped in decaying inner cities. The available jobs are usually temporary, low-paying, and dead-end, and too often unlikely to offer a better standard of living than welfare.

We cannot rely on general economic improvement to remedy this underinvestment in human beings. We will need a combination of measures that upgrade workers' skills, provide relevant training, and lead to permanent jobs at reasonable wages.

This should not entail a proliferation of new government programs —or the steadfast retention of all existing ones. The poor track record of some CETA programs should prompt a search for better alternatives that result in lasting gains in employment and earnings. A well run public employment program could provide useful public services *and* worthwhile job experience for the hard-to-employ.

We lack effective methods of tapping the resources of private industry for our human investment programs. The current employment tax credit program is poorly designed, and few employers have bothered to use it. But surely, as part of an investment-oriented tax cut, we can look for ways to strengthen financial incentives for employment and training.

The current attack on the Trade Adjustment Assistance program should encourage us to consider more general ways to deal with worker dislocation, whether caused by trade or technological change. Instead of concentrating on income maintenance, such a program should explicitly encourage training or other actions that improve employability. We will need to experiment with different combinations of services, to learn just what government can do to smooth the adjustment process for workers. But the case for government involvement is a strong one. Good adjustment programs will reduce the pressures for ill-fated rescues of "losing" industries.

LABOR-MANAGEMENT-GOVERNMENT COOPERATION

The comprehensive approach I have outlined—combining investment in plant and equipment, research and development, public infrastructure, and human resources—should form the basis for a rational industrial policy.

In each of these areas, attention should be given to the special needs of the small business sector, typically the source of our most innovative and most rapidly growing industries.

The inner city ventures of the Control Data Corporation, for example, illustrate one promising way of making urban areas commercially attractive to small business. The company has enlisted public and private backing for its projects to establish business development centers in low-income neighborhoods. The centers provide training, computer, and mailing services, and other shared facilities that new businesses need, but often cannot afford on their own. When tried in St. Paul, Minnesota, such a center attracted dozens of new businesses which proceeded to grow rapidly. By addressing the specific impediments to small business growth, such public/private activities will accomplish much more than broad tax breaks intended to lure firms to economically distressed areas.

Government should be facilitating cooperative efforts by business and labor to improve productivity and foster industrial development. In scores of plants, labor-management committees have worked out solutions to specific industrial problems outside the scope of collective bargaining. Some of the more ambitious initiatives produced new training programs to alleviate skill bottlenecks; others led to the design of more efficient production processes. In communities such as Jamestown, New York, joint committees have encouraged these activities at the plant level and greatly strengthened labor-management relations. With modest government resources, we can assist a variety of labor-management initiatives and increase awareness of their achievements.

4.

LABOR'S VIEW OF REINDUSTRIALIZING AMERICA

Lane Kirkland

It is a coincidence, I suppose, that 100 years ago when the Wharton School was founded, the fledgling unions of the United States felt that they had better get together and organize a strong, central trade union federation, which they did in the same year, 1881, and in Pittsburgh.

Very shortly thereafter, a myth emerged that has been repeated to this day by men who ought to know better, and who assiduously preach the value of checking one's sources before one quotes. The myth is that when asked what labor wants, Samuel Gompers simply said, "more."

I want to give the exact quotation, which is the only one that he ever made from which that misstatement could possibly have been derived:

> What does labor want? It wants the earth and the fullness thereof. There is nothing too precious, there is nothing too beautiful, too lofty, too ennobling unless it is within the scope and comprehension of labor's aspirations and wants. We want more schoolhouses and less jails. More books and less arsenals. More learning and less vice. More constant work and less crime. More leisure and less greed. More justice and less revenge. In fact, more of the opportunities to cultivate our better natures, to make manhood more noble, womanhood more beautiful and childhood more happy and bright.

That was from a paper delivered before the International Labor Congress, Chicago, in 1893. And that is the only source of that observation.

We are concerned about the economic magic plan now being put forward by the new Administration. Many of our friends, who fought with us to establish many of the programs at risk today, are yielding to the old, old political doctrine that one should never kick a man when he's up. Our resistance to that Administration program goes back to the point that Gompers made. It is our apprehension that this program means less schoolhouses and more jails, less books and more arsenals, less learning and more vice, less constant work and more crime, less leisure and more greed, less justice and more revenge.

The AFL-CIO supports the proposition that inflation must be reduced; the number of jobs increased and the unemployed put back to work; that productivity must be improved, industrial strength restored, and Federal programs made more effective and efficient. America needs policies, including an industrial policy, that meet the nation's needs with fairness and equity.

During the seventies, the U.S. economy experienced extended periods of high unemployment, massive layoffs, and plant closings. The growth of the economy slowed, inflation increased, and our balance of payments worsened. These events would have been bad enough if they had been purely cyclical in nature, with the economy rebounding after a downturn. Underlying these setbacks, however, was a much more serious and enduring problem: the industrial base of the U.S. economy was in fact *eroding*.

During the seventies, the U.S. share of the world market for manufactured goods declined 23 percent, and our share of our own domestic market also declined. As a result of this deindustrialization, at least two million industrial jobs have been lost. There has been no *coherent* national policy to reverse this ominous trend.

Now, in the eighties, the need to reindustrialize the American economy has become widely acknowledged. There are, however, distinctly different concepts about how to do it.

One approach that is receiving almost faddish attention emphasizes removing the allegedly excessive burden that government places on the private sector. Its adherents call for general business-tax cuts and a reduced role for government in the economy. In other words, we should return to a more laissez-faire environment for business. Industries and regions that are experiencing economic difficulties would be left to sink or swim, their fate supposedly determined by the benign invisible hand of the competitive market.

This approach ignores the radical departure from the ideal competitive market that has taken place in the real world. Decisions of large firms to relocate abroad can have disastrous effects upon domestic industries and communities. Moreover, domestic firms increasingly face competition from foreign producers that are heavily subsidized by their governments.

We just do not believe that you can write off major industries in this country without paying for it dearly in the future. Nor do we believe that whole cities and regions of America can be allowed to decay, without serious social and economic consequences. It is the height of arrogance to talk in abstract, theoretical terms about letting certain industries disappear and then putting everyone else to work making microchips.

We feel it is important that the United States remain a diversified industrial nation, not one that just depends upon one or two industries or upon a so-called "service economy." I do not believe that our standard of living will or can be improved if we allow basic industries to erode, nor would the world be better off if each country simply specialized in the production of one kind of product. No other country has accepted that idea.

On the contrary, the countries that have been most successful in outperforming us economically have taken the opposite course of action. They have generally approached their economic problems with a coherent industrial policy, in which government, labor, and business all play key roles. Industries that are considered important to the nation's growth are not allowed to atrophy in order to demonstrate any doctrinaire faith in the theoretical principles of free market economics. New industries are often given government assistance, even though market conditions alone would prevent them from getting started.

It is clear that the success of foreign competitors has not resulted from a rigid adherence to the free market myth. On the contrary, they have accepted and responded to the need for a coordinated national industrial policy. Furthermore, they have recognized the importance of including representatives from labor, business, and government in the formulation of industrial policy. Instead of blindly clinging to economic prescriptions based upon an industrial structure that existed 200 years ago, we should adopt similar procedures in order to stem the erosion and begin the revitalization of U.S. industry.

But conservatives argue that all we have to do to achieve growth rates comparable to our foreign competitors is to cut taxes across the board. They argue that taxes are so burdensome here in the United States that the incentive to save and invest has diminished, thereby causing a long-term slowdown in economic growth.

This notion does not square with reality. As a proportion of gross domestic product, taxes in the United States amount to 30 percent. In France, they are 39 percent; in Germany, 38 percent. Yet these countries have achieved higher rates of growth. If there is a relationship between taxes and growth, it appears to be positive rather than negative, as the supply-siders would like us to believe.

While we are constantly bombarded with tales of the dire consequences of deficit spending, the truth is that from 1977 to 1979 the

United States had the lowest ratio of government deficit to gross domestic output of any of the 7 leading industrialized countries. For the United States, this ratio was 1 percent, while for Germany it was 3 percent and for Japan it was 6 percent.

Thus, the idea that we have grown more slowly than other industrial nations because of excessive taxes just is not true. A general tax cut is not the answer to our problems.

The track record of general business-tax cuts demonstrates that they are generally ineffective in stimulating investment or productivity. Despite several huge business tax cuts during the 1970s, including liberalized depreciation allowances, an increased investment credit, reduced corporate tax rates, and reduced taxation of capital gains, investment as a proportion of GNP remained substantially constant. In effect, businesses were being rewarded for doing no more than they would have done anyway. As a result, the corporate share of Federal budget receipts declined from 19.5 percent in 1969 to 14.1 percent in 1979, while corporate profits as a percent of GNP increased during this period.

The only assured result of across-the-board tax cuts is that corporate cash flow will increase. Instead of increasing capital investment here in the United States, businesses tend in practice to raise dividends, invest abroad, or purchase other companies.

Carefully targeted tax benefits may be appropriate tools for reindustrialization, but huge across-the-board tax cuts are not. For example, almost all of the benefits of the proposed 10–5–3 depreciation program would flow to big businesses which tend to be less labor intensive than small businesses. Almost one-fifth would go to oil companies and one-third to regulated utilities.

The proposed 10 to 18 year depreciation schedule for building, which does not approximate the actual useful life of buildings, is perverse incentive that is more likely to lead to disproportionate speculation in buildings than to modernization of equipment. By artificially stimulating the needless turnover of buildings, this scheme would only accelerate the movement of industries and jobs away from older regions of the nation.

Tax policy—if it is to be a tool for reindustrialization—must be structured in terms of precise and planned goals. It must be flexible and selective, not across-the-board.

In place of general across-the-board cuts in depreciation, we need a new, targeted program as part of an overall reindustrialization policy. To that end the AFL-CIO has proposed the creation of a tripartite National Reindustrialization Board—including representatives of labor, business, and the government—which would determine the amount and type of any tax incentive or accelerated depreciation allowance granted to any company on a case-by-case basis with some type of certificate of necessity. Investment credits would be made available only for increases in investment levels, and tax subsidies would be clearly targeted to industrial sectors and regions where they are needed.

This Board would also direct the activities of a financing agency, patterned after the Reconstruction Finance Corporation of the thirties and forties, which would be authorized to make and guarantee loans to finance approved reindustrialization ventures. Private pension funds should be permitted and encouraged to make investments in such financing arrangements to support and expand industrial employment in the United States.

A common thread that runs through the economies of countries that have grown faster than our own is their adoption of a coordinated industrial policy that systematically includes the views of labor, industry, and the public. By contrast, we have too long been at the mercy of a series of economic schools, each of which believes that it alone can see the unseen hand. It is time to take our economic life into our own hands, by dealing directly with our many concrete visible problems and sectoral and structural needs. It is time for the United States to formulate a national industrial policy and abandon the irrational attachment to laissez-faire policies that threaten to bring about the wholesale condemnation of entire industries and regions.

We also insist that, to succeed, any plan for economic recovery must be fair and equitable. But the Administration's proposed cuts in social programs will have a disproportionately large and negative impact on unemployed workers, on the poor, on the needy, at the very time that its proposed tax cuts will have a disproportionately large and beneficial effect on the rich, and on affluent and highly profitable businesses.

Add to this a deregulation policy that weakens the impact of laws protecting the consumer, the environment, and the health and safety of workers—and it is clear that the Administration's proposals do not meet the essential tests of fairness and equity in public policy. Nor will they achieve the goals of reducing inflation, creating jobs, improving productivity, and restoring the nation's industrial strength.

Rather, they require more sacrifice from those who have little, and they give more to those who already have much. They substitute unrestrained market power for social responsibility and human concerns. They short change sound economic growth and sound industrial policy by cutting back programs to achieve energy independence, to rebuild the nation's transportation system, to safeguard the environment, and to revitalize urban areas, along with other basic public investment programs that contribute to the nation's social and economic progress.

Let me turn now to some related questions: How are we to know whether funds allocated from pension reserves to the investment program that I have suggested will go to serve the most efficient undertakings in the country? I do not know how we can have that assurance today under the method that is now used to invest these funds. They are in the hands of corporate trustees, primarily and essentially the major banks, and the judgment as to what is efficient use of them and what is not is usually in the hands of a few men. I presume that it would still be in the hands of human beings, and human beings would still occasionally make mistakes. What I propose is that we establish a mechanism by which people can make sure that their pension money which is derived from their work, is set aside for their future, and heavily depends upon their being able to continue to work in this country—that such pension money will be used for the welfare of working people and for the welfare of the nation.

I cannot blithely accept the proposition that we can just write off the auto and steel industries. I think it is an arrogant man who says he can see the future 20 years from now as to whether we have enough steel production capacity, particularly if we do some of those things that this country ought to do in terms of finding energy alternatives. The steel demand in a real all-out synthetic fuels drive would be tremendous. I presume that the steel demand, if we really undertook to revive the coal ports, would be tremendous, and so also with adequate rail facilities. I think it is quite conceivable and probable within a very few years that we will be straining our capacity to produce steel. I do not believe in forecasting by taking a slice of time out of today. Our brethren from the forecasting profession have not done very well in the past, and I am not sure that I want to bank the future of this country on their predictions.

I also believe the automobile industry can turn around; I am not going to embrace the proposition that you can write off an industry that employs one out of six people in this country. The automobile is essential still to a continental economy where one of the real problems, in terms of employment and concentrations of unemployment and youth unemployment, is the simple fact that when a kid looks for a job with an employer, the first question he is asked is do you have a car and can you drive. This country needs an automobile industry. It must have one and it is all very nice to talk about letting Chrysler collapse, then you let Ford collapse, then you have one big giant company and then you have an antitrust issue trying to break up General Motors. All of these laissez-faire and tax gimmick solutions simply remind me of an old variation of Murphy's Law that all of our problems are created by solutions.

The AFL-CIO continues to support the basic concept of tripartite labor-business-government national industrial policy development, which I proposed last year. I was, to a degree, persuasive to the previous Administration on the establishment of a national reindustrialization board. One of the missions of this board would be creation of a financing agency which would be a channel for safe and useful pension fund investment, as well as other funds aimed to effectuate an industrial policy. The fate of a particular industry is, to a large extent, affected by the general level of economic growth and demand. Certainly it is also affected by the character of the competition and by the price of hiring the money. I suggest that it warrants examination at a time when we have the proposition put before us that the way to beat inflation is to hold down the price of hiring labor and increase the price of hiring money. I confess I never quite understood that. One thing I would certainly do is reverse the policy that is now being advocated as a cure to all of our ills—more Friedmanism and more money supply control and let interest rates run sky high. If we reversed these misguided policies, they would have a profound effect on industrial revival, help the housing industry, the auto industry, and help revive many of our basic industries. The housing industry is getting killed by high interest rates and tight money. I do not subscribe to the tight money proposition. At least it does not make sense to me to think that the cure of inflation is control the money supply. I had always thought that the aim was to balance the money supply and the supply of goods, but if, in the process of tightening and reducing the supply of money, you kill the production of goods, and that would put you well on the way to a downward spiral. The really important thing is whether money and goods are in balance.

We are killing the goose that lays the golden eggs. We are killing the housing industry and all its suppliers, including the steel industry. We don't have a ship building industry; we build very few American ships here. Railbeds are going to hell: There are sections of rail in this country where a freight train cannot go faster than 30 miles an hour without jumping the track and if that is not a concrete, finite, visible place to deal with the productivity question, I do not know where you are going to find it.

If we are going to do all these things, it is going to take a very high degree of public investment, I believe, and we are moving in the opposite direction.

I grew up in the South in a semirural area and I am not really receptive to the proposition that government is some sort of burden that is on your back. When I grew up, I remember, there were dirt roads one foot outside of the city limits, there was a paved main street in town and that was it. There were outdoor privies everywhere. You went to the well for your water one-half mile outside of town. You had kerosene lamps. If you had a farm, there was a gully on it about 80 feet wide and

50 feet deep and every time it rained it got about two feet wider and two feet deeper, and the land was being washed away. The Social Security system was the county poor farm. And all this existed and it was real and visible.

It was not private enterprise that stopped all those things. It was private enterprise that *did* all those things.

The kerosene was replaced by electricity from the Rural Electrification Administration. The roads were paved by a highway program. The gullies were cured and the land regained by the Soil Conservation Service. The poorhouse was wiped out by Social Security. And the basic ingredient of a big new industry in that part of the world was created by the Civilian Conservation Corps. Practically every pine tree that you see in that state was planted by the CCC. And now that is what the pulp and paper industry lives on. They are thriving on a product which is there because of having government on their backs.

So I think it is crazy to stop basic public investment. It does not make sense to abolish or curtail REA, curtail the highway programs, tinker with Social Security and undermine those public investment programs because they have a price. They also have a tremendous value in terms of a better, stronger economy and in terms of human welfare, human dignity, and human freedom.

★ ★ ★ ★ ★ ★ ★ ★ ★ ★ ★ ★ ★ ★ ★

PART TWO

POLICY AREAS

Capital Formation ☆ ☆ ☆ ☆ ☆ ☆

5.
STIMULATION OF
CAPITAL FORMATION:
ENDS AND MEANS

Marshall E. Blume, Jean A. Crockett, Irwin Friend[1]

This paper addresses the benefits and costs of governmental policies to stimulate capital formation. The potential benefits would derive from an improvement in the growth rate of productivity, and especially of output per unit of total input, which would permit growth in economic welfare and would aid in the effort to control inflation. The substantial rate of productivity growth during the 1950s and 1960s made possible the steadily rising standard of living which many Americans now expect. The dramatically lower growth rate of the 1970s cannot support these expectations. Wages have risen at rates far in excess of productivity gains, yielding workers little in the way of higher real income—except to the extent that the shares of other groups are thereby reduced—but contributing very substantially to the inflationary process.

The first section of this chapter places productivity growth in perspective as a factor contributing to the rise in living standards and discusses on a general level the costs of government intervention in terms of allocational efficiency, equity considerations, and those social benefits and costs which are not accurately reflected in the market place.

The second section discusses the recent trends in productivity growth, the factors which may have contributed to the sharp decline in the growth rate after 1973, and the extent to which this decline may be accounted for by a lower rate of capital formation. Empirical studies of the relationship between capital inputs and productivity, including new findings based on cross country data, are reviewed in order to clarify the potential of increased capital formation for increasing productivity growth. Reasons for the considerable differences in findings among various studies are explored, with particular reference to the concept of productivity used, the scope of the measure of capital inputs used, and the methodology for combining the various components of labor and capital into overall aggregates.

The third section reviews and evaluates alternative policies for stimulating capital formation, while the fourth section presents our conclusions.

1. BENEFITS AND COSTS

As previously indicated, the primary benefit of increased capital formation lies in its contribution to productivity growth, which in turn facilitates a rise in the standard of living and the control of inflation. Apart from productivity growth, there are few options open to us that can contribute jointly to these twin goals.

One such option may be the reduction of involuntary unemployment, which not only increases output but has other social benefits as well. However, the potential gain from this source is sometimes overstated, to the extent that the skills of the added workers are lower than the average for those already employed. Furthermore, it is not clear how reductions in unemployment below, say, 5½ or 6 percent can be achieved without accelerating an already unacceptably high rate of inflation. A second option, without much offsetting cost, is to eliminate fiscal disincentives to the entry or retention in the labor force of the elderly and the poor and to reduce market imperfections that limit employment opportunities for women and minorities. A third option, by no means costless, is the improvement of health care and safety, so that fewer hours of work are lost through illness, accident, or disability. Finally, it is possible that a reduction in personal income taxes might induce longer and/or more productive hours of work among the middle and upper income classes, but there is little substantive evidence to date to support the belief that this effect would be large or necessarily positive.

While options such as these, which serve to increase the total number of hours worked, can make some contribution to economic welfare, we remain primarily dependent on productivity growth for a substantial, sustained rise in living standards. The causes of productivity change are not simple; and capital formation, while important, is only one of them. Furthermore, there are large differences in the extent to which different types of capital formation contribute to productivity growth. Among the questions to be addressed are: (1) How much increase in productivity growth can we reasonably expect from a given stimulus to capital formation? (2) How does this depend on the type of capital formation stimulated? (3) What complementary policies may enhance the impact of stimulus to capital formation? Finally, we must consider the costs of government policies to stimulate capital formation and attempt to evaluate both the relative effectiveness and the relative cost of policy alternatives.

Apart from situations involving externalities, that is, situations in which the social benefits and/or costs of an activity differ from the private benefits and/or costs, it is generally accepted that overall economic welfare is reduced by any government intervention that distorts the free market allocation of resources among economic activities or between leisure and productive labor or between current and future consumption. In particular, the private benefits that influence the allocation of productive resources among alternative uses depend on after-tax returns, while the social benefits are related to before-tax returns. Thus, taxes which redirect the use of resources reduce economic welfare below its overall potential. Purely economic considerations must, of course, be balanced against social and political values and humanitarian considerations in the policy decisions of government. But taxes which affect the allocation of productive resources must be justified carefully in terms of externalities or of noneconomic gains.

In considering policies to stimulate capital formation, we are talking about the diversion of resources from current consumption of private or public goods in order to increase the potential for future consumption of such goods. We do not, however, begin from a free market situation, but from one in which the allocation of resources is already heavily influenced by government policies. The undoing of certain existing interventions may be more relevant to productivity growth than the introduction of new interventions.

In the first place, the overall tax rate (corporate and personal) on returns from equity capital is higher, except perhaps for the very wealthy, than on other types of income. This is particularly true in an era characterized by high inflation, unless the capital gains on equity implicit in the reduced real value of debt are sufficient to offset not only the loss in real value of liquid assets, but also any unfavorable tax effects.[2] The result is that individuals below the highest income brackets may contribute less to the provision of equity capital than they would if the tax disadvantage of income from such capital were reduced or removed. This is particularly important to the extent that equity capital is believed to be especially relevant for financing the kind of technological innovation that promises most for productivity growth.

In the second place, the favorable tax treatment of mortgage interest on owner-occupied homes, in combination with the failure to tax imputed income, reduces the cost of capital for residential construction relative to that for plant and equipment.[3] The result is that a higher proportion of the saving of the middle and upper-middle income classes may be channeled into residential construction, and a correspondingly lower proportion into corporate securities which finance business investment, than might otherwise be the case. But residential construction has little, if any, direct effect on the efficiency of any group of workers. While subsidies to improve the housing of the poor may well be justified on social grounds, it is more difficult to defend the present large subsidy to the housing of the middle class in these terms.[4] The tax deductibility of interest on consumer debt, in the absence of any income tax on the services of consumer durables, provides a similar kind of tax advantage and tends to divert resources into the production of consumer durables.

Third, it appears that regulations relating to environmental protection and worker health and safety are more stringent and thus more costly for new than for existing plants. This differential may have discouraged the retirement of inefficient plants and diverted business investment from areas with potential for large productivity gains into minor modifications of existing facilities that provide only marginal productivity gains. In this connection it is interesting to note that the major shortfall in capital formation after 1973 occurred in plant rather than equipment.

Thus, there are several reasons to believe that existing tax and regulatory policies significantly distort the free market allocation of resources. Policies to stimulate capital formation which operate to reduce such distortions are costless, and indeed beneficial, in terms of allocational efficiency, except to the extent that the existing distortions can be rationalized in terms of externalities. Policies which stimulate capital formation by techniques that further distort the free market allocation of resources impose offsetting efficiency costs.

In evaluating tax policy proposals, efficiency considerations must, of course, be balanced against equity considerations. A tax structure favorable to property income, while it can be expected to stimulate capital formation, also tends to increase the inequality of the income distribution, since the relatively wealthy receive most of the property income. Whether or not this redistributional cost is worth paying depends on the expected efficacy of the tax change in terms of promoting substantial and fairly certain improvements in productivity growth. For reasons indicated below, the reduction or elimination of the present tax disadvantage for income from equity capital might be expected to have especially strong implications for productivity. In view of the substantial amount of corporate stock which is now held by the retired, who have been particularly hard hit by inflation (in terms of income from sources other than Social Security), there might be equity advantages as well as disadvantages in such a change. Increases in the investment tax credit and in accelerated depreciation also may be expected to have relatively strong impact on capital formation per dollar of tax loss, but they fail to discriminate among investments in terms of potential for productivity gain and their implications for allocational efficiency are questionable, to say the least.

Any specific tax change should, of course, be evaluated in the context of the overall tax system. In principle, a properly orchestrated program of tax reform could stimulate productivity growth without reducing the share of low income workers in after-tax income or increasing the budget deficit. For example, a reduction in corporate plus personal taxes on equity income might be combined with reductions in Social Security taxes, which fall disproportionately on low income earners, and a limitation or cap on the tax exemption of mortgage interest on owner-occupied housing and of interest on consumer debt. Efficiency might then be improved, not only by directing additional resources into productivity-enhancing investment, but also by widening the margin between the after-tax earnings of workers with low skills and the benefits available to them from unemployment insurance, Social Security, or welfare.

Other trade-offs must be considered, as well, in evaluating policies to raise productivity. The social benefits of reasonably clean air and pure water and of safety from toxic wastes and job-related hazards must be weighed against the efficiency costs of government regulation. The special social value of housing services relative to other consumer goods must be weighed against productivity losses resulting from the tax subsidy to housing, which tends to divert into residential construction funds potentially available to finance business investment. The productivity loss from any reduction in government support of research, education, and transportation must be weighed against the productivity gains from capital formation stimulated by the tax cuts made feasible by these particular reductions in government expenditures.

2. RELATIONSHIP OF CAPITAL FORMATION TO PRODUCTIVITY GROWTH

Studies of productivity growth show a great deal of diversity, both in methodology and in empirical findings. There is general agreement, however, that growth in the 1970s was sharply diminished, as compared with the 1950s and 1960s; and this is true not only for the United States, but for industrialized countries generally. The year 1973 shows up as a convenient division point, in part for cyclical reasons. To the extent that the decline can be attributed to the somewhat slower rate of net capital formation observed after 1973, then the appropriate remedy would seem to lie in policies encouraging investment. To the extent that the results cannot be so explained, other complementary remedies may be required. Capital formation, however vigorously stimulated, may prove an inadequate tool.

HISTORICAL TRENDS IN PRODUCTIVITY

It is of some interest to investigate whether the seeds of the productivity slowdown were already apparent in earlier periods, suggesting that long-term forces were at work which accelerated rapidly in the 1970s, or whether a clear break in trend occurred early in the 1970s. The identification of shifts in the long-term trend is complicated by the strongly cyclical behavior of productivity measures. Traditional economics tells us that the marginal product of production workers falls in periods of excessive pressure on plant capacity. Observation of business behavior tells us that nonproduction workers are largely retained in their positions during cyclical declines of limited duration; and since they are underutilized, their marginal productivity drops in such periods. Empirical evidence clearly substantiates negative effects on productivity during recessions.[5]

Evidence is quite mixed as to whether some change in long-term productivity trends can be discerned in the period immediately preceding 1973. The years 1965–1972 were characterized by a generally high level of prosperity, in contrast both to the subsequent 1973–1978 period and to the preceding 1957–1964 period. The rate of growth in the capital stock was, if anything, unusually high by historical standards. However, the growth rate of the labor force was also unusually high, so that the capital-to-labor ratio grew relatively slowly. The most carefully detailed studies suggest that—with the notable exceptions of mining, public utilities, and construction—there was little evidence of any general decline in cyclically-adjusted productivity growth *within* industrial sectors before the early 1970s, especially if allowance is made for the change in age-sex mix of the labor force.[6] However, changes in the mix of demand among industrial sectors may also affect productivity growth, as normally measured; and these shifts appear to have been less favorable in 1965–1972 than in earlier post-World War II periods.[7]

If we search for events specific to the early 1970s that may have served to depress productivity growth in the years following 1973, a number of possibilities come to mind. The activities of OPEC are perhaps the most obvious. Second, the regulations relating to environmental protection and worker health and safety, which had been enacted in the late 1960s and early 1970s, were beginning to have a substantial impact by 1973.[8] Third, research and development expenditures ceased growing in real terms around 1969, remaining at or below the 1969 level for the next eight years.[9] In 1974–1975, the first major recession in many years produced a considerable psychological shock, perhaps conducive to risk-averse investment policies. The persistence of inflation, which had been accelerating since the mid-1960s,[10] became embedded in popular awareness, inducing a widespread upward revision in inflationary expectations, as well as widespread uncertainty about inflation, and generating behavior responsive to such expectations and such uncertainties. The long process of adjustment by which surplus agricultural labor found its way into more productive urban employment seems to have reached its end in the 1970s.[11]

At the same time the baby boom generation entered the labor market in rapidly increasing numbers, as did women workers of various ages.[12] Thus an abnormally high component of the work force was lacking in on-the-job training, an important component of labor efficiency. The postwar generation, while surpassing their elders in number of years of schooling, had been exposed to an educational regime that deemphasized certain basic skills highly relevant to economic performance. Furthermore, this was a generation that grew up in affluence, with very different attitudes toward both work and saving from those which the depression of the 1930s had impressed upon the age cohorts now reaching retirement.

In view of the above considerations, it seems unduly simplistic to attribute the striking decline in productivity growth after 1973 exclusively to the moderate reduction that occurred in capital formation. Similarly, it may be unduly hopeful to believe that the problem can be cured by sufficiently vigorous measures to stimulate investment.

EMPIRICAL STUDIES

How much of the decline in productivity growth of the 1970s can be attributed to the slowing of capital formation and—the other and more interesting side of the coin—how much improvement in productivity growth can we expect from stimulation of capital formation? Empirical findings from major studies are surprisingly diverse in their measurements of the growth rate of capital inputs, the growth rate of productivity and the contribution of the first to the second. However, none of the studies reviewed here indicated that more than half of the decline in productivity growth after 1973 could be accounted for by the decrease of roughly one percentage point per year that occurred in the growth rate of the capital stock. In most cases the empirical relationships implied that considerably less than half of the decline could be so explained.

Before examining several of the studies in detail, we consider some of the major differences in concept and in methodology that are responsible for the diversity of results.

First of all, three different concepts of productivity are used. The most common is the average product of labor, defined simply as the ratio of total output to total labor input.[13] A second concept is the marginal product of labor. This is the productivity measure most closely related to the economic welfare of workers, although it is less than satisfactory to the extent that market imperfections obstruct the achievement of equality between compensation and marginal product. The third concept is total factor productivity, defined as output divided by a value-weighted sum of labor and capital inputs. This is the concept most closely related to the economic welfare of society as a whole. All three measures are imperfect to the extent that they fail to allow fully for improvements in the quality of output or to take account of output that does not enter the market economy.

It is easy to see that capital formation may affect the three measures differently. For example, if we think of the housing stock as a capital good that produces housing services without complementary labor input, then a higher level of the housing stock implies a higher average product of labor, since total output is larger with no change in labor input. But neither the marginal product of labor nor labor compensation is affected, since no worker produces any more than he would have produced with a smaller housing stock.[14]

Restricting ourselves to those capital goods which are complementary to labor in the process of production, it is still not necessarily true that an increase in the capital to labor ratio will raise the marginal product of labor; and in the absence of any improvement in the quality of capital goods—that is, in the absence of technological advance—there is no reason to expect an increase in total factor productivity.

It is important to distinguish two cases in which the ratio of capital to labor rises. First, there may be a shift in demand mix that is favorable to capital-intensive industries. Such shifts apparently accounted for much of the growth in the average product of labor during the early postwar years; and the diminution or reversal of such shifts appears responsible for some of the subsequent decline in productivity growth thus measured. Once productive resources have adjusted to such a demand shift and producer equilibrium is reestablished, the marginal product and the compensation of labor of given skill will, of course, be equated across industries, and the change in demand mix will have reduced the overall demand for labor, while raising that for capital. Therefore the presumption is that (for any given labor supply) the marginal product of labor will fall, even though more labor is now allocated to industries in which its average product is high. While the marginal product of capital may rise, depending on long-run supply elasticity, there is not necessarily any effect on total factor productivity.

The second case of a rise in the capital to labor ratio involves a change of input mix within individual industries; and this should indeed lead to a rise in the marginal product of labor. In the absence of technological advance, such an increase represents a movement along a static production function, presumably induced by a shift in the relative prices of capital and labor inputs. As the marginal product of labor rises, that of capital declines; and while some redistributional effects may be expected, there is no reason to believe that total factor productivity or overall economic welfare will be increased.

Changes in overall economic welfare are predominantly related to changes in the quality of inputs, rather than their quantity, and to changes in organizational efficiency, including in particular the efficient allocation of productive resources among alternative uses. This suggests that we should be concerned with improving the quality (efficiency) of the capital stock and with its optimal allocation, rather than exclusively preoccupied with augmenting its quantity. We should reduce existing allocational distortions rather than create new ones. Since technological innovation is continually occurring, most new capital formation tends at the same time to raise the overall efficiency of the capital stock, but it is important to be aware that some kinds of investment have far greater potential than others for doing so.

Time trends in the quality of capital, reflecting technological advance, have been strongly favorable to the historical rise in living standards. Time trends in the quality of labor, reflecting education, skills acquired on the job, and worker motivation, have been generally favorable, although as indicated above, some recent developments may have had a negative impact. Time trends in the quality of the third major productive input, land, may be conveniently measured in terms of the magnitude of labor and capital inputs required to extract a given level of basic raw materials—mineral and agricultural—and to ensure a given quality of such natural resources as air and water, which are essential to human life and health. It is clear that these trends have now become a significant negative force, which was brought sharply to our attention in the 1970s.

It follows from the above discussion that movements in the average and marginal product of labor may diverge. In particular, the effect of any increase in the *quantity* of capital—as distinct from an improvement in its quality—will generally be to raise the average product of labor, but not necessarily its marginal product. Total factor productivity is not expected to be favorably affected by purely quantitative changes in the capital stock; and for this reason its growth rate has been lower historically than the growth of labor productivity.

A second major difference among the empirical studies reviewed lies in the extent to which quality changes in labor or capital are commingled with quantity changes in the measures of input growth used. If, in aggregating the various components of labor, different skill levels are weighted by rate of compensation, then an improvement in quality, represented by a shift of workers from lower to higher skill categories, will show up as an increase in aggregate labor input. For example, if a youth without job experience has a performance equivalent of 80 percent of that of an adult, while an adult with a college degree has a performance equivalent of 1.2 adults with no education beyond high school, and if labor input is measured by the number of adult high school-educated equivalents, then (for a given total of hours worked) an increase in the proportion of youths will reduce measured labor input, while an increase in the proportion of workers with college educations will increase measured labor input. Similarly, if weights based on the rate of return earned on various types of capital goods are utilized in measuring total capital input, then an improvement in the quality of capital, represented by an increase in the proportion of relatively efficient capital goods earning a high rate of return over cost, will show up as an increase in aggregate capital input. Clearly the greater the extent to which quality upgrading is incorporated in the measures of input quantity, the more rapidly will these input measures grow and—given the growth rate of output—the less rapidly will productivity measures grow.

Finally, the scope of both the capital measure and the output measure differs among studies, and this affects significantly both the growth rate of labor productivity and the impact of capital formation upon productivity growth.

At one extreme Denison (1979) measures output as national income in the private domestic non-residential business sector. Other authors prefer to use a gross output measure, although it is somewhat less relevant to economic welfare. Wachter and Perloff (1980) omit the farm sector, but include residential services. Kendrick (1980) includes both sectors, and Christensen, Cummings, and Jorgenson (1980) use the gross private domestic sector, including the imputed value of services of consumer durables (as well as new purchases of such durables) in their output measure. To reduce cyclical effects, Denison and Wachter and Perloff use "potential" rather than actual output.

Denison finds annual growth in average labor product to be 2.5 percent per year in 1964–1973, while Wachter and Perloff find it to be 2.6 percent per year for the 1965–72 period. Both studies use cyclical adjustments and apply efficiency weights in aggregating components of labor input. Kendrick finds a growth rate of 2.1 percent per year for 1966–73 without cyclical adjustment or internal weights for labor components. Christensen, Cummings, and Jorgenson find a rate of 1.7 percent for 1965–73, without cyclical adjustment and using weights for labor components that reflect educational level, but not demographic mix. Thus they obtain a larger growth rate for labor input (and a smaller growth for productivity) than they would have either by unweighted aggregation, or by using weights that reflect demographic mix as well as education. Denison has the narrowest output coverage, using net income in nonresidential business, while Christensen, Cummings, and Jorgenson have the broadest coverage, using gross private domestic business, including the imputed value of the services of consumer durables as well as housing.

For the post-1973 period, Kendrick finds the growth rate of average labor product declining to 1.1 percent per year in 1973–78, a drop of one percentage point. Wachter and Perloff find a growth rate of 1.2 percent for 1974–78, a drop of 1.4 percentage points. For marginal labor product they find a drop of 1.3 percentage points. Denison shows an extremely large decline for the 1973–76 period.[15] Christensen, Cummings, and Jorgenson do not present data after 1973. In spite of the differences among studies, it is clear that the growth rate of average labor product declined sharply after 1973 to an extremely low level.

At the same time the growth rate of capital inputs declined by about one percentage point, whether we use Denison's estimate for nonresidential structures and equipment or Kendrick's broader-based estimate. There are modest differences in level between the two studies. Christensen, Cummings, and Jorgenson (using a very broad concept), show close agreement with Denison's estimate of a 4.4 percent growth rate for the period preceding 1973, while Wachter and Perloff (using a concept fairly similar to Denison's) show close agreement with Denison's estimate for the period following 1973 (i.e., 3.1 vs. 3.3 percent per year).

We are now in a position to consider what the implications of the various studies might be as to the impact on average labor productivity of a decline of one percentage point in the growth rate of capital inputs, given the growth rates in other factors that actually occurred in the two periods under comparison.

Applying the simplest and most commonly used production function, the Cobb-Douglas,[16] it can be shown that the growth rate of output is a weighted average of the growth rates of the various factor inputs, with weights under producer equilibrium equal to earnings shares, plus a term reflecting those efficiency changes over time that are not incorporated in the input measures. The greater the extent to which efficiency weights are used in aggregating the components of labor and capital, the smaller the residual term will be, since improvements in input quality that represent a shift from lower to higher efficiency categories will be treated as an increase in input quantity. For any given growth rate in labor (and other) inputs, the impact on the growth in average labor productivity of a given change in the growth rate of capital inputs is the same as that on the growth rate of output itself and is simply equal to the earnings share of capital.

From Denison's study the earnings share of non-residential structures and equipment is about .11, in relation to net national income originating in the non-residential business sector. A decline of one percentage point in the growth rate of this relatively narrow concept of capital would thus imply a decline of only 0.1 percentage points in the growth rate of average labor product.

For a similar capital concept, the work of Perloff and Wachter (1979) implies an earnings share of about .20, in relation to gross private domestic non-farm product; but it should be noted that when *gross* output is allocated among productive factors, the share of capital is augmented by the inclusion of depreciation allowances and indirect business taxes imposed on the capital goods covered. A one percentage point decline in the growth rate of capital inputs now implies a decline of 0.2 percentage points in the growth rate of average labor product, but much of this lost output would have been required for additional replacement as the additional capital goods depreciated.

For a capital concept including residential structures, Kendrick's study implies an earnings share of almost 30 percent of gross private domestic product, suggesting that a decline of 0.3 percentage points in growth rate of average labor product would result from a decline of one percentage point in capital formation. But we have argued that the housing stock makes no direct contribution to marginal labor product, since complementary labor inputs are not utilized in the production of residential services. Thus the figure of 0.3 percentage points would appear to overstate the impact on the growth in marginal labor product and in the economic welfare of labor.

For a very broad concept of capital, including land and consumer durables as well as residential structures, Christensen, Cummings, and Jorgenson find an earnings share of a little over 40 percent, implying that a reduction of about 0.4 percentage points in the growth rate of average labor product would result from a drop of one percentage point in the growth rate of capital inputs. Since consumer durables and land, like residential structures, make very little contribution to marginal product of labor outside the farm sector, it must be assumed that the impact on the growth rate of marginal labor product would be considerably less than 0.4 percentage points.

As an addition to this body of time series results, a new analysis of a cross section of up to 16 countries was undertaken. The appendix to this report contains a detailed description of this analysis. Over the period from 1965 through 1978, growth rates in productivity were positively and significantly related to growth rates in capital, holding other relevant variables constant. Initial regressions indicated that a change of one percentage point in the growth rate of the capital stock was associated with roughly a 0.3 percentage point change in the growth rate of average labor productivity; but an adjustment for errors in variables raises this figure to 0.4. These results fall within the range derived from time series studies for the United States.

The best cross sectional relationships measure growth in capital by a linear regression upon time of the logarithm of net capital formation and hold constant not only the growth in the quantity of labor, but also the change in the quality of labor as measured by the difference between the growth rate of the labor force and the growth rate of the total population, a variable which has not previously been used in productivity studies. The argument is that if the labor force is growing at a faster rate than the total population, the new entrants are less skilled than otherwise.

We now combine the results of these studies to compare the late sixties and early seventies with the period beginning in 1973. We find that the decline of about one percentage point in the growth rate of capital inputs that is found by both Denison and Kendrick, using somewhat different time periods and somewhat different capital concepts, could be expected to account at most for a decline of 0.4 percentage points in the growth rate of average labor product and considerably less for marginal labor product. Yet the estimates of the declines that actually occurred in the growth rate of average labor product range from a minimum of one percentage point (Kendrick) to 1.4 percentage points (Wachter and Perloff), and a much larger figure is obtained by Denison for the cyclically depressed 1973–76 period.[17]

The clear indication is that the decline in growth rate of the quantity of capital inputs falls far short of explaining the events. It follows that the contributions to productivity growth of changes in the quality of inputs and/or in organizational and allocational efficiency must have been substantially curtailed. This view is supported by the estimated decline in growth rate of total factor productivity, which basically reflects quality factors not incorporated in input measures. Kendrick finds a decline of 0.8 percentage points or about one-half; Wachter and Perloff, who use a measure of aggregate capital based on quality weights, find a decline of 0.54 percentage points, or about one-third, cyclically adjusted; and Denison finds a negative growth rate for the 1973–76 period.

In terms of our primary interest in the contribution of capital formation to productivity growth, the data suggest that there may have been a shortfall, not only in the growth rate of capital inputs, but also in the effectiveness of investment in improving the quality of the capital stock. Further support for this hypothesis may be inferred from our cross sectional finding that differentials among countries in the growth rate of capital had a considerably weaker impact on differentials in productivity growth for the 1973–78 subperiod than for the 1965–72 subperiod. This suggests that the contribution of new investment to the quality of the capital stock may have been reduced quite generally in the later period, and not just in the United States.

There are several reasons to suppose that investment in the 1970s did less than might normally be expected to augment efficiency. First of all, a great deal of the new investment simply served to offset the depletion of natural resources. The inputs of capital and labor that are required to extract fuels and metals from the earth increase as low-cost sources of supply are exhausted, but these increments do not show up in larger final outputs. The investment required to implement energy conservation does not generate an increment in output. The investment required to maintain existing levels of air and water quality and safety from toxic wastes does not raise the level either of measured output or of economic welfare, more broadly defined.

Other capital expenditures may have increased welfare, without affecting output as presently, though imperfectly, measured. Such investment would include outlays that serve to safeguard workers from occupational hazards or that actually reduce pollution levels.

Government regulations to protect workers and the environment may have a further effect on productivity growth. Crandall (1980) points out that they may lead to the postponement of new projects, which are subjected to more stringent standards than existing facilities, making controls more costly. It therefore may become economical to keep older facilities in operation beyond the time when they might otherwise have been replaced. The impact of such delays in replacing old facilities falls primarily on that segment of investment which involves substantial technological innovation and which therefore may have the most to offer in terms of productivity gains. In this connection it is interesting to note that investment in plant in the 1970s slowed much more sharply than that in equipment. Uncertainty as to interpretation of the laws and indecision or reversed decisions on the part of regulatory agencies may have contributed to postponements.

Other factors in the 1970s may have had a particularly unfavorable impact on major investment projects involving substantially new products or techniques. The unsatisfactory performance of research and development expenditures after 1969 is one such factor. A second is the decline, actual or perceived, that may have occurred in the after-tax rate of return on equity capital. This may be an important consideration because risky projects tend to depend relatively heavily on equity financing, and highly innovative projects are subject to unusually large uncertainties.

With respect to research and development, overall growth in constant dollar expenditures essentially ceased after 1969, although expenditures financed by business and universities continued to rise slowly, offsetting the decline in Federal government expenditures. Griliches (1980) estimates that the growth rate in the stock of technologically significant knowledge generated by research and development expenditures and not yet fully exploited by embodiment in new capital goods was very much lower in 1973–77 than in 1960–65. Depending on assumptions, growth in the later period ranged from about one-half to one-fifth of the rate in the earlier period. The meaning of this decline in terms of productivity growth is extremely difficult to quantify, but clearly the implications for improvement in the quality of the capital stock are unfavorable.

With respect to the availability of equity capital to business, the accelerating inflation and widespread inflationary expectations of the 1970s may have tended to accentuate the unfavorable impact of a tax structure which favors debt relative to equity and favors housing investment and purchase of consumer durables relative to investment in plant and equipment.[18] Inflation reduces the real after-tax return on equity unless the capital gains implicit in the reduced real value of debt and the favorable tax effects associated with higher nominal interest payments are sufficient to offset fully both the loss in real value of liquid assets and the unfavorable tax effects of depreciation calculated on original rather than replacement cost and of inventory profit calculated on a first-in-first-out basis. For risky projects unable to obtain much debt financing, the net effect of inflation probably is to make equity investment less attractive and thus to make the funding of highly innovative projects more difficult. It may be noted that the cross country regression study mentioned earlier finds that the uncertainty of inflation has a significantly negative effect on productivity growth in the 1960s, though not in the 1970s.

A second effect of inflation in the United States, at least since the mid-1970s, has been to make housing an extraordinarily attractive inflation hedge for the middle and upper-middle income groups.[19] Capital gains are not taxable until realized, and then frequently at favorable rates.[20] Interest payments are deductible, offering some protection against bracket creep. Thus inflation has combined with tax policy to increase the incentives for investment in housing relative to investment in the financial assets that support plant and equipment expenditures. The high interest rates of the last two years, on the other hand, may have had a more unfavorable effect on housing than on business fixed investment.

For the reasons given above, it would seem to be a plausible hypothesis that the decline in growth rate for those capital projects that embody substantial technological innovation may have been considerably greater in the 1973–78 period than the overall decline in growth of capital inputs. If it is fair to assume that such projects have unusually high potential for enhancing the quality of the capital stock, then we might expect a shortfall to have occurred in the rate of quality improvement, reinforcing the deleterious effects of slower growth in the quantity of capital inputs.

In conclusion of this section, we return to the questions posed earlier:

(1) How much increase can we expect from a given stimulus to capital formation? It appears that, abstracting from improvements in the quality of the capital stock, an increase of one percentage point in the growth rate of capital inputs will produce at most an increase of 0.4 percentage points in the growth rate of average labor product, a considerably smaller increase in the growth of marginal labor product and probably no change at all in total factor productivity. However, most capital formation can be expected to produce some improvement in the overall quality of the capital stock, since new capital goods are generally more efficient in terms of measured output than existing capital goods. Any improvement in quality of capital will serve to augment the effects indicated above for a purely quantitative increase.

(2) How does the increase in productivity growth depend on the type of capital formation stimulated? Clearly the composition of new investment, broadly defined, is a primary determinant of the extent to which the quality of capital will be enhanced. Investment in housing (or consumer durables) makes little or no direct contribution to the efficiency of employed labor. Investment undertaken to preserve environmental quality or to conserve energy or other scarce raw materials, while it may be necessary to maintain present living standards, does not raise them. This is a case of running harder to stay in the same place. The potential for improving the quality of capital arises primarily from technological innovation that permits larger output for given input. Stimulation of investment in capital goods that embody such innovation will make the greatest contribution to productivity growth.

For purposes of affecting the composition of investment in a direction favorable to productivity, it would be useful to reduce the extent to which the tax structure penalizes equity financing of business and subsidizes housing investment and purchases of consumer durables. Such a change would be costless, and in fact beneficial, in terms of allocational efficiency, except to the extent that externalities associated with housing investment may be lost. Such externalities may be important for low income housing, but it is much harder to make a case for a massive tax subsidy to middle and upper income housing. Equalization of the tax rate on returns from equity capital with rates on other income would have a significant redistributional cost, in terms of its impact on the share of after-tax income received by workers in the lower half of the income distribution, a group already severely hurt by inflation and by the rapid increase in Social Security taxes. Other changes in the tax structure might be undertaken to mitigate this effect. In any case, careful consideration must be given to the trade-offs between efficiency and equity that may be involved.

(3) What complementary policies may enhance the impact of stimulus to capital formation? Clearly the stimulation of research and development activities should add to the availability of investment opportunities with a high potential for raising productivity, and thus should contribute to the rate of improvement in the quality of capital. Furthermore, to the extent that new plants are postponed because more stringent and more costly regulatory requirements apply than is the case for existing facilities, a more even-handed regulatory approach might improve the contribution of increased investment to the quality of the capital stock.

3. COST-BENEFIT ANALYSIS OF DIFFERENT ALTERNATIVES FOR STIMULATING CAPITAL FORMATION

The most common proposals for the stimulation of capital formation, especially plant and equipment expenditures, have included various forms of abatement of personal and business taxation, a reduction in government expenditures and regulation of business and an easing of monetary policy, though the last option in the present period of marked inflationary pressures would presumably require offsetting fiscal policy. To appraise the relative advantages of different tax changes obviously requires, first of all, an evaluation of the impact on new investment of a dollar of tax revenue foregone. However, different types of tax changes may also have significantly different consequences for two other policy objectives, economic efficiency and an equitable distribution of income, totally apart from their effect on the volume of capital formation. While we shall, in view of the orientation of this paper, pay most attention to the tax effectiveness of the various tax measures examined, we shall also discuss briefly their implication for economic efficiency and distribution of income. Subsequently, we shall consider the implications of other proposals for the stimulation of capital formation. It should be noted that measures to stimulate capital formation may impact quite differently the various forms of investment (such as type of plant and equipment, business inventories, housing, and so forth) and that the effect of increased capital formation on productivity will depend on the particular form that investment takes.

Prior to engaging in a fairly rudimentary cost-benefit analysis of proposed changes in tax and other government policy, it should be emphasized that in view of the state of the art, the margin of error in quantifying the economic effects of changes in policy is extremely large. Frequently, the judgments or estimates which have been made in the literature have been based on incomplete theory (that is, without adjustment for uncertainty effects on optimization behavior) or questionable reliance on econometric models (that is, where insufficient attention is paid to the inadequacies of a limited number of aggregate time-series observations for distinguishing among alternative explanations of econometric interrelationships).

In the following analysis, we shall use three different sources of information to examine the likely impact of changes in government policy on the economy, with particular reference to capital formation. These include theoretical models appropriately modified by empirical evidence wherever possible, a wide range of econometric models which, unfortunately, frequently lead to dramatically different conclusions, and surveys of business officials and market investors designed to elicit how the respondents would react to specified changes in government policies. None of these sources of information is very satisfactory, but jointly they may help to illuminate the range of likely outcomes.

WAYS IN WHICH GOVERNMENT POLICY MAY AFFECT CAPITAL FORMATION

The various fiscal and monetary measures which have been proposed to stimulate capital formation would be expected to operate either through changes in the propensity to save, or the propensity to invest, or both. Theoretically, the propensity to save of any economic unit might be affected by government policy impacting disposable income, after-tax rates of return on assets, and the market value of net worth, while the effect of policy on the propensity to invest would depend on the way it impacts the marginal efficiency of investment and the cost of capital. In less than perfect markets, the saving of any economic unit might also depend on its investment opportunities, and similarly its investment might be partly dependent on its own saving.

If it is assumed that the totals of government taxes and expenditures are held constant, the primary way changes in policy may affect saving and investment is through their influence on the after-tax rates of return and cost of capital (which also may affect the market value of net worth). However, though the direction of the effect on investment of an increase in the after-tax rates of return or a reduction in the cost of capital to business which might be brought about through appropriate policy is unambiguous, this is not true of the effect on saving of a change in after-tax rates of return on assets.

While for many years it has been realized that the effect of a change in real interest rates on saving and consumption[21] depends not only on a "substitution" effect (which is positive for saving and negative for consumption), but also on an offsetting "income" or "wealth" effect, it has only been in the past decade or so that the relative importance of these two effects has been rigorously related to measurable characteristics of households' utility functions. There is fairly strong evidence that the assumption of constant relative risk aversion is, as a first approximation, a fairly accurate description of the utility function of a representative household or of the market place, with a Pratt-Arrow measure of relative risk aversion well in excess of one.[22] The implications of such a utility function for the combined "substitution" and "income" effects of a change in interest rates on savings is of particular interest.

It has been shown under certain simplifying assumptions that with constant relative risk aversion the relative size of the "substitution" versus "income" effects of changes in interest rates on saving will depend on the magnitude of the Pratt-Arrow measure of relative risk aversion.[23] If it is higher than one, the total or combined effect is negative; if less than one, the effect is positive; and if equal to one, there is no effect. It may help to understand this result if we observe it implies that a high risk averter (relative risk aversion over one) will increase present consumption more with a decrease in the riskiness of return than for a corresponding increase in expected return. This is so since a high risk averter prefers a steady flow of consumption at a lower level than a more erratic flow at a higher level.[24]

Since the empirical evidence points to an overall measure of relative risk aversion of well over one, theory might seem to indicate that saving is negatively related and consumption positively related to changes in real after-tax interest rates—a result opposite to that implied by classical economics. However, when taxes are introduced into the analysis, the theoretically expected effect on household saving of changes in real after-tax interest rates associated with changes in personal income taxes will depend not only on the magnitude of relative risk aversion, but also, among other things, on the differential impact of taxation on income from different sources and on whether households consider as part of their wealth the capitalized value of future transfers from the government. Moreover, a change in personal taxes affects personal disposable income and therefore is likely to affect both personal consumption and saving in the same direction, so that the relevant question from the viewpoint of the personal sector is how the change in taxes would affect the allocation of personal disposable income between saving and consumption. The nature of this allocation again depends on the magnitude of relative risk aversion and other factors. Thus, the results implied by theory depend on a number of assumptions, and these may or may not be warranted.[25] The underlying theory is referred to here mainly to emphasize that there is no theoretical presumption in favor of the classical result.[26]

Empirical studies of either household or private saving, which includes corporate saving, have been inconclusive as to the direct effect of real after-tax interest rates or rates of return on the propensity to save. Some studies of U.S. times-series data point to statistically significant negative effects, some statistically significant positive effects, and still others to no discernible effect.[27] In unpublished research which we have carried out, we experimented with a number of real after-tax interest rate series, different periods, different saving specifications, and instrumental variable as well as simple least-square solutions. Our conclusion was that the estimated interest rate was at least as likely to be negative as positive. The specific relationship depended particularly on the interest rate series used, and there were no strong reasons to assume that one series was better than another.

Sometimes, the higher household saving-income ratios in a number of foreign countries with lower tax burdens on individuals than in the United States are cited as evidence that a cut in individuals' tax rates would stimulate saving. However, no comprehensive study of the determinants of international differences in saving behavior, including tax effects, has been carried out, reflecting the difficulty of obtaining reliable information on and holding constant the relevant economic and noneconomic variables across different countries. The occasional attribution of the substantially higher household saving rate in Japan than in the United States to the difference in their tax burden seems difficult to justify even on the basis of casual empiricism, since the only noteworthy difference in the comparative taxes on individuals in these two countries seems to be their different treatment of capital gains.[28] While the absence of a capital gains tax in Japan might help to explain a relatively greater demand for common stocks, it would not be expected to have a substantial impact on total household saving, and even the effect on net stock accumulation should be limited in view of the relatively moderate effective (as distinguished from nominal) capital gains tax in the United States, estimated in recent years to be about 5 percent.[29]

More relevant casual empirical evidence on the impact of taxes on household saving than supplied by the usual type of international evidence would seem to be provided by the long-term historical data in the United States. Not only do these data avoid some of the problems associated with international comparisons, but they cover periods of major change in effective personal tax rates from relatively negligible to very high levels. In spite of this change, the ratio of personal saving to personal disposable income showed little secular variation from the early 1900s to the period after World War II.[30]

Thus, neither theory nor the available data provide a satisfactory basis for determining the sign or magnitude of the direct effect on saving of an increase in after-tax real interest rates which might stem from a decrease in personal income taxes applicable to property income.[31] Yet, it is our judgment, on the basis of all the evidence, that the effect is likely to be small. Similarly, in a theoretically rigorous uncertainty model, it is not possible to state what effect such a decrease in taxes, and the associated change in real interest rates and after-tax real rates of return, would have on the market value of assets which directly affect savings.[32] On the other hand, while there is no strong reason for anticipating that higher real after-tax interest rates would generate much additional savings, a reduction in personal income taxes might be associated with a positive effect on the cost of equity, and therefore a negative effect on the propensity to invest, and hence perhaps on realized saving and investment.[33]

Of course, even with the totals of government taxes and expenditures held constant, there is another potentially significant way in which changes in government tax policy might affect total private saving, namely, through the effect of such changes on the distribution of income between individuals and corporations and among different socioeconomic groups of individuals. Corporations have a substantially higher propensity to save than individuals, so that lowering the relative burden of taxes on the corporate sector would tend to raise the overall propensity to save. A rise in the corporate saving-income ratio will probably be partly offset by a decline in the household saving-income ratio, reflecting lower direct saving by stockholders, but, except perhaps in the very long run as higher corporate saving is associated with higher household wealth, it is unlikely that the offset will be anywhere near complete.[34] Similarly, while there is considerable dispute as to the relationship between the average and marginal household propensities to save, we expect that an increase in total household saving would result from a shift of after-tax income from wage earners to recipients of property income,[35] both because of the direct effect of income levels on the saving-income ratios and because people with higher assets at a given level of income may have accumulated these assets through a greater propensity to save. A given change in the burden of taxes as between corporations and individuals (for example, increasing personal taxes proportionately and applying that increase to offset a proportionate decrease in corporate taxes) would probably have a substantially larger effect on total saving in the short run, and perhaps even in the long run, than a comparable change among different groups of individuals.

The one other government action which could favorably affect the total propensity to save is a marked reduction in government expenditures. The effect on the saving propensity would obviously be greatest if not associated with a reduction in taxes. However, even with a compensating reduction in taxes, the total saving propensity would be raised significantly, since the private sector has a much greater propensity to save than the government.[36]

As distinguished from the difficulty of substantially increasing the overall propensity to save,[37] it is much easier to increase the propensity to invest through a wide variety of fiscal and monetary measures and changes in other government policies which adversely affect investment decisions. Thus, a reduction in the taxation of corporate income, whether this took the form of lower income tax rates, liberalized depreciation allowances, or investment tax credits, would obviously increase the after-tax marginal efficiency of new investment and probably also reduce the cost of capital.

Several other kinds of government action may affect investment favorably. First, a reduction in government regulation of business, particularly in the form of mandated investment, would also increase the marginal efficiency of new investment, especially in plant and equipment. Second, decreased government expenditures, in addition to the effect on saving noted above, would reduce the government's demand for funds and lower the cost of capital. Lower government spending would also alleviate inflationary pressures which have raised business risk, lowered real earnings, and may have increased the real cost of capital.[38] A monetary-fiscal policy mix which combined relatively easy monetary policy with low government expenditures and relatively high taxation (especially of the nonbusiness sector, if the objective is to stimulate business investment) would also lower the cost of capital.

The relative advantages of the different approaches to the stimulation of saving and investment will be considered in a subsequent part of this paper. We should emphasize here, however, that our interest is in the stimulation of capital formation, not of saving or investment propensities *per se*. It seems reasonable to assume that the way in which many proposed changes in government policy can appreciably affect aggregate investment and saving under present circumstances (and probably the foreseeable future), when the national income and utilization of labor and capital resources are well below full employment levels, is likely to depend more on its impact on the inducement to invest than on the propensity to save. The personal saving-personal disposable income relation is likely not to be very sensitive to moderate changes in the valuation of assets, and even less so to moderate changes in the rate of return on assets.[39] However, given the level of inflation, the relatively high cost of capital (at least in nominal terms) and the disruption in the capital markets, the problem of financing this additional investment through additional saving is likely to be more of a constraint on investment than would normally be true in a recessionary period. Measures to increase corporate saving and, even more important, to cut the government deficit, could be used to finance an increase in private capital formation.

In the long run, we believe that the sum total of corporate, personal, and government saving propensities, which are considerably less sensitive than investment to the rate of return on financial assets, will largely determine the level of capital formation. This is especially true if reasonably full-employment conditions are maintained. Thus, to stimulate capital formation in the long run would probably require measures directed at promoting the propensity to save. Again it would appear easier to accomplish this through measures designed to increase corporate, and especially government, saving rather than household saving, though in the long run the effect of an increase in corporate saving on household saving is not altogether clear. Both in the long run and short run, different measures to stimulate saving or investment will, of course, impact differently the various forms of capital formation, with policies designed to affect saving behavior likely to have more uniform effects across the various forms of capital formation than policies initially directed at investment behavior.

While the discussion thus far has emphasized the difficulty of increasing total saving and investment in the long run through many of the fiscal and monetary measures which have been proposed, it should be noted that it would be easier to stimulate one form of capital formation at the expense of another. Thus, if growth and related social policy considerations dictated a substantial reorientation of new investment out of housing and consumer durables and into plant and equipment, this could be accomplished by appropriate government policies directed at the relative profitability and cost of financing of these two forms of capital formation.

ABATEMENT OF PERSONAL VERSUS BUSINESS TAXATION

On the basis of the preceding discussion, there is no substantial reason for expecting that a reduction in personal income taxes, even if directed disproportionately to recipients of property income, would have a significant effect on the households' saving-income ratio or overall investment-income ratio, except perhaps through the effect of such changes on redistributing income from the lower to upper income groups.[40] Reductions in personal income taxes which are proportional to income, thus maintaining the current degree of progressiveness of the after-tax income distribution, would probably have very little effect on the saving or investment propensities of households. It would seem that only to the extent that the personal tax structure is changed so as to make the after-tax income distribution less progressive or more regressive[41] would the aggregate propensity to save be increased, and even then the effect would be minimal, according to economists who believe in permanent or life cycle theories of consumption.

Apparently, the main economic justification for lowering personal income tax rates would have to be based on considerations other than aggregate capital formation, such as the effect of income incentives on increasing the supply of labor, or the effect on economic efficiency of equalizing tax rates on different types of income or economic activity, or stimulating one type of capital formation at the expense of another. The effect of income incentives on the supply of labor is still controversial, though a strong positive relationship has been adduced by "supply-side" economists.[42] There is probably more general agreement among economists about the qualitative gain in allocational efficiency that would result from equalizing tax rates on different types of income, so that the tax structure would be neutral with respect to production decisions.

Thus, it would appear that a reduction in business income taxation is generally likely to be more effective in stimulating capital formation, at least on plant and equipment,[43] than a corresponding reduction in personal income taxation. This may be especially true in an inflationary environment in view of the much higher saving propensity of business organizations and the adverse impact of inflation on investment decisions.[44] While changes in personal income taxes do not appear likely to affect appreciably the aggregate propensity to save or invest, differential changes can have substantial effects on saving or investment in specific forms such as saving in common stock[45] or investment in plant and equipment. Though substantial attention has been paid, especially by the financial community, to the potential utility of changes in capital gains taxation as against other tax changes for stimulating stock prices and plant and equipment expenditures, no definitive results are available.[46] Even if the level of plant and equipment expenditures is not affected appreciably, however, a reduction in capital gains taxation might be associated with a significant increase in allocational efficiency.

GENERAL CORPORATE TAX REDUCTION VERSUS DIRECT CORPORATE TAX INCENTIVES

Apart from a reduction in personal income taxes, the new Administration in Washington has seemed to favor a marked liberalization of depreciation allowances as the other major change in tax policy for encouraging capital formation. In this section, we shall consider the tax effectiveness of this approach to the reduction of corporate taxes relative to other approaches which have frequently been proposed, including notably investment tax credits and a general reduction in corporate income tax rates. In the long run, as suggested earlier, an increase in the ratio to national income of corporate capital formation, which consists of plant and equipment and inventories, would largely depend on either increasing the national propensity to save, or diverting capital formation from housing or consumer durables in the household sector to investment in the corporate sector. Generally, as previously mentioned, any decrease in the burden of taxes on corporate income at the expense of income tax rates in the household sector will increase the overall propensity to save, in view of the relatively high saving propensity of the corporate sector. The type of investment in the corporate sector whose stimulation is of most interest is, of course, plant and equipment expenditures.

Turning now to the effect on the propensity to invest in plant and equipment of a reduction in corporate income taxes through the different approaches which have been suggested, most econometric models indicate that investment tax credits are more effective per dollar of tax revenues than accelerated depreciation and more effective still than corporate income taxes.[47] However, the range of estimates among models is extremely large, with a number of models indicating very little effect of any of these approaches.[48]

Another potentially valuable source of insight into the likely differential effects of these different tax changes comes from surveys of business firms. In perhaps the most comprehensive and recent of these surveys, conducted by the Rodney L. White Center for Financial Research in early 1980,[49] all corporations listed on the New York Stock Exchange were asked to estimate what effect five different tax changes would have upon the future level of their plant and equipment expenditures, assuming that in each case the dollar amount of their Federal tax liabilities was reduced by 10 percent.[50] The tax changes considered were a decrease in corporate taxes on income paid out as dividend income, a general decrease in corporate taxes, a permanent increase in the investment tax credit, an extension of the permanent increase in the investment tax credit to buildings, and liberalization of depreciation methods. It should be noted that in view of lags in the investment process, the responses on the impact of these tax changes on plant and equipment expenditures are probably best interpreted not as initial-year effects, but as average annual effects in the future (until the new optimal level of capital stock is achieved).[51]

Corporate officials indicated that in their judgment, the most effective of these tax changes for purposes of stimulating their plant and equipment expenditures was liberalization of depreciation methods, followed closely by a permanent increase in the investment tax credit and a general decrease in corporate taxes. An extension of a permanent increase in the investment tax credit to buildings was judged to be somewhat less effective, with a decrease in corporate taxes on income paid out as dividends considered the least effective of these changes. For the largest NYSE corporations, the liberalization of depreciation methods and a permanent increase in the investment tax credit were both considered more effective in stimulating business capital formation than a general decrease in corporate taxes, but again a general decrease in corporate taxes was only moderately less effective. The other tax changes do not appear to be as effective for the largest NYSE corporations as for the smaller listed companies.

The most surprising result is that a general decrease in corporate taxes is estimated to be nearly as effective in stimulating plant and equipment expenditures both for the largest and other NYSE corporations as a permanent increase in the investment tax credit or the liberalization of depreciation methods. The greater apparent effectiveness of the liberalization of depreciation methods over permanent increase in the investment tax credit, at least for the smaller NYSE corporations is also somewhat surprising, but it may reflect to some extent the favorable prospects for this type of legislative action.

It should be noted that while corporate officials may be able to estimate with some precision the relative size of the direct effect of different types of tax changes on their investment behavior, they may find it more difficult to gauge appropriately the indirect effect of these changes on their cost of capital. As a result, they may understate somewhat the overall effectiveness of a decrease in corporate taxes on income paid out as dividends, if in the period in which the tax change was instituted investors preferred dividends to retained earnings.

The actual level of the increase in plant and equipment expenditures which respondents indicate would be associated with a 10 percent reduction in their Federal income tax liabilities would be on the order of 7.7 percent of their annual fixed investment outlays if the reduction in taxes took the form of liberalization of depreciation, moderately less if the reduction in taxes took place as a result of a permanent increase in the investment tax credit, and somewhat less still with a general decrease in corporate taxes. A 10 percent reduction in Federal income tax liabilities of all U.S. corporations would have amounted to $9.3 billion in 1979, while a 7.7 percent increase in corporate plant and equipment expenditures would have amounted to $14.7 billion.[52] A 7.7 percent increase in gross plant and equipment expenditures amounts to a substantially higher increase of 35 percent in net expenditures, which represent additions to the productive stock of capital. However, this increase in net expenditures represents only about a 1 percent growth in the corporate gross stock of plant and equipment and less than a 2 percent growth in the corporate net stock.[53]

It is possible of course that, while there is no obvious reason for any important bias to enter into the respondents' estimates of the relative size of the effect of different types of tax changes on investment behavior, their estimates of the actual level of tax effects might be biased upward. On the other hand, the estimate of a roughly $1.50 increase in plant and equipment expenditures associated with a $1.00 permanent increase in investment tax credit is of the same general order of magnitude as indicated in a different type of survey conducted in the fall of 1979 based on a much smaller sample. In that year the prospects for this type of legislative action did not seem favorable, since the Carter administration seemed to be advocating that any reduction in taxes on capital formation take the form of integration of corporate and personal dividend taxation.[54] Moreover, the indication that a $1.00 reduction in corporate taxes as a result of increased investment tax credits would generate $1.50 of plant and equipment expenditures is intermediate between the lower effect implied by the Wharton econometric model and the higher effect implied by the Hall-Jorgenson model, but closer to the latter.[55] It should be noted that the model effects used hold constant the general level of business activity, so that any induced effects on capital investment of change in overall business activity associated with the tax changes are not reflected. It is quite likely that such induced effects would not be reflected in the survey responses.

For most size and industry groups, there were no significant differences in the impact of the different tax changes on corporate plant and equipment expenditures. Two exceptions might be noted, however, even though they are not particularly surprising. The utilities indicated they would be much less affected by these tax changes than other corporations, presumably because the public utility commissions set utility rates largely on the basis of after-tax rates of return. Also, as might be expected, the fixed capital investment of wholesale and retail trade firms would be much more favorably affected than other industry groups by extension of the investment tax credit to buildings, since a relatively high proportion of their fixed capital formation takes the form of structures.[56]

Our assessment of all the econometric models, survey data, and theoretical considerations leads us to conclude that from the viewpoint of stimulating plant and equipment expenditures, direct corporate incentives either through an increase in the investment tax credit or liberalization of depreciation methods are likely to be more effective per dollar of tax revenue than a general decrease in corporate income taxes. However, since the differences between these measures and a general decrease in corporate taxes is not very large, and a reduction in corporate tax rates would have less distortionary effects, it is not clear that any one of these different approaches to corporate tax reduction is to be preferred over the other. Our survey data as well as some of the econometric models suggest a $1.00 reduction in taxes either as an investment tax credit or in the form of liberalized depreciation will be associated with more than a $1.00 increase in plant and equipment expenditures, though the evidence is by no means conclusive.

Before leaving the subject of the efficacy of different ways of reducing corporate income taxes, it should be noted that all of them imply, in the absence of other changes in the tax structure, an increase in the inequality of the income (and wealth) distribution among different households.

NON-TAX IMPEDIMENTS TO CAPITAL FORMATION

In addition to tax effects, the most important impediments to plant and equipment expenditures, according to the 1980 survey of NYSE corporations cited earlier, are inflation, cost and availability of external financing, government regulation, and inadequacy of profits and internal funds. Cited somewhat less commonly were unsound fiscal and monetary policy (especially high government spending), inadequate depreciation allowances, uncertainty (mainly about future needs and about the economy), inadequate private saving, and a miscellaneous category that included a wide range of more specialized problems. Clearly, many of these reasons (for example, taxation and inadequate profits, inflation and the high cost of financing, and the like) are not independent of each other.

An attempt was made to quantify roughly the effect of two of these other impediments to capital formation, inflation and government regulation. According to the survey data, a halving of the inflation rate from the 10.5 percent annual average rate expected by the sample firms over the next five years would increase real plant and equipment expenditures by roughly about 6.0 percent. In those instances where the respondents indicated an effect of reduced inflation on prospective plant and equipment expenditures, about the same number attributed the effect of reduced inflation to its impact on the cost of financing as to its impact on uncertainty of sales, prices, wages, and profitability. The effect of changes in the inflation rate on real capital outlays was not substantially different between the largest and small NYSE corporations, though for the largest firms this effect was somewhat more likely to operate through the cost of financing than through uncertainty.

Changes in government regulation are the last of the impediments to business capital formation for which the survey attempted to obtain the estimated impact of specified changes in present policies. When the NYSE corporations were asked "If all government regulations either requiring or significantly affecting your plant and equipment expenditures were nullified," how their "*total* plant and equipment expenditures would change from what they would have been otherwise," the net effect on total investment was estimated to be only of the rough magnitude of 2 percent.

However, when the question was changed to ask "How would your new level of plant and equipment expenditures compare with the level of *nongovernment-mandated* plant and equipment expenditures that would have been made?", the effect is more substantial, with the net effect on nonmandated fixed investment estimated at roughly 5 percent. Since the total level of expenditures on plant and equipment in 1979 is estimated at $258 billion, at that level of expenditures the increase in *total* real fixed capital outlays by U.S. business associated with the elimination of government regulations affecting such outlays is estimated to amount to about $5.2 billion annually in the near future, while the increase in *nonmandated* outlays may approximate $12.9 billion annually. The $12.9 billion figure is of course more relevant to the effect of higher outlays on increased productivity as usually measured.

The effects of government regulations on plant and equipment expenditures described above operated mainly, as might be expected, through the effect of regulations already enacted on the expected profitability of new investment. However, it is interesting to note that the uncertainty as to the potential effects of future regulation on profitability of current investment also played a significant role in deterring plant and equipment expenditures.

The types of government regulations specified most often as deterring nonmandated capital outlays were environmental regulations largely administered by the Environmental Protection Agency. Such regulations were mentioned in 43 percent of the responses. Next in importance were safety regulations, mainly under the aegis of the Occupational Safety and Health Administration, which were mentioned in 22 percent. No other single type of regulation was referred to by a high proportion of the respondents.

There was only one noteworthy difference among the different industry and size groups in the relative impact of government regulations on plant and equipment expenditures. The petroleum companies indicated that elimination of such regulations would have a very much greater stimulating effect both on their nonmandated and total capital outlays than was true for corporations generally. Largely as a reflection of the large size of the petroleum companies, the capital expenditures of the largest corporations as a group appeared to be somewhat more sensitive to government regulation than the corresponding outlays of the smaller companies.

Obviously, measures to restrain inflationary pressures and to curtail government regulations (especially EPA and OSHA) would have significant, if not major, desirable effects on capital formation. Restraining inflation would facilitate business planning and cut down on the riskiness of investment and the cost of capital, thus stimulating capital formation and enhancing allocational efficiency. If an excessive braking of economic activity is avoided, costs would be minimal. Clearly a curtailment of government regulation of business does involve some real costs, but it is our belief that significant curtailment is possible without excessive cost.

One important, though perhaps not entirely surprising, conclusion that emerges from these responses by corporation officials on impediments to capital formation, as well as from most other careful analysis, is that while public policy can stimulate plant and equipment expenditures, the results of any single policy action are not likely to be dramatic. It will require a comprehensive program embracing a wide range of public policy measures to bring about a major increase in the stock of plant and equipment. Such measures would probably have to include some form of business tax incentives to encourage plant and equipment expenditures, some relief from regulatory restrictions on business, and perhaps most important some relief from inflationary pressures and the associated uncertainties.

4. CONCLUSIONS

The preceding discussion in this paper and the analysis on which it is based lead us to the following conclusions:

(1) Any feasible increase in capital formation brought about by appropriate changes in government policy is likely to make only a

moderate contribution to productivity. However, even a moderate contribution to productivity would be highly useful, both for its desirable long-run effect on the standard of living and its favorable effect on future inflation. Policies which stimulate plant and equipment expenditures are likely to have more effect on productivity than those which stimulate other types of investment, and certain types of plant and equipment outlays may be especially effective both for enhancing productivity and furthering other social objectives.

Moreover, some policies which encourage plant and equipment expenditures—for example, a decline in corporate income taxes, particularly if it is not targeted to specific capital outlays—are likely to increase allocational efficiency in view of the relatively high rate of double taxation applicable to income generated by corporations. Such an increase in allocational efficiency might be expected to raise productivity totally apart from the impact of higher capital formation.

(2) It is possible to raise significantly the realized level of aggregate capital formation in the short run by policies designed to stimulate the propensity to invest. However, in the longer run an appreciable rise in the level of capital formation as a whole would depend on policies favorably affecting the propensity to save. Any long-run stimulation of investment in one form (for example, plant and equipment expenditures) would require either stimulation of saving as a whole or constraints on investment in other forms (such as housing or consumer durables).

(3) There is no convincing scientific evidence that the propensity to save by the household sector of the economy can be raised by increasing after-tax rates of return through appropriate tax policy. In other words, saving does not appear to be very sensitive to real after-tax interest rates, and even the direction of the interest rate effect is not at all clear. (Of course, saving in a specific form is sensitive to the rate of return it offers as compared to rates of return in other forms).

(4) However, there is one government policy which would have a highly favorable effect on the overall propensity to save, and that is a marked reduction in government expenditures. A reduction in government expenditures without a reduction in taxes would reduce government dissaving, while reduced expenditures offset by reduced taxes would shift disposable income to the private sector, which has a much higher propensity to save.

(5) Apart from reduced government expenditures, other measures which can increase the level or productivity of investment in plant and equipment, both in the long run and short run, include a decrease in the tax burden on corporate income, some relief from regulatory restrictions on business, and other policies designed to provide some relief from inflationary pressures and the associated uncertainties. The

two most effective corporate tax changes for purposes of stimulating plant and equipment outlays for a given reduction in government revenues appear to be an increase in the investment tax credit and liberalization of depreciation allowances. However, a general decrease in corporate taxes would also stimulate corporate capital outlays and, though probably not as effective in raising plant and equipment expenditures as those tax changes directly tied to such outlays, would be expected to be more effective in improving the economy's allocational efficiency.

(6) While in theory it would be possible to increase capital formation by an appropriate mix of changes in monetary and fiscal policy holding government expenditures constant (for example, a combination of easier monetary policy and higher taxation of personal income), this is hardly a practicable alternative under present or foreseeable circumstances.

(7) Though changes in fiscal policy, specifically a decline in government expenditures and a reduction in corporate income taxes, appear to be the most promising approach to the stimulation of capital formation, and especially plant and equipment expenditures, they do raise one major problem—the effect of such changes on the distribution of income and wealth.

A very substantial reduction in corporate income taxes without other changes in the personal tax structure would significantly increase the inequality in the distribution of personal disposable income and wealth. As an offset, it might be desirable to cut down on personal taxes, not by an across-the-board proportionate reduction in personal income taxes, but by a cut in income or other taxes, or changes in tax subsidies, targeted to benefit more heavily the lower end of the income distribution. More extensive changes in the tax structure, such as the institution of some system of graduated consumption taxes, might be useful in helping to maintain a balance between equity considerations and saving incentives.

Similarly, a very substantial reduction in government expenditures could impinge adversely on important social programs and affect the poor more heavily than the rest of the population. Clearly it will be necessary to ensure that reduced government spending does not have an undesirable effect on the truly needy, but we believe that major cuts in the budget can be carried out within this constraint. Such cuts might well include not only substantial cuts across the board in most government programs (including those involving guaranteed loans), but also a more realistic indexing of government and Social Security pension payments and a moderate increase in the Social Security retirement age.

A basic assumption which underlies the goal of increasing the capital stock is that increases in the capital stock generate increases in productivity, but as documented earlier, there is considerable debate as to how much the growth of capital stock contributes to increases in productivity. The purpose of this appendix is to examine a cross section of countries to provide further insights into the validity of this assumption and, anticipating that there is a positive relationship, to measure its magnitude. In addition, this section will attempt to determine whether there were any substantial changes in this relationship over the period from 1965 through 1978, a period which includes the dramatic increase in the price of energy, the escalation of inflation, and the floating of exchange rates. Finally, this section will examine whether the relationship between capital growth and productivity growth in the United States differs in any substantial way from the relationship in other countries.

The Model: The empirical work will be undertaken in the context of a generalized version of a Cobb-Douglas production function. Further work should examine other types of functions. Specifically, it will be assumed that output X is a function of the capital stock K and labor L of the form

$$X = A \, K^{a_0 + a_1 g_K} \, L^{\, b_0 \, + \, b_1 g_L} \tag{1}$$

where A is a function of time; a_0, a_1, b_0, and b_1 are constants; and g_K and g_L are respectively the growth rates of the capital stock and of labor. If a_1 and b_1 were zero, (1) would reduce to the usual Cobb-Douglas production function, where a_0 is the elasticity of output with respect to capital and b_0 is the elasticity of output with respect to labor.

The more generalized form of the production function as given by (1) allows the exponents of K and L to vary with the growth rates of capital and labor. (These exponents can be interpreted as elasticities.) It might be hypothesized, for instance, that a rapidly growing economy will have, on average, newer production facilities than a less rapidly growing economy. Everything else equal, newer facilities would embody the more recent advances in technology. In addition, a growing economy may find it politically easier to shift resources away from declining industries. A positive value of a_1 would be consistent with this hypothesis as well as numerous others. For reasons of symmetry, the exponent of L was made a function of g_L.

A finding that a_1 was positive would indicate that a competitive equilibrium in the capital and labor markets would not necessarily be socially optimal if business did not recognize the impact of new investment upon the aggregate growth rate of output in calculating the benefits

Stimulation of Capital Formation

of this investment. Put another way, if externalities were associated with capital accumulation, private decisions by themselves would not be expected to lead to socially optimal decisions, and it would be the appropriate role of the government to determine through the political process the socially optimal growth rate of capital. If, however, a_1 were zero, the desirability of altering the capital growth rate from its competitively determined level would have to rest on some other argument.

To estimate the parameters of (1) over a sample of countries would require that all the domestic currencies be converted to a common currency. Since converting all currencies to a common base is fraught with potential difficulties, it would be desirable, if possible, to avoid having to make such a conversion. It turns out that (1) can be converted into another form which does not require such conversions.

To highlight the productivity role of capital, divide (1) by L to obtain

$$\frac{X}{L} = A \, K^{a_0 + a_1 g_K} \, L^{b_0 - 1 + b_1 g_L} \tag{2}$$

Taking the time derivative of (X/L) and dividing by (X/L) yields

$$\frac{d \frac{X}{L}}{\frac{X}{L}} = \frac{\frac{\delta A}{\delta t}}{A} + (a_0 + a_1 \, g_K) \frac{\frac{\delta K}{\delta t}}{K} + (b_0 - 1 + b_1 \, g_L) \frac{\frac{\delta L}{\delta t}}{L} \tag{3}$$

or

$$g_{X/L} = g_A + a_0 g_K + a_1 g_K^2 + (b_0 - 1) g_L + b_1 g_L^2, \tag{4}$$

where g_Y is defined as $(\delta Y / \delta t)/Y$.

In regression form, (4) was estimated over a cross section of countries using Organization for Economic Cooperation and Development data covering the years 1965 through 1978 to estimate the relevant variables. It should be noted that in estimating (4) there is no need to convert domestic currencies to a common currency. For purposes of examining the stationarity of the coefficients, the overall period was divided into two subperiods: 1965–1972 and 1973–1978.[57] The year 1973 was the year in which energy prices began their dramatic increase, inflation rates escalated, and the flexible exchange rate regime was fully instituted. Thus, if there were substantial nonstationarities in the parameters of (4), this division might be expected to highlight such changes. Depending upon the time period and the specific variables used, the number of countries ranged up to 16.

Two primary measures of productivity were used: The first was the ratio of real national income to the number of persons in the civilian labor force. This measure is similar to the usual measures of productivity, except that some authors replace real national income by real GNP, or the civilian labor force by the number of hours worked. The results using real GNP were not much different from those based upon real national income, and thus these results will not be reported here. Since the number of hours worked was not available by country, we were unable to determine the sensitivity of the results to the substitution of this series for the civilian labor force. Finally, national income, as well as all series in local currencies, was converted to real terms using the deflator for the gross domestic product.

The second measure of productivity was the ratio of real national income to the total population, or per capita real national income. This measure reflects the material well being of society as a whole and, at least under one set of circumstances, may even reflect the output per unit of labor input more accurately than the first measure. For instance, consider a household of two persons with one employed spouse. The other spouse, while not technically employed, may provide substantial service to the working spouse which facilitates his or her productivity as conventionally measured. This second measure would properly attribute two units of labor input for the real national income generated by the household. Now, if the second spouse decided to join the labor force, the first spouse would lose some support services, perhaps reducing somewhat the real national income generated by his or her efforts. Moreover, if the second spouse were no more, and perhaps less, skilled than the first, the entry of the second spouse into the work force would cause a decline in the value of the first measure of productivity. Such a decline would be interpreted as a decrease in productivity, when in fact the family unit is producing more for the same labor input.

Although this second measure of productivity can be justified as being more accurate than the first in the above situation, it can certainly be criticized in that it treats the unemployed infant or retired person as if he or she provided the same support services to a working person as the unemployed spouse. What this discussion suggests is that there are conceptual problems with both measures of productivity. Therefore, theoretical considerations alone cannot dictate which measure is the preferable one. In cases like this, it is useful to run the empirical tests using both measures and to let the data determine which provides the better fit.

Finally, the growth rates of each of these productivity measures, as well as the civilian labor force and the total population were estimated. Specifically, the logarithms of each of these annual series were regressed on time to yield estimates of the continuously compounded rates of growth. Separate estimates of the growth rates were obtained for the overall period 1965–1978 and for each of the two subperiods.

The growth rate of the capital stock was estimated in three different ways, none of which is fully satisfactory. The first was by a linear regression upon time of the logarithm of net capital formation, which was defined to include increases in stocks. The continuously compounded rate of increase in net capital formation would equal the growth rate of the capital stock if the age distribution of the capital stock remained unchanged. If the average age of the capital stock were increasing (decreasing), this measure would tend to understate (overstate) the growth rate of the capital stock.[58]

The second was the ratio of the annual net capital formation to capital consumption or economic depreciation, averaged over the relevant sample period. The assumption in this measure is that the capital stock is a constant multiple of the annual level of economic depreciation, an assumption which is similar to the assumption underlying the first measure.

A third measure estimated the growth rate of the capital stock in year t as the ratio of net investment in year t to the sum of net investment over the 10 prior years. The assumption here is that the ratio of the sum of the 10 prior years of net capital formation to the total value of the capital stock is constant over time.

Preliminary work indicated that the second and third measures had little if any explanatory power. In regressions of productivity growth on measures of labor growth and either of these last two measures of capital growth, the R^2s adjusted for degrees of freedom ($\bar{R}^2$s) were often negative and, in comparison to the regressions using the first measure of productivity, always considerably smaller. For example, for the overall period, the $\bar{R}^2$s were at most one-third of the $\bar{R}^2$s for the regressions involving the first measure. Thus, the reported regressions will be based upon the first measure of capital growth.

The growth rates of the first measure of productivity, which was defined as the ratio of national income to the civilian labor force, were regressed upon the growth rates of capital, the growth rates of the civilian labor force, and these rates squared. Separate regressions were calculated for the overall period and for each of the two subperiods. In no case did the squared terms significantly improve the fit of the regression.[59] This result is consistent with the hypothesis that growth itself does not shift the production surface of an economy. Likewise, the squared terms in the regressions of the growth rates of the second measure of productivity on the growth rates of capital, the growth rates of total population, and these rates squared did not significantly improve the fit of the regressions. This second measure of productivity was defined as the ratio of national income to the total population.

In view of the insignificance of the squared terms, only the linear forms of the regressions will be analyzed in depth. Table 5–1 contains the various regressions of the growth rates of productivity on the growth rates of the capital stock and on the growth rates of population. The $\bar{R}^2$s are quite large for cross sectional analyses. In the overall period and in either of the subperiods, the $\bar{R}^2$s are greater when the quantity of labor input is defined as the civilian labor force: for the overall period, the $\bar{R}^2$ is 0.80; for the 1965–1972 period, 0.93; and for the 1973–1978 period, 0.67.

An examination of the residuals for each of the regressions disclosed no extreme residuals. This result suggests that the functional relationship between capital growth and productivity growth in the United States did not differ in any substantial way from the relationship in other countries.

Although the fit using the civilian labor force appears better than the fit using the total population, the coefficients on the growth rate of the civilian labor force are troublesome. For example, the coefficient for the overall period is -1.071. This coefficient can be interpreted as the elasticity of productivity growth with respect to the labor force growth. Taken at face value, this coefficient of roughly -1.0 would imply that a 10 percent increase in the civilian labor force would lead to a 10 percent reduction in productivity or output per unit of input. The net result would be no change in national income.

In contrast, the coefficients on the growth rate of labor input in regressions using total population as the measure of the labor input are insignificantly different from zero. If the coefficients were in fact zero, an increase in the population would lead to no change in productivity and thus real national income would increase as the population increased—a more plausible result. Yet, as measured by $\bar{R}^2$, these regressions do not fit the data as well as those which utilized the civilian labor force as a measure of labor input.

One explanation of the peculiar results using the civilian labor force is that the quality of labor is not being held constant. Such a possible effect has already been discussed. A potential measure of this change in quality is the growth rate in the civilian labor force less that of the total population. When this variable is included, the troublesome coefficients on the growth rate of the civilian labor force become insignificantly different from zero, regardless of the time period or the explicit measure of labor input (table 5–2). The negative coefficients on this difference variable in the regressions using the civilian labor force appear to be quite large in absolute value. Part of the explanation may be that the increase in the labor force over that which is due to population growth may represent part time, and possibly less skilled, workers; so that this difference in growth rates may overstate the true increase in the quantity of labor supplied.

In these expanded regressions, which include the growth rate of the labor force less the growth rate of the total population, many of the coefficients and t-statistics are the same regardless of the measure of productivity. The reason is that there is a mathematical relationship between the sets of regressions.[60] Nonetheless, this mathematical relationship would not force the coefficient on the growth rate of the civilian labor force to approach zero.

For the purpose of this paper, it is interesting to note that there are no substantial changes in the coefficients on the growth rate of capital when either this difference variable, or a wide array of other variables are added. The additional variables that entered significantly will be discussed below.[61] The relative stationarity of these coefficients on capital growth suggests that any measurement error in the growth rate of capital is not strongly correlated with potential measurement errors in the other variables in the regression. If so, the classic errors in variables model would hold as a first approximation and the coefficient on the growth rate of capital would be biased towards zero, suggesting that the regressions would understate the true effect of capital growth. Thus, the coefficients on the growth rate of capital should probably be interpreted as minimal values.

For the 1965–1978 period, the estimated coefficient on the growth rate of capital was 0.304 in the regressions that included as a variable the differences in the growth rates of the civilian labor force and the population. The growth rates of capital are obviously measured with error, which would generally lead to a bias in the estimate of 0.304. If the standard error in measuring the growth rates of capital were .015 or 1.5 percentage points, a very rough adjustment would imply an unbiased estimate of 0.4.[62]

As already mentioned, the estimated coefficients on the growth rate of the civilian labor force in the regression of the growth rate of productivity, defined relative to the civilian labor force, on this variable and on the growth rate of capital were implausible for the overall period 1965–78 and the second subperiod 1973–78. If the civilian labor force measured the input of labor with an independent error, there would be induced a negative correlation between the measurement errors in the growth rate of productivity and the growth rate of the civilian labor force. Moreover, if as a first approximation, the growth rates of the capital stock and the labor input were uncorrelated, the large negative coefficients on the growth rate of the civilian labor force could be rationalized as consistent with a standard errors-in-variables problem. When a variable measuring the quality of the labor force was added to the regressions using the civilian labor force, the estimated coefficients on the growth rate of the civilian labor force took on plausible values and the fit of the regressions improved.

In magnitude, the coefficients on the growth rate of the civilian labor force, holding constant the quality of the labor input, are roughly of the same size as the coefficients on the growth rate of the total population in the regressions which used this measure of labor input, whether or not the quality of labor is held constant. Theoretical considerations discussed above suggest that the civilian labor force may measure labor input with more error than the total population. If the labor force were growing through part time, and perhaps less skilled, workers, the differences in the regressions using the two different measures of labor input would be consistent with these theoretical considerations. Taken at face value, the estimated coefficients imply that, holding the growth rate of capital and the quality of labor constant, the level of productivity is unaffected by the growth rates in labor.

Probably of greater significance is the potential nonstationarity of the parameters of this model. Thus, for 1965–1972 period, the coefficient on the growth rate of capital is 0.482; but in the later 1973–1978 period, the coefficient drops to 0.167. Likewise, the coefficient on the quality of labor variable decreased from -0.634 to -0.934 over the same period. The coefficient on the growth rate of the labor force is insignificantly different from zero in both periods. A formal test of the changes in the value of these two coefficients from the 1965–1972 period to the 1973–1978 period indicated that the changes were statistically significant.[63] Moreover, this particular division of the 1965–1978 period is associated with the greatest change in the coefficient on the growth rate of capital. Using any other year end from 1969 to 1974 to divide the overall period leads to a smaller estimated change.

The final analysis carried out for this study was to determine whether, holding constant the growth rates of capital and labor as well as the quality of labor, there were any statistically significant relationships between the growth rate of productivity and some other variables which might, on a theoretical basis, affect the growth rate of productivity. Of the variables examined for the 1965–1972 period,[64] only the standard deviation of the annual rate of inflation, as measured by the gross domestic product deflator, was significantly related to the growth rate of productivity, holding constant the other relevant variables. The coefficient on this variable was -0.63 with a t-value of -3.85.[65]

The standard deviation of inflation in this period ranged over the countries analyzed from a low 0.007 to a high of 0.031. This range implies an expected difference of 0.015 or 1.5 percentage points in the growth rate of productivity between the country with the least uncertainty as to inflation to the country with the most uncertainty, everything else constant. Of the variables examined for the 1972–1978 period, the annual ratio of the number of farm workers to the total civilian labor

TABLE 5–1
Regressions of the Form *

$$g_{X/L} = a + bg_K + cg_L$$

DEFINITION OF L	DATE	a	b	c	$\bar{R}^2$
A. Civilian Labor Force	1965–1978	0.032 (8.25)	0.378 (4.83)	−1.071 (−4.67)	0.80
	1965–1972	0.023 (7.39)	0.507 (11.71)	−0.393 (−2.83)	0.93
	1973–1978	0.030 (7.87)	0.184 (3.89)	−1.096 (−5.25)	0.67
B. Total Population	1965–1978	0.024 (5.59)	0.332 (4.67)	−0.283 (−0.06)	0.69
	1965–1972	0.018 (4.40)	0.436 (10.63)	0.405 (1.16)	0.88
	1973–1978	0.023 (6.37)	0.148 (3.85)	−0.209 (−0.54)	0.49

NOTE: t-values are given in parenthesis below the respective coefficients.

*See text of Appendix for explanation of symbols.

TABLE 5–2
Regressions of the Form

$$g_{X/L} = a + bg_K + cg_L + d\triangle g$$

Where $\triangle g$ Is the Growth Rate of the Civilian Labor Force Less the Growth Rate of the Total Population

DEFINITION OF L	DATE	a	b	c	d	$\bar{R}_2$
A. Civilian Labor Force	1965–1978	0.024 (6.68)	0.304 (5.09)	0.258 (0.61)	−1.77 (−3.41)	0.88
	1965–1972	0.020 (4.86)	0.482 (9.74)	0.019 (0.04)	−0.634 (−1.04)	0.93
	1973–1978	0.025 (6.37)	0.167 (4.09)	−0.293 (−0.77)	−0.934 (−2.37)	0.76
B. Total Population	1965–1978	0.024 (6.68)	0.304 (5.09)	0.258 (0.61)	−0.518 (−2.47)	0.75
	1965–1972	0.020 (4.86)	0.482 (9.74)	0.019 (0.04)	0.385 (1.52)	0.89
	1973–1978	0.025 (6.37)	0.167 (4.09)	−0.293 (−0.77)	−0.227 (−1.22)	0.51

NOTE: t-values are given in parenthesis below the respective coefficients.

force, averaged over these years, was positively related to the growth rate in productivity, holding constant the other growth rates, but the t-value was only 1.82. All other variables had smaller t-values.[66]

In sum, this new empirical analysis is consistent with a positive relationship between the growth of productivity and the growth of capital over the 1965–1978 period. However, it appears that following 1973, the increment to productivity from an increment to capital has declined. This decline in the contribution of new capital to productivity appears to be a world wide phenomenon and not just a problem confined to the United States. Further work is required to determine the reason for this decline.

NOTES

1. Marshall Blume had primary responsibility for the Appendix of this study, Jean Crockett for sections 1 and 2, and Irwin Friend for sections 3 and 4.

2. The calculation of depreciation on original rather than replacement cost and of inventory profits on a first-in-first-out basis lead to unfavorable effects of inflation on corporate taxes. Tending to offset these is the favorable tax effect associated with rising nominal interest payments.

3. This point is well known in the housing literature, but may not be as widely recognized elsewhere. To illustrate with a numerical example, consider an individual with $50,000 which he may invest either in stock in a corporation with a debt-equity ratio of 1 or in a home worth $100,000, which he would occupy subject to a $50,000 mortgage. In the absence of distortions due to the corporate and personal income tax structure (and abstracting from differences in risk), we would expect that in equilibrium the net rental value of the house, after depreciation and property taxes, would equal the net earnings before interest on $100,000 worth of plant and equipment owned by the corporation, say $16,000. If the yield on debt is 12 percent, the return to the investor would be $10,000, either from investment in corporate stock or from investment in the house (after payment of $6000 in mortgage interest).

Now consider what happens to after-tax returns under a tax structure such as ours. For convenience, we assume a 30 percent effective corporate tax rate (after allowing for the favorable tax effects of accelerated depreciation and the investment tax credit) and an investor in the 50 percent income tax bracket. If the investor buys stock, his share in earnings after corporate taxes is $7000 and he would receive $3500 after personal taxes with 100 percent payout. His after-tax rate-of-return would be 7 percent in this case; or with 100 percent retention he

Stimulation of Capital Formation

could earn 14 percent, but in the form of retained earnings, not cash. If he invests in the house, he receives a service flow worth $16,000, less $3000 after taxes in mortgage interest payments. With property taxes of, say, $2000, he receives a further tax saving of $1000, for an after-tax return of $14,000, or 28 percent. In equilibrium, the after-tax rates-of-return must, of course, be equalized. Thus the share of plant and equipment in the asset mix must fall until its relative before-tax yield is high enough to eliminate the differential in after-tax rates-of-return. This may involve substantial allocational inefficiency.

Apart from tax effects, other types of government policies may have important implications for investment in housing. Historically, the Federal Housing Administration and Veterans Administration programs and the housing programs of the early 1960s were favorable factors, while more recently the excessive dependence on restrictive monetary policy to control inflation has had clearly unfavorable effects.

4. It is also possible that there may be favorable indirect effects of improved housing on labor quality, although there is little hard evidence to support this for the United States.

5. Nordhaus (1972) finds statistically significant cyclical effects on labor productivity in six of the twelve industrial sectors he studied. Gollop and Jorgenson (1980), using a much finer industry break, find much lower growth rates of total factor productivity for a number of industries in the depressed years 1957–60 than in other subperiods of the 1947–73 time span studied. Sixty percent of the 45 industries analyzed showed negative productivity growth in this period. Denison (1979), using aggregate data, finds no change between 1948–64 and 1964–73 in potential (i.e., cyclically corrected) output per unit of total input, but a considerable decline in actual output per unit of total input.

     6. Denison (1979), pp. 92–93; Nordhaus (1972), p. 506; Wachter and Perloff (1980), p. 120.

     7. Nordhaus (1972), p. 517.

     8. Crandall (1980), p. 93.

     9. Denison (1979), p. 123.

10. The acceleration during the 1970s may have been due to several factors, including sharp increases in energy prices, poor world harvests in particular years, and the floating of exchange rates.

11. There appears to have been a disequilibrium that persisted over many years, in which the marginal, as well as the average, product of labor was lower on the farm than elsewhere.

12. The growth rate in number of persons aged 16–24 rose from 0.48 percent per year in 1965–72 to 7.53 percent per year in 1972–78. (Wachter and Perloff [1980], p. 119, ff.)

13. Labor input may be measured as (1) number of hours worked,

either unweighted or weighted by level of skill; (2) number of hours paid for, which leads to understatement of improvements in efficiency by failing to take account of the rising trend in paid holidays and vacations; or (3) number of persons employed, which leads to understatement of improvements in efficiency by failing to take account of the rise in the proportion of part time workers and the decline in the length of the standard work week.

14. This abstracts from long-run indirect effects in which the quality of labor might be improved by better housing.

15. This was a depressed period in which cyclical effects on productivity appear to have been unusually strong, so that Denison's cyclical adjustment may have failed to eliminate them fully.

16. It should be noted that the Cobb-Douglas production function is more plausible for homogenous industries than for aggregates of industries that are highly diverse in capital intensity and other characteristics.

17. Kopcke (1980), in comparing the period 1950–65 to the period 1965–78, attributes half of the decline in the average product of labor to slower growth of capital, especially non-residential structures. However, he subtracts unutilized capacity (as estimated from Federal Reserve Board data for manufacturing), as well as capital for pollution abatement, from his measure of the capital stock. This measurement technique must produce a considerably larger estimate of the decrease in growth rate of the capital stock after 1973 than the one percentage point found by Denison and by Kendrick. See Denison's comments on Kopcke's paper.

18. Even in 1970, it may be noted that the value of housing stocks plus stocks of consumer durables was much higher relative to the value of plant and equipment for the United States than for such other highly developed countries as Canada, Germany, Japan, the United Kingdom, France, and the Netherlands, according to the data developed by Christensen, Cummings, and Jorgenson (1980). Of the countries they studied, only Italy had a marginally higher ratio than the United States.

19. A cross sectional analysis of family behavior since 1970 by H. S. Rosen (1979) suggests that the proportion of households owning homes would fall by more than 4 percentage points and the amount of housing consumed by homeowners would fall by about 15 percent, if the favorable Federal income tax treatment of owner-occupied housing were eliminated. Patric H. Hendershott finds that the user cost of owner-occupied housing for an individual in the 30 percent tax bracket fell from about half of that for corporate structures in 1964 to less than one-tenth in 1978. (Research Summary in the *NBER Reporter*, Spring 1980, p. 5). In this connection it is interesting to note that in constant

dollars residential construction as a percentage of non-farm plant and equipment expenditures rose from 36.2 percent in 1965–1970 to 40.7 percent in 1971–1978. The increase in residential relative to non-residential structures was still larger, since the decline in growth was much sharper for plant than for equipment during the 1970s. The figures are, of course, even higher for the 1950s, when a period of unusually high demand for residential construction was generated by the combination of (1) a housing shortage built up over nearly two decades in which family formation considerably exceeded the number of dwelling units constructed and (2) the availability of favorable financing terms under the VA and FHA programs.

20. Capital gains on owner-occupied housing are likely to be more attractive to middle and upper-middle income groups than capital gains on corporate stock for several reasons: (1) Once a specified age has been reached, $100,000 in capital gains on one's house can be realized without tax liability, while stocks must be held until death if capital gains taxes are to be avoided completely. (2) Rollover provisions are more flexible for housing than for stocks. (3) Capital gains on stock represent in part a return of capital reinvested in the corporation through retained earnings. No such prior reduction in the return available for immediate use is involved in capital gains on housing. (4) Capital losses are considerably more likely to occur on stocks than on housing, at least in terms of the record of the last 15 years. This may lead unsophisticated investors to feel that the capital gains component of their return on housing is less risky than the capital gains component of their return on stock. On the other hand, greater diversification is possible through stock ownership, although to approach the maximum tax shelter, stockholders may be locked into their more successful stocks for many years and this tends to limit portfolio diversification.

21. It should be noted that net investment in consumer durables is normally considered in economic theory as saving rather than consumption. One reason for this is the very high degree of substitutability between durable expenditures and other forms of saving (See Friend and Jones [1960]). However in the U.S. national accounts, all expenditures on consumer durables are included in consumption. In this paper, the treatment of consumer durables will be made explicit whenever it is important to do so.

22. Friend and Blume (1975). The Pratt-Arrow measure of relative risk aversion is estimated in this paper to be in the neighborhood of two.

23. E.g., see Merton (1969), which assumes all resources come from nonhuman capital or wealth; and Losq (1979), which allows for stochastic wages as well as stochastic returns from nonhuman wealth. See also Jones (1980) and Modest (1981).

24. This is implicit in a model developed by Jones as an expansion of his Ph.D. dissertation.

25. A number of important considerations not included in these theoretical papers are discussed in Crockett and Friend (1979).

26. Theory does, however, provide a theoretical presumption that saving in specific forms, with independently distributed returns, is positively related to relative interest rates.

27. See Weber (1970), Boskin (1980), Howrey and Hymans (1978), McLure (1980), and Modest, (1981). A recent paper by Gylfason (1981) finds a significant negative relation between quarterly consumption and nominal interest rates, holding expected inflation constant for the period 1952–78. However, when the years 1965–78, the period of most variation in interest and inflation rates, are analyzed separately, this relation disappears. Tests for serial correlation suggest that the results for this period are more reliable than those for 1952–65. Moreover, the adaptive expectations model used, where expected inflation is determined by inflation of the current and previous quarters, is highly questionable as a basis for inferring the relevant long-run real interest rate.

28. According to New York Stock Exchange (1981: 24), dividend income is taxed somewhat more in the United States while interest income is taxed somewhat more in Japan.

29. See Friend and Hasbrouck (forthcoming).

30. See Friend (1963: 666–667). Including net investment in consumer durables in saving, there was a moderate increase in the ratio of personal saving to disposable income from the 1900s to the 1950s, while excluding consumer durables there was an insignificant decrease.

31. As noted earlier, the theoretical effect on personal saving of an increase in after-tax real interest rates resulting from a decrease in personal income taxes may be somewhat different from the effect of an increase in real interest rates in the absence of taxation. One reason is that a reduction in tax rates on property income increases the variance as well as the expected value of after-tax returns on risky assets held by investors. Another is that the two types of interest rate changes may lead to different wealth effects on saving.

32. Friend and Hasbrouck (forthcoming). Under certain assumptions, theory would imply that a reduction in personal tax rates on property income might decrease the market value of assets and hence increase saving if the real before-tax risk-free rate was higher than .019 with the reverse effect if the risk-free rate was below .019 (using reasonable parameter values for the other variables involved). Estimates of the risk-free rate have ranged between .01 and .03. For a brief discussion of different views of how a decrease in the market value of wealth, distinct

from any change in the total future income stream, would increase saving, see Blume, Friend, and Crockett (1978: 36–37).

33. Friend and Hasbrouck (forthcoming). The tax effect on the cost of equity depends on the assumed effect on and value of the risk-free rate and on the assumed symmetry of tax effects on property income including capital gains and losses.

34. Feldstein (1973), Feldstein and Fane (1973), Tanner (1979), and Howrey and Hymans (1978).

35. Such a shift in income might also be associated with some shift away from saving in the form of housing to saving in other forms.

36. The low level of substitutability in the United States between one set of measures of household and government saving is documented in Howrey and Hymans (1978).

37. It is theoretically possible and there is some evidence (Friend and Jones [1960]) to suggest that stimulating saving in specific forms, such as private and public insurance and pensions, may increase the overall propensity to save (i.e., there is less than perfect substitutability among different forms of saving by the same economic unit). Though the evidence is far from conclusive, it does provide some support for proposals to provide tax incentives for households to set up their own pension or retirement plans.

38. Friend and Hasbrouck (1981).

39. For an analysis of the effect of lower corporate income tax rates on the cost of capital, see Blume, Friend, and Crockett (1978: 83–85).

40. Not only is the effect of lower personal income taxes on the propensity to save through higher real after-tax riskless interest rates indeterminate, but so also is their effect on the propensity to invest through changes in the overall cost of capital. See Friend and Hasbrouck (1981, forthcoming).

It should be noted that studies which indicate that reduction in personal income taxation of property would promote saving make the highly questionable assumption of a substantial positive interest elasticity of saving (e.g., Becker and Fullerton [1980]).

41. The present tax structure in the United States—all taxes levied at all levels of government—appears to be either essentially proportional or mildly progressive over the whole range of income classes, except for relatively high rates at both income extremes. (See Holland [1977].) A substantial change in the currently progressive Federal income tax could make the entire tax structure regressive.

42. Thus Michael K. Evans (1980) finds a substantial negative effect of taxation on labor supply. However, Albert Ando in that same Conference raises serious questions about the structural equations on which

this finding is based, and more fundamentally on the Evans model as a whole (1980).

43. This may not be true of investment in housing and consumer durables.

44. For the effect of inflation on business investment decisions see Blume, Friend, and Westerfield (1981). The evidence on the effect of inflation on household saving is conflicting. For example, Warren Weber (1975) finds no statistically significant effect for the United States while Howard (1978) and Juster and Wachtel (1972a, 1972b) find positive effects. If there are positive effects, they apparently weren't substantial enough to perceptibly stimulate saving in 1979 and 1980, a period of the highest sustained inflation in the United States for more than a half century, but with a relatively depressed personal saving to income ratio. There was evidence of positive effects in 1974–75 when the spurt in inflation was presumably unexpected. Modest (1981) concludes that while theory would suggest that households would react to uncertain inflation by increasing their saving, empirical analysis suggests the opposite result.

45. Blume and Friend (1978: 94 ff.).

46. Time series data which have generally been used for this purpose are quite suspect. Survey data indicated a preference by stockholders in the late 1970s for a dollar of dividends versus a dollar of retained earnings (which may have reflected the sorry performance of retained earnings over the preceding decade) and not surprisingly an even greater preference for a dollar of capital gains (Blume and Friend [1978]).

47. One notable exception is Evans who concludes "Our results in the supply-side model have shown that, for the same revenue-producing change, the corporate income tax rate cut has greater efficiency than a change in depreciation allowances, which in turn has a greater effect than a change in the investment tax credit" (1980: 2.2).

48. Holland (1977: 184–7). See also Auerbach and Summers (1979), which is based on the Data Resources, Inc. model. Perhaps the most striking example of the enormous variability in the range of estimates obtained from different models is provided by Robert S. Chirinko and Robert Eisner (forthcoming).

49. Blume, Friend, and Westerfield (1980).

50. It might be noted that in response to a general question about the most important impediments to capital formation, about twice as many respondents referred to business taxation as to personal taxation.

51. Lower corporate income taxes or higher investment tax credits would be associated in theory with a higher expected rate of return or lower user cost of capital and therefore with a higher optimal or equilibrium level of capital stock for corporations. Once the new equilibrium

level is attained, net plant and equipment expenditures would no longer be affected, but gross expenditures would remain higher than they would otherwise have been.

52. See U.S. Department of Commerce, *Survey of Current Business,* (1980: S–1, 14) for 1979 estimates of total new plant and equipment (P. & E.) expenditures and total corporate profit tax liabilities. The 1979 estimate of new P. & E. expenditures is shortly to be revised sharply upward, but revised estimates for 1947–77 have already been published in the U.S. Department of Commerce News Release BEA-80-68, November 12, 1980. The 1979 estimate of total new P. & E. expenditures used here, amounting to $258 billion, is obtained by adjusting the estimate in the July, 1980 *S.C.B.* (S–1) by the ratio (1.46) of the revised estimate for 1977 to the previously published estimate for that year (the corresponding ratio was 1.42 in 1976). To obtain the final estimate of new P. & E. expenditures by corporations in 1979, the total of $285 billion by all U.S. business has been multiplied by the ratio (.74) of the corporate stock of fixed capital to the total business stock of fixed capital at the end of 1978 (U.S. Department of Commerce, *Survey of Current Business* [1979] resulting in a figure of $191 billion.

53. See U.S. Department of Commerce, *Survey of Current Business* (1980, 14) for data on corporate depreciation and (1979: 62) for estimates of the corporate stock of plant and equipment.

54. Blume, Crockett, and Friend (1978). In that earlier survey, respondents were requested to hold constant the general state of the economy. An earlier study by Robert Eisner and Patrick Lawler (1975) indicated that responses to McGraw-Hill capital expenditure surveys pointed to very much smaller tax effects on plant and equipment expenditures. However, the McGraw-Hill survey elicited data only on the first year effects and was characterized by the theoretically questionable finding that the capital outlays of the bulk of corporate respondents were unaffected by significant changes in tax policy.

55. Klein and Taubman (1971) and Hall and Jorgenson (1971), especially pages 52 and 233. See also *Statistics of Income Corporation Income Tax Returns* (1965: 130). Other econometric models have implied a wide variety of estimated impacts of investment tax credits, but generally intermediate between the Wharton and Hall-Jorgenson models. These models typically indicate that investment tax credits are more effective per dollar of tax revenue than accelerated depreciation and more effective still than corporate income taxes (see Holland 1977: 184–6).

56. The higher proportion of structures in fixed capital formation of wholesale and retail firms as a whole than in manufacturing is documented in the *Survey of Current Business* (U.S. Department of Commerce [1979: 62]).

57. For the overall period 1965–78, the regressions were based upon the following 14 countries: Canada, United States, Japan, Australia, Belgium, France, Germany, Greece, Italy, Netherlands, Norway, Spain, Sweden, and United Kingdom. In addition to these countries, the 1965–72 regressions included Switzerland and Austria, and the 1973–78 regressions included Finland.

58. Despite these potential biases, which in some circumstances could be large, it is interesting to note that the correlation between the growth of net capital formation and some direct estimates of the growth rate of the capital stock is high. Christensen, Cummings, and Jorgenson (1980) provide direct estimates of the growth rate of the capital stock for the 1960–73 period for eight countries from which this study obtained estimates of the growth rate of net capital formation for the 1965–72 period. The correlation between these two series was 0.89, which is significant at the 5 percent level.

59. The explicit test was of the null hypothesis that the coefficients on the squared terms were jointly zero.

60. Consider the regression in which productivity is measured in terms of total population:

$$g_{X/P} = \alpha + \beta g_K + \gamma g_P + \delta (g_C = g_P) + \epsilon$$

where the subscripts C and P refer respectively to the civilian labor force and the total population respectively and ϵ is a mean-zero independent disturbance. It can be shown that the least square estimate of $g_{X/P}$ is identical to the least square estimate of g_X less the least square estimate of g_P. By substituting $(g_X - g_P)$ for $g_{X/P}$, adding g_P to both sides, subtracting g_C from both sides, and finally rearranging terms, one can rewrite the above regression as

$$g_{X/P} = \alpha + \beta g_K + \gamma g_C + (\delta - \gamma - 1)(g_C - g_P) + \epsilon$$

Thus, the relationship is established.

61. These additional variables were not available for every country. When not available, the specific country was dropped from the regression.

62. This adjustment is based upon the classical errors-in-variable formula and assumes that the growth rates of capital is uncorrelated with the other independent variables in the regression, and the measurement errors are independent mean-zero errors. That adding additional variables of various types to the regression does not appreciably change the estimated coefficient on the growth rate of capital is consistant with this assumption. The cross sectional standard deviation of the estimated growth rate of capital for the overall period is 0.031 or 3.1 percent. A standard deviation of the measurement error of 0.015 would

imply a cross sectional standard deviation of the true growth rates of 0.027. Thus, the adjusted estimates of b would be given as

$$1 + \frac{(.015)^2}{(.027)^2} \quad 0.304 = 0.40$$

63. The data for the two periods were stacked one upon the other and the following regression run

$$g_{X/C} = 0.023 + 0.465g_K - 0.319\delta g_K - 0.149g_C$$
$$\phantom{g_{X/C} = } (8.17) \quad (11.95) \quad (5.48) \quad (0.54)$$

$$-0.454 \, (g_C - g_P) - 0.561 \, \delta(g_C - g_P), \quad \overline{R}^2 = 0.94$$
$$(-1.08) \quad\quad\quad (-2.08)$$

where δ is a dummy variable taking on the value of 0.0 if the data points came from the first part of the sample and 1.0 if from the second part. The remaining variables are defined in footnote 60.

The estimates of the growth rates of the capital stock from the 1973–1978 period probably contain more measurement error than the corresponding estimates from the 1965–1972 period due to the differences in the number of observations upon which the estimates are based and the generally greater volatility of the net capital formation series after 1973. Part of the shift in the estimated coefficient on the growth rate of capital may be due to such differences in the size of the measurement error, but in view of the work of others documented in section 2, these differences are probably not sufficient to obviate the apparent shift in the value of the coefficient on the growth rate of capital.

64. The other variables examined were: (a) the average annual ratio of farm workers to the civilian labor force, (b) the average annual inflation rate, and (c) the average annual ratio of government revenues to national income.

65. The explicit regression was

$$g_{X/C} = 0.031 + 0.430g_K + 0.218g_C$$
$$\phantom{g_{X/C} = } (7.67) \quad (11.83) \quad (0.75)$$

$$-1.051(g_C - g_L) - 0.633 \, \sigma(\pi), \quad \overline{R}^2 = 0.97,$$
$$(-2.46) \quad\quad\quad (-3.85)$$

where $\sigma(\pi)$ is the standard deviation of the annual inflation rates and where the other variables are defined as in footnote 60.

66. The other variables examined were: (a) the average annual ratio of the number of male workers to the civilian labor force, (b) the average annual ratio of capital formation in the form of residential housing to gross capital formation, (c) the average annual ratio of community, social, and personal services workers to the civilian labor force, (d) the

average annual inflation rate, (e) the standard deviation of the annual inflation rate, and (f) the average annual ratio of government revenues to national income.

BIBLIOGRAPHY

Ando, Albert. "On Evans' 'Supply-Side' Model." In *Proceedings from the Conference on the Supply-Side Effects of Economic Policy, October 24–25, 1980.* Washington: 1980.

Auerbach, Alan J. and Summers, Lawrence H. *The Investment Tax Credit: An Evaluation.* National Bureau of Economic Research, Working Paper No. 404. Boston: National Bureau of Economic Research, (November) 1979.

Becker, Charles and Fullerton, Don. *Income Tax Incentives to Promote Saving.* National Bureau of Economic Research, Working Paper No. 487. Boston: National Bureau of Economic Research, (June) 1980.

Blume, Marshall E. and Friend, Irwin. *The Changing Role of the Individual Investor.* New York: John Wiley and Sons, 1978.

Blume, Marshall E.; Crockett, Jean; and Friend, Irwin. *Financial Effects of Capital Tax Reforms.* Monograph Series in Finance and Economics, Monograph 1978–4. New York: New York University Graduate School of Business Administration, 1978.

Blume, Marshall E.; Friend, Irwin; and Westerfield, Randolph. *Impediments to Capital Formation.* Philadelphia: Rodney L. White Center for Financial Research, The Wharton School, University of Pennsylvania, (December) 1980.

Boskin, Michael. "Taxation, Saving and the Rate of Interest." *Journal of Political Economy* 2 (April, 1980).

Chirinko, Robert S. and Eisner, Robert. "The Effects of Tax Parameters on the Investment Equations in Macroeconomic Econometric Models." In *Symposium on Saving, Investment and Capital Markets, March 26–28, Duck Key, Florida.* Cambridge, Mass.: Ballinger Publishing Co., forthcoming.

Christensen, Laurits R.; Cummings, Dianne; and Jorgenson, Dale W. "Economic Growth 1947–73: An International Comparison." In *New Developments in Productivity Measurement and Analysis,* edited by John W. Kendrick and Beatrice N. Vaccara. Studies in Income and Wealth, Vol. 44. Chicago: University of Chicago Press, 1980.

Crandall, Robert W. "Regulation and Productivity Growth." In *The Decline in Productivity Growth.* Federal Reserve Bank of Boston, Conference Series No. 27. Boston: Federal Reserve Bank of Boston, 1980.

Crockett, Jean and Friend, Irwin. "Consumption and Saving in Economic Development." In *Research in Finance,* edited by Haim Levy. Vol. 1. JAI Press, 1979.

Denison, Edward F. *Accounting for Slower Economic Growth: The United States in the 1970s.* Washington: The Brookings Institution, 1979.

Eisner, Robert and Lawler, Patrick. "Tax Policy and Investment: An Analysis of Survey Responses." *American Economic Review* LVX (March, 1975): 206–212.

Evans, Michael K. "An Econometric Model Incorporating the Supply-Side Effects of Economic Policy." In *Proceedings from the Conference on the Supply-Side Effects of Economic Policy, October 24–25, 1980.* Washington: 1980.

Feldstein, Martin S. "Tax Incentives, Corporate Saving and Capital Accumulation in the United States." *Journal of Public Economics* 2 (1973): 159–171.

Feldstein, Martin S. and Fane, George. "Taxes, Corporate Dividend Policy and Personal Saving: The British Postwar Experience." *Review of Economics and Statistics* LV (November, 1973): 399–411.

Friend, Irwin. "Determinants of the Volume and Composition of Saving." In *Impacts of Monetary Policy, Commission in Money and Credit.* Englewood Cliffs, N.J.: Prentice-Hall, Inc., 1963.

Friend, Irwin and Blume, Marshall E. "The Demand for Risky Assets." *American Economic Review* LXV (December, 1975), 900–922.

Friend, Irwin and Hasbrouck, Joel. "Effect of Inflation on the Profitability and Valuation of U.S. Corporations." Rodney L. White Center for Financial Research, Working Paper No. 13–81. Philadelphia: The Wharton School, University of Pennsylvania, 1981.

———. "Comment on Inflation and the Stock Market." *American Economic Review* LXXII (forthcoming).

Friend, Irwin and Jones, Robert. "The Concept of Saving." In *Consumption and Saving.* Vol. 2, Study of Consumers Expenditures. Philadelphia: The University of Pennsylvania Press, 1960.

Gollop, Frank M. and Jorgenson, Dale W. "U.S. Productivity Growth by Industry, 1947–73." In *New Developments in Productivity Measurement and Analysis,* edited by John W. Kendrick and Beatrice N. Vaccara. Chicago: University of Chicago Press, 1980.

Griliches, Zvi. *R and D and the Productivity Slowdown.* National Bureau of Economic Research, Working Paper No. 434. Boston: National Bureau of Economic Research, (January) 1980. Also published in *American Economic Review* 70 (May, 1980): 343–348.

Gylfason, Thoraldur. "Interest Rate, Inflation and the Aggregate Consumption Function." *Review of Economics and Statistics* LXIII (May, 1981): 233–245.

Hall, R. E. and Jorgenson, Dale W. "Application of the Theory of Optimum Capital Accumulation." In *Tax Incentives and Capital Spending,* edited by Gary Fromm. Studies of Government Finance. Washington: The Brookings Institution, 1971.

Hendershott, Patric H. "Research Summary." In *National Bureau of Economic Research Reporter.* Boston: National Bureau of Economic Research, forthcoming.

Holland, Daniel M. "The Role of Tax Policy." In *Capital for Productivity and Jobs.* The American Assembly, Columbia University. Englewood Cliffs, N.J.: Prentice-Hall, Inc., 1977.

Howard, David H. "Personal Saving Behavior and the Rate of Inflation." *Review of Economics and Statistics* LX (November, 1978): 547–554.

Howry, E. Philip and Hymans, Saul H. "The Measurement and Determination of Loanable-Funds Savings." *Brookings Papers on Economic Activity* (3, 1978): 655–685.

Jones, Emerson Philip, Jr. "Intertemporal Financial and Monetary Equilibrium." Ph.D. dissertation, Massachusetts Institute of Technology, 1980.

Juster, J. Thomas and Wachtel, Paul. "Inflation and the Consumer." *Brookings Papers on Economic Activity* (1, November 1, 1972a): 71–121.

———. "A Note on Inflation and the Saving Rate." Brookings *Papers on Economic Activity* (3, November 3, 1972b): 765–778.

Kendrick, John W. "Survey of Factors Contributing to the Decline in U.S. Productivity Growth." In *The Decline in U.S. Productivity Growth.* Federal Reserve Bank of Boston, Conference Series No. 22. Boston: Federal Reserve Bank of Boston, 1980.

Klein, Lawrence R. and Taubman, Paul. "Estimating Effects within a Complete Econometric Model." In *Tax Incentives and Capital Spending.* Washington: The Brookings Institution, 1971: 197–242.

Kopcke, Richard W. "Capital Accumulation and Potential Growth." In *The Decline in Productivity Growth.* Federal Reserve Bank of Boston, Conference Series No. 22. Boston: Federal Reserve Bank of Boston, 1980.

Losq, Etienne. "A Note on Consumption, Human Wealth and Uncertainty." In "Essays on the Theory of Finance." Ph.D. dissertation, University of Pennsylvania, 1979.

McLure, Charles E. "Taxes, Saving, and Welfare." In *Theory and Evidence.* National Bureau of Economic Research, Working Paper No. 504. Boston: National Bureau of Economic Research, (July) 1980.

Merton, Robert C. "Lifetime Portfolio Substitution and Uncertainty: The Continuous-Time Case." *Review of Economics and Statistics* LI (August, 1969): 247–257.

Modest, David M. "Uncertainty and Optimal Consumption: Theory and Evidence." Mimeographed. Cambridge, Mass.: Massachusetts Institute of Technology, (January) 1981.

New York Stock Exchange. *U.S. Economic Performance in a Global Perspective.* New York: Office of Economic Research, (February) 1981.

Nordhaus, William D. "The Recent Productivity Slowdown." *Brookings Papers on Economic Activity* (3, 1972): 493–536.

Perloff, Jeffrey M. and Wachter, Michael L. "A Production Function-Nonaccelerating Inflation Approach to Potential Output: Is Measured Potential Output Too High?" In *Carnegie-Rochester Conference Series on Public Policy,* 10. (1979): 113–163.

Proceedings from the Conference on the Supply-Side Effects of Economic Policy, October 24–25, 1980. Washington: 1980.

Rosen, H. S. "Housing Decisions and the U.S. Income Tax." *Journal of Public Economics* 11 (February, 1979): 1–23.

Tanner, J. Ernest. "Fiscal Policy and Consumer Behavior." *Review of Economics and Statistics* LXI (May, 1979), 317–323.

U.S., Department of Commerce. *Survey of Current Business.* Vol. 59, No. 8, Part II. Washington: Bureau of Economic Analysis, 1979.

———. *Survey of Current Business.* Vol. 60, No. 7. Washington: Bureau of Economic Analysis, 1980.

U.S., Department of the Treasury, Internal Revenue Service. *Statistics of Income Corporation Income Tax Returns.* Washington: Government Printing Office, 1965.

Wachter, Michael L. and Perloff, Jeffrey M. "The Productivity Slowdown: A Labor Problem?" In *The Decline in Productivity Growth.* Federal Reserve Bank of Boston, Conference Series No. 22. Boston: Federal Reserve Bank of Boston, 1980.

Weber, Warren E. "The Effect of Interest Rates on Aggregate Consumption." *American Economic Review* LX (September, 1970): 591–600.

————. "Interest Rates, Inflation and Consumer Expenditures." *American Economic Review* LXV (December, 1975): 843–858.

6.

FINANCING CAPITAL
FORMATION IN THE 1980s:
ISSUES FOR PUBLIC
POLICY

Benjamin M. Friedman[1]

Increased American capital formation has emerged as a nearly undisputed objective of economic policy for the 1980s. Dissatisfaction with the U.S. economy's poor productivity performance in the 1970s, as well as with the erosion of international competitiveness that began much earlier, but also became more evident in the 1970s with the dramatic declines in the international exchange value of the dollar, has elevated what was once largely a business interest into a much more widely shared goal. In today's environment groups representing labor and consumers also recognize the need for capital investment to create jobs and to raise productivity and hence the population's overall standard of living. On the whole, public discussion has moved from whether more capital formation is desirable to what policies can best achieve it.

An important aspect of capital formation that this discussion has often overlooked, however, is its explicitly financial side. In an economy like that of the United States, each decision to create more physical capital necessarily has a financial counterpart. This financial counterpart may be a single transaction, but in an economy with highly developed financial markets it is more likely to be an entire chain of obligations and transfers leading from an ultimate saver to an ultimate investor. In the end the financial and nonfinancial systems interact so that the allocation of the economy's real resources—whether to make consumer goods or producer goods, for example, or how much and what kind of each—exactly corresponds to its allocation of financial resources.

The financial aspect of the capital formation process is especially important in a public policy context for two reasons. First, the financial transactions associated with capital formation are not merely a reflection of real resource allocations that would necessarily come about in any case. The setting in which the financing of capital formation takes place can also be a key determinant of real resource allocations, including not only the total amount of capital formation, but also its composition. The financial and the nonfinancial elements of the process jointly determine one another, and public policy may affect the ultimate outcome by influencing either. Indeed, financial aspects of private capital formation decisions, like a firm's after-tax borrowing costs, may be much more readily subject to public policy influence than physical aspects like the production rates of the latest machine models.

A second reason why the financial side of capital formation is so important for public policy is that, when financial markets are as fully integrated into the economy's life pulse as they are in the United States, fragility of the financial structure can pose major hazards for the entire economic system. Moreover, there are sound reasons for believing that the considerations determining the actions of individual financial market participants do not adequately reflect potential threats to the system as a whole from too brittle a financial structure at the aggregate level. Financial structure is therefore a kind of "public good" in the familiar sense that an individual's (or individual firm's) actions bear "externalities" potentially affecting everyone else. Because there is no reason for the presence of such externalities to affect directly the decisions of individual financial market participants, there is a role for public policy in providing incentives that will in the end lead to a more satisfactory aggregate financial structure.

The object of this paper is to consider, from the financial perspective, both the setting of and the prospects for American capital formation in the 1980s, and to focus in particular on the opportunities (and pitfalls) for public policy. Section 1 reviews the evolution of investment and saving in the United States during the last quarter-century and emphasizes the connection between the allocation of physical and financial resources. Section 2 examines in detail the financing of investment through the economy's nonfinancial corporate business sector, which historically has accounted for nearly three-quarters of all U.S. investment in plant and equipment. Section 3 develops more fully the concept of externalities associated with private financial actions and the resulting role for public policy. Section 4 focuses on three specific aspects of corporate financing decisions—internal versus external funds, equity versus debt within the external component, and the maturity of the debt —and identifies in each case the issues for public policy. Section 5 provides a brief summary of the paper's principal conclusions.

1. PHYSICAL CAPITAL FORMATION AND FINANCIAL CAPITAL FORMATION

The principal development that has spurred interest in increased U.S. capital formation as a goal for the 1980s has been the economy's deteriorating productivity performance, in conjunction with its declining rate of net investment in productive plant and equipment. The productivity of labor in the U.S. non-farm private business sector increased by 2.6 percent per annum during 1948–65, and 2.2 percent per annum during 1965–73, but only 0.6 percent per annum during 1973–79.[2] Although neither 1978 nor 1979 was a recession year, labor productivity declined absolutely in both, marking the first two-year continuous productivity fall in U.S. postwar history. With a recession in 1980, productivity has now declined for still a third successive year.

In principle, any or all of a number of potential explanations may help to account for the U.S. productivity slowdown.[3] There is evidence that the rate of technical progress has slowed, probably as a result of the trend away from research and development activities undertaken by industry. There is also evidence that both capital and labor resources have become less mobile, and hence less able to adapt to changing technologies and consumer tastes. Demographic factors were rendering the labor force progressively younger, and hence less experienced and less skilled, until the very end of the 1970s. Government regulation has added increased burdens to production, importantly so in many industries. Slower output growth *per se* also typically exerts downward pressure on productivity, and the 1970s were a recession-prone, slow-growth era, at least in comparison with the 1960s.[4]

The increased attention to the nation's capital formation rate, however, has brought into a single focus the role of capital—that is, plant and equipment—in the basic production of goods and services. Although economists investigating the production process have often found the role of capital frustratingly difficult to quantify, both economic theory and empirical evidence make clear that fixed capital is essential to production in the modern economy.[5] Table 6–1 shows the experience of investment in plant and equipment in the United States during the past quarter-century, by five year spans (as well as for the single year 1980, to indicate the starting point for today's policy environment). The table shows not only gross investment in plant and equipment, but also the corresponding net investment after subtraction of capital consumption allowances adjusted to reflect true economic depreciation. The table shows these totals both in absolute dollar amounts and as percentages of GNP in each year.

The experience reviewed in the bottom panel of Table 6–1 in particular suggests clearly why capital formation has received increased atten-

TABLE 6–1
U.S. Gross and Net Investment in Plant and Equipment

	1956–60	1961–65	1966–70	1971–75	1976–80	1980
				Billions of Dollars		
Gross Plant and Equipment Investment	$45.0	$56.6	$92.2	$137.3	$239.3	$295.9
Capital Consumption Allowances with Capital Consumption Adjustment	−33.6	−40.0	−58.0	−97.4	−178.7	−225.6
Net Plant and Equipment Investment	11.4	16.6	34.2	39.9	60.6	69.8
				Percent of GNP		
Gross Plant and Equipment Investment	9.8%	9.4%	10.6%	10.4%	11.0%	11.3%
Capital Consumption Allowances with Capital consumption Adjustment	−7.2	−6.5	−6.6	−7.3	−8.2	−8.5
Net Plant and Equipment Investment	2.6	2.9	4.0	3.1	2.8	2.7

NOTE: Data are averages (except for 1980) of annual flows, in billions of dollars and as percentages of annual GNP. Detail may not add to totals because of rounding.
SOURCE: U.S. Department of Commerce.

tion as the economy's productivity performance has slipped during the 1970s. Although *gross* investment in plant and equipment has moved to a progressively larger share of the nation's total GNP, the corresponding *net* investment has shown a sharp reversal since the late 1960s. Indeed, by the late 1970s the share of total output devoted to net investment in plant and equipment was almost back to the level of the late 1950s, and the growth rate of the capital stock had fallen back accordingly. In light of the economy's declining net capital formation rate, it is hardly surprising that the amount of capital available to each employed U.S. worker has actually declined since 1974 after rising steadily at 3 percent per annum during the previous 25 years.

Moreover, even the dramatic decline in the net investment rate shown in these statistics may understate the true extent of the effective reduction in the economy's productive capital investment. One reason is that at least part of net capital outlays in recent years have gone into special investments that protect the environment, or enhance workers' health and safety, but do not otherwise increase capacity to produce the items included in conventional measures of output and productivity. In addition, the sharply higher price of energy relative to the prices of other inputs to the production process (especially labor) has changed the appropriate mix of those inputs to be used, so that substantial amounts of labor-saving but energy-consuming capital are no longer economical.[6]

Increasing the economy's investment rate is, at one level, a matter of the allocation of real resources. Although additional capital increases the economy's productive capacity once it is available for use, in the short run resources are fixed, and devoting more to any one use means devoting less to something else. Devoting a larger share of output to business fixed investment than the 1980 level of 11.3 percent would require devoting a smaller share to consumer spending (63.7 percent in 1980), or to purchases of goods and services by Federal or state and local governments (7.6 percent and 12.8 percent, respectively), or to residential investment (4.0 percent).[7]

Increasing the economy's investment rate is also a matter of the allocation of financial resources, however. An important key to understanding the functioning of any economy is the truism that, on an *ex post* basis, the economy's saving must equal its investment. Since it is unlikely in a decentralized market economy that *ex ante* plans for saving and investment will precisely balance one another, the market mechanism must influence the decisions of businesses and consumers so as to change these inconsistent *ex ante* plans into consistent *ex post* actions. Financial markets play a large role in this mechanism, generating adjustments in the real yield which the market pays to savers as suppliers of funds and in the cost and availability factors which confront those who demand funds to invest in productive plant and equipment, office buildings, inventories, and residential construction. If plans to supply funds exceed plans to demand funds, the market excess leads to increased availability and a decline in yields. If plans to supply funds fall short of plans to demand funds, the market shortage leads to reduced availability and higher yields. The result is that, *ex post,* saving equals investment.

The function of the financial markets goes even further, however. The individuals or institutions that seek to do investment, in the sense of forming new physical capital, are often not the same as those that wish to do saving, in the sense of spending less on current consumption than the limit their income would permit. It is also the job of the financial markets to transfer available savings from those who have an excess out of income to those who have a deficiency because they are currently undertaking investment for the future. No doubt the financial markets perform many other important functions as well—for example, providing liquidity and a host of transactions-oriented services—but from the standpoint of their role in guiding the mainstream of economic activity, the equilibration of total saving and total investment, and the transfer of available resources from savers to investors, constitute their main activity.

Moreover, these two functions are hardly independent, in that the amount of saving and investing that individuals and institutions do often depends on the facility of the financial markets in executing the relevant transfer. If the financial markets accomplish this transfer in an efficient way that delivers to savers much of the total return available from investment, then, other things equal, the amount of income saved (and, once transferred, devoted to investment) will typically be larger. Alternatively, if the financial markets do not function efficiently, so that much of the return available from investment does not find its way to savers, then, other things equal, the share of output devoted to investment will probably be smaller.

Table 6–2 shows the balance of saving and investment in the United States during the past 25 years, scaled in relation to the GNP as in the lower panel of table 6–1. It is clear from the table that during this period there has been no trend at all in the economy's total gross saving or total gross investment (which equals total gross saving, except for statistical discrepancy) in comparison to total income and spending. The 15–16 percent range has held remarkably steady throughout.[8]

Several important changes have occurred, however. Behind the steadiness of the total gross saving rate, the gross private saving rate has shown some tendency to increase while government as a whole has

TABLE 6-2
U.S. Gross Saving and Investment

	1956–60	1961–65	1966–70	1971–75	1976–80	1980
			Percent of GNP			
Total Gross Saving	15.7%	15.4%	15.8%	15.7%	15.9%	15.3%
Gross Private Saving	15.9	15.7	16.3	16.9	16.7	16.5
Personal Saving	4.3	3.8	4.9	5.6	3.9	3.9
Undistributed Corporate Profits	3.0	2.9	2.9	3.2	4.3	4.1
Inventory Valuation Adjustment	−0.2	−0.1	−0.4	−1.2	−1.2	−1.7
Capital Consumption Adjustment	−0.7	0.2	0.4	−0.0	−0.7	−0.7
Capital Consumption Allowances	9.5	8.8	8.4	9.3	10.4	10.9
U.S. Government Surplus	0.0	−0.4	−0.6	−1.8	−2.0	−2.3
State and Local Government Surplus	−0.2	0.0	0.1	0.6	1.2	1.1
Total Gross Investment	15.7	15.8	15.7	16.0	16.1	15.3
Gross Private Domestic Investment	15.5	15.2	15.5	15.7	16.3	15.1
Plant and Equipment	9.8	9.4	10.6	10.4	11.0	11.3
Residential	5.1	4.8	3.8	4.6	4.7	4.0
Inventory Accumulation	0.6	1.0	1.1	0.7	0.7	−0.2
Net Foreign Investment	0.2	0.6	0.2	0.3	−0.2	0.2

NOTE: Data are averages (except for 1980) of annual flows, as percentages of annual GNP.

Total gross saving and total gross investment differ by statistical discrepancy.

Detail may not add to totals because of rounding.

SOURCE: U.S. Department of Commerce.

moved from a neutral position to that of persistent *dis*saving. Within the private sector, capital consumption allowances have risen, even after adjustment to reflect the true economic depreciation, so as to account for essentially all of the increase in the gross private saving rate. Personal saving as a share of GNP has varied irregularly, as movements in the rate of personal saving out of disposable personal income have sometimes offset and sometimes compounded movements in the share of GNP represented by disposable income itself. Undistributed corporate profits have increased in relation to GNP during the 1970s, but here essentially all of the increase has consisted in artificial profits due to price inflation for firms treating inventories on a first-in-first-out basis. Within the government sector, continually growing surpluses among state and local governments (consolidated to include retirement funds) have offset about half of the growing deficits at the Federal level.[9]

Because of the key role played by the Federal government's dissaving in affecting the economy's overall balance of saving and investment, it is useful to focus on this one development in somewhat greater detail. Total Federal government expenditures have risen steadily as a share of GNP over the last quarter-century, from 18.4 percent during 1956–60 to 22.0 percent during 1976–80. This relative growth of Federal expenditures has itself reflected the net result of two sharp but opposing trends, as Federal purchases of goods and services have represented a steadily declining share of GNP (from 11.2 percent to 7.3 percent) and Federal transfer payments a steadily rising share (6.0 percent to 12.9 percent). Both the goods and services purchases, which represent the government's own use of economic resources, and the transfers, which represent the government's redirection of claims on these resources within the private economy, must be financed.

The Federal government's receipts from taxes and Social Security contributions have also increased in relation to the overall economy over these years, but only from 18.4 percent of GNP during 1956–60 to 20.0 percent during 1976–80. The shortfall from the corresponding growth of Federal expenditures, shown in table 6–2 as a steadily growing negative surplus, has therefore represented a direct absorption of the private saving available to finance investment. To the extent that the government itself has undertaken investment activities, however—including either infrastructure investments like highways and bridges, or directly productive investments like hospitals and power facilities—the familiar private investment data shown in table 6–2 understate the economy's overall investment total.

On the gross investment side in table 6–2, the one clear trend during this period has been the increasing share of output devoted to gross investment in plant and equipment, as already indicated in table 6–1.

Apart from the typically cyclical characteristics of the single year 1980, which depressed homebuilding and induced an inventory run-off, there has been little trend in the other two components of private domestic investment. Finally, net foreign investment—that is, the excess of U.S. investment abroad over foreign investment in the United States—became negative in the late 1970s, so that in recent years (except for 1980) U.S. savers have had to finance less than all of U.S. domestic investment, instead of having to finance more than all of it as in earlier years.

The balance of saving and investment (again, except for statistical discrepancy) shown in table 6–2 makes clear the sense in which increasing the economy's overall investment rate involves the allocation of financial as well as real resources. An increased investment rate also means an increased saving rate. In the absence of an infusion of foreign saving (in other words, a more negative net foreign investment position), increased investment would require either more private sector saving or less government sector dissaving, or both. Moreover, the largest component of correctly measured private saving, adjusted capital consumption allowances, are in effect given by the economic depreciation of the existing capital stock.[10] Hence any increase in private saving would have to come from personal saving or undistributed corporate profits (adjusted for inventory profits), both of which have fluctuated only within a fairly narrow range during the last quarter-century.

2. FOCUS ON THE CORPORATE SECTOR

In the U.S. economy many kinds of institutions as well as individuals undertake investment in plant and equipment, but the dominant source of this investment has traditionally been incorporated firms doing business in nonfinancial industries including manufacturing, natural resource extraction, transportation, communication, and public utilities and other nonfinancial services. As table 6–3 shows, nonfinancial business corporations have consistently accounted for nearly three-fourths of all U.S. plant and equipment investment. No other single readily identifiable group has even accounted for as much as 10 percent of the total—although the miscellaneous category, presumably a catch-all for individuals and unincorporated firms apart from farms, has consistently represented some 10–15 percent. While the remaining one-fourth of investment is hardly unimportant, any major increase in U.S. fixed investment activity is likely in large part to involve the nonfinancial corporate business sector.

Just as the corporate sector bulks large in the nation's total plant and equipment investment, investing in plant and equipment represents a large share of the corporate sector's activity. As table 6–4 shows, nonfi-

TABLE 6-3
Distribution of U.S. Investment In Plant and Equipment

	1956–60	1961–65	1966–70	1971–75	1976–80	1980
			Billions of Dollars			
Total Investment in Plant and Equipment	$45.0	$56.6	$92.2	$137.3	$239.4	$295.9
Nonfinancial Corporate Business	31.8	40.2	68.4	100.4	177.2	217.9
Farms	3.5	4.2	5.8	9.2	16.4	17.8
Nonprofit Institutions	2.3	3.4	4.4	5.3	6.5	7.4
Financial Corporations	0.9	1.2	2.3	5.7	7.5	10.0
Other	6.6	7.6	11.3	16.7	31.8	42.9
			Percent of Total Plant and Equipment Investment			
Total Investment in Plant and Equipment	100.0%	100.0%	100.0%	100.0%	100.0%	100.0%
Nonfinancial Corporate Business	70.6	71.0	74.2	73.2	74.1	73.6
Farms	7.7	7.5	6.3	6.7	6.8	6.0
Nonprofit Institutions	5.2	5.9	4.7	3.8	2.7	2.5
Financial Corporations	1.9	2.1	2.5	4.1	3.1	3.4
Other	14.6	13.5	12.3	12.2	13.3	14.5

NOTE: Data are averages (except for 1980) of annual flows, in billions of dollars and as percentages of total investment in plant and equipment. Detail may not add to totals because of rounding.

SOURCE: Board of Governors of the Federal Reserve System.

nancial business corporations typically use far more funds for physical investment than for financial investment, and plant and equipment is by far the dominant focus among corporate sector physical investments.[11] The table also shows that the increase in total U.S. plant and equipment investment as a share of GNP indicated in table 6–1 has been entirely due to the corporate sector. The increase from 9.8 percent of the nation's output devoted to gross investment in plant and equipment in the late 1950s to 11.0 percent in the late 1970s has simply reflected the corresponding increase from 6.9 percent to 8.1 percent in corporate sector plant and equipment investment in relation to GNP.

TABLE 6–4
Uses of Funds by U.S. Nonfinancial Corporate Business

	1956–60	1961–65	1966–70	1971–75	1976–80	1980
			Billions of Dollars			
Total Uses of Funds	$42.3	$62.1	$102.1	$163.0	$274.0	$297.3
Physical Investment	35.1	47.7	79.7	112.8	196.9	224.6
Plant and Equipment	31.8	40.2	68.4	100.4	177.2	217.9
Other	3.3	7.5	11.3	12.4	19.7	6.7
Financial Investment	7.2	14.4	22.4	50.1	77.1	72.7
Liquid Assets	−0.4	2.3	1.2	11.5	11.8	13.8
Trade Credit	4.8	8.0	13.9	23.5	40.8	31.9
Other	2.8	4.1	7.2	15.1	22.6	27.0
			Percent of GNP			
Total Uses of Funds	9.2%	10.3%	11.7%	12.4%	12.6%	11.3%
Physical Investment	7.6	7.9	9.2	8.6	9.1	8.6
Plant and Equipment	6.9	6.6	7.8	7.6	8.1	8.3
Other	0.7	1.2	1.3	1.0	1.0	0.3
Financial Investment	1.5	2.4	2.6	3.8	3.5	2.8
Liquid Assets	−0.1	0.4	0.1	0.9	0.5	0.5
Trade Credit	1.0	1.3	1.6	1.8	1.8	1.2
Other	0.6	0.7	0.8	1.2	1.1	1.0

NOTE: Data are averages (except for 1980) of annual flows, in billions of dollars and as percentages of annual GNP.

Detail may not add to totals because of rounding.

SOURCE: Board of Governors of the Federal Reserve System.

TABLE 6-5
Sources of Funds to U.S. Nonfinancial Corporate Business

	1956–60	1961–65	1966–70	1971–75	1976–80	1980
				Billions of Dollars		
Total Sources of Funds	$46.1	$68.6	$108.1	$175.0	$301.0	$328.8
Internal Funds	31.7	45.5	63.1	91.1	169.9	196.7
Undistributed Profits	9.9	13.1	18.4	31.3	70.3	80.2
Capital Consumption Allowances	21.6	31.3	46.7	70.8	118.5	149.7
Inventory Valuation Adjustment	−0.9	−0.5	−4.0	−16.5	−28.7	−45.7
Foreign Earnings	1.1	1.6	2.0	5.5	9.8	12.5
External Funds	14.4	23.1	45.0	83.9	131.0	132.1
Equity Issues	2.0	0.7	2.5	8.8	5.7	9.5
Bonds and Mortgages	6.8	8.7	19.3	32.6	45.8	51.6
Trade Debt	3.6	7.1	12.7	21.7	34.0	29.3
Other Debt	3.1	5.3	11.4	17.9	38.6	40.2
Other Sources	−1.1	1.4	−1.0	2.9	6.8	1.5

Percent of Total Sources

Total Sources of Funds	100.0%	100.0%	100.0%	100.0%	100.0%	100.0%
Internal Funds	68.8	66.4	58.4	52.1	56.4	59.8
Undistributed Profits	21.6	19.1	17.0	17.9	23.4	24.4
Capital Consumption Allowances	46.8	45.6	43.1	40.5	39.4	45.5
Inventory Valuation Adjustment	-2.0	-0.7	-3.7	-9.4	-9.5	-13.9
Foreign Earnings	2.4	2.3	1.8	3.1	3.3	3.8
External Funds	31.2	33.6	41.6	47.9	43.5	40.2
Equity Issues	4.4	1.0	2.3	5.1	1.9	2.9
Bonds and Mortgages	14.7	12.6	17.9	18.6	15.2	15.7
Trade Debt	7.7	10.4	11.8	12.4	11.3	8.9
Other Debt	6.8	7.7	10.6	10.2	12.8	12.2
Other Sources	-2.4	2.0	-0.9	1.8	2.3	0.5

NOTE: Data are averages (except for 1980) of annual flows, in billions of dollars and as percentages of total sources.

Other external sources category includes change in corporate profit taxes payable, hence may be positive or negative.

Detail may not add to totals because of rounding.

SOURCE: Board of Governors of the Federal Reserve System.

Like any other entity within the economy, nonfinancial business corporations can use funds for investment or other purposes only to the extent that they either have these funds available internally or find external sources. As table 6–5 shows, until the late 1970s the corporate sector increasingly financed its investment in physical and financial assets by raising external funds. (The total sources of funds in table 6–5 differs from the total uses of funds in table 6–4 by a statistical discrepancy which over time grows about in pace with the size of the corporate sector, and which represents unreported uses of funds.) Internally generated funds accounted for more than two-thirds of all corporate sector sources of funds in the late 1950s, but little more than one-half in the early 1970s, as the percentage reliance on external sources steadily rose. In addition, close inspection of the underlying year-by-year data suggests that the reversal of this trend in the late 1970s has largely reflected the aftermath of the unusually severe 1973–75 recession as well as the brief recession in 1980.

Among corporations' internal sources of funds, both undistributed profits and capital consumption allowances rose substantially throughout the 1956–80 period in absolute terms, but until the late 1970s neither rose rapidly enough in comparison with the surge in exernal funds to maintain the initial two-thirds internal share. Moreover, throughout this period an ever larger share of reported profits consisted of artificial inventory profits. Further, even in the late 1970s capital consumption allowances continued to increase more slowly than total sources of funds, and hence fell for the first time below two-fifths of total sources.

The corporate sector's external sources of funds have consisted almost entirely of debt. Despite the existence in the United States of the world's largest and most liquid secondary market for corporate equity securities, together with a well-developed investment banking industry capable of underwriting and distributing primary issues of new securities, nonfinancial business corporations have consistently determined the equity/debt mix of their sources of funds almost entirely according to the internal/external mix.[12] In addition, during the period of enlarged equity issuing activity in the early 1970s and again in 1980, many of the new equities issued were typically preferred shares (which are essentially equivalent to debt, except for the tax treatment), and even then one industry (public utilities) accounted for much of the total.

Hence the corporate sector's ever increasing reliance on external funds until the late 1970s really amounted to an increasing reliance on debt. Within the various categories of corporate debt, however, the late 1970s slowdown relative to the growth of total sources involved only the bonds and mortgages and the (mostly intercompany) trade debt. Since 1975 nonfinancial business corporations have actually increased their percentage reliance on (largely short-term) "other debt," including mostly bank loans and commercial paper, thereby renewing a trend that has now prevailed throughout the past 25 years except for a brief interruption during the early 1970s.[13]

In the same way that an increase in the economy's overall investment rate would require an increase in its saving rate, in the absence of a reduction in its financial investment an increase in the corporate sector's use of funds for investment in plant and equipment would require an increase in its internally generated funds or its external funds, or both. If past patterns of financing continue, then an increase in internal funds would imply additional reliance on equity, while an increase in external funds would imply additional reliance on debt. At least in principle, however, an increase in external funds could mean debt or equity, just as whatever additional debt corporations issued could consist of either long- or short-term instruments.

3. FINANCIAL STRUCTURE AS A PUBLIC GOOD

Almost any kind of financial system is capable of transferring resources from ultimate savers to ultimate investors. The special feature of competitive financial markets is that, in so doing, they also perform an important allocative function. At the aggregate level the market mechanism determines the overall amount of the economy's income to be saved, and hence the overall amount of its output to be devoted to augmenting the physical capital stock. At the underlying level of the micro-unit, the same process enables a multitude of individuals and institutions to allocate the total amount saved and invested efficiently among countless potentially productive projects.[14]

This key role in efficiently allocating the economy's scarce resources constitutes the fundamental rationale underlying the very existence of competitive financial markets. In centrally planned economies, for example, the fiat approach is also generally capable of commandeering resources from various sources and transferring them to designated applications. Without competitive markets, however, the efficiency of the resulting resource allocation rests entirely on the centralized information gathering and decision-making process.[15] By contrast, a competitive market system utilizes each individual market participant's information (and preferences) in arriving at the prices of and yields on the full range of financial assets and liabilities. These prices and yields in turn provide the signals and incentives that induce individual savers to direct their savings toward the ultimate real investments that the market as a whole considers most valuable.

When individuals (or the intermediary agents acting in their behalf) decide which firm's equities to buy, or to which firm to lend via securities or other loan arrangements, they do so on the basis of the prospects for return and the apparent risks associated with that firm's equities or debt claims. For firms in nonfinancial businesses, however, the prospective returns and risks associated with its securities mostly reflect the returns and risks associated with the firm's underlying real activity, based on its physical assets, its human resources, its organization, and other features of its business. If a firm's managers believe that it can expand in ways that will generate unusually high returns, even after allowance for risk, they will be prepared to pay a greater than average return in order to attract financial resources. If savers (or their agents) similarly assess the firm's prospects, they will advance financial resources to the firm on that basis. Because the economy's overall financial resources are scarce, mirroring the scarcity of real resources, each firm's ability to attract funds to finance its expansion necessarily limits the expansion of other firms. By allocating financial resources in this way, the competitive market system ultimately determines not just the overall rate, but also the specific directions of the economy's real expansion.

The efficiency of the financial resource allocation process—and hence of the economy's chosen growth path—is not a matter of concern to the individual saver or to any one firm, however. The nature of a competitive system is that each participant pursues only his own objectives, yet in so doing contributes to the establishment of signals and incentives which steer all participants in the direction that best contributes to the efficiency of the overall outcome. For the system to operate effectively, therefore, any aspect of individual decision-making that matters for the overall outcome should also influence the prices and yields to which the individual decisions respond. If financial decisions at the level of the micro-unit bear aggregate-level implications that these prices and yields do not reflect, then the resulting "externality" will prevent the system from directing individual financial decisions so as to constitute, in total, the most efficient overall outcome.

The primary area in which modern financial markets may be subject to such externality problems is that of risk. To be sure, market participants acutely analyze the risks associated with any specific individual borrower or firm raising either debt or equity funds, and the yield or prospective return set by the market as a whole in principle does reflect such risks in each case. Moreover, the market tends to price these risks in ways that systematically vary between individuals and business firms, among both individuals and firms according to a rich variety of criteria, and from one stage of the economic cycle to another.[16] What the financial markets may not price, however, is the collective risk to the economy as a whole associated not with any individual borrower's debt *per se* but, instead, with the economy-wide aggregate debt position.

In industrially advanced economies with highly developed financial markets, a complex financial structure typically supports most real activities—including especially the basic business sector. As is clear in table 6–5, nonfinancial business corporations in the United States typically finance much of the expansion of their productive plant and equipment by raising external funds in the debt markets. Moreover, in most cases these funds came not from individuals but from intermediary institutions, which in turn raise their funds by issuing their own liabilities to individuals or to still further intermediaries.[17] At every level of this process, each market participant's leverage position may be entirely satisfactory in the sense that liabilities are well in line with assets, yet most participants' assets are in reality just others' liabilities.

The fact that most of the assets are simply someone else's liabilities lends a pyramid, or chain, characteristic to the resulting financial superstructure. At its base, of course, are physical assets with real values of varying degrees of stability, together with presumably default-free claims on the Federal government. Beyond that base, however, nonfinancial events causing the default of any one link in the chain have the effect of invalidating the assets of the next link, and therefore threaten further defaults due now to financial circumstances. The more complex and interwoven is the superstructure in comparison to its underlying base, the greater is the risk that such a default situation initially due to nonfinancial events could cumulate, thereby threatening a major rupture to the system as a whole.[18]

The implications of aggregate-level financial risk for the growth of the economy are related to, but yet distinct from, the implications of the amount and composition of capital formation addressed above. Because the devotion to net capital formation of a part of the economy's fixed resources at any time increases the economy's future productive capacity, the investment (and savings) rate is an important determinant of how fast the economy grows. Similarly, because different investment projects make different contributions to that productive capacity, the efficiency of any given amount of capital formation also matters for the economy's growth. By contrast, the economy's overall level of financial risk matters primarily for the variability of economic growth, although it may affect the average growth rate also. The effect of a fragile financial structure on the variability of economic growth was most readily apparent in the United States in the decades before World War II, when business fluctuations that were far more severe than any in the postwar experience often followed financial disruptions. Moreover, if the increased pace of investment during business expansions does not completely make up for the shortfall during contractions, more variable growth will mean slower average growth as well.

As table 6–6 shows, in the United States the total amount of outstanding debt issued by nonfinancial borrowers has grown approximately in pace with the economy's nonfinancial activity during the past 25 years. Except for a short period in the 1950s, the economy's aggregate nonfinancial debt-to-income ratio has exhibited essentially no trend.[19] Within the stability of the total, however, the composition has steadily shifted toward greater private sector indebtedness, and reduced government sector indebtedness, relative to the economy's total output and spending. Between 1955 and 1980 the combination of some movement in the overall total, and this large change in composition, resulted in nonfinancial private borrowers' outstanding debt rising from only two-thirds of a year's total income to well over a full year's income. Although some of this increase merely reflects the growth of the nation's physical capital stock (including residential capital) relative to income, to a large extent it also indicates more heavily leveraged financing of that capital.[20]

Moreover, in addition to this increase in the private sector's relative indebtedness, the financial system has continued to become more extensively intermediated.[21] The share of total private sector holdings of credit market debt claims accounted for by financial intermediaries has risen steadily during this period, from 69.8 percent at year end 1955 to 81.5 percent at year end 1980.[22] From the perspective of aggregate-level risk, therefore, a growing superstructure of financial intermediation has compounded the effect of greater leverage.

Finally, not all kinds of debt liabilities are equally fragile as assets in the portfolios of lenders who hold them. Although it is possible to draw a number of distinctions among different debt instruments along these lines, the greater exposure associated with short- in contrast to long-term maturities is the most readily apparent. Here the effect of nonfinancial business corporations' increased reliance on short-term debt, as indicated in table 6–5, has led over time to a steady reduction in the average maturity of these corporations' outstanding debt. As table 6–7 shows, the short-term share of U.S. nonfinancial business corporations' outstanding debt rose from only one-fifth of the total at year end 1955 to well over one-fourth at year end 1980, so that during these years the corporate sector's outstanding short-term debt more than doubled in relation to GNP.

As the combination of greater leverage, more intermediation and shorter maturities continue to increase the U.S. economy's aggregate-level financial risk, the externality associated with individual financial decisions that do not take this aggregate-level risk into account becomes

TABLE 6-6
Outstanding Debt of U.S. Nonfinancial Borrowers

	1955	1960	1965	1970	1975	1980
				Billions of Dollars		
Total Debt of Nonfinancial Borrowers	$549.9	$726.4	$1011.7	$1431.3	$2280.6	$3899.7
Federal Government	230.0	236.3	262.4	300.8	446.3	742.8
State and Local Governments	46.3	72.0	103.1	149.2	222.9	321.1
Households	137.2	218.4	343.6	481.2	772.3	1430.9
Corporate Nonfinancial Business	104.2	153.9	223.4	376.4	629.5	1048.4
Other Nonfinancial Business	32.1	45.9	79.3	123.7	209.7	356.6
				Percent of GNP		
Total Debt of Nonfinancial Borrowers	134.1%	144.0%	141.8%	143.6%	142.7%	142.8%
Federal Government	56.1	46.8	36.8	30.2	27.9	27.2
State and Local Governments	11.3	14.3	14.4	15.0	14.0	11.8
Households	33.4	43.3	48.2	48.3	48.3	52.4
Corporate Nonfinancial Business	25.4	30.5	31.3	37.8	39.4	38.4
Other Nonfinancial Business	7.8	9.1	11.1	12.4	13.1	13.1

NOTE: Data are year end outstanding amounts, in billions of dollars and as percentages of fourth quarter GNP.
Detail may not add to totals because of rounding.
SOURCE: Board of Governors of the Federal Reserve System.

TABLE 6-7
Outstanding Debt of U.S. Nonfinancial Corporate Business

	1955	1960	1965	1970	1975	1980
				Billions of Dollars		
Total Credit Market Debt	$104.2	$153.9	$223.4	$376.4	$629.5	$1048.4
Long-Term	83.1	122.1	174.5	287.8	477.2	756.7
Short-Term	21.1	31.8	48.9	88.6	152.2	291.7
			Percent of Total Credit Market Debt			
Total Credit Market Debt	100.0%	100.0%	100.0%	100.0%	100.0%	100.0%
Long-Term	79.8	79.3	78.1	76.5	75.8	72.2
Short-Term	20.2	20.7	21.9	23.5	24.2	27.8
				Percent of GNP		
Total Credit Market Debt	26.1%	30.4%	32.4%	37.9%	40.6%	38.4%
Long-Term	20.8	24.1	25.4	29.0	30.8	27.7
Short-Term	5.3	6.3	7.1	8.9	9.8	10.7

NOTE: Data are year end outstanding amounts, in billions of dollars, as percentages of total outstanding credit market debt, and as percentages of fourth quarter GNP.

Detail may not add to totals because of rounding.

SOURCE: Board of Governors of the Federal Reserve System.

progressively more of a problem. The role for public policy with respect to the nation's financial markets is accordingly greater. In addition to using the financial system to achieve the amount of overall capital formation judged appropriate on macroeconomic grounds, and protecting the system's competitive aspects so as to promote the efficient allocation of that capital, aggregate-level risk represents yet a third focus of public policy with respect to the financial markets. The containment or reduction of this aggregate-level financial risk is, in effect, a "public good." Moreover, the more capital formation the nation undertakes—and hence the more financing it does—the more important this public good becomes.

4. CORPORATE FINANCE AND PUBLIC POLICY
Three distinct aspects of the corporate financing decision, as illustrated in table 6–5, represent areas in which public policy may exert influence over the amount and composition of capital formation undertaken in the United States, and on the aggregate-level risk associated with financing that capital formation: internal versus external funds, equity versus debt within the external component, and features of the debt, including especially maturity.

INTERNAL VERSUS EXTERNAL FUNDS
To the extent that the competitive market mechanism represents the most efficient available system for allocating scarce capital resources, an emphasis on external sources of funds to finance an increased rate of capital formation would best ensure the direction of that capital toward those industries, and those companies within particular industries, that provide the best opportunity for putting the added capital to productive use. Conversely, the more firms simply redeploy the financial resources that they generate internally, without having to face the market test in attracting new capital, the less role the competitive market system plays in promoting efficient allocations. Similarly, if government distorts capital formation away from market-determined allocations by means of direct or indirect subsidies (or by differential taxation), it substitutes its own more limited information gathering and decision-making system for that of the financial markets.

A corporation relying largely on internal funds is, of course, not entirely exempt from the judgment of the market. The market still prices the company's shares, and shareholders seeking improved returns may exert some influence on the firm's management. In addition, if the market places too low a value on a corporation's shares, it sometimes becomes attractive for new ownership, prepared to provide new management, to acquire a controlling interest. Even so, the imperfections of the dominant modes of corporate governance suggest that external funding in competitive markets is likely to enhance the efficiency of business capital formation.

Public policy could contribute to promoting externally financed corporate capital formation in two complementary ways. First, if the corporate sector is to raise additional external funds, it is necessary that those funds be available. As the balance of saving and investment shown in table 6–2 makes clear, an increase in investment not financed by increased undistributed corporate profits (or by reduced residential investment or a shift to negative net foreign investment) requires either an increase in personal saving or a reduction in government dissaving, or both.

Much recent discussion has focused on tax incentives to stimulate personal saving by raising after-tax returns, although the historical variation of personal saving as a share of total income (see again table 6–2) does not suggest any clear connection between such returns and the personal saving share.[23] By contrast, the Federal government's progressively larger budget deficits in relation to GNP have clearly absorbed ever larger amounts of private saving that would otherwise have been available to finance investment. As table 6–8 shows, net funds raised by the Federal government have steadily increased, not just in relation to GNP, but as a share of the total funds raised by all nonfinancial sectors in the U.S. credit markets. In addition, the government's use of its sponsored financial intermediaries has increasingly absorbed still more funds, which these intermediaries then have usually passed on to noncorporate borrowers for purposes other than investment in plant and equipment.

One major way for public policy to promote externally financed capital formation, therefore, would be to reduce the government's claims on the economy's real and financial resources. Between the late 1950s and the late 1970s, the share of real economic resources absorbed by the Federal government rose by about 4 percent. Because the government did not finance that increase with increased taxes (and because of the growth of government intermediation), the share of total credit market resources absorbed by the Federal government, either directly or indirectly, rose by more than 18 percent. Reducing the Federal deficit (even if just in relative terms) would release these resources, as would reducing the sponsored credit agencies' scale of activity.

The mere availability of savings, however, does not automatically mean that individuals (or their agents) will be willing to transfer them to nonfinancial business corporations for use in financing investment in plant and equipment. Hence a further major consideration for public policy along these lines is the corporate sector's ability to attract external funds. Corporations must show prospects of earning a sufficient rate of return on that investment, after due allowance for risk, to render such applications of financial resources competitive.

Hence corporate profits are hardly beside the point, even if the ultimate objective of public policy is to enhance capital formation largely financed from external sources. Through a combination of taxation and related means, policy could help to reverse the erosion in the after-tax profitability of fixed business investment, and thereby importantly affect the corporate sector's ability to attract the external funds necessary to finance additional capital formation.[24]

EQUITY VERSUS DEBT

As table 6–5 shows, during the past 25 years U.S. nonfinancial business corporations have used debt instruments to raise almost all of their external funds, so that the internal/external mix of their financing has also largely determined the equity/debt mix. The consequence of this financing pattern has been the rising corporate sector leverage discussed in Section 3.[25] A substantial increase in externally financed capital formation would only further erode corporate sector balance sheets if this pattern continued, and the resulting aggregate-level financial risk to the economy would accordingly rise further.

Nevertheless, a corporation's choice of whether to issue debt or equity securities, as well as a saver's choice of bonds or stocks for his portfolio, is hardly independent of public policy influence. The likely avenues of policy influence in this area lie with the tax code's treatment of the respective costs and returns associated with debt and equity instruments. Probably the greatest such single influence in the United States in recent years has been the discrimination between debt and equity forms of pay-out at the corporate level under the corporate profit tax.[26] Because the tax code allows interest payments (but not dividends) as a deduction from corporate profit taxes, in most circumstances a corporation can reduce the total taxes due from its operations by financing its assets with debt instead of equity. Moreover, the interaction of the tax code and accelerating price inflation has made this discrimination all the more powerful in recent years, as nominal interest rates have risen to reflect the inflation premium necessary to compensate lenders for the reduction in the real value of their principal.

It is impossible to know the extent to which the tax code's discrimination in favor of debt and against equity has accounted for the observed pattern of corporate external financing. Even so, it is clear that eliminating this discrimination would at least remove corporations' current *dis*incentive to finance with equity. There probably exists no perfect

TABLE 6–8
Total Net Funds Raised in U.S. Credit Markets, According to Borrowing Sector

	1956–60	1961–65	1966–70	1971–75	1976–80	1980
			Percent of GNP			
Total Net Funds Raised	9.3%	11.4%	12.0%	16.3%	19.3%	16.0%
By Nonfinancial Sectors	8.4	10.1	10.2	14.3	16.4	13.5
U.S. Government	0.2	0.9	0.9	2.1	2.8	3.0
State and Local Governments	1.1	1.0	1.0	1.2	0.9	0.9
Households	3.5	4.1	3.1	4.5	6.2	3.9
Corporate Nonfinancial Business	2.6	2.4	3.9	4.6	4.0	3.4
Other Nonfinancial Business	0.6	1.1	1.0	1.3	1.4	1.2
Foreign	0.4	0.5	0.3	0.6	1.1	1.0
By Financial Sectors	0.9	1.3	1.8	2.0	2.9	2.5
Federally Sponsored	0.2	0.2	0.6	1.0	1.7	1.8
Other	0.7	1.1	1.1	1.0	1.2	0.7

Percent of Total Net Funds Raised

Total Net Funds Raised	100.0%	100.0%	100.0%	100.0%	100.0%	100.0%
By Nonfinancial Sectors	90.3	88.3	85.1	87.2	85.1	84.4
U.S. Government	2.6	7.9	7.4	12.9	14.5	18.9
State and Local Governments	12.0	9.0	8.7	7.1	4.6	5.6
Households	37.8	36.2	26.1	27.4	31.8	24.1
Corporate Nonfinancial Business	28.1	21.1	31.5	27.8	20.7	21.9
Other Nonfinancial Business	6.4	9.6	8.5	8.1	7.1	7.3
Foreign	3.4	4.3	2.8	3.9	5.6	6.6
By Financial Sectors	9.7	11.7	14.9	12.8	14.9	15.6
Federally Sponsored	2.3	2.0	5.2	6.4	8.6	11.3
Other	7.4	9.7	9.7	6.4	6.2	4.3

NOTE: Data are averages (except for 1980) of annual flows, as percentages of annual GNP and as percentages of total net funds raised.

Detail may not add to totals because of rounding.

SOURCE: Board of Governors of the Federal Reserve System.

way of completely neutralizing the tax system in this regard, but there has been no shortage of proposed steps that would advance this objective at least in part. These ideas have ranged from simply abolishing the distinction between the treatment of interest and dividend payments at the corporate level to fully integrating the corporate and individual income tax systems. Indexing the tax code to eliminate the effects of inflation, a suggestion often made for other purposes too, would be especially relevant in this context.

Moreover, in light of the deterioration in corporate sector balance sheets that has already occurred, and which would otherwise continue and even increase with an enhanced capital formation rate financed externally, there is even a case for going beyond merely restoring neutrality. Under the circumstances a positive incentive in favor of equity financing (or, alternatively, a penalty to debt financing) would be a plausible objective to guide public policy. The rationale for this reverse discrimination lies in the externality associated with each individual corporation's financing decisions. Although the market presumably prices fully the incremental risk to the corporation's own securities associated with additional borrowing, there is no way for the market to price the added aggregate-level risk resulting from the further compounding of the economy's overall financial superstructure. To the extent that the containment or even reduction of aggregate-level financial risk represents a public good, positive discrimination in favor of equity financing would be a way of achieving it.

FEATURES OF THE DEBT
Even if public policy does lead U.S. nonfinancial business corporations to increase their historically minimal reliance on external equity financing, the major part of the external funds required to finance any new surge of corporate capital formation will almost inevitably take the form of debt. To the extent that considerations of aggregate-level risk create greater externalities when corporations issue one kind of debt instrument rather than another, there is again a role for public policy in augmenting the markets' own systems of incentives. In addition, there is room for public policy initiatives to broaden the U.S. debt markets in ways that would make debt funds easier overall for corporations to raise.

In deciding on the maturity of its debt instruments, a typical corporation takes into account the relative costs of short- versus long-term financing, including not only currently prevailing interest rates, but also its expectations of interest rate movements in the future. At the simplest level, the relevant comparison is not between today's 20-year bond rate and 90-day paper rate, but rather between the bond rate and the (risk-adjusted) expected cost of renewing short-term paper for 20 years. In reality the comparison is far more complex, because a decision to issue short-term paper today still leaves open the possibility of issuing long-term bonds in the future. The available empirical evidence indicates that, in deciding the maturity of debt offerings, U.S. corporations respond to interest rate considerations along just these lines.[27]

The Federal government is also a borrower in these markets, however, and evidence suggests that the government has at least some significant ability to influence the relative interest rates on short- and long-term instruments by the management of its own debt.[28] Because lenders are not indifferent to the varying risk characteristics of securities of dissimilar maturity, the more the government issues short- instead of long-term debt, the higher will be short- relative to long-term interest rates, and vice versa. During most of the post-World War II era, the Federal government progressively shortened the average maturity of its outstanding debt. The mean maturity of privately held U.S. Treasury securities outstanding fell from 116 months at year end 1945 to 71 months at year end 1955, and only 29 months at year end 1975. The net effect of this policy was to reduce long- relative to short-term interest rates, thereby encouraging corporations (and others) to finance with larger maturities.

Since 1975, however, the government has changed its debt management policy so as instead to emphasize long-term issues. By year end 1980 the mean maturity of privately held Treasury securities had risen from 29 months to 45 months, and it is continuing to rise. By *raising* long- relative to short-term interest rates, the new policy encourages corporations to finance with short maturities. This point is especially important in an era in which, because of the high level and volatile nature of the rate of price inflation, fewer lenders are willing to devote major shares of their portfolios to long-term fixed-income securities.

One way for public policy to pursue the objective of containing or reducing aggregate-level financial risk, therefore, would be to reverse the debt management policy pursued since 1976—that is, to return to the policy which prevailed almost throughout the first 30 years of the postwar era. Even a neutral debt management policy, which simply preserved the current maturity structure of the outstanding Treasury debt instead of lengthening it, would prevent the government from exerting ever greater pressure on the corporate sector to finance an increased capital formation rate with short-term debt.

Finally, despite the great depth and diversity of the U.S. financial markets, these markets make available only a limited range of vehicles for transferring capital along the chain from ultimate savers to ultimate investors. For example, although price inflation and inflation risk have continued to be a major (perhaps *the* major) focus of attention among both borrowers and lenders in the United States for at least a decade, the market has yet to evolve any vehicle by which savers can pay a price to transfer inflation risk to someone else.[29] Similarly, although the asymmetry of the conventional call feature greatly increases the inflation risk to the lender, almost all long-term corporate bonds issued in the United States continue to bear the standard call deferment of either five or 10 years depending upon the business of the borrowing corporation.[30]

Often the reason why the financial markets are slow in introducing new instruments, especially in well-developed markets like that in the United States for corporate bonds, is that no one issuer is prepared to pay the cost of pioneering an innovation. Here, too, there is an externality in that the set of market incentives confronting the individual decision-making unit do not encompass the full set of benefits (or costs) attendant on the decision to be made. A potential role for public policy in such circumstances would be to assume the pioneering role, introducing limited amounts of particular new kinds of securities so as to open new markets that private borrowers could then tap to raise funds to finance capital formation.

5. SUMMARY OF CONCLUSIONS

Capital formation implies the allocation of both physical and financial resources. The resulting constraints apply both to the economy as a whole and to its individual sectors. For the overall economy, increased investment is possible only if there is increased private sector saving or reduced government sector dissaving. For the nonfinancial corporate business sector, which accounts for nearly three-fourths of all U.S. investment in plant and equipment, increased investment is possible only if corporations generate more funds internally or raise more funds externally.

In a system of highly developed competitive financial markets, several considerations guide the effort of public policy to promote increased capital formation. Policy may affect the total amount of capital formation undertaken by influencing private saving or by controlling government dissaving. Policy may also enhance the efficient allocation of that capital formation by protecting the competitive nature of the financial markets. In addition, because there is an externality associated with the contribution of individual financing decisions to the economy's aggregate-level financial risk, the containment or reduction of that risk is itself a public good.

Three specific aspects of the corporate financing decision—internal versus external funds, equity versus debt within the external component, and features of the debt, including especially maturity—present opportunities for public policy aimed at enhancing the nation's capital formation. First, by reducing the government's dissaving and hence its claims on the economy's financial resources, policy can make credit market funds available for corporations to finance their investment externally, thereby both stimulating the overall amount of capital formation and also taking advantage of the allocative efficiency of the competitive market mechanism to achieve a productive composition of that capital formation. At the same time, by using the tax system to augment the rate of return on corporate sector assets, policy can also enable corporations better to compete for such funds once they are available. Second, by eliminating or even reversing the current tax discrimination in favor of debt, policy can encourage corporations to rely at least in part on equities in their external financing, thereby reducing the economy's aggregate-level financial risk. Third, by neutralizing or even reversing the current emphasis on long-term securities in managing the Federal government's own debt, policy can encourage corporations to issue long- instead of short-term debt instruments, thereby further reducing aggregate-level financial risk. Along the same lines, policy can also play a role in pioneering markets for new financial instruments, like bonds providing protection of the investor's purchasing power, that private borrowers can then use to finance private capital formation.

NOTES

1. This paper draws in part on my earlier research. I am grateful to the National Bureau of Economic Research, the National Science Foundation and the Alfred P. Sloan Foundation for support of that research. I am also grateful to Stephen Taylor for helpful discussions that contributed to the preparation of this paper, to Gerald Silverstein for supplying unpublished Commerce Department data, and to Seymour Himmelstein, Michael Wachter, and Susan Wachter for comments on an earlier draft.

2. These data are from U.S. Council of Economic Advisers (1981).

3. See Kendrick (1979) for an analysis of these factors, including an effort to quantify their respective contributions.

4. See Gordon (1979) for an analysis of the effect of output growth on productivity in a cyclical time frame.

5. See Lucas (1970) for an early review of the literature of empirical production functions, with emphasis on the difficulty in empirically identifying the contribution of capital. For a more recent example of this problem in an applied policy context, see Perry (1977).

6. See Jorgenson (1978) for an analysis of the influence of relative prices on production and productivity, in the context of the post-1973 rise in energy prices.

7. The remaining major spending categories of the GNP, inventory accumulation and net exports, are probably not subject to policy decisions in this context.

8. The single-year high and low were, respectively, 16.6 percent (1965) and 13.4 percent (1958) for total gross saving and 17.3 percent (1956) and 13.8 percent (1958) for total gross investment.

9. The appearance from the table that the Federal deficit for 1980 was the largest in relation to GNP during the 1956–80 period is misleading, however. In fact the relative deficit was larger in 1975 and 1976 (4.5 percent and 3.1 percent, respectively) and in 1958 (3.0 percent).

10. The fact that adjusted capital consumption allowances are given does not mean that allowable depreciation does not affect saving when the allowance affects taxes payable.

11. Other physical investments undertaken by nonfinancial business corporations include inventories, residential dwellings (essentially all multi-family), and mineral rights.

12. During three years in the 1960s nonfinancial business corporations' total net equity issuance was actually negative, as repurchases exceeded gross new issues.

13. In fact the interruption was limited to the two years 1975–76, and was almost certainly a reflection of the 1973–75 recession.

14. See Baumol (1965) for a classic description of this process in the context of the equity market. Much of Baumol's analysis applies to the debt markets as well.

15. See Bergson (1978) for an analysis of the equivalent of "profits" in centrally planned systems.

16. See Jaffee (1975) for an analysis of the variation in risk premiums on debt securities.

17. For example, a manufacturing firm may borrow from a bank, which issues a certificate of deposit to a money market fund, which issues shares to an individual. Such chains may involve many more transactions, of course.

18. Minsky's work has emphasized this aspect of the distinction between gross debt and net debt; see, for example, Minsky (1972, 1977). See also Kindleberger (1978) for a lively historical account in support of this idea.

19. See Friedman (forthcoming) for an analysis of the debt-to-income stability phenomenon, and Friedman (1980) for a descriptive overview of the behavior of the debt-to-income ratio since 1918.

20. See again Friedman (forthcoming), especially figure 3.

21. See Gurley and Shaw (1960) and Goldsmith (1958, 1969) for

analyses of the relationship between increasing levels of financial intermediation and the development of the economy.

22. These data are from the Board of Governors of the Federal
Reserve System.

23. As Feldstein (1978) has explained, in principle the effect of
higher returns could either increase or reduce saving. See Boskin (1978)
and Howrey and Hymans (1978) for differing views of the empirical
evidence on this question.

24. The concept of "profits" that matters in this context is the rate
of return gross of interest payments. See Feldstein and Summers (1977)
for estimates of the U.S. corporate sector's gross and net rates of return
during recent years.

25. See Ciccolo (forthcoming) for a careful analysis of changes in
the U.S. corporate sector's balance sheet since early in this century.

26. See McLure (1979) for a comprehensive review of the U.S.
corporate tax structure in this context.

27. See Friedman (1979).

28. See Roley (forthcoming).

29. See Bodie (1980) for a detailed analysis of the inflation risk
associated with different kinds of securities in the United States, and
Friedman (1980) for a set of international comparisons.

30. See Bodie and Friedman (1978) for an analysis of the call feature
on U.S. corporate bonds.

BIBLIOGRAPHY

Baumol, William. *The Stock Market and Economic Efficiency.* New York: Fordham University Press, 1965.

Bergson, Abram. "Commentary." In *New Challenges to the Role of Profit,* edited by
Benjamin M. Friedman. Lexington: D.C. Heath and Company, 1978.

Bodie, Zvi. "Financial Innovation for Stable Real Retirement Income in an
Inflationary Environment." *Journal of Portfolio Management* VII (Fall, 1980):
5–13.

Bodie, Zvi and Friedman, Benjamin M. "Interest Rate Uncertainty and the Value
of Bond Call Protection." *Journal of Political Economy* LXXXVI (February, 1978):
19–43.

Boskin, Michael J. "Taxation, Saving and the Rate of Interest." *Journal of Political
Economy* LXXXVI (April, 1978): S3–S27.

Ciccolo, John H., Jr. "Changing Balance Sheet Relationships in the U.S. Corpo-
rate Sector." In *The Changing Roles of Debt and Equity in Financing U.S. Capital
Formation,* edited by Benjamin M. Friedman. Chicago: University of Chicago
Press, forthcoming.

Feldstein, Martin. "The Rate of Return, Taxation and Personal Savings." *Economic
Journal,* LXXXVIII (September, 1978): 482–487.

Feldstein, Martin and Summers, Lawrence. "Is the Rate of Profit Falling?" *Brookings Papers on Economic Activity* (1, 1977): 211–227.

Friedman, Benjamin M. "Substitution and Expectation Effects on Long-Term Borrowing Behavior and Long-Term Interest Rates." *Journal of Money, Credit and Banking* XI (May, 1979): 132–150.

———. "The Financing Must Come—But From Where?" *Harvard Business Review* LVIII (September-October, 1980): 52–56.

———. "Postwar Changes in the American Financial Markets." In *The American Economy in Transition,* edited by Martin Feldstein. Chicago: University of Chicago Press, 1980.

———. "Debt and Economic Activity in the United States." In *The Changing Roles of Debt and Equity in Financing U.S. Capital Formation,* edited by Benjamin M. Friedman. Chicago: University of Chicago Press, forthcoming.

Goldsmith, Raymond W. *Financial Intermediaries in the American Economy Since 1900.* Princeton: Princeton University Press, 1958.

———. *Financial Structure and Development.* New Haven: Yale University Press, 1969.

Gordon, Robert J. "The 'End-of-Expansion' Phenomenon in Short-Run Productivity Behavior." *Brookings Papers on Economic Activity* (2, 1979): 447–460.

Gurley, John G. and Shaw, Edward S. *Money in a Theory of Finance.* Washington: The Brookings Institution, 1960.

Howrey, E. Philip and Hymans, Saul H. "The Measurement and Determination of Loanable-Funds Saving." *Brookings Papers on Economic Activity* (3, 1978): 655–685.

Jaffee, Dwight M. "Cyclical Variations in the Risk Structure of Interest Rates." *Journal of Monetary Economics* I (July, 1975): 309–325.

Jorgenson, Dale W. "The Role of Energy in the U.S. Economy." *National Tax Journal,* XXXI (September, 1978): 209–220.

Kendrick, John W. "Productivity Trends and the Recent Slowdown: Historical Perspective, Causal Factors, and Policy Options." In *Contemporary Economic Problems 1979,* edited by William Fellner. Washington: American Enterprise Institute, 1979.

Kindleberger, Charles P. *Manias, Panics, and Crashes.* New York: Basic Books, Inc., 1978.

Lucas, Robert E., Jr. "Capacity, Overtime, and Empirical Production Functions." *American Economic Review* LX (May, 1970): 23–27.

McLure, Charles E., Jr. *Must Corporate Income Be Taxed Twice?* Washington: The Brookings Institution, 1979.

Minsky, Hyman P. "Financial Stability Revisited: The Economics of Disaster." *Reappraisal of the Federal Reserve Discount Mechanism.* Washington: Board of Governors of the Federal Reserve System, 1972.

———. "A Theory of Systematic Fragility." In *Financial Crises: Institutions and Markets in a Fragile Environment,* edited by Edward I. Altman and Arnold W. Sametz. New York: Wiley-International, 1977.

Perry, George L. "Potential Output and Productivity." *Brookings Papers on Economic Activity* (1, 1977): 11–47.

Roley, V. Vance. "The Effect of Federal Debt Management Policy on Corporate Bond and Equity Yields." *Quarterly Journal of Economics,* forthcoming.

U.S. Council of Economic Advisers. *Annual Report.* Washington: U.S. Government Printing Office, 1981.

7.

PRODUCTIVITY AND CAPITAL FORMATION

Otto Eckstein   Robert Tannenwald

The U.S. economy is embarking on a policy experiment to see if the slide in productivity performance can be reversed. This chapter provides some econometric exercises to review the record, suggest what is feasible, identify realistic goals, and help point the way toward desirable policies. It does not attempt to deal with every facet of our productivity performance. Little is said about such issues as the role of regulation in disrupting business progress, the shortsightedness of current business incentive systems, the diminished support of research and development efforts by both public and private sources, the diversion of top quality manpower out of manufacturing industries, or the merger and acquisition movement created by the tax laws and the norms of the financial community. Nor is this the place to fully analyze the role of U.S.-Japanese economic relations in the decline of American productivity performance.

UPDATING THE PRODUCTIVITY EQUATION
To analyze the impact of capital formation on productivity, one must have a theory. Economics has long advanced the hypothesis that productivity, defined as output per manhour, depends on (1) the capital to labor ratio—the amount of capital provided for each worker; (2) the degree of resource utilization, with high industrial operating rates yielding more output per manhour, but with an overly tight labor market creating work disincentives and the use of less qualified workers; and (3) the industrial composition of production, recognizing that there are cyclical swings and long-term trends moving workers from low- to high-productivity industries.

In recent years several other factors have come to be recognized as influences on productivity. They include (1) the level of pollution abatement expenditures which are assumed to be partially diverted from capital formation for modernization or expansion; (2) the surge of energy prices since the Organization of Petroleum Exporting Countries, which is leading to the adjustment of production processes to conserve high-cost energy, adjustments which partially come at the expense of other investments and innovations; and (3) the level of the personal tax burden, with excessively high marginal tax rates leading to less work effort, or diversion of effort to moonlighting and other underground activity which are unmeasured and untaxed.

Most of these ideas are embodied in equation 1 (table 7–1). The capital to labor ratio is measured by the depreciated stocks of producer's durable equipment and non-residential structures, divided by the labor force that would be available at full employment. The change in this ratio is plotted in figure 7–1.

Resource utilization is measured by three variables, reflecting a rather sophisticated theory of short-run productivity. The Federal Reserve's measure of the utilization rate of manufacturing capacity has an important and strongly positive influence, as in all previous studies.[1] The "surprise" component of final demand (figure 7–2) has a strongly negative effect. When demand is surprisingly low, as in recession, business is likely to have misplanned production and to wind up with surprisingly high costs and ineffective utilization of labor. Finally, the

TABLE 7–1
The Productivity Equation

INDEPENDENT VARIABLE	COEFFICIENT	STANDARD ERROR	T-STATISTIC
Constant	−1.272	0.262	−4.856
Time Trend	0.00609	0.000916	6.649
Index of Labor Market Tightness	−0.000547	0.000242	−2.259
Output Surprise	−0.000440	$9.984E^{-5}$	−4.403
Energy Prices	−0.0629	0.0157	−4.000
Tax Burden	−0.344	0.118	−2.916
Pollution Abatement	−8.407	2.167	−3.880
Capital to Labor Ratio	0.0442	0.0129	3.420
Capacity Utilization	0.223	0.0577	3.858
Demographic Composition of Labor Force	0.761	0.379	2.008
Industrial Mix of Employment	−0.958	0.5064	−1.892
Rho	0.862	0.0593	14.55

R-BAR SQUARED: 0.9989

DURBIN-WATSON STATISTIC: 1.8917

STANDARD ERROR OF THE REGRESSION: 0.00558 Normalized: 0.02667

Equation corrected for first-order autocorrelation.

EQUATION 1

LOG (JO%MHNF) = 1.272 + .00609 ★ TIME − .000547 ★ JLMTITE
− .000440 ★ (((QSTAR − LETOUTPUTPABE)/LETOUT-
PUTPABE) + .07) ★ 100
− .0629 ★ (WPI05/WPIIND)
− .344 ★ (TP + .5 ★ TW)/YP − 8.407 ★ PABE/GNP
+ .0442 ★ (KNEPDENR72/1 + KNECNR72/1)/((1 −
RUFE/100) ★ LC)
+ .223 ★ (UCAPFRBM) + .761 ★ EM20&/EHH
− .958 ★ (ET + ESV + EFIR)/EHH

Where: JQ%MHNF = BLS index of output per manhour, non-farm business sector
TIME = A time trend beginning in 1947:1, increasing by 1 each quarter
JLMTITE = Data Resources, Inc. Index of Labor Market Tightness ★
LETOUTPUTPABE = Real final sales less imputed rent and compensation
of government employees, adjusted for pollution abatement expenditures
QSTAR = Expectations variable for real output, a Koyck lag of LETOUT-
PUTPABE with a lambda of .9
WPIO5 = Wholesale price index for fuels
WPIIND = Wholesale price index for all industrial products
TP = Personal tax and nontax payments
TW = Contributions for Social Insurance
YP = Personal income
PABE = Pollution abatement expenditures
GNP = Gross national product
KNEPDENR72 = Net effective capital stock—producer's durable equip-
ment (1972 dollars)
KNECNR72 = Net effective capital stock—non-residential structures (1972
dollars)
RUFE = Unemployment rate at full employment
LC = Civilian labor force
UCAPFRBM = Capacity utilization, manufacturing, total
EM20& = Number of employed males over 20
EHH = Total employment—household survey basis
ET = Total employment—wholesale and retail trade
ESV = Total employment—service industry
EFIR = Total employment—finance, insurance, and real estate industries

★ For explanation of Index, see DRI *Review,* February, 1978. Details available on request.

DEPENDENT VARIABLE: Natural Log of Productivity

ESTIMATION INTERVAL: 1954:1 to 1980:4

NUMBER OF OBSERVATIONS: 108

Data Resources, Inc. Index of Labor Market Tightness, a composite measure of nine labor market indicators reflecting the workweek, manufacturing turnover, the employment ratio, and unemployment changes, has a negative effect on productivity (figure 7–3). Thus, when the labor market becomes tight, there is a decline of worker productivity, that is, some evidence of diminishing returns.

The demographic factor in labor supply also is a long-recognized influence in productivity. The percent of workers who are adult males still seems to make a difference to productivity (figure 7–4). The industrial mix of employment also has a role, as measured by the percentage of employment in the service, trade, and financial industries. As figure 7–5 shows, the share of employment of these industries has been rising rapidly and continues to do so.

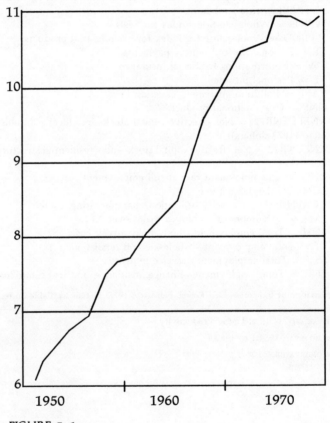

FIGURE 7–1
Capital/Labor Ratio

The percent of the GNP devoted to pollution abatement expenditures, as measured by Department of Commerce surveys, also is a significant variable. As can be seen from figure 7–6, the major move in this area came in the late 1960s and has seen little change since then. Thus,

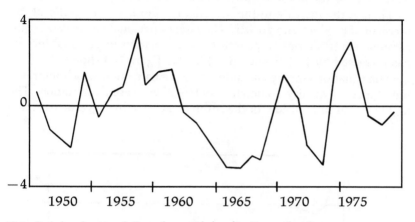

Note: Scaled and centered. Formula provided earlier in equation 1.

FIGURE 7–2
The "Surprise" Element in Final Demand

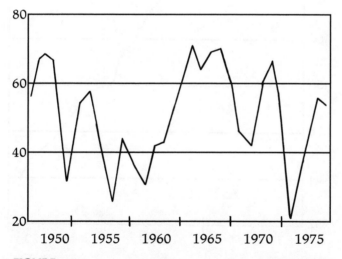

FIGURE 7–3
Data Resources, Inc. Index of Labor Market Tightness

it does not seem to be a new factor in the productivity slowdown of the last seven years.

The energy factor is measured here by the ratio of the composite Wholesale Price Index for fuels, related products, and power to the Wholesale Price Index for all industrial commodities. This is the dramatic new factor in the productivity analysis, as figure 7–7 shows.

Finally, the increase in the personal tax burden is a significant depressant of productivity growth. The ratio of personal income taxes plus personal contributions to payroll taxes in relation to personal income has increased by 39 percent since 1965, as figure 7–8 shows.

The equation employs an autoregressive correction which improves the statistical quality somewhat and removes serial correlation. The highly significant t-value for the autoregressive term suggests that there

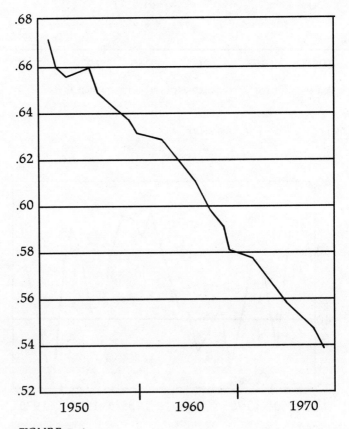

FIGURE 7–4
Ratio of Employed Adult Males to Total Employment

are missing elements in the analysis, and that further research would be amply justified. The time trend, the independent thrust of productivity created by improved education, worker health, disembodied technology, possible changes in the work ethic or other factors, is a large 2.5 percent a year.

ANALYSIS OF THE PRODUCTIVITY SLOWDOWN

Equation 1 can be evaluated with the data of the three productivity periods to allocate the causes of the slowdown. Figure 7–9 shows the productivity slowdown as measured by a five-year moving average. Table 7–2 shows the decomposition of productivity growth. It can be seen that the 0.5 percent a year slowdown in 1965–1973, compared to the

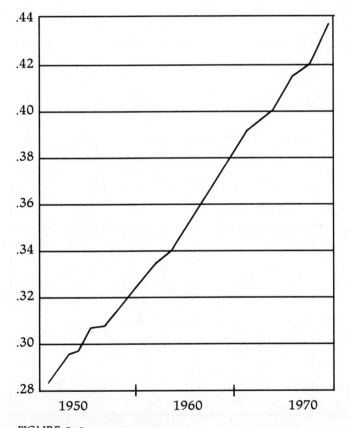

FIGURE 7–5
Ratio of Employment in Trade, Service, and Financial Industries to Total Employment

previous decade, was mainly due to the introduction of pollution abatement expenditures, a worsening of the industrial mix of employment, and small changes in demography, resource utilization, and energy prices. The capital to labor ratio was a very positive factor in these years: a capital goods boom in the late 1960s was partly triggered by favorable tax incentives and high activity levels created by the Vietnam War.

The dramatic slowdown in productivity trend from 2.2 percent to 0.8 percent after 1973 can also be explained by this analysis. The surge of energy prices reduced the productivity trend by 0.8 percent a year, compared to a very small negative effect in the preceding interval. The capital to labor ratio contributed only 0.4 percent a year to productivity after 1973, compared to the extraordinarily high 1.1 percent contribution in the previous interval. Other changes were small, with the nega-

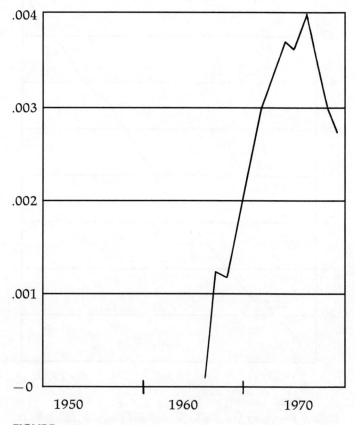

FIGURE 7–6
Ratio of Pollution Abatement Expenditures to GNP

tive effects of higher resource utilization and unfavorable demand surprises offset by a somewhat looser labor market which helped the efficiency of labor. The industrial mix, demography, and a rising tax burden continued to have negative effects, but no worse after 1973 than in the previous interval.

PRODUCTIVITY PROSPECTS
Before turning to the role of accelerated capital formation in any future productivity recovery, let us examine the probable role of the other factors which have an important influence.

The demographic factor will have little or no effect from now to the mid-1980s, as the share of young workers in the labor force stabilizes. Resource utilization is likely to have a very small impact on productivity over the next several years. Demand management policies are likely to

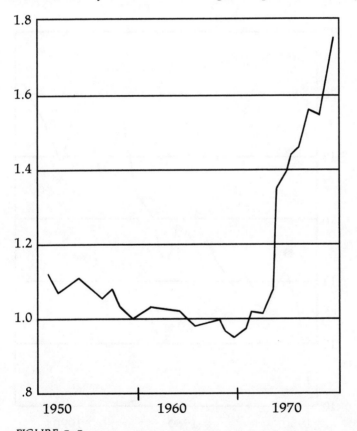

FIGURE 7–7
Ratio of Wholesale Price Index for Fuels to Wholesale Price Index for All Industrial Commodities

be on the tough side, and high real interest rates will also help to keep demand at modest levels. The labor market, therefore, will remain somewhat loose, which will help productivity, while utilization of industrial capacity will be a bit subpar.

The effect of pollution abatement expenditures is also likely to be relatively small, and could conceivably turn positive. Certainly the percentage of the nation's resources devoted to pollution abatement will not be increasing under the new policies, and might even fall a bit. On the other hand, the country is not going to abandon its decade-old campaign to reduce the volume of dangerous substances introduced into the living environment by industrial processes.

The shift of employment to the service industries is likely to continue. This is a fundamental historical trend that has long been recog-

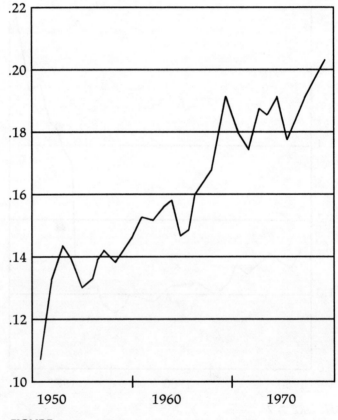

FIGURE 7–8
Personal Tax Burden

nized. It should also be recalled that productivity measurement is particularly difficult in the service industries, and that output may be understated. Certainly the rate of technological change is just as great in such fields as finance and communications as it is in manufacturing, mining, or construction.

Energy prices are not likely to be as damaging a force in the years ahead as they have been since 1973. The 95.7 percent change in relative energy prices from 1973 to 1980 could not be repeated. The DRI long-term projections call for an annual rate of increase of the relative price of energy of 5.0 percent in 1980–1986, including the large rise in 1980,

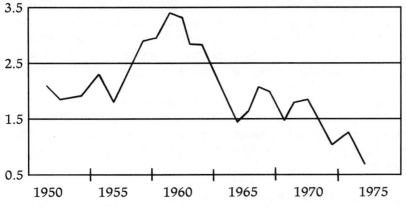

FIGURE 7–9
Percentage Change in Productivity (Five-Year Moving Average)

TABLE 7–2
The Composition of Productivity Growth (Average Annual Percent Change)

	1973–1980	1965–1973	1955–1965
Time Trend	2.5	2.5	2.5
Economic Utilization	−0.1	0.1	0.2
Labor Market Tightness	0.2	−0.1	−0.1
Output Surprise	−0.1	0.2	0.2
Energy Prices	−0.8	−0.1	0
Tax Burden	−0.1	−0.1	−0.1
Pollution Abatement	0	−0.3	0
Capital to Labor Ratio	0.4	1.1	0.7
Demographic Composition of Labor Force	−0.4	−0.4	−0.3
Industrial Mix of Employment	−0.6	−0.6	−0.4
Non-farm Productivity Growth	0.8	2.2	2.7

NOTE: Columns may not sum because of residual in equation.

Productivity and Capital Formation

compared to 9.9 percent in the previous interval and no change at all in earlier decades. Of course, this is one of the riskiest elements in productivity forecasting. Renewed political troubles in the Middle East would boost world oil prices by larger amounts, and with domestic oil prices decontrolled and natural gas moving toward decontrol, the price of domestic energy would move with world markets. On the other side, the relative price of oil may remain stable, leaving only rising gas and other sources to raise the composite energy price.

The 15-year surge in the personal tax burden is probably coming to an end with congressional passage of at least a portion of President Reagan's program. But even these proposals amount to little more than indexing of the tax system against inflation. The average effective personal tax rate is not projected to decline, just to stabilize at a relatively high level. Thus, no lift to productivity can be expected from this source, but at least the negative effect of the last 15 years is likely to be brought to an end.

Adding up all of these factors, the productivity trend is likely to improve by 1.2 percent a year, for the interval 1981–1986 compared to the poor performance in the years since 1973. This is a healthy improvement and provides a good base for a program of accelerated capital formation.

TAX INCENTIVES AND CAPITAL FORMATION

The DRI 800-equation Model of the U.S. Economy can be used to analyze the different means available to stimulate capital formation. The Model uses the Jorgenson theory of investment as its point of departure, with modifications made necessary by the economic circumstances of the last 15 years. These modifications include a more explicit measure of the cost of capital which takes into account the particular sources of finance, the debt service burden created by a company's balance sheet in relation to its cash flow, the investment required for pollution abatement, and the "surprise" element in output as compared to output expectations. The DRI Model has been used quite extensively for this kind of analysis, and a particularly widely cited set of results was published in the Joint Economic Committee study paper, *Tax Policy and Core Inflation*. [2]

The two principal tax incentive proposals, the 10–5–3 proposal submitted by President Reagan, and the Senate proposal developed last year by Senator Lloyd Bentsen and the Senate Finance Committee, show the same improvement in productivity for the six years, a boost of 0.3 percent a year to 2.2 percent. However, there is a difference in timing. The 10–5–3 proposal, because of its generosity to buildings, has to be staged in and therefore has a small initial effect. The Bentsen proposal, on the other hand, does not require such staging, and therefore actually provides a substantially larger incentive in the opening years. As a result, the Bentsen proposal boosts productivity by four-tenths of a point by 1982, whereas the 10–5–3 proposal only adds 0.1 percent. On the other hand, once 10–5–3 is fully effective, it adds five-tenths of a point for 1985 and 1986, whereas the Bentsen proposal by that time only adds three-tenths of a point.

These boosts in productivity of 0.3–0.5 percent may seem disappointing relative to the hopes with which some of them are advanced. The average real share of business fixed investment in the GNP is boosted to 11.1 percent in the Bentsen proposal by the end of the period. Under 10–5–3, the investment share reaches 11.3 percent by the end of the period, beyond the previous peak performance achieved by the modern U.S. economy, with a particularly large boost for buildings, of course. Thus it is a major accomplishment. I recognize that the President's proposals are estimated to have much larger effects in the Administration's own calculations. Treasury Secretary Donald Regan has testified that he looks for an investment share of 16 percent in the years ahead, implying a much more dramatic boost in the capital to labor ratio and in the productivity trend. While such estimates are not impossible, they are on the optimistic side. An investment share beyond 12 percent requires major structural changes in the U.S. economy, with a far greater ability to produce capital goods and construct buildings than we now possess. Also, if such a rise of investment is to avoid an explosion of industrial wages and prices, new wage-setting arrangements would have to be achieved, both in the construction and capital goods industries.

Nor should we underestimate the power of the restoration of a 2.0 percent a year productivity trend. Such real improvement would permit a significant resumption of rising living standards, and given the new budget and tax policies, would allow major increases in the real spendable earnings of American workers.

BROADER ISSUES

Econometric study of worsening productivity performance can carry the analysis only so far. It is a framework for giving some preliminary weights to the relative importance of traditional economic factors, but it does not provide the reasons for the underlying changes. Let me touch on a few of the causes.

Shifts in the industrial mix of employment have accounted for a loss of productivity performance of 0.6 percent a year for the last 15 years. The service industries, including finance and retail and wholesale trade, employed 28 percent of the labor force in 1950 and 44 percent of the labor force in 1980. A very large part of all employment growth occurred in these sectors in the last three decades.

Some of the swing to services is inevitable, derived from the patterns of consumption that prevail at the high income levels of a postindustrial society. Consumers devote increasing purchasing power to travel, eating out, financial services, medical care, as well as increased educational and cultural activities. While auto factories and steel mills may be closing, we are opening museums, concert halls, hospital wings, gourmet restaurants, and boutiques. The productivity of an opera singer, a doctor, a sculptor, a chef, or the buyer for a mod clothing chain is difficult to measure, yet the official data somehow throw them all into the pot of GNP, stir well, and derive a composite output per personhour printed to three decimals.

But not all of the employment shifts out of goods production into services has such historic inevitability. Some of it is due to a needless decline in the economic performance of U.S. manufacturing industries created by public policy neglect and management failures. Let me cite just a few.

For most of the last thirty years, the United States has maintained an overvalued exchange rate. Following the exchange rate realignment of September, 1949, the United States allowed its principal industrial competitors in Europe and Asia to maintain super-competitive exchange rates, initially as part of a deliberate program of economic recovery, later on as a stubborn misbelief that the prestige of the United States was tied, somehow, to a fixed and costly exchange rate.

The toll of a falsely valued dollar becomes ever greater with the passage of the years. Manufacturing industries lose the opportunity to modernize as potential markets abroad are lost, profitability is diminished and foreign producers take over the American market. Equally important, the best human material entering the managerial classes ceases to be attracted to manufacturing industries and builds careers instead in such fields as investment banking, consulting, and other service occupations. Once the financial markets correctly assess the poor prospects of the traditional manufacturing industries, the cost of capital increases, completing the circle to guarantee a continuing industrial decline.

For a few years in the late 1970s, the dollar was valued sufficiently cheaply to let U.S. industry regain some of its lost position. The OPEC debacle of 1973, Watergate, weak economic policies, and relatively poor trade performance weakened the dollar. The result was real export growth of over 12 percent a year for the years 1979–1980. But that happy period now seems to be drawing to a close all too soon.

The United States produces half the oil it consumes, and so the dollar is less damaged by the second round of OPEC increases than the currencies of continental Europe and Japan. Great Britain has shown in these years just how damaging the strong petropound can be to manufacturing. On the other hand, Japan has demonstrated that a determined industrial country can pay for its oil imports if it shows sufficient aggressiveness in its export policies and performance. The pound is ruining British industry, the yen is giving various Japanese industries world domination. The United States is in an intermediate position.

The new monetarist approach to economic policy also is strengthening the dollar greatly. During the period of transition to noninflationary money growth, interest rates are very high, attracting capital inflows. Inflation prospects also improve, serving to keep the dollar very strong.

As a result of these international developments, U.S. export performance is likely to deteriorate over the next few years compared to the brief period of extraordinary success just behind us. This change will deteriorate the mix of employment once more, retarding productivity growth.

Domestic developments have also hurt productivity performance needlessly. The mix of employment has been damaged by the industrial relations system of the postwar period. The three-year wage contracts adopted after World War II, many of them with escalators and some with annual productivity factors, have led to a relative wage shift in favor of workers in the traditional heavy industries. High relative labor costs have been quite damaging to their international competitive position. The market economy has adjusted to this relative wage change: new factories have tended to locate far away from the heavily unionized Midwest region. Industries with little or weak unionization have grown much faster than the unionized sectors. And consumers have flocked to foreign products that are priced more competitively. From the point of view of productivity, at least as measured by the standard statistical methods, these shifts have been costly. Capital-intensive industries are high-productivity sectors, and if they languish, national productivity performance is reduced. There are also major social costs to this adjustment process. Migration may provide young workers with new opportunities in the Sun Belt, but older workers and older communities are left behind to suffer from the vicious circle of regional decline.

Management policies have also been adverse to productivity performance.[3] The links between true business quality and financial performance have been loosened by increased layers of management in the typical multiple-enterprise corporation. Acquisition is more exciting than modernization, and research and development has gone out of style in an era of executive compensation tied to annual results and stock valuations based on the preliminary estimates of quarterly earnings streams. Many of these destructive tendencies are reinforced by the tax laws and accounting conventions.

Public policies have made their own unique contributions to the productivity slowdown. Crudely administered regulations have diverted capital and management from developmental to defensive goals. Highly cyclical monetary policies have created periodic gluts of financial capital to fuel speculative activities, followed by disruptive periods of financial stringency. Income benefit programs have paid little attention to the incentive to work. Excessive personal tax burdens have driven work underground where it is not measured by the productivity statistics.

These lists could go on and on, of course. The main point is that the productivity issue has finally been recognized all through our society. The steps are being taken, in private and public policies, to put the development process back on a normal track. The step-up of capital formation, to be fostered by new investment incentives in the corporate income tax, is likely to be accomplished. It is not sufficient to do the job, but it is one strategy that we fully understand and has reasonably predictable results. It is an essential centerpiece of any program to renew productivity growth. Demographic changes and an improved world oil outlook also help create the opportunity for a productivity turnaround.

NOTES

1. See Kuh (1960) and Wilson and Eckstein (1964). Recent important productivity analyses include Denison (1979); Norsworthy, Harper, and Kunze (1979); and Siegel (1979).
2. U.S. Congress, Joint Economic Committee (1980).
3. For a sympathetic critique, see Hayes and Abernathy (1980).

BIBLIOGRAPHY

Denison, Edward F. *Accounting for Slower Growth.* Washington: The Brookings Institution, 1979.

Hayes, Robert H. and Abernathy, William J. "Managing Our Way to Economic Decline." *Harvard Business Review* LVIII (July-August, 1980): 67–77.

Kuh, Edwin. *Profits, Markups, and Productivity—An Examination of Corporate Behavior Since 1947.* Washington: Joint Economic Committee, U.S. Congress, (January) 1960.

Norsworthy, J. R.; Harper, M. J.; and Kunze, K. "The Slowdown in Productivity Growth." *Brookings Papers on Economic Activity* (2, 1979): 387–421.

Siegel, Robin. "Why Has Productivity Slowed Down." *Data Resources Review* (March, 1979): 59–65.

U.S., Congress, Joint Economic Committee, *Tax Policy and Core Inflation,* 96th Congress, 2d Session, April 10, 1980.

Wilson, Thomas A. and Eckstein, Otto. "Short Run Productivity Behavior in Manufacturing." *The Review of Economics and Statistics* 46 (February, 1964): 41–54.

DISCUSSANTS

Finn M. W. Caspersen

First, I would like to qualify my remarks by noting that talking about capital formation is very different if one does not talk about human capital. I think in many respects that human capital is the most important issue, as the leverage factor of educating or training a human is far more important to overall productivity than fiscal capital.

Second, I would like to say that I personally have little faith in any government policy of emphasizing capital accumulation which utilizes cushioning, either on a regional or industry-wide basis. Similarly, I have little or no faith in any government policy based on picking-the-winner, spotting-the-winner, or breeding-the-winner, to utilize Professor Ball's concept. In our system, unlike others, the political process is too pervasive to hope to have any sort of dispassionate analysis of what, how, and when to do it. We differ from other countries in that respect, but that is a fact of life.

Further, I see no evidence whatsoever that any group of people acting in concert can successfully pick-a-winner. Indeed, all the evidence is to the contrary. The only appropriate way is to let the market work its usual function, let the winners come to the fore and the losers fail.

We have heard that other countries have succeeded in such policies. I query this. I think that if you looked at Japan, you would find some very deep questions as to whether their economic policies have worked. Indeed, many of their leading intellectuals feel that they have not.

Third, I would like to talk a little bit about the Administration's supply proposals. It is very important to understand that the Administration first arrived at a philosophy and then arrived at economics to fit that philosophy. Whether or not that is good or bad is an entirely different question, but any discussion of their proposals has to be understood in that framework. Basically, it means that they are pretty well tied to them, far more so than perhaps political expediency would suggest.

From an analytical viewpoint, there is a real question if, even in normal times, such a supply economics would be successful, let alone whether we have the time now to let it be successful. There is a further question of whether we have the resources to let it be successful. The Administration's policy is much akin to a shotgun vis à vis a rifle, and I would suggest that many of the solutions advanced in this section are far more rifle-like and would be far more successful utilizing far fewer resources.

The standard Administration viewpoint is that in past situations, when you raised the tax rate it came out of the saving rate and, therefore, it follows logically that when you lower the tax rate it will go right back into the saving rate. This is a very open question, logically; with the lower standard of living, large parts of that tax decrease may in fact go into consumption. This is just a pragmatic approach, but I think it is fairly accurate.

The political system that we operate under basically mandates relatively gradual, transitional changes. We are not going to have radical changes, but we will have changes of magnitude, that is what we are discussing here. I would also suggest that for changes to come, they are going to need more than a business constituency to be implemented. This has serious ramifications for both the political process and how-to-target the tax break. You need a constituency, but more than just business.

I would like, at least in part, to challenge something that has been taken as a given. From dealing with the consumer on a day-to-day basis, both on the debit side and on the depositary side, I would disagree with the concept that the consumer pattern saving has not changed. I do this completely from *ad hoc* evidence, with all its limitations, but it is quite clear to me that the consumer has reacted to the current inflation by increasing his or her borrowing and decreasing his or her saving. This has had profound effects on the economy.

Further, the nature of consumer saving has changed. The one area that the consumer has been able to save in, the sole area that has kept up with inflation, has been the consumer's house. This is not an overly productive employment of capital, yet it is locked there right now and there are some very difficult problems unlocking it. But until we create a new environment and new tax laws, it will continue to be locked in with an adverse effect on capital formation and productivity.

There is one possible solution to the consumer saving problem which I view as fairly important. I do not think you can get an appropriate tax change through the Congress of the United States unless consumers are rewarded for increasing saving, and I am not sure at all that the traditional tax exemption for saving works. The tax exemption is basically oriented towards the upper-middle and upper income groups, and is basically a regressive concept. Similarly, I am not sure that the other concept being bandied about now, an open, portable Individual Retirement Account that is available to somebody who is covered by a regular pension particularly works for the same reasons, with the additional problem of the difficulty of getting assets out.

Perhaps we have to find some way of converting the idea of an investment tax credit to a consumer tax credit. I would further suggest that, psychologically, this is very important to the American consumer. We must break the back of the concept that the only way to stay ahead of the game is to spend and borrow, and instead, we need some way to stimulate a significant amount of real consumer savings.

I am optimistic. While there is some disagreement, I think if we all sat down, we could all agree that we *do* need productivity increases, we *do* need some new policies, and we *do* need capital accumulations. We would not have had the same consensus three to five years ago. And based on that, I think there will be a long-run solution!

Lacy H. Hunt

Capital formation is the key to economic expansion and a rising standard of living. For any state of technology with realistic expectations about the marginal productivity of labor, economic prosperity requires an increase in the economy's capital stock.

In recent years, however, capital stock enhancement has been severely limited. An expanding labor force, coupled with weak investment expenditures, has led to declines in labor productivity in each of the last three years. An economy suffering from falling productivity cannot expect to enjoy a higher standard of living.

To reverse this pattern, increased investment expenditures are essential. However, there is conceptual disagreement about the inducement to invest. In one corner, we have the Keynesian theorist; in the other corner, the supply-side theorist. Both parties would agree that the major inducement to invest is after-tax profits. However, this is where the similarity ends.

THE KEYNESIAN VIEW

According to Keynes, businessmen are motivated to invest by "animal spirits"—the expectation of future yield from capital investment. Therefore, increases in saving actually reduce investment. This analysis is based on the notion that increased savings in the current period can only occur if consumption is reduced. Weakness in consumption, and thus aggregate demand, would reduce investors' expectations of the future yields on alternative investments, thereby reducing perceived investment incentives.

To Keynes, the motivation to save was quite different from the motivation to invest, and the interest rate was not the mechanism or the "invisible hand" that equated the two. Instead, Keynesian economic growth is predicated on the acceleration principle. That is, increases in demand and output necessitate increases in plant and equipment. Investment is induced by increases in aggregate demand.

There is something to be said for the Keynesian analysis. However, an uncertain environment, with the future cost of money defying the laws of probability, a continuing upward ratcheting of the price level, and an ongoing escalation of the tax rates, does not provide a stable climate for investment incentives. Unfortunately, this uncertain environment is the classic description of U.S. economic history since the mid-1960s.

When a broader analysis includes government and financial markets, the problem becomes even more complex. The demand-management approach advocated by Keynes may indeed stimulate the economy, but along with increased aggregate demand, there may be some changes in the composition of demand. More specifically, increases in government spending may be financed by greater government borrowings, placing upward pressure on interest rates. As a result, corporations may reduce borrowings for new plant and equipment. Eventually, government spending supplants private investment through the classical "crowding-out" process, and when government spending supplants private investment, the economy does not experience the same improvement in its productive base that would result without government intrusion.

In basic terms, we can look at the last 15 years as a moving frontier of production possibilities, where overall policy has shifted the economy toward consumption and away from capital goods. Unfortunately, this government-induced change, in the mix of our output, has diminished the potential for future economic growth, a better standard of living, and gains in productivity. There are other ensuing ripples from this shift. Weak productivity, for example, raises long-term questions about the international competitiveness of U.S. industry. Already, this problem is too painfully evident in the automotive, steel, and textile industries.

THE SUPPLY-SIDE VIEW

I strongly believe that recent economic history has repudiated the Keynesian demand-management approach to fine tuning the economy. Table 1 tells the sorry story. Investment for productive plant and equipment as a percentage of GNP has moved downward since 1973 and the saving rate has decreased as the effective personal tax rate has risen. In addition, important and once prestigious firms face bankruptcy, and the rate of growth of government spending is out of hand.

The supply-side approach advocates moving the economy up the production possibilities curve, that is, shifting toward capital goods and away from consumer goods. In short, government policies or lack thereof which promote increased investment in plant and equipment will provide a sound basis for future economic growth.

Supply-side recommendations include: (1) cutting personal taxes, (2) increasing depreciation allowances, (3) decreasing the size of government, and (4) removing regulations which interfere with natural market forces. Essentially, the supply-side doctrine espouses "turn the economy back to the marketplace."

CUTTING PERSONAL TAXES

A reduction in personal income taxes is often considered to be a demand-management technique. The argument states that a one dollar reduction in personal income taxes will increase consumption by nearly 95 cents, but savings by only 5 cents. However, supply-side evidence indicates that the potential gain in savings is likely to be much greater than 5 cents on the dollar. According to Table 1, nearly every time the effective personal tax rate increased, the saving rate declined, and the recent record increase in Social Security taxes appears to be pushing the saving rate down even further. Consumers have maintained their standard of living and consumption by reducing savings, and the saving rate is largely the residual of the tax rate. Assuming that the impact of changes in the tax rate is symmetrical, we may infer that every 1.0 percent *drop* in personal tax rates will lead to nearly an 0.8 percent *increase* in the saving rate.

To the extent that the supply curve for labor is upward sloping, a drop in the effective tax rate is tantamount to a rise in wages. This will lead to a greater supply of labor, without a corresponding increase in the wage rate paid by employers. The ensuing rise in output and income would increase tax revenues, offsetting some of the revenues lost. Also, incentive to invest in nonproductive tax shelters would be diminished, thus freeing funds which could be employed more productively.

The increased saving which would result from tax cuts would be used in part to buy financial assets. This would drive up security prices and reduce interest rates. The reduction in the market rate of interest, coupled with positive expectations, would serve as an inducement to invest. Thus, funds saved by the household sector will be ultimately used to purchase new capital, thereby improving the productive base of the economy.

INCREASING DEPRECIATION ALLOWANCES

The supply-side proponents also argue that more favorable depreciation schedules would induce investment expenditure. The logic of this argument is that increased depreciation allowances will decrease corporate income taxes. However, the cash-generated profits of the firm would remain unchanged. As a result, the effective rate-of-return on depreciable assets would be increased, and thus investment in these assets would increase.

DECREASING THE SIZE OF GOVERNMENT

According to the supply-side doctrine, the role of government in the economy should be reduced. Between 1976 and 1980, Treasury receipts increased by over 68 percent. Despite this huge surge in revenues, the Treasury accumulated a deficit for the five year period of $240 billion. The funding of this deficit in the financial markets has caused severe pressure on interest rates. As a result, the Federal Reserve has experienced much difficulty in attempting to control the money supply and, at the same time, maintain order in the money markets. Interest rates have hit record levels and the gyrations in rates have created an aura of uncertainty. Clearly, such an environment is

TABLE 1

	New Investment in Plant* and Equipment as a Percentage of		Savings Rate	Effective Personal Tax Rate**	Productivity Percentage Change
	GNP	Consumption			
1973	6.2%	10.9%	8.6	15.4	2.0
1974	6.1%	10.0%	8.5	16.2	−3.1
1975	5.3%	8.4%	8.6	15.1	2.2
1976	5.1%	8.1%	6.9	15.7	3.6
1977	5.2%	8.2%	5.6	16.1	1.8
1978	5.2%	8.2%	5.2	16.5	−0.3
1979	5.3%	8.5%	5.3	17.3	−0.9
1980	5.1%	8.1%	5.6	17.3	−0.3

*New investment for plant and equipment minus expenditures for pollution abatement.
**Includes Social Security taxes.
SOURCE: U.S. Department of Commerce; Fidelity Bank—Economics Department

not conducive to investment. High long-term financing costs and uncertainty about future costs have caused both lenders and borrowers to shy away.

REMOVING REGULATIONS

Excessive government regulation has increased the cost of production, which is shared both by the corporate and household sectors. The cost to the corporate sector has reduced profits and profit expectations from alternative investments, thus impinging on the innovation and execution of otherwise profitable endeavors.

In summary, the role of government must be reduced. If a supply-side prescription is adopted, the natural market forces inherent in our economy will provide the incentives for new investment, increased productivity, and improvements in the standard of living.

Rudolph A. Oswald

In any discussion of capital formation and investment, it is important to have correct facts. Proponents of general tax cuts and liberalized accelerated depreciation allowances for business in order to stimulate investment have been suggesting that investment has been seriously lagging in the U.S. economy in recent years. However the U.S. Commerce Department's Bureau of Economic Analysis has recently released revised data which show that corporate profits and investment in the national income and product accounts have been much higher than previous data indicated—and that their share of national income and GNP has been at postwar peaks.

For example, profit as a percentage of national income was revised upward from 7.0 percent to 8.0 percent for 1978 and from 7.5 percent to 8.5 percent for 1979. Similarly, non-residential private fixed investment as a proportion of GNP was raised from 10.4 percent to 11.2 percent in 1978 and for 1979 from 10.8 percent to 11.6 percent, which was the highest rate of investment during the past 30 years. Thus, arguments for across-the-board tax subsidies through tax cuts to increase business profits and to stimulate investment are not supported by the actual data on profits and investment.

Cash flow—profits and depreciation set-asides is a good measure of business resources for paying dividends and expanding investment in plant and equipment. It is now at historic high levels. In 1979, cash flow of corporations was 15.7 percent of national income, a share higher than in any year after 1950. In the first three quarters of 1980, cash flow increased again, in spite of the recession, and at 15.2 percent of national income was again substantially above the 13.3 percent average for the past 30 years.

I recognize that inflation creates some problems in measuring profits and depreciation, but it is important to recognize also that inflation reduces the real burden of corporate debt. The declining debt burden offsets the higher cost of replacing and adding to plant and equipment. The business tax reductions of recent years, such as the investment tax credit and accelerated depreciation, have also offset some of the effects of inflation. The declining burden of debt and the tax cuts have offset the higher costs of replacing plant and equipment.

Age of plant and equipment is often taken as a proxy for technological progress. Plant and equipment have become increasingly more modern since World War II. The average age of plant and equipment in U.S. manufacturing, according to the Commerce Department, has fallen from 7.4 years in 1950 to 6.3 years in 1979, the lowest level in the postwar period. (This is on a net basis, after set-asides for depreciation.) The average age of equipment—excluding plant—has varied between 4.4 and 5.3 years since 1950, and now stands at 4.5 years.

The average age of equipment falls during times of expansion and rises during recessions. So it was at its lowest levels in the expansion of the 1940s and the 1960s and fell again in the four years of recovery from the 1975–76 recession. A 1978 McGraw-Hill survey found U.S. plant and equipment reasonably up-to-date with durable goods manufacturers reporting 49 percent of the plant and equipment less than five years old, and non-durable goods manufacturers reporting 39 percent of their plant and equipment less than five years old.

Finally, let me suggest that there is no evidence of an economy-wide shortfall of savings or "capital shortage" deterring investment and lowering growth in productivity. Savings have been high in recent years, but speculative loans for corporate acquisitions and for the speculation in commodities and real estate have diverted funds from productive investment. These big claims in credit markets have an adverse effect on the economy because they do not produce new capacity; they do not produce improvement in productivity; they do not create new production or new jobs.

The big oil companies offer a particularly horrendous example of big profits being used *not* for productive investment, but for a reshuffling of ownership by these corporate giants. The *New York Times* of March 16, 1981 reported big oil companies, with about one-third of all corporate profits in the United States, are putting their profits into buying existing business rather than finding more oil. The *Times* noted that a growing number of economists worry that these acquisitions are not an efficient use of capital. I worry about that too, and I also worry that these

TABLE 1
Investment

Year	GNP	Non-Residential Private Fixed Investment		Investment in Non-Residential Producers Durable Equipment	
		Billions of Dollars	As a Percent of GNP	Billions of Dollars	As a Percent of GNP
1949	$ 258.3	$ 24.4	9.4%	$ 15.7	6.1%
1950	286.5	27.3	9.5	17.8	6.2
1951	330.8	31.3	9.5	19.9	6.0
1952	348.0	31.3	9.0	19.7	5.7
1953	366.8	34.5	9.4	21.5	5.9
1954	366.8	34.2	9.3	20.8	5.7
1955	400.0	38.5	9.6	23.9	6.0
1956	421.7	44.0	10.4	26.3	6.2
1957	444.0	47.0	10.6	28.6	6.4
1958	449.7	42.0	9.3	24.9	5.5
1959	487.9	45.9	9.4	28.3	5.8
1960	506.5	48.5	9.6	29.7	5.9
1961	524.6	48.0	9.1	28.9	5.5
1962	565.0	52.2	9.2	32.1	5.7
1963	596.7	54.8	9.2	34.4	5.8
1964	637.7	61.0	9.6	38.7	6.1
1965	691.1	72.7	10.5	45.8	6.6
1966	756.0	83.1	11.0	53.0	7.0
1967	799.6	83.9	10.5	53.7	6.7
1968	873.4	90.7	10.4	58.2	6.7
1969	944.0	101.3	10.7	64.6	6.8
1970	992.7	103.9	10.5	65.2	6.6
1971	1077.6	107.9	10.0	67.4	6.3
1972	1185.9	121.0	10.2	76.9	6.5
1973	1326.4	143.3	10.8	92.3	7.0
1974	1434.2	156.6	10.9	100.7	7.0
1975	1549.2	157.7	10.2	102.3	6.6
1976	1718.0	174.1	10.1	115.3	6.7
1977	1918.0	205.5	10.7	140.9	7.3
1978	2156.1	242.0	11.2	163.3	7.6
1979	2413.9	279.7	11.6	183.4	7.6
1980	2626.5	295.4	11.2	186.8	7.1

SOURCE: Department of Commerce, Bureau of Economic Analysis
Updated from February 18, 1981 release.

Discussants
151

TABLE 2
Shares of National Income Profits and Cash Flow

Years	Corporate Profits After Taxes Percent of National Income	Corporate Cash Flow* Percent of National Income
1950–59	7.6	12.5
1960–69	7.0	13.5
1970–79	7.0	14.0
1950–79	7.2	13.3
1978	8.0	15.1
1979	8.5	15.7
1980 (1st 9 mos.)	7.8	15.2

*NOTE: Cash flow equals corporate profits after taxes, plus depreciation allowances as estimated by Federal tax returns.

SOURCE: U.S. Department of Commerce, Bureau of Economic Analysis data.

big oil companies are raising the concentration of economic and political power in the United States.

Briefly here, I have tried to open up the "capital formation" issue so as not to be tied up in the tired rhetoric of "capital shortages" and the need for more trickle-down economics. We in the labor movement will continue to press for a healthy, growing, full employment economy with widely disbursed and rising buying power in the hands of the great mass of consumers. This is the best way to stimulate sales, production, and employment, and thus to create business profits and incentives for investment and capital formation.

Theodore F. Brophy

The problems of high inflation, sluggish economic growth, and high unemployment, with their undesirable economic and political side effects, have not come upon us suddenly and do not affect the United States alone. Over the past few years, a consensus has formed among business executives, government leaders, economists, academicians, and labor leaders that these economic difficulties either stem from or can be traced directly to government policies that were or have become inappropriate in the changing economic environment of the 1970s and 1980s. However, as yet no clear consensus has been reached within this group regarding the changes that are needed to reverse these ills. It is my judgment that two important steps we must take are: (1) to make fundamental changes in our tax laws to stimulate capital formation, saving, and investment, and (2) at the same time significantly decrease the rate of growth in Federal government spending to reduce the percent of GNP expended by our Federal government.

Clearly, government policy has failed in at least five key areas: (1) excessive and ineffective regulation when measured by cost-benefit; (2) cost-of-living indexing of government expenditure programs which tend to perpetuate inflation; (3) a steeply progressive income tax system which leads to "bracket creep" in times of high inflation, and depreciation procedures based on historical cost and so-called "useful life," which form a disincentive to capital formation; (4) tax and social programs which have encouraged overreliance on government, discouraged savings, and created work disincentives; and (5) large continuing government deficits which have resulted in related increases in the money supply. The common thread that runs through these policy failures is the fact that they either perpetuate or directly worsen inflation. They also contribute to the decline in productivity which adversely impacts our competitiveness in the world marketplace.

This interlocking cycle of inflation, slow economic growth, poor productivity performance, and inadequate capital formation must be broken. A program for breaking this cycle has been put forward by President Reagan. It has five principal components: reduction in government spending, regulatory reforms, renewed support for the Federal Reserve's policy of stable and noninflationary money supply growth, reductions in personal income tax rates, and accelerated depreciation for U.S. business. I would like to focus the balance of my remarks toward the tax aspects of this program.

Perhapsthe major factor behind the nation's inadequate capital formation in recent years has been the structure of our Federal tax laws, exacerbated by the global inflationary force of energy prices.

Our Federal tax system contains many counter-investment inefficiencies and inequities that become more prominent during times of high inflation.

- Investment income is taxed at a burdensome rate because inflation creates illusory, but taxable, capital gains on equities and other assets.
- Dividends and interest income, for the most part, are subject to double taxation.
- The progressive nature of the individual tax rate structure strips real income from taxpayers whose wages have just kept pace with inflation and reduces their ability to save and invest.

An important shortcoming of the current approach to capital recovery is that it is based on the so-called "useful life" concept, which classifies assets into categories for depreciation purposes according to purely technical considerations. This fails to take into consideration critical economic factors such as obsolescence, the impact of new technology, and changing competitive conditions. An even more serious defect of the current capital recovery procedure is the fact that in a highly inflationary environment, write-offs based on original cost do not provide sufficient deductions to recover replacement costs.

During the 96th Congress several significant proposals emerged that would provide a major change in the tax treatment of capital recovery. The 97th Congress is now considering a Reagan administration proposal called Accelerated Capital Recovery System (ACRS), which contains many of the concepts from the 10–5–3 system. All these proposals would:

- significantly enhance business cash flow, an important component of private saving,
- improve rates-of-return on capital investments,
- provide urgently needed relief to our capital markets and the precarious financial condition of many U.S. corporations,
- simplify the current tax depreciation rules, something that would be particularly beneficial to our smaller businesses, and
- make great strides towards ending the dependence on the "useful life" concept.

There is evidence that tax cuts and spending restraints together cannot only improve the economy, but also increase governmental revenue.

An example of a successful program on a local government level is the experience of New York State and City over the past several years. In 1975 New York had the second highest state and local tax burden in the country (nearly 40 percent above the national average) and was on the brink of bankruptcy. Income taxes, particularly in the highest brackets, were cut, and real estate taxes were frozen. At the same time fiscal austerity was imposed in the budget area. As a result of these actions, tax collections have increased dramatically (for New York State 18 percent annually since 1977) and there has been significant real growth in the city's economy. New York City, now living within its financial means, is poised to reenter the long-term bond market for the first time in many years.

Second, we can point to instances at the national level when investment-oriented tax changes have had a favorable impact on our economy. The Revenue Act of 1978 reduced the maximum capital gains tax for individuals from about 49 percent to 28 percent, and the corporate capital gains tax rate from 30 percent to 28, thereby making it more attractive from a risk/reward standpoint to invest in capital assets. Evidence to date shows that this has had a very positive impact on the new issues market, the venture capital industry, and the stock market as a whole. Equally important, a Treasury Department study indicates that this rate reduction caused a new revenue loss in 1979 of $100 million rather than the $1.7 billion that had been forecast. The lower tax rate generated much more economic activity than had been anticipated.

We must depart from the philosophic trend of "income redistribution" that has been maintained over most of the postwar period and embark on a new era that focuses on creating a larger income pie for everyone.

Sustained real economic growth for our nation will:

- lower inflation,
- create new jobs,
- reduce the percentage of our citizens at poverty levels, and
- raise standards of living in general.

SUMMARY REPORT

Capital Formation

Jack Guttentag

The general case for encouraging capital formation is that it increases productivity, which is essential to rising real income per capita.

There was some disagreement among panelists on the importance of capital formation as an influence on productivity relative to several other factors such as energy prices, inflation, and personal tax rates. Nevertheless, it was generally agreed that a slowdown in capital formation has been a significant factor in recent declines in productivity. (Capital formation can be measured in many different ways, some of which point in different directions, but the consensus was that the most relevant measures show a decline in recent years.) The desirability of increasing capital formation, especially plant and equipment spending, was not questioned, although there was considerable disagreement as to different policies for bringing it about.

One policy to increase capital formation commanded almost complete agreement among panelists, namely, a reduction in government spending. Such a reduction would, other things being the same, reduce inflation, which would lower investment risks. Studies were cited showing that inflation significantly depresses capital investment in plant and equipment. Lower government spending would also increase the availability of loanable funds and reduce interest rates, thereby lowering the cost of capital. However, specific types of government spending may contribute importantly to capital formation (for example, expenditures on infrastructure, such as roads or research and development). And some government spending, on education and training for example, may directly benefit productivity.

There was also a consensus for relying mainly on private markets to allocate capital among competing users. There was no support for the idea of a national investment board which would make case-by-case decisions on capital allocations. This reflected panelists' concern about intrusion of politics in the decision process, and about possible bias toward propping up declining industries and ailing firms.

The panel generally favored reducing corporate taxes as a means of increasing capital formation by improving after-tax rates-of-return. Lower corporate tax rates may also raise total saving. Liberalized depreciation allowances and investment tax credits appear to have a somewhat larger effect on plant and equipment spending, per dollar of revenue loss, than a decline in general tax rates. The latter, however, because they reduce the discriminatory effect of double taxation on equity investment, may provide greater encouragement to investment in new technology. Liberalization of rules that prohibit expending of patent purchases also would encourage investment in new technology.

A general reduction in corporate tax rates also lessens the incentive for corporations to finance with debt rather than equity, reducing their overall leverage, and their exposure to unforseen shocks.

The panel split badly on the effect of personal tax rates on capital formation and productivity. In particular, the statistical evidence on the relationship between personal tax rates and personal saving was subject to sharply divergent interpretations. There also was no agreement on whether enactment of the Kemp-Roth (or similar) tax cuts in the near-term future would stimulate capital formation, or only inflation. The panel agreed, however, that favorable "supply-side" effects were more dependable in the case of lower corporate taxes than in the case of personal taxes. On the other hand, high personal tax rates clearly stimulate growth in the so-called "underground economy," with consequent revenue losses to government, inequities between those who participate in the underground economy and those who do not, and erosion of private morality.

The panel generally agreed that plant and equipment investment would be stimulated by reducing government subsidies to housing. However, one type of subsidy directed through specialized thrift institutions is already being phased out under the Depository Institutions Deregulation and Monetary Control Act of 1980. The major remaining subsidy is the interest deductibility of home mortgage payments, which some panelists would limit. It was agreed however, that such a proposal might not be politically feasible.

Panelists were sensitive to the impact of measures to increase capital formation on the distribution of income and several suggestions which would cushion this impact, such as a reduction in Social Security taxes, were proposed.

Energy ☆ ☆ ☆ ☆ ☆ ☆ ☆ ☆ ☆

8.
POLICIES FOR ENERGY INDEPENDENCE

Robert R. Nathan

In the intervening seven-and-a-half years since the October 1973 oil embargo, some real progress has been made in coping with the energy crisis, but relative to the severity of the problem the progress has been quite limited. Organization of Petroleum Exporting Countries oil pricing has contributed to serious inflation in the United States and in many other oil importing nations. Mitigation of that damage is not in sight.

The massive dollars spent for U.S. oil imports (some $80 billion in 1980) has served to undermine our balance of payments and weaken the dollar. Tight money and very high interest rates have strengthened the dollar temporarily, but have weakened the domestic economy. Many of the less-developed nations that import oil cannot both pay for oil and finance development. They have borrowed heavily from financial institutions, including U.S. banks. The economic and financial consequences of OPEC have been very damaging.

Except for large new discoveries and rising output of natural gas, the production of domestic sources of energy has ranged from disappointing to despairing. Much was expected of nuclear power, but compared with clearly feasible goals and huge energy requirements, nuclear power output has lagged badly. The outlook for nuclear power continues to be bleak because of confusion, uncertainty, and weak public leadership.

Conversion from oil to coal for electricity generation moves at a snail's pace. President Ford in 1974 set an annual goal of 1.5 billion tons of coal production by 1985. In 1977 President Carter reduced that goal to 1.2 billion tons. Both of these targets have become about as realistic as the proverbial snowball in Hades. We have the reserves and could readily develop the production and transportation facilities, but again action falls far short of promise.

Except for the temporary upturn when Alaskan North Slope oil came on line in 1977, U.S. oil production tended downward over the past decade and, at best, will remain level over the next few years, despite record numbers of drilling rigs at work onshore and offshore.

Natural gas had usually been discovered as a by-product in drilling for oil. Now that gas prices have increased immensely and will rise more as gas price decontrol proceeds toward a total free market in 1985, the search for new gas reserves has become more targeted, and the results have been more fruitful. The outlook is certainly brighter for natural gas, but not nearly bright enough to make a major dent in the continuing need for large oil imports.

The belated and barely perceptible start toward substantial development of synthetic fuels may well be derailed by President Reagan's retrenchment of government commitments to share risks inherent in developing synthetic fuels. There are plentiful supplies of coal, shale, tar sands, and other sources of synfuels, but huge investments will be required and the risks are very large. A tendency to greatly curtail or to terminate a role by the government is almost certain to doom synfuel prospects for at least the next decade.

Public programs and outlays for research and development activities relating to new sources of energy, to more efficient energy use, and to environmental protection do not begin to match the intensive efforts in the 1960s associated with space exploration. The energy crisis has been referred to as the moral equivalent of war, but the production effort to date is hardly compatible with that view. It may be true that dollars alone will not solve complex problems, but rhetoric alone without dollars will surely yield no results. Much more research and development will enhance nuclear power safety and permit much higher use of coal with less threat to clean air and pure water.

More progress appears to have been achieved in conservation than in expanding new domestic sources of energy. After 1973 many industrial and commercial enterprises responded to much higher oil and other energy prices by discovering and applying new fuel-saving devices and procedures. As a result, energy use per unit of industrial output has declined significantly over the past several years. Residential use of energy has also become more efficient in response to rising energy prices and to patriotic appeals.

Gasoline consumption of automobiles and trucks did not fall perceptibly until gasoline prices approximately doubled in 1979–80. Starting in 1979, there was a pronounced shift in demand to more fuel-efficient cars and a reduction of automobile mileage. I hope this portends a continuing marked drop in the massive use of gasoline in the United States. To reduce substantially our dependence on imported oil and thereby improve our economic and energy independence and strengthen our nation's security, we must continue to curtail consumption of oil at a rapid and sustained rate.

The key question is "to what degree can the market place be relied upon to deal effectively with the energy crisis: exclusively, or substantially, or only slightly, or not at all?" To date, neither the private sector nor the public sector can claim high honors for scintillating performances in dealing with energy.

For many decades the oil industry explored and exploited fossil fuels in the United States effectively, efficiently, and generally profitably, but not always under vigorous competitive conditions. The first major antitrust suits by the government were initiated against the large oil companies and considerable concentration of productive capacity and marketing channels evolved and persisted.

Competition did prevail in varying degrees in the United States among different sources of energy, such as wood, water, coal, oil, and gas. Tax incentives, in the form of cost depletion and intangible expenditure allowances, encouraged the discovery and development of oil and gas reserves. Only when oil reserves became more and more difficult to find did it become clear that prices were too low to stimulate new discoveries. And they were too low to discourage consumption of this valuable, nonrenewable fuel. But for many years it was not U.S. government policies that kept prices down. Rather, unprecedented large discoveries of oil around the world, especially in the Middle East, tended to keep prices low. Thus, low-cost foreign oil supplies kept U.S. oil prices below levels that would have restrained demand for oil and would have stimulated the development of alternative energy sources.

Many oil importing nations pursued sound energy policies of raising prices to consumers through very high sales and excise taxes on gasoline and other petroleum products. Long before OPEC, gasoline in many European nations retailed at three to five times prices in the United States. Of course, the United States was self-sufficient in petroleum and even exported oil, but there were distressing signals that we were heading into trouble. Studies were conducted and reports were published warning that the future prospects for domestic oil reserves were increasingly bleak. These findings were either ignored or criticized by the oil industry. Proposals for even modest increases in gasoline taxes were resisted by the industry. Those who most vigorously opposed our following the logical pattern of other countries are now the most severe critics of earlier government policies. Domestic oil prices were restrained in recent years by government actions, but price control is now over for oil. Prices for natural gas are in the process of decontrol.

A great deal of nonsense is uttered by groups seeking to place blame for past failures. On the one hand, some critics charge the oil industry with practices that adversely and seriously affect the national interest. These charges are often made without evidence, but with vehemence and, sometimes, with impact. On the other hand, some oil industry leaders foolishly contend that if only the government would get off the backs of the oil industry, the United States could now and for the foreseeable future produce all the oil the country needs. Most expert observers disagree totally with this simplistic view and are convinced that even with substantially higher oil prices, pretroleum production in the United States will inevitably trend downward. That means that the total supply of oil will not increase in any significant degree even with substantial rises in prices. That does not mean that costly secondary and tertiary recoveries or costly drilling, very deeply and very far offshore, will not be undertaken as prices rise, but it does mean that substantially greater supplies of oil will not be forthcoming as a result of greater or total reliance on market forces. The supply elasticity of oil is not high. In essence, higher oil prices will yield limited increases in oil production.

To increase the production of alternative sources of energy, higher prices of oil products to users should have some impact. But higher prices for gasoline and other oil products should be achieved through higher taxes rather than higher producer prices, which in turn will bring huge windfall profits and then windfall taxes. Gasoline prices in the United States, although very high by past U.S. standards, are very low by international standards. They would have to at least double to equal retail prices in other large oil importing nations. Such higher prices can be reached reasonably soon and with minimum inflationary impact through the taxing mechanism. As proposed by the late Arthur Okun, revenues from such taxes could be funneled back to states and localities on condition that sales taxes (or even property taxes where there are no sales taxes) be reduced in like dollar amount, and thereby counter the general inflationary consequences of higher gasoline prices.

By resorting to higher taxes on oil products, OPEC pricing would cease to be the principal determinant of U.S. domestic petroleum product prices. As demonstrated in 1979–80, the conservation response to much higher gasoline taxes would be significant. Also, higher gasoline and other oil prices should serve to stimulate production of alternative sources of energy. Of course, resistance from the oil industry, the automobile industry, and even consumer interests can be expected unless inflationary offsets are provided. The time is long overdue for substantially higher taxes on petroleum products, especially at the consumer level.

Can and should we rely entirely on market forces to develop alternatives to oil supplies? Can safety and environmental considerations with respect to nuclear power and much greater coal use be left totally to the market place? Can the private sector be expected to assume all of the risks involved in early and large-scale developments of facilities to produce synthetic fuels? Will private enterprise alone support the needed research and development efforts for the early and substantial reduction of our dependence on oil imports? Can nonintervention by government be warranted when so much of the world's oil reserves are controlled by an international cartel whose pricing and production decisions are determined by political rather than economic factors? These are not frivolous questions. They need careful thought. Solutions will not be found in polarized antiintervention policies nor will they be found in government controls embracing all energy issues.

There is almost universal agreement that major shifts from oil to other fuels in the production of electricity has not been occurring at a satisfactory rate when weighed against the costs inherently associated with continued heavy reliance on oil imports. But general concensus that this conversion process must be accelerated will not get results. Both nuclear power and substantial increases in the use of coal pose safety and environmental problems that cannot be ignored or brushed aside by antigovernment slogans. Nor will these problems be resolved by exclusive reliance on market forces.

I am convinced that continuing dependence on large-scale imports of oil poses greater danger to our system, to our economy, and to our very existence than does increased reliance on nuclear power. Such conclusions entail political decisions and not just economic determinations. They go far beyond pure market place responsibility. Some dangers are associated with greatly expanding the production of nuclear power, as demonstrated by the ineptness that was evidenced at Three Mile Island. But these risks can be greatly reduced. The safety record to date has been remarkably good, but there can be further improvement and greater security assurances. We can and must improve these technological factors and the managerial disciplines, that would greatly reduce the prospects of another Three Mile Island problem.

Actual safety and public confidence would increase if nuclear power production were limited to a small number of the best managed, best operated, and best equipped public utilities whose energy output would then be made available to other utilities through the national grid system. The concentration of managerial and technical talents in a small number of firms would minimize the degree of risk, as compared with policies that allow nearly every utility that wants to get into the act to produce nuclear power.

Of course, such selectivity tends to be alien to those who believe that the market place can solve anything and everything, including all environmental risks. Clearly, an agency of the Federal government, hopefully with the advice of the electric utility industry and perhaps of state regulatory commissions, would determine the list of eligible nuclear energy producers. I believe it is as unreasonable and perhaps irresponsible to attack all government intervention in the field of nuclear power as it would be to demand that this important area be developed exclusively through government ownership and government operation. The extremists opposed to nuclear power have achieved some of their success in arousing public opposition just because of excessive claims and demands of other extremists who call for no government intervention in this difficult, but very important, problem area.

Currently, the prospects are not entirely favorable for completing all nuclear projects now under way. Even more bleak are the prospects for initiating new nuclear projects. There are strong advocates who want to get rid of every nuclear power facility, even those already in operation. Unfortunately, among the supporters of nuclear power are some ardent spokesmen who go so far as to ridicule any talk of possible risks or dangers associated with this important source of electric power. Common sense and cool heads do not appear to be prevailing today. The cooler heads seem to stand aside and let the polarized extreme views capture the headlines. That is regrettable because the need for nuclear power will become more urgent, whereas the safety and environmental issues will not disappear.

Government has an important role in establishing sound and workable nuclear safety regulations. Without such regulations there will be little hope for further nuclear power, and that would be most unfortunate. We need not spell out a precise program to reestablish confidence in nuclear power, but we do need to recognize that government has critical functions to perform to maximize safety and protect the environment. This must be achieved without making the production of nuclear power so costly and so involved in red tape as to, in effect, help the antinuclear forces achieve their objectives.

If President Reagan is going to rely on simplistic solutions or pure rhetoric to expand the nuclear power program in this country, he will not succeed. Above all, the tearing down of every vestige of confidence in and support for government policies and actions will be a serious disservice to the whole energy subject, and especially to the cause of nuclear power. It seems inconceivable that government licensing and regulation of nuclear power would be terminated, but in the spirit of 1981 that perhaps could happen.

Serious environmental questions are also raised by the prospect of substantially increased use of coal. The best scientists differ greatly about the risk factors associated with expanded nuclear power facilities and with the substantial conversion to coal for the production of electricity. For the average layman this diversity of expert opinion is very distressing. If noted experts cannot agree, how can the general public arrive at rational and sound conclusions in these complex areas. Reasonable persons cannot entirely ignore the dramatic and exaggerated contentions about the dangers to life from nuclear accidents and the disposal of nuclear waste.

As an example, I too am worried about charges that acid rain has ruined thousands of lakes. I do not believe for one minute that the market place will take care of that issue. Also, how can political forces be mobilized to support the increased use of these two very significant contributions to increased energy independence, especially if no governmental role is allowed? With all due respect for Milton Friedman's facile mind, his oversimplified and anecdotal solutions will not convince many thoughtful persons and legislators that nuclear energy and vast increases in coal use pose no problems and that there is nothing to worry about as long as evil Uncle Sam is put to sleep. We might all be charmed into peaceful slumber and told that the market place will take care of everything, but it will not work, even in 1981.

Let us take a hard look at coal. This country has tremendous reserves of coal, enough for hundreds of years even if we export large quantities. In the past we produced great quantities of electricity from coal. Many manufacturing industries generated their own heat and power from coal for decades. But those quantities were of a different order of magnitude. Also, the sensitivity of people to clean air and clean water and other environmental objectives has changed drastically. We want a healthier environment, and most of us are prepared to pay a price. But, environmental standards can be made so rigid as to raise the economic and social costs to a level that can precipitate economic suffocation with reduced production, fewer jobs, declining income, lower living standards, and worse inflation. A reasonable balance is very difficult to achieve. Such a reconciliation between reasonable environmental objectives on the one hand and economic and social costs on the other is not readily determined in the market place. Nor will they be readily achieved under a variety of proliferating government policies and activities. As with so many problems, government and business must cooperate and coordinate their actions rather than confront each other as bitter adversaries.

One of the more interesting energy topics in Washington concerns the scheduled deregulation of natural gas prices. As of now, a law calls for the gradual deregulation of gas prices with full freedom by 1985. The new Administration has floated a trial balloon suggesting immediate or accelerated deregulation, as was done recently with oil. In the case of oil, the date of total price deregulation was advanced by President Reagan from its original October, 1981 schedule to February, 1981. The change involved only seven months, whereas for natural gas the control period could be shortened by as much as four years. Also, added profits accruing to the oil companies will in part be siphoned off by the government through the so-called Windfall Profits Tax.

Interestingly enough, the natural gas industry is not an advocate for immediate decontrol of natural gas prices. In fact, the industry has indicated to the Reagan administration that it has grave doubts about such action at this time. Part of its policy derives from its concern about the enactment of higher Windfall Profits Taxes for natural gas. But the industry also recognizes how disruptive it could be to raise natural gas prices by as much as two dollars per thousand cubic feet at the wellhead within a very short period of time. Many analysts now conclude that the price of natural gas to produce the Btu. equivalent of a $40 barrel of oil would be somewhere in the $6 or $7 range per thousand cubic feet of gas. That would represent an astounding cost increase to all users. Storms of protest and huge profit increases in the industry would take place simultaneously and bring strong pressures for high Windfall Profits Tax legislation. Also, it certainly would add strongly to the nation's inflationary forces at a time when it is desperately important to slow the pace of general increases in prices.

Whether decontrol of natural gas at this time would significantly increase the discovery of new reserves is highly questionable. A huge effort is under way already to find new gas reserves and has had considerable success. The recent increases in prices of natural gas, coupled with assured large increases over the next four years, provide very attractive incentives to those seeking new gas reserves. Also, because drilling rigs are in short supply, increased drilling can be achieved only gradually. Therefore, there would appear to be little justification for early price decontrol of natural gas on grounds of stimulating further production. If higher gas prices would encourage greater conservation of this very desirable fuel, or would increase efforts to find alternative sources of fuel, that could be accomplished by placing excise taxes on this important product. In any case, the present schedule of decontrol should assure those investing in alternative sources of energy that in very few years natural gas will be selling at least at $6 or $7 per thousand cubic feet in 1981 dollars. That should be sufficient incentive for more drilling for gas once the supply of rigs catches up with demand.

It is commonly agreed that natural gas is a most desirable fuel from the point of view of cost, efficiency, cleanliness, ease of use, ready transportability, and safety. Given these highly favorable features, is it good policy not only to discover every possible reserve of gas in the United States, but also to exploit those reserves as quickly as possible? Would it be an appropriate objective to reduce our reliance on imported oil by using our natural gas reserves speedily and totally? Or should nuclear power and coal be the principle substitutes for oil imports? It would seem to be in the best interest of the country and of coming generations to stretch out the use of natural gas, rather than consume all of it before alternative sources with equal beneficial characteristics are developed.

It is doubtful whether the market place can resolve that issue. It seems essential that the government adopt policies designed to increase reliance on coal and nuclear sources to the extent that reasonable environmental problems can be resolved, rather than rely on more natural gas. The natural gas industry itself has expressed the view that a combination of some natural gas and more coal can be substituted for oil to produce electricity, with significant reductions in the adverse environmental impacts associated with coal. That certainly ought to be encouraged, but, again, there are serious doubts whether market forces alone will expedite these and other constructive programs.

Most persons would agree that conservation is the most feasible and cheapest single step to decrease oil imports. That does not mean that the energy crisis can be solved by conservation alone, soon or over the long run. Beyond doubt, the United States is far less efficient in the use of energy than most, if not all, oil importing nations. There is much room for large savings of oil through further conservation measures, and we ought to go all out to achieve these savings. That is true for other sources of energy as well.

As already noted, the rise in oil and all energy prices starting in 1974 did result in substantially greater efficiency in energy use in many industries. OPEC prices quadrupled soon after the embargo. Large industrial users of oil were hard pressed to offset these higher costs in order to remain competitive. Some of them soon learned to use oil and other energy sources much more efficiently. The rise in gasoline prices after the embargo seemed to have only a modest and transient impact on the market for gasoline. But, the doubling of oil prices in 1979 and 1980 led to the first major and significant conservation in the use of gasoline. It took a jump of about 70 cents per gallon in just a few months to reduce mileage driven substantially and to achieve a large shift in demand from gas-guzzling large cars to fuel-efficient compacts and subcompacts. The shift to fuel-efficient cars is affecting the demand for used as well as new automobiles.

Some persons question whether there is an ongoing role for government in programs and policies to achieve greater fuel efficiency. Those who strongly oppose all government intervention contend that such intervention will hurt more than it will help. This kind of rigid ideological posture makes little sense, because reasonable efforts by government to get more energy conservation are essential. The government has spurred residential and business surveys on energy consumption and pressed for the development of conservation programs by public utilities. Community-wide efforts of this nature have had an impact and should be broadened and continued. Research and development efforts on conservation financed by public funds have been evaluated favorably. The fact that higher fuel prices trigger greater conservation does not preclude other efforts. The market place does not offer the only answers. Some public programs may involve the stimulation of voluntary efforts; others may entail compulsory standards. Fruitful conservation programs by government should not be terminated because of the strong bias against government intervention.

As indicated earlier, serious consideration should be given to a tax program that will increase the cost of gasoline and other oil products to achieve more conservation. We know from the 1979–80 experience that there is a high degree of demand elasticity for gasoline. Surely over the next decade gasoline prices will increase as OPEC increases the price of crude oil and oil products. Oil gluts will be temporary in nature, but as prices soften during these transient periods, gasoline demand may again increase. It is even possible that demand might even increase for larger cars. But we cannot ignore the longer term downward trend in world oil supplies or the more certain increasing longer term reliance of the United States on imported oil. Nor should we neglect the impact on our balance of trade and balance of payment of scores of billions of dollars in oil imports. Of especially grave consequence is the insecurity of the United States when so much of our energy availability depends on the production and selling policies of OPEC.

The sooner and the greater the decline in oil imports, the better off the United States will be. Why should the United States depend on cartel-influenced oil pricing policies for greater conservation, when taxes on gasoline can bring early and persistent drops in oil imports? Other industrial nations have followed this policy for decades and their fuel efficiency in transportation makes the United States look like a terrible waster of a precious and scarce resource. We ought to legislate at least a 50 cent tax per gallon of gasoline and add further sizable increments annually until the demand for gasoline falls dramatically and until alternative fuel sources for motor vehicles are developed.

Of particular significance are policies designed to facilitate and encourage the development of new sources of energy. In many of these programs the risks are great and large financing is required, especially if rapid progress is needed. In reviewing President Reagan's budget proposals, it is distressing to note the large number of energy-related programs in which substantial reductions of governmental outlays are proposed. The list includes programs related to alcohol fuels development, biomass projects, fossil energy research, solar subsidies, energy conservation, and support for synthetic fuels projects. Some of these programs are to be entirely eliminated, such as solar subsidies and alcohol fuel subsidies. Others are to be reduced by 50 percent or more in the next few years. Such widespread and substantial energy-related budget reductions are not in the public interest and reflect the view that there is no energy crisis, and/or that most government programs are not needed.

Given unlimited time, the chances are somewhat favorable that private industry will exploit many new fuel potentials effectively. But time is urgent for economic and political, as well as security reasons. If we are going to reduce the inflationary forces in this country, we cannot continue to be dominated so heavily by OPEC pricing decisions. If we are going to strengthen our dollar and improve our trade and payments balances, we must move rapidly to replace much of our oil consumption with nuclear energy and coal, and new, renewable energy sources.

Assumption of risks is an essential element in our enterprise system. However, during the last decade or two, there has been less inclination by corporations to assume business risks. Inflation may be a critical factor in this respect. But inflation itself is in part attributable to OPEC pricing. That makes it all the more urgent to deal aggressively with the risk issue through various incentives and risk sharing by government. We need to determine not only whether government should assume any risks, but also how such sharing should be structured; that is, either through financial participation, such as loans at concessionary rates, or minority equity participation by government, or funding by public agencies set up for these purposes, or through guaranteed marketing arrangements. Serious consideration should be given to various means of moderating risk so that venturesome businessmen will greatly speed up the development of new sources of energy.

Of particular significance is the massive size of outlays required for research and development programs, pilot plants, and production facilities. Many large outlays will be doomed to failure. The pace of technological change makes the risk factor so costly as to discourage private companies from assuming such risks alone or in concert with other corporations. All these risks are made even more discouraging by the very high level of interest rates that may persist for years to come. Rather than becoming more favorable, the prospects for a large synthetic fuels program, rapid rise in solar energy, and increases in other renewable sources are becoming more and more uncertain, if not bleak.

Government support programs now underway should be monitored and evaluated rather than tossed aside on pure ideological grounds. New constructive and effective ideas for dealing with the risk factor are needed, not negative attacks on all proposed government policies and programs.

There is another important area where the public role must play an important part and that relates to international arrangements. To avoid the worst kind of dog-eat-dog scrambling, the United States and other oil importing nations are tending to work together to facilitate maximum production of old sources of energy, to engage in common efforts to achieve much more efficient use of scarce energy resources, focus more sharply on new sources, share technical know-how, and share limited supplies when serious scarcities emerge. These are justifiable public goals and policies and should be accorded high governmental priorities.

Many functions that are exclusively or largely in the government sector are importantly related to the energy crisis. With few exceptions, local mass transit is publicly owned and operated, principally by large city governments. This includes subways, city bus systems, suburban rail lines, public school buses, and other government operated vehicles. Airlines, intercity bus service, and trucking are largely in private hands. Railroad freight operations are generally under private sector control. Harbors are largely in the public sector, but merchant shipping is mostly under private ownership and operation. Governmental regulation in differing degrees influence fares, safety standards, routes, and services in many transport modes.

The transportation industry is a large energy user. Market forces have already brought improved fuel efficiency in private passenger car operations. Fuel is a significant cost factor in many modes of transport and higher prices will bring greater economy of use. Taxes can and should play a role in speeding and enlarging the reduction in fuel use in this sector. That objective requires public as well as private policies and actions.

It is difficult to conclude that all these varied programs or any potentially important part thereof should be discarded because of the expectation that the market place will provide the full solutions. This contention has practically no validity in the international arena, and is dubious in many domestic programs. Rather than abandon government policies and activities, the governmental programs should be geared to take advantage of market forces. Projects and programs should be structured in ways that would benefit from the effective forces that are truly generated by competition and free markets. But realistically, we should recognize that where the private sectors are dominated by cartels and monopolies, there is less to be gained by depending on the market place for efficiency in resource allocation, price flexibility, and high productivity than where vigorous competition prevails.

Concentration of economic power and the effective functioning of the market place often are largely incompatible. Yet, we see increasing horizontal concentration of ownership of supposedly competitive raw material resources. The large oil companies have acquired commanding positions in the ownership of large coal companies and of uranium mining enterprises. This tendency is justified by oil companies on grounds of possessing huge financial resources, having technical expertise, possessing strong managerial talents and experience, and being in positions to shift resources to meet national and foreign needs promptly and efficiently. But that does not satisfy one of the most essential ingredients of a well-functioning market place, namely, aggressive competition, and, especially, price competition. We may be in danger of overselling market place performance at a time when the market cannot do the job promised, not so much because of government regulation, but more importantly, because of anticompetitive business practices. The active pursuit of competition had better not be neglected in the energy field or in other key sectors where failure and frustration will lead to more government involvement if the market place fails to function much better than it has.

The issues already identified are illustrative rather than comprehensive. They can be multiplied many times over, not only for identifying the basic and difficult problems we face in coping with the energy crisis, but also more broadly in considering government-private roles and relationships. A basic objective in role determination should be to achieve agreed upon goals with optimum benefits at minimum costs. We can often agree on goals, but the "means" of pursuing these goals is very important because that is where the toughest troubles and sharpest differences are encountered. It is in the specific programs and implementation procedures where significant economic impacts can be encountered and failure or success occurs. Costs and benefits are especially difficult to measure, particularly when such intangibles and qualitative elements are involved as freedom of choice, environmental values, national security, international relations, monopolistic practices, equity elements, limited information, political manipulations, and a host of other factors that affect our daily lives. The means are especially important because our economic and political systems are not simplistic and most often do not function in textbook fashion.

There is little point in wasting time on the totally polarized views of, on the one hand, complete governmental intervention through ownership of all or much of the nation's basic energy resources or, on the other hand, the total or near-total absence of governmental intervention, whether it concerns pricing, taxation, conservation standards, environmental practices, subsidies, financial support for mass transit, or concessionary financing in developing new sources of energy. Although there are many supporters of extreme views, they are not going to prevail. The more realistic and responsible task is to find that degree of balance between public and private roles which will secure the optimum benefits of both the competitive enterprise system and the public support for essential and constructive governmental policies and programs. That, of course, depends on the interpretation of what is essential and constructive in the government sphere. That interpretation varies from time to time, and usually the pendulum tends to move too far in one direction and then there is overcompensation by excessive moves in the other direction.

It is an especially difficult balance to achieve because in our society the determination of public views is often not clearly quantifiable. Also, there is interplay between the role of the private and public sectors that is generally ignored. Many government functions are undertaken because of the inherent inability or weakness of the market place to perform effectively. It is clear to most Americans that the nation's defense, city fire departments, police forces, highway construction and maintenance, school systems, and other functions cannot be left to the market place. Less evident are the basic reasons for the Social Security pension system, Medicare, unemployment compensation, rights of workers to bargain collectively, bank deposit insurance, antitrust legislation, Federal Reserve Board control over the money supply and varied bank operations, international trade policies, laws on child labor and other fair labor standards, protection of the environment, controls over rates and services of public utilities, and endless other government roles. The rationale for many of these government functions differs greatly from one activity to another. But, very often government intervention is predicated on the commonly accepted fact that the poor performance of the private sector is intolerable. Most often, manmade impediments to the effective operations of the market place are the reasons for government intervention. The antigovernment groups fight against the introduction of most of these public policies and activities and continue to fight for their termination. Seldom do they acknowledge, let alone seek to strengthen, the market place so that government intervention can be minimized.

Deficiencies in the market place are at least as much attributable to anticompetitive practices in the private sector as they are to government intervention and regulation in economic matters designed to prevent or correct the deficiencies. The calls for getting the government out of economic matters are frequently made by those who preach competition, but practice monopoly.

Criticisms of government performance are often warranted. There are large gaps between the goals of legislation and regulation and the actual results that flow from implementing laws and from regulatory processes. The government seems to be less efficient and effective than in the past, but that can be said for the private sector also. It is overly simplistic to blame all the private sector inefficiencies on government regulations, as many business leaders are inclined to do.

Neither the private nor public sectors has proven to be consistently efficient or effective in dealing with the important and complex issues in energy. We need the best performance from both sectors, based on strong lines of communication, solid information, institutions for reconciling or, at least, airing differences of views, and substituting constructive discussions for name-calling and accusations with respect to failures. This will not be easy after several years of political campaigns in which the major theme has been an anti-Washington thrust. Carter and Reagan not only campaigned against government services and performance, but they also continued the antagonism in office. The 1976 Carter campaign was strongly focused on the deficiencies of government and the need to clean up the mess supposedly created by the bureaucracy. Although that theme persisted during Carter's term in office, not much change of a basic nature took place. Reagan's campaign was in the same vein and probably more vehement. The early months of the Reagan administration reveal the persistence of a rigid antigovernment posture and the seeming assumption that, except for defense, much, if not most, of what the government does is unnecessary, or wasteful, or badly performed.

In cutting back government funds and organizations for the synthetic fuels program, reducing funds for mass transit, reducing or eliminating incentives to substitute solar and other potential fuels for oil, and talking about the vast unexplored and unproven oil reserves in the United States, President Reagan calls for less and less of a government role in dealing with the energy crisis. The President's clearly articulated signals point toward going much too fast and too far in abdicating the presidential responsibilities in the public interest. Perhaps Reagan and his Administration will, in time, moderate some of their views as the realities become more apparent, but that is highly uncertain. The ideological rigidities against governmental roles are unprecedented, at least for the last half-century. In the meantime, the pace toward an increased degree of energy independence may become even slower than in recent years, and that pace has been highly unsatisfactory.

Two general observations need to be made on the subject of industrial policy. One relates to energy policies and the other to the relationship of energy policies to a general industrial policy. The two are inevitably interrelated. First, our economy is completely dependent on energy, and it is and will continue to be importantly affected by changes in energy supply and prices. Second, policies pursued in the field of energy will provide strong signals as to what to expect in other specific industrial sectors, as well as in broader economic policies affecting the economy, encompassing such subjects as tax incentives, international trade arrangements, interest rates, research and development support, specific productivity efforts through labor-management cooperation, procompetitive programs, careful review of regulations and regulatory practices, and the like.

Everything I have stated is based on the deep conviction that the United States has had and continues to have an energy crisis. This energy crisis calls for an all-out effort in all segments of the economy. Clearly, the private sector role will be critical in overcoming this crisis. The private sector should be encouraged and, where necessary, helped to play that major role effectively in achieving the energy solution. The Federal government and, in fact, all levels of government, have strong obligations to adopt policies and programs that will facilitate increased energy output by the private sector from traditional sources, will expedite further rapid improvement in the efficient use of energy, and will encourage and support the development of new sources of energy. Government must take into account the need for incentives, because profit prospects strongly affect investment and operating decisions in the business world.

On the other hand, the idea that the energy crisis can be solved by exclusive reliance on the private sector and the market place is wholly unrealistic. We are faced with a powerful cartel which has achieved a more than tenfold oil price increase in a few years. Nor will world oil production be decided by market forces alone. The market place cannot take full account of security considerations either of the United States itself or of the sharing agreements among all the western powers. Different sources of energy are not totally substitutable for each other and market competition alone will not soon sort out and adopt the patterns of supply and demand of these sources of energy. The fullest feasible dependence on competitive forces will be desirable, but this highly concentrated sector, supercharged with political and social factors, cannot be expected to solve the energy crisis, absent governmental policy formulations and incentive programs. Nor can the market deal with issues of equity, environment, conservation, international trade matters, longer term public interests, and different competitive patterns under different economic systems.

In fact, we need better public policies and much better implementation of those policies if the private sector is to play its major role efficiently and effectively. The essential role of government cannot be ignored. And, it is not an either/or approach that is required. Rather, important inputs from both the public and private sectors are essential. The major problem is to identify all the key issues and then to determine how these issues can best be dealt with. The "get the government off the back of business" syndrome is not going to help the process. Time is too urgent to pursue a "let nature take its course" policy. The investment magnitudes are so huge and the risks with respect to new energy sources are so great that new approaches of a cooperative and innovative nature are needed. Ramifications of energy policies will be felt in all sectors of business and all segments of our society. In essence, it is a crisis of such proportions that all kinds of inputs need to be given serious attention. We should be sensitive to problems resulting from excessive government, and we need to be realistic about holding government's role to the minimum levels needed for success, but that government role should not be ruled out arbitrarily.

The act of formulating a new general industrial policy in the United States inherently involves governmental policies and actions. That this country has faced severe problems in this increasingly internationalized business environment is hardly debatable. Over the post-World War II years, as labor-intensive and nonmechanized industries disappeared, there was much concern about jobs, capital flows, trade liberalization, and productivity. Much deeper concerns emerged as basic U.S. industries producing steel, automobiles, and high technology products such as televisions, radios, watches, and cameras became less and less competitive in domestic and world markets. Those companies and workers affected by increased imports and losses of export markets sought government trade protection and other assistance. At the same time, many of them joined the chorus calling for less governmental action. Probably much of the antigovernment sentiment coming these days from the business community stems from a state of shock over our competitive weaknesses as well as a lack of constructive proposals and innovative actions by business to change the directions of our economy toward more growth, better productivity and improved competitive capabilities among U.S. industries.

We do need to formulate new industrial policies, especially to encourage and stimulate the private sector, to preserve and strengthen competition, to fight inflation successfully, to modernize our plant and equipment, and to restore growth and vigor to our enterprise system. These policies inevitably entail government policies and some government intervention. We cannot succeed if we undermine confidence in the role of government, nor should there be exaggerated promises that the private sector alone can achieve the millenium by curing all our economic ills. Yet, that is precisely what many industrial and financial leaders are doing with respect to energy, as well as broad industrial policies. Therein are grave pitfalls and dangers of deep disillusionment that could be harmful to the enterprise system for years and years to come.

9.

ENERGY, PRODUCTIVITY, AND THE NEW U.S. INDUSTRIAL POLICY[1]

Robert S. Pindyck

1. INTRODUCTION

Deterioration in the performance of the American economy over the past decade has been along several dimensions: reduced productivity growth, reduced growth in real disposal incomes, higher rates of inflation, and higher rates of unemployment. Energy is often singled out as deserving much of the blame for these problems (as is the economics profession). While its importance and effects need careful assessment, there is no doubt that energy has had a significant role in the performance of the economy. Furthermore, its role has been a dual one, so that the design of a new U.S. industrial policy must be concerned with energy in two very distinct ways.

First, productivity growth in the energy sector itself has declined considerably in recent years, partly as a result of government regulation, and partly for other reasons. This in turn has helped drag down productivity growth in the economy as a whole. As a result, "energy productivity" has been viewed as an important goal in itself.[2] Restrictive government regulations of the energy sector are being reassessed and reformed, and the energy sector has been singled out (rightly or wrongly) as a target of "preferential" policy for the coming decade (notably via large government subsidies for synthetic fuel development). Now we must carefully consider just what role the government should have in the energy sector. In particular, is there any justification for large-scale subsidization of certain supply technologies? Should the government use a tax or tariff to reduce import dependence, and is a strategic stockpile desirable? And, what is the proper role and timephasing of price decontrol, the Windfall Profits Tax, and assistance to low-income energy consumers?

Second, we now live in an era of rising energy prices, and this has important implications for economic growth and stability, income distribution, and the design of economic policy. To begin with, rising energy prices must necessarily reduce real national income—that is, the "standard of living"—for the country as a whole, and some groups within society may suffer particularly large losses. Also, because of the linkage between the use of capital and the use of energy, rising energy prices will affect investment demand, as well as the utilization and productivity of the existing capital stock. Finally, sharp and unexpected increases in energy prices can destabilize the economy; the price increases that occurred in 1974, 1979, and late 1980-early 1981 have significantly depressed real output and income, and exacerbated both inflation and unemployment. This means that we must design economic policy to make it responsive to rising energy prices, so that their adverse effects are no larger than necessary.

This chapter addresses both of the ways in which energy is relevant to economic policy and the design of a new industrial policy. We begin with the energy sector itself. The next section briefly reviews the effects that price controls have had on energy production and consumption, and explains why this country went the route of controls. Section 3 discusses the synthetic fuels program, an example of a "preferential" policy. We will argue that this program is inherently wasteful, inefficient, and in the long run counterproductive, and that the lessons learned from synthetic fuels may be applicable to "preferential" policies in general. Other issues relating to the role of government in the energy sector are discussed in Section 4, and that section also summarizes the changes needed in American energy policy.

In Section 5 we turn to the relationship between energy and macroeconomic activity. There we explain the ways in which rising energy prices necessarily reduce real potential national income. We also discuss the destabilizing effects of sharp and sudden increases in energy prices —price "shocks"—and their impact on inflation, output, and employment. This provides the basis for the discussion of economic policy in Section 6. There we argue that the use of certain kinds of "supply-side" policies can be a particularly appropriate way to respond to the economic impact of rising energy prices, but we must specify those policies clearly, and recognize their limitations.

2. GOVERNMENT INTERVENTION IN THE ENERGY SECTOR IN THE 1960S AND 1970S

The energy sector is important in its own right, even if we ignore its linkage to the economy as a whole. As Lester Thurow recently pointed out, productivity growth in the "mining" sector declined from an annual rate of 4.3 percent over the period 1948–1965 to −4.2 percent in 1972–1978, and this in turn accounts for 10 percent of the recent national productivity decline.[3] Furthermore, almost all of this decline in mining productivity can be attributed to oil and natural gas production. Here one underlying cause is depletion of the potential reserve base, but another cause may be past regulatory policy.

Any discussion of government intervention in energy markets must begin with the sorry history of price controls. Two separate price control policies have been in force in the United States—the long-standing regulation of the price of natural gas by the Federal Power Commission (FPC), and later by the Federal Energy Regulatory Commission (FERC) of the Department of Energy after that new agency was established, and the more recent crude oil price controls-entitlements program. Of interest to us here is first, the inefficiency effects of those controls, both on energy markets and, by creating energy shortages, on the economy as a whole, and second, the reasons that these controls were put and kept in place. This last issue is particularly important, since as we will see, the politics of past energy policies has important implications for the choice of future policies. However, before discussing the political and economic reasons for price controls, it is useful to review the effects that they have had.

Consider first the regulation of natural gas markets. The average price of natural gas at the wellhead has been regulated since 1954, but those regulations became "effective" (in the sense that regulated prices were below prices that would have prevailed had the market not been regulated) beginning only around 1962.[4] From 1962–1970 natural gas prices continued to deviate more and more from world market prices, and from the thermal-equivalent prices of competing fuels (such as home heating oil) in the United States.

Not surprisingly, the demand for natural gas was artificially stimulated by these controls, and the supply of natural gas was artificially repressed. The result was that from 1962–1970 the average reserve-production ratio for natural gas fields in the United States fell from about 20 to about twelve. The deviations of regulated natural gas prices from free market prices became even greater in the 1970s, and by 1971 the United States began to experience outright shortages of natural gas in wholesale and retail markets in different regions of the country. At first those shortages were limited to agricultural and industrial consumers in the North Central part of the country, but over time they grew, and during the winter of 1976 the country experienced natural gas shortages that caused plant shutdowns leading to the layoffs of approximately 1.1 million workers during those months. It became clear at the time that energy shortages can have a severe impact on an industrial economy like ours, more so even than large increases in energy prices. By restricting the production of other goods and creating supply bottlenecks throughout the economy, energy shortages can reduce GNP and (as occurred in 1976) increase unemployment.

In addition to the clear effects of shortages, the regulation of natural gas markets imposed other indirect costs on the American economy. Because natural gas price controls substantially subsidized the consumption of gas by those able to obtain it (mainly households, but also industries in some parts of the country), it artificially increased their consumption. Since those unable to obtain natural gas had to shift to oil or electricity, price controls likewise artificially increased the demands for these fuels. Over the 1974–1978 period, the net effect was to increase the demand for energy in the United States by one to two million barrels of oil-equivalents per day. In addition, price controls severely limited the supply of natural gas, since even the prices for new contracts were held well below world levels. The net result was to artificially increase oil imports in the United States by at least two million barrels per day. The indirect cost becomes clear if one remembers that those higher imports had to be paid for—through a reduction in the international value of the dollar, and corresponding increases in the prices of all other imported goods. Although critics of deregulation argued that it would be inflationary, in fact in the long run the controls themselves were far more inflationary.

The Natural Gas Policy Act of 1978 was a step in the right direction with respect to natural gas regulation. It significantly increased the regulated wellhead prices of many categories of natural gas, and it provided for further increases in the future, leading to the deregulation of most categories of gas by the middle or late 1980s.

But the Act contains some significant flaws, some of which were foreseeable, and some of which were not. First, by delaying deregulation of certain categories of gas, it may actually cause natural gas production (at least for these categories) to be *less* over the next five years than might otherwise have been the case. Second, by creating some 20-odd categories of natural gas and subjecting each category to separate regulations, it creates a bureaucratic nightmare that is also likely to depress gas production. Related to this, it does not provide the incentive necessary for the exploitation of potential high-cost gas reserves. Finally, world oil prices have increased much faster than people expected at the time the Act was passed, and as a result regulated new contract prices are now at about half the Btu.-equivalent prices for oil, thus further creating the incentive for producers to delay production until 1985. For these reasons, complete deregulation of natural gas markets in the near future is preferable to waiting until 1985 to let prices increase.

Let us now turn to the crude oil price controls-entitlements program. It is important to understand that the effect of this program was not only to reduce the domestic price of crude oil and refined oil products, but also to act as a *tax* on domestic oil production, and a *subsidy* for imported oil. Recall that under its provisions, domestic producers received an average price for their oil below the price paid by refiners, which was in turn below the world market price set by the Organization of Petroleum Exporting Countries. In order to refine a barrel of domestic crude oil, producers purchased an "entitlement," which was the tax on domestic production. At the same time, refiners importing crude oil at the world price received entitlements, financed by the payments from domestic producers, and which in effect provided a subsidy for imported oil. Ironically, crude oil regulatory policy in the 1970s put the U.S. government in the business of subsidizing oil imports from OPEC.

What were the effects of this policy? When OPEC sharply increased world oil prices in the winter of 1974 and summer of 1979, crude oil price controls combined with price controls on retail product markets led to shortages of gasoline. Furthermore, those shortages, which were only about 5 or 10 percent of total demand on a nationwide basis, were made still worse by additional government regulatory activity. In an attempt to "allocate" the shortages around the country, the Federal Energy Administration (FEA) in 1974 and the Department of Energy in 1979 simply concentrated the shortages and shifted them about the country, so that at any one time, some regions of the country had large *surpluses* of gasoline, while others had shortages on the order of 30 or 40 percent of demand.

Gasoline lines were both obvious and aggravating, but the more serious effect of crude oil regulatory policy was less well-perceived by the public, and perhaps by the government. That effect, as in the case of natural gas regulation, was to artificially stimulate demand, and artificially repress crude oil exploration, development, and production. Again, this meant an artificial increase in our level of oil imports—by about three million barrels per day over the 1976–1978 period. And that in turn put downward pressure on the value of the dollar, leading to increases in the prices of all imported goods, and contributing to general inflation.

Certain aspects of the price controls-entitlements program caused economic inefficiency in other ways as well. Two examples are the "Small Refiner's Bias," a provision in the program that permitted smaller refiners to purchase fewer entitlements (thereby subsidizing them), and the "Exceptional Relief Program," a provision that provided outright subsidies to refiners whose estimated profits fell below historical levels—for whatever reason. The benefits involved in this latter provision have been estimated to total some $300 million per year. The result has been to subsidize highly inefficient refiners, and to discourage the construction of large new refineries.[5]

In summary, regulation of natural gas and oil markets has resulted in shortages, increased import dependence, increased inflation, and inefficiencies in the production of fuels. In addition, it has resulted in the wasteful consumption of energy resources that have been artificially priced below their true value. Finally, by causing shortages and making us more dependent on insecure supplies of imported oil, they have created the incentive for the government to adopt various subsidization programs—such as the synthetic fuels program to be discussed shortly —which in turn have the effect of increasing long-run energy costs more than necessary, and contributing still more to inflation. Why, then, were these policies in effect for so long?

The problem has been a basic conflict in the objectives of American energy policy. On the one hand there has been a desire to keep the price of energy to consumers down, and on the other hand a desire to stem what was becoming an uncontrolled growth in oil imports.[6] The pressure to keep the price of energy low was not surprising; consumers are displeased to see the price of anything rise, and in the case of energy they could express that displeasure through their votes. At the same time, the desire to limit the growth of oil imports grew as those imports made us increasingly vulnerable, both politically and economically, to the demands and decisions of a small number of oil exporting countries, and also contributed to inflation by reducing the value of the dollar through their impact on our trade balance.

As explained earlier, until recently American energy policy favored the low-price option, but the basic conflict still remains, and the approach taken to resolve that conflict during the last year-and-a-half of the Carter administration is one that is bound to be counterproductive in the long run. Unfortunately there has been a great temptation to find a "cheap fix" to the energy problem—cheap in terms of *political cost,* if not in terms of *real economic cost.* I will argue that the far-reaching program initiated by the Carter administration to provide government subsidies for a plethora of nonconventional energy supplies is exactly the kind of "cheap fix" that is politically attractive, but that should be avoided.

I discuss the synthetic fuels program in more detail in the next section, but first it is important to stress that there are two alternative ways that Americans can pay for the higher cost of their energy. One way is to pay *directly* through higher prices at the gasoline pump, and the like. The second way is to pay *indirectly,* through increased tax revenues that are allocated to synthetic fuel production or conservation subsidies, through increased general inflation, generated in part through an artificially-induced growth of OPEC imports, and sometimes through the cost of lost time spent waiting in lines resulting from outright shortages of fuels.

Paying for energy directly is by far the more efficient way. First, it gives consumers a direct incentive to conserve; there is little incentive to lower the thermostat or drive a smaller car if part of one's energy bill is paid for through taxes or through general inflation, since no one can reduce that portion of the bill by consuming less.

Second, producers receive payment directly, and this gives them the incentive to minimize production costs, producing lower cost fuels today, and moving towards higher cost fuels only as it becomes necessary in the future. Thus, when energy is paid for directly, the fuel mix of the future—whether it will include shale oil, or liquified coal, or solar energy, or wind power, or whatever—is determined on *economic* grounds, so that its long-run cost is minimized. If instead we pay for our energy through our taxes, the fuel mix of the future will be determined on political grounds, with projects financed by the government based on the congressional districts in which they are to be built, the political connections of the particular corporations seeking subsidies, and so forth. This is bound to lead to a wasteful allocation of resources, and a much higher cost of energy.

Then why did the Carter administration—and the Congress—create the synthetic fuels program? The reason is a simple one—it is politically cheaper to have the public pay for its energy indirectly. In this way the public (or at least part of it) *thinks* it is getting cheap energy—something for nothing. In addition, congressmen *know* they will be getting large-scale construction projects for their districts, and they will *appear* to be "doing something" about the energy problem. In fact the public will end up paying even more for its energy, although the payments will be disguised because they will take the form of higher taxes and greater inflation.

3. THE SYNTHETIC FUELS PROGRAM AS "PREFERENTIAL" POLICY

In his televised energy address on July 15, 1979, President Carter stated, quite correctly, that the United States had become intolerably dependent on insecure supplies of imported oil. Unfortunately his prescription for the problem was the synthetic fuels program, under which large-scale government subsidies would be used to "speed up" the production of a variety of nonconventional energy supplies. Those subsidies are to take a variety of forms: direct subsidies to help finance "demonstration plants" as well as actual operating plants, various kinds of tax credits, and loan guarantees and interest subsidies. The program is a good example of a preferential policy—pick a developing industry, preferably one involved in new technologies, and plow money into it to accelerate its movement down the "learning curve."

But does the program make sense? I believe the answer is clearly no, and that by any rational economic criterion, the synthetic fuels program is bound to be inefficient and wasteful, is unlikely to contribute significantly to the solution of our energy problems even by 1990, and could exacerbate our existing economic problems. Furthermore, such a program is particularly undesirable today, when the need to limit government expenditures overall will impose severe restrictions on other far more important areas of government activity.

It is important to stress at the outset that the problem here is not that synthetic fuels and other nonconventional energy supplies have no promise as components of our future fuel mix. In fact some of these technologies have considerable promise. It is highly likely that, as energy prices continue to rise in the future, some of these new sources will become commercially viable and will eventually displace conventional oil and natural gas as major fuels. But as they become economical they can be, and should be, produced by private companies without a program of government subsidies.

Of course proponents of synthetic fuel subsidies usually argue that "market imperfections" make them necessary. The arguments basically boil down to claims that these energy sources have certain special characteristics, that is, advanced technology, large capital requirements, long lead times, and various uncertainties, and that these characteristics make private sector commercialization difficult or impossible without government assistance. But these claims are simply fallacious.[7]

Consider, for example, the question of "advanced technology." It turns out that those energy sources that are likely to receive the largest subsidies involve technologies that are in fact well understood, and do not involve fundamental scientific advances. Remember that shale oil was produced in Britain in the 1850s, and liquified coal was produced in Germany during World War II, and is being produced today in South Africa. What makes these energy sources (and others such as solar energy, biomass, and wind power) "nonconventional" is simply that they are expensive—much more expensive than conventional sources.

It is true that the commercialization of some of these energy sources involves large capital expenditures, but this has also been the case for many other projects undertaken by the private sector. In some instances, plans for synthetic fuel projects have been made involving two or more companies on a joint venture basis (as has been the case for related projects such as the Alaska Pipeline and off-shore oil exploration), and even where individual companies are involved, there is no reason why financing cannot be handled through the private capital markets. And while these projects tend to be large and scale economies are involved, those economies are not so great or far-reaching as to justify the formation of government enterprises on "natural monopoly" grounds.

It is also true that the lead times involved in the construction and licensing of operating plants for some of these energy sources is large, perhaps five to 10 years. But this has commonly been the case in many other private ventures. The long lead time involved in the design, development, testing, and licensing of the Boeing 747, for example, certainly did not prevent the commercialization of that aircraft. In fact, there are no theoretical reasons or empirical evidence that would have us believe that private capital markets are biased against large projects with long lead times.[8]

Next we come to the issue of uncertainties. There is no question that the commercialization of some nonconventional energy supplies involves real risks, but we must ask whether those risks justify government subsidies. One form of uncertainty that is often cited is uncertainty over ultimate production costs. Cost uncertainties are significant, but they are no more significant than for a wide range of projects that have been routinely undertaken by private industry with no government involvement.[9] Furthermore, when such uncertainties are present, large-scale government subsidies are even more likely to lead to *cost inflation,* both for individual projects (since cost is likely to depend positively on the speed of commercialization), and for the overall portfolio of projects (since firms have an incentive to understate expected costs in order to obtain the subsidies).[10]

Another form of uncertainty is on the revenue side, and has to do with the future price of oil. Given the instability of the world oil market, the price of oil 10 years from now is indeed highly uncertain. It is quite conceivable that oil prices could double or triple over the next decade as a result of political turmoil in the Persian Gulf, or prices could drop considerably if major new discoveries occurred. But this in no way implies that synthetic fuels should be subsidized. In fact if anything, uncertainty over the future price of oil will *increase,* not decrease, the *private* incentive to develop synthetic fuels.

To see this, remember that shale oil or liquified coal is substitutable for conventional oil. This means that *each stage* in the private commercialization of a particular synthetic fuel technology represents an "option" on ultimate production of a product whose price will just be the price of oil at the time. Those stages of commercialization include, for example, construction of a demonstration plant, purchase of mineral rights and perhaps water rights, environmental certification, construction of the basic operating plant, and finally actual operation. (Each stage is an "option" because the project can be abandoned should the price of oil become too low, and the costs of the remaining stages, including ultimately the variable cost of operation, can be saved.) And like a call option on shares of stock, the value *rises* as the volatility of the price of oil (or the price of the stock on which the option is written) rises. As a result, uncertainty over the future price of oil can make synthetic fuel commercialization *even more attractive* to industry, and certainly does not lead to a need for government involvement.

There is only one form of uncertainty that can form a real impediment to commercialization, and that is over government regulatory policy. From the point of view of the private sector, serious problems can arise when there are uncertainties about possible future price regulation or taxation, or uncertainties over environmental controls that will apply after a project is completed.

It is not surprising that companies would be unwilling to take the risk of developing new energy technologies if they perceive a probable government ceiling on their upside profit potential. Companies are willing to take downside risk, but only when the upside potential is commensurate. Similarly, the problem is not so much with current environmental restrictions, but rather the fear of unpredictable and perhaps irrational revisions of those restrictions in the future.

But these are uncertainties that the government created and that the government can remove. What is needed is not only the removal of controls on current and future energy prices, but also a commitment that energy markets will be allowed to operate freely in the future. As for environmental regulations, the government should revise those that are unnecessary, and clarify those that would apply in the future. These changes would put private companies in the position to develop economical synthetic fuel technologies efficiently, and without any need for government subsidies.

There are other reasons why the synthetic fuels program is undesirable. An important one is that large cost overruns are more likely in government-subsidized program, and *much* more likely in a government-managed program. This means that the final cost of synthetic fuels could easily turn out to be several times more expensive than recent estimates would have us believe. (It is interesting that President Carter, who was highly critical of cost overruns in government agencies and government procurement, supported a program that provides almost every incentive for cost overruns.) Remember that as the program now stands, the size and form of the particular subsidy will be linked to the difference between production costs and the world prices of conventional energy supplies. For companies receiving subsidies, this removes the usual incentive to hold down costs.

Another problem is that the synthetic fuels program runs the risk of locking us into the wrong technologies. The point here is that it is private industry, and not the Department of Energy or a government Synfuel Corporation that is in the best position to determine which new energy technologies are most economical and most promising, and to manage their commercial development most effectively. It is private industry that is best able to respond quickly and efficiently to any technological and economic developments that might arise in the future. And perhaps most important, private industry is much better able than any government bureaucracy to stop the development of a particular project if it later turns out not to be as promising as it once appeared. Unlike a government agency, a private company is usually unwilling to continue to pour money into what has clearly turned out to be an unprofitable project just because it is in a particular congressional district, or because the company wants to "save face."[11]

Finally, the synthetic fuels program creates an inefficiency by converting direct purchases of energy into indirect ones. As I explained earlier, when energy is paid for through taxes, consumption is artificially inflated. There is now a growing body of statistical evidence indicating that increases in energy prices can have a significant effect on reducing demand, particularly after some time has passed after the price increase.[12] A subsidy program removes part of this price incentive, and thereby contributes to the growth of energy consumption. By subsidizing the commercialization of synthetic fuels rather than utilizing the price mechanism, the government would in effect be asking taxpayers to finance the difference between the high cost of producing synthetic fuel supplies and the lower price that consumers would be asked to pay for energy.

It is worth recalling that when the Windfall Profits Tax on crude oil production was first proposed, the tax revenues were to have been earmarked to go back to the public in the form of general tax relief. If that had been the case, the Windfall Profits Tax would have become what it was originally intended to be—an instrument for corrective income redistribution. Instead, much of those tax revenues have been channeled into synthetic fuels, so that they are returned as subsidies to many of the large companies that were paying the tax in the first place. As a result, the redistributive objective of the Windfall Profits Tax has been perverted.

Usually "preferential" policies are justified as providing "help" for industries that show "promise." In the case of synthetic fuels, the justification has instead been a need to reduce import dependence (a dependence created in large part by government regulation of energy markets). But although the justifications may differ, other "preferential" policies are likely to suffer from the same shortcomings as the synthetic fuels program. Such policies involve inherent inefficiencies, and before they are adopted, it must be clearly demonstrated that the market really cannot work without them, and that they will result in a significant net public benefit.

4. THE ROLE OF GOVERNMENT IN THE ENERGY SECTOR

Our discussion in the last section should not be taken to imply that there is no role for the government in the energy sector. In fact, the government has an important role to play, but it should be based on a set of guiding principles. Those principles are best illustrated by considering the changes needed in American energy policy.

Of primary importance is the *decontrol of energy prices.* President Reagan's decontrol of crude oil prices shortly after taking office is to be applauded (although those controls were due to expire anyway by October, 1981). As discussed earlier, the Natural Gas Policy Act of 1978 was a step in the right direction, but new contract field prices of natural gas are still well below free market level, and with decontrol scheduled under the Act for 1985, there is an incentive to withhold production. Natural gas markets should be fully decontrolled as soon as possible. Although this could result in as much as a doubling of new contract prices, *average* field prices (and therefore average wholesale prices) would rise only gradually. Furthermore, in many parts of the country the pipeline plus retail (gas utility) markups account for more than half the cost of gas for residential consumers, and since these markups will remain subject to Federal and state regulation, the increases for these consumers will be proportionately smaller.

The decontrol of natural gas markets will require congressional legislation to override the Natural Gas Policy Act, but the Administration should push for that legislation as forcefully as possible. That legislation is important, not only to remove the direct and indirect inefficiency costs of price controls, but also to signal a commitment to refrain from regulation in the future. As discussed in the last section, that commitment is needed so that developers of new high cost and high risk energy supplies need not fear that their upside profit potential will be regulated or taxed away if energy prices continue to rise.

Related to a policy of decontrol, the United States should be committed to free trade in energy markets. This means that importers of crude oil should never be "urged" (or told) not to purchase on the spot market as they were in the spring and early summer of 1979 (and which contributed to our gasoline shortages that year). Similarly, importers of natural gas should be free to strike any contract they wish with Mexican or Canadian suppliers.

There is a widespread fear in the United States that production cutbacks in some of the OPEC countries might lead to fuel shortages in this country. Sudden production cutbacks are indeed a possibility (and I will discuss their economic effects later). But it is important to remember that shortages in retail markets can only result from government attempts to control the prices of fuels below market-clearing levels. It is exactly such controls (combined with government attempts to allocate regional supplies) that caused gasoline lines in the United States in 1974 and 1979. Because they allowed prices to rise to market-clearing levels, the other major industrial nations escaped this problem, even though some of them are far more dependent on imports than the United States.

This means that should major cutbacks in OPEC production occur in the future, the very thing *not* to do is impose price controls. (Remember that the crude oil price controls-entitlements system came into being in 1974 as a response to the OPEC oil price increases.) On the contrary, maximum price flexibility should be maintained.

At the same time, we must recognize that sharp increases in fuel prices will indeed impose a significant burden on the poor.[13] In our 1977 article, Robert Hall and I suggested expanding the present food stamp program to cover fuel expenditures as the most promising way of helping the poor in this area. This would mean some increase in food stamp allotments, so that home heating bills (or that portion of a family's rent allocated to fuels) could be covered under the program. If the expanded food stamp program were aimed at the lowest 20 percent of the income distribution, the additional cost to the taxpayer would be modest, and certainly much less than subsidizing the energy consumption of all consumers as we have been doing in the past.

Another important principle for American energy policy is that *the government should stay out of commercialization.* As explained in the last section, it is private companies, and not the government, that should be involved in the commercialization of new energy technologies, and private companies do not need and should not receive government subsidies for the production of particular energy supplies. This rule should apply to the full gamut of nonconventional energy sources—shale oil, liquified or gasified coal, solar energy, biomass, wind power, and so on. If any of these energy sources are economical or become economical, private companies will have all the incentive they need to produce them, and there is simply no role for government subsidies.

Related to this, the government should not in any way choose the fuel mix of the future. One of the serious problems with the synthetic fuels program is that it puts the government in the role of deciding which fuels will be produced commercially in the future, and that is likely to mean that the fuel mix of the future will be based on political and bureaucratic grounds, rather than economic, cost minimizing grounds.

No one today can accurately predict what energy sources will turn out to be most economical 10 or 20 years from now. As a case in point, the claim has been made by some that oil and natural gas supplies will dwindle over the next 15 or 20 years, so that these fuels will account for a relatively small proportion of our total energy consumption in the year 2000.[14] This claim may turn out to be correct, but it may also turn out to be totally incorrect. At this point we simply do not know what the potential is for further oil and gas discoveries in the United States, and in other areas of the world, such as Latin America, particularly in the face of rising prices. The statistical, geological, and econometric evidence here is mixed, and it indicates that there is considerable uncertainty over supplies of oil and gas that would be forthcoming with higher prices. Those supplies may turn out to be very significant, and from sources that would not have been predicted several years ago.

This means that the fuel mix of the future should be determined by energy producers on economic grounds, and should be financed by energy consumers, not by the government. Any fuel mix that is artificially imposed—whether it consists of solar energy, "conservation," or synthetic fuels—can only increase the long-run cost of energy for all of us.

Although the government has no role in commercialization, it has a very definite role in the *support of energy research*. The stress here is on the word *research*. Although the government should keep out of the development and production phases of energy supply, government support of basic research is a good economic policy. Technological advance in the area of energy is critical, and needs to be encouraged. Government funding is warranted because basic research into new energy technologies has a high social value that is greater than the incentives facing private firms that might consider supporting research themselves. The ideas and techniques developed in publicly-supported research can be and should be made freely available, and the private sector can then be counted upon to commercialize those new technologies that make good economic sense.

There is one other area where the government has an important role to play, and that is to raise the cost of energy, as seen both by producers and consumers, to its true marginal social value. This can be done by the imposition of a *tariff on imported oil.*

Even with the complete deregulation of energy markets, our dependence on imported oil would still remain significant. As is explained in some detail in the next section, an energy price shock, brought about by a sudden reduction in OPEC oil production, could have severe macroeconomic consequences, and that creates a social cost that can only be reduced by government intervention. Furthermore, our current import level creates a political and strategic dependence that is undesirable.[15] For these reasons it would make good sense to further reduce our dependence on imported energy, and thereby reduce the potential economic impact of any sudden increases in world energy prices.

The most effective means of doing this is to impose a tariff on imported oil. Such a tariff would raise the price for all oil in the United States, *both for consumers and for producers.* This would give consumers an added incentive to conserve, and it would give producers an added incentive to produce—*efficiently,* choosing those energy sources (oil or others) and those technologies that are most economical. The net result would be less domestic energy consumption, more domestic production, and a lower level of imports.

Unfortunately, in the short term the macroeconomic effect of a tariff is the same as that from an OPEC-induced increase in the price of oil —it is inflationary and recessionary. Therefore it is essential that two things be done to eliminate this adverse effect. First, the tariff must be phased in gradually, perhaps over a three-to-five year period. (As explained in the next section, gradual increases in energy prices are much less damaging than rapid increases.) Second, the tariff must be matched dollar-for-dollar with cost-reducing tax cuts. The leading candidate for such cuts is the Social Security payroll tax. A decrease in this tax has exactly the same effect on prices and output as a reduction in the price of energy, and therefore can be used to perfectly offset the tariff. At the same time, revenues from the tariff would be earmarked for the Social Security program, so that the only change would be in the source of its funding, and not the amount.

Related to the oil import tariff is the development of the strategic oil reserve, which should be another important component of energy policy. A strategic reserve can have two functions. First, in the event of an all-out war or military action that disrupted most shipping and trading of oil, the world oil market might cease to function as such, and shortages could occur in the sense that imports might be unavailable at any price. Strategic reserves could then be used to prevent such shortages.

Short of a major military conflict, strategic reserves are not needed to prevent shortages, since such shortages would not occur in the absence of government controls. But a *sharp* increase in energy prices resulting from an OPEC production cutback could be economically damaging to this country. The second function of a strategic reserve is its use to smooth out price increases in the wake of such a production cutback.[16]

However, it is important to point out that strategic reserves are most effective when implemented multilaterally. The point here is that when a stockpile is released, no matter where it happens to reside, it adds to the supply of oil in the world market and thereby reduces the world price. As a result the benefits are enjoyed by *all* importing countries, even if they do not have stockpiles of their own, but the benefits to the country holding the stockpile are likewise reduced. If only the United States owned and released a stockpile in the wake of a crisis, its imports of oil would fall, but the impact on world oil prices—and prices faced by American consumers—would be small. But if most or all of the major Organization for Economic Cooperation and Development nations maintained large stockpiles of oil which, as part of an international agreement, flowed into the market during a major production cutback, this would significantly reduce any sharp price increases and resulting economic damage.

5. RISING ENERGY PRICES AND THE ECONOMY

Our discussion so far has been limited to the energy sector itself, and the ways in which various government policies can affect that sector. Energy is also important because of its relationship to the economy as a whole. The likelihood is that energy prices will continue to increase over the coming years, and those increases may be sharp and unexpected as in 1974 and 1979, rather than gradual and predictable. Energy price increases reduce the level and growth of real national income, add to inflation, and raise unemployment. Even with a rational energy policy, rising energy prices will therefore impose a burden on the economy, and make the choices and trade-offs for economic policy all the more difficult.

I will argue that rising energy prices have important implications for American economic policy, and that the macroeconomic impact of any future energy price "shock" will depend strongly on the chosen policy response. First, however, it is important to summarize and clarify the ways in which energy price increases affect the economy.[17]

An energy price increase can have two very distinct and different effects on an industrial economy such as ours. First, the increase has a *direct* effect by reducing the total real national income available for domestic consumption and investment, and no economic policy can change this. Furthermore, it does not matter whether the cost of energy increases because it is imported and a cartel raises its monopoly price, or because depletion makes domestic energy sources more difficult to tap. Either way the higher cost of energy will mean a lower real national income, which in turn means lower real wages, profits, and consumption levels.

Second, energy price increases that are rapid and unexpected also have an *adjustment* effect. An energy price shock will raise the rates of inflation and unemployment, and reduce investment levels. Adjustment problems occur because of important rigidities that characterize our economy—rigidities in prices, in the use of inputs to production, and in wages. The adjustment effect cannot be eliminated entirely, but it can be significantly reduced through the proper use of economic policy. The wrong policies, however, can magnify adjustment problems, so that they become a serious threat to economic growth and stability.

Let us examine these two different effects of energy price increases in more detail. We begin with the direct effect—the reduction in real national income. The question of interest is how large must this reduction be.

The answer depends on the role and importance of energy in the economy, both in terms of its magnitude as a cost share of GNP, and in terms of the ability of household and industrial consumers of energy to use less when it becomes more expensive. The cost share of energy as a fraction of GNP sets an upper bound on the extent to which an increase in the price of energy will depress real national income; with *no substitution possibilities* (that is, if energy demand were completely price-inelastic), the drop in real national income will be $S/(1-S)$ times the percentage price increase, where S is the share of energy in GNP, and is about 8 percent in the United States. This impact would be smaller the more elastic the demand for energy. A reasonable estimate of the overall price elasticity of energy demand in the United States is about -0.6, and this would imply that a 10 percent increase in the price of energy would reduce real national income by about 0.6 percent.[18]

The impact would be smaller to the extent that we could produce much of our own energy at low cost. But unfortunately, a growing share of our energy is produced at a cost close to or equal to the world price. This means that in terms of economic impact, we are not much better off than an importing nation like Japan or West Germany, since the labor and other resources devoted to energy production deprive the economy of the use of goods and services exactly as would be the case if the energy were imported. In fact it is for this reason that the production of synthetic fuels in the United States cannot provide an economic buffer against a rising cost of energy.

It should be kept in mind that while a slowly rising price of energy will depress real national income, it is likely to have only a small effect on real GNP, and therefore on productivity, particularly if much of the energy is imported. The reason is that GNP is a measure of final output, and not the real flow of goods and services available for domestic use. If the elasticity of substitution between energy and other inputs to production is small, domestic production will be largely unaffected by higher energy prices. The problem is that more of that production must be bartered away for the more expensive energy, and this is why real *income* falls. Paradoxically, the larger the elasticity of substitution between energy and other inputs to production, the *larger* will be the reduction in *real GNP* resulting from an energy price increase, but the *smaller* will be the reduction in *real income* (and thus in our standard of living).

For this reason it is important to focus on the real income losses connected with energy price increases, and not GNP or productivity losses. To take an example, measures that speed up the replacement of energy-inefficient capital (for example, gas-guzzling cars) with energy-efficient capital can *reduce productivity,* because they accelerate the use of energy-efficient, but labor-inefficient technologies. But for an oil importing country, this means a reduction in imports and improvement in the terms of trade, so that output may fall, but *income will rise.* [19] In the long run, the problem with steady increases in energy prices is not that they will drain away our output and productivity growth, but that they will drain our real incomes and living standards.

The impact of rising energy prices on real national income is significant in magnitude, but it is far from catastrophic in terms of its implications for the health of the American economy. If energy prices were to rise at 5 percent per year in real terms for the rest of the century, this would reduce real national income growth by about 0.3 percent per year. Using 3.0 percent as a "consensus" estimate for real annual growth in potential national income over the next 20 years, this would mean a loss of about a tenth of our total normal growth in real income. But a growth rate of 2.7 percent is one that we can live with, and even that could be increased somewhat if we can succeed in restoring part of our nonenergy loss in productivity growth.

The problems become more serious, however, if energy prices rise in sharp, unexpected jumps as during the past decade, rather than along a smooth and predictable path. Let us turn now to the adjustment effects that accompany an energy price shock—further reductions in real income, reductions in output, and increases in the rates of inflation and unemployment.

These adjustment effects come about because of the rigidities that characterize our economy. For example, prices of goods other than energy do not fall rapidly to reflect changes in relative scarcities, and inputs to production cannot be shifted quickly given the new price of energy faced by industry. Perhaps most important, real wage rates often fail to fall quickly to the lower equilibrium level consistent with higher energy prices and reduced national income. Labor thereby prices itself out of the market, full employment becomes uneconomical, and the unemployment rate rises and level of real output falls.[20]

Consider the inflationary effect of an energy price shock. There is no economic law that says that prices in general must rise when the relative price of one good rises. If there were no rigidities and equilibrium could be quickly restored, the prices of most other goods would fall slightly after the price of energy rose. But for the U.S. and most other countries, the tendency is for sympathetic movements of prices in general when energy prices rise. As we saw with the 1974 and 1979 shocks, sharp increases in energy prices led to a burst of inflation throughout most of the industrial world.

One of the main reasons for this is the linkage between wages and prices, a linkage that makes the real wage rate downwardly rigid. The problem is simple—the message that real wages must fall is one that workers would rather not hear. Furthermore, since for many workers wages are automatically linked to prices through both explicit and implicit cost-of-living escalators, the message can indeed be ignored. In recent years, wage-setting processes have been increasingly based on the custom of recognizing recent increases in the cost of living. Such processes push wages up when they must inevitably fall relative to the cost of living, and thereby cause an inflationary spiral—and an increase in unemployment as workers price themselves out of the labor market.

An energy price shock will also cause a reduction in real output. One reason for this is the inability of the economy to come back to equilibrium quickly at a lower real wage level. As explained above, this means that after a shock employment will fall as firms lay off workers rather than take losses, and this in turn implies a drop in real output.

Real output is also adversely affected because of the dampening effect that an energy price shock has on investment. First, sudden changes in input prices can, in general, create uncertainty about the profitability of private investment, and combined with the higher interest rates that accompany a suddenly higher price level, this can bring about a slowdown in investment demand. Second, there is evidence (and it is reasonable to expect) that energy and capital tend to be complementary inputs to production in the short run (although they are substitutable in the longer run). This means that a higher price of energy will reduce industry's demand for capital, and again cause a short-run drop in the demand for investment.[21]

6. ENERGY AND ECONOMIC POLICY

These effects of rising energy prices seriously complicate the design of economic policy. To begin with, the combination of higher inflation, higher unemployment, and lower real output that follows an energy shock is the worst of all worlds. There are sure to be social and political pressures on the one hand to pursue contractionary policies in an attempt to fight inflation, and on the other hand to use expansionary policies to stimulate output and reduce unemployment.

Monetary policy is a good example of how this conflict can prove disastrous. In 1974 the Federal Reserve gave in to the temptation to use strenuous monetary deceleration as a means of "treating" the rapid inflation that followed the energy shock. The result was a recession that was far worse than it needed to be. The inflationary burst following an energy shock is inevitable in the short run, and monetary policy should not be used to try to offset it. Instead, money growth should be smooth and predictable so as to provide a stable economic environment, and to control inflation in the longer run. This is particularly important in view of the negative impact that the shock will have on investment demand; sharp and unpredictable increases in interest rates will only exacerbate that impact.

A similar conflict arises with respect to fiscal policy. On the one hand there is pressure to lower tax rates to make up for the loss in real income brought about by higher energy prices, but on the other hand real government revenues may decline in any case because of a reduction in the real tax base. It is essential that fiscal policy be based on the recognition that higher energy prices necessarily imply a decrease in real national income. It is not possible to maintain real growth in government expenditures *and* cut taxes enough to maintain real growth in consumption, when the total resources available for domestic purposes have been reduced by higher energy prices. If the government chooses to keep expenditures in real terms at their preshock levels, then tax *increases,* not decreases, will be needed sooner or later. With constant tax rates, government expenditures must share in the decrease in real national income.

Unfortunately, when real income falls after a price shock, there is an unhealthy tendency for the share of government in the economy to rise. The role of government and the size of the government's share in GNP should be determined by broad social and economic considerations. The reductions in real national income that follow a price shock should be spread evenly and proportionately across all sectors of the economy, including the government sector. Otherwise government budget deficits will grow out of control, leading to still further inflation, and a more than proportionate drop in real income levels outside the government sector.

It is also desirable to use special incentives to stimulate investment in the aftermath of an energy price shock. As explained earlier, increases in energy prices tend to reduce investment demand, and this in turn can retard potential GNP growth for years to come. Proinvestment policies, such as investment tax credits and accelerated depreciation, should be used to stimulate investment demand. Such incentives can help to achieve capital-energy substitution earlier and thereby further reduce energy consumption (and soften the impact on real income), since *new* capital is likely to be much more energy-efficient. Finally, proinvestment policies can also help at least somewhat to offset inflation by adding to productive capacity and thus increasing aggregate supply.

Cost-reducing tax policies, which lower prices and raise output by reducing costs of production, are also desirable. In effect, such supply-side policies provide a way for the government to introduce the flexibility that the economy seems to lack in the short run. Reducing payroll taxes is the leading candidate for this kind of policy. A payroll tax increase has much the same effect as an energy price increase—it causes more inflation, which in turn feeds back into wages, then into still more inflation, and so on. That is why a payroll tax *cut* is the natural antidote for an energy price increase. Unfortunately the scope for this policy response is limited by the magnitude of existing payroll taxes. Furthermore, such tax reductions would require politically difficult modifications of existing fiscal institutions, since the Social Security payroll tax is now earmarked for a single purpose. In any case, it is sad to note that we are now moving in exactly the wrong direction, with major payroll tax *increases* scheduled.

In summary, while it is impossible to eliminate the inflationary and recessionary impact of an energy price shock, there are policies that can and should be used to ameliorate that impact and prevent it from becoming worse than it need be. Such policies include moderate growth of the money supply, restraint on fiscal expansion and government budget deficits, investment incentives, and, where possible, reductions in payroll taxes.

7. CONCLUSIONS

As I said at the outset, the role of energy in the design of economic and industrial policies is a dual one—such policies must be concerned with efficiency and productivity in the energy sector itself, and with the relationship of the energy sector to the economy as a whole, particularly with respect to the effects of rising energy prices. As a result, the scope of this paper has been rather broad, shifting from such problems as the role of government in the commercialization of new energy technologies to the use of monetary policy in the wake of an energy price shock.

In the hope that the numerous policy recommendations contained in this paper have already been stated sufficiently clearly and forcefully, I will not summarize them here. Instead, for those readers who found themselves in clear agreement with most or all of these recommendations (and I hope there are more than a few), I should point out that until recently government policies have almost without exception gone in the opposite direction. Of course changes are now occurring, or at least they seem to be. At the time of this writing, the Reagan administration has proposed cuts in the synthetic fuels program, crude oil prices have been decontrolled, investment incentives appear likely, and there is at least a recognition of the importance of restraint on fiscal expansion and stability in the growth of the money supply.

On the negative side, natural gas price controls may remain in effect until 1985, large expenditures on synthetic fuels are likely even if some cuts are made, a tariff on imported oil seems to have been ruled out by the Administration, and payroll tax increases are on the books. It will take some time to determine whether real policy changes are possible or likely. In the meanwhile our energy sector is not as productive as it could be, and our economy remains vulnerable to sharp increases in energy prices.

NOTES

1. The chapter is based on research supported by the Center for Energy Policy Research of the M.I.T. Energy Laboratory, and that support is gratefully acknowledged.

2. See, for example, the various papers in Sawhill (1979).

3. See Thurow (1980), p. 44–45. Thurow also shows that an additional 8 percent of the national productivity decline is attributable to reduced productivity growth in electricity and gas utilities, which in turn is the result of reduced energy consumption (caused by higher prices), and is therefore unavoidable.

4. For a detailed discussion of natural gas regulation and an analysis of its effects on gas markets, see MacAvoy and Pindyck (1975) and Pindyck (1977, 1978). For a detailed history of government energy policies beginning with the Truman administration, see Goodwin (1981).

5. These and related regulatory rules are discussed in Weiden-

baum (1981), chapter 7. The welfare implications of oil price decontrol are analyzed in Arrow and Kalt (1979). Also, see the Ford Foundation Study (1979).

6. This conflict was described in a 1977 article by Hall and Pindyck (1977). Also, see Pindyck (1980a).

7. These arguments were examined in considerable detail in a research project that Paul Joskow and I conducted at the Center for Energy Policy Research of the M.I.T. Energy Laboratory, and a more thorough discussion is presented in Joskow and Pindyck (1979). A related analysis of synthetic fuel subsidies can be found in Schmalensee (1980). Finally, for a financial analysis (including an analysis of the risk characteristics) of several specific synthetic fuel technologies, see Majd (1979).

8. And, as Schmalensee (1980) points out (p. 12), "even if such a bias could be demonstrated, . . . the rational policy response would not be to use that bias as an excuse to single out the energy supply sector for special treatment, but rather to attempt to offset biases against large investments with long lead times throughout the economy."

9. The characteristics of these cost uncertainties are analyzed for some specific technologies in Majd (1979). Also, see Jacoby *et al.* (1976) on this point.

10. See Schmalensee (1980), pp. 26–28, on this point. As he points out, loan guarantees and other forms of subsidies that shift risk to taxpayers can be particularly inefficient. "Information about the real cost of risk-bearing is hidden; design decisions are biased toward capital intensity; both design and operating decisions are biased toward risky alternatives; and a disincentive for follow-on investments is created."

11. As Weitzman (1980) points out, synthetic fuel development should be based on a series of *sequential decisions,* rather than a "crash program" or once-and-for-all choice.

12. For a discussion of some of the statistical evidence, and an analysis of energy demand in the United States and in other countries, see Pindyck (1979).

13. For an analysis of the impact of rising energy prices on different income groups, see Waverman (1979) and Wright and Cox (1980).

14. This was a major theme of Stobough and Yergin (1979), as well as other studies and reports.

15. For a discussion of some of these problems, see Deese and Nye (1981).

16. For analyses of the use of a strategic reserve and the design of an optimal oil import tariff, see Hogan (1981), and Tolley and Wilman (1977).

17. For a more detailed discussion of the macroeconomic effects of

rising energy prices, see Pindyck (1980b), Hall and Pindyck (1981), Helliwell (1980), and Solow (1980). For a discussion of international differences in these effects, see Hall and Pindyck (1981) and Fieleke (1981).

18. This is discussed in Hall and Pindyck (1981). For estimates of energy demand elasticities in the United States and elsewhere, see Pindyck (1979).

19. This example is due to Nordhaus (1980). For more on the relationship of energy to output and productivity, see Berndt (1980), Nordhaus (1980), and chapter 8 of Pindyck (1979).

20. For a more general view of the problems that rigidities like these cause for our economy, see Scitovsky (1980).

21. For a discussion of both the meaning of and statistical evidence regarding capital-energy complementarity, see Berndt and Wood (1979).

BIBLIOGRAPHY
Arrow, Kenneth J. and Kalt, Joseph P. "Why Oil Prices Should Be Decontrolled." *Regulation* (American Enterprise Institute, September, 1979): 13–17.
Berndt, Ernst R. "Energy Price Increases and the Productivity Slowdown in United States Manufacturing," in *The Decline of Productivity Growth*. Federal Reserve Bank of Boston, Conferences Series No. 22. Boston: Federal Reserve Bank of Boston, 1980.
Berndt, Ernst R. and Wood, David O. "Engineering and Econometric Interpretation of Energy-Capital Complementarity." *American Economic Review,* 69 (June, 1979): 342–354.
Deese, David A. and Nye, Joseph S. eds., *Energy and Security,* Cambridge, Mass.: Ballinger Publishing Company, 1981.
Fieleke, Norman S. "Rising Oil Prices and the Industrial Countries." *New England Economic Review* (January, 1981): 17–28.
Ford Foundation. *Energy: The Next Twenty Years,* Cambridge, Mass.: Ballinger Publishing Company, 1979.
Goodwin, Craufurd D. *Energy Policy in Perspective,* Washington: The Brookings Institution, 1981.
Hall, Robert E. and Pindyck, Robert S. "The Conflicting Goals of National Energy Policy." *The Public Interest* 47 *(Spring, 1977): 3–14.*
———. "Energy and the Western Economies." *Technology Review* (April, 1981): 32–40.
Helliwell, John F. "The Stagflationary Effects of Higher Energy Prices in an Open Economy." Resources Paper 57, Department of Economics, University of British Columbia. Vancouver: October, 1980.
Hogan, William W. "Import Management and Oil Emergencies." In *Energy and Security,* edited by David A. Deese and Joseph S. Nye. Cambridge, Mass.: Ballinger Publishing Company, 1981.

Jacoby, Henry D.; Linden, Lawrence H.; Adelman, M. A.; Ball, Ben C.; Greenwood, Ted R. I.; Hammond, Ogden H., 3rd; Myers, Stewart C.; Nyhart, J. Daniel; Wood, David O.; and Zimmerman, Martin B. "Government Support for the Commercialization of New Energy Techniques." M.I.T. Energy Laboratory Technical Report EL76–009. Cambridge, Mass.: November, 1976.

Joskow, Paul L. and Pindyck, Robert S. "Synthetic Fuels: Should the Government Subsidize Non-Conventional Energy Supplies?" *Regulation* (American Enterprise Institute September, 1979): 18–24.

MacAvoy, Paul W. and Pindyck, Robert S. *Price Controls and the Natural Gas Shortage.* Washington: American Enterprise Institute, 1975.

Majd, Saman. "A Financial Analysis of Selected Synthetic Fuel Technologies," M.I.T. Energy Laboratory Working Paper EL79–004WP. Cambridge, Mass.: January, 1979.

Nordhaus, William D. "Policy Responses to the Productivity Slowdown." In *The Decline of Productivity Growth,* Federal Reserve Bank of Boston, Conference Series No. 22. Boston: Federal Reserve Bank of Boston, 1980.

Pindyck, Robert S. "Prices vs. Shortages: Policy Options for the Natural Gas Industry," In *Options for U.S. Energy Policy,* San Francisco: 1977. Institute for Contemporary Studies, 1977.

———. "Higher Energy Prices and the Supply of Natural Gas," *Energy Systems and Policy* 2 (1978): 177–209.

———. *The Structure of World Energy Demand.* Cambridge, Mass.: M.I.T. Press, 1979.

———. "The American Energy Debate," *The Public Interest* 59 (Spring, 1980a): 100–105.

———. "Energy Price Increases and Macroeconomic Policy." *The Energy Journal* 1 (October, 1980b): 1–20.

———. "An Agenda for American Energy Policy." In *Politics and the Oval Office: Towards Presidential Governance,* edited by A. Meltsner. San Francisco: Institute for Contemporary Studies, 1981.

Sawhill, John, ed. *Energy Conservation and Public Policy.* Englewood Cliffs: Prentice-Hall, 1979.

Schmalensee, Richard. "Appropriate Government Policy Toward Commercialization of New Energy Supply Technologies." *The Energy Journal* 1 (July, 1980): 1–40.

Scitovsky, Tibor, "Can Capitalism Survive?—An Old Question in a New Setting." *American Economic Review* 70 (May, 1980): 1–9.

Solow, Robert M. "What to Do When OPEC Comes." In Fisher, S., ed. *Rational Expectations and Economic Policy.* Chicago: University of Chicago Press, 1980.

Stobaugh, Robert and Yergin, Daniel eds., *Energy Future: Report of the Energy Project at the Harvard Business School.* New York: Random House, 1979.

Thurow, Lester C., "The Productivity Problem." *Technology Review,* (November, 1980): 40–51.

Tolley, George S. and Wilman, John D. "The Foreign Dependence Question." *Journal of Political Economy* 85 (April, 1977): 323–348.

Waverman, Leonard. "The Visible Hand: The Pricing of Canadian Oil and

Natural Gas Resources." Working Paper, Institute of Policy Analysis, University of Toronto. Toronto: September, 1979.

Weidenbaum, Murray L., *Business, Government, and the Public.* Englewood Cliffs: Prentice-Hall, 1981.

Weitzman, Martin L. "Sequential R & D Strategy for Synfuels," M.I.T. Energy Laboratory Working Paper. Cambridge, Mass.: October, 1980.

Wright, Lindsay, and Cox, Loren C. "The Impacts of Energy Price Increases on Low Income Groups," M.I.T. Energy Laboratory Working Paper EL80-025WP, Cambridge, Mass.: July, 1980.

10.

ENERGY AND SECURITY POLICY

William W. Hogan

INTRODUCTION[1]

Internal political convulsions in the Persian Gulf and a regional war
have created an economic emergency for oil importing countries. Moreover, competition for oil in the volatile Persian Gulf could precipitate
a wider conflict involving the United States and the Soviet Union. The
importance of the oil trade has increased greatly with the sudden jumps
in the economic value of oil. Starting the decade of the seventies as a
topic only for specialists, the world oil system ended the decade as a first
order political-economic-security challenge to the oil importing nations.

Payments for oil imports have drained more than an additional 2
percent of our GNP in the form of higher prices. More importantly, the
evident inability of policymakers to correctly diagnose and treat the
inflation and income distribution problems caused by oil disruptions
was the principal source of the inferior economic performance of the
seventies. Future oil emergencies could be the greatest single threat to
our economic recovery. Furthermore, the evident externalities associated with oil supply disruptions place a burden on government to
devise and implement policies to correct the failings of the international
market. These twin features, overriding importance and a mandate for
government action, make an effective energy security policy a prerequisite and integral part of any new industrial policy for guiding the economy.

This dramatic transition in oil trade has not been sufficient for common agreement on the nature of the changes, on possible future developments, or on the necessary measures to deal with the problems. It is
of the highest importance for the United States, as the largest oil importing nation, to interpret correctly the oil messages of the last decade in
order to fashion a sound program for meeting the energy security

threats of the future. A number of reports and monographs recently published in the United States move us far along in the development of a common description of the problems before us.[2] In this paper we summarize the current state of debate over energy security problems, issues, and policies, at least from the perspective of the United States and other oil importing countries. We consider first the main dimensions of the problem; we then outline the issues that are open for debate and relevant to the design of a new industrial policy.

DEPENDENCE AND VULNERABILITY

Oil importing nations are heavily dependent on the Persian Gulf. In 1979, before the economic slowdown of 1980, the noncommunist world consumed about 50 million barrels of oil per day, and around 17 million barrels per day came from the Persian Gulf. The United States imported eight million barrels of oil per day, amounting to 45 percent of total oil supply and 20 percent of total energy supply. Japan provided a starker example as a country even more dependent on imported oil. In 1979 Japan imported five million barrels per day, or nearly 100 percent of its oil supply and 70 percent of total energy consumption.

This high level of dependence on oil imports is not likely to change soon. Although high oil prices and depressed economies dampened oil demand in 1980, a recent survey by Krapels[3] demonstrates that every responsible forecast of world oil supply and demand, over the next decade and beyond, anticipates a continued high dependence on Persian Gulf oil. There are many steps that can and should be taken to reduce this dependence and minimize its cost, but there are no presently conceivable policies which will remove the problem of Persian Gulf oil from the center stage of policy concern.

Because of the political volatility of the Persian Gulf, we face a high probability of major interruptions of oil supply and precipitous jumps in the world price. We also face the danger of large-scale Soviet Union interventions in the area. This situation increases not only the threat of interruption of oil supply, but also raises the possibility of the diversion of part of the large oil revenues to the aims of Moscow. Our high dependence on oil from the region heightens both of these problems.

The vulnerability to supply interruption is closely linked to the level of dependence on Persian Gulf oil, but it is a separate threat and requires separate policy responses. Too often in the past, policymakers in oil importing countries have blurred the distinctions between dependence and vulnerability. As a result, we have wasted valuable time fashioning energy policies that mismatch ends and means. The problem has been especially acute in the United States where visions of energy independence are viewed through a lens focused narrowly on "Fortress America."

The first step in meeting the challenges in the world oil market is to clarify the distinct dimensions of the oil problem. From the perspective of a special concern with energy and security issues, a common view is emerging.

OIL INTERDEPENDENCE

Each oil importing country can take steps to reduce the problem of oil. But it is a delusion for any country to consider only its own imports as the measure of exposure to the large costs of oil supply interruptions. Even with no oil imports, which would be difficult to achieve and more difficult to maintain, the United States would not be free of the burden of meeting security threats to world oil supplies. The ties to allies would still bind. Similarly, even with a high level of oil imports, a country like Japan need not be as vulnerable to the costs of interruption as it is today. With a large reserve capacity and long-run fuel switching capability, Japan could adjust well to a high level of oil imports. Hence, dependence and vulnerability are separate, but interdependent, issues.

An effective program for energy and security must recognize the essential international character of oil supply and demand. Actions in any part of the world affect outcomes everywhere. Even without the link through oil trade, the broader economic and security relationships of the oil importing countries preclude the withdrawal of any country from meeting threats to oil security. The oil policy of all nations must address the interdependent nature of the oil market.

CURRENT WEALTH TRANSFER

The first order effect of higher oil prices is to increase the transfer of wealth from oil importers to oil exporters. For example, in 1972, oil imports payments were $8 billion and $4.5 billion for the United States and Japan respectively. By 1979, with the growth in both the volume of imports and the price per barrel, these payments exploded to $55 billion and $36 billion. Discounting for the effects of inflation and economic growth, we saw oil imports rise from 0.4 percent of GNP in 1972 to over 3 percent in 1980 for the Japanese. The oil importing countries have a strong interest in reducing dependence on oil imports and moderating the growth in oil prices.

INTERTEMPORAL WEALTH TRANSFER

In addition to the current transfer of wealth, higher oil prices sap the long-run health of the economies of all importing nations. Long-run scarcity and the replacement costs of oil cannot justify current oil prices.[4] Since higher prices foreclose many otherwise productive uses of energy, total world economic output is lower than necessary. Hence, the aggregate economic costs to the oil importing nations are greater than the transfer of wealth to the oil producing nations. It may be difficult soon to lower the real price of oil, but oil consumers should not be lulled into a false complacency with high oil prices based on the producer propaganda that these prices serve our own long-term interests by rationing scarce deposits of oil needed for future generations. Total world economic output would be optimized with a faster depletion of oil reserves.

INTERRUPTION COSTS

Given a smooth transition, however, the oil importing countries, at least the developed oil importing countries, could absorb higher prices, oil wealth transfers, and slowed economic growth without causing an absolute reduction in living standards. The immediate energy-security threat of economic losses springs from the vulnerability to sudden oil supply interruptions. With little flexibility to substitute quickly for any form of energy, a sudden loss in supply can cause major economic disruptions and dramatic increases in prices. Furthermore, our less than adept management of past supply interruptions and price increases contributed to the costs of supply interruptions. A major disruption blocking oil supplies from the Persian Gulf could create an economic catastrophe on a scale comparable to the Great Depression.

OIL POLITICS

Oil has become a political commodity. The economic prominence of oil, especially in the short run, guarantees that economic forces will be only partial determinants of the nature of the oil market. Some oil producers see oil as their major weapon in political negotiations. Oil producers can trade real or imagined economic concessions, in terms of lower prices or favorable conditions of supply, for a variety of political concessions. There is little doubt, for example, that Israel's political position has eroded with the growth in importance of Persian Gulf oil. The political components of oil deals will be more apparent and more important, complicating both the analysis and the resolution of oil threats to security.

However, there are clear limits to the use of the "oil weapon" set by the fact that the oil market is a world market. For example, selective embargoes do not work, as was illustrated in 1973. Economic concessions can be granted in exchange for political ones, but economic "punishment" is a blunt and nonselective instrument.

SOVIET THREAT

Soviet control of Persian Gulf oil supplies would greatly exacerbate the problems facing oil importing countries. The Soviet Union would be much better able than the oil producers to manipulate the conditions of access to oil for political and military advantage. In the extreme case of total Soviet control of the Persian Gulf oil fields, oil importing countries would face an even more effective cartel, manipulating prices and production to maximize the transfer of wealth. This oil wealth would provide a bonanza for Soviet economic and military strategists. Even in the more likely case of Soviet "Finlandization" of the Persian Gulf, oil importing countries would have to pay a steep political bill for an ever tenuous access to oil supplies. Geology provides the fulcrum and geography, plus a large increase in its capacity to project power abroad, provide the lever for the Soviet Union to tip the world balance of power through domination of the Persian Gulf.

FREE RIDERS
Nearly every energy action available to oil importing countries—tariffs, stockpiles, fuel conversion measures, emergency conservation, and the like—works better if done cooperatively. Oil is a fungible good in an international market. Decreasing the demand for oil or increasing its supply anywhere benefits consumers everywhere. The United States, Japan, Western Europe, and other oil importing countries, therefore, can each justify much more aggressive oil market programs if they can be guaranteed that others will follow suit.

Unfortunately, this source of cooperative gain, that we each benefit from the action of others, is also a source of disunity among oil importers. Each country can hope to be a "free rider." If Japan lowers its oil imports, it will soften prices for everyone, including the United States, even if the Americans take no action of their own. The United States would get a free ride. And the smaller the country, the more pronounced the free rider effect. This leaves us with the classic problem of the prisoner's dilemma. Each country hopes that others will absorb the costs while it reaps the benefits. For fear of being exploited, no country acts, and each loses. A major challenge for diplomacy among oil importing countries is to overcome free rider induced policy inaction.

ENERGY ISSUES
These views on the nature of the problem did not develop immediately or easily. Many in the United States still fail to make the distinction between dependence and vulnerability and seek energy security through energy autarky. But these several dimensions of the nature of the problem with Persian Gulf oil supplies are common threads in the evolving view of energy and security. These points of agreement pro-

vide the foundation for the examination of energy issues where controversy remains.

REDUCED DEPENDENCE

Every oil importing country should reduce its oil dependence and oil interruption vulnerability. Numerous studies over the past decade have examined a welter of policies for reducing oil dependence. Lower levels of energy use through conservation and lower levels of oil use through fuel switching could greatly reduce the demand for oil imports. The United States, for instance, could achieve as much as a 40 percent reduction in energy intensity per unit of output by the turn of the century.[5] More importantly, the United States could have zero to negative growth in oil consumption despite a hoped-for 60 percent increase in real GNP.

Subsidies for residential energy conservation, mandatory standards for automobile fuel efficiency, and incentives for conversion to alternative fuels have dominated policy in the United States. But by far the most important conservation policy now adopted in the United States is to allow consumer prices to reflect the price of oil on the world market.

Aggressive efforts to expand domestic oil supply may be in the offing with the Reagan administration. Coupled with the incentive of higher prices, the United States may be able, over the next decade, to halt the decline in domestic oil production. Over the longer term, synthetic fuels and alternative energy supplies may provide sufficient supplements to further reduce dependence on imported oil.

Other oil importers also have ambitious programs to promote alternative sources of supply. Returning to the Japanese example, nuclear power and coal for boilers offer promise of expanding energy supplies. In addition, Japan is investing in the search for new sources of oil that will add to the scale and diversity of world supplies. Between 1973 and 1978, Japan's oil use per unit of GNP dropped by 22 percent.[6] With the price shocks of 1979–80, oil conservation accelerated. There are many cost effective steps available to lessen the degree of dependence, but there is no serious prospect of eliminating Japanese oil dependency.

Although the speed of response may have been disappointingly slow, the reduction of import dependence has been a prime policy objective in all oil importing countries. More problematic is deciding just how far to go with investments in long-run substitutes for oil imports. Higher world oil prices alone provide a lower bound on the economics of import substitution. But the many additional costs of oil imports—exacerbated inflation, balance of payments impacts, wealth transfers, vulnerability costs—create a premium for import reduction.

Each oil importing country should be willing to pay more than the world oil price for oil import substitutes.

There is no precise estimate of this oil import premium. It varies across countries according to the degree of dependence; it rests upon subjective judgments about the likelihood and depth of oil supply interruptions. For the United States acting alone, we estimate that a premium of about 30 percent of the price of oil should be the guide for selecting among substitutes for oil imports. For countries with a greater dependence, or for several countries acting together, even higher premiums would apply.

This premium provides a standard for discriminating among import alternatives. Hence, coal-based synthetic fuels, which may require early public subsidies, would appear to be cost effective at current world oil prices. Gasohol would not. There is a limit to how far any country should go to limit oil imports, but there is not yet agreement on the precise premium. We can look forward to continued debates about the adequacy of individual government efforts to reduce long-run import dependence.

EMERGENCY PREPAREDNESS

This long-run premium will not eliminate vulnerability to interruption of Persian Gulf oil supplies. At any moment, we could suffer a major loss of production and a skyrocketing of oil prices. The appalling state of emergency preparedness is a subject of controversy in the United States. But a number of steps can be taken now to mitigate the costs of a supply interruption. The United States, for instance, should develop a market allocation system to distribute the limited oil supplies that will be available during a major interruption. Such a system would be far superior to the cumbersome gasoline rationing and standby allocation mechanism offered to date as the major tools for managing oil shortages.

But reliance on the market for domestic distribution, which should be compatible with the philosophy of the Reagan administration, should not mirror a similar reliance on the international market to determine the terms of oil trade. The costs of oil supply disruptions or the oil price increases borne by all from any increment to oil demand are large externalities that will not be recognized by the private actors in the market. These transfers of wealth make international energy pricing and security arrangements a natural arena for government intervention.

The enormous transfer of wealth within the United States, as well as to foreign oil producers, will also require a rapid system of emergency income transfusions to mitigate the impacts on the poor. At the same time, economic managers will need to coordinate macroeconomic fiscal and monetary steps to eliminate a large fiscal drag and accommodate the price inflation sparked by oil price increases.

Action now could improve the short-run flexibility for fuel switching. The United States and other oil importing countries have or could have large stocks of coal (and also natural gas for many) available for use during an oil supply disruption. Some energy facilities have dual burning capabilities now. Others could acquire this capability on relatively short notice. All oil importing countries should be expanding this short-term conversion flexibility and stockpiling the appropriate reserves of coal and natural gas to supply the converted facilities during an energy emergency.

Emergency conservation measures such as van-pooling and modified work schedules may provide a quick fix for reducing oil demand. Many of these adjustments will occur naturally in response to the sharp price rise of the market allocation system. But not all preparations or adjustments can occur through the market alone. Governments and companies can take steps now to prepare the conditions so that consumers will have alternatives when prices do rise suddenly.

Finally, the United States and a few other countries have a capability for surging production of oil and natural gas during an oil emergency. The initial expansion of oil supplies might be small, but could be accelerated over time. Surge production from domestic wells could complement the most important source of excess capacity: strategic petroleum reserves.

STOCKPILES

A large stockpile of oil, held in reserve for emergencies, is the most obvious and most convenient source of excess capacity to compensate for abrupt losses of oil supply. Although oil importing countries now hold record levels of stocks, these inventories are far below the optimum levels justified by the precarious nature of world oil supply. Size is among the several aspects of stockpiles that incite controversy.

Size The optimum size of a strategic petroleum reserve continues to be a subject of debate. However, this may be a question for which knowing the answer has little value. We do not need to know how many billions of barrels would be in the optimal stockpile to conclude that the optimum is much more than the few hundred million barrels available in 1981. Strategic inventories of oil are far too low. Calculations done by the Department of Energy and others suggest that the stockpile for the United States should be at least one billion barrels of oil (or oil-equivalent fuels); for all oil importing countries the figure climbs to over three billion barrels.[7]

Fill Rate The debate over stockpile size gains meaning when we turn to the rate of fill of the strategic reserve. As with most remedies in the international oil market, the medicine must be taken now, in the form of higher prices and payments while filling, and the benefits come only later, in the reduction of the cost of interruptions. From the record, it seems that the optimal time to fill the strategic reserve is always six months in the future. In a December, 1980 International Energy Agency communique, for example, the oil importing countries even agreed on reducing the level of strategic inventories as a means of softening pressure then on the world market.

The most active proponents of slow-fill or reduced strategic petroleum reserve size, not surprisingly, are the oil producers themselves. There is power in the control of spare capacity. The oil producers will lose power if the oil importing nations have a cushion against supply interruptions. Hence, every attempt to add to strategic reserves must face the threat and possible reality of retaliation by the oil producers. But if the strategic reserves are not filled soon, we will have little security from this source during the dangerous decade of the eighties.

Public versus Private   As with most oil issues today, therefore, the management of a strategic petroleum reserve is a political issue. Hence, there is a great interest now in the United States in depoliticizing inventory management by moving control from public to private hands. Furthermore, decisions by governments to build up or draw down inventories will strongly affect the decisions of private holders of inventories. Hence, government action may only substitute for private action, with no net change. The proper mix between public and private inventories, and the proper institutions for controlling public inventories, remain as controversial subjects surrounding the development of a strategic petroleum reserve.

Multilateral Coordination   Most analysts believe that coordinated policies for stockpile use will greatly enhance the value of this emergency preparedness tool. Unfortunately, it is easy to conceive of circumstances where individual country incentives will work at cross-purposes to coordinated action. And it is difficult to think of an institution which could overcome these incentives. Often this concern with the difficulty of multilateral coordination has led policymakers to discount any benefits that might accrue from a strategic stockpile. The opportunities, extent, and necessity for multilateral coordination of stockpile policies remain as topics requiring careful study.

TARIFFS

Because of the oil import premium, that is, because the market price does not represent the true cost of oil imports, every oil importing country should take steps to reduce demand and increase domestic supply beyond the automatic adjustments of the market. And the scale of required action multiplies greatly during an oil supply interruption.

In principle, a sophisticated, centrally planned economy could, without resort to prices, orchestrate all necessary conservation and supply actions in order to obtain the appropriate reduction in oil imports. In practice, oil importing countries need higher prices in domestic markets in order to provide conservation incentives for private decision-makers.

The most direct means of sending these higher price signals to the domestic market would be to impose a substantial tariff on oil imports. Since imported oil is the source of the extra cost, imported oil should bear the burden of the tariff. For the long run, we can justify a 30 percent tariff for the United States. During an interruption, the tariff might be 100 percent or more.

This attractive economic instrument must confront responses by the oil producers. There are many reasons to expect that a clumsy import tariff would precipitate retaliatory action by oil producers, rational or irrational, to raise oil prices even more and aggravate, not lessen, all the problems of our dependence on a vulnerable oil supply. Nonetheless, the attractions of using market-like mechanisms to stanch the flow of wealth to oil exporting countries are large and the threat of retaliation in some circumstances (e.g., during a Persian Gulf crisis in which the price of oil has gone to over $100 per barrel) may be low.

There may be other ways of obtaining an approximately similar effect. Taxes on oil products, for example, might be less provocative than tariffs. Even more imaginative policies have been suggested for creating the effect of a tariff without its political liabilities. The details of these policies continue to stimulate discussion among energy analysts. Using a tariff as an ideal to be approached, oil importing countries need to search for practical instruments for regulating the demand for oil imports.

Problems of coordination across oil importing countries are equally severe, and equally attractive, for tariffs as they are for oil stockpiles. The size of the optimal tariff for the United States could double with a guarantee of coordinated action by all oil importing countries.

QUOTAS

In a competitive market, there is natural duality between import quotas and tariffs. A tariff provides price certainty, and the quantity imported results from the interaction of market forces. A quota provides quantity certainty, and the effective tariff, that is, the price of the import tickets, results from the same market forces.

Because quotas focus on quantity, and apparently because of a hope that consumers will not blame government for the resulting price rises, governments have found quotas or quantity targets to be attractive instruments for controlling imports. Conventional wisdom and precedent have established the import targets as the principal vehicle for international agreements on managing oil imports.[8]

But this consensus on targets is misplaced. So far, we have acted cautiously by imposing import targets above the expected level of import demand. While such nonbinding quotas may yield some benefits through the appearance of action, by definition they do nothing to restrict oil imports. Should we accelerate, however, and impose binding quotas, we will founder upon the fallacy of viewing quotas as equivalent to tariffs in the present world oil market.

Since producers exercise market power, the potential response to higher prices, as well as the level of demand, determine the market price. But with a binding quota, oil producers will face an inflexible demand for oil. As long as the quota binds, producers can cut production, raise prices, and enjoy increased revenues without any decrease in demand. Unless we hope to "break OPEC," binding quotas will result in higher prices and lower consumption. But the higher prices will be on the world market, not in the price of the import tickets. The import tickets will be free and the higher revenues will go to oil producers.

In the present oil market, therefore, tariffs and quotas are not the same. With a tariff, or a tariff-like policy, the governments of the oil importing countries are the tax collectors. With a quota, we turn to the oil producers to collect our taxes. The counterproductive binding quota is likely to yield the worst of both conditions; higher prices and lower supply. We must look elsewhere for tools to control oil imports.

CHANGING MARKETS

Still in flux in 1981, the international oil market experienced dramatic changes in structure during the seventies. No longer do the major international oil companies dominate all transactions. According to Neff,[9] the majors' share of the distribution of oil dropped from 90 percent in 1973 to 55 percent in early 1980. In addition to taking charge of production decisions, the producing governments have assumed control of the distribution of the balance of 45 percent of the oil traded on the world market.

Producers now use a variety of government-to-government arrangements, sales to independent oil companies, sales on the spot market, and an amalgam of processing deals to dispose of their export crude oil. Buyers now face a dizzying array of special conditions for purchase, particularly on long-term contracts: direct price premiums, exploration fees or requirements, incentive crudes for other investments, signature bonuses for the right to sign contracts, destination restrictions, use and resale restrictions, anticompetitive clauses, mandatory purchases of low quality crude and products, transportation requirements, and demands for joint processing deals.

Where all this leads, no one is sure. But it is apparent that many oil importing governments and companies see the possibility of gain through contracts with producers that involve much more than arm's length transactions at a designated price. And oil producers see real or imagined opportunities for profit by using access to oil to diversify their economies or extend their control into downstream activities. These trends are likely to continue into the next decade.

It is doubtful whether the changes matter very much. From first principles, more diversity in trading arrangements could work to the advantage of both buyers and sellers. After all, the many special conditions demanded by producers come presumably in lieu of a still higher price. The chief concern is that the loss of control by the majors may remove an important source of flexibility for balancing regional markets in normal times and, more importantly, in redistributing oil during supply interruptions. In the past, the fungible nature of oil supplies, and the integrated systems of the major oil companies, made it impossible to restrict supply to any one country without restricting supply to all countries. Apparently the intent of the destination restrictions on government-to-government deals is to give the producers more power to determine who uses their oil, and to protect favored consumers from the reallocation of supplies during an oil shortage. Both partners in the special deals are preparing themselves for a possible targeted embargo.

To be successful, however, a targeted embargo must leave the favored countries with more oil in total than they would have received through traditional market allocations. And they must be insulated from the shortage-induced price increases. Hence, the protected oil deals must cover nearly all of their oil consumption. If only a fraction of the oil supply to a country is open to reallocation, this fraction can absorb all of the shortage adjustments. Without nearly complete coverage, therefore, the special deals would be futile, not to mention the contravention of the spirit of of international sharing agreements.

Changes in the structure of the international oil market bear watching. But how much these changes affect the aggregate results of market allocation, as opposed to the appearances, is yet to be revealed.

BEDOUINS, BANKERS, AND BORROWERS

The international banking system stands between the enormous new wealth of the oil producers and the financing needs of the oil importing countries. Although this system proved resilient in handling the unprecedented recycling of surplus oil wealth in 1973–74, and again in 1979–80, strains on the system continue to worry both borrowers and lenders.

The first oil shock created an immediate surplus in OPEC of $70 to $80 billion, with a corresponding payments deficit in the oil importing countries. However, the oil producers' absorptive capacity increased apace with the growth in their revenues, eliminating the surplus by 1977. The second oil shock, with prices doubling again in 1979–80, produced a new surplus of upward of $100 billion. Although the international financial system has performed remarkably well to date, with threats of further price increases we cannot be complacent about the ability of existing financial institutions to recycle indefinitely this enormous unspent oil loot. Concern over the increased indebtedness of many less developed countries, and over the exposure of banks that have been carrying much of their debt, has been growing.

Worry over the reliability of the banks and their deposits gives rise to real effects in the oil markets. If the banks threaten collapse, if inflation destroys nominal deposits, or if visible bank accounts invite expropriation, cautious sheikhs will come to value oil in the ground as the only reliable store of value over the long haul. Their logical choice will be to lower production now and save their oil for the future. (That this may yield even greater revenues in the short run only reinforces the decision.) Consumers and producers both suffer when producers do not have access to sound investments that can compete with speculation on oil deposits. Oil importers would do well to consider alternative investment institutions for recycling oil payments.[10]

Under normal conditions, the banking system should be able to recycle whatever surplus appears. There will be painful adjustments for the poorest countries, but the aggregate deficit always just equals the aggregate surplus, and the producers are not likely to stuff their dollars under a rug.

During a major supply interruption, however, large liquid assets concentrated in the hands of a nervous or unfriendly few create conditions for a financial panic that could be as dangerous as the loss of the oil supply itself. Money can move much faster than oil. Whether contrived or accidental, a banking collapse could accompany any flareup in the Persian Gulf. Fortunately, we have experience in dealing with bank failure; if we know what is happening, our bankers can adjust for any rapid movement of funds. But we need to plan ahead. Emergency preparations for dealing with an oil crisis must include procedures for insulating the international banking system.

Under the increasingly customary abnormal conditions, bankers fear the financial collapse of their poorest credit risks: the oil importing developing countries. Here the problems are as much the familiar issues of foreign aid to the impoverished as they are any new dilemmas created by changes in the oil market. However, the condition of the poorest countries does affect the nature and part of the solution of our energy problems.

OIDCS

Oil Importing Developing Countries (OIDCs) suffer the most from oil price shocks:

> Current account deficits in the OIDCs jumped by at least $33 billion, from $27.1 billion in 1978 to over $60 billion in 1980—an enormous shock to absorb over only two years.[11]

Poor to begin with, most OIDCs cannot make the adjustments needed to meet this higher oil bill.

As a first resort, OIDCs turned to private banks and other financial institutions for new capital to finance current consumption. This is a formula for producing bad debts, and the formula works. Banks, anxious to avoid default, refinance the loans, but the situation is precarious. For example, Brazil's interest payments and oil imports together exceed the value of all its exports.[12] As a last resort, the oil producers and the developed countries must come to an agreement on aid to cover not only the cost of oil for OIDCs, but to solve the larger problem of development for the great mass of poor in the world. Oil shocks widened the gulf between rich and poor, but they did not create it. Paying for oil is only one among many problems for the poor nations.

To the extent we solve the problem of development and stimulate the OIDC economies, we will increase the pressure on the world oil market. Forecasts of energy demand for OIDCs, built on an assumption of substantial economic growth, suggest that energy demand by the turn of the century could easily exceed 25 million barrels per day of oil equivalent, as compared to 9.5 million barrels per day in 1972.[13]

A large part of this demand will be for oil, increasing competition for limited supplies and placing greater upward pressure on the price demanded from oil importing countries. If we hope to see the economic growth in OIDCs, we must find ways to produce and finance the necessary oil supply.

One source of new oil supply may be in the OIDCs themselves. Explorers for oil have spent little time in these countries. While not all countries will be equally blessed, it is expected that many OIDCs contain significant deposits of oil. Given the sudden increase in the value of oil, we can justify large new exploration efforts.

The benefits of even modest discoveries would fall to both the lucky owners of the new oil and the consumers in all oil importing countries. Consumers will benefit indirectly from any addition to world production that moderates price and diversifies supply to lessen the likelihood of major interruptions. The fortunate OIDC would benefit directly from the added oil wealth. Being so poor, the new oil income would mean more to them than to anyone else. Hence, part of any future aid package for OIDCs should be to develop energy sources to substitute for or augment the world oil supply.

INTERNATIONAL COOPERATION

The oil producers and others occasionally propose a formal agreement between oil importers and oil exporters to stabilize both prices and supply. Despite the surface appeal of such agreements, there is not much here to benefit the oil importers. Any agreement would certainly call for high price levels, paid now in exchange for promises of stability during future interruptions. But the later benefits would be ephemeral as the producers would find themselves in circumstances where they would be unable or unwilling to comply with the agreement. Added to these problems of enforcing compliance, it would be difficult to limit the agenda for cooperative talks to the narrow issue of oil policy. Any such effort would soon be lost in the morass of the broader north-south dialogue.

By contrast, the rich rewards for cooperation among oil importing countries call for new and stronger international institutions. The International Energy Agency (IEA) and the International Energy Program (IEP) provide minimal benefits to their participants. The IEA offers a forum for discussion common energy problems. The IEA information systems collect and organize data useful for analyzing energy options. And for moderate disruptions of world markets, the IEP sharing plan is in place and could promote limited cooperation among consumers.

For small or truly large disruptions, however, the IEP is likely to be ineffective. No formal sharing agreement exists for supply interruptions below 7 percent, and present antitrust law in the United States prohibits major oil companies, the most important actors, from participating in informal discussions to allocate supplies and avoid the ruinous competition that could lead to increased shortages and higher prices.

If the IEA shortfall rises above 10 percent of expected supplies, the present sharing rules, which shift to a bias in favor of the United States, create strong incentives for important participants (for example, Japan) to back out of the IEP agreement. Unless the participants see the sharing formula as no worse than open competition, they will not be inclined to take the difficult domestic actions needed to reduce their demand for imports. Assuming equally flexible economies, a first approximation of the market allocation would be to share the shortage in proportion to oil (or perhaps energy) consumption. Such a sharing scheme might avoid the price increases and the great transfer of wealth to the oil producers, but leave each country with the oil it would have had without cooperation.

Under the current IEP scheme, importers must share shortages above 10 percent according to the level of imports, not consumption. If it works, this rule benefits those importers with significant domestic production (for example, the United States). If it fails, as it surely will, the rule benefits only those who wish to see higher oil prices in the world market. A political compromise engineered by and for the United States, this sharing rule for large interruptions is counterproductive and should be changed, probably by using the oil consumption sharing standard for all levels of interruption.

Finally, with 20 signatory nations, the IEA is too large and cumbersome an organization to be expected to respond with speed and dexterity to manage international oil crises. We need a more effective tool for meeting the energy and economic challenges of oil supply disruptions. The IEA should be preserved for its acknowledged value as a policy forum. There is nothing to gain from trying to eliminate or replace the existing organization, and with United States support we should be able to correct the egregious flaws in the sharing schemes. But we must find a leaner institution for orchestrating the cooperative actions of the major oil importers.

The Summit mechanism offers a process that seems well suited to fashioning a more effective organization and strategy. The seven Summit nations presently account for over three-quarters of the world oil consumption. And they all have bilateral or multilateral military alliance ties. The oil ministers of the Summit nations meet periodically to develop energy strategies. Past Summit meetings in Tokyo and Venice gave us the feeble attempts at establishing import ceilings. A formalization and strengthening of the Summit energy ministerial group may be the easiest path to creating an international cooperative capability to supplement the IEA and mitigate the economic damages of energy emergencies. And the IEA should be predisposed to adopt any agreement of the Summit nations.

The agenda for international cooperation should cover the full range of problems that now plague our adjustment to the new, world oil regime. In addition to a better concept for a sharing scheme, we need teeth for the sharing program to guarantee adherence under the wrenching pull of chaos in the world market. In addition, a cooperative strategy for stockpile development and use would aid everyone in developing this primary source of excess capacity. And a package of tariff-like policies for normal and disrupted markets may establish the import limitation goal for cooperative negotiation among the oil importing nations. Finally, once we address the critical needs of emergency preparedness, there may be political capital left for the more difficult and more protracted negotiations about the long-run adaptation to our collective energy future.

Cooperative planning for energy emergencies must soon expand beyond the boundaries of normal energy markets. Who, for instance, will take responsibility for developing repair capabilities to restore production destroyed by a convulsion in the Persian Gulf? This is but one small example of the issues outside the normal bailiwick of energy planners. The political maturation of energy issues demands that energy plans mesh with the web of foreign policy and military preparations to meet the security threats made suddenly important by the explosion in oil values.

COORDINATION AND CONFRONTATION

Foreign policy and military preparations lie outside the scope of this cursory sweep of priority energy issues linking the Persian Gulf and the Western economies. This division of labor does not reflect any corresponding separation of the substance of the policy problems at hand. Oil makes the Persian Gulf important, and energy policy can help mitigate the problems associated with our dependence on the Persian Gulf and our vulnerability to supply interruptions. But energy policy may not be even the most important component of a collection of policies needed to manage this critical element of international trade, politics, and power.

The central importance of the Persian Gulf oil supply and our palpable weakness in the region demand new initiatives to redress the balance of power there. The challenge rivals concerns in every other area of Western alliances and strategy. We are in for a fundamental reassessment of how we approach large parts of the world. And none of the proposed plans, whether a redefinition of NATO priorities or the acquisition of bases near or on the Arabian peninsula, appears easy to implement or certain to succeed.

Part of the challenge of the reassessment will be to coordinate policy across many arenas of traditional specialization. Are oil repair facility capabilities adequate to exploit the advantage military planners promise to gain? Are there levers in foreign aid policy that can promote cooperation on the energy front? How will the U.S. coal export policy affect the ability to weather shocks in the oil market? How much difference would settlement of Arab-Israeli differences make to the availability of oil from the Persian Gulf? Can the military balance in the Gulf be altered without major changes in policies and programs in Western Europe and the Western Pacific? These and other questions make it evident that energy policy cannot usefully be separated from broader political and military planning.

Every policy must be subjected to the scrutiny of cost effectiveness analysis in comparison with other alternatives to achieve the same ends. Once compared, for instance, our large military expenditure to protect Europe exposes the folly of the pittance we have devoted in the past to similar ends in the Persian Gulf. But by the same standard, costly—and uncertain—military efforts to protect the oil in the Gulf seem an equal folly for a nation unwilling to endure the discomfort of a modest tax on gasoline. It will be no easy matter to balance hypothetical economic calculations on the energy front with life-and-death choices on the military front, but we should not turn to military solutions unless we also exhaust the home remedies in our energy medicine chest.

Nevertheless, despite our best efforts, at some point a prolonged loss of the oil from the Persian Gulf may be too great for any of the mechanisms we now envision to "manage" energy emergencies. How far can we go before markets, banks, political agreements all collapse? And how much is it worth now to begin thinking about what might happen and what to do? The chaos in Iran created opportunities for the extension of Soviet power. How much time do we have before the Soviets act to exploit these opportunities?

Whether we focus mainly on the political and economic aims of some of the oil producers and the political instabilities within the region which are so costly to us, or whether we address the even more threatening potential of Soviet action in the region, we are led to the issue of the role of Western military power. The United States has moved a substantial part of its Navy to the Arabian Sea, has put ground force equipment in ships at Diego Garcia, and is negotiating for facilities in Oman, Kenya, Somalia, and Egypt. Steps have been proposed to permit more rapid reinforcement of the region. These moves are clearly inadequate to deal with the existing dangers. The Western nations need urgently to consider additional actions.

CONCLUSION

This is a time of great peril at the nexus between energy and security issues in the Persian Gulf. The United States will not find security in energy independence. Neither will oil importers find security in appeasement of the oil producers. Only our own actions can help—actions based on a clear and shared view of the security threat. And because of the major externalities associated with oil supply disruptions, international markets fail and only government action can mitigate the large costs associated with energy security emergencies.

We recognize that oil import dependence is not vulnerability, and vulnerability to oil supply interruptions is the most serious danger. Coordinated action among the oil importing countries will greatly enhance efforts to reduce vulnerability. The first focus of attention for energy policy should be on developing domestic and international measures to mitigate the large costs of supply interruptions. These programs for emergency preparedness and macroeconomic planning should be taken in parallel with far-reaching foreign policy and military steps to redress the balance of power in the Persian Gulf. And eventually the short-run energy measures can phase into longer term adjustments to the new oil market. With the appalling state of our present policies, there is an ample agenda from which to take new initiatives. Action on energy security policy is a prerequisite for progress in assuring political and economic security for most of the world.

NOTES

1. This chapter draws on an earlier draft, which includes contributions from Harry Rowen and was discussed at the Security Conference on Asia and the Pacific (SECAP), January 1980. The author is responsible for all deficiencies.

2. *Persian Gulf Oil and Western Security* (1980), *Reducing U.S. Oil Vulnerability*, (1980), *Geopolitics of Oil* (1980), Nye and Deese (1981).

3. Krapels (1980).

4. For example, applying the usual Hotelling principle, if we assume a cost of $45/bbl for alternative oil supplies, a $2/bbl cost of Saudi production, and a 5 percent real discount rate, then the 1981 $35/bbl oil price can be justified on scarcity grounds only if all the low cost oil reserves will be exhausted by 1987 ($[35-2] = [45-2]/[1.05]^{**}[1987-1981]$)! Since conventional oil supplies are being depleted much more slowly than this, the world as a whole would be better off with lower oil prices and more rapid exhaustion. Of course, the oil producers increase their own wealth, at the expense of the rest of the world, by using their market power to follow the current production and pricing policies.

5. Landsberg (1979).

6. The Committee for Energy Policy Promotion (1980).

7. *Persian Gulf Oil and Western Security* (1980).

8. For instance, at the June, 1979 Summit, President Carter proposed import targets which were later adopted by all IEA countries.

9. Neff (1981).

10. For example, see Levy (1980).

11. Deese (1981).

12. *Ibid.*

13. Bakke (1980). The range of forecasts is 25 to 50 million barrels per day of oil equivalent by 2000.

BIBLIOGRAPHY

Bakke, Dennis. "Energy in Developing Countries." In *Selected Studies on Energy: Background Papers for Energy, The Next Twenty Years,* edited by H. Landsberg. Cambridge, Mass: Ballinger Publishing Company, 1980.

Committee for Energy Policy Promotion. *Japan and the Oil Problem.* Tokyo: Committee for Energy Policy Promotion, (February) 1980.

Deese, David. "The Oil-Importing Developing Countries." In *Energy and Security,* edited by Joseph S. Nye and David Deese. Cambridge, Mass.: Ballinger Publishing Company, 1981.

Krapels, Edward N. "Energy Forecasts: Oil Import Dependence in the 1980s." Paper read at Security Conference on Asia and the Pacific, January, 1980, at Tokyo, Japan.

Landsberg, Hans., Chairman, Energy: The Next Twenty Years Study Group. *Energy: The Next Twenty Years.* Cambridge, Mass.: Ballinger Publishing Company, 1979.

Levy, Walter "Recycling Surplus Petrodollars via Internationally Issued Indexed Energy Bonds." *Middle East Economic Survey,* (April 7, 1980).

Neff, Thomas. "The Changing World Oil Market." In *Energy and Security,* edited by Joseph S. Nye and David Deese. Cambridge, Mass.: Ballinger Publishing Company, 1981.

Nye, Joseph S. and Deese, David, eds. *Energy and Security.* Cambridge, Mass.: Ballinger Publishing Company, 1981.

Persian Gulf Oil and Western Security. Marina del Rey, Cal.: Pan Heuristics, PH80–11–LV902-60G, (November 4) 1980.

U.S., Congress, Senate, Committee on Energy and Natural Resources. *Geopolitics of Oil.* 96th Congress, 2nd session. November, 1980.

U.S., Department of Energy, Office of Policy and Evaluation. *Reducing U.S. Oil Vulnerability.* November 10, 1980.

DISCUSSANTS

Edward J. Carlough

There are two objectives in discussions of energy: to increase supply and induce more conservation. On the supply end, there has never been a free market in terms of energy development in our country. There have always been some forms of government inducement and, in many cases, of government subsidies. Some of the greatest amount of oil and gas exploration in our country occurred within the 27.5 percent oil depletion allowance. Discussing this matter with a representative of the present Administration very recently, he said, "What people don't understand, Ed, is that if we simply turn loose the oil and gas industry, there are five Prudhoe Bays lying out there in Alaska that haven't been discovered yet. When the Administration discovers them, I would suggest that the geologists for the Administration that discovers them be given some form of Nobel Prize." I think, however, that the deregulation of oil and the impending deregulation of gas will probably have more of an effect in our country on the demand side, in terms of conservation, rather than on the supply side or in terms of new discoveries.

Nuclear energy has vast potential, even though it is only utilized to generate electricity. The sad thing is that it has not been used. To quote President Reagan, "In this respect, there isn't anything the government can do at this point except to undo some of the regulations that have inhibited the nuclear industry. . . ." When the accident occurred at Three Mile Island, it occurred in Unit Two. Unit One, which had been producing electricity for central Pennsylvania for many years, was down for maintenance and repairs. It is still down, even though it could have been operating for at least the past eight or nine months; the fact that it does not costs about half a million dollars a day in the importation of electricity by that utility into central Pennsylvania. Given the facts of life, eventually the consumer and the industrial user will have to pay those costs.

There are other areas where the government can be very useful on the supply side. The synfuels have been covered rather well. One really important aspect of the synfuels program is security: simply to show those outside that this country is willing to adopt an activist stance. I think it has its limitations in the short term, as well as a lot of problems in connection with it. A major problem is its heavy use of water and the very real shortage of water in the western states that have the synthetic fuel reserves.

As we look at it from the standpoint of our union, this country simply cannot afford to turn its nose up on any possible form of energy or energy production. It is simply a question of priorities. When we look at the energy consumption of the country, instead of looking at it in terms of barrels of imported oil, we should look at it in terms of how we consume energy and determine the most sensible way to approach the problem.

The automobile accounts for approximately 25 percent of energy consumption in this country, but there is another industry that consumes almost as much as the automobile. Space heating in buildings and appliances in homes add up to about 18 percent of domestic energy consumption, and air conditioning is another 3 percent. When you throw in industrial process heat, such as is used in the paper industry, you are talking about an industry that consumes energy to the degree that the automobile does. It is extremely difficult to change driving habits of Americans. It is not difficult, given the state of technology available to industry today, to make very significant savings in energy conservation, space heating, air conditioning, and industrial process heat. We simply must put more effort in it. The Harvard Energy Report[1] is a good example. Earlier, in 1974, the Sheet Metal Workers' International Association commissioned the Stanford Research Institute in Palo Alto, California and the MITRE Corporation in Cambridge, Massachusetts to run parallel studies on the impact of energy conservation and solar energy on energy savings in this country, and what we could do, together with our contractors and the manufacturers in our industry, to make sufficient inroads on the particular problem. The SRI and MITRE conclusions in 1974 were essentially the same as Harvard's findings in 1978. Although almost 25 percent of energy conservation of the country is in the fields of space heating, air conditioning, and industrial process heat, very little has been done about this problem. In areas where we have gone into conservation, and where insurance companies and others have done it, without government assistance, the savings both in terms of utility bills and their own energy consumption have been tremendous.

A lot of serious problems in the country are ones we have lived with for a long, long period of time, and it will take a great amount of time in the future to try to resolve them. But the current energy problem is new. It really only occurred with the Arab boycott of 1973. What we need to focus on is, first, how we can use the various forms of energy available to us in this country in the best possible way. Second, we must find what we can do more in terms of energy conservation in this country. This is not a matter of turning off the light, but of the sort of energy conservation that in many respects has to do with mechanical input into a building. One of the good things that they did with the Windfall Profits Tax was to put a 25 percent tax incentive on industrial process heat and the use of solar applications in energy conservation. That is one form of conservation that seems to be working and these are the sorts of things that we ought to encourage.

I do not have any great faith in the Department of Energy, though perhaps too much blame was placed on President Carter, but they muddled through for several years. Now with President Reagan, some of the things that I have been reading about his approach to energy make me afraid that we are going to be muddling through a little bit more. What is really necessary is a partnership between the private sector and government. It cannot be modeled on the Japanese model or that of the Federal Republic of Germany. They have their unique characteristics and reasons why, over a period of time, those models evolved and developed. However, if we can learn from their experiences while drawing upon our own unique institutions, perhaps we can make some progress. If the public and private sectors work together, we can at least reduce the antagonism and attempt more sensible cooperation in those areas of energy where our country can truly have a significant impact.

NOTES
1. Stobaugh and Yergin (1978).

BIBLIOGRAPHY
Stobaugh, Robert and Yergin, Daniel. *Energy Future.* New York: Random House, 1978.

Norma Pace

The application of market-oriented economics to the energy problem has been greatly deterred by many factors, including the strength and durability of the OPEC cartel and its impact on U.S. energy supply and demand, government regulations which have hampered both the adjustment to the new energy economics and the development of alternative energy sources, and the firm conviction of many that only the government could provide the solution to the energy problem.

The result is that the solution has languished in the chasm of political ineptitude, fear, misinformation, and lack of trust. The government's price controls of oil and gas at a large discount from world market prices encouraged more consumption when less was needed. It has impeded timely shifts to alternate fuel sources and methods of achieving needed fuel efficiencies. It has created inequities that have required ever more government intervention to correct, and has led to a convoluted program of decontrol of prices that have reduced the efficiency of the consumer energy dollar, while creating a large energy bureaucracy.

Supply-side economics for energy can well be defended by its performance to date. Once the hurdle of gas and oil price decontrol was crossed, activity virtually exploded.

- The number of drilling rigs in operation is at an all-time high;
- More and more imaginative avenues of financing energy development are coming forth;
- Reserves of oil and gas are rising.

THE ROLE OF THE PRIVATE SECTOR
The demand response to higher energy prices (a manifestation of market forces at work) is evident. Consumers are conserving now that fuel prices are headed toward world levels. For example, the paper industry consumes 27 percent fewer purchased Btus. per ton of output than it used in 1972. Gasoline consumption in the United States is 8 percent to 9 percent lower this year than last.

Energy supply, including the use of alternate energy sources, can be provided by the private sector. Funding is not difficult today, because with decontrol the proper payoff does exist for such investments. For example the development of resource recovery systems which convert garbage into a resource, has occurred primarily at the private level. This technology, still in its early stages, has nonetheless resulted in many projects in use, and private funding takes care of most of the financing needs. Supply-side economics can work in energy—it is working and with continued incentives it will do even better. The time has come to shed inhibitions about the ability of the private sector to handle the problem.

In contrast to the recent successes of the market forces, the record of the government in the matter of energy use and production is dismal.

Price decontrol finally came, but the road was full of potholes. The results took more time than required and the eventual cost to customers was much higher than it need have been. Certainly the most recent surge in oil prices could have been moderated by more timely decontrol action.

During the discussion of oil and gas decontrol, a suggestion was made that the excess after-tax income of the oil producers be forced into investment in new energy production. That requirement would have provided a direct link between producers with both know-how and cash with higher energy investments. This suggestion was unpopular with the energy producers, who found it too restrictive on investment; with conservatives, who felt it was an intervention in market mechanisms; and with those who believed that only government could solve the energy problem equitably. It deserved more consideration.

Instead, a slush fund was created for the Department of Energy out of the Windfall Profit Tax, which resulted in mischief: (1) People were given incentives to burn waste paper and wood, regardless of their higher economic value as fiber. (2) Expensive statistical reports were required whose sole purpose was to educate government employees and eventually give them a big club to use with industry—a costly and adversarial approach. (3) A whole series of bureaucratic regulations came forth which had the net effect of pumping money into projects that would have been built anyway.

Conflicting governmental directives given to industry during the past 10 years have created major problems. For example, in the early 1970s industry was ordered out of coal (for environmental reasons) and into oil and gas. Now it is being forced back into coal, even in New England where there is none.

Such false and conflicting signals of the government are too high a price to pay for the solution of the energy problem. Industry gets the rap because it, like Typhoid Mary, is the one that passes the cost of these errors on in higher prices. Efficiency suffers and management performance becomes almost unmeasurable. Management errors are hidden by these dicta of the government and there are times when good management is penalized.

Still, one cannot say that there is no role for government in the solution of the energy problem.

- Government policy that properly blends the environmental, so-cial, and production needs of the nation must be evolved. Market forces alone cannot perform this referee function. However, the mechanism used for regulation is wrong. It should be obvious that a government agency whose sole purpose is to police pollution abatement will maximize that function at the expense of others.

If pollution abatement conflicts with a more urgent need, such as energy production or use, conflicts multiply and the agency finds that its very existence is threatened by the new needs. The sensible response to a changed condition should be a reevaluation of environmental concerns in the light of the new energy situation, but the cumbersome legislative and bureaucratic processes do not permit that kind of efficiency. The role of the Federal government must be reevaluated and redirected toward orchestrating the various needs and priorities of the nation.

- Diplomatic relationships with those countries upon whom we depend must recognize that dependence. Other countries have learned how to live with such dependencies and surely we can as well.

- Our relationships with other energy consuming nations must recognize how our policies affect them. Price controls on oil and gas in the United States have been a sore spot with trading partners and other importers of oil for many years.

- The government can provide some seed money for esoteric technology where the risk is high and the payoff far into the future.

What can the government do about shocks? There always will be shocks, there always have been, and they will have to be dealt with when they occur. We cannot insure ourselves against all eventualities, even though we recognize their possibility. We must also have faith in the imagination and creativity of succeeding generations to tackle problems. Each generation sees its needs and challenges in its own way and each set of solutions takes the economy into new directions, some good and some bad. Our responsibility must be to tackle today's problems with a long-range framework for solutions.

Robert McClements, Jr.

President Reagan said at one point in his Inaugural Address, "it's not my intention to do away with government. It is rather to make it work —work with us, not over us; to stand by our side, not ride on our back. Government can and must provide opportunity, not smother it; foster productivity, not stifle it."

Since the Inauguration, the Administration's basic posture seems to be that government's role in the economy has grown to the point where it is completely out of proportion to the need.

Energy is one of the best areas with which to illustrate the nature of the policy failure which the Administration is attempting to correct. Until just recently, crude oil and petroleum products were subject to Federal price controls, which actually originated with President Nixon's wage and price control program, but which were, in effect, retained because of the concerns generated by the 1973–74 oil embargo.

The rationale sounded good to many people at the time. The controls were necessary, the argument went, to prevent people from being subjected to sudden and massive jolts from too rapid an increase in the cost of energy.

What were the effects? First, consumers were able to buy their gasoline and heating oil at an artificially low price. In effect, government mortgaged future supplies in order to subsidize current consumption. Second, the petroleum industry during the 1970s did not enjoy an exceptionally good track record for return on investment. Part of this can be traced to the psychological impact which the controls had on investors. A controlled industry simply doesn't look like a good investment.

More fundamentally, however, the controls restricted our ability to find and produce more oil. Too many opportunities were rendered uneconomic because of the controls; as the controls grew more and more complicated and cost more and more to comply with, the oil business began to look more and more unattractive, even to those of us in it.

At the same time that government was becoming more and more involved in energy, it was also sending confusing signals as to the nature and extent of that involvement. The rules changed from day to day, and the only thing we knew for sure about government's energy policy was that it was unpredictable.

That unpredictability had major impacts as the petroleum industry attempted to perform risk assessment for energy projects. In many cases, it made the difference in an investment decision and thus some of the industry's capital was diverted out of energy.

At the retail end, the price controls and allocation mechanisms had the effect of freezing marketing and distribution patterns. The market could not adjust itself to changing patterns of demand.

The most visible effect was the one we saw in the summer of 1979 —gasoline lines. Much of that problem, according to the Federal government itself, was traced to the Department of Energy's allocation system, which allocated gasoline according to historical patterns of consumption. These changed faster than the regulators could keep up with and so supply and demand were mismatched in many areas of the country.

One other area to look at is the effect these controls had on the refining industry. The Department of Energy administered an entitlements program, the basic thrust of which was to insure that no refiner was penalized because its access to lower priced domestic crude was limited for one reason or another. In other words, refiners who relied heavily on higher priced foreign crude were subsidized by those who relied less heavily. This protected inefficient refiners at the expense of the more competitive ones.

Today, after all of those years of controls, along with the effects of environmental regulations which have limited the refining industry's ability to upgrade its capital equipment, we have a domestic refining industry which is at a competitive disadvantage relative to foreign refiners. We are not in danger of exporting some of our refining capacity in the same way that we have been exporting our crude production capacity.

What effect might policy change in energy have upon income distribution? There is no question that rising energy prices can have a great deal of impact on lower income groups, for it appears that in many instances that the proportion of income spent on energy is rising. There are, and there need to be, safety net programs administered by government to prevent new fiscal policies from having drastic effects on lower income groups.

Energy is no exception. I do not think it is appropriate for the energy industry to tackle this problem directly, although we do have programs related to conservation which we believe offer some help. The Sun Company also has programs at the local level where we offer assistance to customers having difficulty paying a heating oil bill, for example.

One must emphasize that preventing or easing the problems of rising energy prices is a proper function of government. It is a proper use of some of the revenues received from the Windfall Profits Tax.

But things can change, dramatically and radically, in response to government policy change. In energy, we are seeing a radical change in the industry, indeed in our nation, as a result of policy change relative to market pricing. Energy prices are up, consumption is down, and in 1980 additions to oil reserves in the lower 48 states were at their highest level since 1965. Similarly, for gas, reserves added in the lower 48 states were at their highest level since 1967.

Perhaps the most significant outcome has been the return of competition to the market place. We now have a worldwide competitive market for crude and petroleum products, and progress is being made toward true market pricing for natural gas.

What should be the government's role in the event of another supply interruption? We never know when we may face a major supply interruption and we believe government ought to develop a comprehensive contingency plan to handle such an emergency. Such a plan should include a mechanism for allocation of available supplies.

Finally let us remember that the energy industry, other than perhaps in times of emergency, has the same rights as any other industry operating in a market-driven economy. We have the responsibility to work with government in the process of delineating its role and ours in both normal times and times of emergency.

In any society, government is merely the mechanism by which we make trade-offs between the freedom of the individual and what we generally call the public welfare. I think what Ronald Reagan meant when he said he wanted to make government work is closely related to that concept. I think he meant that government has mismanaged the trade-offs, has sacrificed too much of individual freedoms, and that the rate of return is unsatisfactory. Also, that the freedoms we have as individuals are the source of the public welfare and that they are threatened.

Government cannot be all things to all people. Any trade-off is bound to disappoint or disrupt someone. But we can do a better job of balancing the two than we have in recent years. And we can do it without altering the substance of our institutions and their interrelationships in any drastic fashion.

F. Gerard Adams

Can we formulate a consensus on industrial policy for energy? There is remarkable unanimity among the various participants with regard to the concerns about the U.S. energy economy—concern about domestic supplies and productivity, concern about excessive dependence on imported oil, and concern about the impact of high fuel prices on the health and performance of the U.S. economy. Equally remarkable, however, is the difference in the conclusions with respect to the role of government in energy industry policy.[1] Effectively, the question is: given the energy problem, can we rely largely or entirely on the free market or is there basis, on grounds of theory or practical necessity, to intervene in the operation of market processes? Do we need an industrial policy for energy?

THE RATIONALE FOR INDUSTRY POLICY
In the past few months, we have been undertaking a sizable research effort on industrial policy. Part of this work has involved an evaluation of what economic theory says with regard to general and specific industry policies. It has also included a summary of the policy experience throughout the world, as well as a number of empirical studies.[2]

While we begin with a recognition of the many advantages of the competitive market, economic theory suggests that there are situations in which there is an important role for government intervention. These are largely situations of "market failure," where profit-oriented private entrepreneurs do not take into account the externalities—benefits or costs external to the agent taking the action, and therefore not considered in the profit maximization calculation. Consequently, market mechanisms cannot alone be expected to do the job. Pollution is familiar as a negative externality. The gains to other producers attributable to research and development, or the issues associated with national security, are also externalities from the perspective of the individual entrepreneur.

Our studies suggest that there can be a variety of approaches to intervention. The international evidence shows considerable diversity in the mechanisms of industrial policy, reflecting long-term differences between countries in institutions, economic situation, and tradition of relations between business and government.[3] Industry policies have ranged from attempts to "rescue the losers" in the United Kingdom and Italy and recently in the United States, "picking-the-winners" in France, to broad "visions" of future industrial potentials, as in Japan. The industry policy mechanisms include policy interventions which involve direct public decision-making, but they also include the use of the mechanisms of private enterprise. We can visualize policies which minimize regulations, which utilize incentives to private enterprise and private decision-making, and which nevertheless favor the social objectives being sought. Among these policy mechanisms are tax credits, preferential financing, government purchasing, price guarantees, write-offs, and other means which leave critical decision-making in private hands. We can also visualize forward-looking policies which foster the dynamics of technological industrial development to improve production capacity, efficiency, and conservation.

It is false to paint a "black and white" picture in which all industry policies are inimical to the operation of private enterprise.

AN INDUSTRIAL POLICY FOR ENERGY?
Energy is not just an industry like shoes or, even, automobiles. Energy requires special concern and may well justify specific industrial policies, even if such policies cannot be justified for other industries. This is not a technocratic notion of the supremacy or essentiality of energy. Energy does, of course, go widely into almost all productive activities and into consumption. But the critical issue is that it has proved difficult to substitute for energy, particularly in the short run, as estimates of the energy elasticities, even by such "elasticity optimists" as Robert Pindyck, indicate. This has meant that high oil prices have had an important depressing impact on the nation's real income, have been a major

source of inflation, an important factor in the decline of productivity, and have caused significant distortions to the income distribution. But an equally, if not more important aspect, is the continued dependence on imports of oil from the OPEC cartel, a fact which exposes us to exorbitant prices and the risk of political blackmail. Overwhelming national considerations influence the energy economy. These have no parallel in most other industries for which special preferential policies might be sought.

There are many examples of market failure in the energy field. Market forces left to themselves will not necessarily yield a result for energy which meets national and social needs. For example:

- Technological problems of synthetic energy production or of shale oil production remain serious. The social benefits of solving these problems through research expenditures or the construction of the first full-scale demonstration plants greatly exceed the advantages to the individual enterprise.[4]

- Risks associated with new technology and with other aspects of energy enterprises—such as the risk of deliberate price manipulations by producers whose costs are extremely low in the Middle East, or the risks associated with changes in environmental regulations—are high. The crucial point is not only that risks are high, but particularly that in many cases risks are higher as seen by an individual enterprise than they are for the nation as a whole.

- Adjustments in the energy field are naturally quite slow, because in most instances turnover in capital stock by users or producers is required. There are, for example, many physical, financial, and regulatory barriers to energy conservation investments.

- Political and military security considerations are important, as William Hogan has pointed out, and are not taken into account by the individual enterprise.

- Energy price and availability has far-reaching impacts on income distribution. While we would give priority to the "efficiency" of the market mechanism over the "equity" considerations which often guide public decisions, income distribution—between rich and poor or between the Northeast and the Southwest, for example, cannot be ignored.

- Pollution and safety problems frequently require legislative intervention. Few people could argue that private decision-making can take care of these problems. Just as many would agree that government regulations imposed with little or no regard to cost have been burdensome in many cases.

I conclude that the arguments for industrial policy focusing on energy production and conservation are strong. This does not mean support for all the old policies of regulation or entitlements. *A rejection of old policy is not necessarily a rejection of all policy.* A new industrial policy for energy must combine the best features of the free market and the public policy mechanisms to recognize the relevant social and political considerations.

NOTES

1. With the possible exception of support for a tariff on imported petroleum.

2. For a discussion, see Adams and Klein (1981), and the papers of the Economics Research Unit Industry Policy Project.

3. It is likely to be difficult, consequently, to transfer the tools which have proved useful in one country to others.

4. To assume, as does Pindyck, that synthetic fuel production calls only for well known technologies is not realistic.

BIBLIOGRAPHY

Adams, F. Gerard and Klein, Lawrence R., eds. *Evaluation of U.S. Industrial Policy.* Lexington, Mass.: Heath-Lexington Books, forthcoming.

SUMMARY REPORT

Energy

Anita A. Summers

The views expressed by the paper writers, discussants, and participants in the Energy Panel, as they addressed the charge of this conference—an assessment of the appropriate roles of the public and private sectors—organized themselves in the classic way in which the problem is thought about. Are there market imperfections? Are there externalities—social costs or benefits not reflected in the market? Are there income distributional results produced by the market which our society wants altered? Affirmative answers to all of these came from at least some of the panel, but there was a considerable difference of view on what the role of government should be. Though the existence of market imperfections, externalities, and distributional problems was generally agreed to be an agenda for government action, it was not agreed that these constituted a mandate for action. A more cooperative relationship between government and industry in determining these actions was urged by all.

MARKET IMPERFECTIONS

There was clear agreement that higher prices of energy had had the effect of lowering the quantity of energy demanded. Robert Pindyck, William Hogan, and Norma Pace gave high grades to the effectiveness of the market; Robert Nathan thought that the importance of lowering the demand for energy was only slowly handled by the market, and that earlier government intervention to raise prices would have been preferable.

The panel reviewed the evidence on the effectiveness of price increases on increasing energy supplies. Pindyck, Hogan, Pace, and Robert McClements anticipated substantial supply-side effects as market conditions were allowed to determine price; Nathan thought government involvement was required to stretch out our natural gas reserves, develop nuclear energy, and develop alternative energy sources; McClements argued for government involvement in supplying the required infrastructure for energy development.

Views differed on the appropriate role of government in contributing to the capital investment required in energy development. Pindyck argued that the private sector can handle the large amounts and the uncertainties in the energy industry as it has in other industries—that the cost of capital reflects these characteristics, and that these costs should be undisguised elements of production decisions. But Nathan argued that nuclear and alternative energy sources required government encouragement; McClements thought there should be some government subsidization of small experimental modules (for shale development, for example); Edward Carlough embraced government encouragement for the development of all sources of energy, particularly solar; and Pace thought government was needed to provide seed money for research and development.

There was general agreement that there was a too large, and too unstable, regulatory environment. Fewer, and more important, stable regulations were urged.

There was, then, general agreement on two points related to the role of government in correcting market imperfections: that the market works well on the demand side—price effectively reduces energy usage—and that there needs to be a smaller and more stable set of regulations. On the supply side, most argued for some government involvement, but the recommendations ranged from very minor subsidization to sweeping participation.

EXTERNALITIES

The major views expressed were that there were two major costs imposed by our present sources of energy, not handled by private markets. First, our dependence on imported oil has created significant national security problems. There was strong agreement, therefore, that government was needed to raise tariffs (or other taxes) in order to increase the price of imported oil. Second, Hogan expressed concern about our vulnerability to the interruptions of energy supply that our dependence on foreign oil has created. He urged a government program of emergency plans for coping with sudden interruptions. This was an area of consensus.

Two other externalities frequently mentioned in the energy area, pollution and safety, were considered only in passing.

DISTRIBUTIONAL EFFECTS

It was recognized by all that the increased use of market pricing in energy would result in higher prices. There was general recognition that some government policy was called for to respond to the problems created for low income people by these higher prices. Pindyck suggested some equivalent to food stamps for heating costs; Nathan suggested lowering other taxes for this group.

In summary, market forces were strongly embraced for increasing energy supplies and reducing demand. Freeing prices and other deregulation was expected to accomplish much in eliminating the energy "shortage." On the demand side, there was virtual unanimity on the effectiveness of higher prices. On the supply side, there was disagreement on the effectiveness of higher prices alone pulling forth adequately larger supplies. All of the participants embraced government control over the price of imported oil on national security grounds, most wanted government participation in resource development, and all wanted a more cooperative climate between business and government in energy policies.

Strategies for Training and ☆ ☆ ☆ Retraining

11.

DEMOGRAPHICS AND AMERICAN ECONOMIC POLICY

Peter F. Drucker

INTRODUCTION

It is predictable—and practically certain—that, barring nuclear war, the proportion of the American labor force engaged in blue collar, manual work in manufacturing 25 years hence, around the year 2005, will not be much larger than the proportion now engaged in farming, that is less than 10 percent and not much more than 5 percent of the total labor force. Where there are now still 20 million people employed in manual manufacturing work—a full fifth of the total labor force—the figures will be between 7 and 12 million in another 25 years.

The events that will make this come true have all happened irreversibly, in this country as well as in the rest of the world. Economic policies, whatever they might be, cannot change them.

What economic policies can determine, however, is whether the United States of the year 2005 will be a major, and indeed *the major,* manufacturing country of the world with manufacturing production the higher the more the labor force engaged in manual manufacturing work goes down—thus paralleling the development in American agriculture, where a drop in the proportion of the labor force engaged in manufacturing from 30 percent to 5 percent since the end of World War II has been accompanied by a near-tripling of farm output. Or will America decline as a manufacturing nation parallel to the decline in its manufacturing labor force? The policy decisions have not been made yet—but will have to be made within the next few years.

1. DEMOGRAPHIC REALITIES

We are in the midst of four major demographic changes. Three of them are domestic—and occurring equally in all developed industrial countries. One is external, and is taking place in the Third World.

(1) The supply of new entrants available for traditional manufacturing jobs during the next twenty years in the United States will be, at most, one-third or so of the supply available during the last twenty years. One-third is the *upper limit* of the range. The *lower limit* might be zero.

One factor is the "baby bust" which started in 1960 and which reduced the birth rate by 30 percent—as unprecedented a drop, by the way, as had been the jump of the birth rate in the "baby boom" a dozen years earlier. As a result, the total number of people reaching the age of entrance into the labor force during the next twenty years or so will be about 30 percent lower than it was in the seventies, when the babies of the "baby boom" reached adulthood.

But equally important is the shift in the years of schooling. The great majority of the people in the American work force who are now reaching retirement age, that is the people aged sixty-five to seventy now, finished school with a junior high school degree or less. By contrast, fully one-half of the young men and two-fifths of the young women entering the labor force now have stayed in school beyond high school. They will thus not replace the people who retire, but will be available only for different work and different jobs.

The supply of traditionally schooled people for blue collar work in manufacturing will drop to zero by the year 2000. For, of the young people entering the labor force, fewer than 3 percent now do not go on to high school. In other words, to assume that there will be available as many as one-third of the present number assumes that the educational level of manual workers in manufacturing will go up to high school or higher—which is quite unlikely except as the result of catastrophic prolonged depression. Whatever people may or may not learn while sitting in school, their expectations change. And the expectation level of the American high school graduate is a good deal higher than traditional blue collar manual work on the traditional assembly line—and so is his capacity. The high school graduate on the assembly line, no matter how poor his school record, is both underemployed and a conspicuous waste of a major resource, deeply disappointed and a threat to social stability.

It should be added, as a further reason why one-third of the present supply of labor for traditional manufacturing work must be considered so high a figure as to constitute the extreme upper end of the range, that the competition for people available for traditional blue collar work will be intense, with sharply increasing demand for them in such services as health care. This demand will have to be satisfied from the available domestic supply. Bringing bedpans to the patient and removing them cannot be farmed out to a developing country where the labor resources are, but must be done in the local hospital. Nor can cleaning the streets be done "offshore." And since these employments do not compete with low-wage countries—precisely because the job has to be done where the patient is or where the streets are—the wages of low-skill manual work in services and especially in public services must go up where manufacturing, restrained both by foreign competition and by consumer resistance to exorbitant prices, could not compete.[1]

The inescapable fact is thus the scarcity, indeed nonexistence, of young people—that is of people born after 1960—for traditional blue collar jobs in general, and in particular for manufacturing jobs where international competition (especially with exports constituting a large and growing source of manufacturing employment accounting for at least 10 percent and probably 12 percent of all American manufacturing jobs) sets a limit to labor costs which it does not set to labor costs in services.

By 2000 or so, labor for traditional blue collar work in manufacturing must be assumed to be not available in the United States.

(2) The central employment problem in the United States in the next twenty years—and especially in the next eight to ten years—is to find jobs for people with long years of formal schooling and with resulting expectation for knowledge jobs and career opportunities. The supply of people entering the labor force with education beyond high school, and especially with college education and beyond, during the next twenty to twenty-five years is going to be at least double what it had been at any time before 1970. And the special conditions which created extraordinarily high demands for highly-schooled people entering the labor force between 1970 and 1980, that is for the first ten cohorts of the "baby boom" generation, are unlikely to continue much beyond the early eighties. After that period, only rapid growth of the American economy and especially very rapid growth of highly knowledge-intensive industries could provide jobs for the highly-schooled new entrants into the workforce.

The number of young people with advanced schooling and with advanced degrees, that is college or better, will crest between now and 1985. All the children of the "baby boom" who are going to go to college are already in college, and most of them have already graduated. The entering classes into colleges today already come from the "baby bust" years. But a substantial number of "baby boom" children are still in graduate and professional schools and will enter the labor market between now and the mid-1980s when the last cohort of the "baby boom" will reach age twenty-five. Only then will the pressure ease—but probably not by much. The number actually attending institutions of higher education and getting advanced degrees may even still increase. Conversely, the proportion might fall somewhat—it is likely, after all, that the income differential between people with advanced degrees and people without advanced schooling will narrow, and perhaps significantly so. But even with a drop in the number—or even the proportion—of young people entering the workforce after advanced schooling, the number will still be substantially higher than it was in the fifties and sixties, when the young adults reaching maturity represented the very lean baby years of the thirties and forties. In other words, a supply at least double that of people with advanced degrees before 1970 is the minimum expectation for the next twenty years. And it is quite likely to be substantially higher still.

The combined effects of "baby boom" and "educational explosion" first hit the labor market in the seventies. But in those years there was a tremendous shortage of people with higher schooling, and especially of college educated people. And thus the first ten large cohorts of highly-schooled young people were absorbed without difficulty and indeed with a minimum of structural change in jobs and employment.

In the first place, for long years the only young people available had been the products of the very lean birth years, the products of the "baby bust" which began in the late 1920s and continued until 1948 or 1949. Secondly, of these young people, only a fairly small proportion stayed in school beyond high school until the sixties or so; despite the "G.I. Bill," the "educational explosion" did not start until the late fifties. Finally, in the fifties and sixties young educated women did not, except for teaching school, enter the labor force in large numbers or stay in it long beyond marriage.

From now on employment opportunities for educated people will largely have to come from *new knowledge jobs.* And the rapid aging of the existing workforce will not help at all; as said before, eight out of every 10 jobs vacated through retirement are blue collar, low-skill jobs for which advanced schooling has disqualified the majority of young people entering the labor force now and in the foreseeable future.

Where a developing country, for example, Mexico, will have to find up to three times as many traditional manual and low-skill jobs for its young people entering the labor force every year during the next twenty years as it has ever had to find before, *the United States—and every other developed country—will have to create up to 50 percent more knowledge jobs and career opportunities for highly-schooled people every year for the next twenty years than this country ever had to create before.*

(3) Demographics are changing the composition of the workforce as much as its structure.

Male married adults, working full time, are indeed still the largest single group—but no more than a large minority. And though they still contribute a majority of the hours worked—precisely because the adult married males tend to work full time—their share in the total number of hours worked is shrinking and will continue to shrink. The American work force is rapidly becoming exceedingly heterogeneous.

For we have all but unmade what the nineteenth century considered its two proudest social achievements: that married women do not hire out for work, and that older people retire and are paid for not working.

It was the great dream of the nineteenth century that the working man's wife would not have to go into the factory or out to domestic service, but could stay home and take care of the children.

Similarly, before the middle of the nineteenth century there was no "retirement." Indeed a "retirement plan" would have been pointless—very few people reached the age at which they could or should have "retired." Altogether, it is nothing but romantic nostalgia to talk about "how well earlier societies treated their old people and how much they respected them." One cannot treat well or respect something that does not exist.

By 1900, and certainly by 1920, the increase in life expectancy had created the world's first substantial supply of people surviving beyond ordinary working age. And then "retirement" became a major employee benefit.

During the last twenty-five years both of these nineteenth century achievements have turned into "discrimination," into "reactionary obstacles to progress" and into "outmoded symbols of age-old oppression." Within another ten or twenty years we will have returned—in the name of "progress"—to the demographic realities of the preindustrial world: women participate in the labor force as much as men; and people do not retire at any given, preset chronological age.

But while we are engaged in unmaking the nineteenth century, we will not return to the earlier policies and practices without fundamental changes—changes that have not yet been reflected in public or managerial policies.

In all of history, men and women, while fully equal in their labor force participation, worked at separate tasks. In the return to full labor force participation by women, however, men and women are not differentiated in their tasks. That men and women work on the same tasks is still, it must be said, an experiment—it will probably take a hundred years or so before we know whether it is successful or not. But it changes fundamentally the character of the workforce and of work.

Similarly, in unmaking the nineteenth century achievement of mandatory retirement at a given age, we are not returning to the earlier system, in which people, almost without exception, worked until they died or became disabled. Prior to 1850 "retirement," that is leisure without work for a relatively healthy person, was virtually unknown. The able-bodied and able-minded—and even those with substantial impairments—worked until they dropped. And the ones who had to stop working because they were no longer able to do so rarely lived very long. There was not enough food available, except among the very few rich.

In fact, all the existing provisions for the care of elderly survivors were introduced because earlier generations did not, and could not, take care of them. All religions preached honoring one's parents—precisely because earlier civilizations did not, and in most cases could not practice it. Maltreatment of the older people was the rule and the reason why philanthropists or governments made provisions for their upkeep, and in the last analysis why they set up pension plans.[2]

As we unmake the mandatory retirement of the nineteenth century, the ability to control one's working life as one grows older will be an increasingly important "employee benefit." This will increasingly include switching to a second career in one's forties or early fifties. It will include the ability to retire early, though on a reduced standard of income and living. It will include the ability to come back into the labor force full time, or part time, and so on. But mandatory retirement at any age substantially below normal life expectancy (which would now mean mandatory retirement below one's mid-seventies) will soon be a thing of the past.

In numbers, people who would not have been considered part of the American labor force only twenty years ago, that is women and older people over sixty-five, will, by the mid-1980s, constitute one-half or more of the American workforce. But they will not, like the traditional workforce, be mainly full time employees. They will, in large numbers, be part time employees—both among married women, especially married women with children (and especially in noninflationary times) and among the older workers. They will also not be "permanent" employees in many cases, in the sense that they will not necessarily stay in the same job for many years or look for "employment security." The older people especially are likely to be in and out of the labor force. Married women who work have, we know, very low turnover. But they, too, are less likely to want to stay in the same job for many years, in part because they still are likely to move when their husbands get transferred or moved, in part because they are more likely than men to have to adjust their working lives to their family demands.

The American workforce is thus going to be increasingly heterogeneous and increasingly different from the workforce which all our figures, especially governmental ones; our personnel policies; our training policies; and our benefit plans still assume: the homogeneous workforce mainly composed of adult male heads of households engaged full time in blue collar work.

(4) As important as any demographic development within the United States—or within developed industrial countries altogether—is that in the *developing countries,* within the next fifteen or twenty years, the one overriding problem will be to find work for young people qualified only for traditional manual blue collar work, and especially for manual work in manufacturing industries producing for export.

More than half of the population of the developing countries is today under fifteen years of age. By the year 2000, the majority of the population in the developing countries will be below twenty-five years of age or so, no matter how fast the birth rates are dropping in those countries—and they are dropping quite fast in most. In almost every developing country the number of jobs to be found, if there is to be no social catastrophe or no social collapse, will be at least twice, and in many countries (for example, Mainland China) three times the number for whom jobs had to be found ten years ago. And in most of these countries the abundant supply of young people will have to find jobs in manufacturing work, if they are to have jobs at all.

Yet very few of these countries have the domestic market to absorb manufactured goods, let alone the purchasing power.[3]

In other words, the only jobs for these young people, qualified for traditional manufacturing work and needing jobs, is manufacturing work for export.

Wages in these countries are therefore bound to go down rather than to go up.[4]

In most, if not all, developing countries, the next twenty-five years will inevitably be years of "immiseration," regardless of political or economic "system." The labor force will increase faster than the market possibly can. Real wages in these countries—probably most extreme in Mainland China—will thus, of necessity, be lower in the year 2000 than they are now. Indeed, it will take another ten to twenty years—that is until 2010 or 2020—before real wages can begin to go up in these countries as population stabilizes and begins to approach a zero growth rate.

In other words, during the next twenty years the developing countries will have to build manufacturing industries and will have to try to build them for export. Even if they do so fast and successfully, demographics will still cause intense social pressures and conflicts. And even if highly successful in their industrialization drives, these countries will still not be able to increase the real wages and the real purchasing power of their laboring masses. Thus labor costs will not go up; they must go down. They will, therefore, become increasingly able to compete in manual blue collar production with the developed countries, almost irrespective of their productivity per man, or per manhour.

While the developed countries, and especially the United States, will not be able to maintain traditional manufacturing industries on the basis of manual work, simply because manual workers will not be available, they would also not be able, if manufacturing remains based on traditional manual blue collar labor, to compete on cost—no matter how successful they may be in raising productivity in traditional blue collar manual work.

2. ECONOMIC REALITIES

(1) The first reality which the United States has to accept is that American economic potential and production can no longer be based on native Americans doing manual labor. It must be based to the fullest extent possible on knowledge workers. And to the extent to which knowledge workers cannot provide the human resource needed for manufacturing production—and for manual work in mining, transportation, and in many services as well—the American economy will have to use non-American manual labor. This might mean importing the labor to the United States in quantities larger than in any time in our earlier history, and larger than during the periods of unrestricted immigration prior to World War I. Or the work requiring manual labor and not capable of being based on knowledge work, that is on automation, information, and feedback, and on low-entropy processes, will have to be farmed out to where the labor is—that is to developing countries.

(2) The second reality which we will have to face is that creating and *providing jobs for knowledge workers* will be the overriding social priority in the United States for the foreseeable future. The employment of knowledge workers rather than of blue collar workers will, of necessity, be the center of economic and social policy.

This in turn means that capital formation will become the central economic demand and priority, perhaps overriding all others. For knowledge work is capital-intensive.

(3) But—and this is also a reality that needs to be faced—there will inevitably be *islands of redundancy,* areas where manual workers will become unemployed, either as the result of the decline of an industry still based on manual work, or of its shift to automation. The total numbers of redundant workers will be very small.[5]

But workers made redundant by structural change tend first to be the least skilled people—skilled people have mobility and are therefore likely to have left a decaying industry or a declining company long before either reaches the end of the road. They are likely to be older people. And they are likely to be highly concentrated in areas of industrial decay. They are the workers in Flint, Michigan, in Youngstown, Ohio, in Chester, Pennsylvania, and so on—workers in old industrial cities in which there are few alternative employments for the simple reason that an industrial area that is in decay does not attract new businesses, but will, on the contrary, intentionally or unintentionally, repel and reject them. The only way for such an area to reverse the adverse trend is to convert redundancy into an opportunity and to mobilize all its resources to attract new industry rather than to hold the old ones.

In number, redundant workers will be but a fraction of the farmers who were made redundant in the great transition of farming that began at the time of World War II. But unlike the farmers, redundant blue collar workers are concentrated, organized, and seen as collectives rather than as individuals. They have political power precisely because they are concentrated in a few areas in which they usually have the casting vote. They are highly visible and highly vocal. They are, as a rule, unionized. And the decline of a company or of an industry, at least a decline that is based on traditional manual production methods, threatens the income and power, if not the very existence, of the labor union. In other words, the redundant manual worker, unlike the redundant farmer of yesteryear, cannot be disregarded. His redundancy has to be converted into an opportunity for him—or at least it has to be accepted as a responsibility of society—or else the very small absolute number of redundant manual workers will endanger, and indeed perhaps block, America's transition to leadership based on her abundant human resource, the knowledge worker; on the new productive technologies of automation and low-entropy process; and on the potential for capital formation in a rich country with stable overall population.

(4) Finally, we have to accept the heterogeneity of the labor force as a reality and have to base managerial and public policies on it.

Human resources supply, both in terms of quantity and of quality, will increasingly become the central economic factor on which the country and each employer within it will have to base long-range strategy and plans.

And the paid workforce, instead of being overwhelmingly adult males working full time, is increasingly going to contain women and older people, working part time as well as full time, and working continuously as well as intermittently. This surely means that policies with respect to the human factor, whether Social Security, retirement rules and pensions or taxes, or management policies such as those in respect to benefits, are increasingly inappropriate, becoming obsolete, and may even do harm.

(5) The external economic reality, that is the world economy and the country's place in it, will also be increasingly different from the economic assumptions which American government policy, American economists, and American business still consider "reality."

The economic reality on which economic policies must base themselves are as follows:

(a) Regardless of productivity per hour or per worker, "developed" countries and their industries cannot possibly compete in manually-based work and manually-produced goods with Third World countries. If they attempt to do so they will inevitably "develop down"—Great Britain is the obvious example.

(b) Regardless of wage levels, Third World countries and their industries cannot produce at lower cost or better quality than "developed" countries basing manufacturing production on optimizing knowledge, that is on automation and/or low-entropy processes. The knowledge-based developed country is bound to grow faster. And the "gap" between the Third World and such developed countries as optimize their human resource supply is almost certain to increase, even for a rapidly industrializing Third World country.

(c) Economic reality in the world economy means that both competition and cooperation are increasingly aspects of the human resource—competition between knowledge and manual work, and cooperation through "production-sharing" between knowledge and manual work.

3. THE POLICIES WE NEED AND THEIR IMPLEMENTATION

(1) The first need is one that is rarely considered. Yet without considering it, we are almost bound not to develop the right policies and not to take the right actions. It is the need for statistical information that adequately represents reality—our present figures and the concepts underlying them do not.

We need, first, employment figures that show not only the total number of people at work, but their *full time equivalent.* Even more, we need *unemployment* figures that show full time equivalents. Our present figures grossly misrepresent a work force in which part time work is playing as big a part as it already does—let alone the bigger part which it will almost certainly play in the future.

The employment figure, in particular, grossly inflates actual unemployment. Whether in the Congress, in government or in the media, a figure of, say, "8 percent unemployment" is read to mean

that 8 percent of the adult married males who are heads of households and available for full time work are out of work and actively looking for it. In fact, the full time equivalent of such a figure is probably well below 5 percent, if not lower. Similarly, the "full employment budget" needs to be adjusted to a full time equivalent figure—otherwise it leads to grossly inflationary policies (as it seems already to have been doing).

We also need figures that show us how many people actually do work. The present figures, as is by now generally conceded, grossly underrate the number of people working and the hours they work, if only because the "underground economy" has become big and is still growing. However, since one cannot get reliable figures on "illegals," we need to do away with the causes of the "underground economy," that is especially with tax penalties on working on the part of older people, before we can hope to get the reliable data needed to make effective policy.

But we also—and just as urgently—need data that indicate the need for capital formation to create the knowledge jobs required; the actual capital formation and the shortfall (or surplus) in capital formation. These, rather than traditional figures of consumer incomes and money supply, are the critical macroeconomic figures in a society in which jobs for knowledge workers—and that means capital-intensive jobs—are the fundamental "full employment need," and in which rapid shifting to new capital-intensive technologies is the key to economic prosperity and competitive strength. We need a "full-investment budget" to parallel the "full-employment budget".

(2) We need to think through an industrial policy which clearly aims at obtaining and maintaining leadership in manufacturing for the United States by optimizing the yield from the existing supply of human resources and of technology rather than relying on yesterday's —no longer existing—supply. Of course we might find enough jobs for our knowledge workers in service industries—though I doubt it. But it is highly doubtful that a major economy could survive, let alone prosper, without a manufacturing base—and surely not in wartime.

For a wide range of existing manufacturing work this will mean either rapid automation of an existing process or its replacement by low-entropy technology using organic processes as its model (for example, reverse osmosis or bacterial action). Predictably the major growth will not be in doing what we are already doing in a different way, but in applying new technology for new work in new processes and for end products that do not exist today.[6]

(3) Work that cannot be automated, either because we do not have the technology or because we do not permit automation, will not be done by native American labor. The only choice we have is whether

such work will be done by "guest workers," that is by immigrants from the developing world. We would need a larger number thereof than any country in Europe, including Germany, has brought in during the period of the "guest worker" migration from the South to the industrial North. Alternatively, such work would be farmed out to where the labor is, that is to the Third World. And then we need a policy that makes sure that we do not become dependent on productive facilities which, in the event of war, we could not control and safeguard.

Stated thus bluntly, the conclusions are quite clear: production-sharing, that puts the work where the labor is, is vastly preferable in every respect to having 30 million guest workers stream into the United States—and that might be the number needed.

Production-sharing is already the fastest growing sector of the international economy. From shoes to transistor radios, the bulk of American consumer products is already produced in a process in which at least one phase of production is performed offshore, where the labor is. But so far little attention has been paid to the strategic implications of this development. A good deal of the production-sharing of crucial goods is being performed in Southeast Asia or in West Africa, areas of the world which would be hard to safeguard and to control in the event of war. It would be strategic and political folly to increase beyond petroleum our dependence on areas vulnerable to enemy attack.

We need a policy that aims at production-sharing within our own hemisphere, especially in Mexico—the one country in the hemisphere, by the way, which will have the greatest need to find jobs for young people qualified for traditional manufacturing work (and for little else) —in the Caribbean, and along the north coast of South America.

There is need for an active foreign economic policy which builds partnerships in production-sharing based on the mutual complement of needs: the U.S. need to place labor-intensive steps of production where the labor is, and the developing country's need for jobs for its manual workers and for a market for their output. And these partnerships, in sharp contrast to traditional free trade, will have to be adapted to strategic realities, that is with countries and areas the United States could hope to defend in case of war.

(4) But demographics also require new domestic policies.

Neither of the traditional industrial policies for declining industries, that is protectionism or the "cushioning" of which labor unions now talk a good deal, can possibly work. Either will actually speed the decay of a company or of an industry. It could only create greater and faster unemployment.

Protectionism assumes the existence of a domestic labor supply. It protects the standard of living of that labor supply at the expense of the consumer. But the American reality in the next twenty-five years—as well as the reality of every other developed country—will be the absence of such a labor supply. Protectionism cannot, therefore, achieve what it is meant to achieve, namely to protect. It can only mean that the consumer pays more for imports. It cannot keep out the imports or enable domestic industry to compete with them.

Similarly, "cushioning" is not possible. The term usually means a policy which slows both the decline of an old industry and that of its traditional employment. It is possible (although not easy) to "cushion" so as to make the transition to full automation less painful for an industry and to make it faster. It is possible, in other words, to "cushion" an industry at the expense of the present manual labor force. It is not possible, however, to cushion the labor force itself. Any attempt to do this would only mean a more rapid decay of that industry. "Cushioning," bluntly speaking, would benefit neither an industry nor its labor force. The only possible beneficiary would be an existing union leadership.

(5) The only policy that can work is one that aims at the fastest possible conversion from traditional labor-intensive manual methods of production to automated processes and to "production-sharing," in which labor-intensive stages of production that cannot be automated are being performed by non-American labor, whether imported "guest workers" with all the attendant social and political problems, or by taking the work where the labor is—that is to developing countries.

This then means that we need *redundancy planning.* We need to anticipate redundancies and to take responsibility for placing workers made redundant by structural technological changes and by structural human resource changes into new jobs.

It is virtually impossible to place 5000 men, if their placement is attempted in the aggregate. It is relatively easy to place 5000 individuals, one by one, even in a depressed area—as Youngstown, Ohio, has proven, where most of the workers made unemployed by the closing of the largest steel mill in town did find alternative employment within a year or so. And it took them a year only because they had to look for these jobs themselves.

We know from earlier experiences in both Japan and Sweden (on this, see Drucker, 1980) that organized systematic attempts started when the shutdown of the steel mills first became a near-certainty, that is six months or so before the actual closing, and then on the basis of finding a job for one individual at a time, would have placed almost every one of the workers made unemployed by the shutdown within a few weeks, if not without any break in his employment pattern.

Redundancy planning need not aim at finding a job for everyone. Younger people, people with less than five years or so of seniority, require neither the emotional nor the economic security which redundancy planning offers. In fact, they have greater mobility than redundancy planning could give them and, as all earlier experience shows, would not accept, as a rule, jobs found for them through redundancy planning. And older people who have a pension to fall back on, that is people past fifty-five or sixty, do not require, as a rule, a job—or at least not right away. The promise that in case of redundancy the employer will attempt to find work for the employee—though not necessarily at the same wage rate, it should be emphasized—is needed for the two-thirds of the employes who are between twenty-five and fifty-five years of age, have families which depend on them for support, and cannot easily move. For those, however, we need emotional and psychological security. For those, neither the Western approach of unemployment insurance nor the Japanese approach of "lifetime employment" is adequate. The former gives the economic security needed, but fails to give the necessary psychological security. The latter gives psychological security, but imposes on the economy a rigidity which in a period of rapid demographic and technological change is a handicap and might well become unbearable.

Redundancy planning combines the psychological security that is needed to make rapid technological change acceptable, and indeed desirable for a good many employees, with the flexibility and mobility needed by the economy in a time of transition.

Redundancy planning may also be the one way in which the community can prevent decay when old industries go down or when they have to change their method of production and with it their labor force. Redundancy planning should enable a community to attract new industries. It has what will increasingly become a major attraction, namely workers available for manual work—workers already trained and used to working discipline. What it usually does not have is the community spirit that looks to change as an opportunity. Decaying communities, as a rule, *talk* about attracting new industry, but do everything in their power to keep newcomers away. They want to remain a "textile town" or a "steel town" or an "automobile town." Redundancy planning endows the community with the capacity to welcome change as an opportunity and with it the capacity to attract new industries. It shifts the focus from the decline of the community to its opportunities. It makes a "growth community" out of a decaying community.

But redundancy planning, it should be said, is not something the central government can do—other than give tax incentives and underwrite pension plans. Redundancy planning can work only if the focus is on the individual employe, his or her capacities, experiences, training, and strengths. Governments have to handle aggregates. They have to handle "1500 steelworkers" rather than John Smith or Jane Robinson. Governments cannot take the telephone and call up the personnel manager in the next plant or the next town and say, "Here are six or seven people with considerable skill in doing this kind of work. They are likely to become available within the next few months. Do you have jobs for them and could you set up interviews for them?"

Wherever tried, redundancy planning worked because the individual employer took responsibility, preferably with the cooperation of the local government and of the labor union.

(6) There is urgent need to adapt management policies to the heterogeneity of the work force. (On this too see Drucker, 1980.) There is urgent need to shift from uniform benefits to options that suit the individual and his or her needs.[7]

There is need to organize for "continuous training" of all employees and especially of "knowledge workers."

So far, the only ones who have formally made such a commitment are the Japanese—and it is in no small measure responsible for their success. But we, too, have, in practice, without such formal commitment, moved quite far toward "continuous training," as witness the constant seminar and meeting activity for knowledge workers and for managers on all levels. With the shift to automation, continuous training will become crucial. Workers, by and large, welcome the shift from being machine operators to being machine programmers—at least no case of resistance has yet been reported, either in this country or in Japan or in Germany, not even in such highly unionized companies as General Electric. But there is need to train employees and to continue training. There is need to train the supervisor who is likely to be a greater problem and to offer more resistance than the workers themselves.

There is need, above all, to realize that the labor force of today—and even more the labor force of tomorrow—represents a tremendous resource of knowledge and experience which has to be continuously tapped and continuously upgraded. We need to shift from the traditional approach of the nineteenth century which saw in labor a "cost," to the approach which so far only the Japanese have taken, the approach of seeing labor as a "resource" and therefore as a "profit center" rather than a "cost center." (For an approach see, for instance, Dahl, 1979.) This means that the employees themselves have to be organized to be responsible for their own continuous improvement in knowledge and skill, in performance level and in quality, and also for continuously improving tools, information, methods, and systems. There is need to organize the human resource around continuous learning and continuous training.

And this need will become even greater as second careers, especially for knowledge workers in their forties and fifties, become commonplace.

CONCLUSION

The developments which will ensure the decline in the proportion of the labor force engaged in manual manufacturing work are major structural demographic changes. They have occurred and are irreversible. Everybody in the American labor force twenty years hence is now born (although not necessarily living in the United States).

Regardless of wage levels, America cannot maintain a manufacturing base resting on traditional manual work and worker. The manpower needed would not be available *at any price.* Even the English "solution" of a low-productivity, noncompetitive traditional manufacturing industry kept from extinction through protectionism and subsidies is not open to the United States.

Conversely, even the most rapid drop in birth rates in the developing countries could not reverse the surge of people qualified and available for manual work in manufacturing at wage rates so low as to offset any conceivable labor-productivity differential. And the educational shifts which are as important for the supply of labor as total quantitative figures, as well as the qualitative changes which might be summarized by saying that we are engaged in unmaking in the developed countries the great social achievements of the nineteenth century, have also occurred and cannot be unmade or even substantially revised in as short a period as twenty-five years.

But at the same time the technologies have become available, for example, automation based on the microprocessor and on feedback control of the process; or low-entropy flow processes based on membrane-reverse osmosis or on genetic manipulation of microorganisms—that would enable the United States to build industrial leadership and the lowest cost manufacturing base on its *one* demographic advantage: the large, if not abundant, supply of people entering the labor force with substantial, if not advanced, schooling. Indeed as recent events, such as the successful competition of "microchips" made by the Japanese in automated processes and with high-cost, but highly educated Japanese labor, with the "chips" made for American producers by exceedingly cheap labor in poor, underdeveloped, but overpopulated countries (for example, Nigeria) have proven, a fully automated process, despite its high capital investment and high income of the knowledge employee, results in lower costs and better quality than any manual process, however low the workers' wages and incomes.

Can "supply-side economics" work under these conditions? To the extent to which supply-side economics means a lower burden of taxes and especially a lower burden of taxes on capital formation, it would certainly be helpful and a step in the right direction. But in its fundamental assumptions, supply-side economics still accepts (as does, of course, Milton Friedman as well) the Keynesian "invisible hand"—the direct, automatic "multiplier effect" of consumption on investment. And there is no evidence for this Keynesian "law" in the economic performance of the last half-century in any country. The investment needed to create the jobs for the labor force of the twenty-first century, knowledge workers engaged in industrial production parallel to the knowledge workers now constituting the bulk of America's productive farmers, is such that *only* massive saving can provide it. We need to "rediscover Say's Law," that is, we need to accept again, as few supply-siders do so far, that it is not investment that follows consumption, it is consumption that follows investment. And this means that low taxes by themselves only help negatively: they do not impede. A positive fiscal policy needs taxes that transfer income from consumption into saving—it may be no accident that this was Japan's underlying fiscal strategy from 1950 until 1979 or so.

It follows from the demographics of the United States that "cushioning" old labor-intensive industries can only hasten their decline. Cushioning as the term is now being used, especially by labor union leaders, implies saving *both* the industry and the jobs of its present employees. But demographics inevitably will make "saving an industry" dependent on the most rapid disemployment of traditional, that is present, manual workers and their replacement by automation employing different, that is, "knowledge" workers.

While jobs for knowledge workers will become America's first priority in employment policy, the country will also need to place workers made redundant by structural change, especially if it succeeds in "reindustrializing America"—that is, in recapturing competitive strength and leadership in manufacturing (and without it, leadership in service industries would hardly work and the country would be almost indefensible in times of war). The total numbers of redundant workers will be small—maybe, at any one time, around 1 percent of the workforce. The number will actually be smaller than the number of people that were made redundant each of these last thirty years by the shift in farming from a "manual" and largely unskilled task into a capital-intensive, knowledge-intensive, and most nearly "automated" industry. But the redundant industrial workers will be highly visible, concentrated in a few industrial areas, and unionized.

We will therefore need a policy for the placement of redundant workers—or rather for the placement of redundant workers between the ages of thirty and fifty-five. Such a policy might rest on a national commitment; but, to be effective, it would have to be decentralized and local.

The first reaction to this will predictably be a demand for massive "training." It is the wrong reaction and is bound to lead to the kind of failure and frustration which have been the lot of all such "training programs" since World War II (such as the Comprehensive Employment and Training Act [CETA]). Successful training, especially of low-skilled people with limited horizons, *follows* placement; it must be tied to a specific job and, preferably, be done in conjunction with it, if not on it.

What is thus needed is *redundancy planning* centered on the organized placement of redundant workers—and that is done, as all experience proves, locally, in the individual community by the individual employers and for an individual rather than for a "problem" or a "category".

Over the next twenty-five years the decisive factor for American economic policy is not going to be economic theory. It is not going to be economics altogether. It is metaeconomic events, that is the structural changes in the supply of the human resource, both quantitatively and qualitatively, which then in turn make compelling both use of the new technologies wherever they can be applied, and "production sharing," that is the shifting of labor-intensive stages of production to developing countries where the labor supply exists, for those manual processes to which the new technologies cannot be applied.

NOTES

1. It is fashionable today to explain away this disagreeable conclusion by counting on an increase in the number of women joining the labor force in traditional blue collar jobs. Alas, this "increase" is a statistical illusion. The labor force participation of women in the United States looks quite a bit lower than that of men, but is only because the women *over fifty*, by and large, are not in the labor force, or at least not in the paid labor force. The labor force participation of women under fifty, whether working full time or part time, is already as great as that of the men of the same age cohort. The percentage figure for labor participation of women will thus go up as the older women reach the age at which they are no longer considered as being "available"—a process that will substantially be over by the early 1990s—when the actual number of women newly entering the labor force will go down as a result of the drop in the birthrate.

2. We made, however, one mistake in providing for "retirement." We equated "retirement age" with "chronological age" from birth. We

should have fixed "retirement age" as a function of life expectancy rather than as a function of longevity. This was clearly seen by some of President Roosevelt's advisers, by the way, when the United States first went into Social Security in 1935—and if we had followed them we would have avoided a great many problems, and would have no "Social Security crisis," for instance.

3. Brazil might be the one exception. Mexico may have some purchasing power, but surely not enough to create employment for a population that is likely to double within the next thirty years and may reach 120 million by the year 2010, as against 60 to 70 million now. Mainland China has the population, but surely not the purchasing power.

4. In economic and social theory there have been two competing schools regarding wage trends. One, with Marx, has preached the "Law of the Immiseration of the Proletariat"—that is the continuing decline in real wages and real purchasing power of the working man; the other one, beginning with the economists of the Austrian School around 1860, proclaimed that income and purchasing would "trickle down" from the top with increasing productivity. We now know that these apparently incompatible theories assume different demographics. If the supply of labor increases faster than the market, Marx's "immiseration" holds good. And it does that whether the "system" is "capitalist," "socialist," or "communist," or what have you. If the population increases less fast than the market, then the "trickle down" theory can work. Historically Europe, in the course of its development, went through an "immiseration" period—most pronounced in the England of the eighteenth and early nineteenth century, which Marx considered to be the one and only prototype of industrialization under the "capitalist system of production." The United States, by contrast, practically throughout her economic history, saw the market expanding faster than production, so that the "trickle down" theory pertained—which explains more than anything else the difference in social conflict, social bitterness, and class consciousness between Europe and America.

5. A hundred thousand workers made unemployed by the shutdown or bankruptcy of a giant company like Chrysler represent only one-tenth of 1 percent of the American labor force, or less than one-half of 1 percent of the blue collar force employed in manual work in manufacturing. Compare this with the average turnover of jobs in this country, which runs to 3 to 5 millions *a day*—and 100,000 workers, no matter how big they look in the headlines, are hardly a factor in the country's macroeconomics.

6. The technical means for this are at hand. The miniprocessor makes possible genuine automation of a very substantial part of manufacturing processes and perhaps of the great majority thereof. The mini-

processor, in its impact on manufacturing technology, can be compared to the fractional horsepower motor which transformed the industrial landscape 100 years ago and created modern manufacturing industry. By the year 2000, the bulk of conventional manufacturing in the United States will, of necessity, be done in automated plants and with automated processes. Today's machine operator will have become a machine programmer, by and large. Similarly the sciences for low-entropy technology using low temperatures, low pressures, and modelled after organic processes rather than after the model of the machine that has dominated technology since the late seventeenth century, already exists in large numbers. The "growth industries" of 2000 are likely to be manufacturing industries using low-entropy processes, e.g., reverse osmosis based on membrane technology, genetic engineering, and bacterial or enzymatic transformation.

7. A present, up to two-fifths of the benefits paid by the American economy may not really benefit the recipient and are economic and social waste. They are likely instead to create resentment and dissonance. The individual employee knows perfectly well that the money that is being paid for him or her into health insurance or a pension plan, even if ostensibly "paid by the employer" and "free to the employee," comes out of the employee's pocket. Or rather, the employee knows perfectly well that he or she would not use that money, if available to him or her, for health insurance or a pension plan, but for other needs that are more important and of greater benefit to the individual employee and his or her family.

BIBLIOGRAPHY
Dahl, Henry L., Jr. "Measuring the Human ROI." *Management Review* 68 (January, 1979): 44–50.
Drucker, Peter F. *Managing in Turbulent Times.* New York: Harper and Row, 1980.

12.

THE HUMAN RESOURCE CONSEQUENCES OF INDUSTRIAL REVITALIZATION

D. Quinn Mills

INTRODUCTION

Industrial revitalization policy implies a tilt of public policy and private endeavor away from personal consumption and government expenditure, and toward investment, especially in manufacturing. Accompanying the emphasis on investment is a stress on modernization and improved labor productivity.

Associated with industrial revitalization will be a considerable amount of technological and human change. Some production processes will see the introduction of robots on a large scale. Other processes will be altered by new materials and means of doing things. Some plants will be closed down. New facilities will, to a large degree, be located at new sites. Some people will lose jobs while others gain them. Difficult problems of adjustment will accompany these changes. Already there are comments that major technological advances are being delayed due to an inability to deal with the potential human consequences of the changes involved.[1]

The broad human resources issue facing a reindustrialization effort, therefore, is whether we can develop a society with a high tolerance for change in the industrial workplace.

BACKGROUND

Underlying the concern for industrial revitalization in the United States is the poor productivity performance of recent years. A few brief tables

TABLE 12–1
United States Output Per Hour of All Persons,
Private Business Sector

Annual Percentage Change—

1948–53	1954–67	1968–73	1974–80
3.98	2.91	2.37	.64

SOURCE: *Economic Report of President,* 1981, p. 277, and Current Economic Indicators, for 1980.

TABLE 12–2
Levels of Labor Productivity, 1960
and 1977

Real Gross Domestic Product per Employed Civilian, 1960 and 1977

	1960	1977
United States	100	100
Canada	87	92
France	61	92
Germany	56	85
Italy	40	63
Japan	27	69
United Kingdom	57	62

SOURCE: U.S., Executive Office of the President, Council on Wage and Price Stability. *Report on Productivity.* Washington: July, 1979.

TABLE 12–3
Manufacturing—1972–1978

	Percentage Change		
	Output	Employment	Output/Hour
France	22.2	−2.2	33.4
Germany	12.5	−12.0	36.0
United States	18.6	6.5	11.7
Japan	21.6	−4.7	33.0

SOURCE: U.S., Department of Labor, Bureau of Labor Statistics. "Manufacturing Productivity Rates." Washington: July 9, 1979.

give the general dimensions of the American productivity performance compared to past performance of the U.S. economy and compared to several of our major trading partners abroad. Table 12–1 indicates that the rate of growth of output (adjusted for inflation) per hour worked has decreased substantially since the end of World War II. In fact, each of the past three years (1978, 1979, and 1980) have registered a small absolute decline in output per hour in the private business sector of the American economy. Table 12–2 indicates that despite the poor performance of the U.S. economy in recent years, the absolute level of labor productivity in the American economy continues to exceed that of our major trading partners. But table 12–2 also indicates that since 1960 the American advantage has been shrinking steadily. Within the next few years it is quite possible that American absolute levels of productivity will be exceeded abroad. In fact, they are now being exceeded in some manufacturing industries abroad.

Finally, table 12–3 indicates that in manufacturing, a sector of the economy that is particularly important in the international context, the lag of American productivity increases in the 1970s has been particularly dramatic. The table is of considerable significance because it allows us to determine the source of the productivity lag in the American economy. Specifically, manufacturing output (in real terms) rose in the United States in the mid-1970s at about the same rate as in France, Japan, and Germany. Because the American manufacturing sector is much larger and more diversified than the manufacturing sectors of the other nations, this is a very good performance. But, as the last column of the table indicates, labor productivity in the United States grew at only one-third the rate of the three other nations. Column 2 of the table indicates that this was because American firms were adding employees during the period in question while manufacturers in other countries were reducing employment. Thus, the American manufacturing sector grew at comparable rates to the other nations, but failed to achieve the productivity increases that workforce reductions permitted abroad.

The superior productivity performance of foreign manufacturing sectors in the last decade is commonly attributed to more rapid rates of innovation in production processes and to greater investment in capital equipment than have occurred in the United States. But this is only part of the matter. The acquisition of skills by individuals is also a major element of investment, the cost of which is borne in varying proportions by business, individuals, and the government.

A skilled, competent workforce is as important to economic growth and wellbeing as is physical capital. The United States has, in fact, benefited from a relatively large, skilled labor force for many years. But today, the United States gives evidence of some substantial and continuing difficulties in the human resource area. Shortages of personnel in certain key occupations are apparent, and will probably increase in the future. The country faces a paradox of education: the average years of schooling of the labor force continues to rise, but the basic capabilities of much of the younger labor force seem to be declining and the skill content of many jobs is being decreased. The result is that despite more formal schooling, there is less capacity in the labor force, and also less satisfaction with jobs. Unemployment rates remain relatively high by post-World War II standards, so that there is continuing concern for job security among much of our labor force. Finally, some elements of the labor force seem virtually unemployable, even should there be a substantial increase in the level of economic activity.

This paper asks the question: what policies toward human resources are necessary to accomplish industrial revitalization? Although differing schemes for revitalization strategies have been advanced, it is possible to generalize to some degree about the human implications of revitalization, regardless of how it is achieved. In particular, what human resource problems are likely to be encountered as the United States achieves a rate of productivity growth in manufacturing that is closer to the rates of our foreign competitors? How will these problems be resolved?

GROWTH AND CHANGE TO 1990: HOW MANAGEABLE IS IT?

The Bureau of Labor Statistics forecasts the growth and change of the American economy and its labor force. These forecasts are made available to the public, and are used in government and business planning and by educators in the design of school curricula and the counseling of students concerning career choices. The Bureau's forecasts are living documents, in that they are periodically updated as conditions change or new developments are foreseen. The forecasts are extremely valuable. They provide an overall context in which the impact of different scenarios for developments in certain sectors of the economy can be evaluated. And, for some purposes, the interesting questions are discovered by contrasting the projections made by the Bureau with possibly divergent developments.

The Bureau's present projections for the development of the American economy to 1990 do not suggest major problems on the human resources side of the American economy. Employment growth is reasonably vigorous in most sectors of the economy, including the manufacturing sector. Productivity increases are expected to resume at a rate only some small amount below the long-term rate of productivity increase in our economy. And while different industries show divergent prospects for growth, there is not a wide divergence, so that the churning of employees among advancing and declining industries is not especially great.

Specifically, the Bureau's forecast (table 12–4) shows an increase of 16.1 percent in total employment in the American economy from 1980 to 1990. Manufacturing employment rises at a lesser rate, and durable goods manufacturing growth is double that of nondurables. But the important aspect of the projection is that both durables and nondurable manufacturing shows a net increase in employment. These projections are based on the expectation of an economy that is reasonably vigorous, having about 4.4 percent of the labor force unemployed in 1990. Table 12–5 gives some additional detail of the employment projections for 1990. The motor vehicles industry is anticipated to add 14.9 percent more employees by 1990. Employment in steel production will decline by 6.3 percent, but employment in steel fabrication will increase by 28 percent. Aircraft production employment will fall, but electrical machinery employment will increase by 16.7 percent. Many nondurable industries also show substantial increases in employment, especially industrial chemicals and plastics. Industries such as paperboard and apparel, which seem today to be likely victims, with autos and steel, of competition from imports, are shown in these forecasts to have net increases in employment.

Employment projections depend critically upon the expectations which are built into them regarding productivity increases. The higher the estimated productivity increase, the lower the projected employment level associated with any particular amount of industrial production. Table 12–6 shows the productivity increases implicit in the Bureau's projections of employment level by several major sectors of the economy. Specifically, the Bureau projects a 2.3 percent productivity increase for the economy as a whole from 1985 to 1990 (shown on the table as 2.2 percent, an arithmetic calculation made by the author by taking the difference between the expected rate of growth of output and the expected rate of growth of employment). Manufacturing productivity growth rates are expected to rise from roughly zero today, to 2.0 percent per year in 1980–85 and to 2.7 percent per year in 1985–90. Productivity increases in contract construction, which have been strongly negative in recent years, are expected to be positive (at 1.1 percent per year) henceforth through 1990 (on average).

These productivity estimates may be correct, or they may be either too high or too low. Some persons might think them too high. The estimates presuppose a reversal of recent U.S. productivity trends, and are based upon a higher level of economic activity (and lower unemployment rates) than we have had in recent years.

BLS is on customary ground in forecasting stronger real economic

TABLE 12–4
Industrial Employment Projections 1980–1990

	Percent Increase
Total	11.1
Government	13.6
Private	
Manufacturing	11.1
Durable	13.6
Nondurable	7.3
Contract Construction	13.0
Transportation	7.5
Communication	13.0
Public Utilities	5.4
Wholesale Trade	6.8
Retail Trades	20.4
Finance, Insurance, and Real Estate	26.0
Other Services	34.6
Private Households	−18.4

SOURCE: U.S. Department of Labor, Bureau of Labor Statistics. *Employment Projections for the 1980s,* Bulletin 2030, (1979), p. 32. The figures for 1980 from which projections are made are themselves projections made in 1979.

TABLE 12–5
Industrial Employment Projections 1980–1990

Manufacturing	11.1
Durable	13.6
Motor Vehicles	14.9
Basic Steel	−6.3
Fabricated Structural Metal	28.0
Aircraft	−9.1
Electrical Machinery	16.7
Nondurable	7.3
Fabrics, Yarns, Threads	0.0
Apparel	8.8
Paperboard	8.6
Industrial Chemicals	16.7
Plastics	18.3

SOURCE: Bureau of Labor Statistics Bulletin 2030, pp. 30–31. (See note to table 12–4.)

TABLE 12–6
Productivity Projections

| | Annual Average Rate of Change | | | | | |
| | Gross Product Originating | | Total Employment | | Implied Productivity Change | |
	(1) 1980–85	(2) 1985–90	(3) 1980–85	(4) 1985–90	(5) 1980–85	(6) 1985–90
All	3.9	3.4	1.9	1.2	2.0*	2.2*
Manufacturing	3.7	3.4	1.4	.7	2.3	2.7
Durable	3.9	3.5	1.7	.8	2.2	2.7
Nondurable	3.4	3.1	.8	.6	2.6	2.5
Contract Construction	2.9	1.8	1.8	.7	1.1	1.1

*Actual Bureau of Labor Statistics estimates are 1980–85, 1.9 percent 1985–90, 2.3 percent (Bulletin 2030, p. 20).

SOURCE: Columns (1–4) Bureau of Labor Statistics, Bulletin 2030, pp. 28 and 32; columns (5 and 6) author's calculations.

growth for manufacturing in the 1980s than in the 1970s, and in coupling the growth forecast with a stronger productivity performance in the 1980s than in the 1970s. The BLS scenario appears to be favorable to the economy, and manageable in terms of potential human resource problems. The BLS scenario shows growth at rates which will not create substantial labor shortages, and will not result in major reductions in the manufacturing workforce.

The most interesting questions arise, however, if these projections are erroneous, as I think they may be. Reindustrialization policy may result in more rapid technological advance than BLS anticipates, so that productivity rises more rapidly, and skill shortages develop in key occupations. Also, economic growth is likely to be less robust than either BLS or the current Administration project. What may occur is a combination of high productivity growth and slow real output growth in manufacturing. This is the probable consequence of reindustrialization policy.

This is not to say that if productivity were to grow more slowly (as the result, for example, of limiting technical progress), employment levels would remain higher. Instead, job losses due to import competition would be greater.

There is, I think, no likely escape from a long-term decline in the number of manufacturing jobs in the United States. If technological progress proceeds at a reasonable rate, there will be a slow, but steady, reduction in total manufacturing jobs of the magnitude estimated above. If technological progress is slowed dramatically, by capital shortages, worker resistance or management choice, then job losses (due to import competition) are likely to be at a faster rate.

The reindustrialization effort is not, in my view, one that is likely to add manufacturing jobs on balance in the next decade. It is, instead, an effort to slow the long-term rate of decline of manufacturing jobs.

Should manufacturing productivity increase at a faster rate than anticipated, and should manufacturing growth be less strong than forecast by BLS (which can occur only in the context of substantial technological advances), then employment in manufacturing is likely to decline. Manufacturing has for years been declining as a percentage of total employment in our economy. It is likely that it may now begin to decline in absolute terms as well. Let us assume an annual real growth rate of 1.5 percent in manufacturing, and a 2.5 percent rate of productivity growth. The combination of these two developments would release some 250,000 persons per year from manufacturing payrolls. Continued over a decade, manufacturing employment in this country would shrink some 2.5 million persons. This is not an unlikely scenario. Table 12–3 above suggests that American productivity performance in manufacturing is more likely to increase through reduced employment than through increased output. This was the experience of the 1970s abroad, and it is likely to be mirrored in America in the 1980s.

There are several reasons to believe that productivity in manufacturing may make a more substantial jump in the near future than is now being anticipated. First, there is a consciousness developing of the size and significance of the U.S. productivity lag in manufacturing. Companies are beginning to treat productivity improvements as an end in themselves, not simply as a resultant of a benefit to cost calculation involved in profit maximization. Several companies now establish productivity targets for managers, as Japanese companies have done for years. Behind this approach lies the expectation that productivity advances will pay off in the market place in the future in ways not now evident in the pursuit of short-term earnings goals. Thus, productivity improvements are becoming an end in themselves, with a potentially magnified impact on productivity gains.

Second, the United States in many major industries now experiences a technological lag, allowing American companies to move quickly to enhance productivity because the applicable technology is existent and the impediments to application are in the area of implementation, not in research and development.

Third, there is a growing recognition of the need for further financial incentives, especially in the form of more favorable tax treatment, for investment. Government may be expected to act to increase the cash flow which is available for investment purposes to firms.

Finally, recent expenditures data indicate that the investment necessary for a sudden increase in productivity is already beginning to occur. In January 1981, the Commerce Department revised its capital spending figures for 1980 and revealed that the level of investment in high technology capital goods reached a $17 billion annual rate in the third quarter of 1980 (up three times from the previous estimate).

The combination of a recognition of the need to pursue productivity improvements as a primary corporate objective, the availability of productivity-enhancing technologies, and the willingness of government to provide financial support to the effort, suggest that in manufacturing, at least, a discontinuous advance in labor productivity may be in the making.

Some additional evidence with regard to the likelihood of a rapid productivity advance, and also some suggestions about its possible consequences, may be obtained from a brief review of BLS's employment projections by occupation. Table 12–7 gives forecasts of employment by major occupation groups for the entire economy and for the period 1978–1990. The projections show an increase of some 20 percent in total employment (somewhat larger than the forecasts in table 12–4 because of the longer period covered in table 12–7). Table 12–7 identifies broad categories of professional, technical, and skilled occupations. In general, there is a rough balance between the rate of growth of employment as a whole, and that of the skilled trades. Thus, craftspersons are forecasted to increase in numbers at just below the overall rate for all employees. Similarly, professional, technical, and kindred occupations grow more slowly than the whole, and managers, officials, and proprietors at just about the overall rate. Once again, these projections (as those made on an industry-wide basis) give little reason for concern that the ordinary operation of the institutions of our economy would not result in providing the human resources necessary to accomplishment of the forecast economic growth.

But there is some evidence in table 12–7 of a more troubling circumstance. Computer specialists were forecast by BLS to increase by some 31 percent from 1978 to 1990. Recent tentative revisions (shown in the table in parentheses) have increased that number to 110 percent. A similar upward revision (though perhaps not so large) should be made in the estimates for mechanics and repairers, a significant number of whom will, in the future, be working on computers and computer-associated equipment. Also, while machinists are expected to increase at almost exactly the same rate as employment as a whole, a rapid shift

TABLE 12–7
Occupational Employment Projections—1978–1990

	Percent Increase
All Occupations	20.80
Crafts and Kindred Workers	20.03
Construction Trades	19.21
Electricians	24.57
Excavating, Grading Machine Operators	35.19
Metalworkers	21.80
Machinists	20.66
Mechanics, Repairers	29.66
Professional, Technical, Kindred	18.32
Engineers	21.46
Electrical	22.54
Computer Specialists	30.79 (110.00)*
Managers, Officials, Proprietors	20.76

SOURCE: U.S., Department of Labor, Bureau of Labor Statistics. "Occupation-Industry Matrix," January, 1980.

*Author's estimate from data provided by Bureau of Labor Statistics.

to numerically controlled equipment will alter to a substantial degree the capabilities required of machinists.

The revisions of the estimated increase in numbers of computer-associated occupations indicate that the advance of technology in the workplace is becoming more rapid than we have anticipated. Further, it indicates that what had appeared to be a manageable degree of change associated with a slow growth in productivity may in fact become a more rapid and less readily manageable alteration in the required skill composition of the workforce.

The labor market implications of this possibly discontinuous jump in the application of new technology to the workplace are substantial. They will be substantial in clerical occupations, as well as in manufacturing. They may well result in much more rapid rates of productivity growth than are expected. They will alter labor force requirements substantially. They will cause shortages in certain occupations, and surpluses in others. There will not be one problem, but two: shortages and surpluses, which periods of change always bring together.

Many companies are already realizing that the labor market is changing. Manufacturing companies have often operated on the assumption that good people were always available, and that while the opposite situation can occur in limited instances, it is always an exception. Believing in the capacity of the market to supply persons, the initial response to shortages was to devote more resources to the processes of recruitment and selection. The result has been a more rapid churning of the labor force in certain critical specialties among companies and a coincident rapid increase in salary levels. Recognizing that a recruitment solution may not be achievable, companies are beginning to abandon the assumption that the market will supply good people, and are instead looking for opportunities for training and development.

The opposite problems of excess supply are also being encountered. Rapid technological change is outdating the skills of many employees, and substantial layoffs in the import-impacted industries are no longer viewed as temporary. The result is a major problem of displaced workers.

There is the likelihood that these difficulties are going to increase in the future. BLS does not now predict such a situation, but it is at least a growing possibility. Put in its simplest form, the issue is what will be the labor force implications of a successful industrial revitalization strategy if it is accompanied by more rapid productivity improvements than we anticipate today, and these improvements are achieved through rapid introduction of new technology?

A successful industrial revitalization effort will impose substantial pressures on the labor market. To a degree these pressures are transitional in nature, arising from the shift in technology which is likely to accompany a revitalization effort. But the transition will also leave a more permanent legacy, in that manufacturing as a whole is likely to enter a period of secular employment decline.

In summary, a revitalization effort will confront two different types of problems: shortages in some occupations, and falling employment levels in manufacturing generally. Both must be dealt with because both problems, unresolved, have the potential for disrupting the revitalization effort. Shortages will disrupt revitalization by limiting the rate of growth in key sectors of the economy, and by creating inflationary pressures in the labor market. Unemployment, or redundancies (to use the British term), will disrupt the revitalization effort by undermining support for it among workers and trade unions. A consequence may be efforts on the shop floor, in collective bargaining, and in Congress to place restrictions on the rate of innovation in American industry.

The problems of providing a labor force with the skills newly required by technological change are probably the more tractable of the two types of difficulties. Problems of growth are more pleasant (though not necessarily less difficult) to manage than those of decline. The incentives for individuals to obtain skills in growing occupations are usually substantial. Rising relative compensation makes more bearable the efforts by individuals needed to learn new methods. But certain difficulties lie in the question of whose responsibility it is to bear the costs associated with training and development. I return to these issues in the next section of this paper.

SKILLED EMPLOYEES: WHOSE RESPONSIBILITY ARE THEY?

A successful industrial revitalization effort envisions increased capital investment, new technology, and American firms recapturing a larger market share in the international market place. This strategy depends to a significant degree on the availability of persons able to design, operate, and maintain the new technology. Also, the current rapid expansion of employment in critical occupations is generating labor shortages. As industrial revitalization progresses, this problem will become more acute. Upon whom and what processes do we depend to overcome the obstacles: the individual responding to the signals of the market place? The employers? Or the government?

The market is indeed providing incentives for persons to seek skills in many of the occupations which industrial revitalization will require. The current salary spiral for computer personnel is well known. But the salary spiral is occurring among only a small group of companies, and in the broader context, the market's signals are less clear. In many companies there has been a steady erosion of wage differentials which favor skilled occupations during the 1970s. A major factor in causing this erosion has been pay increases made on a cents-per-hour basis in response to increases in the cost of living. Whether as a result of formal cost of living allowances (formulas tied to the Consumer Price Index) or as a result of adjustments made on an *ad hoc* basis, there has apparently been a substantial reduction in skilled pay differentials in recent years. It is therefore increasingly difficult to retain skilled employees in their occupations, and to induce other employees to acquire those skills. I am not able to ascertain from aggregate data the degree to which this compression of pay levels is a common problem. Statistics by broad occupation group, and covering all industries from the post-World War II period, do not show a major reduction of skilled-unskilled differentials. But a substantial compression in manufacturing (and in particular in durable goods manufacturing) in which formal cost of living escalators are common is not necessarily inconsistent with the overall data.

It is, of course, within the discretion of employers and unions to reestablish differentials through the collective bargaining process, or through the employer's policies of wage administration where there is no collective bargaining. Such reestablishment may be difficult for the companies, however, because of the additional labor costs imposed on top of those already generated by substantial cost of living wage increases. And increasing skill differentials may be difficult for the unions because of the large numbers of less skilled people who often dominate the unions' internal political processes.

On balance, therefore, it cannot be assumed that the incentives favoring skill acquisition will be forthcoming in terms of pay differentials in the industrial environment.

Even where pay differentials are substantial, the market place may not be an effective mechanism for resolving skill shortages. This is particularly the case where training periods are substantial. In the traditional cobweb pattern of adjustment which characterizes scientific specialties, the time lags between market incentives to acquire certain skills and the times necessary to be educated in them are such that in today's world, the skills needed may have become substantially obsolete before they can be placed on the job market in large numbers.

It is ordinarily expected that when shortages of skilled personnel develop, employers will train persons to fill the positions. Often this occurs, but not always. While it may seem counterintuitive, shortages of skilled people may well result in lesser training by employers. This is because initial training costs are often substantial. Where there are serious labor shortages, competitors will hire away people trained by other firms. Thus, a firm which trains people bears the training costs, yet risks losing its newly-trained people to other companies. Where this occurs, providing training can become a competitive disadvantage for a firm.

Often companies do provide considerable training to employees in skills which are in short supply. But the willingness of companies to provide training is constrained by several factors. First, there are constraints arising from limitations on a company's ability to pay. Employers whose wage bills and other costs are rising rapidly are often short of cash for physical investments and are also generally short of cash for investment in human resources. There is, in many instances, an imbalance between the incentive to invest and the ability to do so. Substantial wage increases provide an incentive to an employer to invest in labor-saving machinery in order to increase labor productivity and lower labor costs. But high wage bills can also so reduce profitability that retained earnings are not available for investment, and external funds cannot be obtained.

The United States now faces what is in some ways the worst of both worlds with respect to the balance between investment incentives and investment capability. Industries with ready access to the capital markets for debt or equity (as indicated, in part by price/earnings multiples on corporate stock), face what are relatively slowly rising labor costs, on average. High technology firms, located to a large degree in the Sun Belt, nonunionized for the most part, and employing many relatively low-paid assemblers, have little incentive from rising labor costs for improvements in production techniques, but have reasonably ready access to capital markets for such funds as they wish to obtain. Industries with little access to debt or equity markets (due to low profitability, poor prospects for growth, and high existing debt burdens) face rapidly rising labor costs (due in many instances to cost of living allowances), so that earnings are not available for retention and reinvestment. Thus, the market tends to provide capital where the incentive for labor-saving innovation is least, and denies capital where it is greatest. This is not to say that the market makes a perverse connection between the two, so that high need for labor-saving investment becomes a cause of restricted access to the capital markets. But instead, a combination of other factors results in the paradox just described.

Thus, sole reliance on the labor market to provide skills in short supply may be misplaced. And this is likely to be the case whether the labor market envisaged is either internal or external. The internal market is compromised at this time due to the compression of pay differentials between skilled and unskilled employees, which reduced incentives for skill acquisition. The external market is compromised by the imperfect connection between the perception of pay incentives (ordinarily well-reflected in the external market) and the availability of training and its duration.

The labor market does not resolve this problem. The market instead signals the developing shortage of skilled persons through rising vacancies and through rising salary levels. These signals tell companies to slow down their growth or to substitute persons with other skills for the shortage occupations. Rising job vacancy rates and increasing pay also signal individuals to attempt to acquire the skills that are in short supply. Where training is available, there will be an inflow of people. But where training is difficult to obtain, shortages can continue and worsen. In the long term, training opportunities will probably emerge, and companies will adjust to shortages, so that a rough balance of supply and demand is created. But in the process, economic growth may have been slowed and costs increased. The market has yielded a form of solution, but it has been an imperfect process due to lags in information and perverse incentives in the provision of training.

The attempts of companies to sustain or develop training programs are also being constrained by a sluggish economy. For example, the American machine tool industry once relied to a substantial degree for the training of skilled tool makers and supervisors on the apprenticeship program conducted by our largest machine tool firm. In 1974–75, under the impact of a very severe capital goods recession, the company terminated the program. In the recovery of the capital goods industry that has occurred since, the program has not been revived. Perhaps this is because the intense competition for skilled persons now makes it likely that the firm will bear the costs of training only to lose a substantial proportion of the graduates to its competitors.

In the construction industry, apprenticeship levels have remained largely unchanged for several years, while employment has increased substantially (by one-third). In part, this reflects the relatively slower growth (or actual decline) of the unionized sector of the industry, where most of the formal training is done. Attempts of the nonunion sector of the industry to formalize multi-employer training programs have been tied up in disputes between the Labor Department, the construction contractors, and the Department of Justice over the appropriate pay scales for apprentices and the application of the antitrust laws to various proposals for determining wage scales for apprentices.[2]

These various impediments suggest that the government has a role with employers, unions, and individuals in providing training opportunities for skill shortage occupations and for bearing training costs. The market place does not provide perfect information on the demand for human skills, especially in highly technical occupations. There are, in fact, no human capital markets as efficient as the financial capital markets. Labor markets external to the firm, and those internal to it, often send conflicting signals to the individual seeking to decide on whether or not to invest in human skills. Further, institutional arrangements (including the freedom of employees in whom the firm has invested training to take employment elsewhere) which have no exact analogue in physical capital, limit the training provided by employers.

If employers and workers are to be assisted in responding to market signals, processes for anticipation of shortages have to be established and actions must be taken by companies and individuals. The attempt to forecast occupational requirements, imperfect as they may be, have an important function in this regard.

The government is deeply involved in the provision of education and skills to individuals through the public schools. Also, the government has, in recent years, begun to attempt to redirect training opportunities provided under the Comprehensive Employment and Training Act to directions suggested by private enterprise. While the government may arguably not have carried out its training responsibilities with any particular success in recent years, it remains a central part of the process by which persons acquire occupational skills in our society.

A SAFETY NET: HOW IS IT TO BE PROVIDED?
The problems of economic decline are of a different sort. If U.S. manufacturing were to achieve labor productivity growth of 5 percent per year in the 1980s, then manufacturing employment would not rise by 2.3 million, as BLS has predicted, but would instead fall by some 2.5 million. This assumes, of course, that the volume of real output in manufacturing is as BLS had projected it. But the combination of these two assumptions is not all that farfetched. It is what occurred abroad in the 1970s, though not in the United States (See table 12–3 above).

What follows here may be considered a form of scenario approach. I am not prepared at this time to forecast a rapid increase in manufacturing productivity, and a consequent substantial decline in employment. However, since there is a possibility of rapid productivity increases and significant employment decline, it is important to assess its possible consequences.

Industries experiencing secular declines in employment often develop substantial resistance from employees to technological change that is labor-saving. The United States has experienced this phenomenon in railways, publishing, maritime, mining, and other industries in recent decades. The first indications of such developments on a large scale in manufacturing are now becoming visible. Plans by large companies to introduce robots into some plants are being greeted with suspicion by employees.³ Transference of production to more modern plants in different geographic regions is becoming a focus of legislative efforts by some communities and unions in an effort to slow the rate of job loss. Should the insecurities engendered in employees by rapid technological advances not be relieved, then social resistance to productivity improvements could become substantial.

In autos and steel, employee and community resistance to economic change is currently being answered by the response that the failure to modernize threatens the loss, not just of some jobs, but perhaps all. This is currently a persuasive argument, coming as it does in the context of rapid import penetration and a weak domestic market. But if the domestic market recovers in these industries, then resistance to job loss due to modernization may become more difficult to overcome. This may seem paradoxical, but is not. Extreme stress permits responses which less extreme conditions cannot be made to justify.

On balance, the current position of several major American industries is so evidently poor, due to the economic recession in the United States and due to competition from abroad in our domestic markets, that resistance among employees and their local communities to job loss due to technological change is muted. But this circumstance may not survive a pick-up in demand in the domestic economy. Should resistance to technology become more widespread and active, the country's industrial revitalization program could be severely constrained. For these reasons, it is important to consider means by which industrial revitalization's impact may be cushioned where it threatens to adversely affect substantial numbers of people and their communities.

Industrial revitalization will, in the longer term, benefit all Americans. But in the short run, a successful strategy is likely to impose substantial costs of readjustment on many people. How are these costs to be minimized, and who is to bear the responsibility for seeing that this is done? A failure to anticipate human dislocations due to reindustrialization, and to provide for means to cushion their severity, may well result in a backlash against technological advance itself. Thus, the ultimate success of the reindustrialization effort may hang on the degree to which the hardships it is likely to impose are mitigated.

In the broadest context there are two alternative means by which the human costs of reindustrialization can be distributed. In essence, the matter goes to the issue of job security. Security for the individual employee whose job is altered substantially or eliminated by technological advance can be provided either within the firm or within the context of the broader society. We have come to think of the former solution as that which is suggested by the Japanese concept of the lifetime employment system. In this concept, employees are virtually guaranteed a position with the firm, despite changes in the content of their jobs. Possibly this approach provides the maximum protection to the individual employee; although this can only be the case where the existence of the firm or of a successor firm is guaranteed (perhaps by the state or by the banking community). It is not a solution, however, that recommends itself to an American audience without substantial reservations. In part, guaranteed employment with a single firm appears unduly costly and impractical within a market place as competitive as that of the United States.

Instead, Americans are most likely to look to the safety nets that can be provided for displaced workers by the public authorities and by the companies for which they once worked. The provision of the safety net is an important element in assisting the success of reindustrialization policy. An effective safety net contributes to reindustrialization policy in the following ways:

1. It lessens the likelihood of growing resistance to technological advances on the part of employees who fear for their jobs.
2. It lessens the hesitancy of individuals to invest in schooling and training for occupations when the long-term future of those occupations is uncertain, and thereby it increases the incentives for the accumulation of human capital.
3. It shifts some of the potential burden of the costs of readjustment for employees from the firm (which might otherwise bear a portion of those costs) to the society at large. In so doing, it releases resources for investment by the firms.

Safety nets may have at least two aspects. One aspect is income support. In this aspect, the safety nets operate as transfer, or entitlement, programs. A second aspect is retraining and readjustment. In these respects the safety nets operate to improve human capital accumulation in the nation. Most programs that currently can be considered safety nets for the consequences of reindustrialization stress the former rather than the latter objectives. This is unfortunate.

The Trade Adjustment Act, for example, provides income support for employees certified by the U.S. Department of Labor to have lost jobs, temporarily or permanently, due to increases in imports. The Trade Act of 1974 provided for funds for job search and special training programs. Recent studies indicate, however, that while the income support seems effective, the services provided for retraining and relocation were of little value.[4]

This experience points out one of the most difficult aspects of reliance on publicly provided safety nets. On balance Americans are likely to opt for a system of employment security that does not stress the individual's connection to a specific firm, but rather to opportunities in the economy as a whole. But what is the economy as a whole to mean? Many persons conceive job security as being able to remain in the same community in which they currently live. If security of this sort is to be provided, then an industrial location policy which can reverse current trends becomes necessary. Currently jobs in the United States are migrating to the south and west, sometimes following the movement of population, sometimes in advance of it.

There is no industrial location policy currently in prospect that will significantly reverse this process. In the wake of the migration of jobs, laid-off employees are drawing unemployment insurance, or supplemental benefits, or Trade Adjustment Assistance. For many, these benefits provide a welcome means to continue to live in their current residences, and to search for alternative job opportunities in the local area. Unfortunately, benefits also permit people to wait for recall to the jobs they previously held, even when there will be no recalls. When layoffs are substantial, people may become effectively locked into a very difficult existence, in which jobs are not available, while the weakness of the local housing market prevents people from selling out and following job opportunities elsewhere. As benefits expire, the funds which could possibly support relocation also disappear. In this cycle, income support funds have contributed not to a readjustment by those laid-off, but rather have helped to drive them further into very difficult circumstances.

This is all too common a development in the United States today. It bespeaks the failure of our society to assist people in making the transitions that current economic developments require. It demonstrates that financial assistance alone will not contribute substantially to resolving what are long-term structural problems, involving the relocation of many job opportunities away from current population centers.

Despite the poor record of the relocation and retraining aspects of Trade Adjustment Assistance, these efforts are in the right direction. What is needed is not a retreat into a greater reliance on income support, but instead a much more creative effort to place persons in jobs, including relocation and retraining as necessary. There are reasons to believe that these efforts can be successful.

Federal and Federally-assisted job placement and training programs have been, for a decade, directed at the disadvantaged. They have operated in a very difficult environment. The unemployment rate has been relatively high. Large numbers of young persons have entered the labor force. Economic growth in the country as a whole has been slow, and the areas of rapid growth have been far distant from the concentrations of disadvantaged persons. The record of governmentally-assisted training and job placement has not been very good measured against the problems to which it was addressed. But the difficulties encountered were very significant.

In the 1980s some of these environmental factors will have improved. Economic growth is likely to increase after 1981. Labor force growth, from domestic sources, will slow to approximately one-half the rate of the 1970s. The unemployment rate is expected to decline slowly. The worst of the large-scale layoffs in automobiles and related industries may be behind us. Finally, training and replacement efforts directed at persons who have lost their jobs due to the industrial shifts of the economy will have a different clientele, instead of the disadvantaged. Specifically, those affected by industrial change are likely to be persons who have substantial work experience and possess the work-related social skills which accompany experience. They will be somewhat older than many of the disadvantaged. Their educational background is likely to be somewhat better. As such, they constitute a potentially more successful group in the labor market.

The proper place to attack the problem of the disadvantaged is in close cooperation with the education system. Basic skills need to be developed, and the education system is the best place for these skills to be imparted. The large growth in proprietary education shows what might be done in the schools. The problem of school dropouts can be dealt with at the local level more effectively than through national level remedial efforts in the context of employment and training programs. Programs in the public schools, funded in part by private companies, exist in many cities and provide guidance for other efforts.

It is time to loosen the connection between training and job placement activities and the disadvantaged, and to redirect public employment and training efforts to a broader segment of the population. Programs for the disadvantaged should be integrated backward into the schools, and forward into the companies, stressing the role of labor market intermediaries as facilitators of the transition from school to work, in place of the training and income support aspects of current employment and training programs.

The training and placement activity of recent years has created systems and persons with expertise in training and job placement. This resource should not be disparaged simply because it has not been overly successful in what has been an unduly difficult mission. Systems and people who have learned training and placement in working with the disadvantaged may be able to do a very good job in assisting the displaced workers of the 1980s.

Trade adjustment assistance should not be limited to persons affected by imports. The system should instead stress relocation and retraining benefits, instead of income support. Persons who lose jobs due to industrial relocation, technological advance, or the impact of imports should be able to draw benefits. Unemployment insurance funds should be used to provide planning and programming assistance for relocation and retraining efforts. Unemployment insurance funds have not, on balance, been used imaginarively in dealing with unemployment in this country. Malcolm Lovell has pointed out there is now an opportunity for a more imaginative use of those funds.

The out-placement of persons who have lost their jobs is not solely a public responsibility. It is first the responsibility of the persons themselves, but the companies involved have a substantial responsibility as well. The country has a right to expect business to meet these responsibilities, although it would probably be a mistake to establish any particular requirements by statute. The difficulty with statutes is that all too often the result is that the procedures called for are met, without the substance or imagination necessary to accomplish the true purpose.

Funds are scarce for large-scale public programs to assist the unemployed. Should there be a reallocation of effort from the disadvantaged to the industrially displaced? The answer is yes. Training and relocation programs have done only limited good for the disadvantaged. They promise a far higher payoff with the industrially displaced. On balance (with the exception of public service jobs), training and employment programs have not served as a significant alternative to income support for the disadvantaged. Nor do they give the promise of doing so in the future. In consequence, at this juncture in our economic history, income support programs are preferable for the disadvantaged, while employment and training programs should be redirected toward the industrially displaced. It was estimated above that over the next decade, there will be released on net from the manufacturing labor force some 2.5 million persons. The total number of persons who will lose jobs in manufacturing as industry relocates, and as older firms cease production and new ones start, will be much greater. The magnitude of the retraining and readjustment effort required to facilitate the shift of jobs which will accompany a revitalized, but smaller, manufacturing sector will therefore be substantial.

In the absence of a successful retraining and relocation effort, industrial revitalization may not be achieved. If there cannot be found some job security for persons in the economy as a whole, then there will be very substantial resistance to economic change. The alternative to successful relocation strategies is probably import restriction and public subsidies for distressed companies and areas. While in an individual situation there may be strong considerations favoring such policies, on a broad basis they are suicidal.

CONCLUSION

An industrial revitalization policy must be accompanied by well thought out policies with respect to the human requirements and consequences of industrial revitalization. Specifically, attention should be given to the problems of skill development and potential job loss. Unthinking reliance on the market place and current programs and procedures is likely to make the transition to a more productive economy more lengthy and difficult than it otherwise need be.

Business must provide the leadership with respect to skill development. The private sector of the economy is in the best position to ascertain which skills are in growing need and are likely to be in short supply. Information as to developing needs should be transmitted to the educational system. Further, business should support the school system in obtaining new technology for training to be provided within the schools. A major opportunity now affords itself as many families obtain computer equipment for their own use at home. If the schools are able to obtain similar equipment in order to familiarize students with the use of computers as a learning device, then the combination of home and school experience with the new technology may help to produce a generation with very substantial skills in the new electronic technology.

There continues to be a major role for the universities, despite the oft-heard chorus that American society now invests too much in higher education and sends too large a portion of the nation's young people to college. Even if this indictment were true, technical specialties involving high technology are not in overabundance, but instead are in short supply. When computer technology first appeared, the major companies assisted the universities in defining the specialities in which degrees should be offered in the new technology. A similar need now exists for guidance from the business sector with respect to the development of educational programs and the allocation of resources to them.

Loans to college students to pay for their education are now under attack as an unduly expensive Federal subsidy. Also, such loans are felt to be unnecessary when there is said to be a surplus of college educated persons. But in those areas in which there is no surplus, but instead a severe and growing shortage, as in high technology specialties, there is a strong case for continuing government educational loans as a device to encourage students to pursue careers in the new technological specialties.

Incentives and disincentives which currently affect the decisions of individuals to obtain training in short skill areas need to be reviewed. Unions and companies need to review the incentives to acquire and use skills which are currently provided under labor contracts. Where incentives have shrunk dramatically, they may require reestablishment. Efforts to provide a skilled labor force in American industry should not, and need not, become a matter of adversary proceedings between unions and companies. It would be very unfortunate for the reindustrialization effort if they were to become so.

Finally, the safety nets by which government and the private sector attempt to insulate workers from the adverse consequences of international competition and technological advance require review and strengthening. Public income support programs which minimize the incentives for persons to acquire new skills should be reduced in favor of those that provide incentives for the development of needed skills. In many instances, the greatest advances may be made in conjunction with private enterprise. For example, companies should be prepared to do more for displaced employees in terms of attempting to achieve successful outplacement for them. It is not enough, and it will not further the nation's attempted economic revitalization, for companies to conceive their obligations as not extending beyond the releasing of redundant employees upon the income support programs now administered by the government. These programs, as currently structured, cannot bear the load of such a heavy obligation.

Finally, programs which attempt to insulate workers from the more extreme effects of changing technology and international competition, may, if improved, offer an opportunity by which people can obtain new skills to fit the changing requirements of industry. Such programs should not be viewed simply as entitlement programs which are competitors with capital investment for scarce public and private funds. Instead, carefully designed and operated safety nets have a major contribution to make to the success of industrial revitalization and enhanced physical investment. In this way, safety nets and capital investment become, and in fact are, complements in a revitalization strategy.

NOTES

1. Fletcher L. Byrom, Chairman of the Board and Chief Executive Officer, Koppers Company, Inc., comments delivered at the Wharton/Reliance Symposium, Philadelphia, March 23, 1981.

2. See Gitter (1981).

3. See, for example, "Mixed Feelings," Bureau of National Affairs, *Daily Labor Report* 242 (December 15, 1980): A–1, ff.

4. Corson and Nicholson (1980).

BIBLIOGRAPHY

Corson, Walter and Nicholson, Walter. "Trade Adjustment Assistance for Workers: The Results of a Survey of Recipients under the Trade Act of 1974." Princeton: Mathematica Policy Research, 1980.

Gitter, Robert. "The Determinants of Firm Apprentice Mores in the Construction Industry." Report to the U.S. Department of Labor, Employment and Training Administration. Washington: 1981.

DISCUSSANTS

Malcolm R. Lovell, Jr.

No free society can move vigorously to meet the challenges of a new industrial period without being sensitive to the needs of the workers who have or will become redundant in the transition process.

The bulk of American programs aimed at training and retraining the American worker have focused on the disadvantaged, specifically, blacks, Spanish-speaking, untrained women, and youth, and not on workers with labor force attachment adversely affected by layoffs and plant closings caused by changes in technology, demand, foreign competition, and other forces beyond the individual worker's control.

Some U.S. programs, such as the basic unemployment compensation system, the extended benefits program, and the Trade Adjustment Act and related programs, although providing an important economic cushion, have sometimes discouraged workers from seeking employment in different areas or new industries. In other instances, they have rewarded workers adversely affected by one economic factor, that is, foreign competition, while remaining insensitive to workers adversely affected by another economic factor, that is, movement of industries from one part of the country to another.

National priorities in the eighties regarding training and retraining workers should focus on those redundant workers with labor force attachment. If this is not done, political resistance of substantial magnitude will impede not only America's free trade policies, but also national economic policies allowing free flow of capital to the country's most competitive industries.

Although there are a number of ways in which a policy to encourage the reemployment of redundant workers can be carried out, there are two which the writer believes deserve special attention at this time:

The first approach (which is currently being recommended by the Reagan administration) is to remove the disincentives currently built into the unemployment compensation system. A step in this direction would be to tighten the work requirement so that as time passes, an individual, to be entitled to continued unemployment compensation eligibility, would be required to consider jobs other than at his/her former wage or skill level.

A second approach (which is not now receiving active consideration) is Federal legislation authorizing state unemployment insurance systems to use their funds for other than benefit payments. This would occur if, in the judgment of the governing body, such alternate uses could, over time, help people with labor force attachment currently drawing unemployment insurance to move more rapidly into new employment. Such alternate uses of unemployment insurance funds might include job search allowances, lump sum payments to people moving to different communities and/or industries, and the payment for specified training clearly recognized as a prerequisite for an available job in another industry or locality.

I do not recommend that activities to enhance the employment opportunities for the disadvantaged be dropped. However, I do advocate that a much stricter standard as to the value of these activities be applied, and that the primary goal of these efforts be to increase a participant's earning capacity, over time; not to provide a temporary income transfer payment which might postpone an individual's own efforts to seek a level of nonsubsidized employment for which he/she was qualified or could so become.

John T. Joyce

I would like to concentrate my remarks on seven points that are central to labor union concerns. Not all these points are directly related to training, but they are important. The first several points are keyed to the outlooks presented by Quinn Mills and Peter Drucker. While their views differ somewhat, it is clear that both see what Dr. Mills expressed as the need for an increased level of tolerance on the part of the American workforce for experimental change. If we are going to get that increased tolerance, we are going to have to establish a political and economic approach that has credibility with U.S. workers. We do not have it now, and my first several points really relate to this question of politico-economic credibility. I believe my comments reflect not only my own views, but, based on my travels around the country, reflect an emerging consensus of the workers that we represent.

(1) The economic situation is not as perilous as the Administration and its clients would have us believe, but it is true that both unemployment and inflation are much too high.

(2) Similarly, I think we have an illustration of rhetorical overkill on the question of the "death of liberalism." I neither think it is dead, nor do I believe our economic problems flow from liberal policies. The primary problem, it seems to me, is that excessive reliance has been, and is being, placed on monetary measures and other macroeconomic approaches. Our problem is not a much-lamented general economic malaise, but economic disruptions in specific sectors of the economy. No real attention has been given to the specific sectors of the economy which have been the primary driving forces of inflation: food, energy, medical care, and housing. It also seems to me that to try to cope with those problem areas by dealing with the economy in a general way, in a society as complex and heterogeneous as ours, is a mistake. It is similar to the kind of mistake a doctor would make if he had a patient who had an abcessed tooth, a cracked rib, and maybe an ulcer, and decided that what was needed was a heart and lung transplant. Well, if I were performing that kind of operation, I would toss in a lobotomy as well: If the patient survives, he is going to get well enough to recognize that his tooth still hurts, his rib is still cracked, and he still has the ulcer; I would just as soon he didn't remember who the doctor was.

(3) My third point continues the second in terms of the proposed supply-side solution. Measures like the tax program, and oil decontrol especially, mean a massive shift of wealth to those who are already wealthy. The benefits, if any, to the working people in the United States and the working poor, projected over the longer run, may just be pie in the sky. As to "deregulation," while we need more sensible administration of regulations than we have seen recently, those in the business community who think that American workers are ready to replace government on their backs with big business had better fasten their seat belts because they are in for a far, far rougher ride than they had anticipated.

(4) I think that the whole notion of "government intervention in the private sector" is an unfortunately misleading mind set. In case no one has noticed, governments have "intervened" since the dawn of civilization. It is, in fact, the job of government to govern and the question is not one of whether government should be involved, but rather what the appropriate role of government intervention is to be. That role will vary considerably depending on the situation and the circumstances. As John Dunlop has pointed out, the appropriate governmental role in providing the engineers that we need in the immediate future is for government simply to act as a catalyst. In the case, however, of ghetto youth, the government is going to have to underwrite employment and training. While it is true that the rate of success has not really been that good

in these programs, we must also recognize that we have been dealing with this problem over a relatively short period of time. I do not think we have been looking for the solution long enough. It would be a terrible mistake, having invested so much time, energy, and money providing training and employment for the disadvantaged, to junk the whole investment now.

(5) The welfare of workers, not the efficient distribution of goods and services, has to be seen as the reason for which we have an industrial system. We seem to have our ends and means reversed. We cannot be cavalier about having 100,000 auto workers and 300,000 construction workers out of work because they are a relatively small proportion of the overall workforce. I think that if we continue to run through these alternating cycles of high inflation, countered by doses of heavy unemployment, we are going to see an increasing radicalization of the American workforce, both to the right and to the left. While I do not believe this polarization to political extremes will involve a majority of the workforce, determined minorities can disrupt a society. If we continue in the way we are going the anger, frustration, and fear that I see as I travel around the country is going to get dangerously close to that critical point where it will not be possible to have an industrial relations system in this country as we know it today.

(6) In terms of training, it really serves no useful purpose for us to focus on program specifics today. I think that, as John Dunlop has mentioned, the process is what is important, and we must recognize that in a society as complicated as ours, it is going to require government, management, and labor collaboration in varying degrees and ways in different sectors of the economy. For example, in construction, it does not seem to me that we need government funds to train the average person as a construction worker. If, however, our society and our government, as the agent of society, would like us to undertake part of society's task in providing economic opportunities and on-the-job training for those people that society itself has failed, then the government must help subsidize the necessary programs.

(7) I think that the role of collective bargaining in our economy has to be increased rather than reduced, and that labor may be more helpful than some might think. For example, in our own industry, the masonry segment of the construction industry, we took a look and found that in a multi-billion dollar industry, only about $3 million was spent in a year on masonry research. That is a ridiculously small fraction of 1 percent. So we got together with the employers and signed a national agreement with them to provide one penny an hour, for all hours worked by bricklayers and other trowel tradesmen, to go into a national masonry research and development program.

Collective bargaining can be irksome to both sides, but there are many positive aspects of it as well. I think that with imagination, we can figure out ways to use collective bargaining in order to meet some of the many problems that we all share.

Let me conclude by saying that I would hope that the training and the retraining programs which are going to be needed should be designed and operated so that they will help reestablish in our society the value and the presence of craftsmanship. There are two reasons for this: the first, that the product of craftsmanship enriches our society, and the other is that the quality of one's work can enrich one's life. After all, we do not live to work, we work to live.

SUMMARY REPORT

Strategies for Training and Retraining

Robert C. Holland

The session began with four broad generalizations: First, the panel agreed that investment in human resources deserved major attention in any industrial policy. Otherwise, we shall be running serious risks of production losses, inefficiencies, and social and political disorder.

Second, our panel emphasized the importance of the powerful demographic changes underway and in prospect in the United States over the next several decades: we will be facing a markedly different labor force. Specifically, there will be fewer young people and more old people. There will be a higher average level of years of schooling, and also there will be a flow of immigrants which will need to be absorbed within the labor force.

Third, with good education, training and placement programs, with high rates of capital investment and with other elements of a good industrial policy, our panel could contemplate a continuing manufacturing sector in our economy, employing an increasingly skilled labor force and producing world class products.

We talked not of one labor force, but four distinguishable ones, each with its specific training and job placement needs. First of all, there is the *experienced, advantaged worker.* For a member of this group, a high level of capital investment is needed to surround him or her with advanced technology and make his or her output competitive. For those already employed, further skill training should take place as needed inside the company. In this era of rapid economic change, however, staffing redundancies will develop from time to time. Existing types of work will be wiped out by change. Therefore, we need "redundancy planning," that is, we need arrangements to place the redundant workers in other suitable work assignments—either within their company, within their community, or within their industry, or if need be elsewhere in the economy. We hope to rely first on the company to arrange for new placements of its redundant workers. When that is too big a task for the company alone, we look for tripartite arrangements between government, labor, and management, primarily on a local level, but if needed on a regional or industry-wide scale. For large concentrations of redundant workers, financing assistance from the Federal level may well be called for. (An example of an imaginative use of an existing fiscal structure to help ease the problem of redundancy would be permitting more flexible use of state unemployment funds.)

The second labor force discussed is the *advantaged first-time job entrant.* These are mostly young people, and it was felt that for very many of them the educational system is not providing the basic skills necessary to perform well in the jobs that are available in the market. These workers thus need entry level training, and that is best done on the job. It was felt, however, that it is often uneconomic for individual firms to provide such training because of "raiding." (There is a built-in disincentive for a company to spend much of its resources in new employee training if the skill shortage which encourages a firm to provide training would also tend to encourage other firms to hire away those newly-trained workers.) To offset this disincentive, it was suggested that groups of firms in the same community or industry might share in the training program and its costs. Furthermore, the trainees themselves might share in the costs, such as by accepting an apprentice-type wage.

The third group consists of the *disadvantaged, first-time job entrants.* Though this will be a relatively shrinking minority in the long run, it still presents a serious problem in the short run (of perhaps five years). The panel felt that it is very important to continue efforts to train and employ the disadvantaged, trying to learn from past program failures and replicate successes. These need not be large-scale programs; they could well be at the local level. The consensus was that businesses and unions are the best sites for training since that training needs to be job specific to be most effective. In general, however, it was conceded that most of these programs will probably need government financing assistance. The costs per trainee are typically too high to be borne by business and unions alone.

The fourth and last group of workers talked about are the *older workers,* past 65. They are becoming an increasingly important part of the labor force. The panel felt that it was important to continue to offer them job opportunities so long as their health permitted, though not necessarily in their prime-age jobs. Employment of older workers makes satisfying use of their existing talents, and lowers the net cost of maintaining the old age population. No targeted training programs were proposed for older workers; it was felt that older workers will place themselves fairly well if we strip away the legal, institutional, and regulatory barriers to designing jobs that they can handle and that are worth doing. For example, we need to moderate the tax and Social Security rules that offset so much of any compensation earned by a pensioner over age 65.

Let me conclude by relating our consensus to the framework of thinking set forth in the background paper for this symposium. In only two aspects did our panel favor a general supply-side approach to the problems of training. One was the removal of disincentives for older people to work. The second was in the encouragement of greater capital formation. Otherwise, our panel favored specifically targeted training and placement programs designed to give a helping hand to workers with a problem.

As to the relative importance of growth versus equity as a broad objective to be served, our panel overwhelmingly favored measures for moving people into a position to earn and to produce, rather than simply to receive.

Regulation ☆ ☆ ☆ ☆ ☆ ☆ ☆ ☆

13.
REGULATORY DYNAMICS
AND ECONOMIC
GROWTH

F. M. Scherer

Our panel was asked to analyze the links between public regulation, broadly construed, and America's ability to achieve a high rate of economic growth. In order to determine how regulatory policies ought to be changed for the 1980s, it is important to understand the effects they have had in the past. My analysis will emphasize this point. It is divided into two parts, the first focusing on regulation as conventionally viewed by economists and another on antitrust policy, which is perceived as regulation by lawyers and business leaders, but less so by economists. The issues are in many respects quite different, so my approach to them differs correspondingly. In both parts, the central concern is with economic dynamics, and in particular, with the question of whether governmental intervention in the market place has impaired the economy's economic growth rate or growth potential, conventionally measured. Secondary attention is devoted to the equally important issues of regulation's positive contributions, measured and unmeasured, to economic well-being, and how current institutions might be improved.

REGULATION AND ITS COSTS
Economic regulation, like most phenomena, has had its ups and downs in American history. In Colonial times, the settlers brought with them from Europe what Jonathan Hughes has called "the governmental habit."[1] There was extensive regulation of prices and service conditions for toll roads, bridges, inns, public warehouses and markets, bakeries, labor contracts, and much else. With the adoption of new governmental forms and the freedom offered by a seemingly limitless frontier, these

species of regulation gradually faded away, and the United States enjoyed, during the first half of the nineteenth century, about as close an approximation to laissez faire as one is likely to find in modern world history. But new, large-scale technologies brought abuses and cries for reform, and the result was the emergence during the century's last three decades of "public utility regulation" in such supposed (but not always demonstrably) natural monopoly fields as railroads, gas works, street railways, and electric power provision.[2] Scandals in the meat packing industry precipitated, in 1906, the creation of the Food and Drug Administration, forerunner of much subsequent Federal regulation aimed at enhancing Americans' health and safety. The crisis of the 1930s led to greatly increased Federal government intervention to deal with a host of perceived problems, including regulation of the quantity and accuracy of information provided to investors and consumers. The 1960s saw Federal regulation extended to questions of equal employment opportunity and the control of raw energy (that is, natural gas wellhead) prices. In 1970 the Environmental Protection Agency was created to usher in an era, President Nixon predicted, when America "pays its debt to the past by reclaiming the purity of its air, its waters, and our living environment."[3] With these and many other landmark actions, the scope of regulation, and especially federal regulation, has grown.

Many and perhaps most of these Federal government intrusions into market processes were responses to genuine problems and laudable goals. The unregulated natural monopolies and oligopolies of the late nineteenth century exploited their power to charge high prices, causing allocative inefficiencies, excessive costs owing to excess capacity and deficient frugality, and income redistributions with which the electorate was palpably distressed. Monopolistic price discrimination in favor of large shippers and against the small man intensified support for railroad regulation. More subtle and pervasive forms of discrimination against women and minorities led to later employment opportunity regulations. Economies of scale, the high cost individual consumers incur attempting to compile information on technically complex goods and services, and the public goods character of already existing information underlay many disclosure regulations and procedures to certify the safety and efficacy of such products as pharmaceuticals and food additives. Environmental pollution regulation was the solution to the classic market failure occurring when the entity responsible for an effect bears at most a tiny share of its costs. Occupational and highway safety regulations are in part motivated by a more subtle kind of market failure: the tendency for individual actors in the market place systematically to overdiscount the consequences of adverse events with a low probability of occurring.[4] And finally, a good deal of regulation has been introduced simply because lawmakers have been persuaded, rightly or wrongly, that the consequences of unfettered market processes were somehow unacceptable to the mass of consumers or to specific, well-organized influential groups.

Observers across a broad ideological spectrum would agree, I suspect, that much (though far from all) regulation has meritorious goals. Even then, however, there is a serious question of efficacy: how well are the goals achieved, and how much does it cost?

COSTS: STATIC AND DYNAMIC

Clear thinking demands that the costs of regulation be separated into three categories: redistributions of income, actual resource use and deadweight losses attributable to the misallocation of resources, and the retardation of economic growth. Income redistributions are not costs in the strict sense of the word. Peter may feel badly deprived as a result of some regulatory action, but Paul's joy in being correspondingly enriched may be equally great, and it is difficult to tell whether society as a whole is better or worse off on balance. The costs of resources (for example, for catalytic mufflers, safety inspections, and form-filling) directly required to comply with regulation are straightforward, though not always easy to measure. Also a drain on the quantity of goods and services available for consumption, but still more difficult to measure, is the set of deadweight losses induced by the misallocation of resources, for example, when distortions in the freight rate structure cause a shipment to move by high-cost truck rather than low-cost rail, or when a person loses a week of work because regulation has made some efficacious drug unavailable.[5]

Even more difficult to pin down are the effects regulation has on economic growth. The distinction here is subtle but important. Suppose an essentially unregulated economy can sustain a GNP of $1 trillion at some moment in time and can grow over time at a real rate of 3 percent per annum. Now introduce into the economy swiftly and without friction regulations that, because of their direct costs and allocative distortions, reduce measured GNP by 4 percent, that is, to $960 billion.[6] If nothing else changes, the economy will grow and, within a year and 131 days, it will have returned to the $1 trillion preregulation GNP level. Two decades after the imposition of regulation, real GNP will be $1.75 trillion instead of the $1.82 trillion it would have been in the absence of regulation. The regulations impose a continuing 4 percent burden. Suppose however that, in addition to their 4 percent burden, the regulations also retard the real growth rate by .5 percent per year. Then GNP after 20 years will be only $1.58 trillion—$170 billion less than with costly but growth-neutral regulation. It does not take long for a modest growth impairment to become much larger and more burdensome than the deadweight losses (in our 20 year example, $73 billion) attributable to current and continuing costs.

The key dynamic questions, therefore, are two: Is there any plausible set of mechanisms by which regulation might retard economic growth rates, as well as imposing static burdens? And second, is there any evidence that regulation has in fact had a growth-impeding effect in the United States?

One can certainly conceive of plausible regulation-growth linkages. Regulation might divert research and development expenditures and/or investment outlays into avenues with little measured productivity growth potential. It might reduce profits and therefore the ability or willingness to invest in new plant and equipment. It might deflect managerial energies from productive endeavors into fighting the government or filling out forms. It might enhance uncertainty and hence induce defective or shortsighted decisions. Or it might simply create a milieu attractive only to play-by-the-rules, undynamic executives, as may have been the case in the railroad industry.

Regulation might also have an apparent impact on observed growth rates without impairing the basic long-run growth rate (that is, the 3 percent assumed in my example). This could occur if the regulations were introduced only gradually, each year adding "unproductive" costs or deadweight losses and hence reducing GNP by a partial increment instead of imposing the "once and for all" 4 percent blow assumed in my original example.

THE EVIDENCE

That regulation has somehow impaired growth appears to have been an important premise of President Reagan in his February 5, 1981 "State of the Economy" address. In a context that stressed the nation's productivity slump problems, he observed:

> We invented the assembly line and mass production, but punitive tax policies and excessive and unnecessary regulations plus Government borrowing have stifled our ability to update plant and equipment. When capital investment is made it is too often for some unproductive alterations demanded by Government to meet various of its regulations.[7]

The President is correct in his emphasis on the dynamics of productivity growth as a key element of the current U.S. industrial malaise. Apart from double-digit inflation, to which it is undoubtedly related, the slowdown in productivity growth is perhaps the nation's most critical economic problem. Output per hour of work in the private business sector, which increased at an average rate of 3.0 percent per year between 1947 and 1969, has since then grown at an annual rate of only 1.2 percent. Had productivity continued to rise at a 3 percent rate, all else equal, real GNP in 1980 would have been 21 percent higher than it actually was. This is an enormous shortfall.

However, it is much less clear that regulation is a major culprit. On face, the numbers show that ongoing costs and deadweight losses from regulation could not have made the difference. Even if Murray Weidenbaum's 4 percent annual cost had materialized entirely between 1969 and 1980, which clearly did not happen, it could have accounted for at most a fifth of the 21 percent shortfall. A tenth, or two percentage points, is a more plausible upper bound estimate.

The question therefore arises, could regulation also have impaired the base rate of measured productivity growth? Certainly, the allocation of some investment and research and development funds was affected. According to Department of Commerce surveys, business investment outlays for pollution abatement between 1973 and 1977 totalled $31 billion, or 5.3 percent of aggregate new plant and equipment expenditures.[8] A McGraw-Hill survey reveals that capital investments in safety and health facilities during 1974 and 1975 were roughly 0.8 percent of total business investment. Another survey indicates that business firms devoted 4.4 percent of their privately financed research and development outlays and 0.5 percent of Federal contract expenditures to pollution abatement projects.[9] These outlays may well have displaced investments more "productive" in the conventional sense. Yet if rational capital budgeting procedures were applied, even under the extreme assumption of a totally inexpansible investable funds supply, the projects displaced would have been those with the lowest prospective yields, not the inframarginal projects making larger contributions to productivity improvement. This, plus the relatively small percentage magnitudes involved, plus the possibility of raising new funds for attractive projects at the margin suggests that the impact of regulation-induced pollution and safety investments on the base rate of growth is not likely to have been enormous.

It is also debatable whether the effects of regulation on investment and innovation are *necessarily* detrimental to productivity growth, even if the benefits of cleaner water and air and safer working conditions are omitted from the growth calculation. My own research on economies of scale in 12 major industries revealed that pollution control mandates were the shock that induced widespread scrapping of open hearth steelmaking furnaces to install basic oxygen furnaces and the replacement with more modern equipment of half century-old cement kilns.[10] In both cases, productivity was enhanced as a result. The downsizing of American autos, spurred first by governmental miles-per-gallon regulations and then by soaring fuel prices, will eventually have important productivity consequences: the modernization of plants and tooling that had been allowed to fall badly behind Japanese practice. And in the realm of more traditional regulatory institutions, the participants at a Brookings conference a decade ago concluded that, although regulation probably impeded technological change in rail and truck transportation, innovation had been accelerated in airlines and perhaps also in communications and electric power generation.[11]

Additional insight is provided by a statistical analysis of productivity growth in a sample of 87 industry sectors encompassing 94 percent of all U.S. manufacturing activity in 1973 as well as the agriculture, crude oil, railroad, air transport, communications, and electric-gas-sanitary services sectors.[12] The dependent variable LPG is the annualized percentage rate of labor productivity growth from 1973 to 1978—that is, from business cycle peak to peak. Explanatory variables include the following:

$\Delta K/L$ The annualized percentage change in a sample industry's gross capital/labor ratio from 1973 to 1978.

RDCAP   1974 research and development expenditures embodied in capital goods used by a sample industry, divided by 1974 industry output.

RDPROD   1974 research and development expenditures on products sold by a sample industry, divided by 1974 industry output.

ENV   The fraction of a sample industry's mid-1970s capital investment outlays devoted to pollution control, health, and safety mandates.

The last of these four independent variables, which is included to test the effects of regulation, was estimated from Department of Commerce and McGraw-Hill surveys. Its values ranged from .023 to .230.

With t-ratios in parentheses, the simplest regression containing all four explanatory variables is:

$$(1) \ LPG = -3.36 + 0.361 \ \Delta K/L + 0.995 \ RDCAP$$
$$(0.55) \quad (3.43) \qquad\qquad (2.22)$$
$$+ \ 0.260 \ RDPROD + 3.41 \ (1 - ENV);$$
$$(1.79) \qquad\qquad\qquad (0.52)$$
$$R^2 = .206, \ N = 87.$$

The capital stock and research and development variables have positive and statistically significant coefficients. The environmental investment variable (specified in terms of investment *not* devoted to environmental matters) has a positive coefficient, but falls far short of statistical significance. To the extent that it can be relied upon, it implies that moving from one extreme (ENV = .023) of the observed distribution to using 23 percent of one's investment for environmental purposes led to a 0.71 percentage point decline in annual productivity growth, all else equal. The mean value of ENV was 0.072, implying an annual productivity growth sacrifice of 0.25 percentage points.

The effect of environmental outlays can be tested with firmer theoretical support by defining a new capital to labor ratio change variable $\Delta(K_o+I/L)$, in which the capital part of the change, benchmarked to December 31, 1972 gross capital stocks K_o, is the sum of 1973–77 new capital investment outlays I. With this substitution and excluding for the moment the ENV variable, we obtain the regression:

(2) LPG = -1.96 + 0.431 $\Delta(K_o+ I/L)$ + 1.017 RDCAP
     (2.17)   (3.84)   (2.36)
    + 0.287 RDPROD;
      (2.02)
    R^2 = .227, N = 87.

We now transform the capital to labor change variable by multiplying 1973–77 investment outlays I by $(1 - ENV)$, obtaining net investment INET *not* devoted to environmental purposes. To the extent that mandated environmental investment detracts from productivity, we expect that a capital to labor ratio change variable using this net figure will explain productivity growth better than the gross index used in equation (2). The new regression is:

(3) LPG = -1.89 + 0.445 $\Delta(K_o+INET/L)$ + 1.056 RDCAP
     (2.18)   (3.94)   (2.45)
    + 0.288 RDPROD;
      (2.03)
    R^2 = .233, N = 87.

There is in fact some improvement in the proportion of variance explained; R^2 has increased by .006 relative to equation (2). But the changes are quite small and statistically insignificant. This, plus the statistical insignificance of $(1 - ENV)$ in equation (1), suggests that the effect of environmental investment mandates on productivity growth during the 1970s was at best "noisy" or erratic and probably small on average, although appreciable negative impacts may have occurred in some industries.

A COMPARISON: THE CASE OF WEST GERMANY
An assessment of the directly observable costs provides little basis for concluding that regulation has been a leading contributor to our nation's

recent economic growth problems. There remains, however, the possibility that regulation has impeded growth in more subtle ways, such as by diverting or stultifying managerial energy. I do not know how to explore this hypothesis directly. However, insight into its importance may be gleaned through the indirect vehicle of international comparisons.

My specific focus will be the Federal Republic of Germany, or West Germany. My reason for choosing it is that I know it better than the alternatives, having lived there doing economic research between 1972 and 1974 and having maintained continuing contact with West German scholars and business executives.[13] It seems as good a basis for comparison as any nation, enjoying a level of economic development similar to that of the United States, roughly comparable per capita income, and political and economic philosophies not greatly different from those of the United States.

What first prompted the idea of an international comparison was the observation that my business acquaintances in West Germany grumbled as much about the pervasiveness of government regulation as business leaders in the United States. I cannot pretend to have quantified a "coefficient of grumbling" and standardized it for differences in national culture. I cannot even claim to have made a systematic study of comparative regulatory burdens. The most I can offer here are some systematized qualitative observations. I shall organize them according to the detailed tally of U.S. regulatory burdens compiled by Weidenbaum.[14] Following each heading are his best estimates of 1976 costs in the United States and my comments on the analogous West German scene.

Federal regulation of milk markets ($985 million). Prices for milk and other agricultural products in West Germany (and the Common Market) are supported by the government at generous levels, encouraging surpluses and resource misallocation. A perennial scandal is the "Butterberg" ("butter mountain"), a surplus stockpile occasionally sold off to the Russians at less than half the domestic price. The crop price support system there is like the one the United States abandoned in 1973 for an approach that allows decisions at the margin to be influenced by market prices. It is almost surely more wasteful than the U.S. system.

Regulation of drugs ($213 million). Until 1978, West German drug testing regulations were much weaker than their U.S. counterpart. They allowed, for example, the continued sale of a drug that had been banned in Sweden, Finland, Belgium, Australia, Holland, and the United Kingdom because of its believed thalidomide-like side effects on unborn infants.[15] In 1978 they were substantially amended to lower the threshold of risk for potentially unsafe products. However, they lack the U.S. emphasis on proving efficacy as well as safety.

Automobile safety and damage regulation ($3.7 billion). According to a recent U.S. study, there is "extensive safety and noise regulation" with respect to autos in West Germany.[16] Many of the items on Murray Weidenbaum's cost tally list, with the notable exception of catalytic mufflers, are standard equipment on most, if not all, German cars, which suggests either regulation or the satisfaction of a market test. Mandated equipment standards are enforced through required biennial inspections by the Technischen Überwachungsverein (TÜV). They are more rigorous than any I have observed in the United States (for example, under Massachusetts, New Jersey, and Maryland state regulations).

Occupational Safety and Health Administration ($3.23 billion). Under West German principles of governmental decentralization, federal regulations concerning occupational health and safety (and many other regulations) are enforced primarily by the local *Gewerbeaufsichtsamt* ("Industrial Supervisory Office"). Regular and stringent workplace inspections are said to be made.

Equal Employment Opportunity Commission ($345 million). There is no governmental agency in West Germany similar to EEOC. However, Article 3 of the German Constitution requires that men and women be equally entitled to jobs and prohibits discrimination in pay and working conditions on the basis of sex, religion, political beliefs, and ethnic or national origin. Officials of the local Labor Offices are, among other things, responsible for preventing discrimination in the workplace against *Gastarbeiter* ("guest workers," typically from Turkey, Yugoslavia, and Spain).

Davis-Bacon Act ($240 million). I know of nothing comparable in West Germany.

Regulation of universities ($176 million). Universities are almost entirely public in the Federal Republic. There is extensive governmental regulation and control. Professorial appointments are made under a uniform procedure more elaborate than any I have seen in the United States. Salaries are regulated under a national tariff.

Costs of reducing pollution ($8.6 billion). Population density in West Germany is 10 times that of the United States, leading to intense interest in environmental protection. Through diligent efforts dating back to the 1950s, air pollution has been reduced greatly, and such industrial rivers as the Rhine, though hardly recommended for swimming, are clean enough to serve as a treated city water source. Industrial outlays for pollution control amounted to 4.3 percent of total 1976 business investment—1.3 percentage points less than the U.S. figure for that year.[17]

Consumer credit regulation ($1 billion). Under federal regulations governing all types of price disclosure, banks and other credit-granting institutions must spell out their credit terms in detail.

Transportation regulation: land ($3.807 billion). The railroads are nationalized in Germany; truck transport is private. Regulation of both and their intermodel competition has waxed and waned over time in severity. Most recently, according to Boyer, the Federal Transport Ministry has rejected so many proposed rate changes that the joint carrier-shipper tariff commissions have become "little more than advisory groups."[18] To protect the railroads, entry into common carrier trucking is stringently limited by permit, so that the right to operate a truck is worth $40,000 on the open market. This has reportedly led to resource misallocations and an "easy life" for truckers.[19]

Transportation regulation: air ($1.02 billion). Scheduled intranational air service, except in the Berlin corridors, is provided primarily by Lufthansa, largely owned and controlled by the state. Fares during the 1970s were much higher than on U.S. routes of comparable distance. Without referring explicitly to Lufthansa, George Eads found that nationalized European carriers "squandered" the cost savings from more stable cartelized route structures through generally deficient cost control.[20] With the concurrence of the U.S. State Department, the Berlin routes were "rationalized" a few years ago into exclusive franchises for the flag carriers of the occupying powers; so that Pan American has all the Frankfurt-Berlin flights, British Airways all the Bonn-Berlin flights, Air France all the Paris-Berlin flights, and so on. Regulation may be weaker than it was in the United States until recently, but the problem of abuse is greater. It is not uncommon, I am told, for scheduled Berlin flights to be cancelled on short notice when few passengers are booked.

Federal Power Commission ($58 million). Electric power and gas supply companies are largely state-owned and subject to political control in rate setting. There are few domestic natural gas sources, so the distortions identified by Paul MacAvoy are largely irrelevant. Murray Weidenbaum's estimates apparently include no losses for crude oil price regulation. West Germany had nothing like the U.S. controls system. When the Organization of Petroleum Exporting Countries raised prices in 1973 and 1974, product prices were allowed to rise freely. Low-income families were compensated for the adverse income effect through the social security system. The West Germans have experienced regulatory and judicial delays in nuclear power plant siting similar to those familiar in the United States.

Cable television ($1 billion). The Comanor-Mitchell loss estimate cited by Weidenbaum emphasizes the lessened availability of cable TV owing to prices held high by regulation. In West Germany, there is *no* cable TV providing independent programming. The television broadcasters are nationalized. In recent years, proposals to establish competitive private TV networks have been successfully resisted by the public television interests within and outside the government.

Import quotas ($4.7 billion). West Germany has been vigorously free trade-oriented. What few import restrictions there have been until recently were largely attributable to political compromises made with more protectionist member nations in the Common Market.

Federal paperwork ($25 billion). If America invented mass production, Prussia (for example, Ernst Engel and L. von Bortkiewicz) invented the government statistical survey. The German government, like others, devours paper. The German individual income tax form is at least as complex as its U.S. counterpart. Registration with the *Einwohnermeldeamt* ("resident registration office") is an experience not readily forgotten; those seeking vicarious insight are advised to read Zuckmeyer's classic, *The Captain from Köpenick.* The Statistical Yearbook of West Germany is about as crammed with survey data as its U.S. analogue. Some alleviation of the reporting burden is probably achieved through close cooperation between the German Federal Statistical Office and industry associations.[21] Corporate financial disclosure is less extensive than under our Securities and Exchange Commission mandates.

Any such comparison of regulatory instruments would be misleading if no mention were made of certain special West German institutions. One is the practice of codetermination *(Mitbestimmung),* under which management and workers meet in formal councils to discuss mutual problems and, more recently, labor representatives have been given mandatory seats on boards of directors. Second, worker layoffs and plant closings are much more tightly regulated in Germany than in the United States. Temporary cutbacks must be coordinated with the Labor Office; severance pay and notice provisions for permanent layoffs must conform with the applicable laws.[22] Third, the zoning laws are stricter and more stringently enforced. Plant expansions are often constrained by the designation of adjacent land as green areas. New residential housing is required to mesh aesthetically with the surrounding architecture. Finally, landlord-tenant relations are also more heavily regulated. One cannot simply evict a tenant under normal circumstances; suitable alternative housing must be found. Disputes over allegedly excessive elevation of rent are referred to officials of the Housing Office. Considerable amounts of time and money are spent in attempts by prospective tenants to obtain available rent-suppressed apartments.[23]

From this brief survey, it is hard to escape the impression that governmental regulation and other interventions are scarcely less pervasive in the lives of West German business persons and consumers than they are in the United States. The sum of 1976 U.S. regulatory costs in the fields covered by Weidenbaum's detailed statistical estimates is $54 billion. West Germany lacked substantially similar regulation in fields comprising only about 10 percent of that sum (that is, drugs, equal opportunity, Davis-Bacon, natural gas, and import quotas), and it made up for the disparity with regulations much less common to or totally absent from the U.S. scene. One might suppose that a heavy toll on economic vitality and growth would have been taken. Perhaps so, but it is scarcely evident from comparative U.S.-F.R.G. growth statistics, as the following data on growth rates in real gross domestic product per employed civilian show:[24]

	1950–73	1973–77
United States	2.1%	0.3%
West Germany	5.0	3.3

Similarly, output per hour in manufacturing remained near its 1950–73 average at 5.5 percent in West Germany during the turbulent conditions of 1973–77, while it dropped from 2.7 to 1.5 percent in the United States. If regulation saps economic growth, Germany has somehow found a way to minimize the damage.[25]

THE HOSTILITY DYNAMICS OF U.S. REGULATION

One possibility is that regulation is exercised in a less costly and clumsy way in the Federal Republic, that is, that U.S. regulators do not conduct their business as intelligently as their German counterparts. There is a grain of truth in this, but it misses the central point. That point was brought home to me at an advisory committee meeting I attended not long ago. Discussion among the members, most of whom were business leaders, had turned to the question of strengthening a graduate studies career path for persons who might join the staffs of regulatory agencies. To this the head of a well known corporation retorted, "That's the last thing we should be encouraging. The worst mistake John F. Kennedy ever made was to bring smart people into the regulatory agencies."

Paradox or not, the speaker was right. Business enterprises in America have a long tradition of resisting regulation unless it could be turned to their advantage. Wharton's Edmund James put it graphically nearly a century ago:

> Private companies do not, perhaps, use their works as mere resting places for political henchmen, but they do what, in some respects, is still more corrupting and ruinous in its influence on our policies, they go into the business of buying votes of councilmen and legislators by the wholesale. . . . The . . . gas companies . . . always join hand in hand with every other

monopoly in the community . . . in order to prevent any investigation or regulation of monopolistic abuses.[26]

The ideal, of course, is to have proindustry legislation passed. But if that fails, one attempts to "capture" the regulatory agency, either through superior information or by seeing to it that friendly regulators (or, when all else fails, eunuchs) are appointed. As James' contemporary and co-founder of the American Economic Association, Henry Carter Adams, observed, "Public corruption . . . is no accident. It is the necessary result of the idea that the best thing to do with a public official is to lay him on the shelf out of harm's way."[27]

The sin of which President Kennedy was accused was to install in office Federal regulators who could and did think independently. The practice was continued and extended under subsequent Administrations. The consequence was a scenario I observed many times during my brief tenure at the Federal Trade Commission. An intelligent, highly motivated staff had been recruited. They took their mandate, statutory and implied from legislative oversight hearings, seriously. They identified what they considered to be potential problems and began a study, usually by approaching their counterparts in industry for information. Sometimes they were successful, but often they were not because one or more industry members had organized the resistance and managed to erect a stone wall blocking access to information. On other occasions, they were lied to about industry practices or the feasibility and costs of some proposal. When regulatory agencies are staffed with secondraters, lying is often an effective defensive tactic. But when the regulatory agency staff come from "establishment" schools, they usually have a friendly counterpart in industry and can learn what the truth is.[28] On still other occasions, the staff found their industry counterparts negotiating with one face and attempting to undermine the negotiations with the other by telling a different story to commissioners or friends on Capitol Hill. When these kinds of things happen, hostility escalates, information requests turn into complex subpoenas, proposals for industry corrective action become increasingly stringent or extreme, and eventually someone loses patience and reaches for the only remaining weapon: "Sue the bastards!"

I have the impression that things work differently in West Germany, although the differences are not as great as those of day versus night. Europeans have a virtually unbroken tradition of extensive government involvement in business affairs. They have lived with it, and they accept it. To be sure, business leaders seek to have laws and regulations written that suit industry preferences. They are no more ready to volunteer information that will sharpen regulators' insight into their operations than their American counterparts are. But when a regulator comes forward and asks for information or points to a problem, they are less apt to adopt stonewalling tactics and more willing to sit down and work cooperatively toward a mutually acceptable solution. The result, I am persuaded, is less costly regulation that is more effective in achieving the goals underlying its creation.

IMPLICATIONS
Perhaps the most important implication of my analysis is that we should not delude ourselves. If I am right, the costs of regulation are not a principal cause of flagging productivity, and so cutting back on regulation is not going to do much toward restoring industrial vitality. Rather, we should find where the real problems are and solve them—for example, a deficient propensity to save and invest, excessively shortsighted decision-making horizons attributable to inflation and misguided managerial incentives, widespread primary and secondary education system failures, and the diversion of technical talent from civilian to military research and development along with inadequate and unstable encouragement of scientific and engineering career paths. Focusing singlemindedly on regulation as culprit is almost certain to divert energy away from curing other problems as least as important. And it may create a scapegoat mentality which, when ultimately proven wrong, will lead to backlash effects worse than the disease whose cure was sought.

This does not mean that regulation is a barren area for reform and improvement. There is much bad regulation; many and perhaps most of our regulatory agencies are overstaffed, except at top talent levels; and much can be done to make good regulation less burdensome and more efficacious. The key to improvement lies in enforcing three principles: (1) Regulation ought to be imposed only when a problem widely perceived as compelling is unlikely to be corrected through the natural workings of the market. (2) There should be constant awareness that regulation imposes costs as well as conferring benefits, and these must be balanced. (3) It is results benefiting the public, not the sound and fury of litigation, that matter.

It would be naive to suppose that these principles will be easy to enforce. President Reagan's Executive Order 12291 is commendable in its emphasis on weighing benefits against costs.[29] But the complex formal apparatus it establishes to ensure that regulatory impacts are properly analyzed is hardly cause for optimism. Nor can one draw encouragement from the Reagan administration's backup strategy for avoiding what it acknowledges to be a potentially cumbersome bureaucratic problem:[30] appointing to regulatory agencies officials who are distinguished mainly by their lack of enthusiasm for the regulatory missions of the agencies they will lead. Regulatory burdens may be minimized by doing nothing, but that course of (in)action is by no means congruent with a pragmatic problem solving approach that best serves the public interest.

Principles and generalizations are cheap and worth every penny of their cost. To enhance my contribution at least slightly, I shall be more explicit about some specific opportunities for regulatory reform. The array of possibilities is enormous. My selection criterion will again be Weidenbaum's tally of costs. Thus, Federal paperwork, pollution control, import quotas, and land transportation regulation come to the fore, in that order.

Federal paperwork. By far the largest paperwork cost burden stems from tax record-keeping. It could be reduced appreciably by simplifying the tax laws. Since this is something everyone applauds and no one supports in detail, I pass on to less important matters. Probably second in costliness are the various censuses. There can be little doubt about their value. But especially for the Census of Population, costs could be reduced and accuracy enhanced by moving from a total count to a more carefully controlled sample. Problems may come from the insistence in Article I of the Constitution that there be an "enumeration," even though the "manner" is to be directed by Congress. If need be, an amendment could be passed. It might be the most popular Constitutional amendment in U.S. history.

Of greater interest are the vast array of special surveys, questionnaires, and the like used to illuminate what is happening in the economy and to inform regulatory processes. There is a fundamental conflict here. Bureaucrats tend to place high value on the information they are collecting and discount heavily the costs imposed upon informants. Business firms care much about the costs, but are often even more concerned about the power accurate information can put into the hands of would-be regulators and lawmakers.[31] Stalemates therefore ensue: bureaucrats ask too much and business respondents seek to provide too little. Some conflict resolution mechanism is needed. The mechanisms I have observed first hand worked badly. Neither the Office of Management and Budget nor the General Accounting Office had the technical competence to resolve complex contested issues of burden. On important disputes, OMB is susceptible to capture by business interests, while GAO has shown a proclivity to dive for the cover of reports damning both sides, but dodging the tough decisions. A problem solving approach would be preferable to the present essentially adversary-adjudicative system. Thus, for important surveys, a committee representing data collecting, data providing, user, and public interest constituencies could be formed and given a mandate to devise a cost effective reporting approach. Good will on all sides cannot always be assumed, and impasses might sometimes occur. But I suspect that in more cases than not, better solutions would be achieved than under currently applicable institutions.

One further set of observations must suffice. The confidentiality rules governing much Federal data collection lead to two serious costs: duplicative surveys by agencies unable to use each others' data and the nonuse of data collected at great expense, but unavailable to academic researchers or government study groups. Many of these rules have little or no sound logical basis. It is ludicrous for Census data on corporate persons to be kept confidential forever, whereas source records on human persons are made available after 72 years. Three improvements are needed. First, rules should be developed and codified to establish diverse classes of business information with suitably graduated confidentiality terms for each class. Second, *bona fide* scholars should be given access, as they were in the past, to confidential Census data. Stringent penalties could be enforced to deter breaches of confidentiality. Third, mechanisms should be devised to ease the flow of confidential data among agencies for public information (as distinguished from ajudicative or regulatory) purposes.

Pollution control. Governmental regulation and control of pollution is necessary and desirable is accepted, I believe, almost universally. The difficulties lie in implementation. Specific source-oriented and technology-prescriptive regulations adopted by the Environmental Protection Agency and bodies with similar responsibilities virtually assure that the marginal dose of pollutant eliminated in one situation will cost much more than the marginal dose eliminated in another situation. Thus, the regulation is inefficient, since the same amount of pollution could be curbed by relatively more control where control is inexpensive and relatively less control where it is costly at the margin. Furthermore, because the benefits of lower pollution have not been systematically measured, regulation has been pushed too far for some emissions and localities, while it may not have been tough enough for others. The regulators, to be sure, have a difficult problem. The process is intrinsically adversary. Manufacturers, auto owners, farmers, and municipal waste treatment operators do not like to incur additional costs to lessen their emission of pollutants. Their incentives are wrong, and because they often possess superior information about emission levels and control possibilities, they also have incentives to mislead the regulators. Nevertheless, a better regulatory job can be done by continuing the already evident movement in certain new directions. First, the mandating of specific technical "fixes" should be replaced whenever possible by effluent charges proportioned to the social costs caused by pollution.[32] Second, and closely related, there should be intensive research on the benefits of effluent reduction to facilitate well informed cost-benefits analyses and help set appropriate effluent charges.[33] Third, to ensure that progress along those lines continues, proposals to reduce the technical staffs of environmental regulatory agencies should be resisted. Rather, those staffs should be strengthened. Fourth, to the extent that effluent charges prove impractical, the use of "bubbles" encompassing multiple emission sources, the trading of emission allowances among entities, and the "banking" of current against future emission allowances should be expanded greatly to equalize as closely as possible the marginal costs of lessening pollution from diverse sources. In this way, a higher level of emission control can be achieved, perhaps even at a lower expenditure of resources.

Import quotas. Here, as "voluntary" auto import restrictions are added to the trigger price mechanism in steel and much else, we are moving in the wrong direction. But having said that, I part company from my more theologically pure economics profession colleagues. Trade restrictions clearly reduce the efficiency with which resources are allocated. They also redistribute income toward producers and away from consumers. However, the central theme of this paper is that over the longer run, dynamic effects can be much more important than static inefficiencies. In my view, a primary consideration in determining whether such industries as autos and steel should be given protection is whether the protection is the best way of assuring, and does in fact assure, that basic problems will be corrected so that the industry is able to stand successfully on its own feet without protection in the foreseeable future. In this respect, the Reagan administration's handling of the auto problem and the Carter administration's behavior with respect to steel represented the worst of both worlds: they provided protection without assuring that industry problems would be solved. In steel, the *quid pro quo* should have included agreements on a time-phased program to modernize or close outdated steel works, build modern new facilities, retrain or otherwise enhance the continued employment opportunities of laid-off workers, and reduce excessive wage costs that do much to impair the U.S. industry's international competitiveness.[34] In autos, the package should have included understandings on future progress toward improved fuel economy and pollution control, productivity improvements through modernization, possibly radical restructuring of Chrysler to maximize its chances of long-run viability, and significant attenuation of wage differentials that let the average auto worker earn 74 percent more per hour (including benefits) in 1978 than manufacturing workers generally.[35] On the cases in point here, the horse is now out of the barn. But in the similar cases that are bound to appear in the future, protection should be given if and only if it will lead to changes that eliminate the need for continuing protection.

Land transportation regulation. For some time, economists favoring the existing structure of regulation have been a rarity, and I am not among the exceptions. I applaud the progress that has been made toward deregulation and hope it will continue, despite opposition from politically powerful groups. For trucking, I see no need for regulation of anything other than safety and weight standards and fraud against poorly informed, powerless, individual household goods shipment consumers. Easy entry combined with application of the antitrust laws assure satisfactory performance in other areas. For railroads, natural monopoly may exist with respect to low-value commodity shipments in some geographic areas. Backstop regulation should be retained to deal with cases of severe abuse.

To sum up, there is much room for improvement in the way we regulate. The improvements must come on both sides of the table. Government regulators must learn to balance costs and benefits. Business executives must somehow learn that if they have lost the battle in the legislative forum and must operate under regulatory laws they would prefer not to have, almost everyone will be better off if they accept the inevitable and adopt a cooperative, problem solving stance rather than setting in motion the hostility dynamics identified here. If for political or economic reasons regulation is inevitable—and in terms of broad objectives, as contrasted to details, much regulation probably is—continuing confrontation between government and business is simply not the way to get it done.

ANTITRUST AND ECONOMIC GROWTH

The second, somewhat briefer, part of my analysis addresses the question of how antitrust policy relates to our current economic malaise and what modifications might be undertaken under a new U.S. industrial policy. I confess to some unease at dealing with antitrust in a paper on regulation. In my view antitrust, properly conceived, is the antithesis of regulation: its objective is maintaining markets sufficiently competitive that they will regulate themselves. There is of course many a slip 'twixt the ideal and what actually happens. Yet the ideal is well accepted. During the Ford administration, a conscious decision was made to expand resources for antitrust enforcement as the deregulation program on which President Ford put considerable stress proceeded. Another confession is required: I derived a certain amount of wry amusement from this policy, since I was convinced that, if they could have their pick, the most vociferous business backers of deregulation would have

gotten rid of antitrust rather than regulation. Antitrust is an ugly duck-
ling loved only by academics, the lawyers who make a good living from
it, and perhaps an occasional unusually appreciative consumer.

ANTITRUST AND INTERNATIONAL COMPETITION

It is said by some that our antitrust policies need extensive revision to
be compatible with the more intense international competition to which
U.S. businesses are now exposed. This new view holds that antitrust is
an unnecessary burden because vigorous import competition will do all
the desired policing of prices and quality. Needless to say, there are
many industries in which import competition is inherently insufficient
to have this effect, for example, because of the nontradability of services, high transportation costs, tariffs, or different product design standards. But even in the industries where, by any observer's standards,
import competition has been strong, such competition alone does not
assure pricing behavior consistent with the public interest. This point
is so important that it merits detailed theoretical and factual support.
The steel industry provides an instructive case study.[36]

The United States Steel Corporation was created through a gigantic
multi-enterprise merger in 1901 in a clear attempt to secure monopoly
power. The consensus among scholars is that it succeeded. But in the
antitrust case that resulted, the law went badly astray. Through the
Gary dinners, a strong "follow the leader" mentality was developed
among industry members, and in its role as price leader, U.S. Steel
tended to erect a high-price umbrella under which its smaller rivals
thrived and expanded. This was the most profitable strategy for U.S.
Steel to pursue, for except in its control of superior iron ore deposits,
which it could sell profitably to rivals as well as to its own mills, it had
no cost advantage over rivals. And when that is the case, the theory of
dynamic optimal limit pricing reveals, long-run profits will be maximized by setting prices high and letting rivals take over an increasing
share of the market.[37] Seeing that no rival complained of abusive practices and that U.S. Steel's market share had been declining over time,
the Supreme Court found the Corporation innocent of monopolization
charges. The message sent to industry by the Court was this: cooperative behavior and high prices that lead to declining market control over
time are permissible; tough competition that preserves market control
is not.

Had United States Steel Corporation been broken up in 1920, no
significant scale economies would have been lost, a different pattern of
behavior would almost surely have emerged, and among other things,
the industry's price leader would have been more tightly managed and
cost-competitive than U.S. Steel in fact proved to be. But U.S. Steel

remained intact; it continued to be the price leader; with high costs, it continued to hold a pricing umbrella over other industry members; and with rare exceptions (such as National Steel in the 1930s), the others continued to go along with U.S. Steel's price leadership in one of the most remarkable shows of discipline in U.S. industrial history.

That discipline persisted into the 1950s, when the steel industry implemented a series of price increases that were much criticized for being both unjustified and inflationary, but whose more important longer run consequences were seen at best only dimly. At the time, the European and Japanese steel industries had just finished rebuilding to the point at which they could supply their home demands. The U.S. industry's price increases made the U.S. market an inviting target, and imports grew from 1 percent of U.S. consumption in 1955 to 11 percent in 1965. This had three further consequences. First, imports captured all the growth of the market until 1964, and so U.S. producers had little incentive to make capacity-expanding investments, which in turn made it difficult to modernize the industry's facilities. Meanwhile others, and especially the Japanese, were aggressively expanding and deliberately seeking to realize maximum economies of scale, in the process building what are now the world's most efficient integrated steel works. This combination of developments worsened the U.S. industry's cost position vis à vis importers. Second, bearing this cost disadvantage, the principal producers of steel in the United States, still pursuing a parallel pricing policy, found themselves in the same situation as a group as United States Steel occupied relative to its more aggressive domestic rivals during the 1910s and 1920s. If a jointly-acting group faces a set of rivals (the importers) with lower unit costs, and if the rivals' inroads can be stopped only by charging prices less than the group's full costs, what policy will be adopted? If the group has enough short-term monopoly power to pick and choose, as the steel industry did, the answer almost inevitably is, the high-price, entry-attracting policy. This was done, and imports continued to grow until quotas were imposed in 1969. Third, as a direct consequence of its past choices, the U.S. industry found itself caught between a rock and a hard place. Having established a tradition of industry-wide negotiations with a strong and aggressive labor union that had not yet caught on to the nature of the new game, it found that if it made quick concessions to the union in wage bargaining, its cost disadvantage worsened, aggravating the import problem, while a long strike induced domestic steel users to turn to importers and learn that the products were both inexpensive and of quite satisfactory (indeed, recently, superior) quality.

Voluntary import quotas relieved some of the pressure from 1969 to

1972. One consequence of lessened pressure was relaxation at the wage bargaining table. Steelworkers' average wages (excluding benefits) rose from 36 percent higher than the all-manufacturing average in 1968 to 46 percent higher in 1973 and 71 percent higher in 1978.[38] Competitive pressure from importers weakened the industry's ability to maintain a disciplined high-price front, but did not eliminate it altogether. In 1975, steel makers were hit world-wide by a severe recession. In Europe and Japan, spot prices fell by 30 to 50 percent. In the United States, there was some price shading, but list prices held firm and the average level of transaction prices (ascertained from detailed commodity class value and quantity data) actually rose. This divergence of pricing movements, one (overseas) conforming to the law of competitive supply and demand and another explainable only by the hypothesis of continuing oligopoly discipline, made the U.S. market an exceptionally attractive outlet for foreign steel. Imports soared, leading eventually to the imposition of trigger prices.

There are several morals to this story. First, the Supreme Court's failure to curb the bases of the steel industry's monopoly power in 1920 led to developments that ultimately invited foreign penetration of the U.S. steel market. Second, once import penetration began, it did not quickly elicit a competitive pricing response from the domestic producers. Rather, the continuation of a "full cost" umbrella pricing policy aggravated the industry's long-run problems by allowing costs to rise persistently, by stimulating (absent government protection) continuing import growth, and by ceding to importers the growth that otherwise might have been exploited to build new, modern facilities. True, this train of events ultimately left the domestic industry with greatly diminished, although not vanishing, monopoly power. In the long run, competition does triumph. But in the long run, when an industry behaves the way the U.S. steel industry has behaved, the industry is likely to be moribund.

This point, I would argue, is applicable not only in steel. It generalizes.[39] The more monopolistic the behavior of domestic sellers, the higher the likelihood, and the deeper the probable penetration of import competition into the domestic market. Moreover, it is plainly not true that the threat of import competition systematically curbs monopolistic pricing proclivities. On the contrary, enterprises with appreciable domestic pricing discretion are likely, in seeking to maximize the discounted present value of their profits, to strike a balance between maintaining long-run market position and capturing short-run profits at prices that accelerate the flow of imports. When domestic producers operate at a cost and/or image disadvantage relative to potential importers, the balance tips in favor of a pricing strategy that encourages imports, at least until the import penetration is so deep that no monopoly power remains.

All this suggests a considerable degree of skepticism toward the assertion that antitrust is irrelevant in a world of increased international trade. At the very least, the proponents of such a view ought to come forward with some facts. Until contrary evidence is presented, I am inclined to read the record as indicating that our current difficulties in remaining competitive internationally are, in part, the result of antitrust enforcement that has been too timid.

THE ROLE OF STRUCTURAL ANTITRUST

Antitrust attempts to keep markets competitively self-regulating in two main ways: by influencing structure (that is, through merger law and, when monopolization is found, divestiture) and through rules governing conduct, notably, the prohibition of price-fixing agreements and certain discriminatory or abusive practices. Among these, the structural provisions raise more interesting issues from the standpoint of efficiency, international competitiveness, and growth. I shall therefore emphasize them, and especially the links between structural antitrust and dynamic performance.

Much theoretical and empirical work has been done on the relationships between market structure and technological innovation, which is the most important single contributor to increases in industrial productivity. The subject is complicated, and a good deal remains to be learned. Here it is possible to present only three broad generalizations that suppress many details and exceptional cases.[40] First, it seems well-established that there is no single uniquely favorable firm size for technological innovation. If anything, smaller enterprises do better than their share of GNP might imply in originating bold new technical concepts, but relatively large organizations are needed to carry out some of the most ambitious developments. Second, once one leaves the extremes of atomistic competition or tight monopoly, the rate of technical progress is linked only weakly to the degree of market concentration (that is, whether oligopoly is "tight" or "loose"). Within limits, some degree of concentration appears conducive to the more intensive conduct of research and development and more rapid productivity growth. The behavioral relationships are complex, and market structure is probably not nearly as important an influence as the richness of an industry's science base or such idiosyncratic variables as the quality of entrepreneurship. Thus, in the range of oligopoly market structures, structural antitrust probably makes little difference either for good or ill. Third, firms with a protected dominant or monopoly position are believed, under most circumstances, to be relatively sluggish innovators.

In such instances, structural reorganization achieved through antitrust might improve dynamic performance.

Note however the word "protected" here. It compels two elaborations. For one, the juxtaposition of monopoly with protection from new competition may owe its existence to regulation. Some would argue that this is the most common case. I believe a careful historical analysis would show that American Telephone and Telegraph Company, although a brilliant originator of scientific discoveries, has been slow at bringing into widespread practical use such important innovations as microwave relay, satellite relay, electronic switching, pulse code-modulated all-data transmission systems, advanced PBX designs, and the like. A sufficient remedy in such situations might be the deregulation of new entry, toward which we have already progressed a considerable distance in telecommunications. Antitrust may be superfluous.

Nevertheless, things are not quite so simple. Firms with a dominant (that is, near monopoly) position may be slow innovators when new technological competition is absent, but when a small rival threatens their market share by introducing a significant new product, the incumbents are likely to pursue a "fast second" strategy.[41] They accelerate the development of their own countervailing products, launch them with a marketing effort exploiting all the accumulated advantages of incumbency, and perhaps accompany the effort with pricing tactics and other behavior designed to stop the usurper in its tracks. If the "fast second" strategy is successful with some frequency, it creates the antitrust analogue of Catch 22. To maintain a rapid pace of technical advance, it is important that dominant incumbents be challenged by smaller innovative rivals. But the would-be challenger, seeing how the incumbent has reacted to previous incursions, may come to assess its postretaliation prospects as sufficiently bleak that it elects not to make the effort. If this happens with some regularity, the dominant firm can rest on its oars, and the rate of technical progress will be unacceptably low.

This "fast second" problem was, or at least should have been, a central issue in the antitrust suits between International Business Machines Corporation and various makers of peripheral computer equipment. In my view, the way IBM reacted to the so-called PCMs' entry could have had a major chilling effect on other would-be challengers. I say "could have had" because, as nearly as I can tell, it did not in fact have that effect. IBM has had to face a continuing stream of technical challengers, and this has done much to ensure a rapid rate of technical advance in computers. I am not sure why others continued to try. Perhaps the technological opportunities were so rich and the markets so large that challengers were confident they could do well, no matter how aggressively IBM reacted. It may also be that IBM was sufficiently chastened by the antitrust suits arising from its behavior in the early 1970s, or at least as important, that would-be challengers believed it would be chastened, that the challengers perceived the risks as acceptable. That events worked out in this way was not inevitable, however. At least in principle, a consistent pattern of "fast second" behavior can have expectational effects detrimental to technical progress. It is a legitimate function of antitrust to be concerned about those effects. I know of no more difficult factual and judgmental problem in antitrust than determining when to intervene, and how much to intervene, to ensure that entry through innovation is open expectationally as well as technically.

Other delicate expectational dilemmas must also be faced. If an enterprise is to bear the costs and risks of significant technological innovation, there must be a distinct prospect of rewards. This means monopoly profits, sometimes substantial. A government concerned about motivating technical progress should be apprehensive about tampering with this reward structure. Yet again, the question must sooner or later arise, how much is enough, and might technical progress actually be impaired if rewards persist for too long? That was the central question in the Xerox monopolization case, in which I was actively involved. The crux of the matter was the pyramiding over time of patents. There were Chester Carlson's original electrostatic concept patents, a second generation of patents on basic inventions from development work by Battelle and Haloid, several hundred more patents resulting from the development of the 914 copier, and a fourth generation covering many hundreds of improvement inventions. By 1975, when the case came to a head, xerography had been a spectacular commercial success for 16 years—a year short of the intended monopoly period implied under U.S. patent law. Yet it was far from clear that the expiration of early patents would be sufficient to allow other firms to break through the accumulated improvement patent logjam. The compulsory licensing decree with which the case was settled was, I believe, a reasonable solution, going neither too far in punishing a company whose performance was, after all, praiseworthy, nor doing too little to open up the industry for the new ideas and business strategies that have been prominent in recent years.

It might be objected, doesn't any such action, however judiciously tempered, impair incentive? The answer in principle is plainly "yes." But in antitrust, as in other fields of governmental action, one must be concerned not only with the direction of effects, but with their magnitudes. I very much doubt whether the Xerox action, settled only after the pioneering company and the technology it created were mature, had much negative influence on other firms' incentives to invest in risky new technologies. It would certainly be unwarranted to postulate a tight causal connection between the Xerox case (or a handful of cases like it) and the decline of innovativeness apparent in numerous American industries. During the 1940s and 1950s, compulsory patent licensing provisions were negotiated or decreed in roughly 100 antitrust cases encompassing a vast array of industries. But despite occasional cries of alarm,[42] the United States experienced during that period an unparalleled boom of industrial technological innovation. Case studies, questionnaire surveys, and statistical analyses show little or no adverse incentive effect from the decrees, except for a probable increase in reliance upon secrecy as compared to patenting for certain inventions.[43] Compulsory patent licensing decrees were imposed much more sparingly during the 1960s and 1970s. It would have taken a major change in business enterprises' aversion to antitrust policy risks for the Xerox decree and its few recent counterparts to have had a serious negative effect when much more widespread use of the same instruments earlier had so little impact.

A good deal more could be said about the links between structural antitrust and the climate for innovation. However, space constraints require me to proceed and deal more briefly with certain additional issues.

For one, antitrust could adversely affect the growth of productivity if it prevented mergers yielding economies of scale, or broke up large enterprises in such a way as to cause the sacrifice of scale economies. This is possible, but it is not a necessary consequence of merger policy or divestiture actions. Most mergers sizable enough to draw an antitrust challenge involve firms already well down their long-run cost curves, and there is considerable statistical and case study evidence that, both in the United States and abroad, large-scale mergers have done little on average to improve operating efficiency.[44] The occasional exception can be found, and one might urge an amendment in either the law or agency procedure requiring that scale economy benefits be weighed against the competition-inhibiting costs of mergers. Difficult evidentiary problems would have to be overcome under such an approach. Such considerations are already taken into account informally, and I believe the gains from a formal policy change would be small.

On the more dramatic, but much rarer, question of divestiture following a conviction for monopolization, the only simple generalization is that anything is possible. My own research on 12 industries revealed that the largest sellers, which are almost always multi-plant operators, were often much larger than they needed to be to realize all applicable economies of scale.[45] In such instances, divestiture need cause no appreciable scale economy losses. But there are also industries in which divestiture would detract significantly from the realization of scale economies. In automobiles, for instance, the most one could achieve, without cutting into scale economy muscle, would be to divide General Motors into two parts, and even then, many difficulties would have to be surmounted. It is questionable whether such a reorganization would bring significant benefits in the form of substantially altered conduct. And from my limited understanding of IBM's structure, I am skeptical whether divestiture could be effected without loss of scale economies, despite claims by some observers that the successors of an IBM broken into three pieces would be even more efficient and formidable competitors than the company as it is presently constituted. In my view, it is not good policy to force reorganizations that cause appreciable scale economy sacrifices. If this view is accepted, the implication is that the antitrust agencies and courts should be meticulous in weighing the costs of reorganization against its benefits. It does not follow that structural reorganization actions are never warranted.

It might be argued that judges and bureaucrats are incapable of performing such weighings. From considerable experience studying scale economies and a good deal less observing judges, I am persuaded that the issues can be crystallized in a way that permits intelligent decision-making by all but the least able jurists. Here, however, we encounter what, from my perspective, is a much more compelling objection to structural antitrust as it is currently practiced: the prodigious complexity, length, and cost of monopolization proceedings. The costs of recent monopolization cases indeed constitute monumental waste. But the solution, I would argue, is not to discard the Sherman Act, section 2, because such prolix litigation is by no means necessary to illuminate the issues, and in fact, it probably clouds them. All the parties involved are at fault: judges for not forcing litigants to the point, government attorneys for attempting to cover every conceivable line of attack, defense attorneys for their rational calculation that delaying a possibly adverse outcome is worth far more than it costs, and Congress for not articulating exactly what goals it seeks to attain through structural antitrust. It is rash to expect that Congress will prove capable of solving the last problem. But I see no reason why it could not pass an amendment to the antitrust laws that reads roughly as follows:

> No party or class of parties in a suit alleging violation of the Sherman Act, the Clayton Act, and/or the Federal Trade Commission Act shall take more than 240 hours of court time to present its direct testimony, cross-examination of witnesses, statements of objection, and oral arguments.

Similar, but much tighter, time restrictions are imposed in hearings before the International Trade Commission. My impression from a recent experience is that, like the prospect of being hanged at sunrise, such constraints provide a remarkable stimulus to concentrating one's thoughts. That, rather than benign neglect, is what American structural antitrust most needs.

CONDUCT ANTITRUST

In the reassessment of U.S. industrial policy, one finds much less objection to the mainstay of conduct antitrust: the prohibitions against price-fixing and similar restrictive agreements. It is worth reverting to our comparative theme and noting that West Germany, whose exports amount to a quarter of GNP, takes a hard line toward price-fixers.

Nevertheless, I should like to suggest for consideration two possible amendments to the law on restrictive agreements. One can find circumstances in which the market fails to induce specialization, and as a result, two or more companies end up producing the same product in economically inefficient quantities.[46] This is wasteful, and it may impair our international competitiveness. One way to approach the problem would be a tightly-drawn amendment permitting a rule of reason approach to proposed product specialization agreements, which would be given advance clearance only when compelling benefits are shown, and where sufficient import or close-substitute competition exists to preclude price-gouging. A recent Canadian amendment provides a useful model.[47] Second, some of our industries are going to have difficulty modernizing when scale economies require that new capacity investment come in very large chunks, when the market is growing slowly, and when large-scale replacement of old equipment is complicated by such characteristics as a low concentration and a wide geographic dispersion of the old facilities.[48] In such cases, permitting investment coordination agreements among an industry's members may facilitate modernization. Again, a rule of reason approach is proposed: there should be compelling benefits that cannot be achieved through less restrictive measures, and no ancillary suppression of price competition should be allowed. I am not certain that the benefits of these amendments would outweigh their costs. The number of meritorious cases might be small, and unless streamlined procedures with good access to information could be implemented, the adjudicative and faulty decision costs could be high. Nonetheless, I believe the issue merits serious consideration.

CONCLUSION

To sum up, as I read the record, antitrust in the United States has not, in the past, been implemented in such a way as to have significant adverse effects on technological innovation, the attainment of scale economies, or other variables affecting productivity and economic growth. If anything, its enforcement has been too timid to maximize our competitiveness vis à vis import threats. Procedural reforms are urgently needed to reduce the enormous costs of major cases. The long-standing ban on product specialization and investment coordination agreements should be reevaluated. And finally, the level of confusion might be reduced if Congress were to reconsider on the basis of first principles and new economic evidence exactly what it wants antitrust to accomplish during the closing decades of the twentieth century.

NOTES

1. Hughes (1977), especially chapter 2.

2. Wharton's Professor Edmund James was one of the intellectual leaders. See his monograph (1886).

3. *New York Times,* December 3, 1970.

4. See Kunreuther *et al.* (1978).

5. To keep the argument clear, I ignore here the benefits of regulation. Regulation may, of course, improve resource allocation or otherwise improve economic efficiency, measured or unmeasured.

6. This is Weidenbaum's estimate. See Weidenbaum and DeFina (1978): 3. Some of the asserted "costs" could more accurately be called income redistributions lacking the burden properties emphasized here.

7. *New York Times,* February 6, 1981. A nit pick on the first phrase: The advent of mass production is commonly believed to have been Eli Whitney's 1798 Federal government contract to produce muskets with interchangeable parts. In fact, Thomas Jefferson wrote from Paris in 1785 about a French gunsmith, M. LeBlanc, who was at the time making muskets with interchangeable parts—an improvement about which, Mr. Jefferson observed, "it may be interesting to Congress to know, should they at times propose to procure any." Gilbert (1958): 437–438.

8. Rutledge *et al.* (1978): 34–35.

9. U.S. National Science Foundation (1978): table 4.6.

10. F. M. Scherer *et al.* (1975): 159–160.

11. Capron (1971), pp. 10–12.

12. The source of productivity and capital stock indices is an updated version of U.S. Bureau of Labor Statistics (1979). I am grateful to Valery Personik for providing the newer data. For a more complete exposition of the analysis excerpted here, see Scherer (1981). Similar results were obtained using a less comprehensive sample of manufacturing industries with physical quantity-based productivity indices.

13. For suggestions and corrections, I am indebted to Juergen Mueller, Joachim Schwalbach, Jörg Finsinger, and a business executive

who must remain anonymous. On many facets of regulation in West Germany, see Mueller and Vogelsang (1979), especially chapter 7.

14. Weidenbaum and DeFina (1978): 10–30.

15. "Die Mutter trägt das Risiko" ("The Mother Bears the Risk"), *Die Zeit,* February 6, 1981: 21.

16. Fuller and Saulter (1980). U.S. regulations are described as "very extensive," suggesting a higher level of severity.

17. *Statistisches Jahrbuch* (1980): 541.

18. Boyer (1977): 6–23.

19. *Ibid.:* 6–44.

20. Eads (1975): 43.

21. But see "Kampf gegen eine nutzlose Statistik" ("The Fight against Useless Statistics"), *impulse,* December 1980: 22–24, in which U.S. statistical data-gathering institutions are cited as a model for Europeans to emulate.

22. On the considerable costs, see "Sozialpläne ohne Rücksicht auf Verluste," ("Social Plans without Regard for Losses"), *Frankfurter Allgemeine Zeitung,* February 24, 1981: 13.

23. On the housing shortages that have come from rent controls, see "Angst vor der Wohnungsnot," ("Fear of the Housing Shortage"), *Die Zeit,* February 27, 1981: 1.

24. Denison (1979): 146.

25. Nor is a lighter tax burden a plausible explanation for the difference. Federal, state, and local tax collections amounted to 22 percent of 1977 GNP in the United States. In West Germany, they were between 24 and 25 percent. Social Security levies were 5.7 percent in the U.S. and 15 percent in West Germany.

26. James (1886): 92.

27. Adams (1887): 528–529.

28. An example: My first working day in Washington, I had breakfast with an old school friend who had become vice president of a major corporation. Among the things we discussed was the FTC's controversial Line of Business program. Having come up through the company's comptroller staff, he was able to explain to me the minor problems the company had with the program and how they could be corrected. A few months later one of his colleagues submitted a sworn affidavit alleging that the company could not possibly comply with the reporting requirements except at prohibitive cost. This was a common experience. Even total strangers told one story in private and a much more damning one in public.

29. "Federal Regulation" (1981): 124–125.

30. See "Deregulation HQ," an interview with Murray Weidenbaum and James C. Miller (1981), especially pages 16 and 23.

31. See Scherer (1979): 1–5.

32. It should be noted that, to the best of my knowledge, the West Germans have made great progress in pollution control without sophisticated effluent charge mechanisms. The main enforcement technique is the penalizing of code violators, but closer cooperation between industry and government has probably lessened some of the problems so much in evidence in the United States.

33. To be sure, research cannot eliminate all the uncertainties. My personal preference, and it is no more than that, is that in doubtful cases of possibly severe danger, regulators should err on the side of stringent control. If, for example, fluorocarbons do dissipate the earth's protection against ultraviolet radiation, we may be most unhappy that we waited until the evidence was definitive before acting decisively.

34. On the last of these problems, more later.

35. The wage problem in autos is not merely a matter of international competitiveness and equity toward consumers forced to pay higher prices as a result of protection. High wages also frighten away other potential employers from cities with a significant auto manufacturing presence, thereby aggravating the structural unemployment difficulties resulting from auto industry layoffs.

36. This material is drawn with revisions from my April 30, 1981, testimony before the House Committee on the Judiciary Subcommittee on Monopolies and Commercial Law.

37. On the theory, see Gaskins (1971): 306–322. For a nonmathematical presentation and application to steel, see Scherer (1970): 236–240.

38. When benefit payments are included, the wage differential in 1978 is 81 percent.

39. For additional case studies of autos and large electrical motors, see my testimony before the House Subcommittee on Monopolies and Commercial Law.

40. For surveys of the literature, see Scherer (1970): chapter 15, and Kamien and Schwartz (forthcoming).

41. See Baldwin and Childs, "The Fast Second and Rivalry in Research and Development" (1969): 18–24; and Kamien and Schwartz (1978): 547–557.

42. See for example "Dangerous Victory," *Wall Street Journal,* January 27, 1956: 6.

43. See Scherer (1959), and Scherer (1977), especially pages 35–84.

44. For a survey of the literature, see Scherer (1980): 118–141. For international comparisons evidence, see Mueller (1980), Cowling *et al.* (1980).

45. Scherer (1975), especially chapters 6–9.

46. *Ibid.,* pp. 297–316.

47. See Stegemann (1977): 533–545.

48. For theory and evidence, see Scherer *et al.* (1975): 35–48, 154–170, and 289–294.

BIBLIOGRAPHY

Adams, Henry Carter. "Relation of the State to Industrial Action." *Publications of the American Economic Association* I (1887): 528–529.

Baldwin, W. L. and Childs, G. L. "The Fast Second and Rivalry in Research and Development." *Southern Economic Journal* 36 (July, 1969): 18–24.

Boyer, Kenneth D. "West Germany: Search for *Marktordnung.*" In *Foreign Regulatory Experiments: Implications for U.S.,* edited by James R. Nelson. Washington: U.S. Department of Transportation, 1977.

Capron, William M., ed. *Technological Change in Regulated Industries.* Washington: The Brookings Institution, 1971.

Cowling, Keith *et al. Mergers and Economic Performance.* Cambridge: Cambridge University Press, 1980.

Denison, Edward F. *Accounting for Slower Economic Growth: The United States in the 1970s.* Washington: The Brookings Institution, 1979.

"Deregulation HQ: An Interview on the New Executive Order with Murray L. Weidenbaum and James C. Miller III." *Regulation* (March/April, 1981): 14–23.

Eads, George C. "Competition in the Domestic Trunk Airline Industry." In *Promoting Competition in Regulated Markets.* Washington: The Brookings Institution, 1975.

"Federal Regulation." *Weekly Compilation of Presidential Documents* 17 (February 23, 1981): 124–125.

Fuller, Mark B. and Saulter, Malcolm S. "Profile of the World-Wide Auto Industry." Boston: Harvard Business School, 1980.

Gaskins, Darius W., Jr. "Dynamic Limit Pricing: Optimal Pricing under Threat of Entry." *Journal of Economic Theory* 3 (September, 1971): 306–322.

Gilbert, K. R. "Machine-Tools." In *A History of Technology,* edited by Charles Singer, E. J. Holmyard, and A. R. Hall, Vol. IV. New York: Oxford University Press, 1958.

Hughes, J. R. T. *The Governmental Habit: Economic Controls from Colonial Times to the Present.* New York: Basic Books, 1977.

James, Edmund. "The Relation of the Modern Municipality to the Gas Supply." *Publications of the American Economic Association* I (1886): 54–122.

Kamien, Morton and Schwartz, Nancy L. "Potential Rivalry, Monopoly Profits and the Pace of Inventive Activity." *Review of Economic Studies* 45 (October, 1978): 547–557.

———. *Market Structure and Innovation.* New York: Cambridge University Press, forthcoming.

Kunreuther, Howard *et al. Disaster Insurance: Public Policy Lessons.* New York: John Wiley and Sons, Inc., 1978.

Mueller, Dennis C., ed. *The Determinants and Effects of Mergers.* Cambridge, Mass.: Oelgeschlager, Gunn, and Hain, Publishers, Inc., 1980.

Mueller, Juergen and Vogelsang, Ingo. *Staatliche Regulierung.* Baden Baden: Nomos, 1979.

Nelson, James R., ed. *Foreign Regulatory Experiments: Implications for U.S.* Washington: U.S. Department of Transportation, 1977.

Phillips, Almarin, ed. *Promoting Competition in Regulated Markets.* Washington: The Brookings Institution, 1975.

Rutledge, Gary L. *et al.* "Capital Expenditures by Business for Pollution Abatement, 1973–77 and Planned 1978." *Survey of Current Business* (June, 1978): 34–35.

Scherer, F. M. *The Economic Effects of Compulsory Patent Licensing.* New York University Graduate School of Business Administration, Monograph Series in Finance and Economics. New York: New York University Graduate School of Business Administration, 1977.

———. "Statistics for Governmental Regulation." *The American Statistician* 33 (February, 1979): 1–5.

———. *Industrial Market Structure and Economic Performance.* Chicago: Rand McNally, 1970.

———. *Industrial Market Structure and Economic Performance,* second ed. Chicago: Rand McNally, 1980.

———. "Industrial Technology Flows and Productivity Growth." Manuscript. Evanston: Northwestern University, 1981.

Scherer, F. M.; Herzstein, Sigmund, Jr.; Dreyfoos, Alex; Whitney, William G.; Bachmann, Otto J.; Pesek, Cyril P.; Scott, Charles J.; Kelly, Thomas G.; and Galvin, James J. *Patents and the Corporation,* second ed. Boston: Harvard Business School student report, 1959.

Scherer, F. M.; Beckenstein, Alan; Kaufer, Erich; and Murphy, R. D. *The Economics of Multi-plant Operation: An International Comparisons Study.* Cambridge, Mass.: Harvard University Press, 1975.

Singer, Charles; E. J. Holmyard; and A. R. Hall. *A History of Technology,* Vol. IV. New York: Oxford University Press, 1958.

Statistisches Jahrbuch für die Bundesrepublik Deutschland—1980. Wiesbaden: 1980.

Stegemann, Klaus. "The Exemption of Specialization Agreements." *Canadian Public Policy* 3 (Autumn, 1977): 533–545.

U.S., Department of Labor, Bureau of Labor Statistics. *Time Series Data for Input-Output Industries.* Bulletin 2018. Washington: Bureau of Labor Statistics, (March) 1979.

U.S., National Science Foundation. *Science Indicators: 1978.* Washington: National Science Foundation, 1979.

Weidenbaum, Murray L. and DeFina, Robert. *The Cost of Federal Regulation of Economic Activity.* Reprint 88. Washington: American Enterprise Institute, (May) 1978.

14.

GOVERNMENT REGULATION: PRESENT STATUS AND NEED FOR REFORM

Marvin H. Kosters

INTRODUCTION

Certain areas of the economy, mainly transportation and public utilities industries, have long been subject to economic regulation. Regulation has, however, not historically been limited entirely to these traditional areas. But when other forms of regulation were introduced in the first part of this century, for example in meat packing and food and drugs, they were limited to these specific areas of economic activity. It has been only during about the past decade that regulation intended to further health, safety, environmental, and other goals—social regulation—was extended broadly throughout the economy.

Federal regulatory programs have been extended comprehensively across areas of activity with quite different technical and economic characteristics, and the goals they are intended to achieve are diverse. In its various forms, however, the growth of regulation represents the implementation of a social philosophy that is inclined toward interventionism on a broad scale as a governmental approach to problem solving. The change in public attitudes toward this approach that has taken place, as evidenced by the attraction of political leaders to "regulatory reform" as an issue, seems to be attributable less to any reaction against the social philosophy itself than to questions that arose about the performance of the economic system. Chronic and rising inflation raised the issue to a place high on the national political agenda by the mid-1970s. Concerns about the vitality of the economic system—productivity, international competitiveness, innovation, and investment, along with dangerously persistent inflation—have contributed to sustaining regulation as a public issue.

A growing public perception that regulation might be a source of economic performance problems was nurtured by several developments. The application of research evidence to economic regulatory policy, particularly for airlines, achieved higher visibility through congressional hearings and Administration policy statements. The accumulation of experience with social regulations pointed up many instances in which comprehensive regulations were not tailored to fit particular needs or regulatory prescriptions did not accord with common sense, anomalies that are more or less inevitable in any major regulatory undertaking, but that nevertheless tend to discredit a program. More importantly, perhaps, experience led to a better appreciation of the costs of the newer regulatory efforts. With inflation high on the list of public concerns, government regulatory programs that supported prices or significantly raised costs met with growing disapproval. Increased public interest in regulatory reform developed in the context of the period of extraordinary regulatory growth during the 1970s.

GOVERNMENT REGULATION METHODS AND GOALS

Although there is great diversity in regulatory programs, some common features also extend across most programs. The system of administrative procedures under which most regulations are implemented is one such common feature. Another is the tendency for economic efficiency and growth considerations to be submerged to some extent to procedural and political goals under an administrative process that emphasizes procedural integrity and fairness. Despite these common features, differences among the various regulatory programs are pronounced, and to organize the discussion it is useful to distinguish between those mainly involving economic regulation and those mainly involving social regulation. Even though there are major differences among programs classified somewhat loosely into these two categories, performance can be evaluated and approaches to reform can be sketched out from broadly similar economic perspectives for many of the major programs in each category.

ECONOMIC REGULATION

Prior to the 1930s, Federal economic regulation was mainly limited to the railroad industry, although interstate commerce was subject to the antitrust strictures of the Sherman Act and public utilities were often subject to regulation at the state government level. Federal economic regulation was greatly expanded, however, during the depression years of the 1930s.[1]

The primary rationale for traditional economic regulation is that market power could otherwise be exercised by "natural monopolies" or in markets with few competing firms.[2] The goal of regulation in these circumstances has been to limit the extent to which market power could be exercised by raising prices and restraining output. Price or rate limits are typically set by the regulatory agencies, and rules to control entry and specify conditions of service are also usually established. In establishing permissible price or rate levels, rate-of-return criteria and procedures usually play a central role, although there have been major differences among industries in the application of these concepts and procedures. Traditional economic regulation of transportation and public utilities industries can be discussed in this framework, although price regulation in a variety of other forms has also been practiced in other sectors of the economy.

In many of the industries subject to traditional economic regulation, varying degrees of competition are present and the potential for exercise of market power is also a matter of degree. Some industries, such as airlines and trucking, include several firms competing in the same markets. In other industries, such as oil pipelines, competing lines or transport modes exist. Economic regulation has often been applied to markets in which there is significant competition.

Regulatory processes based on a natural monopoly rationale have systematically malfunctioned in markets where extensive competition prevails. Price regulation in industries with several competing firms has induced competition in various dimensions of service quality, retarded innovation, and contributed in other ways to inefficiency. Higher costs and higher prices to consumers, for less favored combinations of services than would be offered under competition, have resulted under regulation. The idea that performance under competitive conditions cannot be improved by regulation is straightforward in theory. The significance of this point for economic regulation is that systematic malfunction has been confirmed in practice by research evidence.[3] This research consensus has shifted the presumption that performance might be improved by economic regulation to a much more limited range of circumstances in which competition in one form or another is lacking.

Increased attention has also been given in analyses of regulatory performance to changes in competitive circumstances over time. Thus, for example, the rapid introduction of new technology has contributed to a recognition of the obsolescence of traditional regulatory approaches to broadcasting, communications and data processing, and financial transactions. While detailed empirical examination of markets can often reveal significant competition from close substitutes or potential new sources, in some markets, such as natural gas pipelines or electrical power distribution, services may be provided by only a single firm.

Market power, even for these examples, may be limited by competition between them or from other energy sources, but for markets served by a single firm, possibilities for improving performance are more favorable and potential for introducing inefficiency less serious than in markets with several competing firms.

REFORM OF ECONOMIC REGULATION

The implication for reform of the preceding discussion is deregulation in markets that would be competitive if regulation were removed. Deregulation efforts should, consequently, be premised on careful analyses in each case of the degree of actual and potential competition. Where competition is adequate, deregulation could be expected to provide a range of services more consistent with consumer wants at lower prices than under regulation, as well as providing industry with more flexibility in adapting to market change.

Considerable progress has been made in initiating deregulation efforts. Federal legislation has been enacted that permits increased flexibility on the way to substantial deregulation for airlines, trucking, and railroads, and that gradually lifts ceilings on natural gas prices and interest rates. Crude oil price ceilings were removed entirely in January, 1981. Several initiatives to loosen regulation of communications and broadcasting have been taken by the Federal Communications Commission (FCC), much like what had occurred earlier at the Civil Aeronautics Board (CAB) and the Interstate Commerce Commission (ICC).[4] These developments should not, however, be viewed as indicating that most of the reforms that are worth making in the economic regulatory area have already been completed.

Although notable progress has been made, much remains to be done. Agency initiatives, which played a critical role in stimulating legislative action in the case of the CAB and ICC, will also be critical under the newly enacted legislation to assure that adequate scope for competition is introduced. In other areas, such as intercity buses and ocean shipping, little agency or legislative activity has begun. New legislation in communications and natural gas regulation will be necessary to permit an enlarged role for the market in those areas. In addition to reforms at the Federal level, however, complementary actions at the state and local levels have a significant role to play. State public utility commissions and local authorities are actively involved in regulation of trucking, buses, and railroads as well as various utilities. Realization of the full potential of reform will depend on whether these regulatory bodies also initiate reforms and make changes complementary to Federal reforms or whether they instead take actions that partially negate reforms at the Federal level.

Although there is more experience and more research evidence to serve as a basis for evaluating performance in economic regulation than in social regulation, many questions remain about transitions to unregulated markets. Indeed, some of the most noticeable and politically sensitive consequences of deregulation may be those associated with such transitions. The most useful and relevant experience at this point is that of the airline industry, although other more limited instances of price deregulation have occurred.

By most measures of domestic airline industry performance—service, rates, costs, and productivity, for example—the air passenger fare and entry deregulation experiment has proved to be successful.[5] Passenger fares declined during the early part of the transition in 1977 and 1978. Traffic growth and operating profits were healthy, but this favorable performance was supported by the general expansion in the economy. Although fares subsequently rose substantially in the face of general price increases averaging more than 10 percent (and much larger fuel price increases), on average they had risen less by 1980 than would be implied by the regulatory fare formulas, and productivity growth under deregulation resulted in a significantly smaller rise in fares than in indices of input costs.

The transition to an unregulated market was accompanied by considerable restructuring of routes and fares, but few communities apparently suffered loss of service without satisfactory replacement, and smaller communities have been supplied with service by commuter airlines at lower subsidy costs than were incurred under regulation. Industrial structure has been affected by merger activity, but such effects have been offset by new entrants in many markets. The maintenance of vigorous competition in air passenger service in the transition to deregulation provides no reason to expect that adequate competition could not be sustained if economic regulation were removed from other industries, such as trucking.

For industries in which markets are served by a single firm, deregulation may not be appropriate as an approach to reform. Reforms of a somewhat different character are necessary, however, in those areas where regulation is continued because competition is lacking. Although the regulatory process applied in these industries has been quite stable, neither the economic impact of the process nor its effects on industry performance have remain unchanged. Rising inflation has introduced cost squeezes in several industries subject to traditional regulation because of the lag between higher costs incurred and rate-setting decisions, and as a result rate adjustments have often been outdated by the time they were granted. The stable rate-setting process (even when more frequent adjustments are taken into account) did not fully accomodate the increasingly rapid rise in costs, particularly in view of disproportionately large energy price increases and the sluggish growth in demand that resulted. The impact on industry performance of traditional economic regulation changed after the mid-1960s, even though the process itself underwent only moderate (mainly accommodating) change.[6]

In order to finance new investment to maintain and expand service, rate-setting practices will need to be accommodated more fully to a high inflation, high interest rate environment. Some relief could be provided by tax changes, such as more rapid depreciation. Because investments in the public utilities industry are relatively long lived, historical cost depreciation procedures have had particularly pronounced effects on real after-tax returns on such investments, since the real value of depreciation deductions has eroded rapidly under high inflation. While changes in the regulatory process and the tax code to more fully accomodate an inflationary environment can make a contribution to encouraging investment in industries subject to traditional economic regulation, such changes would, of course, be second best solutions compared to actually achieving lower inflation in the economy as a whole.

Areas of economic regulation that are somewhat outside the traditional mode include those that set price supports for agricultural commodities, insurance rate regulation, and rent controls. Even in these areas, however, production costs are typically taken into account, although in ways that differ from those based on cost-of-service and rate-of-return proceedings. Regulation of wages departs more significantly from the traditional mode, because rate levels are obviously set on the basis of considerations other than costs of producing labor services, such as equity, fairness, or income concerns. These latter considerations, of course, have also been important factors influencing the existence of more traditional types of economic regulation, and particularly the structure of rates established by economic regulatory agencies.

When income distribution concerns are a primary element in the rationale for price or wage regulation, questions that should be addressed are whether the desired effects on income distribution are in fact being attained, whether they are worth the costs induced by regulatory inefficiency, and whether the desired distributional effects could be more effectively achieved in other ways. In the case of oil price regulation, for example, analysis has indicated that income distribution effects were not commensurate with the large costs induced by the regulations.[7] Federal minimum wages have been shown to be an extremely inefficient policy as an effort to achieve a more equal distribution of income.[8] The case for prevailing wage regulation, such as the Davis-

Bacon Act, has not been made in terms of income distributional considerations, since it is applicable to relatively high-wage construction labor.[9] The general conclusions supported by research on these areas of economic regulation are that they frequently make little or no contribution to more equal distribution of income, that favorable effects that are realized do not justify the substantial costs of these regulatory policies, and that preferable, less costly policies can be applied to achieve comparable income distributional effects.

SOCIAL REGULATION

Social regulation can be distinguished from economic regulation in several ways. It is first of all in the social regulation area that growth has been most pronounced during at least the past decade. The most important and visible of the new agencies created during the 1970s were the Environmental Protection Agency (EPA) and the Occupational Safety and Health Administration (OSHA), but others were created and regulatory activity was greatly expanded in environmental, health, safety, and employment areas.[10]

Second, the rationales for social regulation are quite different from those for economic regulation. For important components of social regulation the underlying rationale is externalities. This market imperfection rationale implies that excessive use is made of "free" or underpriced resources, (such as air and water) for disposal of unwanted by-products of production operations. Because the full social costs of production are not reflected in prices, production and consumption are also excessive compared to levels if full costs were paid by consumers. Inadequate information is the main rationale for another important class of social regulations. Problems of this sort to which regulation has been addressed include: lack of awareness of possible hidden hazards (such as exposure to toxic substances in the workplace or dangers in product usage), inability of consumers to assess risks (such as potential side effects of drugs), and difficulties consumers face in comparing information expressed on different bases (such as effective interest rates on consumer loans, warranty provisions, or provisions of life insurance policies). Effective market performance depends, of course, on well informed decisions, but costs need to be incurred for both production and acquisition of information. Other explicit or implicit rationales include income distribution concerns or fostering equitable treatment in the case of antidiscrimination and pension regulation.

Third, the goals of social regulation, although they are often difficult to measure, are in many instances expressed in absolute and unqualified language in enabling legislation. The difficulty in specifying and measuring goals has led to a regulatory preoccupation with the methods and mechanisms for achieving them (such as detailed equipment specifications or quotas), instead of monitoring of the goals themselves and installing incentives to further them. These regulatory methods have, in turn, made social regulation far more intrusive than has been typical in economic regulation. The absence of carefully specified qualifications concerning the extent or limits to which goals should be pursued in legislation establishing single mission agencies has, on the other hand, resulted in too little attention paid to the costs occasioned by the regulations.[11]

Fourth, much of the real resource costs of social regulatory programs is incurred outside the budget of the regulatory agency. Developing, writing, and enforcing the regulations are often low cost activities compared to the costs incurred by economic units to comply with them. Moreover, the magnitude of compliance costs is subject to no explicit limit and agencies have little incentive to economize on such costs (except, of course, when the economic viability of an industry becomes threatened).

Although substantial deregulation is the obvious prescription for reform of economic regulation where adequate competition is present, deregulation for social regulatory programs intended to mitigate the effects of externalities would be "throwing out the baby with the bathwater." In principle, price incentives could be designed to remedy the market imperfection, but this approach has by and large not been followed. Implementation of such an approach would admittedly not be simple in practice, and realistic reform approaches are consequently usually more complex than for many areas of economic regulation. For social regulatory programs based on rationales other than externalities, still other prescriptions are appropriate.

COSTS OF SOCIAL REGULATION

Estimates of the costs of regulation can be developed and presented in various ways. Cost estimates have been based on resources used to comply with regulation, and efforts have been made to estimate in addition costs attributable to inefficiency induced by regulation. Estimates of annual costs have been developed, and such estimates have sometimes been translated into implications for production and income levels in the economy.[12]

Cost estimates discussed here will be limited to those for two major classes of social regulation, environmental and worker safety and health regulation. A large share of overall regulatory costs is accounted for by programs in these areas, and estimates of resources directly devoted to compliance are available. These costs quite clearly represent real resource costs to the economy, although the estimates are, of course, subject to a range of uncertainty. For many areas of economic regulation, on the other hand, it is difficult to separate real resource costs from components of costs that represent transfers between groups in the economy. For most of the other areas of social regulation, such as equal employment or pension regulation, only fragmentary information is available on costs. Estimates of regulatory costs incurred and financed by government are available for a broad range of regulatory programs,[13] but particularly for many social regulatory programs, these are only a small fraction of total costs to the economy.

Information available on environmental regulatory costs indicates that at least $50 billion in resources is being devoted annually to abatement of air and water pollution and solid waste disposal.[14] Some three-fifths of these environmental regulatory costs have been incurred for air pollution abatement, and about half of these air pollution abatement costs have been for stationary sources. Costs for worker safety and health regulation have apparently been considerably smaller than for environmental regulation, perhaps in the range of 10 percent to 20 percent, currently $5 to $10 billion annually.[15] Significant fractions of total new business investment have been required for compliance in both of these areas of regulations. About 2 percent of investment has been devoted to safety and health regulation in recent years, while for environmental regulation the fraction has declined somewhat to the 4 percent to 5 percent range.

These cost estimates are based on outlays made by business firms and other units for compliance. Conceptually, these cost estimates can be viewed as representing real resource costs, and although all of the costs of regulation are not accounted for by estimates based on outlays, this information can be used to assess the effects of these regulations on measures of economic performance such as productivity.

Estimates of the effects on productivity of environmental and workplace safety and health regulation have been made by Edward Denison.[16] According to his estimates, measured productivity growth was reduced by about a third of a percentage point annually from 1973 to 1976, with these effects tapering off somewhat after the mid-1970s, even though the amount of resources devoted to compliance with regulation continued rising. These estimates were derived by a two step procedure. First, the components of labor and capital services that reduce measured productivity (because the resource costs are not translated into higher real final output) were distinguished from components that do not reduce measured productivity (because the resource costs are already reflected in higher real final output measures). Second, estimates of productivity effects were based on the amount of labor and capital services diverted *from* production activities that would lead to higher measured output *to* regulation-induced activities which were necessary to comply with the regulations, but which would not be reflected in higher measured output.

Two implications of this approach to estimating effects of these regulatory programs on productivity growth are worth noting. First, if more resources were diverted to compliance with regulatory standards because of an inefficient regulatory process than would have been necessary to achieve comparable results in terms of pollution abatement and risk reduction, part of the estimated reduction in productivity could have been avoided. Second, the actual effects on productivity growth may have been larger than the estimates suggest if inefficiency induced by the regulatory process was important. Both of these aspects of social regulation will be discussed in sections that follow.

THE PRACTICE OF SOCIAL REGULATION

To assess how well social regulation has performed and to identify reasons for performance failure, it is useful to examine how regulation has been implemented in practice. Regulation of air pollution abatement from stationary sources provides a useful example. This program, first of all, accounts for a very large component of overall regulatory costs. Second, many of the problems that extend across a wide range of social regulatory programs can be illustrated by analyzing air pollution regulation.

Clean Air Regulation The broad outlines of air pollution abatement regulation will first be sketched out to reveal the main concepts employed. The National Ambient Air Quality Standards define "acceptable" air quality levels for six specific pollutants. The primary standards are developed with reference to effects on human health. These standards serve to divide the various areas of the country into two categories with respect to each pollutant, those that meet the standards being "attainment" areas and those that do not being "nonattainment" areas. Different technological requirements for compliance are applied to each category, and different technological requirements are also applied to existing production operations than to new investment or major modifications of existing sources. More stringent standards are applied in nonattainment than in attainment areas and for new than for existing sources of emissions. The broad structure of the system is illustrated schematically in figure 14–1, along with the technological standards that are applied.

Areas in nonattainment status for one or more pollutants are estimated to include over half the population of the United States. Areas in attainment status are also subject to regulations that limit permissible

FIGURE 14–1
General Structure of Clean Air Regulation for Stationary Sources

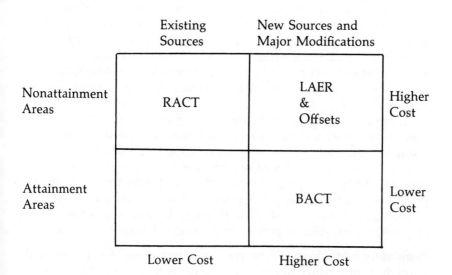

RACT = Reasonably Available Control Technology
LAER = Lowest Achievable Emission Rate
BACT = Best Available Control Technology

- In order of relative stringency, the technology requirements can be arranged as:

    LAER ≥ BACT ≥ RACT

- Other relevant technological requirements are NSPS (New Source Pollution Standards) and BART (Best Available Retrofit Technology).

degradation of ambient air quality, the so-called Prevention of Significant Deterioration process (PSD). There are, in addition, standards for hazardous pollutants, such as lead and asbestos, established under the section of the Act requiring national emissions standards for hazardous air pollutants.[17]

From an economic point of view, the imposition of these technological requirements represents a partial withdrawal of emission rights that were previously exercised by existing sources in nonattainment areas. For potential new investment, they represent capital and operating cost commitments in excess of those that need to be made by existing production operations. The regulatory system confers "squatters rights" in varying degrees on existing production operations, at least compared to new sources. In nonattainment areas, potential new sources not only need to meet more stringent standards, but they also need to arrange for and finance offsets—actual reductions for the same pollutant in the same area from other sources. The higher capital and operating costs entailed for new sources and in nonattainment areas creates economic incentives similar to differentially higher taxes applied to these circumstances.

There is, of course, a certain logic to this pattern of cost differentials. More stringent standards for areas with more pollution take into account, at least qualitatively, the greater reduction in potential harm in such areas for a given amount of emissions abatement. More stringent standards for new sources, on the other hand, take into account the presumably higher costs for retrofitting than for installation in new production facilities. Nevertheless, this regulatory system falls far short of producing an efficient pattern of pollution abatement activity.

Regulatory Inefficiency A program to reduce emissions of unwanted byproducts of production processes into the surrounding air necessarily involves costs as compared to a situation in which emissions disposal is free or underpriced. It is not the imposition of costs, but instead the fact that such costs are excessive that is subject to criticism. Excessive costs, moreover, are not isolated occurrences resulting from inevitable occasional management failures, but rather the systematic result of the regulatory process. This is illustrated in the case of clean air regulation, but many of the features of this system are also applicable to other areas of social regulation.

The way the standards are used to distinguish between attainment categories (and corresponding regulatory requirements that need to be met) is an extremely crude approach to the design of regulatory requirements that express a willingness to spend more for pollution abatement in areas where potential for harm is more severe. Areas that fail to meet the standards by a wide margin would presumably experience considerably more reduction in potential harm from a specified reduction in emissions than those marginally above the standards, and the same logic applies to cleaner areas. Classification only by attainment or nonattainment status (with some qualifications) is an inefficient approach compared to a process in which finer gradations of health risk were taken into account.

Relaxing the air quality standards would be an obvious way to reduce regulatory costs. In view of the evidence as it relates to human health, a case could be made for relaxation in many instances. An even stronger case could be made for modifying the "threshold" and "margin of safety" rationale that currently underlies standard-setting in order to take risks and risk differentials more explicitly into account. The discussion that follows will proceed on the basis of a given set of standards, however, in order to distinguish between relaxation of goals and more efficient achievement of given goals.

The stricter effective standards applied to new sources than to existing plants raises capital and operating costs for new entrants. New investment and modernization that could result in improved productivity are discouraged by pollution abatement costs that are higher than for existing plants. Existing plants are, of course, given a degree of protection from competition by strict new source requirements, and shutdowns and geographic shifts are discouraged to some degree. But older, less efficient, and more heavily polluting plants tend to be kept in operation longer and used more intensively, which can lead to pollution levels that are higher in the interim than if the regulatory hurdle for new investment were lower.

The major problem with the current system is that regulatory activity is not directed toward the offending emissions themselves. It is directed instead toward prescribing detailed specifications for technology to be installed and operated, generally for each source of emissions within a production facility. The main focus in prescribing acceptable technology is on achievement of emission reductions at each source, and indeed this focus is strongly suggested by statutory language. As a consequence, under the equipment specifications prescribed by the standards, differences in costs per physical unit of particular emissions abated are extremely large. Costs per unit of emission reduction achieved that differ by a factor of 100 or more have been estimated, and cost differences by a factor of 10 or 20 among sources within a plant for large quantities of a particular pollutant have apparently been quite common.[18]

These cost differences per unit of pollution abatement mean excessive costs for a given overall level of emission reduction for a given plant or production facility. In addition, unit costs differ widely among plants and among industries. According to studies in which these data have been analyzed, cost savings in the range of 25 percent to 50 percent could frequently be made by marginal cost equalization within plants (depending on the industry and the scope of tradeoffs permitted) within an overall emission ceiling. Tradeoffs among plants and industries would permit even larger cost savings.[19]

There are several reasons for this systematic regulatory failure. The agency personnel developing the standards have little incentive to analyze costs and virtually no encouragement in their legislative mandate to take costs into account. Even if those developing the standards were charged with taking costs into account, defining reasonably effective and economical technology for a half dozen different pollutants, for thousands of sources, in hundreds of plants, in scores of industries, in all areas of the country is inherently a difficult task. The requisite information would be difficult to assemble in the necessary quantity and detail for any agency not intimately familiar with the scientific, technical, and economic data that are dispersed throughout the country. Moreover, the requisite information is, in general, not available for the most effective and economical processes, discovery is a more apposite procedure than estimation. The current regulatory system, however, fails to generate incentives for discovery of such processes.

Other Social Regulatory Programs Legislation establishing social regulatory programs provides for varying and frequently inconsistent degrees of protection for workers or the general populace. In many cases the degree of protection is simply a byproduct of the regulatory treatment applied under the legislation and regulation. Thus, under clean air regulation, health-based ambient standards are set, but for areas well within attainment of such standards stringent technological requirements still need to be met for new investment. Workplace safety and health standards established on the basis of engineering and economic feasibility, an approach that the Supreme Court has decided is consistent with the legislative language,[20] imply levels of protection that vary with "feasibility." Water pollution abatement legislation sets as a goal "zero discharge." And food additives for which evidence of carcinogenicity is developed must be prohibited, no matter how small the risks or how they compare with those from naturally-occurring ingredients.

These disparate approaches to the treatment of benefits under social regulatory programs have not been conducive to establishing realistic and reasonable priorities. Priorities have not been based on analysis of areas where risks were high or where pollution problems were most severe, or problem areas where improvements could be secured at lowest costs. The consequence has been high cost solutions prescribed to secure improvements in some relatively limited areas of economic activity while opportunities for obtaining more widely diffused and less costly improvements in other problem areas were foregone.

The emphasis on technological and equipment installation remedies prescribed for stationary source air pollution abatement regulation is also applicable to the regulatory program for mobile sources. As in the case of technology to improve air quality, wide differences in costs per unit of improvement have been estimated for different industrial processes and levels of technology for water pollution abatement.[21] Standards established by the National Highway Transportation Safety Administration (NHTSA) to improve automobile safety have also been strongly oriented toward installation of specific equipment, such as proposed air bags or other passive restraints, and costs for given improvements in safety have varied considerably.[22] Extensive and detailed equipment specifications have been established by OSHA, but there is little evidence that these standards have contributed significantly to improved workplace safety.[23] In summary, standards prescribing technological remedies have been a common feature of many social regulatory programs, but in many cases the effectiveness of these remedies has been quite limited and the remedies have usually not been cost effective approaches to achieving the goals of the programs.

The application of more stringent requirements to new production processes or products than to those already in existence extends water pollution abatement regulation as well as clean air regulation. A similar disparity in treatment occurs under auto safety and fuel economy regulation. Regulation of safety and effectiveness of drugs is another example. New investment and development of new products have accordingly been discouraged. Overall pollution and risk levels have as a result sometimes been higher than would have occurred if differentially stringent standards had not been applied, while opportunities for lower cost improvements have sometimes been foregone.

Regulations intended to deal with problems involving potentially hazardous chemical substances are only in the introduction phase. These include regulation of exposure to chemicals in the workplace by OSHA and regulation by EPA under the Toxic Substances Control Act and the Resource Conservation and Recovery Act. Since introduction of regulations in this area is at an early stage, there is little experience with their effects. Some aspects of the regulatory process that require testing and approval of industrial chemicals before marketing and use are similar to the process applied to drugs, with new chemicals and new uses subject to more stringent scrutiny than those already in use, but which may pose similar risks.[24]

Considerable evidence on the effects of regulation on innovation in drug development is available, in part because changes in regulation over time and differences among countries have facilitated research in this area. This research has produced strong evidence that regulation has had adverse effects on innovation. Development of fewer drugs and delays in their introduction for general usage have been the adverse side effects of regulations intended to assure their safety and effectiveness.[25] The potential for discouraging innovation in the industrial chemicals area should be recognized in our emerging efforts to reduce the risks of harm from new chemicals that turn out to be hazardous to health.

REFORMING REGULATION
Many different techniques have been proposed to reform the management and implementation of regulation.[26] Most of these approaches can be characterized as either intended to rationalize and improve the management of regulation under the administrative and control procedures of the traditional process, or intended to modify regulation more radically by removing it or by replacing it with incentives to induce the outcomes desired. Some combination of both these approaches may often be appropriate.

Improved rationalization of current processes would require, first of all, developing a more realistic and scientifically-based approach to risks to human health and the natural environment. Legislative and administrative changes to permit some retreat from absolute goals would be necessary, and a combination of scientific evidence and balanced judgment would need to be employed to assess the most likely consequences of different courses of action. Judgments would also need to be made about the value that should be placed by society on reducing risks of various kinds and on reducing the incidence of adverse developments. This approach, for example, would move away from concepts such as zero discharge goals, bans automatically triggered by evidence of risks (no matter how slight), and standards based on thresholds concepts where no evidence of thresholds can be found. A more explicit and analytical approach to risk issues would encourage the establishment of more constructive priorities and reduce the prevalence of lacunae represented by areas where risks are important, but are not addressed by regulatory action under traditional processes.

Rationalization of current regulatory processes would also require more attention to the costs imposed by regulation. Attention should be focused both on assuring cost effectiveness (achieving lowest cost approaches to obtaining given levels of performance), and on achieving a reasonable relationship between benefits and costs (assuring that incurring the costs is worthwhile in terms of the value placed on reduced risks). Under this approach concepts such as "best available technology" could not be defined without introducing economic considerations, and qualifying phrases in regulatory mandates such as "to the extent feasible" could not be interpreted simply in terms of engineering feasibility (even if constrained by industry viability). Development of regulatory policy under this analytical framework would also call attention to priority-setting, and it would help to avoid greatly excessive costs for achieving whatever goals are established.

Cost-benefits analysis should be introduced more extensively into the development and implementation of regulation. Despite conceptual and measurement difficulties, marked improvement in regulatory performance could be achieved if careful analyses were made and applied to regulatory decision-making. Although cost-benefits analysis cannot produce the spur to cost effectiveness and efficiency that private incentives could, it is a valuable tool for improving efficiency, analytically and synthetically.

The structure established by the Reagan administration for reviewing regulatory initiatives represents an approach to reform largely in terms of this first general approach. The two main procedural characteristics of the approach established by the executive order are its process for clearing regulations and its structure for decision-making. Each new regulation needs to receive clearance at both the proposal and final stages, and regulations already in existence are to be identified for review and scrutiny. Policy is established by the Cabinet level Presidential Task Force on Regulatory Relief, and specific regulatory initiatives can be reviewed by the Task Force or ultimately by the President.[27]

The principal substantive requirement established by the executive order is a Regulatory Impact Analysis to be submitted at both stages of the clearance process. These regulatory impact analyses must contain reasonably explicit information on benefits that are to be achieved and on the costs that will be entailed. Information on alternative approaches and why proposed approaches were chosen is also required. The main thrust of the review process, therefore, is more explicit and analytical rationalization of regulatory initiatives as they are developed under current regulatory legislation and procedures.

The second general approach to reform—introduction of incentives or deregulation—would be a more radical departure from current practices, and its applicability might be limited in practice to only part of the range of important regulatory problems. The general principles that would be applied in designing a system based primarily on utilizing incentives, such as effluent fees or marketable permits, are quite well understood.[28] However, the legal mechanisms and institutional arrangements that might be developed are less well understood, and how a transition could be accomplished from current regulatory processes to more use of incentives has also received only limited attention.[29]

Perhaps the most important prerequisite for introduction of incentive-based systems is improved capability for monitoring performance. Improved monitoring would require a redirection of attention on the part of the regulatory agency from such procedures as preconstruction review and permit approval to actually monitoring performance. More effective performance monitoring would make a valuable contribution, of course, to assessing the extent to which the real goals of regulation are being achieved. It would also provide a basis for establishing a rational and effective approach to enforcement and imposition of penalties for performance failures.

Deregulation, where this is practical, could be accomplished directly by removal of legislative authority for regulation. The removal of regulation from air cargo rates is an example of this direct approach.[30] In practice, however, deregulation has often occurred through a combination of introduction of increased flexibility by agency initiatives and enactment of legislation to accommodate further progress toward deregulation.[31] Gradual and deliberate change in regulation in this way has helped to bring the issues into focus for public debate and the opportunity to monitor results has helped to assuage congressional concerns about the effects of deregulation.

SUMMARY AND CONCLUSIONS

In the context of current policy discussions about the need to encourage investment in order to stimulate growth and improve productivity, regulatory policy is certainly relevant, although its quantitative importance is difficult to assess. In traditional areas of economic regulation, much of the research evidence has been developed in terms of efficiency gains that could be achieved by deregulation as compared to the effects of the regulatory process in a stable economic environment. The consensus of this research evidence is that improved performance can be achieved by deregulation of industries in which adequate competition is present.

The influence of economic regulation has not been stable, however, during the past decade-and-a-half of rising inflation. Rising inflation has affected investment decisions through regulatory and tax procedures that fail to take into account the effects of inflation. These effects of inflation have placed rates-of-return under pressure in the regulated industries, with the result that investment has been discouraged by the interaction of rising inflation and a stable regulatory process. Changes in the regulatory process to more fully accommodate an inflationary environment and tax changes to permit more rapid recovery of historical depreciation costs could make a contribution to encouraging investment in industries subject to traditional economic regulation.

Social regulation in the environmental and workplace health and safety regulation areas has had significant, measurable effects on productivity growth according to the research evidence. This evidence is based only on estimates of outlays actually made to comply with regulation, however, and the effects of social regulation are more pervasive than those reflected in increased outlays for compliance. The bias against new investment that results from stricter regulatory requirements for new sources of emissions tends to discourage investment as compared to operation of older, existing facilities. This bias against new investment is present in many environmental and other social regulatory programs, and difficulties in finding or financing actual reductions in emissions, together with the pressure of attainment deadlines, has sometimes virtually precluded new investment in the more heavily polluted areas of the country.

Adjustments in standards by relaxing them could, in many instances, both reduce compliance costs outlays and alleviate the present disparities in regulation-induced costs between new and existing plants and among areas. While some deterioration in some dimensions of the "quality-of-life" would occur in some instances, in other instances—where regulatory hurdles are so high that modest improvement from new investment, more modernization, and earlier scrapping of existing investment are excessively discouraged—the goals of regulation might be achieved more rapidly by selective and carefully considered relaxation of standards. Moreover, in broader terms the overall quality-of-life, taking into account the potential for higher measured real income, would not be adversely affected by relaxation of standards in those instances where essentially "zero risk" or "zero discharge goals" are not worth achieving in terms of the resources that would need to be devoted to such efforts and the income-producing activities that would need to be foregone.

Even in the absence of goals and standards relaxation, however, the potential for increased efficiency in working toward such goals is large. The equipment design specifications orientation of standard-setting is characteristic, not only of environmental regulation, but also of much safety and consumer product regulation. The order or magnitude of the compliance costs involved, particularly in environmental regulation, and the evidence on the potential for cost savings of more efficient approaches, indicate that regulatory management approaches and other reforms could contribute very significantly to reducing the resource costs of regulation without detracting from or delaying the achievement of worthwhile goals.

The evidence at hand does not demonstrate that regulation is the primary source of poor performance in the economy in recent years. Nor does it provide any assurance that reforms are available that can restore performance to rates that were experienced during the first two decades of the postwar period. On the other hand, the influence of regulation on performance has not been negligible, there is evidence of significant regulatory failure, and the evidence on potential for improved regulatory performance is sufficiently striking to show that efforts to achieve constructive reform are well worth making.

NOTES

1. Economic regulatory agencies established during the 1930s include the Federal Power Commission (1930), the Federal Home Loan Bank Board (1932), the Federal Deposit Insurance Corporation (1933), the Commodity Credit Corporation (1933), the Federal Communications Commission (1934), the Securities and Exchange Commission (1934), the National Labor Relations Board (1935), the Federal Maritime Commission (1933), the Agricultural Marketing Service (1937), and the Civil Aeronautics Board (1938), and Federal regulatory responsibilities were extended to trucking under the Motor Carrier Act (1935).

2. For a comprehensive discussion of issues in traditional economic regulation, see Kahn, (1970, 1971).

3. Among the research studies showing these results are Douglas and Miller (1974), Boyer (1977), and Levin (1978). See also Levin (1981).

4. For a review of recent regulatory developments in these and other areas, see *Major Regulatory Initiatives During 1980* (1981).

5. This discussion of developments in the airline industry draws upon Frank (1980) and Graham and Kaplan (1981).

6. Paul W. MacAvoy (1979), and Carron and MacAvoy (1981).

7. Arrow and Kalt (1979).

8. See, for example, Gramlich (1976) and Welch (1978). For a different view, see Levitan and Belous (1979).

9. See U. S. General Accounting Office (1979), and Gould and Bittlingmayer (1980).

10. The social regulatory programs introduced during the 1970s were notable for the new directions they established and for the scope of the regulations they introduced. New regulatory agencies established during the first part of the decade include the Environmental Protection Agency (1970), the Occupational Safety and Health Administration (1970), the Consumer Product Safety Commission (1972), the Mining Enforcement and Safety Administration (1973), the Pension Benefit Guarantee Corporation (1974), the Federal Election Commission (1974), the Nuclear Regulatory Commission (1975), the International Trade Commission (1975), and the Commodity Futures Trading Commission (1975). Legislation mandating new and additional social regulation continued throughout the decade, and it included: the National Environmental Policy Act (1969), the Clean Air Act (1970), the Federal Water Pollution Control Act (1972), the Federal Environmental Pesticide Control Act (1972), the Noise Control Act (1972), the Rehabilitation Act

(1973), the Endangered Species Act (1973), the Magnuson-Moss Warranty Act—Federal Trade Commission Improvement Act (1973), the Equal Credit Opportunity Act (1974), the Employee Retirement Income Security Act (1974), the Safe Drinking Water Act (1974), the Energy Policy and Conservation Act (1975), the Home Mortgage Disclosure Act (1975), the Toxic Substances Control Act (1976), the Resource Conservation and Recovery Act (1976), the Clean Air Act Amendments (1977), the Mine Safety and Health Act (1977), the Surface Mining Control and Reclamation Act (1977), the Quiet Communities Act (1978), and the Comprehensive Environmental Response, Compensation, and Liability Act (1980).

11. MacAvoy (1981).

12. The most comprehensive and widely cited estimates of regulatory costs are those developed by Murray L. Weidenbaum and his associates at the Center for the Study of American Business, Washington University, St. Louis, Missouri. See, for example, Weidenbaum and DeFina (1978) and Weidenbaum (1978). One of the most carefully documented studies following these methods is that conducted by Arthur Andersen and Co. for the Business Roundtable, New York, New York. See Simon and Kosters (1979). For a discussion of regulatory costs in terms of their implications for overall output, see MacAvoy (1979).

13. For a useful and timely compilation of information on agency, budget, and personnel trends for regulatory programs of different kinds, see Penoyer (1981).

14. See Rutledge and Trevethan (1981).

15. Economics Department, McGraw-Hill Publications Company. *Investment in Employee Safety and Health.* Annual McGraw-Hill Survey, annual May releases.

16. Denison (1978, 1979a, 1979b).

17. For a reasonably up-to-date and detailed discussion of the various elements of clean air regulation, see *To Breathe Clean Air* (1981).

18. See, for example, Bodily and Gable (1981); *Analysis of the Cost Impact of Plantwide Emissions Control on Four Domestic Steel Plants* (1979), an EPA-sponsored analysis; "Numerical Examples of Potential Benefits Derived from a Bubble Approach to State Implementation Plan Emission Limits" (1979), an EPA-sponsored analysis; and Ginberg and Schaumberg (1979).

19. See, for example, Maloney and Yandle (1980).

20. American Textile Manufacturers Institute, Inc., *et al.* v. Donovan, Secretary of Labor, *et al.*, Supreme Court No. 79–1429, 49 USLW 4720.

21. See, for example, Green (1979) "Evaluation of the Potential Cost Impact of Plantwide Effluent Limitations" (1981).

22. Gates and Goldmuntz (1978).

23. See Smith (1976) and MacAvoy (1977).

24. "Pre-Manufacture Notification Under the Toxic Substances Control Act" (1981).

25. See Grabowski (1976) for a discussion of the issues and review of the evidence from experience with drug regulation.

26. See Clark, Kosters, and Miller (1980) for a discussion of different viewpoints on a wide range of proposals for procedural reform.

27. For a discussion of the Reagan administration's regulatory reform program, see "Deregulation HO" (1981), and for a comparison of this program with the approach pursued by the Carter administration, see Eads (1981).

28. See, for example, Dales (1968), Montgomery (1972), Kneese and Schultz (1975), Schultze (1977), and Yandle (1978).

29. An extensive and detailed study of the potential application of incentive-based approaches to air pollution abatement in the Los Angeles basin in Southern California has been undertaken by Roger Noll, California Institute of Technology, and his associates.

30. Keyes (1980).

31. Clark, Kosters, and Miller (1980), see especially the various essays on "The Case-by-Case Approach to Regulatory Reform," by Bailey, Breyer, Shay, and Snow.

BIBLIOGRAPHY

Analysis of the Cost Impact of Plantwide Emissions Control on Four Domestic Steel Plants. Washington: Putnam, Hayes, and Bartlett, Inc., 1979.

Arrow, Kenneth J. and Kalt, Joseph P. "Why Oil Prices Should be Decontrolled." *Regulation* (September/October, 1979): 13–18.

Bailey, Elizabeth E. "The Case-by-Case Approach to Regulatory Reform." In *Reforming Regulation,* edited by Timothy B. Clark, Marvin H. Kosters, and James C. Miller III. Washington: American Enterprise Institute, 1980.

Bodily, Samuel E. and Gable, Landis. "Decisionmaking in a Bubble: An Optimization Model for Compliance with Environmental Regulations." Charlottesville: The Colgate Darden Graduate School of Business Administration, University of Virginia, 1981.

Boyer, K. D. "Minimum Rate Regulation: Modal Split Sensitivities and the Railroad Problem." *Journal of Political Economy* 85 (June, 1977): 493–512.

Breyer, Stephen G. "The Case-by-Case Approach to Regulatory Reform." In *Reforming Regulation,* edited by Timothy B. Clark, Marvin H. Kosters, and James C. Miller III. Washington: American Enterprise Institute, 1980.

Carron, Andrew S. and MacAvoy, Paul W. *The Decline of Service in The Regulated Industries.* Washington: American Enterprise Institute, 1981.

Clark, Timothy B.; Kosters, Marvin H.; and Miller, James C. III, eds. *Reforming Regulation*. Washington: American Enterprise Institute, 1980.

Dales, John H. *Pollution, Property, and Prices*. Toronto: University of Toronto Press, 1968.

Denison, Edward R. "Effects of Selected Changes in Institutional and Human Environment on Output per Unit of Input." *Survey of Current Business* 58 (January, 1978): 21–44.

———. "Pollution Abatement Programs: Estimate of Their Effects upon Output per Unit of Input, 1975–1978." *Survey of Current Business* 59 (August, 1979a): 58–59.

———. *Accounting for Slower Economic Growth: The United States in the 1970s*. Washington: The Brookings Institution, 1979b.

"Deregulation HQ: An Interview on the New Executive Order with Murray L. Weidenbaum and James C. Miller III." *Regulation* (March/April, 1981): 14–23.

Douglas, George W. and Miller, James C. III. *Economic Regulation of Air Transportation: Theory and Policy*. Washington: The Brookings Institution, 1974.

Eads, George C. "Harnessing Regulation: The Evolving Role of White House Oversight." *Regulation* (May/June, 1981): 19–26.

"Evaluation of the Potential Cost Impact of Plantwide Effluent Limitations: The Water Bubble Concept." Washington: Putnam, Hayes, and Bartlett, Inc., 1981.

Frank, Robert H. "Productivity Gains Since Deregulation in the Airline Industry: A Survey of Research in Progress." In *Dimensions of Productivity Research*, edited by John D. Hogan. Vol. 2. Houston: American Productivity Center, 1980.

Gates, Howard and Goldmuntz, Lawrence. "Automotive Safety." Washington: Economics and Science Planning, Inc., (November 13) 1978.

Ginberg, Paul and Schaumberg, Grant W., Jr. "Economic Incentive Systems for the Control of Hydrocarbon Emissions from Stationary Sources." Washington: Meta Systems, Inc., 1979.

Gould, John P. and Bittlingmayer, George. *The Economics of the Davis-Bacon Act: An Analysis of Prevailing-Wage Laws*. Washington: American Enterprise Institute, 1980.

Grabowski, Henry. *Drug Regulation and Innovation: Empirical Evidence and Policy Options*. Washington: American Enterprise Institute, 1976.

Graham, David R. and Kaplan, Daniel P. "Developments in the Deregulated Airline Industry." Washington: Office of Economic Analysis, Civil Aeronautics Board, (May 21) 1981.

Gramlich, Edward M. "Impact of Minimum Wages on Other Wages, Employment and Family Incomes." *Brookings Papers on Economic Activity* 2. Washington: The Brookings Institution, 1976.

Green, Robert L. "Water Pollution Controls for the Iron and Steel Industry." In *Benefit-Cost Analyses of Social Regulation*, edited by James C. Miller and Bruce Yandle. Washington: American Enterprise Institute, 1979.

Hogan, John D., ed. *Dimensions of Productivity Research*. Vol 2. Houston: American Productivity Center, 1980.

Kahn, Alfred E. *The Economics of Regulation: Economic Principles.* Vol. 1. New York: John Wiley and Sons, Inc., 1970.

———. *Institutional Issues.* Vol. 2. New York: John Wiley and Sons, Inc., 1971.

Keyes, Lucille S. *Regulatory Reform in Air Cargo Transportation.* Washington: American Enterprise Institute, 1980.

Kneese, A. V. and Schultz, C. L. *Pollution, Prices, and Public Policy.* Washington: The Brookings Institution, 1975.

Kosters, Marvin H. "Counting the Costs." *Regulation* (July/August, 1979): 17–25.

Levin, Richard. "Allocation in Surface Freight Transportation: Does Rate Regulation Matter?" *Bell Journal of Economics* 9 (Spring, 1978): 18–45.

———. "Railroad Rates, Profitability, and Welfare under Deregulation." *Bell Journal of Economics* 12 (Spring, 1981): 1–26.

Levitan, Sar and Belous, Richard. *More Than Subsistence: Minimum Wages for the Working Poor.* Baltimore: Johns Hopkins University Press, 1979.

McAvoy, Paul W., ed. *OSHA Safety Regulation: Report of the Presidential Task Force.* Washington: American Enterprise Institute, 1977.

———. *The Regulated Industries and the Economy.* New York: W. W. Norton and Co., 1979.

———. "Health, Safety and Environmental Regulation: An Agenda for Reform." In *AEI Public Policy Papers.* Washington: American Enterprise Institute, 1981.

Major Regulatory Initiatives During 1980: The Agencies, the Courts and the Congress. Washington: American Enterprise Institute, 1981.

Maloney, M. T. and Yandle, Bruce. "Bubbles and Efficiency." *Regulation* (May/June 1980): 49–52.

Miller, James C. and Yandle, Bruce, eds. *Benefit-Cost Analyses of Social Regulation.* Washington: American Enterprise Institute, 1979.

Montgomery, David W. "Markets in Licenses and Efficient Pollution Controls Programs." *Journal of Economic Theory* 5 (December, 1972): 395–418.

"Numerical Examples of Potential Benefits Derived from a Bubble Approach to State Implementation Plan Emission Limits." Washington: ICF, Inc., 1979.

Penoyer, Ronald J., ed. *Directory of Federal Regulatory Agencies.* Formal Publication 38. St. Louis: Center for the Study of American Business, Washington University, 1981.

"Pre-Manufacture Notification Under the Toxic Substances Control Act." Comments of the Council on Wage and Price Stability staff, Washington, D.C., on the Environmental Protection Agency's Regulatory Analysis, March 13, 1981. Mimeographed.

Rutledge, Gary L. and Trevethan, Susan L. "Pollution Abatement and Control Expenditures, 1972–79." *Survey of Current Business* 61 (March, 1981): 19–27.

Schultze, Charles L. "The Public Use of Private Interest." *Regulation* (September/October, 1977): 10–14.

Shay, Harold H. "The Case-by-Case Approach to Regulatory Reform." In *Reforming Regulation,* edited by Timothy B. Clark, Marvin H. Kosters, and James C. Miller III. Washington: American Enterprise Institute, 1980.

Simon, Michael E. "What We Did." *Regulation* (July/August, 1979): 17–25.

Smith, Robert S. *The Occupational Safety and Health Act: Its Goals and Its Achievements.* Washington: American Enterprise Institute, 1976.

Snow, John W. "The Case-by-Case Approach to Regulatory Reform." In *Reforming Regulation,* edited by Timothy B. Clark, Marvin H. Kosters, and James C. Miller III. Washington: American Enterprise Institute, 1980.

To Breath Clean Air, Report of the National Commission on Air Quality. Washington: National Commission on Air Quality, (March) 1981.

U.S., General Accounting Office. *The Davis-Bacon Act Should Be Repealed.* Washington: Government Printing Office, 1979.

Weidenbaum, Murray L. "Estimating Regulatory Costs." *Regulation* (May/June) 1978): 14–17.

Weidenbaum, Murray L. and DeFina, Robert. *The Cost of Federal Regulation of Economic Activity.* Reprint 88. Washington: American Enterprise Institute, (May) 1978.

Welch, Finis. *Minimum Wages: Issues and Evidence.* Washington: American Enterprise Institute, 1978.

Yandle, Bruce. "The Emerging Market in Air Pollution Rights." *Regulation* (July/August, 1978): 21–29.

DISCUSSANTS

William A. Marquard

We talk far too often about regulation in metaphors of aggression, as if business and government were enemies, or at the very least, adversaries. Some of this adversarial attitude springs from real differences of opinion. However, a large part of it reflects a very basic national problem: our country lacks a national policy with which to deal with Federal regulation. We need a framework to help our policy makers guide legislative and executive efforts in formulating new legislation or in trimming existing regulation. Such a framework and policy must be fashioned and must incorporate several points on which a consensus can be reached.

First, some existing regulation cannot be avoided. It responds to deeply felt needs and frequently performs valuable functions. Equally important, however, is our reluctance to expand the power and intrusiveness of government.

In view of our well-founded reluctance about governmental power, further expansion of its regulatory activities should be the exception rather than the rule. We should start with the assumption that such expansion is normally unwarranted unless the benefits appear to outweigh the costs.

Third and finally, many existing regulations need to be reexamined. Some can be eliminated, while others need significant readjustments.

In suggesting this framework for a national regulatory policy, I have borrowed generously from a statement on Federal regulatory reform made by the Business-Higher Education Forum of the American Council on Education. The following reflects many of their thoughts, some ideas of the Business Roundtable, and conclusions based on my own business experience.

Federal regulation is as old as the Republic, and so are the quarrels about it. Yet, even today, economists by no means agree about the impact of regulation on the nation's productivity and growth. What does seem clear is that our economic system is not functioning as we would like. We are not meeting either our economic or social goals and we may, in fact, be regressing in certain areas.

A national policy on regulation need not restrict productivity improvement or growth. It need not impinge on the economic or social goals we believe are desirable, but, at a time when business is obliged to change so quickly, we need the flexibility to change regulation within an agreed-upon framework.

Without attempting to put a quantitative figure on the effect of regulation, we must subject it and every other economic area to scrutiny and, where necessary, to reform. Beyond whatever percentage we might agree to be the indirect costs of regulation, the loss from products and projects that are stillborn is enormous. What is the cost of managers repelled by wrangling and the prospect of litigation? Who can measure the loss from creativity discouraged so that instead of working in new ways, we continue in tired old ones?

We need to agree on a national policy for Federal regulation. We can and should learn from experience, but we will compound our weaknesses rather than our strengths by looking for villains, whether in business, government, or labor. We must make certain that we impose no burden on growth so great that it will prevent us from reaching our economic and social goals.

There is no virtue in reiterating the vast expansion of the Federal regulatory apparatus. A problem exists, in part, because authors of agency regulations have operated largely by default, and have pursued a piecemeal proliferation of the nation's regulatory burden. Rather than the product of a broad political design expressing a national consensus, Federal regulation has grown out of uncoordinated efforts to solve a mass of separate problems whose very solutions are often in conflict.

Six principles, applicable to executive or legislative oversight, are fundamental to implementing a national policy on Federal regulation:

(1) Unless there is a compelling economic or social objective, there should be no intrusion of Federal regulation. Any statute or regulation that reduces the autonomy and self-management of the private sector must have prior recognition that its objectives are important enough to make intrusion necessary. However compelling those *objectives* may be, the *results* must be monitored to make sure they justify continued intrusion.

This principle goes somewhat further than the analysis of projected costs and benefits. Projecting costs is difficult and neither the regulatory agencies nor industries have a reassuring record. When it comes to quantifying health or environmental benefits, the record is even worse.

We should, as a matter of course, attempt cost-benefit projections, but we must also monitor results.

(2) Equally important is the principle of alternative analysis, the careful determination that alternative means may not achieve important objectives at lower cost or with less intrusion. We need to ask if there is not a cheaper, less burdensome way of achieving the same or comparable benefits. It may, for example, be profitable to build a new plant. But it may be more profitable to renovate an old one.

(3) Agencies should issue no regulations unless they are clearly consistent with the intent of Congress. In recent years, we have seen an erosion of congressional oversight which has allowed some regulators to usurp more than a little congressional authority. Congressional oversight must be made more effective, or otherwise that oversight should be exercised by the executive office, which might, in fact, be a more practicable idea.

(4) We must establish the principle of regular review of existing regulations. Such a review should ensure that the regulations are necessary and that they conform to national policy.

(5) Agencies should be required to issue public reports as part of an ongoing review of their compliance with national regulatory policy. They should also seek public comment and reaction to what they are doing, perhaps through the creation of an independent authority to make such periodic reviews.

(6) We must, almost as a reflex, consider alternatives to regulation itself. Enough time must be provided for those alternatives to work before regulations come to be written. Among those often viable alternatives are *self-regulation,* voluntary efforts with or without special financial incentives; *performance* rather than design standards, encouraging those closest to problems to choose the most effective means of compliance; and *impact statements,* broader than in the past, to include behavioral and human consequences of regulation.

It is easy to opt for clean air, pure water, and an accident-free workplace as it is to be for motherhood. Choosing a sparkling lake over a polluted one, health over sickness, or prosperity over recession is easy enough. Achieving them is a good bit more difficult and turns out to be more costly than we knew. But, just as too many automobiles sometimes threaten us with gridlock, the growth of regulations could lead to immobility through reglock.

As individuals and as a nation, we have recognized the present danger. The shock of that recognition has pushed us into seeking reforms that can ameliorate regulatory fallout. We must, however, go further and enunciate a national regulatory policy within which reform can be truly effective. If we do, and if we exchange our adversary positions for cooperation based on common concern and mutual benefit, we will go well beyond amelioration to something that resembles a real cure.

Esther Peterson

I have alternatively railed against regulation and railed against the absence of a particular regulation. I have no grand plan for integrating regulation into a new industrial policy nor plea on behalf of more regulation generally. Rather, I would like to enumerate a series of "Myths To Be Avoided."

A number of myths about regulation have dominated the public policy debate in Washington for about five years. They include:

(1) A common belief that regulators intentionally complicate straightforward laws for their own devious reasons. The truth is that increasingly complicated technology begets increasingly complicated regulation.

(2) Many congressmen (and others) believe that a Congress lacking the expertise to master the technology being regulated somehow possesses the expertise to judge the adequacy of hundreds or thousands of complex regulations[1] developed by the regulating "technocrats."

(3) Many people believe that regulators act precipitously and without authority. Regulators are usually late in carrying out the will of Congress and generally tend to be conservative. (For example, the much maligned Occupational Safety and Health Administration [OSHA] regulations of the 1970s were based on national consensus standards developed by large corporations.)

(4) The term "regulatory moratorium" is heard with increasing frequency. One must remember that the creation of a "regulatory moratorium" would require congressional committees to approve taking authority away from their own committees.

(5) Experts on the subject of regulation like to tell business audiences that business has had nothing to do with the expansion of regulatory power in Washington. In the area of social regulation this is most certainly a myth, as one industry after another continues to counter the threat of disparate state regulation by supporting the enactment of Federal preemptive legislation, as in the history of Federal consumer laws of the past 15 years.

(6) Implicit in the current discussion of the cost of regulation is the assumption that there is no socioeconomic cost of *not* regulating.

(7) Another popular myth in Washington circles is that a national consensus exists on the "excessive burden of regulation." However, I

know of no recent survey or past data showing a public animus against social or consumer protection regulation.

(8) Another myth, especially cherished in the business community, is that regulators are "out to get" American business. For example, I recently read that fuel economy regulations, rather than the gasoline price/supply picture, were endangering the survival capacity of Detroit. I wonder where our auto industry would be without those regulatory mileage goals.

(9) Perhaps the most popular myth about regulation is that there exists in Washington, D.C. a "black box" which enables us to measure the costs and the benefits of regulation, thereby paving the way for regulatory cost accounting, cost-benefit tests for individual statutes and individual regulations, and ultimately, for regulatory budgets to be imposed upon regulatory agencies. The facts are that since 1974, when President Ford first assumed he was ordering the development of standards to measure the inflation impact of regulations, up to today, government has not been able to expose for public comment any methodology for measuring regulatory costs. Further, almost no work has been done in government, business, or academia toward developing a methodology for measuring the benefits of regulation—a condition precedent to arriving at regulatory net costs. The "black box" myth gives rise to a further subset of myths, including:

- The myth that Federal agencies can be directed to develop meaningful rules for measuring direct and indirect costs of regulation *before* they are given direction on how to do it.

- The myth that agencies or the Office of Management and Budget can mandate the social judgments inherent in a national consensus on measurements of regulatory costs, and the myth that such a system could be accepted and survive without such a consensus being developed.

- The myth that costs and benefits of regulation can be separated in developing criteria for measuring the "burden" of an individual regulation or the "burden" of an agency's total regulatory activity.

- The myth that the procedure for designating which rules shall be measured is independent of the problems of devising the criteria for measuring the costs of regulations. It does not help to tell Federal agencies to consider the magnitude of the capital and operating costs in designating which rules shall be measured for costs. This begs the problems and gives further currency to the myth.

Why am I concerned about these myths? Fools can speak of myths, but they can give no currency to them. Many of the people who currently and unquestioningly accept these myths as reality are not fools —and their acceptance gives currency and plausibility. Unfortunately, as has been demonstrated over the years, public policy can be, and often is, based on myth. In a brief article in the *Washington Post* of November 26, 1980, an OMB official was quoted as saying: "The state of the art of measuring for the costs of regulations is far behind the rhetoric. . . . Regulatory budget today is a buzz-word—a concept beyond the government's present abilities."

Producers and consumers have a common interest in creating the kind of public policy in which cost-effective regulation is the rule. We will not hasten the day of that policy by allowing myths about regulation to create public policy. An enduring, effective industrial policy cannot be so built.

NOTES

1. Example—the number of bills proposing legislative veto.

Almarin Phillips

In the Commonwealth of Virginia, one repeatedly hears politicians and political commentators adopting the maxim, "That government governs best that governs least." The quotation is usually attributed to Thomas Jefferson.

There are a number of things wrong with this view. In the first place, Thomas Jefferson never said it. Second, Virginians do not in fact behave in strict accord with their own maxim. When it comes to government regulations that are beneficial to those having principal political power, regulations are all right. Regulations that are protective of existing vested interests are common and difficult to rescind whether or not they are in accord with the broader social welfare. Grave political consequences would accrue to a champion of true, across-the-board deregulation.

In any case, whether Virginians behave according to the generalization and whether or not Jefferson in fact said it, there seems to be agreement here that we should regulate where the social benefits of regulation exceed the social costs. The discussion here turns out to be more one of how to achieve accepted regulatory goals than of the goals themselves. It is a question of delineating and choosing among the potential alternative mechanisms. Achieving the benefits is seen as important, but it is emphasized that we must simultaneously look at regulatory costs before blindly adopting the notion that, because of recognized benefits, more regulation is better than less or that some regulation is always better than none.

There are many types of externalities that market mechanisms do not take care of in the best of circumstances. Actions of various private parties in the economy confer either or both costs and benefits on other parties. Someone living on a 100,000 acre ranch in a remote part of Arizona might say, "Well, I do not really see the need for all these regulations." The remoteness of one individual from others reduces both the fact and the perception of externalities.

The truth of the matter for modern society is that, increasingly, we are losing "remoteness" and becoming more and more interdependent. Even Arizonans, as New Yorkers, will increasingly discover needs for regulation that have not hitherto existed. Private, unrestricted transactions tend increasingly to involve externalities—what one does with respect to pollution, to the style and construction of buildings, how high one puts a fence, the volume at which one plays a stereo or radio, what one does about smoking or communicable diseases—all involve instances where peoples' welfares are complexly interdependent. Externalities extend all over and they present a problem that cannot be solved by piously saying that markets will take care of everything.

There is no question that the present environmental, health, safety, consumer product regulations, and the like, have had something of a dampening effect on output and growth as conventionally measured. Studies that examine the amount of extra dollars' worth of output capacity that is achieved per dollar of investment conclude that the "incremental capacity investment coefficient" has fallen over the last decade. An increased portion of the investment is going into such things as scrubbers and pollution control devices, conveniences for the handicapped, and worker safety rather than into equipment that would increase the dollars of output as conventionally measured. However, it does not follow that the incremental *social value* resulting from the investment has gone down. Many of the things that we are asking for—cleaner air, less cancer, better working conditions, fewer people killed in mines—are things that do not carry market determined monetary values. In fact, if there had not been a decrease in the conventionally measured increase in capacity per unit of investment, that would be indication that we have not had really any investment of the sort that these regulations were designed to provide.

Let me indicate some areas that are problematic insofar as regulation is concerned: First, there is the regulation of financial markets. Part of this is regulatory, part is technological, but we are living in a world presently where regulations apply to the technology, market structure, and conduct of 40 years past. Regulations originally intended to provide stability in banking and money markets are now inducing instability. Capital formation has suffered and is suffering because of the instability in financial markets. Long-term debt instruments are risky to issue and risky to hold. Equity capital financing is difficult. Mortgage markets and the institutions that serve them are in disarray. Short-term debt financing is increasingly accommodated by the growth in liabilities of institutions other than the deposit financial institutions, whose liabilities are insured. Reform, deregulation, and reregulation are vital necessities.

Second, although an entire section of this book is devoted to energy, I note it in passing. No one could possibly argue that the nature of U.S. energy regulations over the past two decades has done anything other than retard domestic economic growth.

Third, there are ubiquitous regulatory problems in the telecommunications industry. Technology has broken down many traditional industry bounds so that new modes of regulation, or deregulation, must be explored.

There are many other areas that require regulatory attention. Some will require regulation of kinds we do not presently have; some will require getting rid of old types of regulation and increased reliance on market mechanisms. There is no doubt that we will not be able to rely entirely on free market mechanisms.

As a final but important comment, I doubt the efficiency and efficacy of the suggested cooperative business-government regulations. There is much to be feared in such arrangements. The purely economic fears may be minimal, but the political fears are not. To espouse policies that encourage more cooperative relationships between business and government in the present context could yield extremely undesirable consequences. It is not just that milk control regulations, protection of trucking, protection of airlines, of the steel and computer industries, and so forth emerge out of such dealings. We can live with such *economic* inefficiency. The more fatal consequence could be the ultimate stilling of political voices in opposition to these relationships and the course of government generally. Voices in opposition are voices that should be heard for the sake of retaining a democratic society.

William Lucy

Discussions about U.S. industrial policy too often deteriorate into debates over supposedly conflicting mechanisms and goals—"supply-side" versus "Keynesian" economics, "growth" versus "quality-of-life," inflation versus unemployment—and lose sight of the larger concern which transcends quantitative economic analysis: the standard of living of the individuals who make up our economic and political systems. Nowhere is this better illustrated than in the debate over government regulation. We can talk all day about trade-offs at the margin, about the regulatory burden, and about economic efficiency, but we must be careful not to overlook the fact that regulations are made with people in mind—both of our generation and of all those that will follow—and that all issues cannot be reduced to purely monetary terms.

To put the issue of government regulation in a proper framework as part of a U.S. industrial policy which recognizes social as well as economic costs and benefits, I will make three principle points.

First, those who wish to remove the burden of regulation from the backs of business argue that the costs of compliance with regulation are inflationary and that they reduce productivity and restrain growth. But what this argument fails to recognize is that these regulations—the "institutional arrangements" we have made—came into being in response to growing public awareness and concern about serious problems which the market economy had failed to, or would not by its nature deal with—such as pollution of the air and water, illnesses and injuries at the workplace, unsafe consumer products, and public exposure to hazardous chemicals.

While there have been improvements in many areas, these problems are just as real today as they were when the regulations were created. Wiping out these protective regulations will not wipe out all traces of the afflictions they were adopted to prevent. No profit-maximizing firm has any *incentive* to voluntarily provide for environmental controls for a safe work environment or for any other social problem. Before regulations were adopted, the public was forced to pay the price for the externalities of the production process.

This is the critical point that any discussion of regulatory policy must acknowledge: *someone always pays when there are market externalities.* Removing environmental and health and safety regulations only shifts the costs of market failure back onto the public in general, and onto working people in particular, in a terribly cruel and wasteful manner. Either we pay now in preventive practices such as effluent treatment, chimney scrubbers, and labelling of hazardous chemicals, or we pay later when fish die, smog descends on cities, and workers contract cancer. Plain and simple, there is no way we can avoid the costs of regulation—but there are clearly more sensible and less sensible ways to pay.

The labor movement in the United States does not stand steadfastly against any change in the regulatory structure. What we do oppose, however, is a wholesale attempt to shift the costs of the problems that market externalities create onto the backs of working people. To do so is not good public policy (since it leaves us treating the symptoms and not the causes) and it is not even good economics. It is far cheaper—in monetary and in human terms—to prevent an accident before it occurs.

Second, we believe that cost-benefit analysis is an impractical and inappropriate means of assessing the need for, and level of, government regulation.

At this stage in the development of economic analysis, it is clearly an imperfect tool. On the cost side, the only reliable estimates obtainable are those furnished by industry itself—and historically, those cost studies have been overestimated and have failed to account for the possibility of technological changes which would reduce the costs of compliance and improve plant efficiency at the same time.

On the benefit side, while the statement has been made frequently in the past, it bears repeating: the benefits of regulation *cannot* be measured in purely monetary or economic terms. In addition to the economic arguments about increasing productivity, reducing inflation, and improving the standard of living and income distribution, there is a strictly moral question involved here which cannot be ignored: is it fair, is it possible, and is it *right* to put a price on human life, or human suffering—or on human enjoyment?

If regulations are relaxed or rescinded because they fail a cost-benefit test, are the antiregulators willing to pay *all* the costs associated with that decision? Will they pay the fisherman who suffers a loss of income because the lake on which he depends is "clear enough" to pass the cost-benefit test, but produces fish which are inedible? Will they pay for the college education of the children whose father dies of cancer in the factory where the cost in installing air filters was greater than the benefits?

Those who would rescind regulations must also be prepared to deal with the consequences of unforeseen tragedies. Since it is impossible to predict *all* the costs and *all* the benefits of an action, the would-be deregulators must be willing to take responsibility for events which cannot presently be predicted. Grim reminders of what can happen when regulations are not imposed, or are imposed or enforced too late abound: Love Canal, Three Mile Island, and the DC-10 crashes are only the most well known examples.

The third point to be made is that our fundamental economic problems of high unemployment and high inflation are *not* the result of regulation and will *not* be solved through a reduction in regulation.

Since regulations are enacted to make businesses account for the costs of market externalities, they can hardly be called inflationary. Any profit-maximizing business will, of course, attempt to pass the costs of compliance along to the consumers by raising the price it demands for its product. This effect is not inflationary, but merely assigns an explicit, preventive cost to a problem which was previously dealt with (if at all) only after the fact.

Cutting back on regulation will not solve the problems that all the U.S. economy, nor will the supply-side economic policies being pursued by the Reagan administration. Few economists believe that our problems of high inflation and high unemployment can be effectively dealt with by the Administration's supply-side economic program. So what are the alternatives?

One way to deal with inflation is to push the economy into a deep recession for a prolonged period of time. This strategy throws millions of workers into unemployment, idles many factories, and drastically reduces the nation's rate of economic expansion. We in labor feel that the cost of this strategy is far too high.

Labor joins many liberal economists in favoring an alternative strategy. This alternative uses an incomes policy to achieve a reduction in inflation without a substantial decrease in economic growth. Under a mandatory incomes policy every worker and business can afford to exercise wage and price restraint because he or she knows that others must do likewise, and that, as a result, inflation will decline.

A strategy which will ensure long-term growth and at the same time achieve a fairer distribution of income is of no value, however, if the quality-of-life for all Americans does not improve as well. The health and safety of the public must be just as important to this society as rebuilding the industrial base, balancing the Federal budget, and increasing our defense capabilities. As we said, the consequences of regulation are difficult and sometimes impossible to quantify in monetary terms. The costs of not regulating, however, are simply too great a price to pay.

Thirty and 40 years ago, when many of today's plants were being built, we were not aware of many health hazards that were present in the workplace. Today, however, we know about dangerous conditions and dangerous chemicals and the effects of long-term exposure on the people in the factories. *Today there is no excuse not to include health and safety precautions in industrial planning.*

It only makes economic sense in the long run to keep government regulations in force. Either we prevent the pollution and the deaths and the injuries now, or we pay the psychic and monetary costs later, and at a much greater expense. Worst of all, those later costs will be distributed in a horribly unfair manner. It is not the bureaucrats who formulate the regulations, nor the congressmen who established the agencies, nor the corporate presidents and managers who complain about the compliance costs who will pay the most. The ones who will pay are the workers—the people who run the machines, who breathe

the factory air, who operate the unsafe equipment—and their losses will be in death and disease. What is an industrial policy worth if it punishes most of the members of the society who make it run?

CONCLUSION

To briefly summarize, the purpose of government regulations is to protect people from the effects of market failures. Those regulations cannot and must not be assessed on a cost-benefit basis. Eliminating the regulations only shifts the costs to working people and to the public as a whole, to be dealt with in a much more unsatisfactory and inequitable manner. Neither will eliminating regulations solve inflation or unemployment. What is needed is a targeted economic development strategy that includes strong health, safety, and environmental safeguards and ensures the social as well as the economic prosperity of all the members of our society.

SUMMARY REPORT

Regulation

Barbara Hackman Franklin

The objective of our discussion was to answer the questions: What should U.S. regulatory policy be for the 1980s? Must trade-offs be made between economic growth and quality-of-life goals? If so, on what basis and by whom?

We recognized at the outset that social and economic regulation are quite different and defined them for purposes of our discussion as follows: Economic regulation is oriented toward setting prices, service, and entry, thereby changing the economics of competition. Social regulation attempts to correct imperfections in the market, the so-called externalities. Health, safety, and environmental rules are examples of social regulation.

Much of our discussion focused on social regulation, since this is where the most difficult decisions and trade-offs must be made in coming years. The following are the highlights of the discussion, noting particularly the areas of agreement:

- First, there has been a negative impact on U.S. economic growth, productivity, and innovation resulting from too much regulatory activity. However, there were some differences of opinion about the magnitude of cost and the degree to which excessive regulation contributes to U.S. economic problems. The benefits of regulation—cleaner air and water, purer food and drugs, safer workplaces and household products—were also noted.

- There has been no coherent regulatory policy. Each agency has done its own thing, working toward its own goals without much cooperative effort or identification of areas of duplication and conflict. Generally, government has been preoccupied too much with means and not enough with results. In other words, government has promulgated too many design standards and not enough performance standards.

- We agreed on the need for an overall framework, a national regulatory policy. Our country's resources are not unlimited today. Trade-offs between economic growth and quality-of-life goals must be made. Even if we are not making them consciously, we are making them just the same, and we are better off to have a framework for our decision-making.

- There was consensus that a commonsense, problem solving approach to regulation and to setting regulatory goals and priorities is crucial. But there were disagreements about what this meant and how to do it. "What's common sense to you," in the words of one panelist, "is not common sense to me." There was support for a cost-benefits approach. However, some disagreed strongly, saying it is difficult to quantify the benefits and impossible to put a value on a human life.

- Among those who supported a cost-benefits approach, there was agreement that the methodology which should be used was not clear. It was generally agreed that a regulatory action should have to be justified and that the most cost effective approach should be sought.

- There was clear agreement that, no matter what the goals, regulatory activity can be accomplished better and more efficiently than it has been. More flexibility could be introduced and costs could be reduced, perhaps considerably.

- We agreed on the need for alternatives to regulation. Most prominently mentioned were voluntary approaches and real market, financial, and tax incentives for business. Voluntary approaches— hammered out by business and government, consumers and business, labor and business, or all of the foregoing—should be first tried before regulation is determined to be necessary. It was suggested that these approaches might best be forged by the participants behind closed doors rather than in open meetings.

- A clear and urgent need exists to change the overly adversarial relationships that exist between government and business, consumers and business, and labor and business. These relationships must change if communication is to occur through which alternatives to regulation can be found. We were not sure how to do this, but agreed that we had to try.

- Finally, regulatory activity should be monitored and evaluated to make sure it is accomplishing its objectives. Other changes—

amendments of statutes, and the like—should be considered where necessary.

Let me now turn to a summary of our discussion of economic regulation. There was agreement that efforts to deregulate, transportation, for example, have been underway for the last several years and are moving in the right direction. Progress has been made, but results should be monitored to make sure that implementation is completed. Complementary deregulatory efforts are needed at the state and local levels to ensure that the thrust of Federal efforts are carried out. Inner city buses were cited as an example.

Several areas were pointed out as still being "a mess," and as possible targets for future deregulation: the financial area, energy, and telecommunications.

The area of antitrust was also discussed as a part of economic regulation, and there was general agreement on a couple of things. Generally, antitrust statutes probably do not need much reform, but the process does. Cases are much too lengthy and costly, and ways to make exceptions should be found.

With respect to whether American companies are less competitive internationally because of antitrust laws, the following points were made: the Webb-Pomerene Act gives U.S. businesses the export latitude they need, and antitrust laws should not be blamed if U.S. companies are not as good at developing markets for export as they should be. But, there was some expression of support for lessening antitrust strictures, to allow more merger activity so that American companies could achieve economies of size and scale that would be helpful in international competition.

In summary, some regulation will be required in the future in order to maintain a competitive environment and continue our health, safety, and environmental protection. But, regardless of whether supply-side or preferential economic approaches are followed generally, regulation must be more efficient. Goals must be clearer, trade-offs between economic growth and quality-of-life considered more precisely, and alternative solutions sought with more participation by those affected.

International Trade ☆ ☆ ☆ ☆ ☆

15.

INTERNATIONAL ASPECTS OF INDUSTRIAL POLICY

Lawrence R. Klein

THE MEANING

Although it is a topic of intense interest at the present time, there is no apparent precise, scientific meaning of the term *industrial policy*. It is not as precise as fiscal policy, monetary policy, tariff policy, antitrust policy, or a number of other well known areas of economic policy.

In the first place, different names are being used to describe fairly similar policy analysis. They are:

- Industrial Restructuring
- Reindustrialization
- Industry Policy

They refer to contemporary discussion in the United States and in the world at large. I shall focus, in this essay, on the U.S. case, but will also make specific reference to other countries, the world economy, or large blocks within the total world economy.

Rather than try to give a concise and scientifically careful definition of industrial policy or any of its variants, let me try to describe what such policies are and what their objectives are. In a discursive, rather than concise, treatment I shall try to bring out some of the several main issues involved. The term has special importance for the United States because there is widespread feeling that we, as a nation, have lost our competitive edge and are slipping in our role of high strategic economic importance as the world's leader.

A pessimistic view would hold that a *long-run* or *permanent* change has taken place among the world's line up of economic powers. It is entirely possible that America's economic descent is only transitory. Many of the things that are thought to have contributed significantly to the *relative* decline of the American competitive edge are transitory and are already in the process of change, witness the present strength of the dollar and the shift from a current account deficit to surplus. It is not necessarily the case that the United States is suddenly going to change course economically, but many ongoing developments are affecting other countries, and, in a relative sense the United States may emerge in a better position in the near future. The processes that favor the United States in a *relative* sense are demographic shifts in labor force composition, trade union confrontation for higher wage claims, and more inflation.

If the United States can deal with inflation much better from this point forward, and much better than several partner countries, there could be a dramatic relative improvement, both on internal and external account. The dollar should strengthen in the long run and this would help to reinforce the tendency for inflation to decline in magnitude. The dollar depreciation that occurred during 1977–79 has made the United States more competitive. Now it is a question of holding those gains, reducing inflation, and firming the dollar's position on a more lasting basis.

After World War II and the disruption to family life that accompanied it, there was, quite understandably, an explosive "baby boom." In the United States, this surge in the birth rate began at the end of the 1940s and continued into the early 1950s. During the latter part of the 1960s there was an enormous expansion in college enrollments, and a few years later, an increase in labor force, at the low ends of the wage scale and skill level. U.S. productivity was restrained by virtue of the fact that the ranks of workers at the low end of the spectrum were flooded over with relatively untrained workers. Until this cohort can mature a bit, acquire some learning on the job, there is likely to be a low rate of productivity growth.

At present, the young entrants into the European labor force are coming from an age cohort that is somewhat behind the American. Also, female participation may have had a head start in the United States. Our labor force growth rate is expected to come down significantly and *stay down*. It appears likely that main competitors in Western Europe will go through the productivity-real wage concepts and analysis that cut down our own productivity edge. Now we can look at labor supply issues and the rest of the economy to note that we might regain some of our competitiveness as a result of absorbing a more trained and productive labor force.

Trade union pushfulness and aspirations of rank/file workers could lead to more pressures on wage rates outside the United States than within. In the end, growing wage rates and poor training of youthful workers are going to restrain Europe's (and Japan's) competitive challenge on unit labor costs, and goods available for export. For these reasons, we believe that some of the lost competitiveness is misplaced and that there will be an improvement in U.S. exports and inflation rates, as a result of relatively favorable demographic trends. Countries that used to be low cost suppliers of goods to the U.S. market, as a consequence of their low wage patterns, are now becoming more expensive (higher unit labor costs). This will redound to our own trade benefit.

PRODUCTIVITY—THE CENTRAL ISSUE
There are two ways of looking at productivity—measured as output per worker or worker-hour—(1) in terms of levels or (2) in terms of rates of change. The *improvement factor* in economic life is best judged by the rate of growth in productivity. Comparative living levels are shown by the level of productivity, in contrast with its rate of change. One of the most widely used formulas in economics is the relationship among change in wage rate, inflation rate, and change in productivity:

> percentage change in wage rate = percentage change in price level minus percentage change in worker productivity.

This is not an ironclad law, but it is probably the single most important relationship between prices and costs (wage costs). Its validity depends on the stability of labor's share in total output. The formula states that if wage changes can be held to no more than productivity changes, then prices should not change. The excess of wage changes over productivity gains governs the degree of price inflation. It is, therefore, quite evident that productivity plays a key role in assessing and controlling inflation.

Much is said and written about the productivity slowdown in the United States, and this is a real event; nevertheless, it should be emphasized that productivity declines have occurred on a world-wide scale and still have not been turned around. The accompanying table 15–1 shows the extent of productivity decline or slowdown in the different parts of the world. The year 1973 is the breaking point, the year of the oil embargo and escalation of energy prices. Whether measured from 1950 or 1960, the growth rates of individual nations held firm until 1973. The rates after 1973 have declined significantly for all countries listed in the table. Productivity in manufacturing is on a higher level than elsewhere in the economy, and some of the latest figures (1973–1977)

TABLE 15-1
Productivity Growth Rates, Selected Countries

	1950–73	1960–73	1973–77
Real GDP per Civilian Employee			
United States	2.1	2.1	0.3
Canada	2.6	2.4	0.5
Japan	7.8	8.8	2.7
France	4.6	4.6	2.9
West Germany	5.0	4.4	3.3
Italy	5.3	5.8	−0.2
United Kingdom	2.5	2.6	0.4
Manufacturing Output per Hour			
United States	2.7	3.2	1.5
Canada	4.2	4.6	2.1
Japan	9.7	10.0	2.4
Belgium	n.a.	7.0	6.6
Denmark	5.2	5.7	5.2
France	5.3	5.5	4.8
West Germany	5.8	7.2	5.5
Italy	6.6	7.2	2.4
Netherlands	6.2	7.4	4.9
Sweden	5.3	6.7	0.5
United Kingdom	3.1	3.9	−0.2

SOURCE: Edward F. Denison, *Survey of Current Business* 59 (August, 1979): 20.

remain high, but country-by-country there has been a real growth slowdown.

The productivity slowdown in the United States has been debated from many points of view. The American improvement factor is admittedly low in the scale of international comparisons of the above table, but it is to be emphasized that even the fast growing countries also experienced significant setbacks. The events of the 1970s dealt harshly with the economic advancement of the industrial nations.

Since the productivity slowdown is so basic, it is worthwhile examining its possible explanations in order to formulate industrial policy. It is necessary to know what the deficiency is that industrial policy is trying to overcome. Without coming to any definitive, widely accepted, or sharp conclusion, economists dealing with productivity trends cite the following causes for the decline:

(1) Inadequate levels of fixed capital formation, in total volume or in modernization.

(2) Need to reequip industry to deal efficiently with expensive energy.

(3) A reduction in research and development activity or in basic research.

(4) Excessive regulation.

(5) Shifts in the industrial composition of production.

(6) Business cycle downturns. There may, indeed, be other reasons for the falling off in the productivity improvement factor, but these are the leading causes cited, and no single cause appears to be predominant.

The productivity decline and the consequent effects on competitiveness are, especially, international problems; therefore, it is of interest to examine them in more detail in the context of international economic issues. This is done in the sections to follow.

DOMESTIC VERSUS INTERNATIONAL MARKET FOR U.S. BUSINESS

The domestic market in the United States is so vast that it is no wonder that U.S. enterprises look first at home for potential in new areas of sales penetration. It does not always work out that way from the side of production, yet there is a great deal of diversity in such a large country, and more opportunities exist than meets the eye in a cursory appraisal.

In some selected industries or nonindustrial lines of activity, and to a large extent in recent years, some U.S. enterprises have found international markets to be more profitable than domestic ones. In many cases, overseas earnings have become the mainstay of company profits.

But regardless of the comparisons between domestic and international opportunities, the fact remains very clear that the American economy is becoming more open. The United States is still the world's single largest trading country, and the share of exports or of imports in the GNP has grown significantly. In 1956, the export share was 5.67 percent and by 1977 it was 9.30 percent. But until 1970 the share was almost unchanged. The large increment took place in the 1970s. The same is true of imports, which grew from 4.66 percent in 1956 to 9.89 percent in 1977.

The popular conception, referred to already in the introduction, of the international position of the United States, is that we have lost our competitive edge. This attitude was so pervasive that a conference was called, about one year ago, by a broad political and professional spectrum, to look into the question, "Can the United States remain competitive?" The popular view is that our productivity is progressing too slowly, or possibly falling, in relation to others, and that we shall lose competitiveness if we have not yet already done so. The counterpart of the relatively low showing on productivity growth is a relatively high level of costs. Comparisons are most frequently made between the United States on the one hand, and Germany and Japan, on the other. This view of competitiveness is too narrow, and the productivity/cost comparison would probably confirm the existence of U.S. problems when judged against many other industrial countries besides Japan and Germany.

The consequences of our losing competitiveness, if indeed we have, is that the U.S. dollar becomes very unsettled and low in value. It also induces a resurgence of protectionism, either outright or "under the table."

The United States is committed to a stable dollar, in a free market situation, and to the principles of multilateral free trade. Any formal policies to be followed—under the heading of Industrial Policy—need to be examined in the light of these two commitments.

A stable dollar, more than in the case of any other currency, needs to be maintained because it plays the role of *key* currency—not truly a *reserve* currency, but certainly, a *key* currency. This means that the dollar should be held steady. It should not be strongly appreciating or depreciating, but should merely serve as a good solid standard. Many strategic commodities, especially oil, are denominated in dollars; therefore, the United States remains vulnerable to renominations in case of severe depreciation or appreciation, although a different interest group would be pushing for changes depending on whether the situation were one of depreciation or appreciation. Basically, however, the partner world wants *stability* and not wide swings. Perhaps we do not or should not want to retain the key status for the U.S. dollar, but we have little choice at this time. Until a basic reform in the world monetary system is introduced, we shall have to live with the present status for the key currency role.

After World War II, the inefficiency of separate bilateral agreements in a destroyed world became apparent. It was our goal, established with the understanding and cooperation of partner countries, that we would mutually seek to establish, step by step, as conditions permitted, a more efficient system of multilateral free trade. That system has been put in place, imperfect as it must be in any realistic setting, and we would be ill-advised to do anything that would undermine it.

Only last year, we participated in another round of multilateral free trade negotiations, "The Tokyo Round," and we are part of a system that is based on the concept of multilateral free trade, with periodic steps to implement it, subject to setbacks such as quotas (textiles, shoes, televisions, cars) and trigger prices (steel). These are apparent barriers to trade, but there are many more nontariff barriers that are just as restrictive, although they are not apparent; they are subtle and more disguised.

INDICATIONS OF NONCOMPETITIVENESS

Although the American economy is more open and although we now pay much more attention to external factors such as overall current account balance, bilateral trade balances, international capital flows, and exchange rates against the dollar, the share of the United States in the world trade total is declining. Since 1965, the U.S. export share has fallen from about 15 percent to about 11 percent in 1980. This is not a uniform pattern. In some lines we may have increased shares, and in others the fall has been modest, but overall, we have definitely lost.

Other indications of the lack of U.S. competitiveness are the deterioration of the trade balance, from surplus to deficit, and the weakness of the dollar in foreign exchange markets. It is important to take a closer and deeper look at these issues, however, because they are very changeable. Only a few years ago, we were alarmed because our current account balance was seriously in deficit whereas it has suddenly turned into surplus and appears to be holding steadily in that position. Correspondingly, the dollar was weak on foreign exchange markets in 1977–79, but it has suddenly turned strong and has managed to hold that position for some months. At the same time that the U.S. current account turned positive, the balances of Germany and Japan, our most noted competitors, turned negative.

Industrial policy should be formulated mainly from a long-term point of view and not as short-run cyclical stabilization policy; therefore, it is important to sort out the secular or chronic aspects of our competitive position from the cyclical aspects. The table of international magnitudes shows some interesting patterns for the United States.

In total, we used to be a net exporter. A merchandise surplus enabled this country to undertake foreign aid, maintain a modest services surplus, and generally be a leader among nations. As the competitive edge became dull, and as other countries produced high quality goods at low prices, our merchandise balance became less positive and eventually turned negative. At the start of this dynamic process, U.S. goods ceased to be cost effective. The event that finally turned the merchandise accounts strongly negative was the petrol deficit—from 1974 forward. A rapid build-up of net invisible exports, on services account, has finally enabled the total of goods and services to become favorable again after having been negative for a few years. The current account balance also

TABLE 15–2
Some International Economic Statistics
United States

	Exports Goods and Services	Imports Goods and Services	Exports Goods (nonservice)	Imports Goods (nonservice)	Exports Services	Imports Services	Current Account (net)
1960	28.9	23.4	20.0	17.5	8.9	5.9	2.8
1961	29.9	23.3	20.5	17.2	9.4	6.1	3.8
1962	31.8	25.4	21.4	19.0	10.4	6.4	3.4
1963	34.2	26.6	22.9	19.6	11.3	7.0	4.4
1964	38.8	28.8	26.2	21.2	12.6	7.6	6.8
1965	41.1	32.3	27.3	24.0	13.8	8.3	5.4
1966	44.6	38.1	30.2	28.8	14.4	9.3	3.0
1967	47.3	41.0	31.8	30.6	15.5	10.4	2.6
1968	52.4	48.1	35.0	36.8	17.4	11.3	0.6
1969	57.5	53.3	37.9	39.8	19.6	13.5	0.4
1970	65.7	59.0	44.0	43.7	21.7	15.3	2.3
1971	68.8	64.7	45.2	48.6	23.6	16.1	−1.4
1972	77.5	76.7	50.8	57.9	26.7	18.8	−5.8
1973	109.6	95.4	73.4	71.3	36.2	24.1	7.1
1974	146.2	132.8	101.3	104.2	44.9	28.6	2.1
1975	154.9	128.1	110.3	98.1	44.6	30.0	18.3
1976	170.9	157.1	119.5	123.8	51.4	33.3	4.4
1977	183.3	187.5	126.9	150.8	56.4	36.7	−14.1
1978	219.8	220.4	149.1	173.3	70.7	47.1	−14.3
1979	281.3	267.9	184.0	206.3	97.3	61.6	−0.8
1980	339.8	316.5	228.2	242.6	111.6	73.9	0.1

turned positive recently. The largest single component of the strong showing by by services was investment income.

At the present time we can characterize the American position as follows:

- Merchandise is in a chronic deficit position, due mainly to the petrol deficit.

- Agriculture is a powerful generator of a net surplus position; our grain exports dominate our needs for tropical fruits, beverages, and sugar.

- Invisibles are a large earner, especially through investment income, some of which is an offset to the petrol deficit as a result of U.S. based oil company earnings.

- Some manufactured goods such as machinery, jet aircraft, computers, semiconductors, and other high technology products yield a net exports surplus.

- Some raw materials, besides oil and gas, also contribute to our deficit.

For the most part, these are not cyclical issues, but the recent change in the U.S. current account position has cyclical components, in that imports are restrained while we are going through a period of recession, with moderate recovery. Also, this present dollar strength will eventually serve to restrain our exports.

As the net external position of the United States deteriorated, the exchange value of the dollar fell, finally devalued in the early 1970s after the Smithsonian Agreement, and recovery set in when the current account strengthened. Also at work were relatively high interest rates and American political stability in an uncertain world.

The strength of invisibles, in the current account, is led by investment income. This flow is a factor return, based on the larger and widespread foreign investment of the United States. During the period when the foreign capital position was being built up, capital flowed out of the United States. This worsened our balance of payments position, encouraged widespread criticism of foreign investment by the United States, and brought down the exchange value of the dollar.

Now we have finished the era of large international investment by U.S. companies. But the investment eventually has a return, and we are seeing the first manifestations of it. For some time, it is likely to remain significantly positive. Some U.S. companies have located some of their operations abroad, being turned off by domestic American costs, together with receding productivity. The opportunity is great, however, for the local areas where international activity thrives. It does so because these areas have good port facilities and an encouraging attitude for international affairs. But international investment runs on a two way street. We are now seeing large-scale foreign investment in the United States. This country remains attractive in spite of the so-called lack of competitiveness, and, eventually, investment income will be flowing out of the United States as a return on the capital that is presently coming here.

The present net surplus position of the United States is new and not necessarily likely to last indefinitely. True enough, the surplus position was painstakingly achieved, and will undoubtedly not go away again quickly, but the new-found position of net surplus may not last, especially in the face of mounting oil bills. Large as the latter are, we have managed to keep our national head above water. We should be prepared, however, to see cyclical swings and possibly a longer term decline.

Whether or not the overall balance goes one way or the other, there are certain specific activity lines where the balance is definitely negative and where no immediate signs of revival are visible. In automobile, steel, television sets, textiles, apparel, shoes, and a few other lines, the United States is *not* competitive. The affected industries, both from the sides of labor and management, want individual stylized relief. The steel industry wants "trigger price" protection; the automobile industry wants quotas on imports; the television industry wants quotas, too. An economist usually abides by the principles of free trade. It is not a question of wiping out a whole industry in the United States; it is a question of rising to the challenge and becoming competitive. There is no inherent reason why the United States cannot compete in most markets. That is what industrial policy is about, namely, to make such competition effective.

For some time to come the United States will remain noncompetitive in overall energy supply. We may have a natural advantage in coal, and we may supply a great deal of oil towards our needs, but no matter how we look at the problem, there is a long-term need to import oil and oil products. The value of the petrol deficit is large and still growing. The dominant view is that these tendencies will continue in spite of good tendencies towards conservation in a volume sense. There are no alternatives to further conservationist moves coupled with supply enhancement. These joint movements will lessen the needs for oil imports, but a fundamental and significant amount will remain as a fairly steady need. Energy, as an integral part of internationally-oriented industry policy will be dealt with by new methods of petroleum engineering, and of plant level experimentation. Industrial policy for energy should be mainly concerned with methods of paying for large oil bills, while striving to restrain their growth.

UNITED STATES STRENGTHS AND WEAKNESSES

In the preceding sections, I have tried to list the issues and show some of the consequences of having been exposed to them for some time in the past. Now, I want to tackle the problem differently. I want to try to identify the potential winners and losers over the next decade and use industry policy as a means for dealing with these two cases.

Some winners: We do an excellent job in feeding ourselves, but after domestic needs are satisfied, there remains a substantial surplus for exports. In 1980, agricultural exports amounted to some $40 billion. This represented about 19 percent of all U.S. exports. It is a figure that has remained fairly steady, falling by no more than 3 percentage points during the past 40 years.

When looked at from the viewpoint of trade balance, the net position is quite impressive. Agriculture generates a net trade balance of more than $7 billion. This figure hovered in the neighborhood of $5 billion for a long time, but recently it increased. The end is not in sight, regardless of the fate of the grain agreements with the U.S.S.R. and the People's Republic of China. As strong as our net export position has grown, and in spite of a strong supply expansion, output for export has continued to expand. The value of agricultural exports has doubled since 1973, the year of commodity price speculation. It had already tripled since the early 1960s. There is a fair amount of inflation in these trends, but nevertheless, there is good strength with good opportunity for further growth.

This is a good case for a positive industrial policy. We should pick-the-winners in part, at least, from among those that have been recent winners and likely to retain a leading role, both at home and abroad. The U.S. economy should move from strength to strength in search of policies that will further benefit the strong cases, and agriculture is clearly one of these. The United States should vigorously support agriculture, which is our perception of a continuing winner industry. It is not a glamorous one, but it does provide solid foundations.

In keeping with the thought of moving from strength to strength, another success story for the United States has been the production and delivery of jet aircraft, both military and civilian. Not only does this industry show that there are still some industrial sectors where the United States remains very competitive and handily qualifies as the number one producer for the entire world, but it also shows how military research and development can develop spin off by-products for the civilian economy. I would not want, at all, to argue that military research and development provides a desirable route for economy-wide research and development, but I do want to point out that military research and development has some redeeming features of a constructive sort. Other nations can also produce jet aircraft, some military as well as civilian, but no other nation is anywhere near the United States in equipping the world's airline companies.

Competition is beginning to emerge in the civilian field, particularly through the European Airbus, some other production in France and the United Kingdom, and especially in the production of small executive planes. Order backlogs will keep the U.S. industry going for some time to come, but other countries will certainly try to penetrate the hold that we have over this market, and the future distribution of market shares could look far different from the present situation.

Computers are another product line where the United States remains as the dominant producer. But the dominance that the International Business Machines Corporation enjoys in this market on a world-wide basis is being challenged now by Japan, Germany, France, United Kingdom, Italy and other countries. Like the case of jet aircraft, the future may change. There is, perhaps, already more internationally diversified activity in computer production than in jet aircraft production. Japan has already penetrated significantly the market for hand-held electronic calculators. The miniaturization has gone at least as far in Japan as in the United States. The question now is whether Japan will compete as effectively in the main frame business for larger computers as they have in hand calculators. It stands to reason that they could. At the same time, Japan will be joined by Germany, other Western European countries, and the United Kingdom.

A feature in favor of Japanese penetration is that they have shown great skill and ability in miniaturization. The next generation of computers will almost exclusively work on a minibasis, through small terminals or small self-contained computer units. U.S. activity is likely to keep rising for some time, but the total market will rise and others will share in this rise, too. The remaining issue, to be settled in the future, is whether others will also gain a rising market share in comparison with IBM and similar giants.

Closely associated with the main frame and hardware end of the computer market is the provision of software, including econometric packages for use with the new generation of hardware configurations. One reason for the amazing success at IBM is the provision of compatible software with the installation of IBM hardware.

The provision of hardware/software is all part of a larger concept, namely, that of the information industry. By information in this context, we mean a fairly broad flow of visual output in the form of reports, tables, graphs, and automatically printed explanatory texts.

The information industry is interesting to me because the econometrics industry is part of it. There is no doubt that the United States is fully competitive in commercial econometrics, on an international scale, and, indeed, in the whole information sector. This lead will be maintained for a while, but it is quite evident that significant competition is building up in Western Europe, the United Kingdom, Canada, Japan, Australia, and New Zealand. It is also doing well in some developing and centrally planned economies. In the case of econometrics, it is possible to be more definite about the catch-up speed as well as our own speed in getting projects underway. In five to 10 years, probably at the lower end of the range, we can expect partner countries to be as efficient as the United States in supplying econometric information and in the whole information field. We shall remain competitive, but we shall not dominate the field, as in the past.

All the strong areas, where we have been and expect to be promoting winners, have both national and international segments. Emphasis is being placed here on the international aspects; so it is worthwhile looking into the more general possibility of raising contributions to cover deficits elsewhere in the U.S. external account system. At the present time, the international component is growing, and this produces combined decision-making in both the domestic and foreign arenas.

Losers: Potential winners may be presently in the class of losers. It makes sense to help ailing industry in a turnaround operation, but in trying to help industries, we may court the danger of backing the losers that ought to be allowed to go bankrupt. The nation is fully surviving the Penn Central bankruptcy. We should not rush to preserve all the jobs of failing sectors or companies. The bailing-out of Lockheed may prove to have been a wise move, and the Chrysler decision has yet to be justified or criticized. But, all in all, industrial policy should be quite aggressive in trying to support the winners, while being cautious about supporting the losers.

In the case of steel, we chose an illiberal method for trying to keep the industry internationally competitive, namely, by introducing the trigger price mechanism. This is outright protectionism. We might have chosen another route, namely, to have subsidized investment for modernization. This would have been a more positive industrial policy. The refunding of the investment tax credit, as cited below, is a simple device for targeting investment aid to steel, but other policies for support of investment could have worked too.

A similar situation prevails in motor vehicles. Investment that would enable effective competition with Japanese and other producers is to be preferred to quotas or other nontariff barriers to trade. This would be a positive way to help an ailing industry that is presently a loser.

INTERNATIONAL ECONOMIC POLICIES

A way to keep the balance of payments favorable is to expand exports. Cutting back on imports, doing things about the exchange rate, are also part of any rounded program, but it seems best to me to look towards export promotion.

It is one thing to say that it is good to promote exports, to enhance productivity in order to make U.S. goods more competitive, but it is quite another thing to bring these to fruition. That, of course, is what industrial policy is all about. The policy to create an effective export board that will seek out potential markets and advise on the design of American goods for particular export destinations is all to the good, but it is unlikely to be able to turn long-term trends around. Many things must be done at once.

The establishment of one or more United States trading companies, modeled on the successful Japanese variants, is an experiment well worth trying. The overall stimulation of capital formation through fiscal policy incentives should help to advance worker productivity. This is important in restraining inflation and making U.S. goods more competitive. Appropriate fiscal policy—investment tax credits or accelerated depreciation accounting—are economy-wide devices, but they are also directed in the sense that they aim at the business sector, and capital formation in particular. They could, however, be more directed, in terms of industrial policy. If the investment stimuli are made quantitatively more attractive for energy investment, they could be especially helpful in developing oil substitutes, saving on imports, improving the external balance, and strengthening the dollar. Other specific directions for policy would be to make the investment incentives stronger for winner industries or for those losers who show a real chance for recovery. This could be achieved, for example, by imposing differential investment tax credits, having a more generous credit for those sectors whose development was targeted at higher rates. There is precedent for this, in that the original investment tax credit, from the Kennedy-Johnson era, provided for a smaller credit for electric utilities. This may have been a misplaced emphasis, but it was nevertheless a differential, and such variants are possible. In line with my point of view of trying to pick-the-winners in order to compete more effectively in world markets, I would emphasize the use of differential investment tax credits.

A subtle, indirect way of varying the investment tax credit is to make it *refundable* or to provide generous accrual privileges. This idea was proposed in President Carter's economic platform for the 1980 campaign. This means that companies incurring losses will have little or no income taxes to pay; so the tax credit is not meaningful unless it is refundable. The targeted industries for this proposal were steel and autos, both of which were having trouble in meeting international competition on a world scale.

Another fiscal policy in support of our international balance is the proposal to ease the domestic tax burden of U.S. employers abroad. This idea has been introduced in order to make it easier for American enterprise to station personnel abroad, especially to compensate for reduced *dollar* purchasing power since 1971. This seems to be well-motivated, but not a powerful move in its own right.

Some years ago, we introduced Domestic International Sales Corporation (DISC) among our international tax options. This was supposed to encourage the development of export operations of U.S. companies through tax concessions. At present, it is not thought to have been very successful legislation, as far as achieving export objectives are concerned. It may be wrong, however, simply to eradicate DISC. The appropriate issue is to seek tax preference that will encourage export operations.

It is not our purpose here to detail all the policy options and choose the best ones. It is simply to indicate that options do exist and that there is some mileage to be gained in exploring policies for improving the trade and payments accounts, either by increasing exports or by restraining imports.

If policy is to be set along the lines of "picking-the-winners," it will be necessary to devise objective procedures for going as far as we can towards identifying the appropriate target sectors. The areas in which the United States is already strong, as outlined on a very partial basis above, should be kept strong through continued policy encouragement. In addition to agriculture, jet aircraft, computers, and information, we might suggest our looking into microelectronics, fiber optics, laser technologies, bioengineering, and other high technology lines of activity. Many competitors are also singling out these sectors for encouragement, and the United States will have to press ahead with positive policy encouragement, just to keep up with others.

In the past, when the United States developed new technologies, with new products, they immediately attained a large share of the world market. Gradually, competition built up and took away some of our leading market share. Reindustrialization is a policy to attempt to arrest this process of declining market share.

The situation is likely to be different in brand new industrial sectors. The United States, for example, has the lead in the new technologies of bioengineering, but we are not alone in the field. A major company is located in Switzerland. So many countries have had their attention drawn to the exotic possibilities of gene-splicing and related technologies that they are backing, with public funds, research and

International Aspects of Industrial Policy

development in the new field. Bioengineering as a potential winner industry is going to have a great deal of international competition at the very start. The U.S. market share will be large at first, but probably not as large as in semiconductors when it first started. As a nation, we shall have to *win* competitively every point of market share that we seek to establish.

One of the hardest sets of decisions in "picking-the-winners" will be to avoid the true losers and also to try to discern which losing cases are worthy of support for revival. There is every reason to have good expectations for coal, but this was a declining industry with little apparent potential in the 1960s. It would have been hard to think of coal as a target for revival if there had not been such great changes in the pricing of oil. It does appear, though, that coal now merits a risk for development as an oil substitute, as do other fuel sources.

Judicious modeling with joint economic and engineering input using elaborate supply-side models with large input-output sectors would be my way of systematically designing scenarios to identify the winners for the next decade or two. Wharton Model projections for the decade ahead suggest that growth will be above average in communications, health care delivery, light metals, electrical machinery, printing/publishing, and chemicals. These results are generated within the input-output core of the Model and can serve as first round approximations, to be combined with expert technological assessments, in iterative steps to lay out a winning scenario.

PROSPECTS

The international perspectives of industrial policy involve comparisons of relative costs, productivities, and efficiencies. The relevant issue is the movement of various U.S. indicators in comparison with those of others. On an absolute scale, there is every reason to believe that U.S. productivity will recover, first cyclically and then on a fundamental trend path. If the present cutbacks in the U.S. public sector spending for research are only temporary, there is a basis for optimism that our customary advances on the frontiers of technology will continue. Our population composition is becoming more favorable in that we shall not have to absorb an unduly large cohort of untrained workers at the low age end of the labor force scale as we did in the 1970s.

There are good grounds for expecting the American performance to be favorable on a comparative scale in the next five to 10 years. Many of our partner countries will be experiencing some of our problems of the 1970s. The baby boom age cohort and high female labor force participation are now hitting some West European countries. In Japan, higher levels of living and a shorter working week are being sought by the working population. We are finally making good headway with energy conservation. The ratio of Btu. consumption to real GNP has been falling since 1975 and continues to move downwards. Reduced oil imports in response to price increases have been encouraging in showing that we can adjust to new situations well.

The United States shows good evidence of political stability. Vietnam and Watergate are behind us now. We do run some danger of excessive military spending. It is not that we should contract or lack ability to shoulder the burden. It is the case, however, that our allies are very reluctant to match the real expansion that is being set in motion. They plead that deficits (internal and external) and their own sensitive currency rates stand in the way of their full cooperation. So far, this is only a threat and not an absolute obstacle to an improvement in the relative position of the United States.

16.

INDUSTRIAL POLICY AND
U.S. INTERNATIONAL
TRADE

William H. Branson[1]

1. INTRODUCTION AND SUMMARY

During the period since World War II, the U.S. economy has grown relatively slower than Japan, Europe, and recently the developing countries. The result has been movement from the position of dominant industrial country in the world to the position of one of several more or less equal competitors. This was only to be expected, but institutions were built at the end of World War II that did not anticipate it. As a result, the dollar became seriously over-valued in the 1960s, precipitating the crisis of 1971 and the breakdown of the Bretton Woods system by 1973.

During the 1970s, the dollar depreciated relative to an index of major competitors' currencies, in real terms, by about 23 percent. This greatly improved U.S. competitiveness, and stabilized the U.S. share of world exports of manufactures. By 1980, the U.S. was running a large surplus in its trade in agriculture and manufactured goods, offsetting a large part of its deficit in petroleum trade. Thus the adjustment mechanism seems to work fairly well, if slowly, and the U.S. competitive position seems to have been reestablished.

A major economic event in the 1970s was the slowdown in the growth rate of productivity across the industrial world. This is illustrated in table 16–2 in section 2 below, where we see a significant drop in the growth rate around 1973. It has been particularly serious in the United States, where productivity growth seems near zero. This seems to me to be the major economic problem facing the United States. During the period 1950–73, the population learned to expect real product and income per capita to grow by nearly 3 percent per year (table

16–2, part A). But after 1973, it has grown by less than 2 percent a year. This leads to widespread frustration of expectations concerning consumption. Until expectations are adjusted to the new reality, continued inflationary pressure will result as prices and wages are pushed up in claims on real output that add up to more than 100 percent.

Thus trade has adjusted well within an overall framework of productivity slowdown and frustration of expectations. This suggests that concentration on trade problems is missing the major point, which is why did productivity growth slow, and what can or should be done about it?

In this chapter I first review trends in U.S. trade and sketch the current position. This sets the context for a discussion of current policy issues that arise in the discussion of industrial policy, which comes in the second half of the chapter.

The evolution of the U.S. economy is reviewed in section 2, and the current trade picture is discussed in section 3. There, in table 16–9, we see the patterns of surpluses and deficits alluded to above. In sections 4 through 6, trade issues are discussed. The vulnerability or national security argument for protection of particular industries such as autos or steel is evaluated in section 4 and, by and large, rejected. Proposals for export subsidies or credits are discussed in section 5, with the same result. In section 6 I suggest that Trade Adjustment Assistance (TAA) be folded into a general program for cushioning adjustment to change, but only if it is indeed an expanded program.

There are two particular issues of trade policy that should be mentioned here, even though they do not fit into the overall structure of the paper. The first is the question of an "optimum tariff" on oil imports. A tariff imposed by a major importer or group of consumers could, by reducing demand, reduce the world price of the good on which the tariff is imposed. This argument for an import duty is normally rejected, as in the General Agreement on Tariff and Trade (GATT), on the grounds that its general acceptance would simply reduce world trade as import duties rose everywhere. However, in the particular case of oil, there may be a reasonable argument for a tariff imposed uniformly by all major consumers. This policy option was explored by the Carter administration and rejected as unfeasible due to difficulties of coordination with the other Organization for Economic Cooperation and Development importers. It is discussed in more detail in the energy papers in this volume.

The second issue is intervention in foreign exchange markets. The recent literature summarized in Dornbusch (1980) has established that in the short run the exchange rate fluctuates as an asset-market price. Since the exchange rate is also the relative price of traded versus nontraded goods, a freely floating rate can cause significant short-run fluctuations in prices in goods markets. Earlier (Branson [1976]), I argued that this provides a rationale for monetary policy smoothing fluctuations in the exchange rate. This has been the policy generally followed in exchange-market interventions by central banks in the 1970s, and probably should be continued.

The essential point of the paper should be made clear at the beginning, however. The basic point to be made at the start is that the U.S. competitive position seems to be in reasonably good shape. Industrial policy should worry about U.S. productivity growth and industrial structure, not trade.

2. BROAD TRENDS IN THE U.S. POSITION IN THE WORLD ECONOMY[2]

At the end of World War II, the United States was the dominant industrial producer in the world. With industrial capacity destroyed in Europe, except for Scandinavia, and Japan, and crippled in the United Kingdom, the U.S. produced approximately 60 percent of the world output of manufactures in 1950, and its GNP was 61 percent of the total of the present (1979) OECD countries. This was obviously a transitory situation. During the 1950s the European economies recovered and rebuilt capacity, competing with the United States in world markets. Japan entered the competition in a major way in the 1960s, and in the 1970s several developing countries have become significant in terms of aggregate world output and trade in manufactures.

Thus during the 35 years since World War II, Europe, Japan and then the Less Developed Countries (LDCs) have grown faster than the United States in terms of real gross domestic product and industrial output, both aggregate and per capita. This has resulted in a shrinking U.S. share of world output and exports, and a closing of productivity differentials.

As its competitors' capacity grew faster than that of the United States, real depreciation of the dollar was required to keep trade and current account balances in line. This depreciation was delayed by monetary arrangements under the Bretton Woods agreements, which resisted change in the dollar exchange rate. Thus instead of a gradual real *de*preciation, a small real *ap*preciation appeared in the late 1960s, contributing to a growing trade imbalance. Once the Bretton Woods system broke down, a significant real depreciation of the dollar occurred during the 1970s, helping to restore balance in trade among the industrial countries.

By 1980, the United States has moved from a position of dominance to a position of equality or symmetry among groups of industrial countries. Its share of OECD real GNP is now 39 percent, and its share of world industrial production is about 35 percent, compared with 40 percent as late as 1963. The U.S. share of world exports of manufactures has fallen from 29 percent in 1953 to 17 percent in 1963 and 13 percent in 1976. The weighted real exchange rate of the United States (in index terms, 1975 = 100) depreciated from around 83 in 1961 to 117 in 1979. The U.S. economy is now part of a world of nearly symmetric interdependence.

In this section we present data describing and summarizing the change in the U.S. position in the world economy since World War II. First we look at comparative trends in production, then at competitiveness and trade, and finally at exchange rates. These data set the framework for subsequent analysis of U.S. trade policy.

MEASURES OF TRENDS IN OUTPUT

Real Gross Domestic Product per Capita and per Worker U.S. real gross domestic product and real gross domestic product per capita have grown more slowly along trend than those of the other major industrial countries since World War II. In Table 16–1 we show index numbers for real gross domestic product per capita for nine major countries: United States, Canada, Japan, Belgium, France, West Germany, Italy, the Netherlands and the United Kingdom. The data are indexed to 1967 = 100. Among these countries, the United States and the United Kingdom are at the bottom of the growth league. In table 16–2, part A, growth rates of real gross domestic product per capita are given. In terms of per capita gross domestic product, the United States growth rate is slightly lower than that of the United Kingdom, and much lower than those of the other major countries. The growth rate summary in table 16–2, part A shows a general deceleration of growth in the industrial world, throughout the period 1950–78, with the U.S. growth rate consistently slower than the others.

Tables 16–3 and 16–2, part B show index numbers and the growth rate summary for real gross domestic product per employed worker, coming closer to a home-currency productivity measure. The U.S. growth rate in these terms is relatively slower than in terms of gross domestic product per capita. Over the entire period 1950–79, the U.S. growth rate was 1.7 percent per year; the next slowest were Canada and the United Kingdom with 2.1 percent and 2.3 percent. The productivity slowdown of the 1970s is obvious in Table 16–2, part B. Compare the rows for 1960–73 and 1973–79 in the middle of the table. Productivity growth is markedly slower in the latter period in all of the countries

TABLE 16-1
Real Gross Domestic Product Per Capita, Own Country Price Weights
(Index: 1967=100)

YEAR	UNITED STATES	CANADA	JAPAN	BELGIUM	FRANCE	GERMANY*	ITALY	NETHER-LANDS	UNITED KINGDOM
				GROSS DOMESTIC PRODUCT					
1950	69.5	64.9	25.7	60.1	52.0	42.4	43.7	58.3	67.7
1955	78.3	73.2	37.1	69.2	61.3	63.5	56.5	70.3	77.9
1960	80.5	78.0	53.3	76.3	74.4	82.1	71.7	80.0	85.2
1965	93.9	93.7	81.8	94.5	92.3	98.8	89.2	94.8	96.4
1966	98.4	98.4	89.9	96.7	96.3	100.4	93.9	96.1	98.0
1967	100.0	100.0	100.0	100.0	100.0	100.0	100.0	100.0	100.0
1968	103.3	104.0	112.7	103.8	103.5	105.9	105.9	105.4	103.8
1969	105.0	107.8	125.0	110.3	109.8	113.1	111.7	110.9	105.3
1970	103.6	109.1	138.2	117.2	115.1	118.7	116.8	116.9	107.4
1971	105.4	115.3	142.1	121.6	120.2	121.3	118.0	120.4	110.1
1972	110.6	120.7	153.2	127.6	126.2	124.9	120.9	123.2	112.1
1973	115.7	128.3	166.1	135.1	131.9	130.4	128.2	129.1	120.5
1974	113.3	131.0	163.4	140.8	135.3	130.9	132.3	132.7	118.7
1975	111.2	130.5	163.6	137.8	134.9	129.0	126.6	130.3	117.9
1976	116.7	136.3	172.2	144.8	141.3	136.3	133.2	136.0	122.4
1977	121.9	138.0	179.8	146.4	144.8	140.3	135.0	139.0	123.7
1978	126.2	141.6	188.6	149.9	149.4	145.0	137.9	141.4	128.1
1979	128.1	144.3	198.2	154.7	153.6	151.4	144.2	144.1	129.1

*Excluding the Saar and West Berlin in 1950 and 1955.

SOURCE: U.S. Department of Labor

TABLE 16–2
Real Gross Domestic Product Per Capita, and Real Gross Domestic Product Per Employed Person* Own Country Price Weights
(Average Annual Percent Change)

PERIOD	UNITED STATES	CANADA	JAPAN	BELGIUM	FRANCE	GERMANY**	ITALY	NETHER-LANDS	UNITED KINGDOM
A. GROSS DOMESTIC PRODUCT PER CAPITA									
1950–79	2.1	2.8	7.3	3.3	3.8	4.5	4.2	3.2	2.2
1960–79	2.5	3.3	7.2	3.8	3.9	3.3	3.7	3.1	2.2
1960–70	2.5	3.4	10.0	4.4	4.5	3.8	5.0	3.9	2.3
1970–79	2.4	3.2	4.1	3.1	3.3	2.7	2.4	2.4	2.1
1960–73	2.8	3.9	9.1	4.5	4.5	3.6	4.6	3.7	2.7
1973–79	1.7	2.0	3.0	2.3	2.6	2.5	2.0	1.8	1.2
1976–77	4.4	1.3	4.4	1.1	2.4	3.0	1.4	2.2	1.1
1977–78	3.6	2.6	4.9	2.4	3.2	3.3	2.1	1.7	3.6
1978–79	1.5	1.9	5.1	3.2	2.8	4.4	4.6	1.9	.8
B. GROSS DOMESTIC PRODUCT PER EMPLOYED PERSON†									
1950–79	1.7	2.1	6.9	3.4	4.3	4.8	4.8	3.5	2.3
1960–79	1.5	1.9	7.1	3.7	4.2	4.0	4.6	3.6	2.4
1960–70	2.0	2.3	9.5	4.2	4.9	4.5	6.4	4.0	2.7
1970–79	1.1	1.3	4.5	3.2	3.5	3.4	2.6	3.3	2.0
1960–73	2.1	2.6	8.9	4.2	4.8	4.3	5.9	4.1	3.0
1973–79	.3	.4	3.4	2.7	2.9	3.1	1.7	2.6	1.1
1976–77	1.8	.6	4.0	1.4	2.2	2.9	1.5	2.5	.9
1977–78	.2	.2	4.6	2.5	3.5	2.4	2.2	2.2	3.2
1978–79	-.3	-1.2	4.6	3.3	2.5	3.4	3.7	2.6	.4

*Data for the latest year are based on preliminary estimates.
**Excluding the Saar and West Berlin in 1950 and 1955.
†Employment figures for the Netherlands are Dutch estimates of work-years of employed persons.
NOTE: Average annual percent changes are compound rates.
SOURCE: U.S. Department of Labor

Industrial Policy and U.S. International Trade

TABLE 16–3
Real Gross Domestic Product, Per Employed Person*
Own Country Price Weights
(Index: 1967=100)

YEAR	UNITED STATES	CANADA	JAPAN	BELGIUM	FRANCE	GERMANY**	ITALY	NETHER-LANDS†	UNITED KINGDOM
1950	68.2	65.8	29.4	58.0	45.8	41.5	38.6	56.9	68.3
1955	77.7	78.0	40.5	66.8	56.0	56.9	48.6	67.8	76.1
1960	83.4	85.5	55.2	76.2	71.0	76.4	64.6	78.9	84.2
1965	96.8	98.4	83.6	93.3	91.9	94.4	87.2	92.9	94.4
1966	99.7	99.4	90.8	95.8	95.9	100.9	94.3	94.7	96.2
1967	100.0	100.0	100.0	100.0	100.0	100.0	100.0	100.0	100.0
1968	102.2	103.7	112.0	104.4	103.4	106.3	106.9	105.4	104.8
1969	102.4	105.9	124.4	109.4	109.0	112.9	114.4	110.4	106.8
1970	101.6	107.5	137.4	114.5	114.3	118.2	120.3	116.4	109.9
1971	104.3	112.5	143.4	117.8	119.7	121.7	122.6	120.6	115.0
1972	107.4	115.7	156.5	124.2	125.8	126.5	128.9	125.9	116.9
1973	109.9	118.6	167.7	130.3	130.8	132.4	136.9	133.0	123.3
1974	106.7	117.9	167.7	134.4	134.0	135.6	139.8	137.6	121.3
1975	107.0	117.3	170.6	133.9	136.7	137.6	134.0	137.1	121.4
1976	109.7	121.5	180.0	142.1	143.1	146.2	140.7	144.6	125.6
1977	111.7	122.3	187.2	144.0	146.2	150.5	142.8	148.2	126.8
1978	112.0	122.6	195.8	147.6	151.4	154.1	145.9	151.4	130.8
1979	111.7	121.2	204.9	152.5	155.1	159.4	151.4	155.4	131.3

*Data for the latest year are based on preliminary estimates.

**Excluding the Saar and West Berlin in 1950 and 1955.

(3) Employment figures for the Netherlands are Dutch estimates of work-years of employed persons.

SOURCE: U.S. Department of Labor

Policy Areas—International Trade

384

shown. In terms of change in the growth rate, Belgium, France, Germany, and the Netherlands show the smallest decrease. The U.S. productivity growth on this measure fell from 2.1 percent per year in the earlier period to 0.3 percent per year in 1973–79.

Tables 16–1 through 16–3, and the additional data on manufacturing productivity in Branson (1980), document the fact that U.S. growth in output and productivity in manufacturing since 1950 has been slower than that of the other major industrial countries. This is the case even before adjustment for the major movements in exchange rates and the terms of trade in the 1970s. It has permitted a convergence toward the U.S. level of productivity by the late 1970s. The data imply a decline in the U.S. share of world output as the others catch up in productivity terms.

Shares of World Manufacturing Output   Calculation of shares of world manufacturing output is difficult because we have no firm data on the world aggregate. Thus any share calculation gives the share of a given country in total output of a group of industrial countries known to produce perhaps 90 percent of the world total. Share calculations have become even more difficult in the 1970s with the growth of manufacturing in the "Newly Industrializing Countries" (NICs) among the LDCs. Therefore we show here two sets of share data. The first is across an aggregate of 10 major industrial countries since 1950; the second is across an OECD estimate of world output since 1963.

Shares of total manufacturing output across 10 major OECD countries since 1950 are shown in table 16–4. Share data can be computed from underlying data supplied by the U.S. Department of Labor in one of two ways. The first is to use real output data by country, converted to a common valuation using a fixed nominal exchange rate. This is the method used for table 16–4, using 1967 exchange rates. The implicit Purchasing Power Parity (PPP) assumption in this calculation is that nominal exchange rate movements, at least along trend, have followed relative price movements. The second way to perform the calculation would be to use nominal output data and convert them at current exchange rates. If the PPP assumption were correct, the two calculations would be the same. But if the assumption is incorrect, the nominal *cum* current rate calculation will distort the share data.

In table 16–4 we see that the U.S. share of major industrial countries' total manufacturing output has indeed been shrinking—from 62 percent in 1950 to 44 percent in 1977. The countries gaining shares within the table 16–4 subset have been in Europe in the 1950s and 1960s, and Japan in the period since 1955.

The share data of table 16–4 omit manufacturing output in the

TABLE 16-4
Shares of Total Manufacturing Output in 10 Industrial Countries,
1950-77

COUNTRIES	Share of Total, Percentages						
	1950	1955	1960	1965	1970	1975	1977
United States	61.9	58.1	50.5	50.1	43.6	42.5	44.0
Canada	3.5	3.4	3.3	3.5	3.4	3.7	3.6
Japan	2.1	3.5	6.3	8.0	13.1	13.2	13.4
Denmark	0.7	0.5	0.6	0.6	0.7	0.7	0.7
France	7.6	7.1	8.1	8.1	8.9	9.8	9.6
Germany	10.1	14.1	17.2	16.7	17.2	16.5	16.0
Italy	2.2	2.5	3.1	3.1	3.7	4.3	4.3
Netherlands	1.8	1.9	2.2	2.1	2.3	2.3	2.2
Sweden	2.0	1.7	1.9	1.9	1.9	2.0	1.6
United Kingdom	8.2	7.2	6.9	5.9	5.3	4.9	4.5

SOURCE: U.S. Department of Labor

developing countries, including the Southern European OECD. However, a major development of the 1970s has been growth of output in
the NICs. This has brought them into competition with the industrialized countries in markets for manufacturing, raising fears of a "new
protectionism." Table 16-5 provides estimates of the distribution of
world output of manufactures since 1963, including the LDCs.

In the first row of table 16-5 we see the U.S. share of world output
falling from 40 percent in 1963 to 37 percent in 1970 and 35 percent in
1975-76. The rise in 1977 is probably due to the U.S. recovery that was
not matched by European growth. The 1979-80 slowdown has probably
restored the U.S. share relationship. Most of the other developed countries in the top tier of Table 16-9 have also had shrinking shares in the
1970s. In this decade the gainers have been the NICs, shown in the
middle tier in the table. On aggregate, their share has risen from 5.4
percent in 1963 to 6.6 percent in 1970 and about 9 percent in 1975-77.
Thus in terms of share of world output in manufacturing, the 10 NICs
have nearly doubled from 1963-77.

An interesting subset of the NICs is the "Gang of Four": Hong
Kong, Korea, Taiwan, and Singapore. Their share of world manufactures output has risen from 0.4 percent in 1963 to 0.7 percent in 1970
and 1.4 percent in 1976, a tripling in 15 years. Thus the major gainer
during the 1970s has been the industrializing LDCs, with the U.S.
share shrinking from 37 percent to 35 percent of the estimated world
total.

TABLE 16–5
Geographical Distribution of World Industrial Production* Percentages and Index Numbers

	1963	1970	1973	1974	1975	1976	1977
United States	40.25	36.90	36.59	36.30	34.97	35.42	36.90
Japan	5.48	9.28	9.74	9.28	8.88	9.06	9.14
Germany	9.69	9.84	9.19	8.95	8.98	8.97	8.85
France	6.30	6.30	6.25	6.35	6.25	6.25	6.15
United Kingdom	6.46	5.26	4.78	4.61	4.67	4.29	4.16
Italy	3.44	3.49	3.29	3.43	3.28	3.41	3.33
Canada	3.01	3.01	3.08	3.16	3.17	3.08	3.08
Spain	0.88	1.18	1.37	1.48	1.47	1.43	1.56
Portugal	0.23	0.27	0.30	0.31	0.31	0.30	0.32
Greece	0.19	0.25	0.30	0.30	0.33	0.33	0.33
Yugoslavia	1.14	1.25	1.31	1.43	1.60	1.53	1.62
Brazil	1.57	1.73	2.10	2.25	2.47	2.49	—
Mexico	1.04	1.27	1.30	1.38	1.54	1.44	1.45
Hong Kong	0.08	0.15	0.18	0.17	0.17	0.21	—
Korea	0.11	0.22	0.32	0.41	0.51	0.63	0.69
Taiwan	0.11	0.23	0.34	0.33	0.37	0.42	0.46
Singapore	0.05	0.06	0.08	0.08	0.09	0.09	0.10
Total "Gang of 4"	0.35	0.66	0.92	0.99	1.14	1.35	—
Total of 10 NICs above	5.40	6.61	7.60	8.14	8.86	8.87	(9.28)
Other developed countries**	10.99	9.72	9.83	9.73	10.58	9.90	9.29
Other developing countries	8.98	9.59	9.65	10.05	10.36	10.75	9.80
of which: India	1.21	1.11	1.03	1.04	1.15	1.17	1.19
Argentina	0.94	1.07	1.09	1.14	1.18	1.06	1.06
World*	100.0	100.0	100.0	100.0	100.0	100.0	100.0
World (1970 = 100)	66.0	100.0	121.0	122.0	115.0	125.0	129.0

*Excluding the Eastern bloc. Figures for 1970 represent value added, those for other years are based on industrial production indices.

**All other OECD countries plus South Africa and Israel.

SOURCE: *The Growth of World Industry,* and *Monthly Bulletin of Statistics,* United Nations: IMF Statistics; Secretariat estimates.

SOURCE: OECD

TRENDS IN COMPETITIVENESS

With manufacturing capacity and output growing relatively rapidly in Europe, Japan, and the LDCs, a significant improvement in U.S. competitiveness would have been required to hold the U.S. share of world markets. During the period 1950–70, in general, U.S. costs relative to its competitors', adjusted for exchange rate changes, did not decline. The

Industrial Policy and U.S. International Trade

result was a shrinking U.S. share of world trade in manufactures. After 1970, the depreciation of the U.S. dollar led to an improvement in U.S. competitiveness of about 36 percent (1970–79), and the U.S. share of world manufactures exports stabilized at about 13 percent.

In table 16–6 we show a measure of competitiveness for the United States, the ratio of U.S. to a trade-weighted average of fourteen competitors' unit labor costs, adjusted for exchange rate changes. This is an index of cyclically-adjusted relative "normal" unit labor cost, computed by the International Monetary Fund. In the table we see a small improvement in the mid-1960s, which was eliminated by 1969, when the index stood at 151.2 compared with 152.6 in 1961. Then the depreciation of the dollar beginning with the German float of 1969 brought relative unit labor cost down to 100 by 1975 and 93.0 by 1979.

TABLE 16–6
Index of U.S. Weighted Relative Unit Labor Cost, 1975– 100

YEAR	RELATIVE COST INDEX
1961	152.6
1962	151.8
1963	151.0
1964	151.2
1965	148.1
1966	147.5
1967	148.1
1968	151.4
1969	151.2
1970	144.8
1971	137.0
1972	123.9
1973	110.1
1974	105.9
1975	100.0
1976	105.0
1977	103.1
1978	94.6
1979	93.0

SOURCE: International Monetary Fund

With competitors' capacity growing and no significant improvement in unit labor cost, over the period 1950–1970 the United States lost 55 percent of its share of the world market for manufactures. Movements in the distribution of world exports of total manufactures for the period 1953–76 are shown in table 16–7. There we see that the U.S. share fell from 29.4 percent in 1953 to 13.4 percent by 1971. The share has been relatively constant at 13.2 percent to 13.4 percent throughout the 1970s.

1953–1959 Two-thirds of the decrease in U.S. market share since 1950 occurred in this period. The U.S. share decreased by 10.7 percent (36 percent of the 1953 share). Canada and the LDC's together lost another 2.8 percent (23 percent of their 1953 share). Most of the gain went to the centrally planned economies (hereinafter the CPEs), Germany, and Japan,[3] Germany's growth could be attributed to rapid growth in the West European economies, but it should be noted that the rest of Western Europe's market share *declined* during that period, while Germany's increased by almost 6 percent (60 percent of the 1953 share). Clearly Germany was increasing its position in the European market and capturing a larger share of non-European markets. Japan's share increased by 2.1 percent (75 percent of the 1953 share), beginning a trend which continued until 1974. Three of the LDC regions lost market shares while the Middle East's remained unchanged.

1959–1971 During the 1960s the United States lost market share at a slower pace. Germany and the CPEs stopped penetrating markets as the lead passed to Japan and the other members of the Common Market. Japan doubled its share from 5 percent to 10 percent of the world market. The non-German European Economic Community (EEC) countries gained 4 percent of the market. Canada's growth was due entirely to the rapid increase in exports of machinery and transport equipment during 1965 to 1971. Examination of bilateral flows reveals that this was due mainly to the effects of the 1965 Auto Agreement between Canada and the United States.

An interesting pattern developed among the LDCs during this period. Overall they gained only 0.2 percent of the world market. The Middle East and Africa lost; Latin America gained slightly; non-NIC Asia lost; but the NICs more than doubled their market share.

1971–1976 During the final five years the U.S. share remained constant at 13.2 percent. The shares of Japan and Germany changed only slightly. The most dramatic movement was the increase in Asian and NIC shares. All of the growth in the LDCs' share was captured by Asian countries (2.5 percent increase in market share), and half of that was

TABLE 16-7
Distribution of Exports of Manufactures (SITC 5-8)

	1953	1956	1959	1962	1965	1968	1971	1974	1976
Total (million $)	37,738	51,721	61,400	79,330	109,730	150,070	226,670	483,070	585,260
Country					Percent of Total				
Developed*	88.0	83.5	82.1	81.6	82.0	83.1	83.9	83.7	83.1
LDCs**	7.0	6.6	5.3	5.3	5.8	5.8	5.5	7.8	8.0
CPEs†	5.0	9.9	12.6	13.1	12.1	11.0	10.4	8.4	8.9
Developed									
Western Europe	49.0	50.1	53.7	54.4	54.7	53.0	54.7	54.9	54.0
EEC	—	—	31.9	33.5	34.4	34.4	35.8	*44.9	44.0
EFTA	—	—	20.3	19.2	18.4	17.2	17.2	*8.2	8.0
Germany	9.7	12.2	15.6	14.8	15.4	14.8	15.4	16.3	15.5
United States	29.4	23.0	18.7	17.6	15.8	15.8	13.4	13.2	13.2
Canada	5.0	4.3	3.9	3.5	3.7	4.9	4.6	3.4	3.5
Japan	2.8	4.2	4.9	5.5	7.1	8.1	10.0	10.9	10.9
Other	1.9	2.0	1.2	0.6	0.8	1.4	1.3	1.4	1.5
LDC									
Africa††	1.6	1.4	1.3	1.2	1.3	1.3	0.9	0.9	0.6
Latin America	1.6	1.6	1.2	1.1	1.2	1.6	1.4	1.9	1.6
Middle East	0.3	0.4	0.4	0.3	0.4	0.2	0.2	0.5	0.4
Asia‡	3.5	3.2	2.4	2.6	2.8	2.7	2.9	4.5	5.4
NICs‡‡	0.9	0.9	0.8	0.9	1.2	1.5	1.8	2.4	3.0

*Developed Market Economies: United States, Canada, Japan, Western Europe, Australia, New Zealand, and South Africa.

**All countries excluding developed and Centrally Planned Economies.

†Eastern Europe, U.S.S.R., People's Republic of China, Mongolia, North Korea, North Vietnam.

††Excludes South Africa and Rhodesia.

‡Excludes developed countries and CPEs.

‡‡Republic of Korea, Hong Kong, Singapore (Data for Taiwan were not available for the entire period).

concentrated in the three NICs. The growth of Asian exports appears to have been at the expense of the CPEs, Canada, and Africa. Had the data for Taiwan been available, the concentration of market share in the NIC category would be even higher.

Summary   Since 1953 the United States has experienced a major reduction of its share of world trade in manufactures. During the 1950s the gains were made by Western Europe, especially Germany, the CPEs, and Japan. During the 1960s Japan's share increased very rapidly while growth of Western Europe slowed and the CPEs actually lost market shares. In the 1970s the growth centers have been the Asian LDCs, especially the newly industrializing countries. Japan's share has continued to increase, but at a much slower rate than in the earlier periods.

TRENDS IN EFFECTIVE EXCHANGE RATES
The combination of growing capacity in the rest of the world relative to the United States and roughly comparable cost developments led to a significant drop in the U.S. share of world exports in manufacturing from 1950 to 1970. This in turn built up pressure for a devaluation of the U.S. dollar. Under the Bretton Woods system, a dollar devaluation was effectively ruled out, so the U.S. trade balance deteriorated after reaching a peak surplus in the early 1960s. As pressure accumulated, eventually the system broke down in 1970–71 and the U.S. exchange rate moved to reestablish equilibrium. The *real effective exchange rate* was an adjustment mechanism that was frozen during the period 1950–70, but has worked reasonably well since.

In table 16–8 we show index numbers for the U.S. nominal effective exchange rate in column 1, relative wholesale price indexes (WPIs) in column 2, and real effective exchange rates in column 3 for the period 1961–78. The period breaks clearly into two subperiods, 1961–70, where the three series are fairly constant, and 1970–79, where the effective rates depreciate substantially.

During the 1960s, the U.S. WPI fell slightly relative to the weighted average of those of the other industrial countries, from 102.6 in 1961 to 98.4 in 1970. This reflects the stable performance of relative unit labor cost shown above in table 16–6. The effective nominal exchange rate also fell slightly during this period—an *up* valuation or appreciation of the U.S. dollar as other exchange rates moved. The combination of a small relative price improvement and an equally small effective appreciation in nominal terms resulted in almost no movement in the real effective rate. From 82.9 in 1961, it rose to 85.9 in 1965 then returned to 83.0 in 1969. Thus over the 1960s there was essentially no adjustment in the real effective rate as the U.S. lost trade shares.

TABLE 16–8
U.S. Effective Exchange Rates, 1961–79,
1975 = 100

YEAR	(1) Effective Exchange Rate*	(2) U.S. WPI Relative to Competitors	(3) Exchange Rate Adjusted for Relative WPI $(3)=(1)\div(2)\times 100$
1961	85.0	102.6	82.9
1962	84.3	101.7	82.9
1963	84.2	99.7	84.4
1964	84.2	98.2	85.7
1965	84.2	98.0	85.9
1966	84.2	98.4	85.6
1967	84.0	98.7	85.1
1968	82.6	99.0	83.5
1969	82.4	99.3	83.0
1970	83.2	98.4	84.5
1971	85.5	98.3	86.9
1972	93.0	98.4	94.5
1973	101.4	98.3	103.2
1974	98.9	99.7	99.2
1975	100.0	100.0	100.0
1976	95.2	103.1	92.3
1977	96.2	100.9	95.3
1978	106.2	93.9	113.1
1979	108.4	93.0	116.6

*This is the inverse of an index of the weighted average of foreign exchange prices of the U.S. dollar.

SOURCE: International Monetary Fund

Beginning in 1971, nominal bilateral rates began to move substantially, and the U.S. real effective rate began to adjust. From 1970–79 the index of the nominal effective rate fell from 83.2 to 108.4, as shown in column 1 of table 16–8. This is a nominal appreciation of the weighted average of foreign currencies of 30.3 percent $[(108.4/83.2)-1]$ against the dollar, or a devaluation of the dollar of 23.2 percent $[(83.2/108.4)-1]$.

From 1970 to 1974, U.S. price performance roughly matched the average of its competitors, as shown in column 2 of table 16–7. Then from 1975 to 1977, during the recovery from the 1974–75 recession, U.S. prices rose relative to the competitors' index, but this movement was reversed in 1978–79. The movements in relative prices since 1974 have tended to make swings in the real effective rate bigger than in the nominal rate, as a comparison of columns 1 and 3 will show. From 1970–79, the real effective dollar rate depreciated by 27.5 percent, compared with the nominal devaluation of 23.2 percent.

In terms of broad trends, U.S. price performance has been roughly comparable to that of its industrial competitors since 1960. During the decade 1960–70, the nominal effective U.S. rate was essentially constant (with a small upward creep due to an occasional devaluation in one of the other countries), and so was the real effective rate. With capacity growing abroad, the United States lost trade shares. In the 1970s, movement in the nominal effective U.S. rate has brought about a real effective devaluation of nearly 30 percent, and the shrinkage of export shares has been halted. It appears that the real effective rate has worked as an instrument for adjustment, and that its movements have come through movements in the nominal rate with roughly parallel price performance.

3. TRENDS IN THE COMPOSITION OF U.S. TRADE

At the end of World War II, the pattern of U.S. trade was distorted by the fact that industrial capacity had been significantly reduced in the other major advanced countries. Trade in consumer goods provides a good example of this distortion. In every year from 1925 to 1938 the United States was a net importer of consumer goods. But in 1946 the United States emerged from the war as a net exporter, and in 1947 the surplus on consumer goods was $1 billion. As industrial capacity was rebuilt in Europe and Japan, the surplus shrank steadily, and in 1959 the United States again became a net importer, with a deficit in consumer goods that has grown steadily since then. This example is typical of the pattern we see in the long-run data on the composition of trade. During the years since 1950 the composition of U.S. trade has moved back toward its longer run base of comparative advantage. By the mid-1960s we see growing surpluses in trade in capital goods, chemicals, and agriculture, and deficits in consumer goods and nonagricultural industrial supplies and materials. Trade in automotive products switched from surplus to deficit in 1968.

The evaluation of the composition of U.S. trade is discussed in detail in Branson (1980). Here I will summarize the long-run trends briefly, and then focus on two aspects of the picture: (1) the position of U.S. comparative advantage in 1980, and (2) the need to disaggregate below the industry level in studying trade issues.

THE U.S. POSITION IN 1980

The U.S. trade position in 1980 is an extension of the trends detailed in Branson (1980); it is summarized in table 16–9. There we show U.S.

TABLE 16–9
U.S. Trade, 1979–80,
($ billions, annual rates)

Category	1979 Exports	1979 Imports	1979 Balance	1980 (Third Quarter) Exports	1980 (Third Quarter) Imports	1980 (Third Quarter) Balance
Total	185.0	211.5	−26.5	228.1	236.5	−8.4
Agricultural	35.4	17.4	18.0	43.8	18.2	25.6
Nonagricultural	149.6	194.1	−44.5	184.3	218.3	−34.0
Nonagricultural						
Industrial supplies and materials	51.4	109.9	−58.5	62.2	121.5	−59.3
Petroleum	2.0	60.0	−58.0	2.7	69.1	−56.4
Chemicals	14.5	4.5	10.0	17.7	4.9	12.8
Capital Goods	58.2	24.6	32.9	77.6	30.0	47.6
Autos	17.4	25.6	−8.2	16.5	28.1	−11.6
Consumer goods	12.6	30.6	−18.0	16.0	34.3	−18.3
Military	3.0	—	3.0	2.9	—	2.9
Other	7.0	3.4	3.6	9.1	4.4	4.7

Source: *Survey of Current Business*, 12/80

trade in 1979 and in the third quarter of 1980 (annual rate), by major and end-use categories. The patterns of surpluses and deficits are instructive.

The surpluses in capital goods and chemicals have grown since the period just after World War II. These are clear areas of comparative advantage. The deficit on consumer goods we already have discussed; that on autos has existed since 1968. The deficit on petroleum is obvious, and the agricultural surplus became a major element also around 1974.

If we aggregate the data slightly differently, we see more clearly the post-1974 adjustment in U.S. trade. In 1979, the deficit on trade in petroleum of $58 billion was substantially offset by surpluses of $18 billion in agriculture and $13.5 billion in nonpetroleum manufactures, leaving a net trade deficit of $26.5 billion. In the third quarter of 1980, the petroleum deficit was $56.4 billion, but the agricultural surplus was $25.6 billion and the manufactures surplus $22.4 billion, leaving a net deficit of $8.4 billion.

Thus the petroleum deficit is largely offset by *surpluses* in agriculture and manufacturing. Within manufacturing there is a clear division by comparative advantage, with a very large and growing surplus in capital goods and smaller but significant deficits on consumer goods and autos and a surplus in chemicals. In its trade in manufactured goods, the United States is becoming increasingly specialized along lines of comparative advantage.

The U.S. economy has responded to the oil price increase, which is generating a $56 billion deficit by 1980, by expanding its trade surpluses along its lines of comparative advantage. The degree of adjustment is indeed quite remarkable; by 1980 we could nearly balance trade overall, with a $56 billion oil deficit. The movement in the real exchange rate helped, improving the U.S. competitive position. Thus, it appears that adjustment has worked remarkably well in the United States.

The problem is not in the overall trade balance, then. It is in the rate of change of industrial composition implicit in the enormous growth of exports in capital goods and imports of consumer goods and autos. Even steel is balanced by other items within nonagricultural industrial supplies and materials, less petroleum and chemicals. The rate at which industrial composition is changing, and the degree of specialization this might imply, seem to be at the root of perceived problems in trade. Before we turn to these problems in subsequent sections, we should look at a little more data to see the importance of disaggregation.

DISAGGREGATION IN STEEL AND TEXTILES
In the debate on trade policy, the discussion frequently is at a far too aggregate level. One can hear the rhetorical question: "How can the

United States live without a steel industry?" in many congressional hearing rooms. The answer is that the *part* of the steel industry that reflects U.S. comparative advantage in production using technology and skill will do fine in trade; the branches using less skilled labor or even heavy doses of capital will migrate.

In steel, the United States has long had a rough balance in trade in basic materials, reflecting national endowment and transport costs. The growing deficit since the early 1970s has been in the category "other primary metals, crude and semimanufactured."[4] On the other hand, the United States has had a small surplus in "finished metal shapes and advanced manufactures" since 1973. This is probably an area of comparative advantage and expansion. The steel industry will be different in 1990 from that in 1980, but it will still exist in the United States. It will grow along lines of comparative advantage.

A second example of the need to disaggregate is textiles. The growing deficit in consumer textiles is a famous source of trade friction. But since 1974 the United States has had a surplus in industrial textiles.[5] This may result at least partially from the effective protection given the industry in the United States by price controls on petroleum. But the fact will remain that on industrial textiles the United States competes; in consumer textiles specialization and comparative advantage go the other way.

The point has already been stated: the branches of industry that express U.S. comparative advantage are competing and expanding; the others are shrinking and migrating. This is not at all surprising, but the *pace* of change can pose problems of adjustment.

4. VULNERABILITY, SECURITY, AND PROTECTION

International trade generally yields benefits by permitting a country to specialize its production along its line of comparative advantage, and then to trade with the world for a diverse basket of goods—in the United States, mainly consumer goods. In this sense, countries behave similarly to individuals in a market economy. Individuals specialize in selling one form of labor according to their comparative advantage, and with the proceeds they buy a basket of consumer goods from other agents in the system. The gains from a system of specialization and trade are obvious. The entire set of post-World War II institutions—World Bank, IMF, GATT—is organized to support freedom of international trade to permit countries to specialize and earn the gains from trade.

This argument assumes that after a country specializes it can indeed trade for a diversified consumption bundle. That is, it assumes security of sources of supply. If supply of import goods is highly uncertain, specialization becomes vulnerability, and the extreme form of the free trade argument can begin to break down. In a world of massive uncertainty (such as an anarchic state), this argument could lead in the direction of autarky. In U.S. trade policy, it provides a rationale for protection for particular industries on vulnerability, or "national defense" grounds.

Two separate tests must be passed by an argument for protection on vulnerability grounds. First, supply interruption must be plausible. It is not enough to note that effective defense requires chromium, or basic steel, or automotive products. It should also be plausible that the United States could be cut off from supply, implying that there are few enough sellers, concentrated in a hostile or potentially inaccessible area. Second, if the supply cut-off test is passed, the question remains whether to protect the domestic industry or to stockpile. The answers to both questions differ for raw materials and manufactures, so let us consider each in turn.

RAW MATERIALS

The regional distribution of reserves of raw materials as of 1977 is shown in table 16–10, taken from OECD Interfutures (1979: 48–49). There we see the share of the leading three and five countries in total world reserves, and the shares of each of the leading five.

As the Interfutures study notes, the interesting exercise is to identify minerals with a high geographical concentration of reserves located in countries that are potentially unfriendly to the United States. The study identifies four minerals groups which have these properties: platinum, chromium, manganese, and vanadium. Rather than paraphrasing, I will simply quote the analysis of the situation on these minerals:

1. As far as the *platinum-group metals* are concerned, 98.5% of the world reserves are in only two countries—South Africa and the USSR. Moreover, each of these countries specializes in one of the two major metals of the group. South Africa produces more than two-thirds of all platinum and the USSR two-thirds of all palladium. In most present uses—the automobile, chemical, electrical and petroleum-refining industries—substitution of other materials for platinum metals is theoretically possible. Moreover, because of the high unit prices of the platinum metals, they are even now used only when fully justified for technical and economic reasons. All told, any interruption of supplies would be a problem, at least in the short term, for all OECD countries except Canada.
2. More than 96% of the reserves of *chromium* are located in only two countries—South Africa and Rhodesia. Chromium is used mainly for metallurgical, chemical and refractory purposes. As there is no known substitute for chromium in most metallurgical applications nor in certain

TABLE 16-10
Regional Distribution of Measured and Indicated Reserves, 1977

Raw Material	Share of Leading Three Countries	Share of Leading Five Countries	Countries' Percentage Share
Iron	59.4	76.7	U.S.S.R. (30.2), Brazil (17.5), Canada (11.7), Australia (11.5), India (5.8)
Copper	44.9	58.7	U.S. (18.5), Chile (18.5), U.S.S.R. (7.9), Peru (7.0), Canada (6.8), Zambia (6.4)
Lead	47.8	61.4	U.S. (20.8), Australia (13.8), U.S.S.R. (13.2), Canada (9.5), South Africa (4.1)
Tin	50.2	68.1	Indonesia (23.6), China (14.8), Thailand (11.8), Bolivia (9.7), Malaysia (8.2), U.S.S.R. (6.1), Brazil (5.9)
Zinc	45.8	58.6	Canada (18.7), U.S. (14.5), Australia (12.6), U.S.S.R. (7.3), Ireland (5.5)
Aluminum	62.8	74.8	Guinea (33.9), Australia (18.6), Brazil (10.3), Jamaica (6.2), India (5.8), Guianas (4.1), Cameroon (4.1)
Titanium	59.0	74.1	Brazil (26.3), India (17.5), Canada (15.2), South Africa (8.6), Australia (6.6), Norway (6.4), U.S. (6.0)
Chromite	96.9	97.9	South Africa (74.1), Rhodesia (22.2), U.S.S.R. (0.6), Finland (0.6), India (0.4), Brazil (0.3), Madagascar (0.3)
Cobalt	63.0	83.5	Zaïre (30.3), New Caledonia (18.8), U.S.S.R. (13.9), Philippines (12.8), Zambia (7.7), Cuba (7.3)
Columbium	88.5	95.3	Brazil (76.6), U.S.S.R. (6.4), Canada (5.5) Zaïre (3.8), Uganda (3.0), Nigeria (3.0)

Manganese	90.5	97.7	South Africa (45.0), U.S.S.R. (37.5), Australia (8.0), Gabon (5.0), Brazil (2.2)
Molybdenum	74.3	86.9	U.S. (38.4), Chile (27.8), Canada (8.1), U.S.S.R. (6.6), China (6.0)
Nickel	54.5	76.8	New Caledonia (25.0), Canada (16.0), U.S.S.R. (13.5), Indonesia (13.0), Australia (9.3), Philippines (9.0)
Tantalum*	72.7	84.8	Zaire (55.0), Nigeria (11.0), U.S.S.R. (2.9), North Korea (6.4), U.S. (6.1)
Tungsten	69.6	80.6	China (46.9), Canada (12.1), U.S.S.R. (10.6), North Korea (5.6), U.S. (5.4), Australia (2.7)
Vanadium	94.9	97.2	U.S.S.R. (74.8), South Africa (18.7), Chile (1.4), Australia (1.4), Venezuela (0.9), India (0.9)
Bismuth	47.9	60.9	Australia (20.7), Bolivia (16.3), U.S. (10.9), Canada (6.5), Mexico (6.5), Peru (5.4)
Mercury	65.2	78.3	Spain (38.4), U.S.S.R. (18.2), Yugoslavia (8.6), U.S. (8.6), China (4.5), Mexico (4.5), Turkey (4.5), Italy (4.1)
Silver	54.9	76.5	U.S.S.R. (26.2), U.S. (24.8), Mexico (13.9), Canada (11.6), Peru (10.0)
Platinum	99.5	99.9	South Africa (82.3), U.S.S.R. (15.6), Canada (1.6), Columbia (0.3), U.S. (0.1)
Asbestos	81.3	91.8	Canada (42.7), U.S.S.R. (32.3), South Africa (6.3), Rhodesia (6.3), U.S. (4.2)

*1974 Figures

SOURCES: U.S. Bureau of Mines. *Mineral Facts and Problems.*
U.S. Bureau of Mines. *Commodity Data Summaries 1977.*
Bundesanstalt für Geowissenschaften und Rohstoffe, Deutsche Institut für Wirtschaftsforschung. *Untersuchungen über Angebot und Nachfrage mineralischer Rohstoffe,* Vol. VII. Hanover/Berlin: Chrom, 1975. Cf. also Bundesanstalt für Geowissenschaften und Rohstoffe. *Regionale Verteilung der Weltbergproduktion.* Hanover: 1975.

chemical uses, it is a critical material for almost all OECD countries. As long as South Africa's exports continue, an interruption of supplies from Rhodesia would cause only short-term problems. If, however, supplies from both countries, and in particular from South Africa, were disrupted, the supply situation of the Western industrialized countries would become highly uncertain.

3. As long as marine nodules are not being mined on a large scale, *manganese* can also be considered a critical mineral. The bulk of the reserves are located in South Africa and the USSR, but since production is more widely distributed than in the case of chromium or the platinum-group, it would be easier for the OECD countries to adjust in the space of a few years if certain supplies were to be interrupted. Nevertheless, the short-term effects would be serious because manganese is essential for the production of almost all steels, and it has no substitute in its main uses.

4. In many respects the situation for vanadium is different. Even though the USSR and South Africa hold nearly all the reserves, the dependence of the OECD countries is much less. Other materials such as columbium, molybdenum, manganese, titanium and tungsten can substitute for vanadium and, allowing for a lead time of two or three years to start production, the United States could produce ample supplies from domestic reserves—or even be self-sufficient—while Europe and Japan could buy elsewhere.[6]

From the analysis, it appears that platinum, chromium, and manganese could be sensitive materials from a security point of view. The best response would be to stockpile these, if more detailed analysis validates the Interfutures view for the United States.

MANUFACTURES

The steel industry is currently protected by the trigger price mechanism, and protection for the auto industry is under serious consideration, with "voluntary" export restraint by the Japanese a likely candidate. Marina Whitman (1981) has recently advanced a version of the "infant industry" argument for temporary protection of the auto industry. She argues that the amount of investment currently underway in the industry, as it shifts toward smaller, fuel-efficient cars, is so large relative to the existing capital stock that the industry is, in effect, starting over. The argument continues that the domestic market should be preserved until the industry works its way down its new cost curve. I have not heard a similar argument for steel.

The infant industry argument is generally based on the assertion that the entire economy can gain from the development of a particular industry. This would justify a temporary subsidy to the industry while it grows to the size needed to take advantage of the assumed externality that reduces cost. Implicit in the argument is the assumption that the industry is one in which the country in question has a comparative advantage. The infant industry position on autos should be considered as one version of the "pick-the-winners" strategy, with autos implicitly identified as a potential winner. *If* that strategy is adopted, *and if* closer analysis reveals that the auto industry is an area of future U.S. comparative advantage, then the argument could be sustained. But it is hard for me to see why assembled autos are high on the list of skill and technology-intensive components of industry that are the future growth sector in the United States.

The other, and more common, argument that protection of autos or steel is in the social interest, is based on consideration of vulnerability or national security. If the United States is to be secure defensively, it must produce its own steel and autos, the argument goes. Let us see how this meets the test of plausibility of supply cut-off.

In table 16–11 we show data on the world distribution of steel production and exports in 1978. The 12 largest producers, plus four regions, are listed. We see that there is a wide distribution of production. Canada plus the Western Europeans aggregate to a share of 20 percent of production; Japan provides another 18 percent. *If* the U.S. steel industry were to shrink relative to the rest of the world, it would probably be due to the growth in capacity in Latin America, an area still likely to support the United States in any conflict large enough to make the availability of steel questionable. Thus the vulnerability argument does not seem to make much sense in steel.

The data on the world auto industry are summarized in tables 16–12 and 16–13. The last column of table 16–12 shows that in 1978 the Western Europeans together had a share of 27 percent, with the United States at 30 percent and Japan at 22 percent. Since then, Japan has gained and the United States lost until the three areas are probably about even with shares of 25–30 percent. Again, Latin America is a growth area in autos, so that further loss of U.S. share would probably reflect growth in Japan and Latin America. The result is the same as for steel; an effective supply cut-off of access to vehicle production seems extremely remote. It may be sensible to preserve some minimum capacity to produce military vehicles in the United States, but that hardly warrants protection of the entire auto industry.

Thus the vulnerability or national security argument for protection of steel or autos in the United States does not seem to pass the test. This does not mean that the auto or steel industry will disappear in the United States if left unprotected. Rather, based on the discussion of section 3 above, the parts of the industry that are based on the sources of U.S. comparative advantage—skill and technology—will probably

TABLE 16–11
Steel Production and Exports, 1978

Countries	Production*		Exports**	
	Production in Million Metric Tons	Percentage of Total	Value in Million U.S. Dollars	Percentage of Total
United States	252.97	18.54	1680.24	3.52
Canada	26.41	1.94	1088.70	2.28
United Kingdom	43.34	3.18	2054.37	4.30
West Germany	80.07	5.87	8594.76	17.98
Italy	46.05	3.37	3151.20	6.60
France	48.26	3.54	4643.46	9.72
U.S.S.R.	301.63	22.10	—	—
Spain	25.20	1.85	1209.83	2.53
Brazil	19.00	1.39	451.92	0.95
South Africa	12.93	0.95	590.02	1.23
Japan	239.58	17.55	11718.03	24.52
Romania	24.39	1.79	—	—
Eastern Europe (less Romania)	89.14	6.53	—	—
Other Western Europe	80.03	5.86	11863.39	24.82
Asia (Less Japan)	67.81	4.97	560.64	1.17
South America (less Brazil)	7.75	.57	190.24	0.40
Total	1364.56	100.00	47796.72	100.00

*source: U.N. *Yearbook of Industrial Statistics,* 1978.
**source: U.N. *Yearbook of International Trade Statistics,* 1978.

TABLE 16-12
Auto Production, * *1978*

Country	Passenger Cars	Trucks and Buses	Total Units	Percentage of Total
Australia	0.32	0.07	0.38	0.87
Canada	1.14	0.67	1.82	4.16
France	3.11	0.40	3.51	8.03
West Germany	3.89	0.29	4.19	9.58
Italy	1.50	0.15	1.66	3.80
Japan	5.97	3.29	9.27	21.20
Spain	0.98	0.15	1.15	2.63
Sweden	0.25	0.05	0.31	0.71
United Kingdom	1.22	0.38	1.61	3.68
United States	9.17	3.72	12.90	29.50
U.S.S.R.	1.31	0.85	2.16	4.94
Latin America	0.91	0.71	1.62	3.70
Western Europe	0.33	0.05	0.38	0.87
Eastern Europe	2.53	0.24	2.77	6.33
Total			43.73	100.00

* All figures in millions of units, corrected to two decimal points.

SOURCE: *World Motor Vehicle Data,* 1979 edition, Michigan

TABLE 16–13
Auto Exports, * 1978

Country	Passenger Cars*	Trucks and Buses	Total Units	Percentage of Total
France	1.58	0.15	1.73	13.62
West Germany	1.90	0.16	2.08	16.38
Italy	0.63	0.08	0.72	5.67
Japan	3.04	1.55	4.60	36.22
Spain	0.36	0.03	.40	3.15
Sweden	0.20	0.04	.25	1.97
United Kingdom	0.46	0.14	.61	4.80
United States	0.66	0.29	.96	7.56
U.S.S.R.	1.35	—	1.35	10.63
Total			12.70	100

*All figures in millions of units, corrected to two decimal points.

Source: *World Motor Vehicle Data,* 1979 edition, Michigan

grow, while the other branches will migrate to countries where production is most efficient.

5. EXPORT SUBSIDIES OR CREDITS

Discussion of a new industrial policy in the United States will inevitably bring to the surface proposals to subsidize exports, or to provide credit on terms easier than the market provides to exporters. The issue will surely arise in congressional discussion of the Reagan administration's proposal to cut the lending authority of the Export-Import Bank by 30 percent from its present level, for example.[7] In the long run, export subsidies or credits simply shift resources to less efficient uses, with no effect on the balance of payments, and no clear benefit to any particular sector or group in the United States, even the exporters.

LONG-RUN EFFECT OF AN EXPORT SUBSIDY

An export subsidy will, in the short run after its imposition, raise profits, output, and exports in the subsidized industry. The profit increase will also raise the market values of the firms involved. But this cannot be a long-run equilibrium result. The relatively high profits in the newly-subsidized industry will attract capital and labor, and the industry will expand. As it does, prices will fall or costs rise until the profit rate inclusive of the subsidy has been reduced to the competitive profit rate in the economy.

In the new, subsidized, long-run equilibrium then, profits and wages are essentially the same as in competitive industries. The subsidized industry has expanded, pulling resources from elsewhere in the economy. The subsidy is consumed by a loss of efficiency in the economy; the only parties who benefit are the fortunate stockholders at the time the subsidy was passed, and foreign importers if the world price of the subsidized good has been pushed down.

Exports of the subsidized good are increased, but to the extent that this would generate a current-account surplus, the exchange rate will adjust to offset the effect of the subsidy. As exports rise, the current-account deficit shrinks or the surplus increases, and the exchange rate will appreciate relative to its equilibrium in the absence of the subsidy.[8] Thus the balance of payments effects are consumed by a change in the exchange rates that could make imports marginally cheaper as the result of the export subsidy.

Thus the argument for an export subsidy has to be based on a reason for expanding the output of a particular industry, based on the presumption that the industry is at a competitive disadvantage vis à vis other industries in the United States that are competing for the same capital and labor resources.

DEFENSIVE OR COMPETITIVE SUBSIDIES

This analysis also applies to the argument that the United States should subsidize exports or provide a credit advantage because foreign competitors follow these policies. If a foreign competitor's export subsidies would have an effect on the *aggregate* U.S. current-account balance, the exchange rate would adjust to offset this effect. This means, again, that a defensive subsidy must be justified in terms of the *particular industry* being subsidized. An argument to subsidize the sale of electrical generators abroad must be based on a reason why we prefer to sell electrical generators rather than something else.

EXPORT SUBSIDIES AND IMPORT TARIFFS

An argument for an export subsidy could be based on the existence of tariffs on imports. The basic argument of this paper supports the elimination of tariffs, except in cases of national security, rigorously demonstrated. But suppose we accept the fact that tariffs exist. The reduction of imports that follows would appreciate the equilibrium value of the exchange rate, reducing exports. The exchange rate would appreciate until the current account is balanced. One might argue that the reduction in exports should be eliminated by an export subsidy, since the effect on exports was an unintended effect of the import duty. But this argument assumes that a surplus on the current account is a reasonable target for a policy of import duties. The point of the latter, however, is to move resources into import-competing industries, and *out of* export industry. This is on the assumption, of course, that the import duties are imposed for a rational purpose in the first place.

EXPORT-IMPORT BANK

The argument above applies to Ex-Im Bank activities as well as other subsidies. The provision of credit to exporters at terms better than they can obtain in the market could be justified if those borrowers were at a relative disadvantage for some reason. However, there is little reason to assume that recipients of Ex-Im loans are firms that are disadvantaged in the credit markets. The firms to which credit is allocated tend to be major exporters, not small companies trying to break into international trade. And, as the Reagan administration's budget document notes: ". . . a large proportion of the Bank's annual lend-supports exports by a handful of large firms. In 1980 seven firms accounted for two-thirds of direct loans."[9]

The conclusion is that subsidies or differential credits directed specifically at exports are in general not productive policy. A new industrial policy may decide to subsidize some particular industry as part of a redevelopment plan. But there is no apparent reason to focus the subsidy on exports.

6. ADJUSTMENT ASSISTANCE

The trade data discussed in Branson (1980) show a pattern of rapid change in the U.S. economy. For example, the trade surplus in capital goods and deficit in consumer goods are growing at increasingly rapid rates. These data reflect rapid structural change in the economy, change that can impose severe hardship on workers, communities, and shareholders. It is this adjustment that Trade Adjustment Assistance (TAA) is meant to facilitate.

But trade is not the only source of disruption in the economy. There is a continuing turnover of products, firms, and jobs in the economy from domestic, as well as international, competition. The pace of change may well be rising throughout the economy, as well as in the sectors producing traded goods. This need to adjust in a dynamic economy is the reason we have, in general, adjustment assistance programs such as unemployment compensation and manpower retraining.

The question that must be asked is: Why have a special program for assistance to those affected by international trade? Presumably they should be entitled to the same assistance as others who must adjust to economic change. The answer probably lies in a historic compromise involving labor support for tariff cuts, but it seems reasonable to question whether the program should last indefinitely after the tariff cuts are finished.

TAA probably should be merged into an expanded program that cushions the impact of rapid economic change. The program should make a careful distinction between temporary income support and adjustment assistance. Income support along the lines of existing unemployment compensation would provide support during periods of fluctuation in aggregate demand. Adjustment assistance would be aimed at workers who move between firms or geographical localities. In general, adjustment assistance should be provided only to workers who do, in fact, adjust. Too much of past TAA programs have impeded, rather than encouraged, assistance by providing subsidies for unemployed workers who do not move or adjust. The Reagan administration's proposal to make TAA follow the exhaustion of ordinary unemployment benefits, rather than add to them is correct in principle.[10] Unfortunately, the Administration seems also to propose to cut back on adjustment assistance in general, a move in the wrong direction.[11]

Thus, in this period of rapid change and dislocation, a comprehensive program cushioning the effects of change is needed, and TAA should be folded into that. But in the absence of this program, TAA may be a good partial substitute for a large number of workers.

NOTES

1. Thanks go to Uday Mehta for research assistance.
2. This section and the next one are based on sections II and III in Branson (1980), with additions, deletions, and updating.
3. Most of the centrally planned economies' increase was due to rapid postwar expansion of their own markets, i.e., most of the increase was in trade among CPEs.
4. See Branson (1980: table 22) for details.
5. See Branson (1980: table 22 and figure 10).
6. OECD Interfutures (1979: 50).
7. See U.S. Government (1981: 4–41 ff.).
8. See Dornbusch (1980) or Branson (1977) for the analysis.
9. U.S. Government (1981: 4–41).
10. See U.S. Government (1981: 1–30 ff.).
11. See U.S. Government (1981: 1–22, 26).

BIBLIOGRAPHY

Branson, William H. " 'Leaning Against the Wind' as Exchange Rate Policy." Paper read at Graduate Institute of International Studies, Geneva, November 28, 1976. Revised, April, 1981 for publication.

Branson, William H. "Asset Markets and Relative Prices in Exchange Rate Determination." *Sozialwissenschaftliche Annalen* 1 (1977). Reprints in International Finance 20. Princeton: Princeton University, International Finance Section, 1980.

Branson, William H. "Trends in United States Trade and Investment since World War II." In *The American Economy in Transition,* edited by Martin Feldstein. National Bureau of Economic Research Monograph. Chicago: University of Chicago Press, 1980.

Dornbusch, Rudiger. "Exchange Rate Economics: Where Do We Stand?" *Brookings Papers on Economic Activity* 1, (1980): 143–185.

U.S. Government, *America's New Beginning: A Program For Economic Recovery,* A White House Report. Washington: Government Printing Office, 1981. 0–338–363, 1981.

Whitman, Marina V. N., "International Trade and Investment: Two Perspectives." Graham Memorial Lecture, Princeton University, Princeton, N.J., March, 1981.

DISCUSSANTS

Sol C. Chaikin

I want to talk about international trade, its effect on our country, our country's policies, and what I perceive to be the national interest. I am a union organizer and I have no specific training in economics or political science, although I have been exposed to them. I find that many of us who specialize in our chosen fields spend a good deal of time talking about theory and fail to get into the local communities and to live in the real world. Adam Smith spoke words of wisdom 200 years ago, but that was within the context of a world that was 200 years younger. I would like to paint a picture of the world as I perceive it at this moment.

I submit that the world today is a closed trading society. The European Common Market exists to open up trading opportunities within its borders, but not to open up trading opportunities outside of it. Through its sovereign power, France has been a banker for any number of its industries, either through grants of money, soft loans, or restrictive import policies. Though these protectionist policies are distasteful to many people, the government of France has understood for the last decade or more that its responsibility is to its people and to its national strength, and that people at work add to national strength while people out of work, displaced from work, weaken the economic and sociopolitical fabric of a country. England too, to a large extent, has injected itself to create an imbalance. It is the national policy of the British government to keep British steelworkers at work in an uneconomic enterprise. As a result, they pile up huge inventories of steel which cannot readily be sold on the international market. Since they cannot forever accumulate inventory, they have to convert some of the inventory into currency. This means selling it in the United States at prices well below the cost of manufacturing the steel in Great Britain (and certainly well below the cost of manufacturing steel here). Does that mean that we are involved in a free and competitive transaction in the world market among steel producers, sellers, and users?

Let us now look at the command economies of Eastern Europe. Those countries and the problems they pose have been neglected in our discussion. For many reasons, however, the command economies of Eastern Europe are increasing in importance as trading partners in the world. One factor is that they have to respond, I think, to a greater extent to the needs of their own people; to provide them with goods and services which they have failed to provide through their own economic infrastructure. Second, we find that there are apparently plenty of dollars and other local currencies available to lend to those command economies in order to prop them up and keep them going. They are becoming more important on the world scene, and yet when we trade with them, we do not trade in the usual sense. That is, a bargain freely struck between two interests, not necessarily mutually strong or well balanced, but at least arguably an opportunity to bargain back and forth. Rather than dealing in a free market community where there is a price on the value for things, one deals with state trading corporations. If they sell goods to the United States which they produce at less than market value, or at cost, they do so because they absorb the social cost of unemployment by keeping people at work, even at activities which are not necessarily desirable or useful at that moment. Does that mean that we are engaged in free trading?

Japan is also not a free and open trading society. I give the Japanese great credit in that they have been able to penetrate the markets of every one of our western, industrial communities, and at the same time withhold that opportunity to a remarkable extent. There are many of our economic units in the western, industrial societies which, if they could trade freely in Japan, might find a market for their goods in Japan.

Last, there are the newly-industrialized countries and the Third World, developing nations which, from the very beginning, have protected their infant industries. They have, however, invited multinational corporations to come in when it suits their purpose, and subsidized them in every way. The worst kind of subsidy is the exploitation of their local labor, asking in return only that a proportion of the newly-erected production be made available for export. They then provide substantial export subsidies in order to bring to fruition their hopes of entering the export market.

If that is the kind of world in which Adam Smith lived, then I will accept his and David Ricardo's doctrine of comparative advantage, and be willing then to lie back and accept whatever happens. However, this is not that kind of world.

Let me tell you what has happened to the United States in the last seven or eight years insofar as imports of goods are concerned. We must bear in mind that we are also an exporting nation and also that, in some categories of products, there is an excess of import over export. In 1972, the total imports, including fuel oil, into this country were about $56 billion. In 1980, $239 billion of imports came in various industries and various product lines. In industrial supplies and materials, $20 billion came in 1972 and $129 billion in 1980. In capital goods, electrical machinery, industrial machinery, farm tractors, business machines and computers, and civilian aircraft and parts, there was a total of $6.5 billion in 1972, and over $30 billion in 1980. For example, in terms of automobiles, in 1972 there were about $8 billion worth of passenger cars coming into the country, and almost $17 billion of passenger cars came in 1980. In 1972, $2.5 billion worth of automobile parts and engines were imported, while in 1980, $6 billion worth came in. These are just figures, but I would like to translate some of them into reality. Two million jobs have been lost in this country in clothing and apparel alone; hundreds of thousands of jobs have been lost to American workers in the last decade. Left to its own devices, the prognosis for the automobile industry is dire in outlook. This is regardless of the circumstances that created the present problem. Many hundreds of thousands of additional jobs will be lost to American workers directly employed by automobile companies and many more hundreds of thousands of jobs will be lost by companies which offer supplies to that industry. An economy which has not been able to solve the problem of high, increasing, and sustained unemployment over the major part of the last decade could not absorb the additional blows which would flow from a diminution of our employment opportunities in the automobile industry.

The function of sovereign power can be to control what comes into the country and what goes out, but primarily it is to act in the national interest. It is not in the national interest of the United States to have the only free and open market, subject to all kinds of import penetration. If we do not evolve a rational system of fair trade, then any number of things will have an impact on any plans for the economy. Public spending can be cut to the bone, and the devil can be chopped out of the budget, but if two million more Americans become unemployed, the so-called third party cost of maintaining these human beings will cause, not a balanced budget, but a budget with as great or greater a deficit than the previous Administration ever had. There will be very much less in taxes coming into the Federal government and far greater outlays leaving. I am absolutely persuaded that a rational system of fair trade must take into account the annual changes in market conditions and market and import penetration. We ought to use market agreements and review them every year or two years; we ought to be as generous as we reasonably can in regard to the admission of products made overseas, for they add a great deal to our national wellbeing: They add diversity, they add challenge, and they also offer workers overseas an opportunity to work and increase their standards of living. However, to do that without safeguards for domestic employment opportunities, at least to maintain our current standard of living, would be foolish in the extreme.

If Mainland China really tried, they could take over almost all of the labor-intensive industry in the United States over the next 10 or 15 years. Where will the jobs be for the five to 10 million workers displaced? These jobs would be lost, not because of mistakes that their employers and merchandisers made insofar as the lifestyles or the taste of Americans. The jobs would not be lost because management was inefficient and inattentive. The jobs would be lost because you cannot compete in labor-intensive industries against workers earning 15 cents an hour. In the United States, the low earnings of workers are at around $5 an hour, and the cost of labor is an appreciable part of the product.

There is no question but that it is essential to evolve a policy which takes care of the problems and needs of the American community, and which offers workers, employers, and business people overseas an opportunity, limited though it may be, to have their products come in, and their wares sold, and to compete in every way. Adjustments will have to be made over a period of time when it becomes obvious that structural changes have taken place in some industries in which our workers are now employed. Then we must increase help for those who are adjusted out of their jobs through retraining, manpower training, relocation allowances, and things of that nature. We should not, through neglect or conscious policy, cause trauma and distress to millions of workers who will have nowhere else to go when they are displaced and unemployed.

J. Paul Lyet

The perspective that I bring to the discussion of international trade is largely the result of my participation in the President's Export Council (PEC) that was reconstituted by executive order in May, 1979. Though it submitted its "Final Report" last December, former President Carter nevertheless extended its term for another two years. Its pragmatic recommendations focus on the key trade issues which can be resolved most immediately and which afford the greatest prospect of significant expansion of exports during the next few years.

America's international competitiveness has been eroded by inflation, which reduces competitive gains resulting from the depreciation of the dollar. True, inflation is, to a large degree, provoked by the high price we pay for imported oil (almost $80 billion in 1980). But our competitiveness also suffers from a steady decline in the rate of productivity growth. We can reduce inflation through greater productivity, competitiveness, and innovation. For two decades now, other industrial nations have been investing far greater amounts of their GNP in new plant and equipment and technology, and their productivity has been increasing much faster than ours. Strong measures are therefore needed for America to recapture a healthy share of world exports. In this regard, the Council recommended tax law changes that encourage investment, not consumption, including improved capital cost recovery allowances to speed the replacement of obsolete equipment and processes.

The United States needs an aggressive export strategy to coincide with the implementation of an industrial strategy for economic recovery. Both are essential to the stability of the dollar and to our efforts to reduce the burdensome trade deficit. After all, the more positive balance of trade situations of many of our major competitors are due to deliberate policies aimed at achieving trade advantages through the expansion of export markets.

Thus, in a world of increasing economic interdependence, the United States cannot afford to take exports for granted. Foreign trade demands serious commitment from business and labor, and an aggressive export policy and strategy from government.

All of these elements must work together if we are to become export-conscious and export-oriented. We need an integrated trade policy that reflects our determination to compete on more even terms in the world marketplace. This will require the elimination or revision of those governmental actions and policies which result in needless export disincentives. For example, current tax laws concerning Americans working abroad seriously undermine U.S. firms operating overseas. We must clarify the Foreign Corrupt Practices Act to make it enforceable and to eliminate needless uncertainties and anxieties which inhibit trade and complicate investment decisions. We may also need to change some of our antitrust policies. Here, the PEC has recommended adoption of legislation to modify the administration of U.S. antitrust statutes that inhibit export expansion. A final type of disincentive is found in the broad area of export controls. Here, the council recommended a reduction of such controls in all areas, except where they are clearly necessary in connection with specific and identified overriding considerations of national security, foreign policy, or national welfare.

As a necessary corollary to the elimination or reduction of export disincentives, we must also provide strong encouragement and support to enable U.S. exporters to be competitive.

Council-endorsed measures in the incentive colume include:

- A substantial increase of the Export-Import Bank's annual loan authorization;

- The companion need to reduce government-subsidized financing by other industrialized countries;

- Greater reliance on the Overseas Private Investment Corporation (OPIC) as an instrument for facilitating investment;

- Tax policies that encourage U.S. exports—including the enhancement of the Disc Program, (which serves as a partial offset to the elimination or reduction of the value added tax on European exports);

- The maintaining of deferral of foreign source income and the avoidance of any unduly narrow interpretation of foreign tax credit provisions;

- The enactment of legislation to create export trading companies—popularly called excorps—to help small and medium-sized companies enter foreign markets.

Another area of obvious interest to PEC was the reduction of foreign trade barriers to U.S. exports. Here, the 1979 Tokyo-Round Trade Agreements are quite explicit. If they are properly implemented, important new markets will be opened to American exporters. What is needed, therefore, is effective monitoring and enforcement mechanisms to safeguard U.S. trading rights provided for in the Tokyo-Round.

The United States should also determinedly press for further trade liberalization in foreign market areas to which access for American exports continues to be barred or restricted. We also have to vigorously enforce U.S. and General Agreement on Tariff and Trade (GATT) laws against unfair or disruptive imports. The nation must develop a strategy to improve its overall industrial competitiveness, productivity, and innovation. Such a strategy must also take into consideration aiding America's core industries.

With regard to trading with Russia, the Council recommended that normal commercial activities be reestablished upon a significant improvement in bilateral regulations, while for other Soviet Bloc nations, PEC recommended that the United States continue its present policy that differentiates those countries from the Soviet Union so long as they do not divert proscribed American goods to Russia.

The Council approached its task with bipartisan commitment that did much to stifle the capacity for conflict, and it developed a plan for action which would increase exports. While there were, to be sure, minority reports to majority positions, the Council's recommendations were, for the most part, unanimous. A similar degree of consensus, among equally diverse groups, will be required if America is to move with unified purpose to solve its trade-related problems.

Jerry J. Jasinowski

There is a central point on which there ought to be full agreement—that the key to improving American international competitiveness is through actions that improve economic growth and productivity, thereby reducing inflation, as pointed out by Lawrence Klein and by William Branson. Instead of building fences around our industries, we need to break the grip of stagnation caused by the conflicting forces of economic change. Our industry difficulties are largely the result of tensions between two conflicting sets of forces: those which induce rapid structural changes in the economy and those which, at the same time, impede the adjustment process. Rapid increases in energy costs, the growth of U.S. involvement in international trade, technological change and its worldwide transfer, and dramatic demographic shifts are examples of factors accelerating economic change. There are many obstacles to adjusting to economic change, however, including the growth in government regulations, the rising cost of capital, an increase in indexing and other measures that insulate public and private parties, and the tendency for high, fluctuating rates of inflation to increase economic uncertainty.

As a result of these and other factors, we have created an environment that fosters stagnation rather than a climate that enables industry to adjust to rapid economic change. This unresolved tension creates an economic inertia that reduces growth and productivity, decreases economic efficiency, and, along with the acceleration of inflation, introduces an upward bias in the cost structure of more and more of our industries.

The central purpose of improved industry policies, both domestic and international, ought to be to overcome this upward cost bias by facilitating and achieving more rapid and efficient adjustment to the structural economic changes outlined above. This means both broad policies, directly targeted at increasing overall growth rates, and more specific policies for improving the ability of particular markets to compete in international trade. The appropriate policies will also vary depending upon the degree to which the problems to be addressed are domestic or international in their origin.

We know, of course, that our domestic and international policies are linked and that both affect overall domestic economic growth and productivity as well as international competitiveness. Our ability to compete abroad is dependent upon domestic policies that improve productivity and the quality of products. In turn, expanding exports can increase the economic growth of the domestic economy. Because of this dual role, policies to improve international competitiveness must move forward on both fronts.

A large part—perhaps two-thirds—of the problem of U.S. international competitiveness lies in the domestic economy. To be competitive internationally we must be competitive at home. Yet we have been losing shares of our own market at the same time that our relative position in export markets has declined. On the domestic front, there is a growing consensus that broad supply-side policies—reduced Federal spending, tax reductions, and regulatory reform—are necessary to encourage increased investment and increase U.S. economic growth and productivity.

The remaining part of the problem—the other one-third—lies with government policies, both in the United States and abroad, that directly affect trade. These policies can be grouped under three broad headings:

- first, U.S. export impediments and disincentives—ranging from regulations governing the export of hazardous substances to explicit efforts to control exports in order to achieve various national defense and foreign policy goals;
- second, substantial foreign barriers to U.S. goods and services—encompassing both tariff and nontariff barriers that impede U.S. exports and investment; and
- third, inadequate U.S. facilities to support U.S. exports—ranging from the Export-Import Bank to the Foreign Commercial Service.

Given the nature of these trade problems, the appropriate policy response will be more multi-faceted. For the most part, this will mean decreased government interference in international trade. There is a substantial role, however, for government and business to work together to offset the market-distorting measures of other governments in behalf of their industries. The following are some of the major specific actions to be taken to deal with these problems:

- As budget resources permit, and in conjunction with negotiations with our trading partners, the Ex-Imbank should be funded to provide competitive financing for American exports.
- Legislation should be passed to permit the formation of export trading companies to encourage small and medium sized firms, in partnership with U.S. banks, to enter the exporting business.

- U.S. antitrust laws should be clarified, beginning with modification of the Webb-Pomerene antitrust exemption.
- The Overseas Private Investment Corporation (OPIC) should be reauthorized in 1981 with a stronger mandate to support trade.
- Antiboycott regulations and laws should be simplified and the antiboycott statutes and policies in U.S. tax law should be eliminated.
- U.S. tax law on income earned by Americans working overseas should be revised in order to maintain the necessary personnel to market and service our products.
- The Foreign Corrupt Practices Act should be administered, or legislatively changed, to minimize its anticompetitive effects on trade.

Improved international competitiveness for U.S. industry begins with a broad supply-side policy at home: to control inflation and to increase investment, savings, and productivity. This must be coupled with specific actions to eliminate export disincentives, prevent unfair trade practices by our competitors, and supportive measures to expand trade and exports. There is growing support for such policies. Taken together, this mixed strategy can improve domestic economic growth, provide needed productivity gains, and improve U.S. international competitiveness.

Donald E. Petersen

A great deal of public attention is being focused on the difficulties of the U.S. automobile industry, and with good reason. We have enormous problems: designing and engineering an entirely new line of small, fuel-efficient cars; investing billions of dollars to convert manufacturing and assembly facilities to make those products; reducing our staggering unemployment; dealing with a huge increase in Japanese imports; and restoring profitability.

The fundamental issue we must debate is not that of Japanese imports, it is whether the auto industry is central to a prosperous U.S. economy, a strong national defense and American leadership abroad. If it is, we need action on several fronts to get it moving again.

I believe that it is, indeed, central to our national interests. One out of nine American manufacturing jobs is related to the auto industry. The products and services of the industry account for about 20 percent of total U.S. retail sales, 22 percent of our steel, 62 percent of our rubber, and 11 percent of our glass. It is the mainstay of some 2000 U.S. companies that supply parts for automobile production.

Also, the productive capacity of the auto industry and its skilled workforce have been the very heart of our defense capability. It is difficult to see how we can provide leadership abroad without a strong industrial base at home that is anchored by the auto industry.

To revitalize this industry, we need action by management, labor, and government. Management and labor must take steps to make the industry more competitive.

Management will have to increase productivity dramatically, emphasize capital investments in the United States; match or exceed the quality of vehicles made anywhere in the world, continue to develop new technology and utilize the best technology available from universities and other sources, and enable labor to benefit in profitable years.

Labor must be willing to negotiate a new wage and benefit structure that will allow the industry to meet the challenge from vehicles made in countries with substantially lower production costs.

Government needs to establish tax incentives for capital formation, reduce the regulatory burden that drains physical and human resources and inflates prices, and see that Japanese imports are limited temporarily to a reasonable level.

In principle, I am for free trade. So is Ford Motor Company. However, there isn't any free trade in cars and trucks. The theoretical model does not exist in the real world. Furthermore, Japanese imports are not just an American problem. They are a major issue in Europe as well. Even though several European countries already have imposed severe limitations on the number of Japanese cars coming into their markets and the European Economic Community has a common tariff almost five times higher than ours, Europeans are holding urgent discussions about what more should be done. In Latin America and other auto-producing countries, various methods of limiting imports have been applied.

Consider this: the Japanese home market is only about five million units, while their capacity to build cars and trucks is close to 12 million. With severe import restrictions in other countries and only a nominal car tariff here, most of Japan's excess capacity is headed for America.

These facts argue for some form of temporary restraint on Japanese imports to the United States. The method can be voluntary export limits by the Japanese, a bilateral agreement, or in the extreme case, U.S. legislation. The voluntary route would be preferable. For the U.S. industry to complete its $80 billion conversion to fuel-efficient cars, a reduction in Japanese imports for at least five years is suggested. However, in the long term, I am convinced that the best solution is local content requirements for foreign manufacturers to participate in the domestic market. It makes good sense that if you want to have a significant share of a national auto market you should invest in capital facilities there, and make significant contributions to the economy of that country.

If the public and private sector policies I have outlined are not resolved by management, labor, and government working together, U.S. auto manufacturers will be faced with a very unpleasant, but nonetheless realistic strategic option: moving off-shore increasingly to compete with importers from other countries. Ford is not going to pull out of the U.S. market, but, if policies in the United States prevent us from being a profitable manufacturer here, we will be forced to look abroad to obtain more components, and ultimately to produce the entire automobile.

This would be a bad move for America. But under the present rules of automotive trade, and in order to deal with competitive realities, we will have to utilize the most efficient, low-cost resources. Ford Motor Company will continue to have a wide array of cars and trucks to market in North America. The only issue is: where will they be made?

The national debate on U.S. industrial policy should focus on the fundamental question of our national interest in maintaining a strong industrial base. If the public's decision is affirmative, new policies, including trade policies, will have to be established in the public and private sectors to make this happen.

SUMMARY REPORT

International Trade

Irving B. Kravis

The panel on International Trade had before it papers which set out the background against which the international aspects of industrial policy must be considered. They called attention to the fact that there are success stories in American industry with respect to international competition, as well as industries which have been placed in difficulty by import competition.

By 1980, the United States had large surpluses in agriculture and manufactured goods that largely offset deficits in petroleum trade. Within manufacturing, trade statistics clearly indicate that the United States has a current comparative advantage in capital goods and chemicals and a current comparative disadvantage in consumer goods, and nonagricultural industrial supplies and material. The most recent figures reflect a near balance of exports and imports, though it was questioned in the discussion how durable this balance would be if the U.S. economy were to have an upswing or if the dollar appreciated further.

Three broad alternative policies were discussed: (1) To accept the verdict of the market about which firms and industries survive, relying only on broad nonindustry-specific policies to promote growth and productivity. (2) To intervene to save domestic industries threatened by import competition when the industries were "core" defense-related industries (steel, auto), or had workers who would find it difficult to shift to other industries (textiles, auto). (3) To pick-the-winners, recognizing that this involved the nurturing of such industries, rather than their mere identification. There was considerable debate over the second of these possibilities, without visibly affecting anyone's initially stated position. Some felt that other countries controlled trade and that the United States should not try to be the only free trade country. Others felt that the United States had its share of trade restrictions and that in any case the gain from trade was in cheap imports, not in large exports *per se.*

When it became clear that no consensus could be reached on these general issues, it was agreed to shift attention to more specific and less philosophical issues affecting the trade position of the United States.

There was agreement that most of the trade problems facing American industries would be greatly alleviated if domestic policies could be adopted to improve productivity. Mentioned in this connection though not discussed very much, were increased capital formation, reduced public claims on resources, the encouragement of technological advancement and innovation, and the improvement of worker-management communication regarding productivity advances.

The international policies which most people attending the panel meeting were willing to support included the following:

(1) Negotiations to eliminate market distortions such as domestic procurement preferences. (2) The removal of domestic export disincentives, such as the simplification of export licensing, the liberalization of antitrust requirements, and more favorable tax treatment for Americans working abroad. (3) The facilitation of exports by measures such as improved information on trading opportunities and the negotiation of the reduction of what are essentially subsidies in export financing. (4) Protection against U.S. vulnerability to supply interruptions by means such as implementing the Strategic Petroleum Reserve plan. (5) Development of better schemes for worker training and adjustment.

In one view the adjustment and retraining requirements would be so large that—in the absence of import restraints for vulnerable industries—an impossible burden would be placed on such a program. On the other side of the question, it was held that people do adjust to changed economic circumstances, and that many displaced persons would find alternative employment without expensive retraining and adjustment costs.

The possibility of the encouragement of trading companies according to the Japanese model was also mentioned.

It was recognized that any U.S. policy, whether one of export promotion, import restraint, or both, would entail foreign responses that would have to be taken into account. The group was reminded that, to our European trading partners, the United States seems like a powerful, successful competitor, and that a protective policy would bring retaliation.

There were some important questions about international trade that affect industrial policy which the group did not have the time to consider, though they were touched upon. One issue was the question of what constraints, if any, the international economic policies of the

United States place on industrial policy. In one sense, the argument over protection as an industrial policy could be viewed as a debate on whether the often expressed preference for free trade should constrain industrial policy choices. A similar question arises with respect to the maintenance of the U.S. dollar as a key currency. If the dollar is to continue as a key currency, it would be desirable, or even necessary, to maintain a stable exchange rate vis à vis other major currencies. Foregoing the use of exchange rates to achieve equilibrium in the balance of payments might create problems if the chosen industrial policy were one that tended to produce balance of payments deficits or surpluses.

Political Experience ☆ ☆ ☆ ☆ ☆

17.

THE POLITICAL RESPONSE TO THREE POTENTIAL MAJOR BANKRUPTCIES: LOCKHEED, NEW YORK CITY, AND CHRYSLER

Charls E. Walker   Mark A. Bloomfield

1. INTRODUCTION

During the last decade, there have been three heavily publicized Federal loan packages to large, specific economic entities. The Lockheed Corporation, New York City, and the Chrysler Corporation successfully petitioned "Uncle Sam" for financial rescue packages after the private financial markets closed their doors.

It started with the Lockheed Corporation in 1971. The Emergency Loan Guarantee Act authorized a Federal guarantee of $250 million in bank loans for the Lockheed Aircraft Corporation. Four years later, the New York City Seasonal Financing Act authorized the Treasury Secretary to make short-term loans of up to $2.3 billion a year through mid-1978 to help New York City meet its short-term cash needs. In 1978, the Federal government thought it necessary to supplement that effort with long-term Federal loan guarantees totaling up to $1.65 billion under the New York City Loan Guarantee Act. The decade ended, in 1979, with the Chrysler Corporation Loan Guarantee Act, a $3.5 billion aid package for Chrysler, which included the "carrot" of $1.5 billion in Federal loan guarantees and the "stick" of $2 billion in financial concessions from the company's employees, dealers, creditors, stockholders, and other involved parties.

The new "bail-out politics" may be an apt description of the political system's response to serious threats of bankruptcy for a major public or private enterprise. The chosen term is not meant to put a value judgment on the optimal economic answer; that is, whether the economy would be better served with a bankruptcy or a publicly supported rescue from bankruptcy. Instead, the term focuses attention on modern interest group lobbying, on the loss of jobs, the congressional district, state and regional economic impact of a sizable bankruptcy, the political impact of a major bankruptcy for a Member of Congress and the President—or, in short, the direct constituent impact of a significant economic crunch, such as the bankruptcy of Lockheed, New York City, and Chrysler.

In this chapter, the authors review the response of the political system to three recent requests for Federal rescue loan packages. In form, the three rescue plans enacted were similar. The Federal government provided Federal loan guarantees (in the case of New York City also direct loans) on condition that the creditors, shareholders, employees, and others with a stake in the entity's future contribute cash and make concessions to hold off bankruptcy.

A review of the events of the seventies suggests that after the initial precedent of Lockheed, each subsequent bail-out seemed easier; the major political decision was no longer bankruptcy or bail-out but the details of the latter; and the amount of Federal involvement in dollars and control grew.

The votes in Congress tell part of the story. The 1971 Lockheed rescue was not an easy decision. The Senate margin was only one vote; the House vote on final passage was 192 to 189. The first rescue plan of New York, in 1975, involving direct loans, also was a difficult political decision. Ten votes made the difference in the House of Representatives; Senate approval was easier, 57 to 30. Even though the 1975 New York rescue package was sold as a one-shot bail-out, three years later Congress provided additional financial aid in the form of loan guarantees to the City without too much opposition. The Senate vote on the final bill was 58 to 35; the House voted 244 to 157 to bail out New York City a second time. The third Federal bail-out of the decade, this time for the Chrysler Corporation, presented by its proponents as just another Lockheed rescue plan, did much better politically than its predecessor. The House approved the measure by almost two to one; Senate approval was by a comfortable nine vote margin.

Vote margins in Congress, however, tell only part of the story. The political story told in this Chapter suggests that the issue in the Lockheed case really was one of bankruptcy versus bail-out for the ailing company, with secondary emphasis on the choice between a loan guarantee program for all eligible business entrepreneurs versus one targeted to Lockheed. A review of the New York City case suggests a shift from whether or not there should be a bail-out to more concern about the details of a Federal rescue package. In 1975, the critical political variable was the reluctance of President Ford to give his stamp of approval and when it came, the Administration confessed that the delay was primarily a tactical one to force concessions from New York City's creditors, politicians, and unions. In 1978, the focus of the debate was on the amount of the loan and the extent of Federal involvement in the City's affairs, rather than the more basic choice of bankruptcy or bail-out.

Also of significance in a review of the three most recent Federal bail-out efforts is the growing Federal commitment, both in dollars and in the administration of the rescue packages. For example, Lockheed involved Federal loan guarantees of $250 million. The amount of loan guarantees for New York City totaled $1.65 billion and 37 percent of the total $4.5 billion plan. The Chrysler loan guarantees added up to $1.5 billion, but were 43 percent of the $3.5 billion aid package.

The authors illustrate that the current political decision-making process on bankruptcy versus bail-out is biased in favor of the latter. Although the initial political response to each of the petitioners, Lockheed, New York City, and Chrysler, was a stern "no," the conclusion of each case was "yes," and perhaps not the best "yes" from an economic standpoint. The simple reason for the successful petitions for a bail-out is that the significant short-term economic impact, especially the loss of large numbers of jobs, combined with modern interest group coalition politics available to a sophisticated large petitioner, results in favored odds for the grant of Federal loan assistance.

The paper concludes with a recommendation for an alternative approach for the political system to respond to bail-out requests—a modern Reconstruction Finance Corporation (MRFC). It would replace the current "ad hoc" political responses, resulting perhaps in a more optimum economic resolution.

2. CASE ONE: LOCKHEED (1971)

THE ECONOMIC CRUNCH
The drama began on February 2, 1971, in London's Grosvenor House hotel. Lockheed Chairman Dan Haughton was informed that Rolls-Royce, Ltd., was declaring bankruptcy. This was devastating news for Haughton because the British company was the manufacturer of jet engines for Lockheed's new potential big money maker, the L–1011 Tristar commercial jet.

Lockheed already was under financial stress because of recent $480 million in penalties assessed by the Defense Department for cost overruns on the production of the C–5 A military transport aircraft and other defense contracts. A day earlier, Haughton had negotiated a commitment of a desperately needed $200 million to address that new financial burden. However, he feared that the new credit commitment would soon be but a wish, especially since Lockheed's 24 principal banks had already extended the corporation $400 million in credit.

Haughton was right. Soon, two leading banks, the Bank of America and Bankers Trust, announced that no further credit would be extended to Lockheed without a Federal government loan guarantee. The idea of government loan guarantees was not new to the Lockheed situation. In 1970, the corporation's 24 leading lenders raised the issue, but agreed to lend Lockheed $400 million without a government guarantee to complete development of the Tristar. This time, the British government added to the clamor for U.S. government guarantees. The United Kingdom agreed to finance a successor corporation to Rolls-Royce, Ltd., to build the needed jet engines, but only if Lockheed met the terms of its American bankers and obtained loan guarantees of up to $250 million.

In a nutshell, Lockheed needed the contract for jet engines; it needed credit not forthcoming from the private market to go into production of its L–1011 Tristar; and it needed its new passenger commercial jet to stay in business. Lockheed faced an economic crunch. Its allies advocated a Federal loan guarantee. Opponents argued that bankruptcy, not a bail-out, was the proper economic solution.

Four basic arguments were put forth for the $250 million government loan guarantee request. First, a bankruptcy would result in high unemployment spread over 25 states. A U.C.L.A. econometric study calculated a loss of approximately 63,000 jobs. Second, the $1 billion investment in the Tristar by banks, subcontractors, and suppliers would be lost. A Lockheed bankruptcy would also trigger a domino effect of bankruptcies for some of these parties. Third, a Lockheed failure would weaken America's defense capability. Lockheed was a principal supplier of vital military weaponry, including the Poseidon and Polaris missiles. Fourth, some European governments subsidize their commercial aircraft industry and similar U.S. assistance would be desirable to provide for "fair competition."

On the other hand, there were four principal arguments against a Lockheed rescue package. First, the unemployment figures were exaggerated because Lockheed would continue to operate in receivership during reorganization. New jobs would be created at McDonnell-Douglas, which would build more DC–10s to substitute for the canceled Tristars. Other firms would pick up Lockheed's lost business and increase their employment. Second, a successor corporation or a reorganized Lockheed would continue Lockheed's profitable divisions, including its defense products. Third, a Lockheed bail-out would be an unfortunate precedent for other ailing U.S. businesses. Fourth, Federal guaranteed loans would not be costless. Other private borrowers would have to pay higher interest on their loans and marginal borrowers would be "crowded out" of the credit market.

THE POLITICAL RESPONSE: OVERVIEW

The Lockheed loan guarantee legislation was one of the most controversial issues of the 92nd Congress. At stake were ideological beliefs, partisan loyalties, political ambitions, and old friendships; but perhaps most important of all was the constituent economic impact, especially jobs, for the Members of Congress who had to vote on the issue.

The Nixon administration sent to Congress a Federal loan guarantee proposal not necessarily limited to the Lockheed Corporation because such an approach, it was thought, would be easier to sell in Congress. In fact, the final bill with the loan guarantee authority limited to $250 million, Lockheed's estimated financial need, was similar in form to the original Administration proposal of May 13, 1971. In the interim, Congress broadened the program into a $2 billion loan guarantee authority for all eligible major businesses. That was the thrust of the Senate Banking Committee bill reported on June 19. On July 21, the House Banking Committee substituted that broader version of the Lockheed "bail-out" for its own bill. House floor debate began on July 30, but now the House of Representatives stripped the bill down to a $250 million loan guarantee authorization for Lockheed only and passed it by a three vote margin. Then on August 2, the Senate abandoned its own bill, which it had been debating since July 21, and passed the House version without amendment, but more significantly, with only one vote to spare.

THE LOCKHEED LOBBY

A fragile coalition, which came to be known as the Lockheed Lobby, faced one major hurdle. There was no handy precedent for what it sought to do. That was to build an interest group coalition to work with a supportive Administration and congressional proponents to enact into law Federal loan guarantees for one specific economic enterprise, the Lockheed Corporation.

At the core of the Lockheed Lobby was the corporation itself. Its chief executive officer, Dan Haughton, sought to build a coalition of Lockheed's creditors, union supporters, airline customers, and aerospace suppliers. They were the "shock troops" who did the actual lobbying on Capitol Hill. Their overriding theme was the potential loss of 60,000 jobs if Lockheed went bankrupt.

Lending important credence to Lockheed's integrity was the support of two dozen of the nation's leading bankers, also Lockheed's creditors. The key bankers included Bank of America's Chairman, C. J. Medberry; Bankers Trust's Chairman, William H. Moore; and Morgan Guaranty Trust's Chief Executive Officer, John Meyer. At a critical meeting held on July 14, 1971, at the Statler Hilton in Washington, Secretary of the Treasury John B. Connally accurately told the twenty-four bankers: "If we're not unanimous on this thing, there's no sense going on with it."

Labor, often a political opponent of business on Capitol Hill, was critical to the success of any Lockheed bail-out scheme. George Meany, president of the AFL-CIO, publicly announced support of the Lockheed rescue plan, even though some labor leaders regarded Lockheed as "a runaway" because of its overseas contract with Rolls-Royce, Ltd. More, specifically, the International Association of Machinists and Aerospace Workers union raised thousands of dollars for its lobbying effort and claimed to have generated half a million pieces of mail to Congress in one month alone. Aerospace workers in California sponsored newspaper ads urging a boycott of Wisconsin beer and cheese because of the opposition to the Lockheed plan by Senator William Proxmire (D.) from Wisconsin.

In a nutshell, the motivation of the Lockheed Lobby was quite simple. "For us and for Lockheed, it was a bread and butter issue," explained a Machinists Union official. "Our jobs were on the line. For the autoworkers and for McDonnell-Douglas and General Electric, it was something that might happen (perhaps to their benefit) if we lost out." McDonnell-Douglas produced the DC–10, chief competitor to the L–1011, and GE manufactured American jet engines in competition to Rolls Royce, Ltd.

THE LOCKHEED OPPOSITION

In the shadows of the Lockheed Coalition was an uneasy alliance of ideological opponents of business bail-outs, both from the Left and the Right; unions who also criticized Lockheed for "runaway plants"; and Lockheed's business competitors, who would profit if the Burbank-based company collapsed.

In matter of fact, the industry opposition to the Federal loan guarantee program was low key and not effective. The fear of public exposure of antibail-out lobbying by Lockheed's competitors was always omnipresent. When the McDonnell-Douglas Corporation made a public statement that abandonment of the Tristar program would result in 20,000 new jobs on its DC–10 production lines, one Senator compared

McDonnell-Douglas to "buzzards picking over the carcass of Lockheed before there is a carcass."

The rules of the game on Capitol Hill were very clear. Lobbying against a competitor would have been in "bad form."

THE ADMINISTRATION

On May 5, 1971, President Nixon made reference at a San Clemente news conference to the large job loss in California that would result if Lockheed abandoned its L–1101 Tristar program.

On May 13, Treasury Secretary John B. Connally made the specific economic case for Lockheed. Lockheed employed 17,000 people in the Airbus program; 2,000 workers already had been laid off. The payroll for the remaining 17,000 employees was $5 million in a week. In addition, 14,000 persons were employed by the principal suppliers of the L–1101. If Lockheed went "belly up," the $1.4 billion invested in the Tristar airline would be written off as a business loss resulting in large amounts of lost tax revenues to the Treasury. The $1.4 billion investment included $400 million from banks, $350 million from suppliers, and $240 million from airlines with orders or options to buy the Tristar.

Furthermore, Secretary Connally put part of the blame for Lockheed's troubles right at Uncle Sam's feet. The Defense Department recently had made the Burbank company absorb almost $500 million in losses resulting from cost overruns and other contract disputes.

THE CONGRESS

Congressional resolution of the Lockheed issue can be gotten by revisiting the debate in the Senate Banking, Housing and Urban Affairs Committee, the House Banking and Currency Committee, and on the Senate Floor.

The Senate Banking, Housing and Urban Affairs Committee hearings in June and July were a capsule review of the debate that took place on the Lockheed issue. Senator William Proxmire, the ranking Democrat on the Committee, voiced strong opposition to the loan guarantee.

> In 1970, more than 10,000 small businesses failed. Why should the government not guarantee them, since their failure had a greater economic impact than a Lockheed failure would? The answer is obvious. The 10,000 small firms do not have the political clout of the Lockheed Aircraft Corporation.[1]

The interest groups which made up the Lockheed loan guarantee proponents put forth every conceivable argument on their side. Deputy Defense Secretary David Packard argued that "Congress can make a distinction between helping Lockheed and creating a precedent for other companies."[2] The Chairmen of Trans World and Eastern Airlines expressed fear of a financial blow to their companies and loss of competition among producers of planes for the trunk airlines if Lockheed had to terminate the Tristar program. Suppliers of Lockheed gave numerous horror stories of potential economic ruin for themselves. The testimony of a small subcontractor manufacturing infrared ovens for Tristar galleys was a good example:

> Bowmar is typical of the smaller firms whose fortunes rest with the proposed legislation (to date almost $504,000). Should Lockheed enter bankruptcy, this investment . . . might not be recovered.[3]

The anti-Lockheed loan coalition likewise used the forum of the Senate Banking Committee. Fred J. Borch, General Electric chairman, testified:

> The British government by refusing to accept all of Rolls-Royce's obligations to Lockheed, created Lockheed's current problem. Consequently, the British should supply the solution.[4]

General Electric was a major U.S. manufacturer of jet engines and lost the contract to build engines for the Tristar. Leonard Woodcock, president of the United Automobile Workers of America, (UAW), opposed the bill; although, eight years later the UAW was a leading proponent of Federal credit aid for Chrysler. Conservative economist Alan Greenspan put forth free market arguments against the bail-out; economist John K. Galbraith set forth the "liberal military industrial complex critique" of Federal entanglement with a major defense contractor. Ralph Nader also testified in opposition to the bill.

In the course of the hearings, the Committee received testimony from the chairman of the Federal Reserve Board, Arthur F. Burns, and its former chairman, William McChesney Martin, both of whom favored broader legislation to establish permanent loan authority. Mr. Martin succinctly said:

> Some broad guarantee program is needed to aid large companies in trouble when their collapse would result in serious repercussions throughout the economy, including the undermining of investor confidence.[5]

Perhaps, they more than others saw the handwriting on the wall well before New York City and Chrysler surfaced on the political horizon.

At the House Banking and Currency Committee hearings on July 8, Lockheed's bankers made their views known. Their message was clear and to the point. Leslie C. Peacock, president of Crocker National Bank, advised the senators: "I can envision no circumstances other than a guarantee which would provide a proper basis for the extension of additional credit by my own bank."[6]

Bank of America's Chairman Chauncey J. Medberry, III, told the Committee:

> ... to a great extent the federal government shares responsibility and thus the federal government has an obligation to assist the firm through its present liquidity crisis.[7]

On August 2, 1971, the U.S. Senate voted on the Lockheed legislation. Senator Cranston, a key champion of the Lockheed forces, sat next to his colleague from Montana, Lee Metcalf, a Democrat, who had little constituent interest in the issue. Mr. Metcalf had told a Lockheed lobbyist earlier in the day he would oppose the bill. Metcalf turned to Cranston and said, "You don't need me, Alan. You can win without me." Cranston tried to persuade him otherwise. Senator Metcalf passed when the clerk called his name. When the vote was 48 to 47 against Lockheed, the clerk again called on Senator Metcalf. "Lee turned to me and said, 'I'm not the person who's going to throw 60,-000 people out of work,'" Cranston quoted his colleague as saying. Mr. Metcalf then stood up and voted "aye," followed by Senator Marlow Cook (R., Ky.), who hadn't told either side how he would vote, but now came out of the Senate cloakroom and also voted "aye." Vice President Agnew, deprived by Cook of the opportunity to break a tie vote, sent the latter a handwritten note: "You S.O.B. You ruined my moment in the sun!"

An analysis of the vote in Congress on the Lockheed loan guarantee legislation tells us something about the partisan attitudes, ideological reactions, constituent economic concerns, and interest group lobbying. First, the GOP in both Houses provided the narrow margins by which the bill passed. Senate Republicans voted in favor of the legislation, 27 to 17; House Republicans supported the bill 90 to 60. Second, although a majority of the Democrats in Congress opposed the Lockheed rescue plan (in the Senate, 31 to 22, in the House, 129 to 102), Southern Democrats supported the legislation (in the Senate, 9 to 8, in the House, 47 to 34). Third, in every congressional district where Lockheed or one of its large subcontractors had a significant presence, the Members of Congress voted for the guarantee. Likewise, in areas where the McDonnell-Douglas Corporation or the General Electric Company had a strong economic base, the vote was against the loan proposal. The congressional delegations of California and Georgia, where Lockheed had plants, thus, were solidly behind the bill. McDonnell-Douglas had its headquarters in St. Louis. Both Missouri senators and all but one congressman went against the legislation. The exception was Richard Bolling, a Democrat, from Kansas City, the headquarters of TWA, a major Tristar customer and Lockheed creditor.

In a strict accounting sense, the Federal government made money on the Lockheed loan guarantee program. It made a profit of approximately $31 million by the time the loans were repaid.

Critics of the Lockheed guarantees point out that loan guarantees permit the favored recipients to borrow at below market rates. Private borrowers have to pay higher interest rates; other marginal borrowers are denied funds or "crowded out" of the credit market.

3. CASE TWO: NEW YORK CITY (1975 AND 1978)

THE ECONOMIC CRUNCH

New York had been living beyond its means for too long and the day of reckoning came in 1975.

New York City was the noble experiment of American liberalism. For more than a decade, New York City's spending rose twice as fast as the growth of its revenues. By 1975 the total City debt was $12.3 billion compared to $5.2 billion in 1965; the annual budget ran $12.2 billion compared to $3.8 billion in 1965; and $1.8 billion or 14 percent of the City's operating expenditures went for debt service compared to only $374,000 in 1965. The City's government financed the budget gap by massive short-term borrowing or "papering" over its deficit; by putting more and more of its "current expenditures" into the "capital budget"; and through the use of a mindboggling array of fiscal gimmicks, involving millions of dollars.

The 1974–75 recession aggravated the City's fiscal situation. Tax receipts from sensitive City income and sales taxes declined; transfer payments automatically increased with the worsening economic situation. The City's response to the latest financial squeeze, almost a habit by now, was again to float new bonds and notes. Borrowing depends on confidence, a fragile, indefinable quality. All that mattered, however, was that in October 1975 investor confidence in the Big Apple was shot. New York City debt instruments no longer found any takers.

The result was that on October 7, 1975, "Black Friday," New York City almost defaulted on $453 million in maturing bonds. Less than two hours before the regular closing time of the City's banks, the City's teachers union agreed to make an investment providing cash for the City to pay off debts falling due on that day and to meet payrolls. But on December 5, a shortfall of $286 million was expected followed by another $437.8 million in debts due December 11.

What would have happened if the City, or the State, in fact, had defaulted? The truth is that nobody knew. But fear of the unknown is often sufficient to bring about action, desirable or not.

Proponents of a New York City bail-out focused on several dire consequences if the City did go into bankruptcy. The financial strains on banks and other businesses would take an unmeasurable toll on public, investor, and business psychology. The impact on the financial markets would create havoc, including the tightening of credit for other municipalities. There would be endless and costly bankruptcy litigation not necessarily resulting in any faster cleaning up of the City's financial mess, but causing severe local problems for the City and its citizens. Finally, the prevention of a bankruptcy would be cheaper than the vast amounts of Federal, State, and City resources that would be funneled into the Big Apple after default to keep the City functioning.

Opponents of a New York City bail-out argued that the widespread financial repercussions were exaggerated. A domino theory of economic disaster was not supported by the evidence. Only after New York City took the bitter medicine of fiscal restraint would it make sense to ask for Federal assistance. And, Uncle Sam should not set such a precedent; bailing out the Big Apple could result in every city in the country camping on the Secretary of the Treasury's doorstep.

THE POLITICAL RESPONSE: OVERVIEW

Mayor Beame clearly understood the fundamental political problem his city had in obtaining Federal loan assistance. On October 18, 1975, he expressed it to the Senate Banking Committee:

> I know, too, that many Americans hold the curious notion that New York City is somehow not a part of the U.S. Would the French disown Paris? Or the British allow London to become insolvent? Would the Soviets abandon Moscow?[8]

"Yes," was the answer the body politic was prepared to give and that made the New York City bail-out issue one of the most heated legislative battles of the year.

Prospects for Federal help were remote when the City first approached the Federal Administration and Congress in May, 1975. Congress ignored the issue during the summer months. After the near-default on October 17, several influential Members of Congress began to act. The Senate and House Banking Committees developed legislation providing for Federal loan guarantees of City debt instruments.

However, on October 29, President Ford vowed to veto any bill designed to bail out the Big Apple before a default. The political dilemma for New York City's allies in Congress was that they lacked the votes to override a presidential veto and, perhaps, even to pass a bill without White House support. Thus congressional sponsors of New York City's rescue legislation held off floor consideration in the hope that the Administration would reconsider its position. To convince the Administration to support aid for New York City, State and City officials put together another financing package.

On November 25, President Ford announced that the steps recently taken made it possible for him to ask Congress to authorize up to $2.3 billion a year in short-term loans for the city. Congress completed action of the President's rescue plan in five days, substituting it for the earlier proposals drafted by the Congressional Banking Committees. The Administration's proposal was the only one that had a chance of becoming law before a default. There was a large amount of opposition to a New York City bail-out, especially from southern and farm congressional delegations, but President Ford's support influenced enough Republicans to make the difference in the vote. The House cleared the New York City Seasonal Financing Act of 1975 on the morning of December 2, by a narrow margin of 213 to 203; Senate approval followed on December 6 by a larger margin of 57 to 30. The President signed the legislation into law on December 9 without a special ceremony.

NEW YORK CITY LOBBYING

The New York City lobby was led by Mayor Abraham Beame (D.) and Governor Hugh D. Carey (D.). Its supporters were the City's partners in bankruptcy, including creditors, unions, and local politicians, as well as urban-oriented organizations across the country.

The most important aspect of the City lobbying effort was not, in fact, lobbying. It was a series of repeated concrete steps by the City and State to show the Federal government that it was serious about putting the Big Apple's finances in order.

Action began in June 1975 when the State created a Municipal Assistance Corporation, soon known as the "Big MAC," to raise $3 billion from the sale of long-term bonds backed by the State aid payments to the City and City-related state tax collections. The proceeds from the sale of MAC bonds went to finance the City's short-term debt. At the same time, the City was required to balance its budget in three years, except for about $600 million in expenses funded by the City Capital Budget. The City soon increased transit fares, deferred capital expenses, and requested advance payments of property taxes. Enough Big MAC bonds were sold to keep the City solvent for a while, but by September investors lost confidence in the City's financial future and the bond market dried up.

A second State bail-out package was passed by the New York legislature on September 9. It provided for financing of the City through

November; it required the City to develop a three year financial plan; and it also established an Emergency Control Board, a State-controlled group of overseers to take charge of the City's fiscal management.

A third State-initiated rescue plan enacted in November was critical to the final outcome of the subsequent Federal rescue plan, because it convinced President Ford to abandon his opposition and to propose an Administration package of direct loans to the city.

The New York State legislature imposed $200 million in additional New York City taxes and required City employees to contribute to their pension funds. In addition, New York banks agreed to delay repayment of City notes and at lower interest rates; and the City's pension systems agreed to lend City Hall additional funds over the next three years.

However, lobbying also did take place, and Governor Carey was one of its most vigorous and effective lobbyists. On November 7, Governor Carey told a San Francisco audience that a default of New York City would cost the economy an estimated $14 billion in GNP, a decline of $3.5 billion in tax revenues, and a loss of 500,000 jobs next year. Also, he said:

> California represents 10 percent of the country's population. Its share of the Federal budget is equally great. Do you in California want to shoulder the extra hundreds of millions of dollars bankruptcy will resource?[9]

A few days later in St. Louis, Governor Carey argued:

> Can one of the largest industries in St. Louis (the St. Louis Car Division of General Steel Industries) afford to have the largest mass transit system in the world crossed off as a potential future customer?[10]

Mayor Beame also marshalled the support of his colleagues in city halls across the country to plead New York City's case. Mayor Moon Landrieu of New Orleans, representing the U.S. Conference of Mayors, joined by the National Association of Counties, told Congress that if New York City went "belly up," every city in the country would find it more difficult to borrow money.

THE ADMINISTRATION

In May 1975, New York City and State leaders began to seek assistance from the Ford administration. A series of private audiences took place with President Ford, Treasury Secretary William E. Simon, and also with Federal Reserve Board Chairman Arthur F. Burns. The reaction was "don't count on our help."

On September 24, Secretary Simon told the Congressional Joint Economic Committee that he did not think New York City would default. If it did, the City would survive bankruptcy. The impact of a default on capital markets would be "tolerable" and "temporary," and a New York City bankruptcy would cause little, if any damage to the nation's banking system.

After the near-default on October 19, President Ford hardened his Administration's opposition to Federal assistance to prevent a default. On October 29, in a speech to the National Press Club, the President said:

> I can tell you—and tell you now—that I am prepared to veto any bill that has as its purpose a federal bail-out of New York City to prevent a default.[11]

He complained that:

> A guarantee encourages the continuation of "policies as usual" in New York—which is precisely not the way to solve the problem.[12]

Upon President Ford's return from a European trip, he hinted at the Administration's real strategy on the New York City financial crisis. On November 19, the President again repeated; "The bail-out bill now before the House of Representatives is irrelevent because it does not address the current situation, and I would veto it." But, he added, if New York continued "to move toward fiscal responsibility, I will review the situation early next week to see if any legislation is appropriate at the federal level."[13]

In late November the New York State legislature, in cooperation with the City, put together one more rescue plan of increased taxes and reduced expenditures. On November 26, the President submitted the Administration's seasonal direct loan proposal and revealed the reasoning behind his government's seeming intransigence on the matter. "If we had shown any give," President Ford said, "I think they [New York officials] wouldn't have made the hard decisions that they have made in the last week or so."[14]

THE CONGRESS

An understanding of congressional action on the New York City bail-out can be gotten by reviewing the Senate Banking, Housing and Urban Affairs and House Banking and Currency Committees' reports and the debate on the House and Senate floors.

The Committee reports on the House and Senate legislation (S. 2615 and H.R. 10481) foreshadowed the subsequent floor debate in the House and Senate on the New York City bail-out legislation. The majority now emphasized the potentially disruptive impact of a New York City default. Cash was needed to meet payrolls and to keep essential services in operation. Default would make it almost impossible for the City to reenter the private capital markets, because 30 states had laws preventing banks from investing in the securities of a defaulted municipality. Other cities would find it harder to market their bonds; they would have to pay a price for New York City's foolishness. It would have an undesirable impact on international money markets and also on U.S. relations with foreign governments. The minority view disputed the dire predictions of catastrophe if a default took place and objected to rewarding the Big Apple for its fiscal mismanagement. A Federal bail-out would expose Uncle Sam to unwarranted financial risks. Massive Federal involvement in cities' financial affairs would follow. And, a bail-out for New York City would be a dangerous precedent.

Later on the House floor Democratic Representative Thomas L. "Lud" Ashley (D., Ohio), Chairman of the Banking Subcommittee that developed the original bond guarantee proposal, told his colleagues how he would defend the aid package to his Ohio constituents. The Federal cost of maintaining essential services after a default would be higher than the expense incurred now to prevent a default. House Minority Leader John Rhodes (Ariz.) appealed to his GOP colleagues:

> We should make it very plain that this is certainly not a bailout bill. It is a stretch-out plan aimed at giving the City and New York State time to make necessary adjustments in spending and revenue-raising and to balance its budget.[15]

On the Senate floor, Senate Banking Committee Chairman William Proxmire pointed out that the risk to Uncle Sam was minimal.

> This is a repayable loan, with interest well above the market. So when it is repaid—and I am confident it will be repaid—it will cost the Federal government nothing.[16]

Majority Leader Mike Mansfield (Mont.) added a note of reverse jingoism to the debate.

> As far as appropriations to our own people are concerned, what kind of people are we? Give them $15 billion overseas. No questions. A large part of it is wasted. But for our own people, what are we going to do for them? Think it over.[17]

An analysis of the close vote in both chambers, especially in the House, is revealing and confirms Mayor Beame's early recognition that the national attitude toward New York City would be a critical factor. House members from southern and farm states by and large opposed the legislation. No favorable votes were cast by 17 states.

The Senate, which passed the legislation by a larger margin of 57 to 30, was, perhaps, less parochial. However, here again there was strong opposition, especially from Southern Democrats. Only six of the 17 Southern Democrats voting supported the bill; Northern Democrats were in favor of New York City aid, 35 to three.

President Ford's last minute support made the difference, especially in influencing enough Republicans to join him and ensure enactment of a New York City rescue plan. Senate Republicans split 16 to 16. In the House, a small band of 38 out of the 138 Republicans voting supported the measure, and this included all 12 Republicans in the New York State delegation. Still, GOP support in the lower chamber was critical, because House passage was by only 10 votes.

The final vote reflected the close division of opinion of this first "bail-out" of a municipality, four years after a similarly hard fought battle on the Lockheed rescue legislation. The 1971 House vote for Lockheed was 192 to 189, the 1975 vote for New York City tallied 213 to 203. In 1971, the Senate approved the Lockheed loan 49 to 48; in 1975 the Senate margin for the New York City loan was 57 to 30.

EPILOGUE (1975)

On December 14, 1977, Secretary of the Treasury W. Michael Blumenthal reported on the "success" of the New York City Seasonal Financing Act of 1975 to the Senate Committee on Banking, Housing and Urban Affairs.

The City had made substantial progess to correct its financial plight, he said. The workforce had been reduced by more than 60,000 jobs to a new level of 300,000 on the public payroll. A wage freeze was in effect for City workers. New York City had eliminated its operating default. About $4 billion in short-term notes had been converted into long-term MAC bonds. Tuition, for the first time, had been imposed at city colleges and subway fares had been increased by 44 percent. A new $16 million management and information expense control system had been set up.

Secretary Blumenthal informed the Committee that the City had taken out substantial loans. However, all loans had been repaid, often ahead of schedule. Furthermore, the seasonal loans had produced a profit to the Federal Treasury of $30 million.

ECONOMIC CRUNCH (1978)

In November 1977, New York City tried to sell between $200 to $400 million in six month notes in the private market. The effort failed when Moody's Investors Service gave the New York securities its lowest rating; underwriters pulled out; and New York City was still shut out of the municipal bond market.

Thus, as 1978 began, even though New York City had raised taxes, reduced spending, and even balanced the budget under the terms set by State law, it was not able to raise needed capital, and again faced the prospect of a default. The City projected a revenue shortfall of $457 million in fiscal year 1979, $204 million in fiscal year 1980, $903 million in fiscal year 1981 and $954 million in fiscal year 1982.

THE POLITICAL RESPONSE: OVERVIEW (1978)

On January 20, 1978, 20 days after Edward I. Koch (D.), the new Mayor of New York City, took office, he unveiled a "candid and realistic" four year plan to restore the City to economic health. It involved additional workforce reductions, management improvements, a $283 million gap to be filled with new direct State and Federal assistance, continuation of the 1975 Federal seasonal loans, and a new Federal and State loan guarantee program.

What, in fact, happened when Congress cleared legislation on July 27 authorizing up to $1.65 billion in Federal loan guarantees for New York City was the result of interrelated developments in New York City and the New York State legislature in Albany. The New York governments put together a package involving hard compromises by everyone who had a stake in the Big Apple's solvency. It involved a pledge by financial institutions to buy $1 billion in unguaranteed long-term City bonds. The State legislature expanded the borrowing authority of the Municipal Assistance Corporation to $8.8 billion from $5.8 billion. The life of the Emergency Financial Control Board, a State body which supervised the City's financial affairs, was extended. An important new contract agreement involving the City and its 200,000 union employees put a lid on the wage increases. All this was politically mandated before Congress would pass the New York City Loan Guarantee Act of 1978.

In summary, the law provided for the first time for Federal long-term guarantees of up to fifteen years for City bonds, although guarantees on some short-term debt instruments were authorized in the first year of the program. To be eligible for these loan guarantees, conditions were imposed on New York City. There would be annual audits on the City's books. The amount of loan guarantee authority was spaced out over a four year period and either chamber of Congress would be able to veto guarantees in the second and third years of the program. The Federal loan guarantees were restricted to bonds purchased and held by City and State pension funds. There was a requirement that the State of New York and private banking institutions participate in the City's financial plan. And, the State was required to underwrite at least 5 percent of the guaranteed bonds.

THE ADMINISTRATION (1978)

On March 2, Secretary of the Treasury Blumenthal submitted the Administration's rescue plan to Congress. At the House Banking Committee that day, Mr. Blumenthal asserted that New York City in bankruptcy will prove far more expensive to the nation—both in expense and personal sacrifice—than any modest form of assistance.

THE CONGRESS (1978)

Unlike the earlier rescue package, this time in Congress there was no disagreement over the fundamental issue of a bail-out for the Big Apple.

On May 3, the House Banking Committee approved its bill, H.R. 12426, authorizing loan guarantees totaling $2 billion for 15 years on New York City bonds. The vote was 32 to eight, a vote margin much greater than New York City's supporters had expected.

House passage of H.R. 12426 followed on June 8, by an unexpectantly large margin of 247 to 155. Majority Leader Jim Wright (Tex.) urged support for the legislation:

> Flood walls in Florida, water projects for the American West, crop supports for the heartland of America—one dollar for every ten that have gone in taxes to support those vital long-term programs has come from the citizens of New York City. New Yorkers are not here asking for a hand out; they are only asking for a hand up.[18]

On June 15 the Senate Banking, House and Urban Affairs Committee, following the action of the House Committee, approved its aid package authorizing $1.5 billion in Federal loan guarantees for New York City bonds, by a vote of 12 to three. It was a surprisingly large margin.

Senate passage easily followed on June 29 by an almost two to one margin, 53 to 27; Banking Committee Chairman Proxmire was the City's chief antagonist prior to the floor debate and also voted against it on June 29. But, on the floor he acted more as a "devil's advocate" than an opponent. His major objective seemed to be to force as many concessions as possible from City and State officials and from pension fund, union, and bank representatives.

House-Senate conferees hammered out an agreement on H.R. 12426 on July 13 and essentially split the difference on the two versions of the legislation. The House passed the conference recommendations on July 25, 244 to 157. The Senate did so two days later, by a vote of 58 to 35.

EPILOGUE (1978)

In 1980, New York City's budget was truly balanced for the first time in anyone's recent memory. That accomplishment was a combination of a period of fiscal austerity followed by a prosperous City economy, which generated sufficient growth of revenue aided by inflation to bring about a balanced budget. Whether or not the Federal direct loan program of 1975 or the Federal loan guarantees authorized in 1978 contributed more efficiently to that end than a bankruptcy is a question that may never be answered.

3. CASE THREE: CHRYSLER (1979)

THE ECONOMIC CRUNCH

The history of the Chrysler Corporation was always one of swings in profitability. During recessionary periods, there were large losses; during periods of prosperity, the company prospered.

Still, in 1979, Chrysler was the third largest U.S. automaker and the tenth biggest corporation on the Fortune 500 list. The company had assets of $6.9 billion, employed 130,000 workers in nine U.S. divisions, and was involved in electronics, tanks, and boats, as well as cars and trucks. The majority of the company's $4.1 billion payroll was based in Detroit, or just across the Canadian border in Windsor, Ontario. Operations, however, were scattered across the country, including some 4700 dealerships in every state.

Yet, in 1979, Chrysler faced serious financial problems. Whereas Chrysler had 25.7 percent of the domestic market in 1946, that fell to 9.1 percent in 1979. In 1978 Chrysler lost $204.6 million. On July 31, 1979, Chrysler's Chairman John Riccardo announced a second quarter loss of $207.1 million, the largest quarterly loss in the company's history, and greater than the entire loss for 1978.

Where had Chrysler gone wrong? Many attributed Chrysler's problems to its misreading of consumers and the demand for small cars in the late 1960s and the 1970s. In 1976, the company decided against building its own four cylinder engine plant for the Dodge Omni and Plymouth Horizon. Instead, Chrysler contracted with Volkswagen and Mitsubishi for the small car engines. Unfortunately, when demand for new gas-efficient cars increased beyond that contemplated in the contracts, Chrysler was left behind. Also, in recent years Chrysler had postponed a major investment in new cars because the company's executives did not really believe consumers would continue to favor small cars once the gas lines eased up. By mid-1979, Chrysler had the largest unsold inventory in the industry—about 80,000 vehicles, most of them big cars.

In short, Chrysler's difficulty could be found in untimely and questionable management decisions, increasing foreign competition, the impact of emergency shortages on consumer tastes and preferences, and the increasing costs of compliance with Federal regulations of the auto industry.

Four basic arguments were put forth in 1979 for a Federal Chrysler bail-out package. First, there was the enormous impact on employment. Data Recourses, Inc. (DRI), an economic consulting firm, conducted a simulation of a Chrysler collapse and estimated a loss of 500,000 jobs in the short term and 200,000 to 300,000 over a longer horizon. Second, proponents of Federal assistance pointed out that many of Chrysler's troubles were not the company's fault. The Organization of Petroleum Exporting Countries (OPEC) and skyrocketing energy prices were out of Chrysler's control. Third, new government safety, environmental, and fuel efficiency standards disproportionately hurt Chrysler. The larger companies, General Motors Corporation and Ford Motor Company, could spread out the regulatory burden over longer production runs. And fourth, there was a national security argument for help for Chrysler. The company produced the main battle tank for the U.S. Army.

Five major arguments were made in rebuttal. First, the impact on jobs was exaggerated, the lost sales would be absorbed by Chrysler's competitors, including GM and Ford, and the workforce would expand. Second, the impact of changing economic realities, higher energy costs, for example, affected the entire economy. Why should Chrysler be singled out for special accommodation? Third, rising energy costs came about at the same time that Federal regulatory policy pushed the automobile industry toward the production of smaller cars. If Chrysler had been doing its job, it would not be in its current financial situation. Fourth, if Chrysler did go bankrupt, it would go into receivership and profitable divisions, such as the defense-related tank production, would continue to exist as a subsidiary of another corporation or, perhaps, as a new company. Fifth, a Chrysler bail-out would be an unfortunate precedent, a signal that the Federal government was available to bail out losers in the free market system.

POLITICAL RESPONSE: OVERVIEW

The real political issue in the Chrysler case was not the choice of bankruptcy versus bail-out but, rather the amount of concessions the Federal government wanted from Chrysler, its shareholders, its employees, its creditors, its suppliers, and others with a stake in the continued viability of the corporation. This was a far cry from the political debate over the Lockheed loan eight years earlier.

The odds were in favor of the $3.5 billion Chrysler aid package, the largest government bail-out ever of a private corporation, from the beginning. On November 1, the White House agreed on a Chrysler aid bill that doubled the amount of the loan guarantees President Carter had earlier said were acceptable. Proponents pressed Congress to complete action before Christmas, because the company would go bankrupt early in 1980 if it did not get government backing. On December 18, the House by a two to one margin voted for a $3.4 billion aid package, while Chrysler's allies in the Senate held an informal filibuster, hoping for passage of a weaker bill which would help them dilute the tough sacrifices from Chrysler employees required in the Senate Banking Committee bill. On December 19, the Senate voted 54 to 23 in favor of a much modified Senate bill designed to give the Senate bargaining room in the House-Senate Conference. In final congressional action, House-Senate Conferences in a six hour session on December 20, split the difference on the two versions of the bill. Later that evening the House approved the conference agreement, 241 to 124, and at 1:00 A.M. the next morning the Senate followed with a 43 to 34 vote. President Carter signed the Chrysler Corporation Loan Guarantee Act of 1979 into law on January 7.

In summary, the $3.5 billion aid package for the Chrysler Corporation authorized $1.5 billion in Federal loan guarantees, provided the company came up with matching $2 billion in help from its workers, its dealers, its creditors, and other parties involved with Chrysler. The company was required to win concessions from its workers, involving new contract negotiations; to obtain $500 million in new credit from U.S. banks and $125 million in new loans from foreign banks and creditors; to get $250 million in aid from state and local governments; and to receive $180 million in aid or credit from dealers and suppliers. Chrysler also had to sell off $350 million of company assets or other equity, develop an energy saving plan, issue $162.5 million of new common stock to its employees, and make another $100 million of new common stock available to its employees as an option to count against the required wage concessions. The Federal Loan Guarantee Board could begin providing loan guarantees to Chrysler once it had "adequate assurance" of commitment by all parties under the private financing plan.

THE CHRYSLER COALITION

The Chrysler Coalition lobby, made up of the company's executives, suppliers, local dealers, and supportive members of Congress and assisted by professional outside lobbyists, was an example of the prototype modern interest group coalition.

Leading the coalition at first was Chrysler Chairman John Riccardo, and later his replacement, Lee Iacocca. Both men spent up to four or five days a week working on Federal legislation to save their company, meeting with Administration officials and congressional leaders. The argument was simple—the loss of 25,000 jobs.

Chrysler's corporate leaders spent time motivating all parties with a stake in Chrysler's future. Riccardo went to Mississippi for a private meeting with the governors of several Midwestern states, where Chrysler had major plants, to encourage the governors to lobby their congressional delegations. Much time and effort was spent on making the case for Chrysler to the media and press. In late September, Lee Iacocca sent a telegram to leading newspapers and publishers across the country to attend a "special meeting" at the company's headquarters in Detroit. The Newspaper Advertising Bureau sent its own telegram, noting that the more than 4700 Chrysler dealers spent about $120 million in newspaper advertisements and dealer associations spent another $130 million. At the September 25 meeting, Iacocca made the same pitch given to Chrysler's bankers, anxious suppliers, Congress, and Carter administration officials. In a nutshell, "A lot is at stake—the company, Detroit, Michigan, the country," said Chrysler's chief executive officer.[19]

Full page ads followed in 50 national newspapers and many leading magazines outlined Chrysler's situation under the headline, "Would America be better off without Chrysler?" This approach was taken a step further. On December 6, pictures of Chrysler's forthcoming "K-car" compacts were sent to all Members of Congress, with a note from Lee Iacocca. It got right to the point. "Here's the future of Chrysler . . . a 'yes' vote puts them in production in less than 10 months."

Paul Bergmoser, the company executive vice president for purchasing, sent a letter to Chrysler's 19,000 suppliers requesting an "all-out effort" to get in touch with Members of Congress to "let them know how important Chrysler's business" was to the local economy. Chrysler claimed that its operations affected the livelihood of business enterprises in 52 American communities. The company estimated that it purchased $7.95 billion from its 19,000 suppliers, most of them small businesses. Its 4,200 dealers, employing some 150,000 people, were soon mobilized.

Detroit Mayor Coleman Young (D.) made lengthy phone calls on the company's behalf to Stuart Eizenstadt, President Carter's domestic policy adviser, and personally lobbied key Members of Congress. Chrysler was Detroit's largest employer. Minorities made up 28 percent of Chrysler's workforce and 34 percent of the company's blue collar employees. Mayor Young claimed that the company paid black employees $800 million a year, or about 6 percent of all personal income of black Americans. The Detroit Mayor's involvement was a crucial factor in enlisting the Administration's support, especially since Carter feared the loss of black support in his nomination battle with Senator Edward Kennedy (D., Mass.) and faced a difficult reelection campaign.

Douglas A. Fraser, President of the UAW, with 1.4 million members, including some 124,000 Chrysler workers, mobilized union support for the ailing Detroit automaker. He personally lobbied Vice President Walter Mondale, Treasury Secretary Miller, and White House domestic affairs adviser, Eizenstadt. The full membership of the UAW was asked to write Congress showing support for the Chrysler rescue plan from the entire UAW, and not just from Chrysler employees. Mr. Fraser secured support of the AFL-CIO, the umbrella labor movement organization.

A crucial aspect of the success of the Chrysler lobby was its flexibility in tactics. The form of Federal financial aid for Chrysler was much less important than the fact that Federal help was forthcoming.

In 1978, Chrysler first sought relief from Federal regulatory costs, including the Environmental Protection Agency's (EPA) emission standards and the Highway Traffic Safety Administration's fuel efficiency standards. When that approach became politically unrealistic, the company shifted its sights to the U.S. Treasury. On August 9, Chrysler floated the idea of "refundable tax credits" or a cash tax break now against future profits. When the tax route failed to gain political support, Chrysler asked for a Lockheed-style program based on Federal loan guarantees. After all, Chrysler argued, the Lockheed bail-out helped the aerospace company rebound into a viable enterprise and Uncle Sam made a $31 million profit on the deal. Thus, on September 15, Chrysler asked for up to $1.2 billion in Federal loan guarantees. When the magnitude of the loan guarantee requests was termed "way out of line," Chrysler scaled down its proposal to match the Administration's initial $750 million aid package.

When Congress approved the Chrysler Federal loan guarantee program, even proponents were surprised by the lopsided vote in favor of the package. But should they have been, considering the varied constituent elements of the Chrysler coalition? Included was the Chrysler Corporation, the UAW and its union allies, Chrysler's small business allies mobilized by its suppliers and dealers, minority groups led by the NAACP and the Urban League, the U.S. Conference of Mayors, and other urban-oriented organizations. In fact, there was no real organized opposition.

THE CHRYSLER OPPOSITION

Felix Rohatyn, who played a large role in the New York City Federal aid package and acted as Chrysler's investment banker in 1979, successfully summed up the different political realities in these two cases. He said, in 1979, that while many congressmen were "very anti-New York," no one was "anti-Chrysler."

Outside interests did register their opposition to the Chrysler bail-out, but it was a passive act. The National Association of Manufacturers issued a statement objecting to the Chrysler legislation, but it did not actively lobby against it. The National Federation of Independent Business, the National Taxpayer's Union, and the Business Roundtable were recorded against the Federal loan guarantee proposal, but played no effective role on Capitol Hill to prevent its enactment.

In short, perhaps the only active anti-Chrysler lobbyist roaming the halls of Congress was Nader lobbyist Howard Symons. Mr. Symons accurately observed:

> You have a situation where all of the [lobbying] elements push different legislators in the same direction. . . . Each group [of legislators] we would expect to oppose the bill is neutralized by one of these interests or another.[20]

THE ADMINISTRATION

On November 1, Secretary of the Treasury G. William Miller held a press conference.

Mr. Miller's long awaited formal endorsement of a Chrysler bail-out came in the wake of extensive lobbying by the Chrysler coalition and its congressional allies. The Treasury Secretary said several factors convinced the Administration it was time to act. First, the "change in outlook" in the automobile industry was persuasive and also convinced the Administration to increase the requested loan guarantee to $1.5 billion from its initial $750 million figure. Second, the "adverse impact" of a Chrysler bankruptcy in the current economic situation would be quite severe. Six days later, Miller told the House Banking Committee that a Chrysler default would cost taxpayers $2.75 billion and result in 75,000 to 100,000 lost jobs over a two year horizon. A barrage of statistics, complete with charts and graphs, were made available to the committee to show that the cost of a Chrysler collapse would exceed that of the loan guarantee program, a cost to Uncle Sam only if Chrysler defaulted. Third, Secretary Miller urged support of the Chrysler legislation in the name of competition in the automobile industry.

THE CONGRESS

Congressional action on the Chrysler legislation was never in doubt. The prevailing view was that the Federal government had to step in to save the hundreds of thousands of jobs at stake. The only issue was the amount of concessions to come from Chrysler, in particular, the size and terms of wage concessions.

One reason was the very effective lobbying role of the Michigan congressional delegation. Senator Donald W. Riegle (D.) and his staff in

Washington continuously lobbied Riegle's colleagues on the influential Senate Banking Committee. On the House side, Representative James J. Blanchard (D.) spent untold hours trying to convince his colleagues on the House Banking Committee that a Chrysler loan guarantee program was in the nation's interest. Many House members who did not feel strongly about the issue later indicated that they voted "aye" because it was "important" to Mr. Blanchard. Representative William M. Brodhead (D.) lobbied heavily; for example, he reminded the New York delegation of Michigan's support for their bail-out a few years ago.

Other Members of Congress with direct constituent interests in the future of Chrysler spoke out. The large St. Louis Chrysler plant was of particular concern to Senator Thomas Eagleton (D., Mo.). On September 11, he released a preliminary study by the Department of Transportation which concluded that a Chrysler collapse would put between 290,000 to 345,000 workers out of work and cost the government about $1.5 billion in annual unemployment benefits.

Each congressional office received a "fact book" and a list of the Chrysler plants, suppliers, and dealers in the pertinent congressional districts and states. Visits from the Chrysler coalition followed and arguments were targeted to the individual Members of Congress. In the first week of December, 600 to 700 Chrysler dealers came to Washington at their own expense. Republicans and conservatives were told that Federal regulation killed Chrysler and, therefore, the government should now come to its rescue. Moderate Democrats with ties to labor were reminded of labor support for the legislation. "You can latch onto this without looking like you want to save big business," observed Howard Symons from Ralph Nader's Congress Watch. He added, "eleven dealers and Chrysler's vice president for marketing came to see me, can you believe it?"[21]

House debate on the Chrysler legislation illustrated congressional sentiment on this issue. There were few speeches on the floor against the Chrysler aid legislation. Representative David Stockman (R.), the only Michigan vote against the bill, accurately observed there was no organized opposition to this legislation. Mr. Stockman said: "This is a zero-sum game. The losers who are going to get squeezed—the taxpayers, the borrowers—are dispersed out there."[22]

On December 18, before the House passed the legislation by an overwhelming margin, 271 to 131, Speaker Thomas P. O'Neill spoke for the majority point of view:

I don't think we can afford not to take the chance. Laying off 700,000 people, you'll start a chain reaction. And we won't be able to dig ourselves out for 10 years.[23]

Chrysler may survive. In 1979 the Chrysler Loan Guarantee Board approved loan guarantees totalling $800 million. On January 20, 1981, the last day of the Carter administration, the government agreed to guarantee an additional $400 million loan for the desperate Detroit automobile company, provided the company, its workers, its creditors, and its suppliers accept more cost-cutting concessions.

On the other hand, the Chrysler Corporation may still go bankrupt. But, regardless of the final outcome, Congress at no time seriously considered the option of bankruptcy rather than bail-out.

4. CONCLUSION

A quick review of the events of the 1970s suggests that after the initial precedent of Lockheed, each subsequent bail-out seemed easier; the major political decision was no longer bankruptcy or bail-out, but the details of the latter; and the amount of Federal involvement in dollars, as well as on other levels, grew.

This is not to deny that there are precedents of the government's refusal to grant direct loans or Federal loan guarantees. In 1970, Penn Central was permitted to go bankrupt before the Federal government provided loan guarantees to allow the company to continue its operations. President Gerald R. Ford turned down Pan American World Airways' request for emergency subsidies in 1974. However, modern "bail-out politics" biases the political system in favor of a Federal bail-out where there is a significant short-term detrimental economic impact, especially a large loss of jobs. As illustrated in the Lockheed, New York City, and Chrysler case histories, the larger petitioner can mobilize an interest group coalition with significant political impact for the President and especially for individual Members of Congress.

The role of Uncle Sam as a financier of troubled private enterprises, however, is not a new one. After the Civil War, the Federal government poured millions of dollars in land grants and loans into the railroads. During World War I, Congress set up the War Finance Corporation (WFC) to assist private companies and also later to help them reconvert to a peacetime economy. It stayed in business through 1929. In 1932, the Reconstruction Finance Corporation (RFC) was established to help banks, businesses, and cities stave off bankruptcy. It outlived the New Deal and, when it finally went out of business in 1953, had provided loans adding up to $40.6 billion. Today, descendants of the WFC and RFC include the Small Business Administration, the Farmers Home Administration, the Export-Import Bank, the Federal National Mortgage Association, the Commodity Credit Corporation, and numerous housing, community development, agricultural, and maritime financial assistance programs.

When the decade began with the Lockheed Federal loan guarantee program, Arthur Burns, in testimony before the Senate Banking, Housing and Urban Affairs Committee in 1971, observed:

> Traditionally, this country has relied on private financial markets to determine whether credit should be granted or denied. I firmly believe that is a sound principal, and I am concerned, as I know you are, about how we can preserve this principal and at the same time provide standby authority under which the government might backstop the private financial markets in emergencies. In authorizing Federal credit assistance, the Congress has understandably concentrated largely on helping home-buyers, small businesses, farmers, and others who will, in ordinary circumstances, need such assistance far more than big businesses do. In extraordinary circumstances, however, even a large, well-established, and credit-worthy enterprise may experience difficulty in obtaining needed credit, and failure to provide that credit could be extremely costly to the general public—in terms of jobs destroyed, income lost, financial markets disrupted, or even essential goods not produced. We should be able to find a way to deal with this problem without injuring the free enterprise system.[24]

An adequately funded, toughly managed Modern Reconstruction Finance Corporation (MRFC) could offer such an approach. The Modern Reconstruction Finance Corporation would replace the politically determined approach to bail-out requests that now exists, and provide better economic solutions. As the senior author of this paper suggested in 1971 testimony before the same congressional committee:

> Mr. Chairman, a strong case can be made for legislation that can be used to help more than one business concern—a standby guarantee authority that is effective in the long-run as well as the short-term. The collapse of any profitable company is detrimental to the economy. The collapse of a viable major business enterprise should be avoided if it is a temporary situation that can be alleviated at small risk to the government.[25]

The Modern Reconstruction Finance Corporation should incorporate several considerations. First, the authority for the MRFC should be "generic." Any eligible applicant, public or private, could apply for assistance if able and willing to meet the MRFC's terms and conditions. Second, the MRFC could either lend "cold cash" or provide loan guarantees. Third, the MRFC should be run by a hard-nosed, take-charge financial type, accustomed to driving hard bargains and making them stick. The MRFC board should be patterned after the Lockheed and Chrysler loan guarantee boards, which did an excellent job in monitoring those programs. The government should be represented on the board, perhaps, by the Secretary of the Treasury serving as chairman; but the MRFC should have a full-time chief executive officer with a well-rounded background in banking. Most importantly, to avoid even the appearance of politics, no elected officials will serve on the board. Fourth, the MRFC should have no authority for financing itself. It should simply "tap" the Treasury for an amount specified by Congress. The appropriations process should show Congress and the people what this effort costs, contrary to loan or guarantee programs whose real economic impact is difficult to determine. Fifth, the grant of congressional authority to the MRFC should be broad, but very specific in setting terms when assistance should be provided. The terms should be tough and include competitive interest rates. The applicant must be prepared to surrender "sovereignty" in exchange for emergency financing.

Four criteria for MRFC assistance eligibility are suggested. First, the applicant must show that he cannot obtain financing from the private capital markets. Second, the enterprise's continued economic well-being must be judged to be in the national interest. Third, the applicant must be willing to submit to management and financial reorganization. And fourth, the petitioner must prove there is a very high likelihood the loans will be repaid.

Several Members of Congress in the 97th Congress have come to similar conclusions about the need for a "modern" Reconstruction Finance Corporation. For example, on February 24, 1981, Representative Blanchard, a member of the House Committee on Banking, Finance and Urban Affairs, introduced H.R. 2000 (the United States Revitalization Act). H.R. 2000 would establish a U.S. Revitalization Bank to provide loans, loan guarantees, and, with certain limitations, purchases of stock to assist distressed business entities and local governments. The bank's seven member board of directors would be appointed by the President and confirmed by the Senate. It would be capitalized initially by the Federal government at $5 billion appropriated for that purpose, and be authorized to issue its own obligations, backed by its capital and assets, up to five times its paid-in capital. Also, the bank could ask the Secretary of the Treasury to guarantee its bonds subject to an additional appropriation by Congress. The proposal sets forth strict conditions of eligibility for business entities and local governments (limited to assistance for infrastructure improvements). As Mr. Blanchard told his colleagues: "This is a critical issue we must face—the sooner, the better."[26]

In conclusion, an MRFC would be similar to what now exists in the private sector. True, it would be a new "public banker" of the last resort, but extension of lines of credit would be so laden with restrictions that few applicants would queue up. The current odds-in-favor for a bail-out would shift. If a bail-out did take place, its terms would be stricter than the current *ad hoc* political response allows, resulting perhaps in a more optimum economic response.

NOTES

1. "Lockheed Loan Guarantee Bill Cleared on Close Votes" (1971): 152.

2. David E. Rosenbaum, "Lockheed Vote Was the Center of Battle of Lobbyists." *New York Times,* August 8, 1971.

3. "Lockheed Loan" (1971): 152.

4. *Ibid.*

5. *Ibid.*

6. *Ibid.*

7. *Ibid.*

8. John M. Goshko, "Beame Asks Congress to Aid New York City." *Washington Post,* October 19, 1975.

9. Douglas E. Kneeland, "Carey on Coast Critical of Ford." *New York Times,* November 8, 1975.

10. "Carey Tries to Win Over St. Louis Civic Leaders." *New York Times,* November 11, 1975.

11. "Congress Approves Loans for New York City" (1975): 441.

12. *Ibid.*

13. "President to Issue New Statement on Aid to New York City Today: Easing is Seen." *Wall Street Journal,* November 19, 1975.

14. William Clairborne, "To the Brink and Back—Chronology of New York Fiscal Crisis." *Washington Post,* November 27, 1975.

15. "Congress Approves Loans" (1975): 441.

16. *Ibid.*

17. *Ibid.*

18. "New York City Aid Extension Cleared" (1978): 258.

19. Andy Pasztor, "How Chrysler Corporation Orchestrates Support of Bid for Federal Aid." *Wall Street Journal,* September 6, 1979.

20. "Chrysler Aid Speeded by Broad Lobby Effort" (1979): 258.

21. *Ibid.*

22. *Ibid.*

23. *Ibid.*

24. Arthur F. Burns, Chairman, Board of Governors of the Federal Reserve System, statement at hearings before the Committee on Banking, Housing and Urban Affairs, U.S. Senate, 92nd Congress, July 9, 1971, p. 910.

25. Charls E. Walker, Under Secretary of the Treasury, statement at hearings before the Committee on Banking, Housing and Urban Affairs, U.S. Senate, 92nd Congress, July 9, 1971, p. 910.

26. Representative James J. Blanchard, *Congressional Record,* February 24, 1981.

BIBLIOGRAPHY

"Chrysler Aid Speeded by Broad Lobby Effort." *Congressional Quarterly* (November 17, 1979): 258.
"Lockheed Loan Guarantee Bill Cleared on Close Votes." In *1971 Congressional Quarterly Almanac.* Washington: Congressional Quarterly, Inc., 1971.
"New York City Aid Extension Cleared." In *1978 Congressional Quarterly Almanac.* Washington: Congressional Quarterly, Inc., 1978.

18.

THE POLITICAL EXPERIENCE IN ALLOCATING INVESTMENT: LESSONS FROM THE UNITED STATES AND ELSEWHERE

George C. Eads[1]

INTRODUCTION

This chapter examines the recent growth of interest in having the government identify promising new industries and promote their growth, in order to help shift resources out of declining sectors in ways that ease the shock of their decline, and to intervene in various ways to "revitalize" ailing firms, sectors, or regions. This growth of interest is surprising, because it implies a substantially increased interventionist role for government at precisely the time that skepticism of the government's ability to intervene intelligently in the detailed workings of the economy has become widespread. The second surprising aspect is the number of conservatives, well aware of the government's recent record and of its limited abilities to "micromanage" the economy, who find the concept of an "industrial policy" attractive.

It is argued that the call for an "industrial policy" is due in large part precisely to the recognition of the government's failure. Specifically, it stems from the belief that the government's policies would be less disruptive if only they were guided by a clear "vision" and were "better coordinated." The problem is thus seen to be poor management on the part of government, not flaws inherent in government intervention. The experience of other countries, especially Japan, is cited by supporters as evidence of what the United States could achieve if only it could develop an equally effective industrial policy.

This chapter examines the various failures—both of the market and of our political institutions—that might justify an increased government role in channeling the flow of business investment. In general, market failures are found to be minor or nonexistent; political failures, on the other hand, are found to be pervasive. The call for the establishment of an industrial policy thus ends up being a call for the creation of a new set of political arrangements to deal with problems that the existing political arrangements in large measure have spawned.

The key argument is that an industrial policy would, if anything, be more prone to "political failure" than the admittedly flawed set of institutions it is designed to replace. Therefore, while certain measures might be taken to improve the climate for business investment and improve the ability of labor and capital to adjust to changing market conditions, targeted policies of the sort generally considered as constituting industrial policy should be viewed with great skepticism.

Finally, the foreign experience is summarized. This experience does *not* suggest that an industrial policy would be good for the United States. Just the opposite. The foreign experience generally provides lessons concerning what *not* to do in aiding industries and sectors. The highly touted Japanese experience does not show what a pervasive, coordinated industrial policy will accomplish; instead, it illustrates the virtues of flexibility and the importance of concentrating the government's attention primarily on making sure that the general climate for business expansion is favorable.

Thus, the adoption of an industrial policy is *not* a shortcut to solving the critical problems facing the nation. It is a dangerous diversion which might prevent us from dealing with these problems effectively and even exacerbate them.

THE EMERGENCE OF INDUSTRIAL POLICY AS A DOMESTIC ISSUE

Recently, a surprising amount of interest has developed in having the Federal government assume a much more active, explicit, and conscious role in channeling the flow of business investment. Proposals have been made that the government identify promising new industries and promote their growth ("pick-the-winners"); that it help shift resources out of declining industries, and that it intervene to "revitalize" segments of the economy whose weakness is deemed to have critical effect on the nation as a whole. Although each of these proposals has somewhat different aims and attracts different groups of supporters, all reflect a belief that major investment decisions have now become too important to be left to private markets alone.

However, this trend coincides with a growing questioning of the benefits produced by and the costs of the host of "social" regulatory programs initiated over the past decade-and-a-half: programs whose aims include controlling air and water pollution, improving the level of workplace safety, and improving the performance of consumer products as diverse as power lawn mowers and automobiles. This skepticism arises less from a questioning of the aims of such programs than from a recognition that we thus far have failed to achieve their laudable goals in ways that do not unnecessarily detract from the economy's other tasks. The fault lies in the government's inability to admit that priorities have to be set and to develop means of setting them. The "market failures" that led to the need for these programs in the first place have been matched by failures in the institutions we created to carry them out. I will refer to these as "political failures."

This leads directly to the second surprise in the current push for a U.S. industrial policy, namely, the identity of many of those who are in the forefront of the movement. Supporters certainly include the expected groups who generally argue in favor of an increased government role in managing the economy. But the movement has also captured the allegiance of a surprising number of businessmen of a generally conservative stripe—individuals who are no strangers to the recent record of government and who have expressed considerable skepticism about the government's ability to implement complex programs efficiently. Paradoxically, the current state of government policy-making and the consequences it has had for the performance of the economy —particularly investment—is seen by these people as a prime reason why a conscious and well-articulated industrial policy is so urgently needed. To them, many of our current problems stem not so much from any inherent defect in our political processes as from the fact that we have not coordinated these numerous government programs under the guidance of a clear national "vision." What is more reasonable, they ask, than to pull together the vast array of current Federal programs directly and indirectly influencing investment at the firm and industry level and make use of this power to bring about a "reindustrialization" of our economy. To put it bluntly, the choice, as these people appear to see it, is between continuing to muddle on as we have—in which case things will get progressively worse—or to begin to make intelligent use of our powers.

There is a certain appeal to this argument. A major Federal presence, both in directing the course of the aggregate economy and in pursuing social goals, such as the reduction of pollution, is clearly here to stay.

Although achieving these goals need not involve the degree of Federal intervention that has come to characterize current Federal efforts, progress in moving toward more flexible and less intrusive forms of regulation has been painfully slow. Furthermore, the sheer number and variety of the Federal government's interventions do sometimes produce chaos in investment planning at the firm level and seriously distort investment flows at the industry level. Our current *ad hoc* forays into industrial policy are messy, intensely political, and their results sometimes leave much to be desired. The nature of the investment requirements the nation faces during the next decade, and the limited resources at our disposal to meet them, make it extremely tempting to explore techniques which promise, even if only in theory, to allow us to stretch these resources. Finally, reports that other countries, Japan especially, have achieved superior results by engaging in just such explicit policies to channel private investment add credibility to the call for their close consideration by this country.

While the purpose of this paper is to probe the arguments that have been advanced to support the development of an increased Federal capability to channel the flow of industrial investment, it does not develop all the points that bear on these arguments as fully as I might have liked. For example, it might have been useful to describe in detail how Federal policies currently affect investment decisions at the firm level. This is an important point of departure from which to measure the likely results of any attempt to institute an industrial policy. It also helps in part to explain the appeal of such a policy. However, this issue was dealt with extensively in other sessions at the Symposium, so will not be treated in detail here. Instead, I must ask the reader to accept the assertion that the growth of Federal regulation over the last decade or so (and in the term "regulation," I mean to include such things as detailed environmental and energy standards, restrictions on the flow of international trade, and economy-wide formal and informal wage and price controls) has extended to much of industry the detailed control over operational and strategic decision-making that was once characteristic of only a limited segment of the economy, the important infrastructure industries—air, rail, and interstate trucking telecommunications, banking, and energy transmission. Indeed, as I have argued elsewhere,[2] in certain important respects, the degree and character of regulatory control that the Federal government now exerts over some previously unregulated industries like steel, chemicals, and autos exceeds that ever experienced by the "classic" regulated industries. While public attention has focused on the diversion of resources into "nonproductive" compliance activities that this vast growth of regulation has caused, I believe that the consequences for the performance of the economy run far deeper. Specifically, the expansion to general industry of "command-and-control" regulation by issue-specific regulatory agencies has gone a long way towards converting what were once more or less routine business decisions and into negotiations between industry and the government in which a firm's skill in understanding, anticipating, and influencing the government has become an important element in its financial success. Business is reacting to this change in its decision-making environment by expanding its capability to operate in a world of "decision-making by negotiation." This is likely to have important consequences for productivity. But more to the point here, the development of these "political" skills also creates problems for those who, somewhat romantically in my view, envision a high degree of cooperation between business, labor, and government in shaping a consensus about the direction in which the nation ought best to proceed. Any proposals for the development of an industrial policy formulation process which fail to take into account business' improved political skills should be viewed with extreme skepticism.

A second issue that I might have addressed in this chapter is the nature of the investment requirements the nation must meet during the decade ahead. (This topic was also the subject of its own Symposium session, and therefore will not be treated in detail.) The size and composition of these requirements, combined with the poor outlook for economic growth during the early years of the decade and the difficulties of freeing up resources from other claims on their use, provide another reason why a more explicit Federal role in channeling investment seems necessary to some. If the most "productive" new industries can be spotted and funds channeled there, and if funds can be shifted out of declining industries more readily, our limited investment resources can be stretched further. The picture is sobering. In the 1981 *Economic Report* we presented what I consider to be a rather conservative estimate that business fixed investment must be raised about 20 percent from recent historical levels—That is, from about 10.5 percent of GNP to about 12.5 to 13 percent of GNP—if we are to restore productivity growth, meet the energy challenge, and answer even only the most pressing environmental, occupational health and safety, and product safety needs. A quick survey of where these extra resources might come from suggests that the most logical place is consumption. However, restructuring our tax system to reduce taxes that adversely affect investment and increase taxes on consumption is likely to prove difficult and highly divisive. In such a situation, an industrial policy has the appearance of a *deux ex machina*—a way of possibly reducing investment requirements, and smoothing adjustments, thereby lessening the need to address the difficult question of *whose* consumption will be cut.[3]

However, if the current *Economic Report* presents a sobering picture of how much we will need to invest during the 1980s, it also makes the point that an equal (if not greater) need is to improve the ability of our economic and social institutions to adapt quickly and efficiently to change. Unfortunately, if the primary benefit of industrial policy is its potential to stretch our limited investment resources, its primary cost is the almost certain adverse effect it would have on the economy's flexibility and adaptability. Therefore, a knowledge not only of the economy's aggregate investment requirements and the difficulties in meeting them, but also of the composition of these requirements and the massive investment shifts that are implied, is a prerequisite for an intelligent discussion of industrial policy.

The paper therefore concentrates on—but only on two—issues central to the "industrial policy" debate: First, how, even in theory, might a more explicit Federal role in channeling investment improve matters? Second, what does the foreign experience suggest about the likely consequences of our adopting an industrial policy? With regard to the first, I will examine the asserted "failures," both "political" and "market," that lead to unsatisfactory results in each of the three major subareas mentioned: declining industries, industries requiring revitalization, and expanding new industries. With regard to the second, I will briefly review what I understand to be the results of the foreign experience and evaluate the applicability of this experience to the institutional setting of the United States.

HOW WOULD A MORE EXPLICIT FEDERAL ROLE IN CHANNELING INVESTMENT IMPROVE THINGS?

Before anyone should be willing to consider recommending a greater degree of government presence in an existing economic activity, he should first ask: "What precisely is wrong with the way things are operating now?" If problems are found (and this is usually not hard), a second question then is appropriate: "What produced the problems?" Do they flow inevitably from the workings of the market and thus constitute market failure, or do they stem from other sources, for example, from current government involvement? Once the sources of any problems have been identified, and their causes correctly diagnosed, the final question to be answered is: "Will proposed solutions lessen the problems or make them worse?" A high degree of skepticism is appropriate in approaching this question for, as mentioned above, if the last decade has taught us anything, it is that certain attempts by the government to solve legitimate social problems can end up making them worse or, if they do offer even partial solutions, can generate important, though unintended, side effects.

In this section of the chapter, I want to explore the real and alleged failures in the current system by which we permit (and encourage) resources to move from less productive to more productive sectors within the economy. It is my belief that very few—if any—of these failures are due to the improper workings of markets; that some follow from the *success* of markets; that some are by-products of the current level of government involvement in investment decisions at the firm or industry levels; and that many are inherent in the "politicization" of economic decisions that has occurred over the last decade. This diagnosis greatly complicates the process of prescribing more government involvement as a cure. For, to use Pogo's famous expression, "We have met the enemy, and they is us," how is more of "us" likely to be a solution?

In making my diagnosis, it will be useful to separate the potential problems into three classes: those associated with achieving "appropriate" levels of disinvestment from weak sectors; those associated with the revitalization of currently weak firms and industries, and those associated with promoting vigorous growth in promising industries.

ACHIEVING "APPROPRIATE" LEVELS OF DISINVESTMENT

Perhaps the most painful thing for an economy to do is to move resources out of an industry or section of the country when that industry or section has become uncompetitive. Our economy (and, indeed, our society as a whole) is geared to expansion, not contraction. Considerable research exists about growth processes and how to manage growth; very little study has been made of the management of decline.

Yet decline and contraction are an essential feature of a growing economy. In a society with limited resources, these resources must be freed up to move to where they can be used more productively. Otherwise, growth will slow to the level that can be sustained merely by the increase in the aggregate volume of factor inputs—the rate of growth of the labor force, the capital stock, and the stock of usable land. Historically, the growth in the physical volume of these inputs has been far below the growth in output we have typically achieved. The bulk of our progress has come from the rearrangement of existing resources in more productive ways.

Furthermore, the process of contraction occurs all the time. It need not be synonymous with "death." Measured in terms of the proportion of the labor force it employs, our agricultural sector has been contracting virtually since the nation was founded. In the mid-1800s, when the first comprehensive data were collected, nearly half the nation's population lived on farms. By the mid-1970s, the figure was less than 5 percent. Yet agriculture is healthier today than at virtually any time in its history. And the movement of labor off the farm contributed importantly to the economy's ability to expand output elsewhere.

Indeed, massive population movements are an important characteristic of American economic history. They are almost invariably viewed as frightening by the industries and regions experiencing the outflow. New England was once seen as the epitome of a "dying" region as the industries forming its traditional base—textiles, shoes, shipbuilding—moved elsewhere. But it seems to have weathered this adjustment and is now experiencing a rebirth, led by new, high technology industries.

Disinvestment is thus as much a characteristic of an efficient economy as is investment. Why might not market forces handle disinvestment "appropriately"? Two separate sorts of failures appear possible: the failure to generate the right *level* of disinvestment due to excessive myopia, and the failure to recognize—or to give "adequate" weight to —certain costs that inevitably accompany disinvestment.

Myopia Private markets are, by definition, myopic. That is, they require an activity to produce a high return in the future to justify investment today. But might the degree of myopia be inappropriate at times? Consider the post-World War II history of coal production and use in this country. At the end of the war, coal was the nation's dominant energy source, accounting for about 50 percent of our total energy needs. Production peaked at about 700 million tons in 1947, but soon thereafter began to drop steadily. Production bottomed out at about 420 million tons in 1961, and thereafter began a slow recovery.[4] Coal employment, which had reached just over 500,000 in the late 1940s, fell to a trough of 131,000 in 1969.

The sharp increase in oil prices caused this situation to turn around. In 1979, total domestic demand for coal reached 680 million tons. Forecasts have total demand (including coal for synthetic fuel conversion and export) reaching nearly 1.5 billion tons per year by 1990.

During this several-decade cycle, the nation's ability to mine, transport, and burn coal first atrophied and then had to be rebuilt. As noted, the number of workers involved in coal mining fell drastically, causing severe economic dislocation in coal mining regions such as Appalachia. Might not a farsighted government, through the use of appropriate subsidies and other tools, have prevented this disinvestment and the dislocation that accompanied it? Possibly, but it is useful to recall that the vast bulk of the resources freed by the post-World War II decline in coal production found employment elsewhere, often at significantly higher returns; that the coal that will be most sought after in the future is not necessarily the same coal that was attractive during the earlier period; and that the technologies that burn coal have changed so radically over the past 30 years that any coal burning capacity that had been preserved would by now likely be technologically obsolete.

There may indeed be cases where markets may give misleading short-run investment signals. Agriculture is a case in point. There, policies to even out season-to-season fluctuations have proved useful in stabilizing investment, both in the production of crops such as wheat and corn, and in associated industries such as beef cattle. But long swings which reverse are an extremely rare phenomenon. Even rarer still are instances in which the resources preserved are precisely the ones that are later needed when an expansion in demand does occur. The costs arising from the temptation to be overcautious—to hold on to capacity "just in case"—would surely overwhelm any savings to society resulting from extremely rare instances where inappropriate disinvestments were prevented.

It might seem that I am belaboring an obvious point. Perhaps. But an important argument often advanced to justify revitalization of an industry rather than the phasing out of certain of its obsolete capacity is precisely that the preservation of this capacity is essential to the nation's strength, either to permit rapid mobilization in time of war, or to permit surges in peacetime demand to be met from domestic rather than foreign sources. As we observed in the 1981 *Economic Report,* there may be cases in which the explicit development of standby capacity makes sense (the case we cited was redundant transportation and burning capacity for alternate fuels to permit stockpiles of energy supplies other than oil for use during oil supply disruptions). But these cases are few and far between, and the argument that a market is being inappropriately "myopic" when it signals major disinvestment in an industry or region should be viewed with extreme skepticism.

If the case for the unaided market generating inappropriate disinvestment signals is shaky, what about instances in which the government, through its various interventions, is itself the agent distorting the investment decisions? While market signals tend to affect investment and disinvestment over a relatively long time, government actions, especially if taken without due regard for their consequences, can tip balances quite quickly. For example, the implementation of government policies to control air pollution in the Western United States have greatly accelerated what otherwise might have been a slow decline in domestic copper refining capacity.[5] Clean air policies have substantially affected the demand for Midwestern high sulfur coal. Federal energy policies have greatly altered the timing of the current technological revolution sweeping the auto industry. Is there not a case for compensating investment-stimulating policies?

This is a much more difficult question to deal with. In principle, one could design a set of policies that just offset any distortions introduced by other government policies. In practice, such an extreme degree of "fine tuning" of policies is likely to be impossible to achieve. As a technical matter, the optimal "second best" set of policies (that is, the set of policies that are just right given the distortions that already exist) is extremely hard to identify. But even more important, the government is hardly a neutral arbiter in such matters. There is a distinct danger that the political process may cause the government to introduce an inappropriately low degree of myopia into disinvestment decisions. The costs of disinvestment are always short-term, graphic, and concentrated; the benefits of permitting the disinvestment are widely spread throughout the economy, often speculative, and always in the future. The pressures on government officials are inevitably going to be in the direction of preserving inefficient capacity, and statements stressing the determination of these officials to be "tough" and "realistic" are unlikely to be effective, especially in dealing with groups of workers and firms who understand how to use the political process.

These problems are likely to be even more intense if the government is responsible, in whole or in part, for the decline of the industry or region. Unfortunately, this is likely to be the typical case encountered today. Earlier in this chapter I noted that, due to the vast expansion in Federal regulatory activity, the government already affects, in a major way, the financial health of virtually every important firm and certainly every important industry in this country. I also observed that firms are becoming much more sophisticated (indeed, more sophisticated than the government in many instances) in understanding the consequences of this influence. Thus, in almost every case in which an important firm or industry is in decline, the firm or industry and its workers are likely to be able to present a semiplausible case that government actions in some way lie at the heart of the problem. This creates the presumption that the Federal government has a responsibility to "do something" to prevent—or to cushion—the decline.

The same expansion of Federal influence also creates the tools by which this "responsibility" can be discharged: "temporary" trade restrictions, "targeted" investment tax credits, special exemptions from regulation, and so on. If the Federal government ever assumes an important explicit role in preserving industrial capacity on the grounds either that the unaided market is excessively myopic or, more likely, that in doing so it is merely attempting to offset the consequences of its own distortions, the political pressures to preserve inefficient operations will be overwhelming. The result is likely to be a growing herd of white elephants, absorbing an ever-increasing share of the nation's scarce capital. Given the government's ability to secure for itself whatever funds it requires (at least over the short to intermediate term), new and growing enterprises will be increasingly crowded out of capital markets. This is hardly the way to meet the investment needs of the 1980s.

Adjustment Assistance If the market does not systematically fail to produce proper *levels* of disinvestment, and if the aim of correcting government-induced distortions is a weak reed on which to rest policy, what other case can be made to support government involvement in disinvestment decisions?

Though this should not be strictly considered a market failure, the fact that the market does not take into account the income losses that occur when plants close and industries move does create a reason for government concern. If the nation as a whole does indeed benefit substantially from a free flow of resources out of unproductive sectors, it is appropriate that all of us bear some of the costs of activities designed to facilitate this flow. Thus, "adjustment assistance," to the extent it actually promotes adjustment, is an appropriate governmental activity. But several problems should be noted. First, the actual shock of a plant closing, or major industry contraction, even when the plant or industry is a major employer in an area, is almost always less than appeared likely at the time the action was first announced. Studies of the impact of military base closings, of adjustments to major weapons systems cancellations, of steel mill and auto plant closings, and of firm dislocations attributed to imports all tend to confirm this. The size of the adjustment assistance that is appropriate is likely to be exaggerated.

The second problem has to do with the likely nature of the government response. I have mentioned that government is never a neutral arbiter when income losses are involved. Our political system inevitably tries to delay or avoid such losses and, in the process, prevents necessary adjustment from occurring. Our current adjustment assistance programs are certainly poorly designed and need a complete overhaul. They cushion temporary losses of income; they do not facilitate adjustment. However, extreme care must be taken in any overhaul to make sure that additional adjustment-retarding measures are not introduced.

For example, as part of a revised program of adjustment assistance, it has been proposed that plants be required to give advance notice of their intention to close. The argument has been that such advance notice would give government agencies responsible for providing adjustment assistance and the affected communities themselves time to mobilize their resources to deal with the coming shock. A more likely result is that such a requirement would permit the mobilization of political resources to prevent the closing. We should be extremely wary of instituting such a requirement.

"REVITALIZING" LARGE FIRMS, IMPORTANT INDUSTRIES, AND DECLINING INDUSTRIES

Disinvestment can either be the first sign of the death of a firm, industry, or region, or it can be an essential prelude to a rebirth of vigor—a revitalization. But do private markets, supplemented by existing institutional arrangements such as the bankruptcy laws, properly identify the appropriate candidates for extinction and revitalization, provide the appropriate incentives and necessary "breathing space" to permit revitalization to occur, and deal humanely with the resources that are not required by the revitalized entity? In large part, these questions are inseparable from the ones addressed in the section immediately above and have similar answers: markets appear to do reasonably well in assuring needed change; they do less well in providing an appropriate cushion to those dislocated by change. But the well-publicized financial difficulties of firms like the Lockheed Corporation and the Chrysler Corporation and of major cities like New York and Cleveland; the problems being experienced by once-vigorous industries like autos, steel, and rubber; and the apparent decline in the industrial Midwest have combined to generate proposals for new institutional arrangements to deal with such situations "better."

Evaluating these proposals is difficult because the nature of the flaws alleged to exist in existing institutions are seldom carefully specified; the goals the new institutions would seek to achieve, never clearly stated; and the manner in which certain critical difficulties would be surmounted, inadequately addressed. For example, with regard to a large enterprise like Chrysler, we are simultaneously told that it is essential to retain the *threat* of bankruptcy in order to enforce the sort of concessions essential to efficient restructuring of such a complex entity, but that *actual* bankruptcy itself would be a prospect too traumatic for the nation to endure. The trauma is variously described as a major unexpected shock to our financial institutions (which might set off a panic) or the blow to our national prestige from seeing such a giant enterprise fail. In the case of important industries like steel and autos, it is acknowledged that improved productivity is vital if their competitiveness is to be restored, but it is suggested that the shrinkage in their size and a reorientation in their product line as necessary preconditions for these productivity improvements is somehow "unthinkable."

In spite of these ambiguities and contradictions, the proposals deserve careful examination, if only because of the prominence of their supporters. To do this, it will prove useful to attempt to separate various of the alleged virtues of such institutions and analyze each individually. Unfortunately, our attempt at such a separation will be only partially successful, so the reader is warned to expect a certain amount of repetition.

"Tough-Mindedness": Separating the Sheep from the Goats—and Keeping the Sheep, Not the Goats   It is not clear whether the primary fault in existing institutional arrangements is that they would choose the wrong set of survivors or that, if permitted to operate, they might result in some firms not surviving. The aim in a bankruptcy is to preserve the assets of a firm's creditors—if possible, by reorganization; if necessary, by liquidation. It is not difficult to imagine that in such a process, some enterprises in which there was a certain element of public interest might be liquidated, while other less "worthy" enterprises might be successfully restructured. But if the test of market viability is not to be the principal one, what objective criterion is to be used? How is the "public interest" to be valued, and properly inserted into a reorganization or liquidation decision? (It certainly is not to be expected to result automatically from the workings of the political process—unless one is willing to *define* the public interest as whatever the political process happens to spew out.)

In the previous section it was noted that governmental institutions are hardly neutral calculators of costs and benefits. Costs that are concentrated in their bearers and near in time are given excessive weight; benefits that are diffuse and in the future are heavily discounted. The government's virtually unlimited access to capital markets regardless of the merit of the activity being supported removes an important check on the excessive use of the "bail-out." The government's ability to borrow at below-commercial rates creates the unfortunate impression that successful bail-outs are "costless" if loans are eventually repaid years after they were first made. Finally, the claim that the enterprise would have been viable but for the government's own misguided policies creates yet another strong incentive to intervene excessively.

It is useful to recognize that aspects of businesses which the government may have a direct interest in protecting can be protected without preserving the entire enterprise. Indeed, the mere fact of the government's interest may be sufficient to assure these units' survival. There was much concern at the time of the Lockheed debate about the threat to the firm's abilities as an important defense contractor if the firm were permitted to go bankrupt. However, it was clear at the time—and it has become clearer since—that the money-losing civilian aircraft branch of the firm could have been successfully separated from its profitable defense-related activities and the latter preserved. And recent newspaper reports have indicated that Chrysler's important tank production subsidiary has been successfully insulated from the rest of the enterprise in a way that would assure its survival, even if the rest of the firm were liquidated.

A second point, related to the one just mentioned, is the inevitable pressure on the government—heightened by the increased political skills of firms, their workers, and the communities and states within which they are located—to give weight to intangibles such as national pride in making the hard decisions about how a firm or industry should be restructured. Statements to the effect that particular industries like steel are "essential" to the nation's civilian and military wellbeing obscure the question of whether an inefficient, unproductive, and overbuilt steel industry is truly a source of strength to the nation. Markets —and bankruptcy referees—give such intangibles little or no weight. It is not clear how much weight governments should give to them, but I believe that it almost certainly would be excessive.

A third point to remember is that a successful reorganization—as opposed merely to the creation of a permanent ward of the government —often requires that major surgery be performed. If Chrysler does survive, it will be a very different company from the one that first approached the government a couple of years ago. Many plants will have been shut down; others will have been modernized. The dealer network will have been shrunk, and supplier arrangements altered. The wage structure will have been changed. Several units of the enterprise will have been sold off. But these are precisely the things that would have been necessary had the bankruptcy route been followed! Why, then, is the bankruptcy route so inferior, especially since it inevitably involves the risk of creating a permanent ward of the state? The supporters of a Federal role in reorganization must show why having the government, with all the political pressures it inevitably is subject to, is likely to produce a more viable enterprise than the bankruptcy route in a case such as Chrysler.

Political Institutions That Are "Nonpolitical" The proponents of "revitalization" experiments might agree with the above argument and yet say that the institutions they are proposing to create would not fall prey to them because they would be "nonpolitical." Unfortunately, there are no nonpolitical political institutions. Any entity created by Congress, given access to large amounts of government funds, and asked to deal with matters having great political importance could not be nonpolitical. Congress has in the past granted blanket authority to restructure small and medium-sized enterprises where the sums involved were not too great.[6] But to assume that Congress would issue blank checks amounting to billions of dollars in borrowing authority is to ignore reality.

This point is strengthened if, as some have proposed, the new entity was to be given authority to employ the entire arsenal of Federal weapons which can help a firm or industry and injure its competitors: the ability to grant antitrust exemptions, special "temporary" trade relief, exemptions from environmental or occupational safety standards, special depreciation allowances, and so on. A close examination of the concerns that arose during the debate over the proposed Energy Mobilization Board—which would have had far less sweeping powers than those discussed here—should be enough to convince anyone of the impracticality of such a sweeping and uncontrolled delegation of powers.

Reduced *Ad Hoc*-ery   It has been suggested that the decision to help Chrysler signals that *no* large firm will be permitted to fail regardless of the merits of its doing so, and that the proposed new institutional arrangements represent merely a more efficient, less costly way to put this policy into effect. Leaving aside the unfortunate consequences for the economy if true, the number of firms which will be aided cannot be independent of the costs we impose to qualify for such aid. At present, the decision to help Chrysler implies *at most* that the government, after much soul-searching and controversy, finally decided to try to help the seventeenth largest industrial corporation in this country attempt to avoid bankruptcy.[7] The costs to Chrysler of deciding to go this highly visible route have been substantial. Its officers have been forced to appear before Congress to explain why their company deserves help. They have had their decisions exposed to detailed criticism and second guessing by virtually every major financial publication. The company has been forced to accept the Secretary of the Treasury, Chairman of the Federal Reserve Board, the Comptroller General, and their staffs as *de facto* receivers. It has had to comply with a host of nuisance conditions —the requirement that it submit an energy savings plan, a productivity improvement plan, an employee stock ownership plan—all to qualify for Federal aid. The number of employees has been reduced substantially through the closure of numerous facilities. And still, "rescue" is far from assured.

A far different—and more ominous—signal would be given by the creation of a special "revitalization" authority with general powers to receive petitions for aid, work out rescue packages shielded from the glare of publicity and congressional scrutiny, and put them into effect backed by the authority of the government. The current process has certainly been "messy," but its very messiness helps assure that it will not be used very often. That check is invaluable, and should be retained at virtually any cost. In fact, if the nation were indeed to be so foolish as to declare that the bankruptcy of a major corporation is "unthinkable," the threat that the political process will fail to produce agreement on an effective rescue plan may be the principal remaining check on gross corporate inefficiency.

But what about the claim that shifting the responsibility for assembling major Federal "bail-out packages" to a new entity would permit the development of specialized staff expertise somewhere within government? Those at this conference more familiar than I with the specifics of how Federal aid to Lockheed, New York City, and Chrysler no doubt had their own views, but I understand that during the course of dealing with these three episodes, there has been a good deal of institutional learning, especially on the part of Treasury staff. It is not clear how much more "learning" would be possible—or useful. Further, there is the problem stressed by several participants at the Symposium that a highly trained staff of experts would be sorely tempted to go out and look for firms or industries to "save" if sufficient candidates did not present themselves. Highly skilled organizations do not remain highly skilled if not called upon with sufficient frequency.

The Ability to Deal with Emergencies in a Much More Timely Fashion On rare occasions, the discovery that a large firm or city is facing imminent bankruptcy may be sufficiently unsettling so as to threaten the stability of financial markets. In the case of banks, this possibility has been deemed serious enough to cause Congress to grant broad authority to banking regulators to reorganize failed and even "open" banks. Might not the same logic apply to industrial enterprises?

A number of important differences between banks and industrial firms should be noted. History confirms the suddenness with which financial problems can come to light at major banks. Either the bank has managed to conceal its developing difficulties from state and Federal banking supervisors, or a major change in financial markets has suddenly changed the characteristics of certain of the bank's assets. In contrast, the difficulties which beset major industrial enterprises are usually much slower in developing and much more difficult to conceal from investors. To be sure, the extent of Penn Central's difficulties did catch financial markets by surprise, and substantial efforts by the Federal Reserve were required to prevent severe problems in the commercial paper market. But the problems of Lockheed and Chrysler were well advertised, giving investors adequate opportunity to assess the company's prospects and adjust their holdings accordingly.

Second, history also shows the rapidity with which "runs" on banks can develop. Depositors can withdraw large blocks of funds very quickly, turning what might have been a relatively small liquidity problem into an insurmountable one. If assistance can be quickly arranged, runs can be prevented and the problem can be contained.

There is some analogy in the case of industrial firms, but the analogy should not be stretched too far. The "orphan car" syndrome is real, and likely accounts for some of Chrysler's current difficulties. But the demonstrated success of the owners of autos produced by other companies that went bankrupt in obtaining service for their cars suggests that the fears of a total drying up of sales are probably overblown. Similarly, claims I have heard that the potential customers of an airline facing bankruptcy would desert it in droves flies in the face of the experience of carriers like Pan American World Airways, Trans World Corporation, and even Braniff Airways Corporation, who have continued to attract traffic in the face of extended periods of losses. Finally, the phenomenon of creditors suddenly deciding to liquidate their claims and run is precisely what the bankruptcy laws are designed to prevent.

A third difference relates to the quantity and quality of information available to whomever would be designing a restructuring plan. As noted above, banks are subject to continuous close supervision by Federal and state authorities. This supervision may occasionally break down, but it generally can be counted upon to produce an understanding of the portions of the firm's business worth preserving, the strengths and weaknesses of its management, and the capabilities of potential buyers of all or part of its assets. This knowledge, plus the knowledge that any surviving firm will also be under continuing close supervision, helps to create a mood in which knowledgeable individuals can rapidly work out an intelligent restructuring plan.

Such a knowledge base does not exist in the case of large industrial firms, and there certainly would be strong opposition to creating it. While an extended (and public) process of fact finding may not be the ideal way to develop the information necessary to the development of a viable plan, it usually does get developed during the course of such an inquiry. It is hard to see what comparable incentives would exist if an entity were given broad authorities to develop restructuring plans in private.

Finally, the history under which the authority to restructure banks has developed makes it clear that the aims of such a restructuring are narrow: to prevent financial panic and create a viable entity as quickly as possible. If the proposals for the creation of an analogous industrial reorganization authority were similarly narrow, they might be more attractive. But, as already noted, more often than not, narrowly focused proposals are accompanied by broad, vague objectives such as revitalizing firms or industries, almost regardless of their ultimate prospects.

The idea that some entity might be created to backstop the bankruptcy laws in certain narrowly specified cases where grave harm to financial markets might otherwise result is potentially appealing. If creating such an entity is the prime objective of supporters of such concepts as a "new" Reconstruction Finance Corporation, they would do well to focus their attention on how it would operate, what constraints it would face, and how it could be prevented from becoming an all purpose bail-out arranger.

Revitalization Versus Generalized Aid   With the possible exception of the case just discussed, I consider proposals to create new institutions to handle major Federal bail-outs and industry reorganizations on a more or less "routine" basis as both politically naive and economically dangerous. However, the decade ahead will require unprecedented adjustments on the part of many firms, industries, and regions, and the Federal government does have a legitimate role to play in easing the burdens associated with this adjustment, while assuring that they indeed do occur. Programs of liberalized depreciation allowances which better recognize the true replacement costs and premature obsolescence of industrial capital, refundable tax credits which provide aid to new firms or to firms undertaking major investment programs during a period of heavy financial losses, and even a reexamination of our existing bankruptcy arrangements as they apply to very large enterprises may be in order. And, as already noted, a major redirection of the Federal government's labor market programs (especially Trade Adjustment Assistance) is overdue. Finally, there may even be the need for an institution which can help localities or states seeking to mobilize help in dealing with the shock of industrial dislocation to find their way through the Federal maze. The primary requirement for the next decade is flexibility: all institutional proposals should be judged against that standard.

ENCOURAGING THE GROWTH OF NEW INDUSTRIES

The third major investment-channeling activity that government might engage in more actively than at present is encouraging the growth of new industries or, to use the more popular phrase, "pick-the-winners." To private markets, "winners" are industries that grow rapidly and generate substantial profits. What are winners from the government's point of view? One might imagine that they have precisely the same characteristics as the winners identified by the private market. In such a case, the purpose of the government's "picking" them presumably would be to encourage more rapid growth and/or higher profits. To accomplish this, either the government somehow would have to be able to spot potential winners that the market overlooked, or it would have to arrange to channel more resources than the market would into those winning industries the market itself had identified. The government's ability to do the first is highly questionable; the desirability of its doing the second (thereby diverting resources away from other sectors of the economy) is equally questionable.

However, the government is not likely to be content merely to try to mimic and then reinforce the private market—it will have additional criteria by which it judges an industry to be a winner. One might be an industry's ability to generate employment, especially in a locality or region where employment appears to be especially needed. Another might be the industry's potential for generating technological externalities—benefits that the industry itself cannot capture fully through the sale of its products or its processes which will diffuse throughout the economy and raise productivity substantially. (This is precisely why the government rather than the private sector is the source of such a high proportion of the funding for the nation's basic research.) A third criterion might be the possibility that the new industry will generate substantial exports.

Each of these objectives has a certain plausibility. But several caveats should be kept in mind. First, any decision by the government to divert scarce investment funds to the achieving of goals not directly rewarded by the private market will reduce the amount of resources available to support growth elsewhere in the economy. Only if these diverted resources stimulate overall economic activity by more than they would have if they had been left to flow by themselves is the nation's growth enhanced. Second, as noted repeatedly throughout this paper, the government does not approach the task of job creation, export promotion, or technology diffusion as a neutral party, anxious only to correct market failures. It imparts its own biases to the decisions—biases which tend to give insufficient weight to the returns that the resources it diverts could earn in alternative uses.

There is yet another extremely important reason why government likely would find it extremely hard to do well in pick-the-winners. These go to its inherent inability to play the role of a super venture capitalist.

A successful policy of identifying and supporting promising sectors implies a willingness on the part of the government to let some of the firms in the chosen sectors fail. A portfolio of venture capital investments designed to pick only winners typically ends up with a few large winners and many losers. However, the government's necessary sensitivity to income losses, intensified by the fact that it would bear a special responsibility for a chosen sector, makes it difficult, if not impossible, to tolerate such a portfolio. The more likely outcome—one frequently observed in other countries—would be a reluctance to abandon individual firms that fail. This could more than offset any gains achieved by the successful few among the chosen firms.

Second, there could be a tendency to implement a strategy of pick-the-winners by excessive reliance upon policies where the government has broader discretion (for example, trade policies) rather than designing policies specific to the problem at hand. The resulting use of easily available, but not necessarily efficient, policy instruments would produce an unbalanced response and introduce additional rigidities and distortion into the economy. Adding to this tendency would be the policymaker's inevitable recognition that a policy tool designed for one purpose can often be used for another. For example, the economic prospects of an industry that the government wished to single out for "favor" could be indirectly manipulated by changes in the stringency of government regulation. Such changes, however, when motivated by objectives of industrial policy, might be counterproductive to achieving the purpose for which the regulation was intended.

Third, to avoid "wasteful duplication," the government would be likely to centralize the process of picking-the-winners. Such centralization would forgo the advantages or risk diversification that comes from decentralized decision-making and would further heighten the pressures to protect losers among the chosen sectors.

The government does indeed have an important responsibility for creating a set of conditions under which new industries and firms can thrive. And it may also have a responsibility to make it relatively more attractive for such firms and industries to locate in one section of the country rather than another. But its role should be like that of the gardener who prepares the soil so that plants can grow successfully, not that of the hothouse gardener who develops beautiful specimens that cannot survive if exposed to the open air. For winners will not help the country if they require constant Federal nourishment.

THE FOREIGN EXPERIENCE: EVIDENCE FOR OR
AGAINST A LARGER FEDERAL ROLE?

The experience of other countries has been cited as supporting the case for a larger Federal role in the three areas examined: phasing out old industries, reorganizing viable firms and industries in trouble, and encouraging the growth of new industries. Certainly examples can be found where each of these activities is practiced to a much greater extent than presently is the case in the United States. And individual examples of success—or reputed success—can be cited. But does the experience overall give grounds for hope or for caution? I think the latter.

What follows will by no means be a complete summary of the foreign experience in industrial policy. That subject is far too voluminous for adequate treatment in a single short chapter—or even a single volume. Furthermore, I can lay no claim to being a recognized expert in this field. I have conducted no original research. My observations are drawn from three sources: (1) a series of studies of foreign industrial policy experiences prepared as background information for Carter administration reviews of U.S. industrial policy and U.S. policies toward the auto industry; (2) exchanges of national experiences—both written and oral—that occurred in 1979 and 1980 during the meetings of the Organization for Economic Cooperation and Development High-Level Group on Positive Adjustment Policies; and (3) attempts on my part to fill in blanks in the picture, through selective reading, since I left the government in late January. Therefore, I would not be surprised to find exception being taken to some of the generalizations that follow.

Experience in Phasing Out and "Revitalizing" Declining Sectors or Firms   I group these two together because, as I read the history of the overseas experiences, it is impossible to separate them. Virtually every government in major overseas industrialized countries has found it necessary to take a direct role in aiding disinvestment in key sectors. Most allow exceptions from their antitrust laws where this is considered necessary to permit major industry restructuring. Many have strict requirements for advance notice of intended plant closings and for consultation with affected communities and workers. Most have incentives to induce expanding industries to locate in areas facing major plant closures. A few resort to nationalization to prevent "unacceptable" levels of disinvestment.

What are the results? Decidedly mixed. Within Europe, the principal thrust of programs to aid disinvestment seems to have been to retard it significantly. The British case is notorious, but hardly atypical. Here, concern over job preservation has blunted needed moves toward industry rationalization, and has led to an endless series of efforts at revitalization. Reductions in capacity eventually do occur—autos, steel, textiles, shipbuilding, and aircraft are all examples—but usually only after one or two rounds of subsidy and/or nationalization. The present Conservative government claims that it will end these repeated efforts at nurturing "losers," but results have yet to follow rhetoric. British industry continues to be the textbook example of how *not* to aid disinvestment—or to revitalize declining industries or sectors.

In a number of the smaller northern European countries, efforts to rationalize such politically sensitive industries as steel and shipbuilding have not met with success. Often, the claim that currently redundant capacity will be needed "someday" has been sufficient to convince the authorities not to take on the politically difficult task of reducing the size of these traditionally strong industries. In certain of these countries, the actual number of jobs involved is remarkably small, both in the aggregate and as a percentage of the total labor force. But geographical concentration of these jobs has prompted claims that the closing of individual facilities would spell economic disaster for the localities involved, and has enabled the day of reckoning to be postponed and repostponed.

In one of these smaller countries, labor market policies designed to cushion the shock of unemployment have all but destroyed any incentive on the part of workers to relocate or to look for jobs in other industries. This geographically compact country faces the paradox of *both* sharply rising overemployment and sharply rising vacancies. Further, high tax rates have virtually destroyed private capital markets, causing the government's industrial policy to consist principally of trying to replicate the role that these private markets would carry out, if only they existed.

In France, there has been a serious effort in recent years to wean industry of its historic heavy reliance on subsidies. Efforts at "indicative planning," in which explicit "visions" were to be designed to guide industry in setting its investment priorities, have been substantially downgraded. Important progress has been made in permitting the market to force reductions in the size of industries like textiles and steel. But progress has come slowly, and it is still considered an appropriate activity of the state to shelter certain firms and sectors in difficulty, especially if the firm in question or a significant portion of the sector is nationalized.

French industrial policy does seem to be moving away from assistance to entire sectors toward assistance to selected key firms. Further, it appears that the French are attempting to develop a formal mechanism of *quid pro quo*. Through the technique of "development contracts," the government is beginning to agree to restructure its various interventions in exchange for specific promises of productivity improvements (somewhat along the lines of what the new U.S. Secretary of Transportation seems to be proposing for the domestic auto industry). Unfortunately, the relative lack of transparency of the French industrial policy process prevents anyone on the outside from learning just how extensive these development contracts are, what the duties and obligations of each of the parties are, and whether the promised contributions on the part of the assisted firms have indeed been made and the hoped for progress realized. Nevertheless, it seems fair to summarize current French experience as reflecting both an increasing concern about excessive support for chronically sick firms, and an attempt to move toward more limited and targeted assistance.

The Japanese experience warrants a special mention. Although attention has generally focused on Japan's real or imagined successes in promoting growing sectors, its efforts to encourage *dis*investment seem to me to be a more interesting aspect of the Japanese experience to study. The Japanese clearly have their problems. Their distribution sector is a notoriously inefficient "sink" for absorbing labor released elsewhere in the economy. And productivity in their agricultural sector could be improved significantly if further rationalization were permitted. Political barriers, tied importantly to the method by which legislative districts are apportioned, have acted so far to limit restructuring in these two critical sectors of the economy. How much longer the Japanese will be able to continue to avoid facing their problems squarely is an important question for both them and their trading partners to consider carefully.

Yet it is unfair to focus entirely on these problems, even though they are significant. What is more interesting is the degree to which the Japanese society has been able to tolerate—and even encourage—bankruptcies and reorganization. When "recession cartels" are formed, capacity sometimes actually seems to get reduced, in contrast to the general case in Europe which finds capacity preserved in anticipation of the next upswing. Thus, when the recession of 1975 and the higher energy prices that accompanied it placed a number of important industries in jeopardy—electric steel, aluminum, textiles, shipbuilding—these industries were given some encouragement to shrink to a more reasonable size. And when large enterprises have found themselves in trouble, these enterprises have been reorganized and their activities have been pruned.[8]

It has been argued that this is all made possible by the Japanese system of "lifetime employment." This system, which permits a high degree of mobility within large industrial groups, certainly does aid restructuring. Furthermore, the presence of banking organizations in the large Japanese industrial combines clearly facilitates financial restructuring in ways that are not feasible given the arms length relationship between financial institutions and their borrowers that U.S. law requires. But the explanation for the Japanese results appears to run deeper. Lifetime employment covers only about 30 percent of all Japanese workers, according to the figures I have seen. And the real losses in many of the more important reorganizations are quite large—more than merely "paper" reorganizations are involved. If units fail to measure up, they are not supported.

What the Japanese appear to be better capable of doing than some others is distinguishing between the value to their economy of preserving a vital and productive industrial sector—regardless of which products seem to be the leading ones at the time being—and the notion more prevalent in the West of preserving particular producing entities. I believe that those who are looking for the key to the Japanese "miracle" would do well to look at this aspect of the Japanese experience as much as seeking to find any particular adeptness at pick-the-winners.

Experience in Promoting the Growth of New Industries Just as in the case of declining industries and sectors, foreign governments have typically assured a much more active and explicit role in promoting new industries than has been the case in the United States. In part, the reason for this is historical. Governments in countries like France have an extremely long history of singling out firms or industries for favor.

Ironically, the reasons given by most foreign governments today for engaging in such policies relate to the need to compensate for advantages their firms experience relative to those in the United States. Anyone who questions why countries like Britain and France continue to offer support to what appear to be promising new sectors has the example of the U.S. defense and space industries immediately thrown back at them. It is argued that the U.S. has engaged in winner-picking on a scale undreamed of elsewhere and that absent these compensatory efforts, the rest of the world would fall hopelessly behind the United States in technology.

I believe the Europeans have seriously misunderstood the U.S. experience. The fact that there are certain spin-offs from programs designed to produce technology where the government is the major customer may be a fortunate occurrence for the United States. Or it may be, as some have argued, in some part responsible for our present industrial difficulties. However, it is not the same as attempting to force feed civilian-oriented technologies. The attempt to do this has, by and large, proved a dismal failure.

As in the revitalization example, the textbook case is Great Britain. This nation has spent billions of pounds and tried virtually every institutional arrangement imaginable in an effort to pick-the-winners. There has been the occasional commercially successful product, but every independent evaluation I have seen has pronounced the British experiment a dismal failure. Certainly it has failed to produce a viable, high technology industrial sector in Great Britain. And it has drained capital and engineering talent from enterprises that might have been more successful. Commitments to projects have been maintained long past the period where it became clear that they were nonviable. Ultimately, considerations of national prestige have been the driving force in causing support to be continued. In short, the British have clearly shown us how *not* to do it.

As always, interpreting what the French have been doing and what the results have been is a bit difficult. The French clearly have had an explicit policy of promoting French technology and French firms. They have used a very wide range of mechanisms to do this, especially discriminatory government procurement contracts. They have had some success in encouraging certain sectors—computers and commercial aircraft are two where they have directed much effort—but it is not clear how much any success achieved has been due to the efforts of the French government and how much is due to other reasons.[9] Still, the French government clearly intends to continue to identify leading sectors—biotechnologies, offshore drilling, robotics, and telecommunications appear to be four sectors currently enjoying favor—and to support these industries with a variety of instruments. Independent evaluations of the success or failure of this effort are not likely to be available.

As was true of disinvestment and revitalization, Japan's experience in pick-the-winners deserves special attention. One reason for this is that it is claimed that, in contrast to the cases of Britain and France, there have been certain conspicuous successes. But of equal importance, in my view, is the fact that there have not been cases of conspicuous failure. What accounts for each?

The classic Japanese "success" stories cited are in steel, shipbuilding, and autos. In the first two, there can be no doubt that the government played an active and important role. Investment funds clearly were channeled in the direction of both industries. Each was also the recipient of other forms of government aid.

The Japanese auto industry presents a more complex case. By now it is widely known that originally the Ministry of International Trade and Industry (MITI) did not believe that Japan should have such an industry and fought against its establishment. Eventually, however, the fledgling industry did receive at least grudging support in its battle for access to scarce investment funds. (However, the industry was never heavily dependent on loans from either the banks or the government. The balance sheets of the major auto companies are largely free of long-term debt. Growth has been principally financed from retained earnings.) More importantly, significant domestic tariff production was supplied to aid the growing industry. Takeovers by foreign firms were prevented. And the standards and certification process were also used to hinder imports. Various forms of indirect governmental assistance were indeed important in helping the Japanese automobile industry get off the ground. But to a remarkable degree, the industry itself has been largely responsible for its own continued success.[10]

As noted, the Japanese have avoided certain of the conspicuous failures that have plagued the Europeans. After a brief but unsuccessful foray into the commercial aircraft market (with the YS11), efforts were sharply scaled back. There has been a continuing interest in computers, but never the aggressive "force feeding" that is characteristic of the French effort. The important thing to note is that the Japanese, almost uniquely among countries with policies designed to pick-the-winners, have been willing to cut their losses at an early stage if ventures appeared to be commercially unpromising.

But what of the future in Japan? Much has been made of the various "visions" prepared by MITI—most recently, the "Vision for the 80s" published about a year ago. These visions are remarkably nonspecific; they in no way resemble a coordinated "plan" for the future. One knowledgeable observer has characterized them as similar to the science and technology pages in the *Economist.* They provide no useful guidance as to priorities and have little or no direct budgetary significance. Such lack of specificity is appropriate. In the years immediately after World War II, a relatively formal process of allocating scarce investment funds may have been appropriate for Japan. But now the Japanese recognize that they no longer are in a "catch up" situation. If they are to push forward, they will have to create the new technology as much as borrow it. Government funding for research and development, always remarkably low by Western standards, will increase somewhat. But the primary burden to identify winning technologies and to support their development will lie with the private sector. A few well-publicized examples—like efforts in robotics and random access memories—should not obscure the fact that the Japanese government is likely to play less and less of a role in the future in pick-the-winner. Instead, the government will concentrate its attention primarily on providing a favorable climate for growth and innovation. If a winner begins to emerge, it may be able to obtain some indirect support from the government, but the successive rounds of tariff cuts and actions against nontariff barriers (such as discriminatory procurement regulations) have limited the use of the tools that the Japanese traditionally could rely upon. Absent a large military effort, the Japanese will be hard pressed to find ways of engaging in major efforts to support new technology, even should they wish to do so.

To sum up, other countries have certainly engaged in explicit efforts to pick-the-winner. But except where they were clearly playing the game of catch up, efforts have generally been unsuccessful, and even in this case the record has been decidedly mixed. Attempts to spot "industries of tomorrow" far in advance of the market have not proved successful, and attempts to do so have managed to consume considerable volumes of scarce capital.

A related issue deserving attention is the implication of various countries all trying to support the growth of the same industries simultaneously. It was mentioned that Japanese steel and shipbuilding were two cases in which government efforts to promote domestic industries appear to have been successful—at least for a time. But these winners of the sixties became the problem industries of the seventies. To be sure, the Japanese appear to be more skillful than most in reducing the scale even of industries "created" with substantial government help. But what of other countries? In particular, what happens when all countries —including the United States if some people have their way—"pick" robotics or microcircuitry and attempt to force feed it? Is a viable world industry created, or do we end up with significant overcapacity? Who are the ultimate winners in such a game?

Lessons for the United States   This survey of foreign experiences has admittedly been far from comprehensive. Its main lesson is to suggest skepticism concerning reports that the experiences of the Europeans and Japanese provide strong support for a more active U.S. government role in phasing out declining industries; revitalizing firms, industries, and regions; or picking-the-winners. What lessons there are tend more in the direction of emphasizing the importance of flexibility and designing government interventions to minimize their intrusiveness than towards supporting a strong pro-active planning role for government.

CONCLUSIONS

The current performance of the U.S. economy certainly leaves much to be desired. The numerous interventions that make up our present *"de facto* industrial policy" are a crazy quilt of imperfectly coordinated and often poorly thought out activities. Our attempts at rescuing major firms or "revitalizing" major industries may be misdirected and poorly executed. It is not hard to imagine how omniscient, omnipotent policy-makers, sufficiently isolated from "politics," might produce far better results.

However, before we recommend that our government increase its role in channeling the flow of investment, we should be clear about what ought to be the relevant standard for comparisons. Any institution we create to formulate and administer industrial policy will be operated by fallible humans and will be immersed in politics. The issue, therefore, is whether such an institution, prone as it would be to the numerous "political failures" detailed in this paper, would be an improvement over the equally imperfect status quo.

The evidence from our own experience and from overseas should teach us to be wary of promises that something called industrial policy will be a cure for our current economic ills. Improving the understanding of government about the effects of its various policy interventions is certainly a feasible goal. But it takes time and resources to create and nurture the analytical capabilities that this requires. Few administrations have been farsighted enough to undertake such investments. Claims that the creation of a small (that is, inexpensive) expert group would magically bring order out of chaos diverts attention from the more difficult task of institution-building.

It also creates the impression that we can avoid facing certain problems that await us in the coming decade—problems that in part are as difficult as they are because we have refused to face them in the past. The 1980s are going to place extraordinary demands on the adjustment capabilities of the United States and the rest of the world. It will be the decade during which the major costs of adjusting to the higher energy prices of the late 1970s will have to be borne. Further, we will have to take expensive steps to reduce our energy vulnerability by increasing our flexibility to use alternative fuels. The long delayed restructuring of many of our traditional industries—particularly steel and autos—will have to occur at the same time we are "deepening" our capital stock and laying the foundation for the growth of new industries. Trade flows are likely to continue to be a disruptive influence—one that we must learn to accommodate, not shut off. The aging of our labor force will reduce the extraordinary pressures we felt during the mid to late 1970s to create "first time" jobs, but will exacerbate the problem of providing adequate retraining and relocation incentives for experienced workers.

The temptation will be to try to avoid these adjustment pressures or to find "solutions" that appear to permit them to be resolved without making hard choices. Industrial policy, at least as espoused by some of its more enthusiastic proponents, is one such tempting solution. However, as our experience in energy has shown, delaying needed adjustment in the hope that the underlying problem will go away, or trying to "manage" the adjustment too carefully in the hope that we can somehow avoid its pain, only serves to make the economy unproductive in the interim and increases the costs once the inevitability is finally faced up to. In this critical period, the acid test for any institutional recommendations is whether in actual operation they will help facilitate this needed adjustment. Unfortunately, most of the industrial policy proposals I have seen, while claiming to be adjustment-facilitating, would actually retard adjustment. These grounds alone should be sufficient to ensure their rejection.

NOTES

1. Research for this chapter was supported in part by The Rand Corporation as part of its program of public service. The opinions expressed are the author's own and do not necessarily represent those of either The Rand Corporation or its sponsors.

2. Eads (1979).

3. Indeed, that seems to be the virtue that attracts Professor Thurow. See Lester Thurow (1980): 191–192.

4. In 1960, coal represented only about 24 percent of total U.S. energy production—its dominant position had by then been taken over by oil.

5. The fact that social costs, such as air pollution, which were once ignored, are now internalized by business—and passed on to consumers —is not itself an inappropriate "market distortion." Just the reverse is true. The market was inappropriately distorted before these costs were internalized. However, the act of introducing even the "correct" degree of internalization may alter investment signals very rapidly. The transitional costs of this rapid adjustment may be an appropriate concern of government.

6. The Economic Development Administration has had such authority. But EDA is to be eliminated, in part because it became too "political."

7. This was its ranking in 1979 according to *Fortune.* In 1978, Chrysler ranked tenth in size among industrials. I *strongly* disagree with Bloomfield and Walker's assertion that the Chrysler decision was an easy one for Congress—or the Administration—to make. The final vote to aid Chrysler may have been lopsided, but only because the difficult issues had been thrashed out earlier.

8. Phil Trezise, in a personal communication, has urged me not to be *too* impressed with the Japanese experience, pointing out the difficulties in separating secular declines from policy-induced shrinkages. His point is well taken. Yet I do detect in the recent Japanese experience a willingness to allow secular trends to operate—and, in some cases, a willingness to reinforce them. But evaluation is indeed difficult.

9. It might be argued that the Airbus represents a clear success for the French. I question this conclusion. The Airbus was selling quite poorly until the run-up in jet fuel prices made the aircraft more attractive. Until then, it was selling only with the help of extremely heavy subsidies. And the long-term commercial viability of Airbus Industries is by no means yet assured.

10. The Reagan administration's recent success in inducing the Japanese to impose "voluntary" restraints on their automakers may prove the industry's undoing. The actual size of the cutback is also

irrelevant. Whatever its size, the Japanese must find a way to impose it and to assure that it is adhered to. Doing this will inevitably increase the Ministry of International Trade and Industry's power vis à vis the industry. This may account for why MITI has been such a supporter of import restraint and why the industry has opposed it so vigorously.

BIBLIOGRAPHY

Eads, George. "Chemicals as a Regulated Industry." In *Federal Regulation and Chemical Innovation,* edited by Christopher Hill. Washington: The American Chemical Society, 1979.

Hill, Christopher, ed. *Federal Regulation and Chemical Innovation.* Washington: The American Chemical Society, 1979.

Thurow, Lester. *The Zero Sum Society.* New York: Basic Books, 1980.

U.S., Office of the President. *Economic Report, 1981.* Washington: Government Printing Office, 1981.

DISCUSSANTS

Bernard E. Anderson

The concern about industrial policy is stimulated, in part, by what many believe are failures in the U.S. economy during the past decade. The economy, it is said, has lost momentum because of a failure to keep modernizing basic industries. U.S. investment in plant and equipment as a percentage of GNP is among the lowest in the Western world. This same failure is thought to have reduced the nation's competitiveness in exports.

Other elements in the concern about industrial policy include the precipitous decline in productivity, the impact of higher energy costs on inflation, and the economic viability of some of the nation's major industrial enterprises and geographic regions. Many structural changes have occurred in American industry during the past decade, and both the pace and direction of change are expected to generate serious adjustment problems during the 1980s.

In dealing with the political implications of these developments, and in thinking about appropriate public policy responses, it is necessary to recognize that the expected adjustments will involve issues that go far beyond the financial aspects of industrial policy. Among the major issues that must be addressed from a perspective not limited to narrow financial considerations are (1) the location of industrial activity, (2) the national security implications of maintaining specific firms, or industries, and (3) the need for stimulating job creation sufficient to achieve full employment and to increase equity, both in the distribution of economic opportunities and rewards for all segments of our population.

As the nation works its way through the very difficult adjustments that lie ahead during this decade, it is important that our decision-making institutions permit all the vital interests to be represented in the allocation of scarce financial and other resources. And when proposing new institutions for developing and implementing industrial policy, proponents should remember that the United States is a pluralistic society in which the often conflicting claims of different interest groups are moderated through the political process. Although the Lockheed Corporation, New York City, and the Chrysler Corporation cases involved considerable public debate and controversy, the process through which the issues were ultimately decided allowed for a full expression of views by the major interests, including stockholders, financiers, customers, employees, and community representatives. Perhaps there is a better way to resolve the difficulties associated with large private and public organizations that encounter serious financial crises, but an alternative to existing decision-making processes should reflect the pluralistic character of our social and political system.

The appropriate role of government in helping the nation adjust to changing conditions is to create an environment in which private decision-making can be maximized. The government should adopt a set of policies designed to help companies in all industries modernize facilities, hold down costs, and improve their efficiency. Instead of trying to "pick-the-winners", the Federal government should try to create optimum conditions for strengthening competitiveness.

The two objectives of greater industrial competitiveness and improved equity in the distribution of economic opportunities can be achieved through a creative use of the tax system. Tax incentives can provide an efficient and orderly means for chaneling resources to areas where they can be used to maximum advantage, and can help reconcile the potential conflict between industrial change and social displacement. The creative use of the tax system is applicable to human, as well as physical, capital investment decisions, and is a superior instrument to alternative measures.

For example, government policy should also encourage the location of industry in areas of high unemployment. One of the major issues today is the appropriate public policy for stimulating greater economic activity in depressed urban areas. Many efforts to achieve this objective through direct government expenditure programs have not been successful, but there is reason to believe a program of tax incentives might produce more favorable results.

Similarly, there is much discussion today about the problem of youth unemployment and some have suggested that it would be desirable to create a subminimum wage for young workers. A subminimum wage aimed at the youth unemployment problem would be both unwise and unnecessary. Instead, the Targeted Jobs Tax Credit is a better device for lowering the marginal cost of hiring youth, because the tax credit can be aimed at the youth most in need, and would provide a significantly greater financial incentive to prospective employers.

In discussing U.S. industrial policy, it is necessary to recognize the major change that has occurred in the structure of the economy during the past several decades, especially the rapid expansion in the services industries. In 1948, the services producing sector accounted for 54 percent of GNP and had 27.2 million employees, while the goods producing sector accounted for 46 percent of GNP, and had 21 million employees. By 1977, three decades later, services producers accounted for two-thirds of GNP (66 percent), and employment had doubled to 54 million workers; while goods producers had slipped to 34 percent of GNP and 25 million employees.

One implication of these trends is that U.S. industrial policy cannot be concerned exclusively with the basic industries, or with manufacturing. In an increasingly open world economy, the loss of competitiveness in some companies and industries is inevitable. Potentially profitable sectors of the economy need resources to optimize their growth. The nation needs policies that do not impede the flow of resources to areas where the United States has a competitive advantage in production.

Finally, while recognizing the limitations of government in substituting for the market in allocating investment resources, it is also important to recognize the responsibility of government to ease the impact of the adjustment process on labor force groups and communities that may be adversely affected by private investment decisions. Economic growth and development tend to benefit society as a whole, but there are often sectoral inequities that deserve special attention. A rising tide might lift all boats, but it does nothing for shipwrecks at the bottom of the sea. A politically acceptable industrial policy must be one that allows for special efforts to assist workers and communities in their adjustment to industrial change.

Michael H. Moskow

Charls E. Walker and Mark Bloomfield give an excellent and fascinating description of the political influences affecting the Federal government's decision-making in the Lockheed Corporation, New York City, and the Chrysler Corporation financial rescue packages. This description of the political pressures and lobbying activities is extremely useful, but I personally disagree with the recommendation to establish a Modern Reconstruction Finance Corporation (MRFC).

Walker and Bloomfield state correctly that "modern bail-out" politics bias the political system in favor of "bail-out," in large part because jobs are at stake. In the Chrysler loan guarantee, for example, they describe in detail the elements of the politically powerful coalition favoring loans: the Chrysler Corporation, the United Automobile

Workers, small business allies mobilized by suppliers and dealers, minority groups such as the NAACP and the Urban League, as well as the U.S. Conference of Mayors and other urban-oriented organizations. Would establishing an MRFC have prevented this coalition from forming or changed the final decision by the government? It seems more likely that the result would have been substantially the same, regardless of whether an MRFC had been part of the decision-making process, because the coalition had such enormous political power.

The main thrust of their recommendation is that the "current odds-in-favor for a bail-out would shift" if an MRFC were established. In my view, establishing the MRFC is putting out a shingle in an area where, once you put out a shingle, you are assured a great deal of business. If the MRFC were established, it would be subject to enormous political pressure, and loans or "bail-outs" (to use the Walker-Bloomfield term) would be even more common.

Walker and Bloomfield assert that ". . . extension of lines of credit would be so laden with restrictions that few applicants would queue up." I find this view difficult to accept, especially in light of my personal experience in agencies granting funds, such as the Department of Labor and the Department of Housing and Urban Development.

It is instructive to visualize how the MRFC would operate in practice. Let us assume that authorizing legislation is enacted and the "hard-nosed take-charge financial type" envisioned in the paper to run the agency is hired. The agency's first steps would be to obtain a congressional appropriation, hire a staff, obtain office space, and issue implementing regulations. The criteria for MRFC eligibility, such as national interest considerations and probability of repayment, will be explained in administrative regulations. The legislation and regulations will be reviewed by numerous firms, trade associations, consultants, attorneys, and others in Washington and other parts of the United States looking for opportunities to obtain funds from the agency. Congressmen will request that the head of the agency, or his representative, meet with, or respond to, constituents who are interested in requesting loans. Some of these congressmen will have been active in supporting the concept of the MRFC and have served on the congressional committees appropriating funds to the MRFC.

No matter what the initial intentions of the head of the agency, there is a natural tendency over time for this agency to become more generous or less strict in approving loans. Once established, political pressures, including pressures from the agency's own staff, will inevitably lead in this direction.

The establishment of the agency increases the likelihood that some loans will be granted. After all, if the agency approves no loans, questions will be raised as to why the agency is needed. It is unlikely that an agency administering a statute to provide emergency assistance will reject all requests for loans when its existence is being threatened. On the contrary, experience with government programs indicates that the natural tendency will be for the agency to expand its "responsibility" so that it can receive a larger budget, staff, and higher salaries. Opportunities for personal advancement are much more prevalent in expanding organizations, as compared with stagnant or declining organizations.

It is important to recognize that these "bureaucratic pressures" exist in private industry as well as in government. It is a natural tendency for managers responsible for businesses or product lines to seek expansion and growth for some of the same reasons mentioned above. The major difference is that if this expansion becomes unprofitable in private industry, the company will change its direction over time. Profits are an important measuring rod of a business firm's performance. If a company continuously loses money on a product, at some point the company will stop producing the product or make major modifications to improve its profitability. The "market test" provides an important flushing mechanism for unwanted products or services. No such flushing mechanism exists in government to counteract the natural tendencies for expansion.

In conclusion, if Walker and Bloomfield intend to make it as difficult as possible for companies to obtain loans or shift the current "odds-in-favor" of a bail-out, we should not establish an administrative procedure to obtain funds. Once the procedure is established, the incidence of loans will expand no matter who is in charge.

Robert Carswell

I would like to sharpen the messages history has given us on Federal intervention to prevent or manage large bankruptcies, and then to draw some tentative conclusions from my perspective as an on-the-job architect of several of the plans.

The Reconstruction Finance Corporation (RFC) was originally sponsored by President Hoover and established by a Republican Congress to meet a perceived need for Federal credit assistance in several critical areas of the private sector. Its sphere of operations was broadened during the New Deal and War years. When its life was terminated in 1951, all of the major credit assistance programs it had spawned during its 20 year life—with the exception of some wartime lending activities —had been converted into permanent, targeted credit programs. One should note that RFC did extend credit to large institutions in two sectors: banking, where the Federal Deposit Insurance Corporation

(FDIC) was granted, but has rarely used, powers comparable to those the RFC had, and railroads, where specialized agencies were created to grapple with the complex and highly resistant problems. There were no true lineal ancestors to the Lockheed Corporation, the Chrysler Corporation, or New York City programs. Those were not the problems of the thirties and RFC's activities provide little direct guidance.

Penn Central, which came first of the more recent examples, seems a good case of what happens when bankruptcy is the chosen alternative, but the political reality was (and is) a public interest in ensuring that some significant operations continue. It has been 10 years and no final solution is in sight, although most creditors have been paid off 100 cents on the dollar and the bill to the Treasury to date exceeds $4 billion. However, would some kind of a more directed negotiating framework, such as emerged in the other four cases, not have been preferable?

Lockheed, in retrospect, seems to be a case where the bankruptcy downside risks were overstated. Management might well have negotiated a merger or takeover if the Federal guarantee escape route had been removed. The route chosen was successful, but it may well have been much ado about little.

New York City was, and is, far more of a problem in effective government than a credit problem. The essential skills required there are political. The financing terms and concessions were, and are, important, but banking and workout experts cannot by themselves force the world's largest city to face political realities.

Chrysler is a close case. It is not at all clear to me that a Chrysler bankruptcy in the summer of 1979 would have been catastrophic. However, in practical effect the results achieved under the Loan Guarantee Act are the equivalent of a reorganization in bankruptcy. An exception was that the concessions obtained from employees probably would not have been secured otherwise. This type of reorganization also avoided the risk that consumers would not buy cars from a bankrupt company. Hence, the result is that through the Act, Chrysler has been reorganized into a company that has a chance of survival, whereas in bankruptcy it probably would have been liquidated. In any case, even if it should in the end fail, the liquidated value of Chrysler's modernized plants and inventory, on which the United States has a first lien, should be ample to pay the government guaranteed loans.

In the case of the First Pennsylvania Corporation the solution, as in the three other cases, was a government-led reorganization outside of bankruptcy and in place of a liquidation. The FDIC, which under its statute is the substantive equivalent of a Loan Guarantee Board, obtained concessions from the private creditors and contributed sufficient new government credit to permit the bank to continue operations. The theory behind this approach was twofold: (1) the failure of a bank the size of First Pennsylvania might have produced ripple effects damaging to other financial institutions; (2) it would be cheaper in the long run for the FDIC to nurse the bank back to health than to pay off the insured depositors in a liquidation scenario.

These five cases are the record of a decade of government intervention in the economic failure of large, private sector enterprises. The motives behind the intervention and the problems addressed through congressional actions were quite different.

First, the Penn Central approach, which was the least bold and combined a bankruptcy with an ill-conceived rehabilitation program, has also been the least successful and the most costly to the government. This approach minimized the leverage of government negotiators and featured diffused responsibility and continuous congressional oversight. Congress is now beginning to face the cold truth that we cannot afford the legacy of an overbuilt and irrational eastern rail system. Had it been willing to face the truth 10 years ago, a preferable alternative would have been to turn the job of rationalization over to a technically qualified negotiator, who could have used the incentive of new money or guarantees, and the threat of an endless bankruptcy to extract the concessions indispensable to a practical solution.

Second, with the exception of Penn Central, none of the cases is an example of a bail-out in the tradition of British Steel or British Leyland, where the government simply subsidizes continuing losses with no expectation of repayment. Rather, they are examples of reorganizations achieved outside of bankruptcy on the basis of concessions obtained from other participants. At least in the case of the New York City, Chrysler, and First Pennsylvania reorganizations, these almost certainly could not have been achieved in a bankruptcy setting. Thus, they really amount to a recognition that in some situations, for whatever set of economic, social, and political reasons, it may be preferable to try an alternative to bankruptcy.

Third, the situations are sufficiently diverse, the structural alternatives sufficiently varied, and the concessions that must be extracted sufficiently sensitive politically that it is doubtful as to the feasibility of writing an appropriate and embracing set of criteria. How much employment must be at risk? What kinds of labor concessions should be mandated as part of a plan? How big must the floundering enterprise be? Must it be a national company—or is the potentially severe impact of the failure of a shoe factory in Haverhill, Massachusetts enough?

Fourth, the cumbersome nature of the congressional process is itself a practical check on a continuous flow of emergency loan guarantees. Congress has not let a landslide develop; it has, in the same period, ignored anguished pleas for emergency help from real estate investment trusts, Cleveland, and a succession of retailers and thrift institutions.

Finally, there is a real risk in establishing an independent agency with money to spend. If past is prologue, it will find a way to spend the money. Remember that a lineal descendant of one of the RFC emergency lending programs is today offering $3 million credit for community TV antennae. Not to ignore the real economic thunderclouds on the horizon, but unless and until acceptable criteria can be developed, it is better to maintain a competent analysis capability in Treasury, with standby authority to hire experts as needed, than risk creation and unexpected growth of another standby credit agency.

SUMMARY REPORT

Political Experience

Robert H. Mundheim

Our discussion group looked at the political experience of sectoral intervention. We noted that targeted government intervention exists today in many programs and has existed for a long time. Indeed, a 1980 Department of the Treasury study indicates that almost all of the Reconstruction Finance Corporation's financing activities are included in various Federal credit programs active today. Moreover, the relative amounts spent on these activities now exceed (even on an adjusted basis) the expenditures in the heyday of the RFC. Thus, it was concluded that (1) organizations once established persist, and functions once in place do not easily disappear; and (2) governmental intervention on behalf of specific companies is not a novel phenomenon.

Interest in governmental aid to specific companies has been heightened as a result of a number of major failures: the Lockheed Corporation, New York City, the Chrysler Corporation, and the Philadelphia contributions, Penn Central and the First Pennsylvania Corporation. No one disagreed with the assessment that these would not be the only cases calling for government help. There are storm clouds on the horizon. Savings and loan institutions and mutual savings banks, and the auto industry were among the areas mentioned as probable cases with which government will be asked to deal.

Although opportunity for government intervention will occur, there was a general lack of enthusiasm for encouraging the government to respond to and rescue specific failing companies or industries. This does not imply a flat "no," but a presumption that the applicant for aid would have to make a very persuasive case, and that each case would have to be examined on its own.

For example, some panel members were prepared to justify keeping Chrysler from being reorganized in bankruptcy as a way of preserving the company's good will, and thus retaining for a U.S. manufacturer some of the sales which otherwise would probably have been lost to foreign competition. In the case of banks, it was recognized that it is generally cheaper to have the company reorganize outside bankruptcy. Finally, the notion that New York City would be run by a District Judge did not seem appropriate.

In reviewing the five cases, it was suggested that Congress had learned to say "yes" to bail-outs by ever-increasing margins; indeed, one panelist asserted it was no longer a case of bail-out versus bankruptcy, but rather a question of the conditions for a bail-out.

Others pointed out that the setting of the conditions was highly significant and that terms for getting governmental help were getting tougher. Also, the severity of the terms deterred many would-be applicants from coming to Congress for help. For example, it was argued that the price New York City had to pay in order to secure Federal help (including yielding a substantial measure of sovereignty) was a powerful argument around which Mayor William Green was able to rally the relevant Philadelphia players to settle that city's problems without outside intervention.

Nevertheless one panelist, perhaps drawing on his knowledge of effective lobbying methods, remained concerned that Congress and the Executive would be so swayed by short-term political considerations that they would permit governmental aid in situations not justified by cold economic analysis and on terms less stringent than obtainable. He urged the creation of a "toughly managed" Modern Reconstruction Finance Corporation to replace the current *ad hoc* political response to bail-out requests, and to achieve more optimal economic resolutions. In other words, he wanted appeals to Congress sifted through a tough-minded, banker-like organization. Moreover, he thought that this organization could negotiate the conditions for getting aid (the necessary concessions from various interested parties) more effectively than Congress or an Executive agency.

Although they sympathized with the purpose of the suggestions, the other panel members rejected them. It was felt that institutionalizing the bail-out process would only encourage requests. Getting the bail-out would become the game to play. Moreover, as one participant remarked, "with the RFC all set for business, it is natural that those in charge of it would rather make loans than not."

The panel also voiced despair about finding the right people to staff such an agency if it were to act only on a stand-by basis, with a mission of discouraging deals. Further, it was pointed out that many of the decisions on the bail-out of a specific major company, and even more so of an industry, embodied important political questions (desirability of cushioning shocks in a specific city, losing domestic employment to foreign competition), for example, balancing of varying interests, which are appropriately resolved in the political process and not insulated from it.

One statement of the problem is: can we articulate in advance standards to determine the circumstances under which it is appropriate for the government to provide help? No one offered a draft.

In sum, there was a near-consensus of skepticism about MRFC. This would exist certainly as long as the criteria under which it could make its determinations were not spelled out, and until its leader (described as politically savvy, energetic, expert in finance and a hard-nosed negotiator) could be identified (and signed to a long-term contract). Thus, we are perhaps prepared to continue to muddle along for a while longer.

We did not linger long on a program to pick-the-winners. There was no confidence that we could structure procedures for doing so successfully. That did not mean, however, that the panel was unwilling to choose some areas in which it was clear that action was needed and governmental intervention desirable. Railroads were an example of an infrastructure development to which attention must be paid, and energy was another area, but we recognized that another group would deal with that area.

There was also discussion of governmental intervention through the tax system to attack specific social problems—particularly for dealing with the problem of minority youth employment. The panel explored the Employment Tax Credit to encourage employment of specific categories of the population, and again a good deal of skepticism about this form of targeted assistance was expressed. The typical sentiment was that general tax incentives generally worked better. (For example, one panelist supported a prospectively enacted provision by which the government would share losses with corporations by allowing recovery of taxes paid. He saw this proposal as a way to increase the willingness of corporations and their owners to take risks.) Nevertheless, it was thought that the Employment Tax Credit provisions (worked out through a consensus between labor, business, and government and implemented through a mutually recognized cooperative effort) deserved careful review to determine if indeed it was effective in getting the targeted job done.

In summary: in terms of the two alternatives put at the beginning of the conference, our panel tended to react skeptically to the effectiveness of preferential programs. It also recognized, however, that it is not appropriate to be doctrinaire and that we must be open minded enough to consider, on their merits, the specific claims for help which will be made.

★ ★ ★ ★ ★ ★ ★ ★ ★ ★ ★ ★ ★ ★

PART THREE

FORMULATING A
CONSENSUS VIEW

19.

THE CONSENSUS: PROCESS AND SUBSTANCE

John T. Dunlop

In his keynote address last night, Reginald H. Jones said, "the purpose of this symposium . . . is to examine the issues and options and trade-offs, and try to hammer out the building blocks from which a national consensus can be erected." He concluded that "the public is ready for vigorous debate that will lead to consensus on a new industrial policy. What we need is a set of ideas that can be combined into a coherent, workable policy."

The *Business Week* (June 30, 1980) issue and editorial on "A Strategy for Rebuilding the Economy" affirmed that "the reindustrialization program must depend on consensus, not coercion." And President Carter in his Economic Program for the 1980s called, on August 28, 1980, for a new partnership "to foster cooperation between government and the private sector in dealing with the complex issues of industrial policy." The Executive Council of the AFL-CIO in its Reindustrialization Statement of August 20, 1980 said, "it is time for the government to take the lead in developing a new partnership with labor and business to help reestablish a growing, diversified and secure industrial economy."[1] President-elect Reagan, through the Public Affairs Council stated: "By bringing together representatives of business, labor, academia and government, we could develop a dialogue that could lead to a genuine consensus. This, in turn, could translate into action through both federal legislation and voluntary private action. 'Consensus building' is a term you will hear often in the next several years, for it is the only effective way to gain the enthusiastic support of the American people. . . ."[2]

There appears to be broad agreement on the necessity for a consensus in economic policy-making, but little agreement on anything else. As a student and sometime practitioner of consensus building, I wish to assert first a few propositions about the process of consensus building as applied to private and public industrial policies and then, second, to make a few suggestions as to an approach to industrial policies. If you are at all interested in consensus building, I fear there is little place for grandiose plans or patented schemes, except as a point of departure.

*   *   *

Consensus building is problem solving and pragmatic. It relies heavily on the art of listening, and listening perceptively between the lines of formal positions. It is devoted to the quest for irreducible facts, for the actual and the tendential. It requires candor and mutual respect. It exhausts charity, patience, and persuasion. It does not presume rationality or order in the affairs of men and women. It is comfortable with a mixed but acceptable system. It seeks agreement on a few matters rather than on a comprehensive plan.

Consensus building does not depend upon political might or the exercise of governmental or market power. It does not thrive in strident tones or in programs or platforms. It is not congenial to doctrinaire adherence to the left or to the right. It does not rely on Keynes or Laffer. It is not the greatest good for the greatest number since it is sensitive to the interests of internal minorities. It rejects both ideology and central planning and their respective distortions of history.

Experience teaches that the consensus building process requires the following elements:

(1) A continuing forum. An occasional symposium or assembly may launch an effort, or call attention to a problem, or provide a one-time platform for meritorious proposals or an opportunity for preachments. But a genuine meeting of minds or a compromise of vital formal positions or conversions necessitates continuing and regular dialogue among the interests represented in the forum. There must be a continuing discourse on neutral turf or under somewhat dispassionate auspices to reach common ground.

(2) Private or off-the-record discussions. It is impossible for responsible leadership of various groups seriously to explore compromise of positions on economic policy or new approaches to industrial policy in the glare of press or media or with destructive leaks. Responsible leaders come to the forum with official positions enshrined in resolutions, traditions, and policies that are crafted to preserve internal balance or that reflect an ideological view. A hospitality to different views requires delicate discussions and explanations to major constituencies. An open meeting cannot generate a consensus, although it may record periodi-

cally the results of private discourse. There is a responsibility to report to a wider public on such private discussions.

(3) Professional staff work. Continuing discourse is substantially facilitated by professional staff under policy direction which marshals the facts, breaks down the issues, and states dispassionately the areas of agreement and disagreement, including a statement of the reasons for contending positions. Staff that captures policy-making functions by default or ambition usually proves to be a disaster. Carefully prepared sessions of policy-makers are likely to be vastly more productive in reaching consensus than a series of bull sessions.

(4) Consensus on limited issues. It is vital to recognize that consensus on some issues is likely to leave differences on many other questions. It takes experience and sophistication to recognize that groups may agree and cooperate on some issues and disagree and conduct limited warfare on other matters.

Two further observations about the process of consensus building:

Consensus development cannot be a substitute for the formal decision-making processes of the private or public sectors. It can only provide a sense of direction, smooth social conflict, and speed formal processes.

The consensus building process can often be extraordinarily constructive; policies emerge which were not envisaged initially by any participant. Thus, initial substantive proposals for industrial policy, even my own, should be treated as tentative, to be tested and perfected by discourse.

* * *

It is conventional to begin a discussion of economic or industrial policies with a statement of goals and high purpose—economic growth, high employment and reduced inflation, and so on. But it may be more sobering and realistic to start by recognizing that we actually have in place a mixture of measures and private and public activities, perhaps not consistent or coherent, that treat economic and industrial problems. We are not likely to be free to make an entirely new start; we are constrained by the legacy of measures in place and applied each day. The Federal tax laws favor some activities relative to others; states compete savagely in grants and tax concessions to attract industry; regulatory rules or their repeal or revision, as well, change competitive conditions among enterprises; trade agreements and autarkical arrangements in various industries abroad, or their absence, differentially affect various sectors of the economy, and grants, subsidies, and procurement policies have differential consequences on industrial growth and vitality.

Like it or not, we already have a complex of entrenched measures; we are not free to wipe the board clean and begin afresh. Moreover, it has always been thus in our country from the days of canals, railroad grants, and infant industries. A review of industrial policies in other industrial countries[3] reflects more intense activities, but no less diffuse a pattern.

This perspective, rooted in sobering reality, suggests that the search for consensus, at least initially, concentrate on a few elements. Your list may be different from mine, and I am willing to consider any short list that you believe can develop substantive agreement. Here are my four items:

(1) domestic energy production and conservation;
(2) modernization of business plant and equipment and capital recovery in an era of inflation;
(3) public infrastructure that has been neglected, but is vital to industrial growth: road maintenance, bridge repair, coal terminals for export, and the like;
(4) urgent human resource development for engineers and shortage occupations.

The development of the most appropriate mix of private and public policies, not necessarily new policies or involving Federal appropriations, to treat these limited but central problems, should be the purpose of the consensus-seeking exercise. Consensus proposals in some cases would require private or formal governmental action (legislative or Executive) to be made effective.

This limited approach eschews a comprehensive program; it regards experience in a limited arena to be essential to extension to a larger and larger field. But it begins with the here and now and seeks to learn from and to perfect the consensus building process as applied to industrial policy issues. A similar limited approach may be applied in some localities or regions.

NOTES

1. Executive Council, AFL-CIO, "Reindustrialization Statement, August 20, 1980," Press release.
2. Public Affairs Council press release.
3. Conference Board (1980).

BIBLIOGRAPHY

The Conference Board in Europe. *European Industrial Policy, Past Present and Future.* London: The Conference Board, Inc., 1980.

20.

INDUSTRIAL POLICY IN
THE UNITED KINGDOM

R. James Ball

My principal role today is as a reporter of the state and development of industrial policy in the United Kingdom. I do not propose to discuss industrial policy in the abstract, or even to define it, other than to interpret it as a variety of measures and policies that go beyond the simple exercise of what you would call stabilization policy, and what the British would call demand management, and which have medium to long-term effects on the growth of output and the allocation of resources.

INDUSTRIAL POLICY IN THE UNITED KINGDOM
1960–79
In the early sixties it began to be believed that, while managing the overall level of demand was an essential adjunct to the maintenance of full employment, different policies might have to be devised and applied if the underlying rate of growth of the economy was to be increased. Demand management needed to be accompanied by policies aimed at altering the structure of the economy. Accordingly, under the auspices of the newly-formed National Economic Development Council and its executive, the National Development Office, studies were put in hand to consider the "obstacles to growth," the identification and removal of which were to pave the way to faster growth and higher prosperity.

The change of government in 1964 brought in Harold Wilson's first administration, rooted in a belief in a new economic technocracy and committed to consume the country in the "white heat of technological revolution." To this end, a new Department of Economic Affairs was created as a makeweight to the Treasury and as the guardian of industrial affairs. No longer, it was said, would economic policies be so obviously directed toward and inhibited by short-term considerations. Its main product was the National Plan, which purported to describe a path of development for the United Kingdom over subsequent years.

In the event, the Plan turned out to be neither forecast nor plan, as the government was overwhelmed by the familiar incoming tides of rising inflation and a deteriorating current account of the balance of payments. The objectives of the Plan were abandoned. The Department of Economic Affairs sank into insignificance as the Treasury regained its authority. Symbolically, the devaluation of the pound sterling in 1967 marked the last resting place of the extensive, if imprecise, ambitions that had been entertained three years earlier. Industrial policy gave way to sound monetary and fiscal policies, in terms of priority, allied with attempts to pursue an effective incomes and prices policy coupled with trade union restraint.

In parallel, attempts were made to change the industrial structure of the United Kingdom and to promote technological advance. The establishment of a Ministry of Technology was to provide a focal point for the encouragement of technological change. Meanwhile, the Industrial Reconstruction Corporation was set up to promote mergers and rationalization within British industry in order to provide a more coherent base from which to attack world markets. "Big is beautiful" would seem to have been the motto of the hour. It had both successes (the ball bearing industry) and failures (the computer industry).

The Conservative government came in in 1970, committed to the new policies of Selsdon Man (named after an hotel near London where the policies were initially discussed). In future, industry was to learn to stand on its own feet. No longer would public money be wasted in supporting and maintaining uneconomic businesses. Cold showers were to be the order of the day, coupled with a major trip to the Common Market plunge pool, through which the sins of British industry might be cleansed. The Industrial Relations Act was to provide a more appropriate legal background against which industry could operate.

Determination to maintain this posture did not last that long. The collapse of Rolls-Royce, Ltd. put the question firmly and squarely to the government. The policy of not supporting the so-called lame ducks disappeared in what became known as a celebrated U-turn. Against this background, the government struggled with the familiar problems of incomes policy culminating in the confrontation with the miners and the loss of office.

Harold Wilson's second government was immediately confronted with a similar set of circumstances to his first. The United Kingdom inflation rate and the current account of the balance of payments were out of control, partly as a result of the world crisis, but also because of the lax fiscal and monetary policies at home. An attempt to come to grips with the underlying problems of productivity and efficiency was overshadowed by the familiar macroeconomic problems of the past. There was much talk of industrial strategy but, in retrospect, it is difficult to see any more than a series of *ad hoc* actions taken in response to short-term pressures largely stemming from the collapse or near-collapse of familiar companies. If this period had any particular characteristic, perhaps it lay in the Labor Party belief that a new industrial panacea could be found in participation and the workings of the Bullock Committee. In practice, talk of the regeneration of British industry through industrial strategy meant largely the preservation of British industry rather than any serious structural change.

THE CONSERVATIVE GOVERNMENT'S OBJECTIVES, 1979–

The objectives of the present Administration on taking office bear a close relation to those of the Reagan administration, as expressed by Secretary of the Treasury Donald Regan this morning. As in the case of the Conservative Government of 1970, it came in committed to a substantial "hands off" attitude toward industry and toward industrial problems. Once again, it was reiterated, the taxpayers' money would not be used to support lame ducks. Industry must stand on its own feet.

At the same time, it was proposed to create a new balance between the public and the private sectors. Through reductions in both taxes and public spending, money was to be returned to the hands of the people. The tax cuts would help, not only in that money spent by private individuals and institutions would be more productively spent than by the state, but incentives would be increased, encouraging enterprise and supply-side efficiency.

The central thrust of fiscal and monetary policy was to be aimed not at the manipulation of output and employment, but at the control of inflation. Inflation, it was believed, was at the heart of the destruction of British industry, and monetary policy should be directed toward the inflation objective. Industrial policy and strategy became synonyms for intervention and excessive public expenditure. The stage was set for what has been billed on both sides of the Atlantic as the great monetarist experiment.

It is, no doubt, a familiar fact that such an experiment has been conducted, and that the British economy has been laid waste by these monetarist policies. Low output has been produced by savage cuts in public spending, and excessively high interest rates have been reduced by suicidally tight monetary policies.

In reality, nothing is further from the truth. In calendar year 1980, current government spending in the United Kingdom rose by 25 percent compared with a rise in national spending of 15 percent. Even government capital spending rose by 13 percent. Current public spending in real terms rose by 1.4 percent compared with a fall in gross domestic product of about 3 percent.

Government expenditure as a proportion of gross domestic product in nominal terms rose to its highest level since 1975, and the fiscal deficit climbed with it accordingly. The supply of money as measured by sterling M3 and other broader measures of liquidity rose in excess of 15 percent. The high interest rates were not the result of an excessively tight monetary policy, but were the result of an excessively loose fiscal policy, and the strength of sterling supported by high interest rates created further industrial difficulties. Public sector average earnings rose between 25 percent and 30 percent, while even in the depressed manufacturing industry the average level of earnings in the third quarter of 1980 was 20 percent more than a year before. While total output in the United Kingdom fell by 3 percent in real terms, as already reported, real disposable income rose by 2.5 percent. Unemployment rose by nearly a million.

Why? Because the government failed to allow the money supply to grow by 25 percent or government nominal spending to grow by 35 percent? The truth is that the government failed, but its failure did not stem from the application of so-called monetarist policies; it failed precisely for the opposite reason, namely that it failed to make them stick. It failed for the following main reasons:

- The control of inflation was put second to the reduction in taxes, hence the disastrous start in raising the Value Added Tax (VAT) to pay for income tax cuts.
- The government failed to control nominal spending, hence laying the basis for high interest rates.
- Industrial policy was confused with interventionism. The government has now drifted into industrial support without plan or control.

I put it to you that this is a far cry from the media presentation of what is going on in Britain, and even from what most people in Britain think is going on. The notion that the British economy is being crucified on an ideological monetarist cross is simply inconsistent with the facts. My interpretation of events is closer to the remarks made by Secretary Regan to the Joint Economic Committee of the Senate than to the daily reports that, at the time of writing, fill the *London Times*.

INDUSTRIAL POLICY ISSUES IN THE UNITED KINGDOM

The central thrust of Margaret Thatcher's government, as far as the supply-side of industry was concerned, was to combine the control of inflation with the creation of incentives. In many respects, this seems to square with the aspirations of the Reagan administration. Fiscal shifts directed at the supply-side rather than at the demand side of the system were to become the order of the day.

At the heart of the discussions of industrial policy in the United Kingdom has been the so-called problem of deindustrialization. What deindustrialization means is not always clear, other than expressing a general concern with the decline of manufacturing industry in some sense. For some, there is concern at the relative and absolute decline in manufacturing employment, a phenomenon that has been observed not only in the United Kingdom but also elsewhere, notably in the United States. Alternatively, some people have been concerned about the share of manufactures in total output, although here, across countries, the evidence of any strong trend decline in manufacturing is not clear. A further approach has been to argue that deindustrialization occurs, or is occurring, if manufacturing industry is becoming increasingly incapable of competing in world markets, so as to permit full employment at a "reasonable" exchange rate. The problem then appears to become one either of inadequate exports or excessive imports and, in certain quarters of Britain, this leads to the demand for protection of industry in order to prevent further deindustrialization and loss of jobs.

The problem of deindustrialization in Britain has been complicated by the existence of North Sea oil, the precise consequences of which are in some dispute. One version of the story is that North Sea oil will inevitably lead to further rapid deindustrialization. The argument is that the principal result of North Sea oil is import-saving, so reducing the need for manufactured exports to pay the import bill. Consequently the current account of the balance of payments moves into surplus and the exchange rate rises to eliminate the exports by reducing their profitability. Thus, the size of the manufacturing sector that is required, other things being equal, shrinks. It has therefore been argued that the recent strength of sterling is not the *cause* of the recent decline of British industry, but simply reflects the mechanism through which the necessary industrial adjustment is carried out.

This is partly true. There is undoubtedly a "North Sea" element in the behavior of the exchange rate, and in practice some adjustment of the manufacturing base may come about. However, in principle this need not be the case, since the balance of payments savings may be used to purchase additional imports, or be invested overseas, thus offsetting the effect on the exchange rate and on manufacturing industry. Moreover, the behavior of the exchange rate in the United Kingdom has also been affected by the high levels of interest rates which, as already explained, have resulted from the extremely loose fiscal policy.

In this context the behavior of the exchange rate has been central to much of the debate about industrial policy. While it is clear that the nominal exchange rate would probably have been lower had interest rates not been driven up by excessive public sector borrowing, it is a long way from this to the belief that the government could and should have attempted to manipulate the exchange rate downward in order to offset the pressure on manufacturing industry. Many people in Britain believe that it could and should have done this. However, those who support this view completely misunderstand the fact that, if monetary policy is aimed at determining the exchange rate, it cannot also be used directly to influence the rate of inflation. One cannot have one's cake *and* eat it.

A second issue of major concern in Britain is similar to that raised by Lane Kirkland this morning, namely the role of financial institutions, particularly pension funds. There is a fairly strong belief in Britain, which is shared by some industrialists, that the financial system has in some sense not done justice to industry's needs. This has led in some quarters to demands for a special investment facility or bank sponsored by the state which the private financial institutions would be required to fund. Despite the findings of the majority of those who sat in on an investigation into the British financial system under the chairmanship of Sir Harold Wilson, this notion is still current. If a further Labor government is elected in 1984, I would expect to see something of this sort put into practice. In place of the direct nationalization of the banks and insurance companies, the emergence of "directed investment" is a serious possibility.

As far as the United Kingdom is concerned, the principal argument here confuses lack of real investment with lack of finance. The fundamental cause of a relatively low rate of investment in the United Kingdom has little or nothing to do with finance. The central problem is the lack of profitable investment projects. One was interested to note the emphasis placed by Secretary Regan on stimulating saving in the United States as an essential element in increasing productivity and efficiency. The problem in the United Kingdom is quite different. During the seventies, the personal saving ratio in the United Kingdom has increased dramatically. The problem has not been an overall lack of saving, but that high interest rates, affecting private borrowers, have been brought about by the high borrowing of the state. Moreover, a similar pattern of increased saving ratios has been observed elsewhere in other countries during this period, which makes one somewhat uneasy about the view that there is a shortage of saving only in the United States.

A third issue that affects industrial policy and strategy in the United Kingdom is that of participation. Despite the somewhat abortive outcome of the Bullock Report, there is still a strong belief in certain parts of the labor movement that dramatic increases in competitiveness and efficiency might be achieved in British industry if there were changes in the way in which employees participate in their businesses. Even those who support such ideas in principle do not always agree about details in practice, but the idea of major union representation on the boards of companies has not gone away, although it is not a matter of daily debate at the present time. Moreover, the practice followed in Britain on this matter is in principle also determined by European Economic Community legislation.

There remain two other dimensions of industrial policy worthy of note, one of which we share and one of which we do not. The first of these is the increasing emphasis, verging on overkill, on the role of the small business. However important small business may be—and indeed it is important—it must be remembered that healthy small businesses invariably require healthy large businesses in order to survive. As in the case of large businesses, too much attention has been paid to the financial needs of small companies rather than the real obstacles to new product creation and development. To believe that a new race of small businessmen is going to make a major dent in the unemployment rate in the immediate future is quite unrealistic. Secondly, there is the problem of the role, financing, and control of the nationalized industries, which the United States does not share, at least in the same form. On all these three issues confusion reigns, issues which require resolution in the framework of any government policy which purports to deal with the infrastructure of the economy.

LESSONS FOR THE UNITED STATES
In listening to the presentations and discussions of this Symposium, I have been struck by the fact that I have heard the same things in the United Kingdom over many years. It is almost possible for me to supply names and faces to match those who have addressed us here. I am not sure whether in fact that should make me worry about you or worry about me!

The conclusion that I would draw from this is that the problems with which industrial policy seeks to deal are not easily dealt with, particularly within the time constraints that are imposed on possible solutions by the political cycle. Accordingly, humility and realistic aspirations must be set. That, it seems to me, is the major lesson of British experience. The same issues recur with monotonous regularity, not simply, I believe, because they are intractable, but because they are intractable in the time scale within which major observable results are expected. If one is really going to achieve real change along the lines discussed this morning, one must be looking at a five to 10 year program. Moreover, change is painful and, as soon as sectional interests are threatened, the long haul is forsaken for the short-term objective.

To put the matter another way, Reginald H. Jones, in his keynote speech, referred to the need for hard decisions. But the real danger is that the hard decisions, which imply hard consequences, will not be consistent with the political consensus that is required for the decisions to be successfully implemented. If the Thatcher government in Britain fails to achieve its objectives, a matter on which I reserve judgment, it is likely to be as much a political failure as a technical failure of misunderstanding how the economy works. The majority must be convinced that the policies will work, or they never will. Political economy was not called political economy for nothing, even though we forget the fact. The central problem is that, at the end of the day, sectional interests will prevail over national interests, which can only be reconciled in a long run that is never reached. To put it simply, people will, in the end, act like people, and it is that that prevents the hard decisions being stuck to. And, unless those hard decisions are made and stuck to, you are not going to change the structure of your economy.

21.

"WORKING THROUGH"
TO ECONOMIC REALISM

Daniel Yankelovich   Larry Kaagan

In the closing moments of the Wharton/Reliance Symposium, Irving Shapiro, chairman of E. I. duPont de Nemours and Co., Inc., made an astute observation which also sounded an optimistic note. His theme was the changing roles played by America's business leaders in a variety of issues that transcend "the bottom line." He pointed out that at various periods of our history, the popular image of a businessman was that of a single-minded character intent on nothing more than turning a profit, and otherwise disavowing any interest or role in the larger problems that beset the nation. Mr. Shapiro also noted, however, that the last half-dozen years had seen the emergence of business leaders who take a much broader view of their roles. These businessmen have begun speaking, if sometimes contentiously, about issues that affect average citizens. More often than not, they speak from the vantage point of personal concern and social responsibility as well as reflect more traditional business interests.

His observation gives us reason to hope for a better relation between business and the public in the years to come. For just as business has turned its attention to the social impact of inflation, the problems of scarcity and economic competition among various regions of the country and the world, the American people have raised a collective voice to question the adversarial and often destructive link between government and business, to question the obtrusiveness of government bureaucracy, and to raise their expectations of what corporate America can do for the economy, and what an improved partnership between business and government can do for the nation.

These new targets for our attention and the answers demanded by those new questions are what the next several years will be all about in this country. They explain why this Symposium was organized, and go a long way toward explaining why some of the most gifted people from business, labor, government, academia, public interest, and media sectors of the society came together for three days to engage in the kind of dialogue that is becoming more frequent these days.

The three days of the Wharton/Reliance Symposium did not, of course, represent the beginning, middle, or end to the discussion about the hard choices and policy options facing the American people and the American economy. The discussion, of which the Symposium was a significant part, really began in 1973, a watershed year in American history insofar as it synthesized, even for those blind or resistant to other messages, the fateful news of a new era. Although some trends started before 1973, the Arab oil embargo launched a discussion about changing economic conditions, strategies, and the future, first among the few, then among the many, that has yet to be resolved.

As the American people and American institutions continue to struggle their way through that discussion, at every turn more people "face reality." In the period prior to the early 1970s we had grown accustomed to a rising economy, a relatively low rate of inflation, a greater concern with managing demand rather than worrying about supply, world leadership in the economic and political sphere, leadership in the scientific/technical sphere, steady advances in productivity gains, a set of political "rules" geared to a rising economy, and a culture in which the family, role relations between the sexes, and the work ethic seemed fixed, permanent, and predictable.

To a startling extent none of these conditions now obtain. Just 10 years ago in 1971, America suffered its first trade deficit in this century —two years before the explosive increase in oil prices. This event proved the harbinger of a decade of economic bad news—rising rates of inflation, interest levels, government regulation, unemployment, and budget deficits; and falling rates of productivity, research innovation, capital formation, and competitive triumphs for U.S. industry. In 1970 our annual bill for imported oil was $4 billion; in 1980, it was over $90 billion. A decade ago, the portion of the Federal budget earmarked for social entitlement programs amounted to $62 billion; in 1980, it approached $300 billion. And a decade ago, we could look behind us at an uninterrupted string of years during which the productivity of the American economy was unmatched and virtually unchallenged in the world. A mere two decades ago, goods marked "made in Japan" were regarded smugly by American manufacturers, and disdainfully by American consumers.

In the same period of two decades, many of the structures we had relied on to stabilize our faith in the country and confirm the harmonious fit between individual and society have been shaken to their very foundations. For example, in family life, long considered the bedrock of American normalcy, transformations have taken place at a nearly dizzying pace. The unitary image of the American family, with a breadwinning father, a stay-at-home mother caring for several school age children, seemed to evaporate overnight. Since 1970 the fastest growing category of households measured by the Census has been persons living alone or with other unrelated persons. Two-thirds of all mothers are now in the labor force, including more than 40 percent of mothers of children under six years of age. America's traditional optimism about the economic future turned into troubled pessimism. By late 1979, as we manufactured divorces as fast as cars, a 72 percent majority agreed with the glum statement that we are "fast coming to a turning point in our history, The Land of Plenty is becoming the Land of Want."

Since the early 1970s, starting with our failure to pay for the costs of waging the war in Vietnam out of current income, the United States has been growing progressively more insolvent. We have less, but we live as if we had more. We are living beyond our means. Pursuing similar policies, New York City in the 1970s came perilously close to bankruptcy. In the end it was forced to bring its financial house into order. But the country as a whole faces no externally imposed discipline, and continues to "eat its seed corn," consuming far more than it produces.

While the debate about how to correct the economy continues to rage, people are reluctant to accept limits and constraints, either on their economic behavior or on the wide range of cultural and life style options which blossomed between the 1960s and 1980s. In the process of coming to grips with a new world order or the need for a new industrial policy, people require time to digest the full implications of the change in conditions.

We do not know much about how long it takes a society such as ours to reverse direction, and to abandon long-standing expectations. For almost 30 years, Americans had learned to expect a rising standard of living each year, provided that one observed the rules of hard work, sought a better education, lived a respectable family life, and trusted in a bit of luck. But from the time of the Arab oil embargo to the present, Americans have been receiving mixed signals about what to expect in the future. Though far from clear, the message buried in these signals seems to be that we must abandon some of the bad habits of the seventies—and must now begin to produce more and consume less. This new task is not one that Americans will embrace without pain, confusion, and travail.

People do not adapt to new, disagreeable economic realities simply by shrugging their shoulders, accepting the new conditions and saying, "well, we might as well get on with it." While not easily factored into econometric models or programs for industrial revitalization, the process is nonetheless a complex psychological phenomenon that will prove crucial in shaping any public consensus on "what next" for America's economic and social future. The "working through" process is an evolution of phases necessary to the goal of adapting to unsettling news or new realities. Most familiar as the "grief reaction" in response to death or terminal illness, the working through process connotes a complex outpouring of emotionalism, inconclusiveness, and inconsistency.

As the process unfolds one expects to find varied expressions of emotion such as anger, confusion, disbelief, denial, barely suppressed panic, scapegoating, grasping at straws, depression, overreacting, exaggeration, fatalism, instability of attitudes (saying one thing one day, and another the next), lack of realism, inconsistency between attitudes and behavior, and indulging in Pollyanna-ish wishful thinking that everything will turn out to be for the best without requiring any real change. At the early stages of the process, people often overreact or refuse to accept realities that deep down they know to be true.

As aspects of an adjustment process, these are not pathological or abnormal responses: they are the temporary—and perhaps inevitable—human concomitants to unanticipated and threatening changes in the assumptions about how one is going to live one's life. They are signs of the huge amount of effort it takes for people to keep panic at bay when they first feel threatened and before they have made a constructive adaptation to new circumstances.

The working through process also implies movement toward a goal. It is a dynamic process, not a static one. It implies that when the sound and fury have abated and people have had time to digest the implications of new realities, they will do so and find appropriate new strategies for dealing with them. Resolution and consensus can then replace ambivalence, conflict, and instability.

It is probably not an overstatement to suggest that in modifying their economic expectations downward as they are lashed by inflation and the changing eminence of our national economic might, Americans are experiencing a real sense of loss. But the American people, in their heart of hearts, are slowly working toward acceptance of the new realities. People are beginning to realize that energy supplies, in availability and price, will not soon again be what they were: cheap, plentiful, and set apart from the troubles of the larger world. Each year, the public also shows a growing awareness that improvements in productivity are crucial to any attack on inflation, that business must attract capital in order to generate profits and jobs, and even that some measure of personal sacrifice may be required to achieve the desired ends of solvency, stability, and growth.

What, then, separates a growing understanding of the problems from a consensus in support of their solutions? The United States possesses all of the institutions needed to expedite forming a popular consensus: a free press and a wide diversity of other media, an abundance of national and local organizations, political parties, an educated populace, a powerful Presidency now occupied by a skilled communicator, and a large and articulate intellectual community fully prepared to present and debate both issues and policies.

But despite our institutions, there are still some crucial elements missing. Although numerous panels, study commissions, and think tanks advise government officials on policy plans, military leaders on scenarios, and industries on research, technology, and marketing, amazingly little attention has been paid to the task of laying out for the *public* their options—and their role—in the fight against inflation, for example. A clear, objective array of policy choices, the pluses and minuses of each choice, the costs entailed, and the benefits to be gained, would go a long way toward engaging the general public in a debate too long left to arcane exchanges among technical experts.

For to the extent that our problems are soluble at all, they can only be solved by involving the American people as active, responsible citizens ready to face reality and do whatever needs to be done to restore the nation's economic vitality. Economists can devise ways to stem the growth of the money supply, but by technical policies alone they cannot dampen an inflationary *psychology,* or the public suspicion that since oil price fluctuations are created by collusion between the Organization of Petroleum Exporting Countries and the oil companies, we can solve our energy problem by "getting tough" with both.

Americans suspect that none of the choices the nation faces is ideal, and that none will return us to unbridled growth and unchallenged eminence. They also know from their personal lives what it is like to scale down expectations, make sacrifices, choose among options.

In principle, people are willing to make sacrifices for the common good, and at some profound level of patriotism, want to do so. But in practice, we can expect the 1980s to be dominated by intense social conflict. Since the start of the decade we have seen the battle lines being drawn ever more sharply—between haves and have-nots; Snowbelt and Sunbelt; those living on Social Security and those shouldering the taxes to pay for it; those who favor the Equal Rights Amendment and those who oppose it; proabortion and antiabortion forces; those who wish to return to the stricter social morality of the past and those who cherish the new freedom to choose one's own "lifestyle." If, in this climate of social conflict and tension, the nation's leadership is itself divided and unresponsive, then the country's transition to a new era will be extraordinarily painful.

The message of this Symposium is that, after several years of confusion and stock-taking, the nation's leadership is no longer as divided and unresponsive as it was in the 1970s. It has passed successfully through the first phase of the "working through" process. It acknowledges that there was something wrong with America's economic policies in the 1970s. It knows that we cannot continue to live beyond our means. At the same time, it knows that Americans do not want to settle for less, to resign themselves to economic stagnancy just because the challenge is more difficult than it was in the postwar era. It knows that most Americans will support a program of economic revitalization, *if* the sacrifices to launch it are fair and equitably distributed.

This Symposium did not produce a new industrial policy or a new economic program. What it did do is advance the thinking on which such programs must be based. And that we must judge as a significant accomplishment.